Treat this book with care

It should become part of your personal and professional library. It will serve you well at any number of points during your professional career.

5th EDITION

Real Estate

Principles & Practices

MAURICE A. UNGER

Professor
Real Estate and Business Law
University of Colorado

S64

Published by

SOUTH-WESTERN PUBLISHING CO.

CINCINNATI WEST CHICAGO, ILL. DALLAS PELHAM MANOR, N.Y.
PALO ALTO, CALIF. BRIGHTON, ENGLAND

by South-Western Publishing Co.
Cincinnati, Ohio

ISBN: 0-538-19640-8

Library of Congress Catalog Card Number: 73-75650

4 5 6 7 8 K 0 9 8 7

Printed in the United States of America

Preface

The purpose of this Fifth Edition of REAL ESTATE remains basically the same as the previous editions; namely, to provide a sound treatment of theories and practices that have a significant influence on the real estate market locally and nationally. The increasing importance of real property, the growing awareness of the effect of real estate activity, and the crying need for a proper balance between land use and the environmental impact have caused greater numbers of persons, associations, and firms to realize the need for additional knowledge and understanding of the problems involved in real estate.

In order to more completely present the full impact of these problems, this book presents the legal framework, the economic significance, and the social implications, blending these forces with a sound treatment of the practices that make up today's real estate market.

A new chapter has been added: "Real Estate Investment," dealing with the fundamentals of this growing area. The chapter on "Tax Factors in Real Estate," has been completely rewritten to incorporate the changes brought about by the Tax Reform Act of 1969.

Much material has been added reflecting changes in the housing laws. Furthermore, by means of additional footnotes, variations in the laws of the several states are indicated. All statistical data have been updated, and changes in practices have been noted. The emphasis on the broad national coverage of real estate practice continues to be an important feature of this fifth edition.

Continued attention is given in this edition to supporting the subject matter with references to real estate publications on research. References are made to professional journal articles, to magazine articles, to publications of professional societies, to university research, to government publications, to studies made by state associations, and to published books.

There are many persons—students, practitioners, teachers—who, through both oral and written constructive criticism, have contributed materially to the improvements in this book. To all these good people, the author expresses his appreciation and thanks.

Maurice A. Unger
University of Colorado

Table of Contents

PART ONE / AN OVERVIEW OF REAL ESTATE

PART TWO / PROPERTY RIGHTS

PART THREE / PROPERTY OWNERSHIP

PART FOUR / FINANCING REAL ESTATE

PART FIVE / REAL ESTATE BROKERAGE

PART SIX / PROPERTY EVALUATION

PART SEVEN / PLANNING FOR THE FUTURE

Chapter 1

The Economic and Social Impact of Real Estate

Some urban economists have declared that the need for housing in the decade of the seventies will amount to nearly 3 million units annually. Others have expressed doubt that this need can be fulfilled, or even that the need will be this great. Nevertheless, private residential new construction alone in 1972 contributed $54 billion to gross national product, while total construction expenditures reached a whopping $123.6 billion. Undoubtedly these figures will fluctuate between now and 1980; yet it is quite clear that construction and the real estate industry in general will have a substantial impact on the national economy.

At the moment, suburbs are overrunning a million acres of new land each year, and back in March, 1965, President Johnson pointed out to Congress: "Each year, in the coming generation, we will add the equivalent of 15 cities of 200,000 each."

In March, 1973, however, the Census Bureau announced that for the first time in history, the United States in the first nine months of 1971 reached a below-zero population growth level. The 2.08 estimated fertility rate for that period was below the average for a zero population growth "replacement" level. The population is still growing, but the rate of growth is about half the average of the

1960's; whether this will continue remains to be seen. The major economic significance of this lies in the fact that the construction of new residences and new commercial and industrial properties contributes directly to the stock of the country's capital goods. Indirectly, new construction finds its ramifications in nearly every other type of industry, resulting in increased sales of everything from nursery plants to washing machines. New construction is, in the final analysis, the largest fabrication industry in the nation, and 16 percent of all employment is directly or indirectly created by this industry.

It should be recognized that most of the phenomenal growth in residential, commercial, and industrial construction has taken place in and around Standard Metropolitan Statistical Areas. The Bureau of the Census defines an SMSA as "a county or group of contiguous counties (except in New England) which contains at least one central city of 50,000 inhabitants or more or 'twin cities' with a combined population of at least 50,000." In these areas, comprising 1.5 percent of the total land area in the United States, lives 73.5 percent of the population. By 1975 it is anticipated that the population of urbanized areas will be close to 200 million; in 1970 it was over 149 million persons. The concentration of population in the

METROPOLITAN POPULATION IN 8 MULTISTATE REGIONS AND THE 19 LARGEST METROPOLITAN AREAS
1950, 1962 and 1975

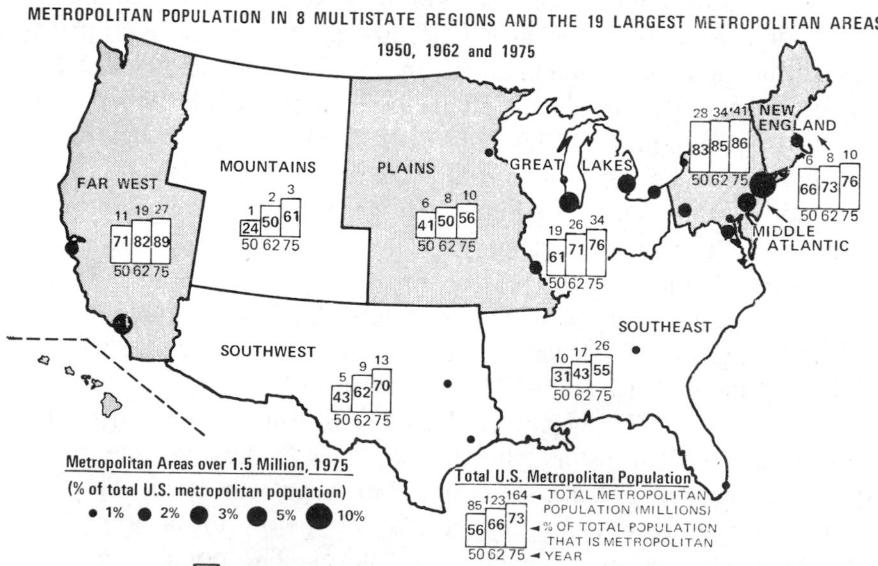

Source: *Looking Ahead,* Vol. 15, No. 5, p. 4, National Planning Association.

metropolitan areas in 1950 and 1962 and the prediction for 1975 can be seen on the map at the bottom of page 2.

It becomes obvious at once that most of the aspects of the real estate business, other than rural real estate, are concentrated about the 248 Standard Metropolitan Statistical Areas, constituting what is broadly classified as *urban real estate*.

CHARACTERISTICS OF LAND

The major physical characteristic of land is its *fixed location*. From this springs a second characteristic, namely, *heterogeneity*. Land is unique. There are no two parcels exactly alike. It is not fungible, that is, no two parcels can be mixed as can two measures of wheat or two barrels of oil. This factor has led to important special legal treatment of land as will be pointed out in subsequent chapters of this text. Land is also *indestructible*. Land does not wear out, except through erosion and depletion. This may affect the value of the land for farming purposes, and perhaps somewhat for residential purposes, but as a general rule land remains the same physically year after year.

In addition to the physical characteristics of land, there are certain economic characteristics. Land is relatively *scarce*. The *improvements* on the land are relatively long-lasting. This suggests that demand has a tremendous effect on both price and intensity of land use, demand being particularly important when the commodity demanded is relatively scarce. *Location* is a third economic characteristic of land. Location, coupled with population and standards of living, tends to produce greater values in one parcel of land as opposed to another.

In this chapter, then, the primary concern is with the economic and social impact of real property transactions with their many facets. Secondarily, the concern is with a broad overview of the many ways in which individuals and business firms engage in the commercial aspects of real property transactions.

RESIDENTIAL HOUSING

From 1970 to the end of 1972 private residential construction (nonfarm) jumped from \$31.9 billion to an amazing \$54 billion, an increase of \$22.1 billion in just two years.

Need for Housing

Three major factors involved in predicting the continuing need for dwelling units are population growth, household formation, and mobility.

Population Growth. Babies are being born at a slower pace than in the 1960's, but population is still growing at a rate of about one percent per year. Every two years our population is raised by an amount approximating the population of metropolitan Chicago and its suburbs. Most of this population increase is moving to urban areas. By the year 1985, some demographers estimate that the total population of the United States will exceed 250 million persons and that a large percentage of the increase will be added to the metropolitan areas.

Bureau of the Census figures show that the rates of births per thousand population fell from 23.8 in 1960 to 18.3 in 1970, and that they continue to decline.

The estimates and projections of the total population of the United States are shown in the chart below:

ESTIMATES AND PROJECTIONS OF THE TOTAL POPULATION OF THE UNITED STATES, 1960 TO 1985

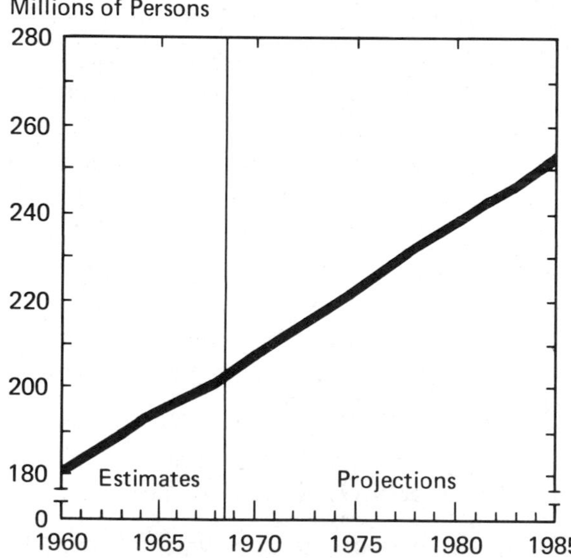

Source: U.S. Bureau of the Census.

Marriages and Household Formation. The Bureau of the Census projections shown in the chart below suggest that total marriages increase rapidly until about the mid-1970's, then more slowly for the rest of that decade. The annual number of marriages is then projected to level off for the first half of the 1980's.

ESTIMATES AND PROJECTIONS OF TOTAL MARRIAGES FOR THE UNITED STATES, 1960 TO 1985

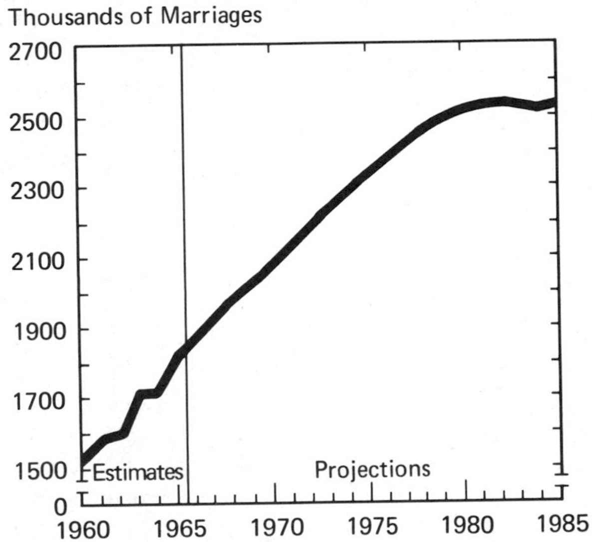

Source: U. S. Bureau of the Census.

Much of the demand for dwelling units is derived from household formation. A *household* is an occupied dwelling unit. Households are divided into two distinct groups: the *normal* household consisting of husband and wife, and the *nonnormal* household, which is generally comprised of bachelors, career girls, divorced persons, widows, or widowers. Very often two or more of these persons, whether related or not, will share the same household.

To a large extent, household formation determines the demand for dwelling space. Between 1800 and 1930 the husband-wife households were about 80 percent of the total new annual household formation. Now the new household formation consists of about 62 percent of husband-wife households and 38 percent of so-called "nonnormal" households.

It has been estimated that by 1985 there will be a total of 84.4 million households of which 59.8 million will be husband-and-wife and 24.6 million "other" households. This is shown on the table below:

Number of Households, Series 1, by Type and Age of Head, for the United States, 1975-85 (Projected)

In Millions

Type of Household and Age of Head	1975	1980	1985
All Households			
Total	70.0	77.3	84.4
Under 25	5.6	6.4	6.5
25-34	15.3	18.6	20.8
35-44	11.7	13.5	17.0
45-54	12.2	11.5	11.3
55-64	11.4	12.1	12.2
65 and older	13.6	15.2	16.6
Husband-wife Households			
Total	50.0	55.0	59.8
Under 25	4.1	4.6	4.5
25-34	12.4	14.7	16.2
35-44	9.7	11.1	13.8
45-54	9.6	9.2	9.1
55-64	7.8	8.3	8.5
65 and older	6.4	7.0	7.6
Other Households			
Total	20.0	27.3	24.6
Under 25	1.5	1.8	1.9
25-34	2.9	3.8	4.5
35-44	2.0	2.4	3.2
45-54	2.6	2.3	2.2
55-64	3.6	3.7	3.7
65 and older	7.3	8.2	9.0

Source: U. S. Bureau of the Census.

These astounding figures do not include an allowance for demolition or for a net increase in the nation's housing inventory. Loss of housing inventory is estimated to range from 250,000 to 600,000 units a year. This loss arises from fire, flood, hurricanes, and highway construction. And with greatly expanded highway construction programs, losses from this source can be expected to rise. For example, by 1975, state and federal governments will have spent $6 billion for *one and a half million acres* in order to complete the 42,500-mile Interstate Highway System.

Mobility. The people in the United States are probably the most mobile that the world has ever known. About one family in five moves each year. This means that approximately 40 million people move every year, many of them to newly developed areas of the country.

The population movement takes place in one of three ways: within the same county; within the same state, but a different county; and to a different state. Movements within the same county are about four times greater than movements either within the same state, but a different county, or movements to a different state. When families move within the same county, likely it is to the suburbs.

The adage "Go west, young man" apparently still holds, but at a slower pace than in the 1950's. In absolute numbers the West has gained, but the rate per thousand has dropped.

For example, the net in-migration to California in the 1970's dropped over fifty percent compared with the 1950's.

Some of the southern states during the 1960's cut losses from out-migration, and a few are showing gains.

The incidence of mobility varies from region to region. In the Northeast, only slightly over 13 percent moved in 1970, while in the West the ratio was almost twice that figure. The high level of mobility in that region might be attributed to the faster pace of suburbanization there.[1]

The net effect of this migration is a decline in demand (hence value) for housing in those areas losing population. At the same time there is an increasing demand (hence value) in those areas with increasing population.

Other Factors Affecting Residential Housing

Gross national product, or GNP, is the total value of all goods and services produced in the nation during a year. *Disposable income* is that amount left to individuals after taxes. The amount of disposable income of individuals has a direct effect on the demand for both older homes and new construction. Costs of construction also influence demand.

---

[1] "A Decade of Suburban Growth," *The Conference Board Record*, V of VIII, No. 9 (September, 1971), p. 49.

Gross National Product. In the early 1960's, residential construction constituted approximately five percent of GNP. Strangely enough, while residential construction outlays increased in absolute terms—that is, the total dollar expenditure increased as a percent of GNP—residential expenditures actually decreased since the boom of the 1920's. For example, such outlays represented 6.6 percent of GNP in 1925 and 6.2 percent in 1926. Today they are about 2.9 percent of GNP.[2] This suggests rather obviously that expenditures for housing are taking a smaller share of the consumer dollar than was the case a generation or two ago.

Disposable Income. Disposable income is extremely important with regard to the economic effects on real estate. Since 1940, disposable income has steadily increased. The percentage of families with more than $7,500 in disposable income has more than doubled since 1947. This means, therefore, that more individuals are in the market for residences simply because they can afford them.

As a general rule, one might say that the proportion of homeowners in any income group varies directly with income. This means the more the disposable income, the more home ownership. This is significant when viewed in the light of the 1956 recession, suggesting that if disposable income decreases greatly and if credit is unobtainable, the real estate industry may have serious difficulties, although in the long run this appears unlikely.

A second general rule with regard to income is that not doubling-up seems to be a result of rising incomes; as incomes rise, there is a tendency for families to move into separate households.

In addition, the higher the disposable income, the more expensive and the better the home demanded. It can also be said that a rise in disposable income speeds up the "filtering down" process. This means that as people's disposable incomes rise, they have a tendency to move to higher priced dwelling units. As individuals move to the higher priced dwelling units, more older homes are made available to persons in lower income brackets, *provided* the prices of older homes do not rise too fast as the result of increased cost.

---

[2] United States Savings and Loan League, *Quarterly Letter,* Vol. 9, No. 1, p. 3. See also Lawrence S. Ritter, "The Political Arithmetic of Recorded National Priorities," *Director's Digest* (October, 1971), Vol. 30, No. 10, p. 1.

Costs. Within recent years, costs of construction have risen more dramatically than the costs of other goods and services. For example, in five years ending in 1970, construction costs rose by 35.4 percent compared with a 21.8 percent rise in the consumer price index. In 1971, building costs rose by 8.5 percent while the consumer price index moved up 5.0 percent.

The median sales price of new homes rose from $18,000 in 1963 to $23,400 in 1970 to $25,200 in 1971. Between September, 1972, and March, 1973, the average cost of a new home jumped $1,200.[3] The increase is partially accounted for by the increase in home sizes. Since 1951, land costs alone have risen about 16 percent per year. The cost of construction, and, consequently, the selling price of homes varies between geographic sections of the nation. The average price tends to be highest in the North Central States and second highest in the West.

One of the major social impacts of the higher cost homes is that new homes are becoming less and less available to lower income groups. At the same time, the prices of older homes have risen closely behind the prices of newer homes, suggesting that older homes are also not readily available to lower income groups. It is further suggested that a continued contraction in homes available for lower income groups might possibly increase political pressure for more direct government intervention in the housing industry.

APARTMENT HOUSES

For statistical purposes *apartment houses* are classified as housing units with more than four dwelling units. In recent years the trend has been toward a greater number of apartment houses. For example, in 1956 the total was 82,300 units; in 1964 the number of units started was 450,000, and in 1971, 779,000.

The chart on page 10 shows some of the characteristics of apartments under construction.

There are a number of reasons given for the increase in apartment living. It appears that large numbers of individuals have become disenchanted with suburbia. Taxes in outlying areas have increased

[3] *The Wall Street Journal,* March 5, 1973, p. 1.

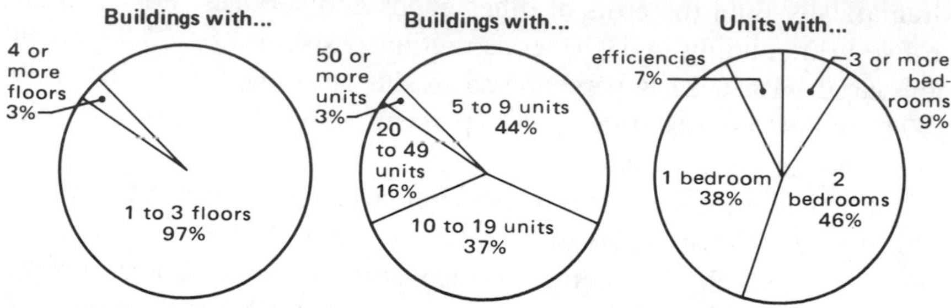

Source: Bureau of the Census, 1971.

rapidly since World War II because of the demand for new schools, parks, and sewage facilities. Commutation tickets have increased together with downtown parking fees and gasoline taxes. Furthermore, builders find apartment-house building attractive because of tax concessions written by Congress into the 1968 Tax Act which permit fast depreciation allowances on new construction.

Perhaps the most important reason for the increase of apartments is the age composition of the population. The median age in the U.S. is now 28 years. Newly formed households are typically demanders of small units, mainly apartments. Furthermore, among younger married people the birth rate has declined recently, leading to an increase in apartment dwelling. The age group over 65 now comprises nearly ten percent of the population. They are demanders of smaller dwelling units and, with increased social security and pension benefits, have the money to pay for these units.

COMMERCIAL PROPERTY

Commercial real estate has been defined as including "all real property acquired for investment except apartment houses, housing projects, and other dwelling units, including stores, shops, and recreational facilities connected with them." [4]

For the most part, commercial building follows the growth and movement of population. Trade is said to follow the customer. Shopping centers are a case in point. A *shopping center* is any area in

[4] Harold Wayne Snider, *Life Insurance Investment in Commercial Real Estate* (Homewood, Ill.: Richard D. Irwin, Inc., 1956), p. 3.

which a number of stores and shops of various types are located and in which a large majority of consumers' wants may be satisfied.

With the flight to the suburbs, the universal use of the automobile, and congestion in the downtown areas of large cities, the shopping center became inevitable. These shopping centers range in size from centers such as Woodfield Mall, at Schaumburg, Illinois, which is the world's largest, to the small nest of stores that can be found in almost any suburban development.

In recent years, shopping facilities have shown an even more marked rise in the relative value of suburban structures compared with those of the central city. The trend has been for a movement of amusement facilities—bowling alleys, drive-in theaters, swimming pools, and others—to follow the suburban pattern.

Office space in central cities has been booming. Millions of square feet of space have been added. Not all growth has been in central cities, however. Various sizes of office buildings or executive parks or complexes have risen in suburban locations. The office building boom has also extended to almost every major city in the United States.

INDUSTRIAL PROPERTY

Industrial property is real estate used in connection with the manufacture of industrial and consumer goods. Industrial goods are goods used for further production, while consumer goods are purchased for immediate consumption. Industrial sites are particularly affected by business conditions in terms of the demand for both industrial and consumer goods.

In recent years there has been a strong trend for industries to move from cities to the suburbs. Much of this movement has resulted from high taxes in the core of the metropolitan areas and lack of space for expansion. Recently some of this movement has ceased as a result of increasing taxes in suburban areas brought about by the need for additional police and fire protection, sewage facilities, water mains, and gas and electric supplies needed to accommodate the new industries.

In no year since 1956 has industrial construction fallen below \$2 billion per year, and in several years it totaled over \$6 billion. One of the current problems relating to industrial construction is the fact that industrial structures are rapidly becoming obsolete due to technological advances. It was suggested some years ago that "in addition to the extensive space required by the machines that have replaced human labor in lifting, stacking, packing, and transportation, greater land area is needed for parking and for terminal facilities required for trucking." [5]

THE SECONDARY IMPACT

In a real sense commercial and industrial properties represent a secondary impact greatly attributable to population increases and home purchases. But this impact is by no means limited to commercial and industrial properties.

Colean and Saulnier in a study pointed this up in their estimate that 100,000 new homes constructed at an average cost of $13,800 would cause the following direct economic impacts:

1. Site improvements, that is, sewage, streets, etc., at $2,000 per home.
2. Other related buildings, that is, religious buildings and auxiliary streets at $3,000 per home.
3. Service expenditures, that is, selling and closing costs at $900 per home.
4. Special outlays, that is, furniture, shrubbery, etc., at $3,000 per home.[6]

They further estimated that the construction of 100,000 new homes results in work to 95,000 on-site workers and 127,000 off-site workers.

SOME SOCIAL IMPACTS

Population pressures bring about demands and economic changes in land uses. Population pressures also raise social costs and diseconomies.

---

[5] Silas J. Albert, "Real Estate Market View Is Brighter," *Realtor's Headlines* (Quarterly Magazine Section), Vol. 30, No. 27 (July 8, 1963), p. 10.

[6] M. L. Colean and R. J. Saulnier, *Economic Impact of the Construction of 100,000 New Homes*, a special study prepared for the United States Savings and Loan League.

A study made at the University of Pennsylvania medical school suggests that urban inhabitants are developing strangely singular mental and physical characteristics. Heinrich Zille, writing of an overcrowded apartment district in Berlin, stated: "You can kill a man with an apartment as with an axe—it takes only a little longer."

Some city dwellers attempt to escape to suburbia whose magnitude is directly proportionate to the congestion of the city complex. Once there, there is a definite difference in the behavioral mechanisms of the in-migrants from the old-established and rooted families. William Whyte in his book *The Organization Man* views organizational living in the outlying areas as mass conformity. The writings of Whyte and others would almost make one believe that suburbs offer complete integration in the community organization with concerted efforts to get along with other people.

With the growth of population, increasing demands are made on our water supply. By 1980 the estimated industrial usage of water alone will be well over 20 *trillion* gallons per year. Currently over 40 percent of the nation is using water that has been used at least once before, and in some cities water is used as much as five times. Water is becoming more polluted, resulting in purification expenses, damage to fish and wildlife, recreation industry losses, and loss due to sickness amounting to an annual cost of untold millions of dollars. In addition, air pollution is making some cities dangerous places in which to live.

"It has been estimated . . . that on an average each year during the seventies an additional $4 billion (above 1970 levels) will be required to improve mass transportation; $10 billion for pollution control; $12 billion to upgrade law enforcement and the judicial system; and $20 billion for improved health and medical care." [7]

Perhaps one of the greatest social costs of larger and larger cities has been pointed out in studies in the field of psychological ecology, the study of the number of people in a given space, their interrelationships and their activities. These researchers have found that the larger the population, the less the involvement, the less the participation, the less the leadership opportunity. All persons—old and young—have more opportunity to serve in a small community. In growing metropolitan areas, people of all ages get less and less

[7] Lawrence S. Ritter, "The Political Arithmetic of Reordered National Priorities," *Directors Digest* (October, 1970), Vol. 30, No. 10, p. 2.

opportunity to become personally involved, with the result that more and more people feel useless and abandoned.

Recently, there has been much written concerning optimum city size and "anti-growth" legislation. For example, Boca Raton, Florida, has an ordinance limiting the number of dwelling units, both apartments and houses, to 40,000, a level expected to stabilize population at 100,000. To do so, a moratorium on building permits is in effect. However, a lower court in San Francisco judged such an anti-growth ordinance unconstitutional, declaring it "reminiscent of the walled cities of antiquity."

A 1972 study by Karvel and Petry strongly suggested that the "optimum city size" be either 100,000 or 250,000. The 100,000 optimum city would provide adequate retail facilities and social amenities, and the 250,000 population city would be designed to support the large industrial firms, the major constraints being a change in our value system, a national dispersal policy for people and industry, and comprehensive central planning. Unhappily they conclude that the idea is likely to prove to be unrealistic and unworkable.

SCOPE OF THE REAL ESTATE BUSINESS

Real Property, Realty, and Real Estate

Real property is defined as the land and, generally, whatever is erected, growing upon, or affixed to the land. Crops requiring annual cultivation are not usually included in this definition. The concept of real property will be more fully discussed in connection with property rights in Chapter 3.

The word *realty* was used historically to connote the land. It is now used in practice as a synonym for real property (which means strictly speaking, the interest in land) or anything which partakes of the nature of real property. *Real estate* is basically a term that has come about as the result of commercial usage. It has two meanings. In common usage it is often employed interchangeably with realty and real property in the sense that it is the thing itself. In the second sense of its meaning, it is the term used to designate those persons concerned with commercial transactions in realty or real property. For example, one might say: "He's in real estate."

Marketing of Real Estate

The average person, when thinking of the real estate business, is apt to think of the marketing or brokerage aspects of the business. The individual contemplating entering the real estate business is also apt to think in these terms, for at present there are nearly 700,000 licensed real estate brokers and salesmen in the 50 states.

Legally, a *broker* is defined as a person who for a compensation negotiates the purchase, sale, exchange, lease, or the rental of real estate or any interest therein. The broker is paid his fee in the form of a commission, which generally amounts to 6 percent of the sale price of the property. By custom and by contractual arrangement, his commission is paid to him by the seller, or if the property is rental property, by the owner of that property.

Real Estate Finance

Real estate finance takes two broad forms: mortgage investing and mortgage lending. A *real property mortgage* is an interest in real property as security for the payment of a debt or the fulfillment of an obligation. These topics will be discussed in detail in Chapter 6.

In mortgage investing, many lenders lend with the expectation of returns on the investment. Some mortgage lenders hope to sell their mortgages to an investor. An insurance company purchasing a block of mortgages in a building project is an example of a mortgage investor. A company that lends money to a builder with the intention of either retaining the loan in its portfolio or of later selling the mortgages to an investor is an example of a mortgage lender. After doing this, the lender collects the monthly payments from the individual borrowers and remits these sums to the mortgage investor. For this he is paid a fee called a *servicing fee*. In addition, the mortgage lender makes a profit from the builder for having found for him the money with which to build.

There are some firms engaged in the business of mortgage brokerage. The function of these firms is to negotiate the sale of mortgages. For example, an individual may own a mortgage that he wishes to sell and convert into cash. The mortgage broker, in return for a commission, attempts to sell this asset to individuals or institutions that might be interested in this sort of investment.

Subdividing and Developing

Subdividers purchase raw acreage and, after having built roads, cut the land up into lots and sell the lots. *Developers* go a step further; they also build homes on the property.

Appraising

An *appraisal* is an attempt to obtain a just and fair valuation of a parcel of real property. (This is probably the most highly specialized field of the real estate business.) The appraiser must have a keen sense of judgment, buttressed by experience and an extensive knowledge of economics, finance, and the law of real property. The individuals engaged in this sort of work may be self-employed, in which case they do their work on a fee basis. Many others are employed by the government or agencies thereof, that is, federal, state, or municipal. Most of those so employed are on a salaried basis. Large business firms, such as insurance companies, banks, oil companies, and chain stores, often employ appraisers in their real estate departments.

Management

A *property manager* acts as an agent for the owner and operates the property for him. His major function is operation of the property so that the owner is able to realize the maximum profit over the economic life of the property. Realization of maximum profit implies the preservation and maintenance of the property over a long period of time.

The most qualified property managers are those having training in the physical, economic, social, and esthetic elements of operation.[8] Professional managers are able to handle the job of operating a building more efficiently than most owners, and their existence can be adequately justified because of their performance of this economic function. The income of the professional manager is generally based on a percentage of the rents collected.

[8] James C. Downs, Jr., *Principles of Real Estate Management* (Chicago: Institute of Real Estate Management, 1967), p. 2.

Often, the one-man brokerage office may find it profitable to take on the management of small properties. However, beyond this, it is often both practical and profitable for the practitioner to add a specialist trained in this area to his staff.

Consultation

With the increasing complexity involved in real property transactions resulting from rapid growth, taxation, and the greater role of government in real estate, the job of consulting or acting in an advisory capacity is growing in importance. *Real estate counselors* determine and advise on alternative courses of action regarding a diversity of problems. For example, an individual lacking knowledge of the subtleties of real estate problems might be wise to seek counsel if he desires to develop property. This counsel might take the form of laying out the development and arranging for financing. Small insurance companies and other investment firms seek the advice of real estate counselors in arranging their mortgage investment portfolios. Industrial firms seeking advantageous sites and others desiring advice with regard to best types of lease arrangements might also seek counsel. Still others attempting to determine the highest and best use of land use the real estate counselors. *Highest and best use* has been defined as that best possible and legal use or employment of land which will yield the greatest return per dollar of investment.

Operators

An *operator* is an individual who buys and sells real property on his own account with the expectation of making a profit. For example, an operator might discover a "sleeper" (a parcel of property underpriced). He might buy this and turn it over quickly for a small profit. Other operators buy *equities.* For example, an owner of a home might have $1,000 of his money over and above a mortgage on a house. The firm for which he is working might transfer him. Where possible, the operator purchases the equity. In short, he pays the owner $1,000 and takes over the mortgage. The operator then attempts to resell the property, sometimes offering it for sale for $1,200 down, thereby making a profit of $200.

Corporate Service

Many of the larger banks, insurance companies, railroads, oil companies, and chain stores have their own real estate departments offering employment in the real estate field. The banks and the insurance companies tend to train mortgage loan men and appraisers. They develop, by this training, all-around real estate investment managers. Some insurance companies develop some of their employees into property managers to handle projects in which they have substantial investments. The chain stores are interested not only in capable appraisers but also, and more important, in men who are able to select the best sites for stores. All of these men must have a knowledge of basic economics, real estate principles, and real estate law.

Syndicate Operation

A *syndicate* is a joint venture that involves two or more people. The syndicate device is used to purchase property when the individual members may have insufficient funds with which to make the purchase. The basis of the syndicate operation lies in the syndicate agreement. This contract usually calls for a statement of the amount invested by the individual members, together with the disposition of the proceeds and capital on the death of an investor; a statement of the property purchased or about to be purchased, if that is the case; and a statement of the appointment of a syndicate manager. More often than not the manager is a professional who is given full control of all matters pertaining to the purchase, management, and selling of the property.

Government

Much of the government activity in the field of real estate deals with aspects of financing. Employment may be found in the Department of Housing and Urban Development and its various related agencies. Appraising work is done by numerous agencies of the government, as well as management of real estate owned or sponsored in some way by the federal government or the municipalities.

Research

Much research into the basic problems of the real estate business is done by various agencies of the government. For example, some work is being done involving the complexities of the housing market. This is just one of the many hundreds of problems being investigated. Much basic work is being done at universities and colleges. The NATIONAL ASSOCIATION OF REALTORS, as well as state real estate associations, and some of the real estate boards in the larger cities and counties have, in recent years, become ardent supporters of this type of research.

Rehabilitation

Rehabilitation consists of remodeling basically sound older buildings with the purpose of increasing the yield of these properties. As will be pointed out in detail in Chapter 29, many such projects are carried out by professional real property managers. However, individuals and practicing brokers also find this a profitable area of the real estate business.

The National Association of Realtors

The National Association of Real Estate Boards, commonly called NAREB, was founded in 1908.

On November 14, 1972, the Board of Directors changed the name from the National Association of Real Estate Boards to the NATIONAL ASSOCIATION OF REALTORS®, effective January 1, 1974. By October 1, 1972, it had reached an active membership list of approximately 106,000 members. The major purpose of this trade association is to encourage high standards of business conduct among its members. In 1913 NAREB drafted its first Code of Ethics, comprising three major parts: (1) the realtor's professional relations, (2) the realtor's relations to clients, and (3) the realtor's relations to customers and the public. The complete Code of Ethics of the NATIONAL ASSOCIATION OF REALTORS is given in Appendix A.

The term "REALTOR" was coined by Charles N. Chadbourn, a member of the Minneapolis Real Estate Board. It was presented to and adopted by the National Association of Real Estate Boards in 1916. The term is owned and controlled by NAR whose ownership has been decided by numerous court decisions, and anyone not duly authorized by the Association is not entitled to designate himself a REALTOR in any manner.

An individual broker belonging to a local member board of the NAR is generally a member of the state real estate association in the state in which the local board is located, as well as a member of the NATIONAL ASSOCIATION OF REALTORS itself.

As NAR grew with the passing years, it was recognized that specialization within the real estate business itself was growing. To fill the need for organizations of specialists, NAR began to sponsor specialized associations, or institutes. Membership in these associations has as a prerequisite membership in NAR. However, the institutes themselves have set other prerequisites for membership. These prerequisites generally take the form of experience, special examinations, and recommendations by other members.

The institutes promote higher professional standards, educational facilities, publications, and, in general, the dissemination of new ideas for their members. The special institutes are:

1. National Institute of Real Estate Brokers.
2. American Institute of Real Estate Appraisers.
3. Institute of Real Estate Managers.
4. Society of Industrial Realtors.
5. Institute of Farm Brokers.
6. The Society of Real Estate Counselors.
7. Women's Council.
8. International Real Estate Federation.

Actually, the main function of the institutes is to raise professional standards. Two of the institutes, for example, the American Institute of Real Estate Appraisers and the Institute of Real Estate Managers, have very high educational, practical, and ethical requirements for entrance. The former, which now requires a college degree or an acceptable equivalent, carries an M.A.I. (Member of the Appraisal Institute) designation, and the latter, C.P.M. (Certified Property Manager). An analogy can be found in the C.L.U. designation of the American College of Underwriters in insurance.

QUESTIONS FOR REVIEW

1. Discuss the physical and economic characteristics of land.
2. One of the demand factors for houses is household formation. Discuss.
3. The age grouping of population may determine the demand for the quality of housing. Discuss.
4. Population pressures are said to create social impacts as well as economic impacts on real estate. Discuss.
5. List and describe five areas of the real estate business.

PROBLEM

1. In the light of the discussion of housing costs in the text, discuss the following conclusions drawn by Richey and Clettenberg:

"There is a large gap between what millions of households can afford to pay for and the cost of providing ownership of what is regarded as adequate housing. Assuming that current zoning and building codes represent the minimums of adequate housing and that ownership is a part of the goal, fewer than one half (41 percent) of the households have the income to meet these goals. This means that 59 percent of the households do not have the necessary income.

"Proposals for bridging the gap involve the lowering of the cost of housing through advanced methods of housing production and land utilization; the filtering down of housing cast off by higher income households; the paying of housing subsidies to the suppliers of housing; and the replacing of the property tax with other methods of taxation; and the raising of the income level of these households by income subsidies, job training, and improved job accessibility. Since it is doubtful that any or all of these programs can completely bridge the gap, we must look to redefining our goals. Home ownership may be too luxurious for many households to qualify. Both used owner-occupied homes and used apartments will enable still additional millions of households to qualify for home ownership.

"Finally, low-income households are very likely being harmed by housing standards that are unrealistically high. Possibly, housing standards should be lowered so as to bring them more in line with ability of these millions of households to pay and the willingness of the taxpayer to support housing and income subsidies." [9]

[9] Clyde W. Richey and Karel J. Clettenberg, "Bankruptcy of Subsidized Housing," unpublished paper, April, 1973, with permission of the authors.

SUGGESTED READINGS

Ring, Alfred A. *Real Estate Principles and Practices,* 7th ed. Englewood Cliffs, New Jersey: Prentice-Hall, Inc., 1972. Chapter 3.

Weimer, Arthur M., Homer Hoyt, and George F. Bloom. *Real Estate,* 6th ed. New York: The Ronald Press Company, 1972. Chapters 5, 6, 7, 21.

Chapter 2

The Real Estate Market and Market Analysis

In recent years there has been an increasing recognition of the need for real estate market analysis. Much of the demand for market studies has come from financial institutions. Where large sums are involved, the financial institutions simply will not finance solely on the assurance by developers that a proposed project is sound. They want much more; often a study or economic analysis proceeding from the nation, to the state, to the local market—with emphasis upon the last.

THE BUSINESS CYCLE

In their constant fluctuation, business conditions tend to rise and fall in peaks and troughs of activity. The National Bureau of Economic Research defines the business cycle as follows: "Business cycles are a type of fluctuation found in the aggregate economic activity of nations that organize their work mainly in business enterprises; a cycle consists of expansions occurring at about the same time in many economic activities, followed by similarly general recessions, contractions, and revivals which merge into the expansion stage of the next cycle; this sequence of changes is recurrent but not periodic in duration; business cycles vary from more than one year to ten or twelve years."[1]

Both the blessing and the curse of our economic society lie in specialization and division of labor, which gives rise to interdependence. We have become a nation of specialists in which each individual is dependent upon the others. It is a rare situation when one man produces an entire product; today many men are engaged in the production of a single commodity. A recession in one part of our economic activity can, therefore, produce chaos in many other parts throughout the entire economic system.

The primitive man with his plot of ground, ax, shovel, and hunting equipment knew no business cycle, no manic variations between the exhilaration of prosperity and the melancholia of a depression. Neither, however, did the primitive man know the benefits resulting from our interdependent money economy.

Phases of the Cycle

For purposes of analysis, the business cycle has been divided into four distinct phases. The first of these phases is called the period of *expansion.* It is here that business activities are on the upswing. Characteristically, more and more durable goods are being manufactured. Demand is increasing. The businessman who formerly needed only three machines now needs and orders ten machines, or he may order larger and more complex machines. Employment is increasing, and national income and savings are up; and more and more money is being poured into new investment, generating a multiplying effect on national income. The future looks bright, and business looks toward further expansion.

But business conditions do not level off and remain at a high point. When the peak is reached, the second phase, the *recession,* sets in. A downswing is now perceptible. Following the recession, the third phase of the cycle, the period of *contraction,* begins. This is the opposite of the expansion period of the cycle. Fewer and fewer durable goods are purchased. The businessman, who in the expansion period bought more machinery, now begins to take his machines out

[1] Wesley C. Mitchell, *What Happens During Business Cycles* (New York: National Bureau of Economic Research, Inc., 1951), p. 6.

of production and orders no new ones. Fewer goods are manufactured; unemployment grows by leaps and bounds; wages drop and with them national income; savings and new investments are small. Conditions become darker and darker.

The length of the stay at the bottom of the trough varies until one day a *revival* period begins after machines have become worn and inventory has declined. This is the fourth and last phase of the cycle. Then it begins all over again.

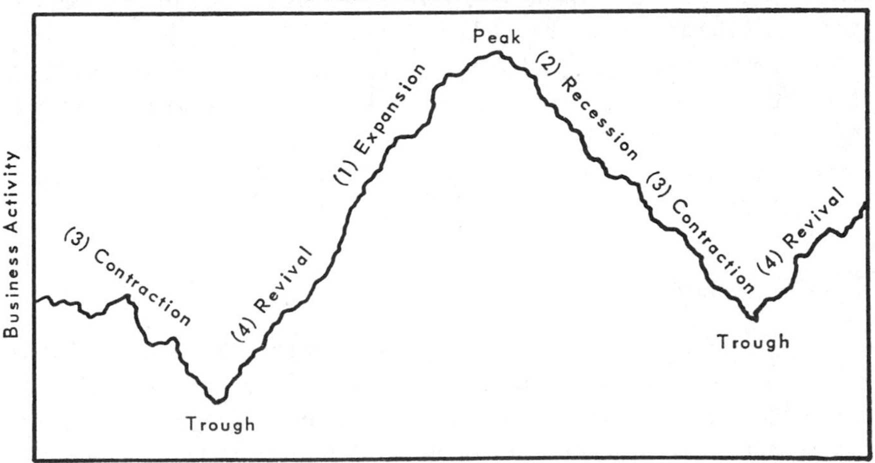

The Four Phases of the Business Cycle

Other Business Cycle Concepts

Although we shall regard the interrelated phases of the cycle as being (1) expansion, (2) recession, (3) contraction, and (4) revival, it should be remembered that many writers on the subject differ in their concepts.

Haberler, for example, lists the phases as: (1) the upswing (prosperity phase, expansion), (2) the downswing (depression phase, contraction), (3) the upper turning point—that is, the turn from prosperity to depression (downturn), and (4) the lower turning point —that is, the turn from depression to prosperity (upturn, revival).[2]

[2] Gottfried Haberler, *Prosperity and Depression* (Lake Success, New York: United Nations, 1946), pp. 268-269.

Schumpeter also believes in a four-phase cycle, namely: (1) prosperity, (2) recession, (3) depression, and (4) recovery. However, in his analysis he divides the "upper" half of his four-phase cycle into two parts: (a) prosperity and (b) recession. He feels that in the prosperity phase employment will continue to increase, but at slackening rate, until the peak of the cycle is reached. In the recession phase, employment decreases until a point of inflection is reached. At this point the cycle moves into the lower half of the cycle which is divided into two phases: (c) depression and (d) recovery. In the depression period employment decreases, but at a gradually decreasing rate, until the trough of the cycle is reached.[3]

Other writers on the subject of the business cycle have analyzed it slightly differently, employing various other terms to indicate the various phases of the cycle; but for the sake of simplicity, we shall employ for purposes of our study the terms used in the four-phase cycle as first outlined.

Cycle Movements

There exists in business cycles time-series movements. These time-series movements or patterns are observable and can be measured by statistical techniques. Although there have been measurements made of numerous movements, the most important for our brief analysis are: (1) secular; (2) major business cycles; (3) minor business cycles; and (4) seasonal variations.

Secular Trend. The *secular trend* is a long-run movement (generally thought of as twenty years or more). A long-run trend is thought of as being smooth and continuous. The main trend influences are difficult to evaluate or isolate because the forces of growth or decline are hidden under the pattern of day-to-day surface developments. In the main, however, such things as population growth, capital accumulation, new markets, and technological improvements are thought by many to affect the secular trends.

Major Business Cycles. The *major business cycles* are characterized by the relatively long length of the expansion and contraction

[3] J. A. Schumpeter, *Business Cycles* (New York: McGraw-Hill Book Co., Inc., 1939), pp. 207-209.

phase. They have varied in length from six to thirteen years. The contraction and expansion phases seem to have no relationship. Sometimes the expansion period is much longer than the contraction period and sometimes seems to be of almost equal length.

Minor Business Cycles. The *minor cycle* is of shorter duration than the major cycle and is generally superimposed on a major cycle. The average duration of the minor cycle is about three and a half years with a range of two to nine years. Generally it is felt that the major cause of a minor cycle is brought about by adjusting of sizes of inventories to short-term changes in the prospective level of sales.

Seasonal Variations. Monthly, quarterly, and weekly data suggest that there exists a regular recurrence of *seasonal fluctuations.* For example, the construction industry is more active during certain periods of the year than other periods, and so is the manufacture and production of various goods such as manufacture of ladies' handbags.

These repetitive intra-annual changes are thought for the most part to be related to climate, holidays, vacation periods, and even differences in the number of working days within a month. These patterns frequently are repetitive because they are entrenched in custom.

Causes of Business Cycles

There are numerous theories given as causes for cyclical fluctuations in business. Generally, however, the causes are categorized as being either external or internal. Some interpreters of the business cycle feel that the wide variations in the cycle result from activities purely outside or external to the economic system. These causes are identified as wars, political situations, new discoveries of important minerals, population growth, technological innovations, and even sunspots!

Other interpreters of business cycles look within the economic systems for causes of the cycle. Basically, the idea is that certain things happen within the system that are self-generating. Machinery, for example, is worn out and must be replaced; thus, an expansion period follows. While the machinery is being consumed, a period of contraction results.

In the final analysis, the variations in the business cycle are probably caused by both internal and external factors. Investment in capital goods, technological changes, population growth, and other factors all play a part in the business cycle.

Government Policies

Theoretically, in a free-enterprise system the "invisible hand" of Adam Smith leads to a self-correction of the business cycle. Smith, the first of the modern economists, felt that each individual in pursuing his own selfish good was led, as if by an invisible hand, to achieve the best good of all. But in a mixed economy of private enterprise, government, and monopoly, the "invisible hand" does not operate as Smith believed it would—at least not in the short run.

The government has entered the picture of the business cycle in an attempt to even out amplitudes of rise and fall from trough to peak and from peak to trough. It is no longer felt that the economic lives of men and material should be wasted as we go from expansion to contraction and from contraction to expansion. Therefore, the government has entered the picture with a *countercyclical compensatory* or *anticyclical policy.*

The countercyclical compensatory policy is designed to do two things. First, if private investment and prices go too high and an inflation is in the offing, an attempt is made to reduce government spending and increase taxes in order to remove money from circulation. It must be kept in mind that government spending has an effect on the price structure much in the same manner as the spending of individuals. Hence, to cut down on government spending and to increase taxes means less money available to purchase goods; therefore, prices will drop.

The second half of the countercyclical policy operates in an opposite manner. If business slumps, the government increases spending and decreases tax collections.

How is this policy effectuated? It may be brought about in part by public works. In times of depression or recession, it is advocated that the government spend for public works. The argument is that in addition to pouring money into the economic system, expenditures in poor times for government buildings and the like are more economical because material and labor are cheaper.

A difficulty with this, however, lies in the proper timing of public works. That is, who is to say when to begin and when to stop; for that matter, it may be impractical to stop at all.

Another argument against public works lies in the fears that are aroused in the private investor. He may fear that the investment or spending by the government will compete with him, and thus he will be disinclined to risk his funds. If this is so, the government expenditure will probably be to no avail.

A second method of the countercyclical policy is the adjustment of welfare expenditures and unemployment compensation. Here, too, government expenditures will increase with bad times; but as conditions improve, the thought is that the expenditures on these items will reduce themselves automatically as people leave the rolls of the unemployed and become employed.

A third phase of the countercyclical policy lies with credit controls, either direct credit controls or through bond manipulations by the Treasury Department and/or Federal Reserve System. Direct credit controls, as far as real property is concerned, may take the form of placing a floor on down payments for real estate purchases. The amount of the floor usually depends upon the purchase price.

The tremendous effect of the monetary policies of the Federal Reserve System on the real estate market is discussed in detail in Chapter 15. There it will be shown how the Federal Reserve raises and lowers the interest rates and thus affects the supply of money for real estate financing.

State and Local Conditions

More often than not the economies of the individual states tend to move in the same direction as the national economy. However, this is not always the case. For example, a state whose economy is predominantly agricultural may, at certain times, be more seriously affected by adverse business conditions than a state whose economy is more diversified. Information with regard to state business conditions can be obtained from *The Federal Reserve Bulletin*, the *Monthly Review* of the federal reserve bank in the district in which the state is located, and from bureaus of business research of state universities.

As previously indicated, the real estate cycle tends to rise and fall with general national and state business conditions. Yet there are times when local booms and depressions occur that do not follow the pattern of general business activity. Some areas seem to be in a state of constant depression. The hard coal regions are a case in point. People have substituted oil for coal; thus demand for coal has decreased, unemployment is the norm, and the localities suffer accordingly; ultimately real estate prices decline. Many of the factors affecting the economy of a state, and consequently demand for local real property, were pointed out in Chapter 1. Some of these are population growth, mobility, and household formation.

THE REAL ESTATE CYCLE

It is necessary to have some concept of the business cycle in order to understand the real estate cycle or what is often called the building cycle. Even though only the barest outline of the business cycle has been given above, the discussion is sufficient to point up the similarities and interrelationships of the business cycle and the real estate cycle.

Although comparatively few studies have been made of the real estate cycle, it is generally agreed that building activity follows to a degree the business cycle in a wave-like movement. It is further indicated that the volume of real estate activity does not necessarily advance with the increases in general business, and declines in real estate activity generally precede general business declines. It appears that the troughs and peaks of the real estate cycle go deeper and higher than those of the business cycle.

Thus, as a warning, one should be cautious in thinking that the volume of business activity necessarily is an infallible guide to conditions in the real estate market.

Length of the Real Estate Cycle

We have already seen that the length of the major business cycles varies from six to thirteen years in length, while the length of the minor cycles varies from two to nine years. The so-called "national building cycle" was first charted by J. R. Riggleman. He based his charts on building permits issued from 1830-1934. Regular fluctuations are noticeable in Riggleman's work, with the cycles running from fifteen to twenty years, or nearly twice as long as the major business cycles. The average length of the cycle is about 17.3 years. It is Riggleman's study that is generally referred to when one speaks of the building cycle and/or real estate cycle.

The postwar cycle, at least in terms of housing starts, seems to be of relatively shorter duration, averaging from peak to trough about 43 months with decreases in housing starts ranging from a —12.5 percent to a low of —46.6 percent and increases ranging from a +20.4 percent to +86.5 percent. This is detailed on Table I below.

TABLE I

Postwar Cycles in Private Nonfarm Housing Starts

DATE OF PEAK (P) OR TROUGH (T)	DURATION (IN MONTHS) OF		PERCENT INCREASE OR DECREASE	PERCENT INCREASE IN FIRST TEN MONTHS OF EXPANSION
	EXPANSION	CONTRACTION		
October 1947 (P)	—		—	—
February 1949 (T)		16	—27.6%	
August 1950 (P)	18		+86.5	+60.4%
July 1951 (T)		11	—40.7	
October 1952 (P)	15		+20.4	+12.0
August 1953 (T)		10	—12.5	
December 1954 (P)	16		+36.5	+13.1
February 1958 (T)		38	—38.8	
December 1958 (P)	10		+44.4	+44.4
December 1960 (T)		24	—35.1	
December 1965 (P)	60		+48.9	+26.2
October 1966 (T)		10	—46.6	
August 1967	10			+64.4

Source: U. S. Department of Commerce, Bureau of the Census.

Recently there has been some feeling that the real estate cycle is predominantly a function of many scattered and local markets, the local markets showing greater degrees of variation than the aggregate, both in amplitude and frequency. Regarding this, Gottlieb makes the following statement:

> While we have extensive data on long building cycles from many individual urban communities—and for aggregates of them—we do

not have many case studies stretching over years of real estate market behavior out of which the demand for new residential building is derived. The full-length case studies show the interplay of variables—sales prices, rent rates, population growth, income, development, construction costs—out of which the long building cycle emerges. I feel deeply that this interplay must be studied in its local setting and not—as has been the case—in aggregated form if we are to understand the process of interaction or measure the influence of the variable at work.[4]

The Rationale of the Building Cycle

Price is determined by supply and demand. The price of an item is that point at which supply and demand are equal, or at equilibrium as it is called. Thus, the price for housing or for rental payments may be said to be at that place where supply and demand are equal, the point where the supply and demand curves intersect if they are shown graphically.

In a sense, real property is unique; it is different from most consumer goods that are produced. This uniqueness results from the fact that the supply of real estate cannot be as rapidly adjusted to its demand as can other consumer products. For example, if the demand for refrigerators declines, the factory producing the refrigerators may immediately shut down or curtail its production, thus affecting the supply of refrigerators. Such an adjustment, however, cannot be made so readily in the real estate business.

In the real estate cycle, if a decrease in demand takes place, prices will decrease, but the supply will remain for all practical purposes the same. Then, as people cease living in single units and two or more families begin living together due to economic pressures, the availability of existing housing increases. This is, in effect, an increase in supply together with a reduction in demand that causes the amplitudes of the real estate cycle to be even greater than those of the business cycle.

What, then, are some of the reasons for the revival in the real estate cycle? If there has been a long period of depression, the supply of buildings will gradually decrease. As buildings depreciate, they are taken off the market. With an increase in general business conditions,

---

[4] Manuel Gottlieb, "Building and Business Cycles," *Proceedings of the American Statistical Association, 1959*, pp. 78-96.

there will be a steadily increasing demand for housing. The doubling-up process reverses itself. People begin living in single units; demand then begins to catch up with supply until the point is reached where demand is greater than supply with a consequent upward pressure on prices.

Finally new construction is planned, and contracts are let. Construction is begun, but lags until such time as construction workers are recruited into the building trades from other jobs that they held during the depression period. There is a further lag from the beginning of construction to its completion. Once building activity is on the upswing, however, it continues even after the peak of general business conditions has been reached. The reason for this is the impracticability of ceasing construction in a stage of partial completion and the lack of knowledge as to supply conditions. This period of completion may last for several years.

There are other things within building activity itself that cause a slowdown in building activity. As building activity increases, costs increase because of diminishing returns and the fact that the supply of materials is not perfectly elastic and the price of materials increases as the demand for them increases. Investment funds may become increasingly more difficult to obtain as the pace of construction activity increases. As a consequence, this, too, will have its effect upon effective demand.

In industrial construction the picture is much the same. In a depression, less and less space is used; but during an expansion period, this space is utilized fully. Existing plants may become obsolete and cause construction of new industrial plants. Population growth causes a slow permanent growth of manufacturing facilities. At the peak of the cycle, construction begins in plant facilities; this, too, causes construction activity to remain at a high point even when the boom is passed.

THE REAL ESTATE MARKET

If someone says: "I have put my house on the market for sale," or "I have put my house on the market for rent," the question immediately arises: What does he mean by "market"? Generally, a *market* is defined as a sphere within which price-making forces operate and in which changes of title tend to be accompanied by actual movement of the goods affected. This general definition is suitable when attempting to explain the term as it is employed to describe the market for grain, the market for refrigerators, or the markets for many other types of goods that are offered for sale. But the term "market" as it is used in real estate means something very much different.

In the first place, a building being offered for sale is quite different from a building being offered for rent. In the second place, there seems to be no commodity exchange. Instead, real estate is offered for sale or rent by owners and brokers and the market tends to act informally. In the third place, because of the fact that real property is fixed, no movement of the goods takes place although there may be a transfer of title. In the final analysis, we find many isolated markets which tend to be connected with and affected by the overall real estate cycle and the business cycle as previously described. We do, however, find in these isolated markets competitive forces at work that do tend to bring about a uniform price for similar properties. Those forces are supply and demand.

What Makes a Good Market

A good market can exist only when competition is able to operate. Competition consists of the buyers bidding against the sellers until a price is established. At times there is said to be a seller's market, and at other times a buyer's market is said to exist. A seller's market exists when relatively few properties are being offered for sale to a large number of buyers. A buyer's market exists when the opposite condition prevails.

Thus, for an efficient market to operate there must be neither a seller's market nor a buyer's market, and both must have knowledge of the conditions prevailing in the market. In addition, and perhaps more important, for competitive forces to operate effectively the product must be standardized and relatively nonperishable. Real estate is not standardized: it is differentiated by location within a housing market area, by size, orientation, mechanical equipment, price, and rental class. Furthermore, the buyers and the sellers often have incomplete knowledge of the market. Thus, the real estate market operates inefficiently as compared with the market for "personal" goods.

Functions of the Real Estate Market

Although it is generally agreed that the real estate market operates inefficiently compared with other markets, it does perform certain necessary economic and social functions.

One function of the real estate market is to determine the use of land. Accordingly, in the long run it has a strong influence on city growth. Since people in the role of investors in real estate are constantly striving to secure the highest return on their investment, they determine how land will be used. Furthermore, returns from land are generally maximized if land is put to its highest and best use. As indicated previously, *highest and best use* means the utilization of property to its greatest economic advantage or the largest return of income over a given period of time. Thus, in the real estate market, competition tends to force land to be put to its highest and best use to insure investors the highest returns. Therefore, it may be said that the real estate market determines how land will be used within the limits imposed by zoning and other governmental and private restrictions.

The other major function performed by the real estate market is the adjustment of space to demand. This adjustment is done on either a long-run or a short-run basis. It might be said that the market rations available space. For example, if there is a sudden demand for space, this will be reflected in the real estate market by an increase in rents. If this demand persists over an extended period of time, an adjustment of space will be made by creation of new housing units to meet the increased demand.

Being aware of the real estate market and its implications, one might next ask: What are the factors that cause a change in prices, and how does one analyze these factors?

Analyzing the Residential Real Estate Market

The residential real estate market is analyzed by weighing certain supply and demand factors, giving relative weights to the factors, and drawing certain conclusions from them.

The first problem in any market analysis is to determine the primary objective of the analysis. For example, an analysis of the condominium market is quite different from an analysis of the single-family residential market. By the same token an analysis of the market for one-bedroom apartments is different from the market for three-bedroom apartments.

Demand Factors. What are the demand factors in the real estate market that may under some circumstances be converted into sales?

Population. The first thing to determine about a community or an area where a study is being made is population trends. Is population rising, static, or falling? Frequently, these figures are obtainable from the Bureau of the Census, a county planning board or state planning board, *Sales Management's* "Survey of Buying Power," or a local chamber of commerce. Often a good estimate can be had by obtaining the ratios of school children and adult population in prior census years. Then, given the number of school children, the present adult population can be approximated and when added to the number of school children, a close estimate may be made of total population. For example, in 1970 the census of a village revealed that there were 1,000 adults and 100 school children, or 10 adults for 1 child. The present count of school children showed 150. One could assume that there would still be 10 adults for each child, or a population of 1,500 adults and 150 children. These figures must be adjusted, of course, to reflect any change in the average size of the family.

Once having obtained gross figures on population, it is important to determine the composition of the population. For example, how many are in the 25 to 34-year-old group, 35 to 44, and so forth? This is important in terms of the reason you are analyzing the market. For purposes of illustration, suppose you are trying to determine if there is a market for tri-level homes. If it turns out that a large portion of the population is over 65, then the project might better be forgotten.

Family Size. Family size is another market factor again depending on the objective of the market analysis. For example, it has been determined that condominium owners generally have three or fewer members in the household. On the other hand, if it is determined that each household in the market area has more than three members, it is probably a bad market for condominiums.

Income, Employment, and Wages. The determination of income of the population is important for purposes of analyzing the possible price of the real estate product. For example, suppose you are analyzing a potential market for $50,000 homes. Obviously, the persons who might buy at this price must have substantial incomes.

Employment is assuredly a dynamic factor in regard to the conversion of latent demand into effective demand, that is, the ability of the individual to convert his desires to purchases. Employment rarely becomes fixed at a constant figure, but is in a constant state of flux. The important thing for the subdivider to keep in mind is the *trend* of employment in the area in which he is planning his subdivision by examining the figures over a period of time. From a positive viewpoint, increasing or steady employment in a particular area is indicative of chances for success for a subdivision when weighed against the other factors that are discussed. Negatively, decreasing employment in an area over a period of time indicates chances for failure, for with decreasing employment demand for housing will slacken.

In order to determine employment trends, data must be obtained. The best sources of this information are state employment agencies. They are able to supply statistics for previous years so that an employment trend can be determined.[5]

Positively, rising wages, when correlated with rising employment and when properly weighed against other factors, indicate that the time may be ripe for subdividing or developing. Conversely, falling wages indicate that the moment is inopportune.

Information relative to wages also may be obtained from state employment agencies. These reports indicate the number of persons employed in an area and the total wages paid over a period of time to these persons. From these figures the average wage of the persons employed over the period is easily determinable.

Marriage and Divorce Rates. Increasing marriages can generally be interpreted as a sign of an increased future demand for housing. By the same token an increased divorce rate often, but not necessarily, is indicative of a decline in the demand for housing units.

---

[5] In Chapter 27 *some* of the same factors will be examined, but with a different objective, that is, the city as an economic base.

Information concerning marriages and the number of divorces granted can be obtained from the office of the county clerk in the county in which the market is being analyzed.

Doubling-Up. The use of one housing unit by two or more families is usually referred to as *doubling-up*. In general, doubling-up increases with a decline of general business activity. Exact information of the amount of doubling-up is almost impossible to obtain. The only practical available sign is in the increasing number of housing vacancies as compared to general population trends. If the population of a city is static or if the population is increasing and if vacancies are on the rise, this may be taken as an indication of doubling-up.

Supply Factors. Demand factors taken by themselves are insufficient to analyze the real estate market. These factors must be considered together with the supply factors. If the demand is high and the supply is even greater, then the time is probably not right for developing or subdividing.

Vacant Units. The normal rate of vacancy for an area is considered to be about 5 percent of the available units. If demand factors are high and vacancies are at normal, then it would probably be an indication that a development is in order. If vacancies are abnormal, for example, 15 percent, it might be indicative that sales in a development would lag until the surplus housing units were absorbed.

In many areas, the local real estate boards maintain records of vacancies. In some areas, the post office is able to supply this information. If these sources do not have the data, it may become necessary to contact a representative number of property managers to obtain a fairly accurate estimate of vacancies. The 5 percent figure given as normal for vacancies is only a rule of thumb and may vary in some localities.

Construction Costs. As costs affect the supply of all consumer goods, so do costs affect the supply of housing. As costs mount, supply has a tendency to fall until there is an adjustment upward of selling prices. Construction cost is a factor, then, that must be weighed before beginning a development.

Here, too, local real estate boards and qualified appraisers should be contacted to determine construction costs. Many boards have compiled accurate records of costs. The building department of the city should also be contacted in order to obtain cost data.

Labor Supply. Another factor to be taken into consideration is skilled labor. A shortage of skilled labor in an area will have a tendency to affect the supply of housing that can be built.

Indicators of Market Activity. Two of the best indexes of market activity are mortgage foreclosures and deed transfer series.

Mortgage Foreclosures. The rate of mortgage foreclosures is a good indication of the status of the local real estate market as well as the national real estate market. Increasing numbers of foreclosures are usually an indication of a decline in real estate activity. Some students of real estate cycles draw a fairly close parallel to the number of foreclosures and the rise and fall in the real estate cycle.

Information regarding mortgage foreclosures can be obtained in the office of the county clerk of the county where the information is being sought.

Deed Transfer Series. Deed transfer series are indications of what may be expected in the real estate market in the immediate future. The procedure is generally to obtain from the county recorder's office the number of deeds recorded by month and year for at least two real estate cycles back. From these statistics relationships can be drawn between transfer activity, income, and foreclosures. In addition, turning points in transfer series may point to turning points in the foreclosure series and thus be a basis for forecasting.

Great care must be taken to distinguish between the gross deed series, bona fide sales, and foreclosures; deeds in lieu of foreclosures; voluntary surrenders; condemnations; non-bona fide sales, which include deeds of gift, deeds given for business convenience, and inheritance. It can readily be seen that these latter deeds might distort a deed series, that is, indicate much market activity when transfers took place only for business convenience.

Weighing the Factors. After having obtained data concerning the various supply and demand factors, it is necessary to weigh these various factors one against the other. For example, ordinarily an upward pressure on rents indicates a strong possible demand for housing units. This factor considered by itself is insufficient and should be weighed against construction costs. If costs are rising, the question is whether they are rising more rapidly than rents. If rents are rising more rapidly than costs and wages are rising and employment is steady, this would be an indication that housing units should sell in spite of rising costs of construction. In the same manner, all of the data in an analysis should be weighed, and consideration should be given to its relative merits.

Index Numbers. The handiest device for weighing supply and demand factors is to create indexes so that the series of data collected may be compared over a time period. The creation of indexes involves conversion of absolute figures to relative figures. For example, if the average home price in a community in 1970 was $20,000 and the average price in 1974 is $25,000, it is simpler and more meaningful to say that the average price in 1974 is 25 percent higher than in 1970 than it is to speak in absolute numbers.

Base Period. Index numbers must be used in conjunction with a base period in order to make the index meaningful. A year selected as the base year should be a "normal" year. For example, it would create bias if a year of abnormal mortgage foreclosures were to be picked for the base year. The base period should be recent since relative prices tend to change over time and distortions are more likely to appear.

As an example, if an individual has run a deed series in a particular county, it might appear as follows:

YEAR	NUMBER OF DEEDS RECORDED IN ORANGE COUNTY	INDEX 1965 = 100
1965	23,356	100.0
1966	28,777	123.2
1967	32,357	138.5
1968	38,133	163.3
1969	43,981	188.3
1970	59,742	255.7
1971	49,595	212.3
1972	42,084	180.2
1973	40,365	172.8
1974	46,032	197.1

To determine, for example, that in 1973 the index number is 172.8, the market analyst will divide the number of deeds recorded in 1973 by the number of deeds recorded in 1965. Then to obtain what amounts to a percentage figure, multiply by 100. For example,

$$\frac{40{,}365}{23{,}356} \times 100 = 172.8$$

Rental Housing Projects. There are essentially five major questions that must be answered in order to test the feasibility of producing a rental housing project.[6] They are as follows:

1. What type and size of family unit is in greatest demand? This requires a close examination of the local market in terms of competitive projects. This also includes a determination of the number of vacancies in the local market, a determination of proposed projects, and a determination of the unit size demanded.

2. Where are the particular locations in which these units will command and continue to command the maximum rentals? There is a tendency for the market to pay for the size and type unit it desires according to the desirability and popularity of the location. In short, higher rentals are obtainable in the choice locations, and lower rentals are obtainable in those areas that are considered to be less desirable.

3. How much does it cost to acquire the land and produce the property? The figures can be obtained from an architect; and, of course, if the costs in terms of the estimated returns are too great, then the project is not practical.

4. How much will it cost to operate the property? This can be determined from a comparison with properties of similar nature. It is customary in rental properties to think of *effective net income*, which is the income the property will return at the proposed rentals, assuming the property is 100 percent rented, less an allowance for vacancy and collection losses.

5. What rate of return on capital does the market demand? This means that one must determine the return necessary to induce intelligent investors to invest in this type of property. As a practical matter, if the rate is 6 percent and the effective net income is $5,000 on

[6] Federal Housing Administration, "How to Test Financial Soundness of Rental Housing Properties" (Washington, D. C.).

a proposed structure which will cost $100,000 to build, then investors will not invest because 6 percent of $100,000 is $6,000. This suggests that intelligent investors are more likely to invest in an alternative investment opportunity where they will be able to receive 6 percent on their investment. This matter will be dealt with more completely in Chapter 25.

THE NONRESIDENTIAL MARKET

The nonresidential real estate market is divided into three broad categories: (1) commercial or business space; (2) office space; and (3) industrial and warehouse space.

In all of these areas the supply of space is more often than not limited by municipal zoning regulations. A *zoning regulation* is a limitation placed on the *use* of land by a municipality. However, the supply outside the borders of urban areas is generally not as limited.

Commercial or Business Space

There are three subdivisions of commercial and business space: (a) the central business district, which is at the heart of the city's retail structure; (b) the outlying or secondary shopping district, which arises as a city increases in population, and covers a broader area (large cities often contain a number of these districts); and (c) neighborhood business streets, which are generally more numerous than secondary shopping districts and are generally located near or next to one another.

In addition, there are, of course, the shopping centers built since World War II. "From 1,000 centers at the end of 1955, the number advanced spectacularly to 4,500 at the close of 1960, to an estimated 12,500 by December, 1970. By 1985 an additional 12,000 are expected to be in operation." [7]

It is important for the real estate practitioner to recognize *why* certain types of retail businesses tend to move to certain areas. To

[7] Delbert J. Duncan, Charles F. Phillips, and Stanley C. Hollander, *Modern Retailing Management* (8th ed.: Homewood, Illinois: Richard D. Irwin, Inc., 1972), p. 95.

do this one must be aware of the traditional classification of consumer goods which are divided into three parts: (1) *Convenience goods,* which are consumer goods purchased frequently and at the most accessible places. Razor blades are an example of this—men in need of a shave don't care where they get the blades as long as they get them. (2) *Shopping goods* are goods for which the consumer desires to compare prices, styles, and quality. A woman shopping for an expensive dress will want to compare prices, styles, and quality at several stores. (3) *Specialty goods,* which are goods infrequently purchased and possessing attributes which induce people to go out of their way to make their purchases. High-grade men's shoes or suits with well-advertised brand names are examples of specialty goods.

Thus, the real estate practitioner should recognize that those stores selling convenience goods should be located close to large numbers of people or where people congregate or pass. Stores handling shopping goods tend to locate in "100 percent" downtown districts and tend to cluster together. Because only a few stores sell goods that can be strictly termed "specialty" goods, they tend to build a reputation above that of competitors and draw trade from wide areas. Thus, they may be found in almost any one of the three commercial or business districts, but they do not necessarily have to cluster together.

Because leases are recorded in the office of the clerk of the county in which the property is located, brokers often have access to this information. Availability of parking space, accessibility of auto traffic, and public transportation are important in analyzing the demand for certain types of space. Some surveys have shown, for example, that customers will walk only 350 to 400 feet from the source of transportation to the store. More important perhaps is a consideration of traffic flows. This is one of the price considerations from the viewpoint of the retailer and, consequently, is of major importance in a determination of the demand for the space. The retailer is not only interested in numbers of possible purchasers but will want to classify them according to sex, their purpose in passing, and their ability to purchase. This latter point suggests that in analyzing traffic flows retailers generally think in terms of the high, the middle, and the low income group classifications which potential customers may fit into.

Office Space

The largest quantity of office space is generally found in downtown central business districts in the skyscraper-type buildings. In addition to office space found in central business districts, there is also such space in secondary districts. Often these districts contain many buildings of the so-called "taxpayer" type. A *taxpayer* is generally a two-storied building with a store on the first floor and office space on the second floor. These properties were the outgrowth of the depression of the thirties and were built by landowners who were seeking only enough profit from their operation to pay the real property taxes.

Businesses rent office space which is often used as a "prestige" item for the business firm. The cost of construction, including land costs, is high and new construction is limited. Financing is difficult to obtain because of the risks involved, and financial institutions are reluctant to lend money on this type of venture unless the prime tenant is a financially strong firm; thus, many institutions regard these loans as "nonstandard." As a result of this attitude on the part of lending institutions, rather large down payments in cash are required for buildings of this sort.

During periods of prosperity, demand for this type of space reaches a high peak and has a tendency to fluctuate with the various phases of the business cycle which have been described previously in this chapter.

Industrial and Warehouse Property

Like commercial property, industrial and warehouse sites are often limited by municipal zoning regulations. With the growth of suburban rings around the standard metropolitan statistical areas, the demand for industrial space has shifted somewhat from the area of the central city to the areas outside the central city. Important in the selection of an industrial site are handy transportation and easy accessibility for workers. Access to power, sewage, water, and other utilities is also important.

In analyzing the market for local industrial and warehouse space, an inventory of available sites is made. In addition, the local analyst should be aware of the local zoning authorities' attitudes on the possibility of "spot" zoning other areas. *Spot zoning* means zoning for activities other than called for in existing regulations. An inventory of this sort, of course, constitutes the supply of available space. Once the supply has been determined, it becomes necessary to investigate the factors within the city as outlined in Chapter 27, "The City as an Economic Base."

QUESTIONS FOR REVIEW

1. What is generally meant by the expression "equilibrium"?
2. How is real property different from other types of consumer goods?
3. List three of thc five questions which must be answered to test the feasibility of a rental housing project.
4. Define *highest and best* use.
5. In determining the market for retail store space, why is it relevant to know the various classifications of consumer goods?

PROBLEMS

1. Prepare a market analysis of your town, your county, and your state, using as a guide the information given in the text.
2. In a market study done to determine a "condominium" market for a community, it was discovered (a) that 67 percent, or 12,400 heads of households, were either under 35 years of age or over 55 years of age; (b) that 35 percent of these 12,400 earned over $10,000 per year; and (c) that the 12,400 households had three or fewer members. It was further determined that these criteria were common to condominium purchasers ($25,000 bracket):

   (1) The family membership was limited to three or fewer.

   (2) The head of the family was either under 35 or over 55 years of age.

   (3) The cash income of the family was in excess of $10,000 per year.

Based on the above, how many prime prospects are there for the $25,000 condominiums?

SUGGESTED READINGS

Ring, Alfred A. *Real Estate Principles and Practices,* 7th ed. Englewood Cliffs, New Jersey: Prentice-Hall, Inc., 1972. Chapter 3.

Ring, Alfred A. *The Valuation of Real Estate,* 2d ed. Englewood Cliffs, New Jersey: Prenticc-Hall, Inc., 1970.

Weimer, Arthur M., Homer Hoyt, and George F. Bloom. *Real Estate,* 6th ed. New York: The Ronald Press Company, 1972. Chapter 9.

Chapter 3

The Nature and Classification of Property Rights

Before one can understand real estate principles or the real estate profession with any degree of completeness, it is necessary to have some understanding of the various means and degrees by which title to real property may be held.

The idea of "property" has had a long and complicated history. Philosophers, economists, and lawyers have all had a hand in the development of the idea of property. Some regard *property* as the rights and interests of an individual in anything subject to ownership. Some regard property as anything having value in exchange. In any event, the right of property can exist only when it is protected by society from encroachment by others. For our purposes here we may look upon the first definition as a working tool.

CLASSIFICATION OF PROPERTY

Property is divided into sets of rights involving land and personal things (*chattels*). Historically, these rights or proprietary interests were classified as analogous to things of a physical nature; namely, (1) land or those things annexed to the land so as to be considered a part of it, and (2) articles of a movable character that were neither annexed as a part of the land nor annexed in the view of the law as a part thereof.

After the middle of the seventeenth century, these two classifications were commonly referred to as *real property* and *personal property*. The names were derived from two types of legal actions: one called "real actions" and the other "personal actions." The first was an action brought by persons who were deprived of freehold interests (interests of indefinite duration) in land, or incorporeal things, such as the rights to the use of another's land. The second or "personal action" was brought to obtain restitution from deprivation of movable goods. The first action was said to "sound in realty" and the second to "sound in personalty."

Real Property

One classification of rights or interests referred to above became known as real property interests. Real property was defined in Chapter 1.

The land, in legal theory, is conceived of as being not only the lot or tract referred to in a deed, but as extending upward over the land to the sky and downward from the lot to the center of the earth. Most attachments to the house or building become a part of the real property and are dealt with under the heading of fixtures.

Personal Property

Just as the first class of rights became known as real property, so the second classification of rights became known as personal property interests. *Personal property* is defined as everything that is subject to ownership and not coming under the domination of real estate; hence, anything that is not attached to the land or any buildings thereon. These articles, that is to say *things* themselves, are called *personalty*. Thus, the interest or ownership of an automobile is a personal property interest. The thing itself, the automobile, is personalty. In practice, "personal property" is used as a synonym for "personalty."

Some property interests in land are treated as personal property. Often these interests are called leasehold interests, for they are created by leases. Leasehold interests are discussed more fully in the chapter on leases.

Sometimes an article of real property may change in character from real property to personal property. For example, trees when growing are to be considered a part of the real property; and the ownership therein is a real property interest. However, when the trees are cut, they are considered as being personalty, even though they may be lying on the particular parcel of real property on which they grew. The interest in the cut trees becomes a personal property interest and is no longer a real property interest.

Fixtures

Just as trees or other types of real property may change in character from real property to personal property, so may personal property change to real property. Articles that have changed from personalty to real property are commonly known as *fixtures*. Confusion sometimes exists as to when personal property becomes real property. For example, an oil burner displayed in the window of a store is an item of personal property. However, once the oil burner is removed from the store and installed in a permanent manner and has become an inherent part of a building, it is then classified as real property. When attached to the building in a permanent manner, it is commonly called a fixture.

The Tests of a Fixture

In determining whether or not an article placed in a building is a fixture, the courts will look into the intent of the parties, the method of annexation, the relation of the parties, and the adaptation of the article.

Intent of the Parties. The courts, upon raising the question of the intent of the parties when an article is placed in a building, ask whether or not the item was attached with the idea (or intent) of making it a permanent part of the building. Refrigerators in apartment houses have been held to be a part of the real estate.[1] The

[1] *Guardian Life Insurance Company* v. *Swanson*, 286 Ill.App. 278, 3 N.E.(2d) 324.

reasoning has been that the refrigerators were installed and were *intended* to remain permanently because their presence increased the rental value of the apartments.

The Method of Annexation. The courts consider the method of annexation of an article to real property and raise the question of whether there would be substantial injury to the real property if the article were removed.

The plumbing in a house must be regarded as a fixture, for substantial injury to the property would result from its removal. There exists, too, what is known as *constructive annexation* in the case of those articles that are not fastened to the realty but are made for use in connection with real property. A key is an example of this.

The Relation of the Parties. Suppose a landlord rents a building to a tenant for the purpose of operating a restaurant and the tenant installs a counter. Could the landlord claim that it was a permanent fixture and that its title had therefore passed to him? He could not, for the court will encourage a tenant to equip himself with the necessary tools of his trade. The tenant, however, must remove the counter, called a *trade fixture*, before the expiration of his lease; otherwise, it would become a fixture. If it became a fixture, it would be regarded as real property and title would pass to the landlord.

The Adaptation of the Article. This test also tends to show the intention of the annexing party. Where an article is essential to the purpose for which the building was intended, it is presumed to be a fixture. This presumption holds true even though the article can be severed from the building.

TITLES TO REAL PROPERTY

A *title* is a legal right referring to the ownership of property One may hold titles to personal property and real property. An *estate* is the interest that a person holds in land.

Titles may be divided into original titles and derivative titles. *Original titles* include those acquired by discovery, occupancy, conquest, or cession. *Derivative titles* are subdivided into titles by descent and titles by purchase.

Original title to real property can never be in an individual, but is acquired by a nation. It may be acquired by discovery. At one time the mere discovery of land, not subject to any civilized nation, vested title in the nation whose subject made the discovery. However, at the present time, discovery gives only the first right of occupancy to the nation.

Title by occupancy comes about when the first nation to occupy a territory not before owned by any civilized nation acquires title thereto. *Title by conquest* arises when one country takes territory from another by force of arms. In such cases only the title to public lands is affected; private land titles usually are recognized. The last method of obtaining original title is by *cession*, which includes all titles derived by grant from one country to another.

Derivative titles are all titles that are not original titles. An individual can hold only by a derivative title. Derivative titles are obtained either by purchase or by descent. *Title by descent* arises when a person obtains land from a relative who dies intestate (without a will). *Title by purchase* includes all methods of acquiring title other than by descent. Technically, the word "purchase" includes transfers by will, voluntary transfers, and involuntary transfers.

Private Grant

Most grants or transfers of property are between individuals. The transfer is effected by means of a deed. A *deed* is an instrument conveying (transferring) the lands of one individual to another. A deed may be voluntary or involuntary. A voluntary deed is made pursuant to an agreement between the parties, and an involuntary deed is made pursuant to an order of the court. Deeds are discussed in greater detail in Chapter 5.

Dedication. A transfer of property by an individual to the public is called a *dedication*. For example, when *A* desires to grant a parcel of realty to the public for a road, he does so by means of a dedication. There must be an intent on the part of the grantor to surrender it to the public, and the public (government) must accept the grant.

Devise. The *devise*, a will or clause in a will conveying property, is a form of private conveyance. Wills disposing of real estate must be in writing and must comply with the statutes of the various states. A more thorough treatment of wills is presented in Chapter 5.

Public Grant

A *public grant* refers to the granting of title to public lands by a governmental body. The authority to grant title to such lands is given by the Congress of the United States, or the legislature of a particular state, either by a special act expressly transferring certain lands to certain parties, or by a general act expressing the means by which individuals may acquire title to public lands. In the first instance the special legislative act serves as evidence of title. In the second instance, persons acquiring title under a general legislative act receive a patent from the government. A *patent*, in this sense, is a complete appropriation of the land it describes and a conveyance of all interests in that land to the grantee. In the exercise of this right, the state must exercise due process of law.

Title from Nature

Title from nature arises from either accretion or reliction. *Accretion* is the increase of land caused by gradual and imperceptible additions thereto caused by the washing of a body of water. *Reliction* (or *dereliction*) is the gradual recession of waters leaving dry land where there had formerly been water.

Title from Civil or Political Relations

Under certain circumstances, title to property may be taken by governments against the wishes of the owners of the property. Details of the circumstances are explained in the following paragraphs.

Eminent Domain. *Eminent domain* is the power of the government, upon payment of due compensation, to take property for public use, or to authorize such taking by a corporation or individual engaged in a quasi-public operation. In the exercise of this right, the taker must exercise due process of law.

Escheat. *Escheat* is a second method of acquiring title from civil or political relations. This is the right of the government to take the property of an intestate (a person dying without a will) who dies without leaving any heirs.

Confiscation. *Confiscation* is the right of a government to take the property of its enemies in time of war. Generally, this right is confined to personal property, but it may extend to real property.

Forfeiture. In the United States, property of an individual may inure to the state by virtue of *forfeiture* for one of two reasons: failure to pay taxes or treason.

Titles from Public Policy

Under certain circumstances, an individual may take titles or use property contrary to the wishes of the owner of the property. Details of the circumstances are given in the following paragraphs.

Adverse Possession. *Adverse possession* is the right of an occupant of land to acquire title against the real owner, when the possession has been actual, continuous, hostile, visible, and exclusive for the legal period. More detailed information is given about this method of acquiring title in Chapter 5.

Prescription. *Prescription* is the right of an adverse user of another's land who continues the use of this land for the legal period.[2] This use results in an *easement*, the right which one individual has in the land or the profit of the land of another. An example of an easement is the right-of-way one may have over the land of another.

ESTATES AND INTERESTS IN LAND

Estates

An *estate* is the interest that a person holds in land. Estates are divided into several types according to the degree of interest held.

[2] In most states, statutes prescribe the time period; a minority of the states still follow the common law.

Estates according to their quantity or duration of interest are divided into *freehold estates* and *estates of less than freehold*. The endurance of an estate of freehold is of indeterminate length. It is distinguished from the estate of less than freehold because the length of the latter is capable of accurate determination. The estates of freehold are generally treated in the legal sense as real property; the estates of less than freehold are generally treated as personal property in the nature of leasehold interests. Estates of the latter type are discussed in Chapter 7.

Estates of freehold are further subdivided into estates of inheritance and life estates. The *estate of inheritance* is one which upon the death of the holder still continues and descends to his heirs, while the *life estate* extends for the life of an individual.

The Fee Tail

The *fee tail* is a limited estate restricting the transfer or alienation of property in that it must pass to the descendants of the property owner. The fee tail, which is both a freehold estate and an estate of inheritance, has been virtually abolished in the United States. It has a certain historical significance, for it insured the passage of land to lineal descendants of the first holder of the estate tail.

Fee Simple

The *fee simple* or the *fee simple absolute*, as it is sometimes called, is an absolute estate. It is the largest estate and most prevalent interest in land; it is the entire property in land—the complete ownership of land. During his lifetime, the owner of fee simple title may do anything he wishes with the land, provided that he does not use the land as a nuisance. Thus, having the complete ownership of the land, the owner may dispose of it entirely by sale or by gift during his lifetime. At the death of the owner, he may dispose of the property by will. If he leaves no will, it will pass to his issue, if he has any, or to his collateral relatives in the event that he has no heirs of his body.

Creation During the Owner's Life. Because the fee simple is the absolute ownership in land, the owner may dispose of the land in any manner he desires during his lifetime. This type of ownership, being the more common, is thus most often subject to transaction. For there to be a valid transfer of real property, there must be a competent grantor and a grantee capable of taking title. The *grantor* is the person by whom a grant (transfer) is made; the *grantee* is the person to whom a grant is made. A competent grantor is usually a person of legal age and sound mind. A grantee capable of taking real property is any person natural or artificial (a corporation), unless excluded by state statute. Some states prohibit some aliens from owning land, Idaho and Arkansas, for example. The deed creating the fee simple will either read "from *A* to *B* and his heirs" or that "*A* bargains, grants, and conveys unto *B*," depending upon the state statutes.

Creation by Will or Descent. A fee simple may be created either by will (devise) or by descent. If *A* dies and by will leaves his property to *B*, then in due course of time *B* will receive from the executor of *A's* estate a deed called an executor's deed. In the event that *A* dies without a will, then an administrator of the estate will be appointed and *A's* heirs will receive from him an administrator's deed.[3] Both of these forms of deed can effect a conveyance of a fee simple.

Since fee simple is the absolute ownership of real property, it follows that all other estates in real property must be held in terms of quantity of ownership or time of holding that are less than a fee simple.

The Fee Simple Determinable

The *fee simple determinable* is a freehold estate, one of indefinite duration, but is less than a freehold estate of inheritance. The determinable fee, sometimes called a qualified fee or a base fee, is an estate in fee that is to continue until the happening of a certain event. For example, *A* conveys property to a church, so long as the realty is used for a church; in the event that the property is not used for a church, the property is to revert to *A* or his heirs. This is a fee simple determinable, and the church will have the fee so long as the property

[3] Although title actually passes upon death, the administrator makes out the deed.

is used for a church. *A* and his heirs are spoken of as having a possibility of *reverter*. If the property ceases to be used for a church, *A* or his heirs get title to the property.

Because one of the essential characteristics of a fee is that it may endure forever, the named event creating the determinable estate must be a contingency, not a certainty.[4]

Fee Simple Conditional

The *fee simple conditional* has been defined as "an estate restrained to some particular heirs, exclusive of others, as to the heirs of a man's body, by which only his lineal descendants were admitted in exclusion of collateral; or to the heirs male of his body, in exclusion of heirs female, whether lineal or collateral."[5] It is called a conditional fee by reason of the condition expressed or implied in the donation of it that if the donee died without such particular heirs, the land should revert to the donor. In short, a limitation was made on a transfer of real property with the implication that if the donee did not produce the particular heirs named, then the title would go back to the donor. If he did produce those heirs, then the donee took the property in fee simple.

Estate on Condition

An *estate on condition* is one which, by the terms of the instrument by which it is created, is subject to a contingency not forming a part of the limitation of the estate. If the estate is to begin on the happening of a contingency, it is called an *estate on condition precedent*; if it is to terminate on the happening of a contingency, it is called an *estate on condition subsequent*. Most states have abolished the estate on condition precedent.

The normal estate on condition subsequent is created as follows: *A* gives land by will to his widow for life, provided she does not remarry. The nonmarriage is the condition subsequent. If she does marry, *A's* heirs may *reenter,* or make a claim for the estate. If they do not make this claim within a reasonable time, the widow may

---

[4] Herbert Thorndike Tiffany, *A Treatise on the Modern Law of Real Property and Other Interests in Land* (Chicago: Callaghan and Company, 1912), Sec. 81.

[5] *Willis v. Mutual Loan & Trust Co.,* 183 N.C. 267, 111 S.E. 163, 165.

retain the estate. This is the big distinction between the fee simple determinable discussed above and the estate on condition. In the fee simple determinable the estate is terminated by the mere happening of the event. In the example above, by the mere fact that the widow remarried while in the estate upon condition, the heirs, or whoever else has an interest in the property, must take some action to terminate the estate.[6]

The Life Estate

The *life estate* is an estate that one may receive either for the duration of his life or the life of another. This latter estate is known technically as a life estate *pur autre vie*. The recipient of the estate for life may receive it either by deed or by will, or in some states by law where estates are granted to either a widow or a widower as the result of the marriage. For example, *A* may by deed convey to *B* for life, and upon the death of *B*, to *C* and his heirs. The grantee of a life estate is generally referred to as the *life tenant*. As life tenant, he may do with the estate almost as much as he could with a fee simple, subject, however, to a number of exceptions.

1. The life tenant may sell. The grantee of a life estate will receive an estate that will terminate upon the death of the life tenant. As a practical matter, upon the sale of the life estate, the life tenant will not be paid nearly so much as the real value of the property because the purchaser will be aware that he may lose possession at any time.
2. The life tenant has a right to receive any rents or profits from the land, but he cannot injure the land to such an extent as to commit waste upon the land.
3. He is entitled to what is technically known as *estovers*, which is the right of the life tenant to take a reasonable amount of wood from the land for fuel and for repairs to any buildings on the land.
4. Like any other tenant, in the absence of any agreement to the contrary, the life tenant is bound to make reasonable repairs,

[6] The possibility of reverter was made assignable by New York Statute effective September 1, 1962. New Jersey and Connecticut adopted a similar statute over 100 years ago.

but he need not make any improvements. If he does make improvements, he cannot recover the cost from the owner of the inheritance.

5. The tenant must pay interest on encumbrances and taxes.

A life tenant may mortgage a life estate, but the mortgage terminates with his death. Upon the death of the life tenant, the mortgage would no longer constitute a lien upon the property.

The life estate, as outlined, is an example of what is commonly called "fee splitting." The absolute ownership of the land was divided, part of the estate going to someone for life and part being more or less held in abeyance during the lifetime of the grantee or the lifetime of another. The problem then arises as to how these interests in real property are dealt with. Commonly, they are called remainders and reversions.

Remainders and Reversions

If *A* conveys to *B* for life and upon *B's* death to *C* and his heirs, *B* has received from *A* a life estate. What, then, has *C* received? *C* has received an interest in the estate called a *remainder*, and *C* himself is called the *remainderman*. Remainders are either vested remainders or contingent remainders. If the remainderman can be determined at the time of the grant, then the estate is called a *vested remainder*. *C*, in the example, can be determined; hence, the interest that *C* has in the estate is that of a vested remainder. Upon the death of *B*, *C* or his heirs will be entitled to the fee simple.

Contingent Remainders. The *contingent remainder* exists when the remainderman cannot be ascertained at the time of the transfer. For example, *B* conveys to *A* for life with a remainder to *A's* eldest son. This is contingent until a son is born, at which point it becomes vested. If the transfer reads to *A* for life and the remainder to the eldest son at the time of *A's* death, then the remainder would still remain contingent until *A's* death, because at that time only can it be determined who is the eldest living son.

Reversions. If, in the examples above, the grant had read "*B* to *A* for life and upon the death of *A* to *B* and his heirs," then it would be said that *B* had a reversionary interest (revert meaning to come back).

Waste

Although the persons having a life estate may use the land and receive the profits from it, they still may not appropriate or injure any part of what is regarded as a permanent part of the land. For example, a life tenant may not take minerals and the like from the land without having committed waste, unless he was expressly permitted to do so by the terms of the grant. The removal or the destruction of a building that is upon the land has been held by the courts to constitute waste. In either case, the life tenant is liable for damages if it is held that he has committed waste. A person having a reversionary interest in the land can bring the action against the life tenant, and the person who has a vested remainder in the land may also bring the action. The contingent remainderman may not bring the action because his interest is a mere possibility and does not ripen until the death of the life tenant.

There is often a possibility of merging the reversionary or remainder interests with the life estate to create a fee. For example, *A* is a life tenant and *B* has a vested remainder. A sale of the fee simple may be made to *X*, if a grant of the life estate is obtained from *A* and a proper deed obtained from *B* of the vested remainder, which will merge the life estate with the vested remainder to transfer the fee simple to *X*.

CONCURRENT OWNERSHIP

Concurrent ownership of property simply means that title to the same piece of property is in two or more persons at one and the same time. This type of ownership is distinguishable from an estate in *severalty*, which is an estate that is held by a person in his own right only, without any other person being joined or connected with him.

The most prevalent type of concurrent ownership is called tenancy by the entireties.

Tenancy by the Entireties

Tenancy by the entireties exists generally only in real property and exists only between husband and wife. When a husband and wife take title together, they are said to hold title as *tenants by the entireties.*[7] The reason for this is the common-law concept that a husband and wife are one person. The deed must be made out to them both at the same time while they are married. If it is made out to them prior to their marriage, no tenancy by the entireties exists. The so-called "grand incident" of the tenancy by the entireties is that the surviving spouse gets title to the entire parcel upon the death of the other. For example, if a couple held a parcel as tenants by the entireties and the husband dies, then the wife receives a fee simple title to the parcel. As tenants by the entireties, neither can sell the property without first obtaining the signature of the other spouse on the deed, and neither can force a partition of the property.

If the husband and wife become divorced, they are then said to hold the property as tenants in common. The reason for this is that the tenancy by the entireties is based upon the common-law theory of the husband and wife being one; after the divorce, there no longer being a unity, there can be no tenancy by the entireties; it must become a tenancy in common.

Joint Tenancy

A *joint tenancy* exists when two or more persons own the same land and have the same unity of interest, time, title, and possession together with the right of survivorship. This latter factor has often been called the "grand incident" of the joint tenancy.

The two or more parties concerned with the joint tenancy are considered as having but one estate in the land. Each is considered to be the owner of the whole. In order for there to be a joint tenancy, the four unities (interest, time, title, and possession) must exist.

1. *Unity of interest* means that the interest of the owners must be of the same duration. For example, if a conveyance were made

---

[7] This is recognized in states of: Arkansas, Delaware, Florida, Indiana, Kentucky, Maryland, Massachusetts, Michigan, Missouri, New Jersey, New York, North Carolina, Oklahoma, Oregon, Pennsylvania, Rhode Island, Tennessee, Vermont, West Virginia, Wisconsin, and Wyoming. There has been an attempt in some community property states to have the husband and wife hold as joint tenants; but title companies have refused to insure these transactions, and its status is in doubt. In Colorado, however, a noncommunity property state, the joint tenancy between husband and wife has been recognized by statute since 1884. In Wisconsin, a deed to husband and wife creates a joint tenancy unless the deed states otherwise.

by the same instrument, to *A* in fee and to *B* for life, there could exist no joint tenancy because one of the four unities would be lacking.

2. *Unity of time* has been construed to mean that the title to the property must vest in the tenants at the same time. One tenant cannot hold the property in possession while another holds it in remainder.

3. *Unity of title* means that both or all of the tenants must have one and the same interest arising out of one and the same conveyance.

4. *Unity of possession* means that each of the tenants must have undivided or equal rights of possession.

The so-called "grand incident" of the joint tenancy is the *right of survivorship*.[8] This means that when a joint tenancy exists, title passes to the survivor upon the death of one of the parties. For example, if *A* and *B* hold property as joint tenants and *A* dies, the title in fee to the entire property passes to *B*. It is for this reason that many of the states have passed specific statutes requiring that the joint tenancy be spelled out in a deed. In Idaho (55-508 ICA) the law states:

> Every interest in real estate granted or devised to two or more persons other than executors or trustees, as such, constitutes a tenancy in common, unless expressly declared in the grant or devise to be otherwise.[9]

To create the joint tenancy the deed should read "to *A* and *B* as joint tenants," or, to be on the safe side, "to *A* and *B* as joint tenants and not as tenants in common."

The joint tenancy, and, of course, the right of survivorship, will be destroyed by a conveyance by one of the tenants to a stranger.

---

[8] In Alabama, Arizona, Florida, Georgia, Kansas, Kentucky, Maine, North Carolina, Ohio, Oregon, Pennsylvania, South Carolina, Tennessee, Texas, Virginia, and West Virginia the right of survivorship in a joint tenancy has been abolished. Thus on the death of the joint tenant, his share passes to his heirs as if it were a tenancy in common, unless the deed expressly states that the property shall go to the surviving grantees.

[9] New York State expresses the same thing thus: Sec. 66. Real Property Law: "Every estate granted or devised to two or more persons in their own right shall be a tenancy in common, unless expressly declared to be a joint tenancy; but every estate, vested in executors or trustees as such, shall be held by them in joint tenancy. . . ."

For example, if *A* and *B* are joint tenants and *B* conveys his estate to *C*, then *A* and *C* hold as tenants in common, without the right of survivorship. If there are four joint tenants, *A*, *B*, *C*, and *D*, and *D* conveys to *X*, then *A*, *B*, and *C* hold as joint tenants to each other and as tenants in common with *X*. If *A* were to die, *B* and *C* would get *A's* share by survivorship and remain tenants in common with *X*.

Tenancy in Common

A *tenancy in common* exists when two or more persons own the same land with undivided interests. Their interests may exist under different titles, or under the same title if it contains words of limitation importing that the grantees are to own undivided shares. There is no right of survivorship in the tenancy in common, distinguishing it from the joint tenancy and the tenancy by the entireties. Also, the tenants may bring a partition action to break up the estate.

Condominium

An ancient concept of co-ownership given a modern dress by virtue of the Housing Act of 1961 is the condominium. A *condominium* is a form of ownership of real property characterized by the fee ownership of individual units, commonly the apartments, coupled with an undivided interest in common with the remainder of the property. Basically the idea is for an individual to own the apartment in which he lives. He pays for it either in cash or by means of a mortgage plus a proportionate annual sum for maintenance and management of the building.

Prior to the Housing Act of 1961, which permitted FHA insurance on condominiums for the first time, there were a number of cooperative apartments which must be distinguished from the idea of condominium. The cooperative apartments are corporations which sell shares of stock to the "tenants." In a cooperative setup, if the corporation failed to pay taxes, the owner could lose his apartment. In addition, the owner could become liable for a tenant's failure to make payments to the co-op. The owner of the condominium can pay off his mortgage, and he cannot be foreclosed upon even if the other owners have not paid. Furthermore, the owner of the condominium can sell without permission of the other owners; but in the case of the cooperative apartments, he must have permission of the other owners. The idea of the condominium is spreading from apartment buildings to business offices in downtown areas.

In order for the condominium to exist, the individual states have to pass legislation permitting city assessors to assess each apartment on an individual basis. This is a prerequisite to the FHA insurance. To date this has been done in a number of states. The first condominium was completed in Hallandale, Florida, in April, 1962. The structure contains sixty units, averaging six and one half rooms per unit with an average unit cost of $23,000 to $25,000.

DOWER AND CURTESY

Dower

In common law *dower* is the right of the wife to a life estate in one third of all of the lands of inheritance that were owned by the husband during the period of the coverture (marriage). Under some of the state statutes, Oregon, for example, the one-third interest provided by the common law has been raised to a one-half interest. This is an example of acquiring title to real property as a result of marriage, and it is also an example of the acquisition of title by law. Dower has been abolished in many states.[10] In some states a property settlement has been substituted in its place. Where dower has been abolished, the wife need no longer join with her husband on a deed conveying the property, unless she holds as a tenant by the entireties or by community property.[11]

Curtesy

In common law *curtesy* is an estate for life given by law to the husband in all of the real property owned by his wife. In order for curtesy to exist, certain conditions must be met. There must be a valid marriage from which there was issue born alive. The husband

---

[10] Colorado, Connecticut, Indiana, Iowa, Maine, Minnesota, Mississippi, Nebraska, New York, North Dakota, South Dakota, Utah, Wyoming, and the community property states.

[11] In Georgia, Tennessee, and Vermont, dower is limited to land owned by the husband at the time of his death.

will then have a one-third interest in all land owned by the wife during the marriage.[12]

Community Property

Community property is a joint interest between husband and wife, existing for the most part in the western United States; namely, the states of Idaho, Washington, California, Arizona, New Mexico, Texas, Nevada, and Louisiana. The law of community property is somewhat technical, but the underlying theory (of Spanish origin) is that the husband and the wife should share equally in property acquired by them through their joint efforts during the marriage. Each has a half interest in the real property. Community property states also recognize the existence of separate property in each of the spouses; for example, that property which may have been owned by one of the spouses at the time of the marriage, acquired later by gift or inheritance, or property purchased exclusively by one of the spouses from separate funds.[13] In the community property states, it is extremely important for the practitioner to recognize the need for obtaining the signature of both parties on an instrument of conveyance, or on any other instrument that might affect the title to real property.

MISCELLANEOUS INTERESTS

Encroachments

An *encroachment* may be best thought of as an overlapping. For example, the most common type of encroachment is that of the eaves of a garage overlapping a property line and extending out over the land and property of another. Branches from trees that extend over a neighbor's property are also classified as an encroachment. When these circumstances exist, the title to the property might very well be considered to be unmarketable; hence, under the general terms of the real property contract when the seller has agreed to deliver

[12] Curtesy continues only in the states of Alabama, Arkansas, Delaware, Hawaii, Maryland, Massachusetts, New Hampshire, New Jersey, North Carolina, Ohio, Oregon, Rhode Island, Tennessee, Virginia, West Virginia, and Wisconsin.

[13] Sec. 31-903, Idaho Code Annotated.

marketable title to the buyer, the buyer may be relieved from the terms of the agreement if the seller is unable, because of an encroachment, to deliver marketable title to the buyer.

Emblements

Emblements are rights in growing crops that a person possesses when the person has an estate in land of uncertain duration. For example, an individual is granted permission to enter upon a parcel of farm property and plant a crop. He takes advantage of the opportunity and plants a crop. The owner of the land may not evict him and take possession of the growing crops. This so-called tenant at will who has planted the crops still has the right to go upon the land to reap his harvest.

Easements

An *easement* is a right in the owner of one parcel of land to use, by reason of such ownership, the land of another for a special purpose not inconsistent with a general property right in the owner.

An example of an easement is a right-of-way over another's property, a party wall, or the right of ingress and egress (entering and leaving) over the land of another. It is, in the final analysis, a nonpossessory right in the use of another's land.

Easements may be acquired or created in any one of a number of ways: by grant, reservation, implied grant, prescription, necessity, or condemnation.

To create an easement by *grant*, an agreement is drawn between the parties, duly signed and acknowledged. It should be recorded in the office of the county clerk of the county in which the property is located in the same manner as any other conveyance.

An easement by *reservation* is generally created in favor of a grantor in a deed. For example, if *A* conveys property to *B*, and *A* desires to retain a right-of-way over the land after the transfer has been completed, he can retain the right-of-way by including in the deed express words that will create the easement in his favor.

A third way that an easement may be effected is through an *implied grant*. Technically, easements of this type are called quasi-easements, but they are usually referred to simply as easements. They may come about in this way: *A* has a house on each of two adjoining lots. On one of them a sewage drain is maintained for the benefit of the other parcel. *A* sells one of the houses to *B* and then refuses to allow *B* drainage through the existing pipe. The courts under circumstances of this kind generally hold that *B* has a right to such drainage, an easement, as a result of an implied grant.

In addition to the above, an easement may be created by *prescription*. For example, *A* uses the land of *B* for a short cut and continues to use the land for the period of time prescribed by the state statute for adverse possession. As a result, he will usually be said to have an easement over the land of *B*. This type of easement is said to arise by prescription.

Another type of easement is that created by *necessity*. This type is created when *A* has a parcel of land and sells the rear part to *B*. If the only way open for *B* to get out onto a highway is over the land of *A*, then *B* is said to have an easement by necessity. There must be an actual necessity, however, or the easement will not exist. But *B* need not use unreasonable means, such as climbing over a mountain, to avoid crossing *A's* land.

In what way, then, are easements extinguished? In the case of the easement by necessity, the easement will be extinguished when the necessity no longer exists. In the hypothetical case given above, if a road is built so that *B* can have a means of egress that is not unreasonable, then the easement will be extinguished and he will no longer have the right to cross the land of *A* to leave his property.

An easement may be extinguished by an express release or by the acquisition by the holder of the easement of the fee. *B*, the holder of the easement (technically he is called the *dominant tenement*), may release the easement or he may purchase the property from the owner, *A* (technically called the *servient tenement*), in fee simple.

An easement may also be extinguished by abandonment. This is brought about when the dominant tenement no longer uses the easement and indicates by his nonuse that he intends to abandon the easement.

License

License is the permission given by an owner of a parcel of real property to perform a particular act or series of acts upon his land.

The recipient of the permission receives no interest in the real property. Generally, the permission may be revoked at anytime by the owner of the property.

QUESTIONS FOR REVIEW

1. List and explain the tests of a fixture.
2. Distinguish between a reversion and remainder interest in real property.
3. The holder of a life estate may not commit waste. How is he restrained and how is the word "waste" interpreted?
4. What is the so-called "grand incident" of the joint tenancy?
5. What is the difference between a freehold estate and an estate of less than freehold?
6. The condominium is sometimes said to have possibilities of restoring the "central city." Discuss.
7. Distinguish between personal property and real property.
8. What is *escheat*?
9. Explain the various ways easements may be created.

PROBLEMS

Although no attempt is being made to create a lawyer out of the student of real estate principles, the fact is that our fundamental concepts of real property come from the law. A study of several cases will enable the student to grasp these concepts more clearly.

1. In the following case, *Ralston Steel Car Company* v. *Ralston,* what type of interest did the court decide the plaintiff had? What difference did it make in this case? How is property classified here?

Ralston Steel Car Co. v. Ralston
112 Ohio 306, 147 N.E. 513 (1925)

The plaintiff, Annie M. Ralston, brought an action against the defendant, Ralston Steel Car Company. Judgment in the lower court was for the plaintiff and the defendant appealed. Judgment affirmed.

Joseph S. Ralston in his lifetime was the lessee of certain real estate in the city of Columbus, under an instrument called a permanent lease, sometimes called a perpetual lease, the tenure of which was for 99 years renewable forever. The estate was insolvent. The widow claimed the lease was real estate and that she was entitled to dower. The creditors claimed it was personal property and therefore the widow had no dower interest in it.

MARSHALL, C. J. Much of the law of real property of this present period is the outgrowth of principles established in England during the feudal period. Classifications and definitions which were applicable then are still employed to a large extent. The obsolete doctrines of the English laws of real property have become the foundations of modern rules, except insofar as their technicalities have been disregarded, and except as they have been modified or superseded by statutory provisions. Property is defined as the right and interest which a man has in lands and chattels to the exclusion of all others.

Blackstone divided property into two classes: Personal, which consists of goods, money, and other movable chattels; and real, which consists of such things as are permanent, fixed, and immovable, as lands, tenements, and hereditaments of all kinds which are not annexed to the person, or cannot be moved from the place in which they subsist.

A hereditament comprehends anything which may be inherited, whether corporeal or incorporeal, and includes both lands and tenements.

These ancient classifications and definitions, which are yet applicable and potent when considered in conjunction with Section 8597, General Code, would seem to leave no doubt that a permanent leasehold is real property.

Blackstone has again divided estates into freehold and less than freehold. He has further described a freehold estate which requires actual possession of the land; again, it is such an estate in lands as is conveyed by livery of seizin. His description is summed up in the following conclusion:

"As, therefore, estates of inheritance and estates for life could not by common law be conveyed without livery of seizin, these are properly estates of freehold."

Estates less than freehold include estates for years, at will, and by sufferance, and in 2 Blackstone 143, the rule is declared that:

"Every estate which must expire at a period certain and prefixed, by whatever words created, is an estate for years."

All authorities agree that in the last analysis the true test of a freehold is indeterminate tenure. Measured by this standard, how can it be said that so-called permanent leasehold is really a lease at all, and what possible reason exists for classifying it as a chattel?

"A grant or lease in fee reserving rent operates as an assignment or sale and not as a lease, although, for some purposes, the relation of lord and tenant, or of landlord and tenant, may be assumed to exist between the parties. Properly speaking, a term of years or other certain period of time and a reversion seem to be indispensable to the idea of a lease."

2. In the following case, *Cook* v. *Whiting,* do you think the decision would have been the same had the timber actually been used for a corncrib? Why?

Cook v. Whiting
16 Ill. 480 (1855)

This action was brought by the plaintiff to recover the value of certain logs and timber removed from his land by the defendant (Whiting). The defendant had sold the land in question to the plaintiff. Prior to the sale the defendant, while still the owner of the land, cut down a large quantity of timber with the intention of building corncribs, fences, and so forth upon the land. It was admitted that the timber sued for was lying upon the premises and not attached to the soil, and that after the sale of the land, the defendant had removed the timber and had sold it. The defendant contended that he had a right to do so, since these felled trees were personal property and did not pass by the deed to the land.

SCATES, C. J. The hewed timbers, posts, and round logs sued for in this case were neither fixtures nor appurtenances to the land, but personal property, and did not, therefore, pass by deed as part of the realty. . . . Here the separation by the act of the owner was complete and he had unquestionably converted it into personalty, though with the intention of reannexing it to the land at some future time. Before this was done, he sold his land and conveyed it; therefore no title to the hewn logs in question passed to the plaintiff.

3. Two sisters and their respective husbands owned adjoining parcels of unimproved property. The defendants built a summer home on what they believed to be their property. Thereafter, a survey disclosed that the building was located 90 percent on the plaintiff's property. The plaintiff brings an action in ejectment and for money damages for withholding possession.
   (a) What is the term to be applied to a situation where a person builds partially on another's land?
   (b) How would you decide this case?

4. *A* had an easement of a road near *B's* land. *B* then raised the road so that *A* could not use the easement. *A* sues *B* to compel him to restore the road. Who wins and why?

5. *A* and *B*, owners of adjoining property, had a common easement. *A*, complaining that the easement area was being used as a general passageway by others, erected a fence and gate which was kept locked so that even *B* could not use it. *B* sues *A* for an injunction ordering *A* not to interfere with his rights. Who wins and why?

SUGGESTED READINGS

Kratovil, Robert. *Real Estate Law,* 5th ed. New York: Prentice-Hall, Inc., 1969. Chapter 3.

Ring, Alfred A. *Real Estate Principles and Practices,* 7th ed. Englewood Cliffs, New Jersey: Prentice-Hall, Inc., 1972. Chapter 6.

Weimer, Arthur M., Homer Hoyt, and George F. Bloom. *Real Estate,* 6th ed. New York: The Ronald Press Company, 1972. Chapter 4.

Chapter 4

Contracts

The contract is the basic legal instrument with which all real estate brokers and their clients eventually become involved. It is the fundamental instrument of the real estate business. Therefore, it is important for the practitioner to have some basic knowledge of contracts as well as the manner in which the contract is specifically applied to real property transactions.

Generally, a *contract* is an exchange of promises or assents by two or more persons, resulting from an obligation to do or refrain from doing a particular act, which obligation is recognized or enforced by law. A contract may be formed when a promise is made by one person in exchange for an act or the refraining from the doing of an act by another. The substance of the definition of a contract is that by mutual agreement or assent the parties have created legally enforceable duties or obligations that did not exist before.

If all the terms of a contract have been fulfilled, it is said to be *executed*. If something in the contract remains to be done, it is said to be *executory*.

In terms of their validity, contracts are valid, voidable, or void. A contract that is binding and enforceable against both parties is a *valid contract.* A *void contract* is neither binding nor enforceable against either party.

A *voidable contract* is an agreement that may or may not be binding and enforceable. In this type of contract, one person usually has an option to avoid or a power to validate the contract. In real property transactions, the question of voidable contracts arises most frequently in cases of contracts with minors—generally under 18 to 21 years of age. As a rule, in a minor's contract—or more accurately, agreement—as long as the contract is executory, the minor is under no enforceable duty; he need do no act of avoidance. However, if the minor receives a part performance and still retains the contract, he must give it up, for its continued retention after his becoming of age operates as a ratification. This means that the agreement will become binding and enforceable.

THE ESSENTIALS OF A CONTRACT

In order for a binding and enforceable contract to exist, certain specific requirements must be met.

The Parties to the Contract

There are always two or more parties to a contract; in real property, the parties are the seller and the purchaser. The parties who enter into a contract may be individuals, partnerships, corporations, or governments. The contract need not be between two individuals, but may exist between any combination of persons or entities having contractual ability. *Contractual ability* means that the parties to the contract must be competent to enter into a valid agreement. The first class of individuals whose competency to contract is in question is minors. To some degree, the relative validity of a minor's contract depends on whether the contract concerns real property or personal property.

Minors' Real Property Contracts. Minors' real property contracts differ from the general rule of law. In general, a minor may disaffirm his contract either before or within a reasonable time after he reaches his majority. *Disaffirmance* is an indication by word or act not to be bound by the contract. The general rule is different, however, in the case of real estate sales. In this case, a minor cannot disaffirm the sale of real estate until after he has reached his majority. However, in some jurisdictions he may recover possession of the property while still a minor; in other jurisdictions the court will require the adult to account to the minor for the use of the property during the term of the latter's minority.

Minors' Personal Property Contracts. In general, when a minor has entered into a personal property contract, he may disaffirm it at his election either before reaching his majority or within a reasonable time thereafter. His contract is said to be voidable. If, after having reached his majority, he does not avoid the contract within a reasonable time, the contract is ratified and is therefore binding. In terms of real property contracts, all of this suggests that great care should be taken to ascertain whether or not the party being dealt with is still a minor.

Insane Persons. The contracts of mental incompetents are generally voidable. As a general rule, the test of mental incompetency is whether or not the individual's mental faculties are so impaired as to render him incapable of understanding the nature or the consequences of his acts in the transaction in question.

If an insane person becomes sane, he may ratify or disaffirm his contract. If a proper court has declared a person to be insane and has appointed a guardian for the insane person, any contracts entered into by the insane person are void. His guardian would have to make contracts for him.

Intoxicated Persons. If an intoxicated person knew that he was making a contract, the validity of the contract is not affected by the fact of his intoxication. If, however, it can be shown that a person was deliberately made drunk in order to induce that person to make the contract, then the contract may be invalidated.

If the person executing the contract was so drunk that he did not know what he was doing, then the contract may be voidable. He may either affirm or disaffirm the contract upon becoming sober but must do so within a reasonable time.

Offer

Not only must the parties to the contract possess contractual ability, but there must also be an offer and an acceptance of this offer. An *offer* is a statement made by one person, referred to as the *offeror*, of what he will give in return for some act or promise of a second person, referred to as the *offeree*. An offer may come to an end at an express time limit, by death of the offeror, or by revocation of the offer by the offeror prior to the time that acceptance is attempted. An offer consists of two parts: the promise and the communication of the promise. Thus, if an offer is not communicated to an offeree, there is no offer, and hence no contract.

In real estate transactions, a property is listed with the real estate broker at a proposed sale price, for example, $20,000. Often the offer is communicated through the broker to a prospective purchaser. Assume for the moment that the purchaser signs a binder or earnest money receipt and in it states that he will pay $18,000 for the property. This action is a counteroffer on the part of the prospect, rather than an acceptance of the original offer, and constitutes an offer to the seller, which he may accept or reject. If the seller says that he will take $19,000, then this is another counteroffer; and the broker communicates that offer to the prospect who may in turn either accept or reject it.

Acceptance

In order to complete the agreement, there must be an acceptance of the offer by the offeree. In a real property contract, the normal transaction contemplates an offer on the part of the seller to deliver possession and title of realty to the purchaser for a price, and an acceptance on the part of the purchaser of this offer and a promise to pay the price. If both parties are thinking of the same thing and there is an offer and acceptance, there is said to be a *meeting of the minds*.

Consideration

The fourth requirement of a contract is the consideration for the contract. Mutual promises may be sufficient consideration, that is, a promise for a promise. The payment of money in return for the conveyance of property is said to be sufficient consideration for a contract. The forbearance by a person of something that he could lawfully do in return for a promise on the part of the offeror is also sufficient consideration for a contract.

In the absence of fraud, the courts will not normally inquire into the adequacy of consideration for a contract. Thus, if a real estate operator purchases a building from *A* for $20,000 and later sells it for $30,000, *A* will not be allowed to say that there was insufficient consideration for the contract.

Legality of Object

In addition to the four parts of a contract outlined above, there must be a legal objective on the part of the contracting parties. In short, the contract must not be in violation of some law or against public policy. In the event that it violates either, then the contract may not be enforceable. A contract, for example, between *A* and *B* whereby *A*, for a consideration, agrees to burn *C's* property is obviously illegal and hence unenforceable.

Real estate contracts ordinarily deal with objectives and objects that are neither illegal nor against public policy and ordinarily are not set aside on this ground.

The Statute of Frauds

The *Statute of Frauds* involves contracts which must be in writing to be enforceable. One section of the statute requires that contracts relating to real property be in writing in order to be enforceable. If *A* agrees with *B* to purchase a lead pencil for the price of $1 and *A* agrees orally to deliver the pencil and then fails to do so, *B* may bring an action against *A* for any damages that he may have suffered. If the same situation takes place, except that the oral agreement contemplates the transfer of real property rather than personal property, and *A* fails to keep his end of the bargain, *B* will be unable to bring a successful action against *A*, for oral contracts concerning many real estate transactions are void under the Statute of Frauds. It is stated, for example, in Section 259 of the New York Real Property Law as follows:

> A contract for the leasing for a longer period than one year, or for the sale of any real property or an interest therein, is void unless the contract, or some note or memorandum thereof, expressing the consideration, is in writing, subscribed by the party to be charged, or by his lawful agent, thereunto authorized in writing.

The other states in the union in their statutes make substantially the same declaration.

Of what then must this memorandum in writing consist to render a contract for the sale of real property enforceable? There are four things that must be done to bring the contract for the sale of real property into compliance with the Statute of Frauds. The memorandum must have a date, the terms of payment, and a description of the property, and it must bear the signature of the party to be charged.[1]

In one case a prospective purchaser gave a check to a seller as earnest money and on the reverse side of the check wrote a statement briefly describing the property and the method by which the balance was to be paid. The seller endorsed the check and deposited it. It was held that this was a memorandum sufficient to bring the contract within the Statute of Frauds. This procedure is not recommended, however.

BINDERS

In many states, the broker uses a rather informal contract known as a *binder*. Upon receiving a deposit from a prospective purchaser, the broker has the prospective purchaser sign the binder, which is, in effect, an offer to the seller, subject to the seller's acceptance. The binder receipts the deposit, describes the property, the terms and conditions of the sale, and otherwise complies with the Statute of Frauds. It calls for the preparation of a more formal contract of sale within a stated number of days.

When the binder is signed by the seller, it may serve as a valid contract provided that it has been properly drawn. The parties will then proceed to the formal contract.

---

[1] The *party to be charged* is the person against whom the suit is brought, but good practice dictates that both parties sign.

BINDER AGREEMENT

Date ......January 8,........ 19--...

Received from ....①Howard Jensen..

of ......②365 Reed St., Borough of Brooklyn, County of Kings, State of New York.........

the sum of .One Thousand 00/100--Dollars

as deposit on account of purchase price of premises ...③at 28 Thomas Street, Village of Patchogue,....

..County of Suffolk,.. N. Y.

on the following terms and conditions:

TERMS:

Purchase Price is $13,000.00...... payable as follows:

$1,500.00...(including above deposit) on the signing of the formal contract as hereinafter provided.

$10,500.00..by taking title subject to a first mortgage in that amount covering said premises, bearing interest at the rate of .7½...% per annum payable .....semi.... annually, principal due ....October 18, 19--..

$............by taking title subject to a second mortgage in that amount covering said premises, bearing interest at the rate of ......% per annum payable .... annually, principal due ....

$............by the purchaser or assigns executing and delivering to the seller on delivery of the deed a purchase money bond and .... mortgage in that amount covering said premises, bearing interest at the rate of ......% per annum payable .... annually, principal due ....

$1,000.00... , the balance, in cash or certified check on delivery of deed.

CONDITIONS:

This deposit is accepted subject to owner's approval of the terms and conditions. If such approval is not obtained on or before five days from date hereof, this deposit shall be repaid to purchaser, but if obtained within such period a more formal contract in the form used by TITLE GUARANTEE AND TRUST COMPANY shall be signed by the parties at the office of ..④Donald Lawyer... at No. .63 Broadway, City of New York at .2 p.m., on ....January 13,... 19--..

The deed shall be delivered on the ..8th.. day of ....February,.. 19--., at ..2 P.M. at the office of ..Robert Counsellor, 15 E. Main Street, Patchogue, New York..............................

SUBJECT to rights of tenants as follows: ....None..

SUBECT, also, to the following: ....None..

The parties agree that ....⑤James Finn...................................

as broker brought about this sale and the seller agrees to pay the usual brokerage commission.

This agreement may not be changed orally, but only by an agreement in writing and signed by the party against whom enforcement of any waiver, change, modification or discharge is sought.

The above terms and conditions are approved and receipt of above deposit is acknowledged.

/s/ ....Roger Owner.................. Owner.

/s/ ....James Finn.................... Broker.

I agree to the foregoing.

/s/ ....Howard Jensen.................. Purchaser.

A Binder Agreement

① The name of the purchaser is inserted here.
② The complete address of the purchaser follows the word "of."
③ A brief, but accurate description of the premises is inserted here.
④ The name of the purchaser's attorney is customarily inserted here.
⑤ The name of the broker should be entered here.

THE CONTRACT FOR THE SALE OF REAL PROPERTY

The binder usually contains a statement that the parties will enter into a more formal contract within a stated number of days. Of what then does this more formal contract consist? The elements of the contract are described and illustrated in some detail in the following pages.

The Date

The contract begins by stating, "This agreement made this...... day of............, 19..." The date has importance when there exist time limits for executing the provisions of the contract or for executing the contract itself.

The Parties

The parties to the contract are generally referred to as the seller and the purchaser. Their names and addresses are spelled out in full. If John Smith is the seller and he is a married man, his wife should join with him on the contract, especially in those states having community property laws, homestead rights, and dower rights. When there is a tenancy by the entireties, the wife should also join on the contract as one of the sellers. It is only when the co-owners sign the contract that they can be forced to convey the real property by specific performance in the manner described later in the chapter.

When property is being sold by a corporation, the president or other officer of the corporation is generally authorized by the board of directors to execute the contract of sale. Under his signature on the contract, he impresses the corporate seal. Usually the board of directors has obtained, by a vote of the common stockholders, the authority to sell the property.

The Description

The methods of describing real property are discussed in detail in Chapter 5. After the names of the parties to the contract, there generally follows this statement:

> . . . the seller agrees to sell and convey, and the purchaser agrees to purchase, all that lot or parcel of land, with the buildings and improvements therein, in the: . . . . (Here might follow the city or the township or even the county; and then a complete description by metes and bounds, by lot and block number, or by government survey.)

Personal Property

In order to avoid any misunderstanding at the title closing that might result from not knowing what personal property items are included with the house, a statement substantially as follows might be inserted:

> All fixtures and articles of personal property attached or appurtenant to, or used in connection with said premises, are represented to be owned by the seller, free and clear from all liens and encumbrances except as herein stated, and are included in this sale. Without limiting the generality of the foregoing, such fixtures and articles of personal property include. . . . (Here a list of the personal property is inserted in the contract.)

Real estate brokers know that sometimes it is the personal property that can give them the most trouble at a closing; therefore, they should be especially careful when obtaining their listings to know exactly what items of personal property are included.

Purchase Price

The purchase price is a most important feature of the contract and should be spelled out in detail for all of the parties concerned. Generally, the method of payment is broken down into its component parts after a statement is made of the total purchase price. For example, if the price of the property is $20,000 and $500 was paid on the signing of the binder, $1,000 to be paid on the signing of the formal contract, $1,000 at the closing of title, and the purchaser to take the property subject to a $17,500 mortgage, then the statement as to the price in the contract would read substantially as follows:

> The price is Twenty Thousand and 00/100 ($20,000.00) Dollars, payable as follows:

a. Five Hundred and 00/100 ($500.00) Dollars, paid as a deposit on the .... day of ...., 19..., receipt of which has heretofore been acknowledged.

b. One Thousand and 00/100 ($1,000.00) Dollars upon the signing of this contract, receipt of which is hereby acknowledged.

c. One Thousand and 00/100 ($1,000.00) Dollars in cash or good certified check upon the delivery of the deed as hereinafter provided.

d. Seventeen Thousand Five Hundred and 00/100 ($17,500.00) Dollars by taking subject to a first mortgage now a lien upon said premises in that amount and bearing interest at .... percent per annum, the principal being due and payable. . . .

Encumbrances and Restrictions

The contract contains a statement that says premises are sold and are to be conveyed subject to:

1. Zoning restrictions and ordinances adopted by any municipal, town, village, or other governmental authority.

Although strictly speaking a zoning regulation is not an encumbrance, it is included in the contract as a restriction for the protection of the seller because under certain circumstances the existence of a zoning restriction will prevent the owner from obtaining specific performance. (Specific performance is discussed in detail in a later section of this chapter.)

2. Encroachments of stoops, areas, cellar steps, trim and cornices, if any, upon any street or highway.

The insertion of the preceding clause ordinarily is interpreted to mean that the purchaser must take title even though these encroachments would render the title unmarketable.

3. Consents by the seller or any former owner of premises for the erection of any structure or structures on, under, or above any street or streets on which said premises may abut.

4. Any state of facts that an accurate survey might show.

This clause is a good one from the seller's viewpoint, especially where no survey has been made on the property or if a survey has not been made recently. However, the purchaser should, if possible,

CONTRACT OF SALE

THIS AGREEMENT, made the 13th day of January nineteen hundred and . . .
BETWEEN Roger Owner, residing at 28 Thomas Street, Village of Patchogue, Town of Brookhaven, County of Suffolk, State of New York,

hereinafter described as the seller, and Howard Jensen, residing at 365 Reed Street, Borough of Brooklyn, County of Kings, State of New York,

hereinafter described as the purchaser.

WITNESSETH, that the seller agrees to sell and convey, and the purchaser agrees to purchase, all that lot or parcel of land, with the buildings and improvements thereon, in the Village of Patchogue, Town of Brookhaven, County of Suffolk, State of New York, described as follows:

① Lot #6 and the easterly half of Lot #7 of The Subdivision Map of Thomas Park, surveyed by Norton Brothers, Patchogue, July 17, 19--.

All fixtures and articles of personal property attached or appurtenant to or used in connection with said premises are represented to be owned by the seller, free from all liens and encumbrances except as herein stated, and are included in this sale. Without limiting the generality of the foregoing, such fixtures and articles of personal property include plumbing, heating, lighting, and cooking fixtures, air conditioning fixtures and units, ranges, refrigerators, radio aerials, bathroom and kitchen cabinets, mantels, door mirrors, venetian blinds, shades, window screens, awnings, storm windows, window boxes, storm doors, screen doors,
②
mail boxes, weather vanes, flagpoles, pumps, shrubbery and outdoor statuary, to the extent that they are located in or upon the premises herein described.
This sale includes all right, title and interest, if any, of the seller in and to any land lying in the bed of any street, road or avenue opened or proposed, in front of or adjoining said premises, to the center line thereof, and all right, title, and interest of the seller in and to any award made or to be made in lieu thereof and in and to any unpaid award for damage to said premises by reason of change of grade of any street; and the seller will execute and deliver to the purchaser, on closing of title, or thereafter, on demand, all proper instruments for the conveyance of such title and the assignment and collection of any such award.
This price is
Thirteen Thousand and 00/100 ($13,000) - - - - Dollars, payable as follows:
Fifteen Hundred and 00/100 ($1,500) - - - - - - - - - - - - - Dollars,
on the signing of this contract, the receipt of which is hereby acknowledged;
One Thousand and 00/100 ($1,000) - - - - - - - - - - - - - - - - Dollars,
in cash on the delivery of the deed as hereinafter provided;
Ten Thousand Five Hundred and 00/100 ($10,500) - - - - - - - Dollars,
by taking the title subject of a first mortgage now a lien on said premises in that amount, bearing interest at the rate of 7½ percent per annum, the principal being due and payable.
October 18, 19--

Dollars,
by the purchaser or assigns executing, acknowledging and delivering to the seller an obligation satisfactory to the seller secured by a purchase money mortgage on the above premises, in that amount, payable

together with interest at the rate of percent per annum payable until when the unpaid balance shall be due and payable.

Any mortgage to be given hereunder shall be drawn with clauses usually used by, and on forms of, Title Guarantee and Trust Company for mortgages of like lien; and shall be drawn by the attorney for the seller at the expense of the purchaser, who shall also pay the mortgage recording tax and recording fees and pay for and affix to such instruments any and all revenue stamps that may be necessary.

A Contract of Sale

Said premises are sold and are to be conveyed subject to:

③ 1. Building restrictions and regulations in resolution or ordinance adopted by the Board of Estimate and Apportionment of the City of New York, July 25th, 1916, and amendments and additions thereto now in force, or if premises are not situate in the City of New York, to the zoning and building restrictions and regulations, if any, of the village, city or town in which the premises are situate.
2. Encroachments of stoops, areas, cellar steps, trim and cornices, if any, upon any street or highway.
3. Consents by the seller or any former owner of premises for the erection of any structure or structure on, under or above any street or streets on which said premises may abut.

If there be a mortgage on the premises the seller agrees to deliver to the purchaser at the time of delivery of the deed a proper certificate executed and acknowledged by the holder of such mortgage and in form for recording, certifying as to the amount of the unpaid principal and interest thereon, date of maturity thereof and rate of interest thereon, and the seller shall pay the fees for recording such certificate.

All notes or notices of violations of law or municipal ordinances, orders or requirements noted in or issued by the Department of Housing and Buildings, Fire, Labor, Health, or other State or Municipal Department having jurisdiction, against or affecting the premises at the date hereof, shall be complied with by the seller and the premises shall be conveyed free of the same, and this provision of this contract shall survive delivery of the deed hereunder. The seller shall furnish the purchaser with an authorization to make the necessary searches therefor.

If, at the time of the delivery of the deed, the premises or any part thereof shall be or shall have been affected by an assessment or assessments which are or may become payable in annual installments, of which the first installment is then a charge or lien, or has been paid, then for the purposes of this contract all the unpaid installments of any such assessment, including those which are to become due and payable after the delivery of the deed, shall be deemed to be due and payable and to be liens upon the premises affected thereby and shall be paid and discharged by the seller, upon the delivery of the deed. Westchester County Sewer System Taxes and ** shall be excluded from the provisions of this paragraph and the installments thereof not due and payable at the time of the delivery of the deed hereunder shall be assumed by the purchaser without abatement of the purchase price.

The following are to be apportioned to the day of taking title:

1. Rents as and when collected.
2. Interest on mortgages.
3. Premiums on existing insurance policies or renewals of those expiring prior to the delivery of the deed, except those which are not transferable.
4. Taxes and sewer rents, if any, on the basis of the fiscal year for which assessed which, unless otherwise herein provided, shall be the dates set forth on the succeeding page hereof.
5. Water rates on the basis of the calendar year.

If the closing of the title shall occur before the tax rate is fixed, the apportionment of taxes shall be upon the basis of the tax rate for the next preceding year applied to the latest assessed valuation.

If there be a water meter on the premises, the seller shall furnish a reading to a date not more than thirty years prior to the time herein set for closing title, and the unfixed meter charge and the unfixed sewer rent, if any, based thereon for the intervening time shall be apportioned on the basis of such last reading.

The deed shall be the usual * ④ Full Covenant and Warranty

deed in proper statutory short form for record and shall be duly executed and acknowledged so as to convey to the purchaser the fee simple of the said premises, free of all encumbrances, except as herein stated, and shall also contain the covenant required by subdivision 5 of Section 13 of the Lien Law, as amended.

The seller shall give and the purchaser shall accept a title such as Title Guarantee and Trust Company will approve and insure.

All sums paid on account of this contract, and the reasonable expenses of the examination of the title to said premises are hereby made liens thereon, but such liens shall not continue after default by the purchaser under this contract.

The rights and duties of the parties to this contract, in respect to partial or total destruction of said premises (including destruction by fire) or partial or total taking thereof by condemnation, are subject to the provisions of Section 240-a of the Real Property Law, except as may otherwise be provided in this contract.

A Contract of Sale (Continued)

The deed shall be delivered upon the receipt of said payments at the office of Robert Counsellor, 15 E. Main Street, Patchogue, N. Y. at 2 p. m. o'clock on February 8, 19--
The parties agree that James Finn
brought about this sale and the seller agrees to pay the commission at the rates established or adopted by the Board of Real Estate Brokers in the locality where the property is situated.
The stipulations aforesaid are to apply to and bind the heirs, executors, administrators, successors and assigns of the respective parties.

IN WITNESS WHEREOF, this agreement has been duly executed by the parties hereto.
In presence of:

/s/ James Finn

/s/ Howard Jensen

/s/ Robert Owner

* Insert form of deed to be used.
** Insert any other assessments as to which similar agreement is reached between the parties.

Title Guarantee and Trust Company, New York, New York

A Contract of Sale (Concluded)

① A complete metes and bounds description may be used here.
② All items of personal property not in the sale are stricken from the contract.
③ Outside of the City of New York this paragraph will not appear.
④ The courts in some states hold that, in the absence of specification in the contract as to the kind of conveyance, a deed without covenants and warranties is sufficient.

seek to have the clause read: "any state of facts that an accurate survey might show, provided the title is not thereby rendered unmarketable."

> 5. Covenants and restrictions of record, if any.

This is an important clause of the contract; without it, there is a possibility of the purchaser's avoiding the contract after having discovered restrictions in the abstract or report of title.

Rights to Road

The contract will also contain this clause:

> This sale includes all right, title, and interest, if any, of the seller in and to any land lying in the bed of any street, road or avenue opened or proposed, in front of or adjoining said premises, to the center line thereof, and all right, title, and interest of the seller in and to any award made or to be made in lieu thereof and in any unpaid award for damage to said premises by reason of change of grade of any street; and the seller will execute and deliver

to the purchaser, on closing of title, or thereafter, on demand, all proper instruments for the conveyance of such title and the assignment and collection of any such award.

Reduction Certificate

The details of the reduction certificate are discussed in detail in Chapter 8. However, if there is a mortgage on a parcel of property which the purchaser is either "assuming" or "taking subject to," he should make certain of the balance due at the time of the closing of title. Therefore, a provision is made in the contract that the seller will deliver to the purchaser a certificate stating the amount due on the mortgage at the time of the closing of title. This is commonly called the Mortgagee's Certificate of Reduction.

The contract will then state:

> If there be a mortgage on the premises, the seller agrees to deliver to the purchaser at the time of the delivery of the deed a proper certificate executed and acknowledged by the holder of such mortgage and in form for recording, certifying as to the amount of the unpaid principal and interest thereon, date of maturity thereof and rate of interest thereon, and the seller shall pay the fees for recording such certificate.

Violations

In most states where the contract is silent in regard to violations of law or municipal ordinances, the purchaser will be required to accept the property subject to any existing violations. Therefore, in order to avoid this, the purchaser will require a clause in the contract to this effect:

> All notes or notices of violation of law or municipal ordinances against or affecting the premises at the date hereof shall be complied with by the seller and the premises shall be conveyed free and clear of the same, and this provision of this contract shall survive delivery of the deed hereunder. The seller shall furnish the purchaser with an authorization to make the necessary searches therefor.

Thus, if it is discovered after the date of closing that violations were in existence on the date of the contract and the purchaser has to pay for such violations, the seller will then be liable to the purchaser for such damages because the clause provides that the covenant will survive the delivery of the deed.

Apportionments

The mechanics of apportionments are explained fully in Chapter 23; however, it is here in the contract that the basis for such apportionments are laid. This is done by the statement:

> The following are to be apportioned to the day of taking title:
>
> 1. Rents as and when collected.
>
> 2. Interest on mortgages.
>
> 3. Premiums on existing insurance policies or renewals of those expiring prior to the delivery of the deed, except those which are transferable.
>
> 4. Taxes and sewer rents, if any, on the basis of the fiscal year for which assessed.
>
> 5. Water rates on the basis of the calendar year.
>
> 6. Coal or other fuel.
>
> If the closing of the title shall occur before the tax rate is fixed, the apportionment of taxes shall be upon the basis of the tax rate for the next preceding year applied to the latest assessed valuation.
>
> If there be a water meter on the premises, the seller shall furnish a reading to a date not more than thirty days prior to the time herein set for closing of title, and the unfixed meter charge and the unfixed sewer rent, if any, based thereon for the intervening time shall be apportioned on the basis of such last reading.

The Deed

The specifications of the deed follow:

> The deed shall be the usual . . (here the type of deed to be delivered is inserted) deed in the proper statutory form for record and shall be duly executed and acknowledged so as to convey to the purchaser the fee simple of said premises free and clear of all encumbrances, except as herein stated.

Marketable and Insurable Title

Often the contract will contain a clause requiring the vendor to deliver either a marketable title or an insurable title. When there is no such clause, the seller is required to deliver marketable title.[2] *Marketable title* is title that is clearly so good that the courts will order its acceptance by a purchaser.

One should be aware of the distinction between marketable title and insurable title. They are not necessarily the same thing. Often, although marketable, a title is not insurable, for the title companies sometimes refuse to insure the title for fear of incurring the expense of defending a lawsuit. Often, too, a title company will insure a title even though it may be, strictly speaking, unmarketable. The instance of the insertion of either marketable or insurable title in a real property contract depends to a large extent on the bargaining position of the respective parties to the contract. In the last analysis, a title is insurable if a title company says it is. One company may say a title is uninsurable; another may state it is insurable.

Delivery of Deed

The contract will contain a clause providing for the delivery of the deed and the payment of the balance of the purchase price at a certain place at a certain time and date. It may also contain a clause stating that "time is of the essence." In the absence of this latter statement, the seller has a reasonable time within which to cure defects of title, and the purchaser can, for good reason, seek to have the closirg adjourned. However, when the contract does contain the statement "time is of the essence," this has been held to mean in effect that delivery of the deed has to be made at the time stated in the contract. Great care should be taken with this statement. If, for example, *A* enters into a contract with *B* for the purchase of a parcel of property on September 1, and at the same time *A* enters into a contract with *C* for the sale of the same premises on September 2, then *A* must insist that the statement "time is of the essence" be included in the contract with *B*. In this manner *A* may avoid any possible damage to himself for failure to deliver the property to *C* at the time stated in the contract between himself and *C*.

---

[2] In the Midwest, "merchantable" is often used synonymously with "marketable."

Risk of Loss

In many states if the premises are destroyed between the execution of the sales contract and the date of closing, the purchaser bears the risk of loss. Some states—for example, Hawaii, Louisiana, Michigan, New York, South Dakota, and Wisconsin—have adopted the Uniform Vendor and Purchaser Risk Act. This act places the risk of loss on the seller when neither title nor possession of the property has passed to the purchaser.

In any event, no chances of risk of loss until closing should be borne by the purchaser. He should insist on a clause in the contract stating in effect: "The risk of loss or damage to said premises until the delivery of the deed is hereby assumed by the seller." The risk may be borne by the purchaser if he so desires; however, he may protect himself by insurance.

Liquidated Damages

In connection with the statement concerning the time of closing of title, there may be inserted in the contract a statement about *liquidated damages*, which is the amount the parties of the contract may stipulate to be paid in case of default. The inclusion of a clause of this type is particularly apropos where rent control is in effect, or if there is a suspicion on the part of the purchaser that the seller will not or will be unable to deliver possession of the premises on the date of the closing of title.

The clause may be inserted substantially as follows:

> In the event that the seller fails to deliver possession of the premises herein at the time of delivery of the deed as called for by these presents, then it is hereby agreed by and between the seller and the purchaser that the seller shall pay to the purchaser the sum of Ten and 00/100 ($10.00) Dollars for each and every day that he shall remain in possession of the premises described herein on and after the date of closing of title called for herein, the sums so paid to be construed as liquidated damages and not as a penalty.

A statement of this type will usually insure delivery of possession at the time of closing. Care must be taken in this case not to make the sum for the liquidated damages unreasonable.

FORM No. 720
Copyright 1947, Revised 1952
Stevens-Ness Law Publishing Co.
Portland, Oregon

① RECEIPT AND AGREEMENT TO PURCHASE

OFFICIAL FORM OF THE IDAHO REAL ESTATE ASSOCIATION

Moscow, Idaho, February 17, 19--

RECEIVED FROM Ronald Yates (hereinafter referred to as Purchaser) the sum of One Thousand and 00/100 - - - - - - - - - - ($1,000.00) Dollars as a deposit and earnest money in part payment of the purchase price of the following described real property situated in Moscow, County of Latah State of Idaho, to-wit: E. ½ of Section 11 Twp. 12 R. 20 W. of Boise meridian
(or any complete legal description)

The following items are to be left upon the premises as part of the property purchased: All irrigation fixtures and equipment, plumbing and heating fixtures and equipment (including stoker and oil tanks but excluding fire place fixtures and equipment), water heaters, electric light fixtures, light bulbs and fluorescent lamps, bathroom fixtures, venetian blinds, window and door screens, storm doors and windows, attached linoleum, all shrubs and trees and all fixtures except storm doors and windows.

The following personal property is also included as a part of the property to be offered for sale for said price: wall-to-wall carpet in dining room of house.

It is hereby agreed that the total purchase price is the sum of Thirteen Thousand Five Hundred and 00/100 - - ($13,500.00) Dollars payable as follows: The sum of One Thousand and 00/100 - - - - - - - - - - - - - ($1,000.00) Dollars hereinabove receipted for and the balance of the purchase price in the sum of Twelve Thousand Five Hundred and 00/100 - - ($12,500.00) Dollars to be paid as follows: (If on contract, state terms generally, and if escrow, also name of escrow holder) Two Thousand Five Hundred and 00/100 ($2,500) at closing of title and Ten Thousand and 00/100 ($10,000) by assuming a mortgage held by the Idaho First National Bank, Moscow, Idaho.

It is further agreed: 1. Seller shall at his expense furnish Purchaser an Abstract of Title continued to a date subsequent hereto showing merchantable title to the above described property vested in Seller, or in lieu thereof, at Seller's option, a title insurance policy insuring title thereto vested in Seller, free and clear of all liens and encumbrances, except the mortgage aforementioned.

It is further agreed that the broker assumes no responsibility in regard to the title and broker recommends that Purchaser have the Abstract of Title or title insurance policy examined by an attorney.

2. The real property is to be conveyed by warranty deed. and the personal property by Bill of Sale, free and clear of all encumbrances except building and zoning ordinances and regulations, building and use restrictions, rights of way and easements, reservations in Federal patents and State deeds and those enumerated in Section 1 above.

3. Sellers shall pay all of the taxes and assessments to date of closing and Purchaser shall pay all taxes and assessments thereafter. Rents, insurance and interest on mortgage or contract indebtedness shall be pro-rated to date of closing. Encumbrances to be discharged by Seller may at his option be paid out of the purchase money at the date of closing.

4. If Seller does not approve this sale within 5 days hereafter, or if Seller's title is not merchantable or insurable and cannot be made so within a reasonable time after written notice containing statement of defects is delivered to Seller, then said earnest money herein receipted for shall be returned to the Purchaser on demand and all rights of Purchaser terminated unless Purchaser waives said defects and elects to purchase; but if said sale is approved by the Seller and Seller's said title is merchantable or insurable and Purchaser neglects or refuses to complete the purchase or shall fail to pay the balance of the purchase price as hereinabove provided, then said earnest money shall be forfeited to the Seller as liquidated damages and not as a penalty and this Agreement thereupon shall be of no further force or effect or the Seller may demand the enforcement of the specific provisions of this Agreement.

5. In the event the improvements on said property should be destroyed or materially damaged between the date hereof and consummation or settlement of this purchase, this Agreement shall, at the option of the Purchaser, immediately become null and void, and said earnest money deposit shall be returned to said Purchaser on demand.

6. Possession shall be delivered Purchaser on or before the 19th day of March, 19--.

7. Purchaser enters into this Agreement in full reliance upon his independent investigation and judgment and there are no verbal or other agreements which modify or affect this Agreement.

8. Time is of the essence of this Agreement. Purchaser's rights herein are not assignable without the written consent of the Seller

Agent, By Lee Brannon Agents for Joe Owner Seller

I hereby agree to purchase the above described property and pay the price of Thirteen Thousand Five Hundred and 00/100 ($13,500.00) Dollars as set forth above and grant to said agent 5 days hereafter to secure Seller's acceptance hereof, during which period my said offer shall not be subject to revocation.

Address 63 E. Main St., Moscow, Idaho
Phone 20195

/s/ Ronald Yates Purchaser

For valuable consideration I/~~we~~ agree to sell and convey to the Purchaser the above described property on the terms and conditions hereinabove stated and agree to pay to the above named agent a commission of Six Hundred Seventy-five and 00/100 - - ($675.00) Dollars for services rendered in this transaction. I/we acknowledge receipt of a copy of the earnest money receipt bearing my/our signature and that of the Purchaser named above. In case the Purchaser fails to comply with any of the conditions of this Agreement, then one-half of the earnest money receipted for shall be retained by the broker, provided the amount to the broker does not exceed the agreed upon commission due and the balance shall be paid to the undersigned.

Dated this 19th day of February, 19--.

②/s/ Joe Owner Seller

STATE OF IDAHO,
County of Latah } ss.

On this 19th day of February in the year 19--, before me Lee Brannon, a Notary Public in and for said State, personally appeared Joe Owner and Ronald Yates known to me to be the person(s) whose name(s) is (are) subscribed to the within instrument, and acknowledged to me that they executed the same.③

IN WITNESS WHEREOF, I have hereunto set my hand and affixed my official seal the day and year in this certificate first above written.

/s/ Lee Brannon
Notary Public for the State of Idaho, Residing at Moscow, Idaho.

BROKER'S COPY — FILE IN DEAL ENVELOPE

Stevens-Ness Law Publishing Company, Portland, Oregon

A Receipt and Agreement to Purchase

① Variations of this form are used in Alaska, California, Colorado, Florida, Idaho, Montana, Nevada, North Dakota, Oregon, South Dakota, and Washington. It is gradually being accepted in a number of other states.

② In community property states, it is imperative to have both husband and wife join on the contract when they are the sellers.

③ In most states the agreement need not be acknowledged unless the desire is to record it.

RECEIPT AND AGREEMENT TO PURCHASE

In some sections of the United States real estate brokers use a contract called the receipt and agreement to purchase.[3] In essence, the *receipt and agreement to purchase* combines the features of the binder and the formal contract for the sale of real property. This is used mainly in those areas of the country where the brokers fill in the spaces on the contract. The attorney, for the most part, does not enter into the picture.

When a broker receives an offer, he prepares a receipt and agreement to purchase. The instrument is dated and states:

> Received from . . . (hereinafter referred to as the Purchaser) the sum of ...... ($......) Dollars as a deposit and earnest money in part payment of the purchase price of the following described real property situated in .... (Here follows a description of the property.)

The contract contains a number of clauses described above and in addition a statement that:

> If Seller does not approve this sale within ...... days hereafter, or if the Seller's title is not merchantable or insurable and cannot be made so within a reasonable time after written notice containing statement of defects is delivered to the Seller, then said earnest money herein receipted for shall be returned to the Purchaser on demand. . . .

After the purchaser signs the receipt and agreement to purchase, the broker submits it to the seller for his signature. If the seller signs the agreement, then a contract for the sale of the property is in effect. Copies are made for the seller and the purchaser and for the broker.

THE CONTRACT FOR THE EXCHANGE OF REAL PROPERTY

Frequently a broker brings about an exchange of real property; it is at this time that the *contract for the exchange of real property*

---

[3] In Michigan substantially the same agreement is used, but called the "Purchase Agreement." In Florida it is called the "Receipt for Deposit—Offer to Purchase and Contract for Sale."

is used. Basically, this contract is the same as the contract for the sale of real property, with only two major changes. In the exchange contract, the parties are not described as the purchaser and the seller, but as the party of the first part and the party of the second part. The contract then states:

> The party of the first part, in consideration of one dollar, the receipt of which is hereby acknowledged, and of the conveyance by the party of the second part hereinafter agreed to be made, hereby agrees to sell, grant, and convey to the party of the second part, at a valuation, for the purpose of this contract, of . . . . . . Dollars.

A description of the property of the party of the first part follows together with a list of any encumbrances that might exist thereon. A statement is made by the party of the second part in the same manner as the party of the first part has made above, together with the valuation of the property. The property is described and followed by this statement:

> The difference between the values of the respective premises, over and above encumbrances, for the purpose of this contract, shall be deemed to be . . . . dollars, and that sum shall be due and payable as follows, by the party of the . . . .

CONTRACT OF EXCHANGE

THIS AGREEMENT made and dated March 23, 19-- between Alfred Kearney, residing on Long Island Avenue, Medford, Town of Brookhaven, County of Suffolk, State of New York.
hereinafter described as party of the first part and Albert Brown, residing at 103 Lakewood St., Village of Patchogue, Town of Brookhaven, County of Suffolk, State of New York.
hereinafter described as party of the second part, for the exchange of real property.

WITNESSETH, as follows:

The party of the first part, in consideration of one dollar, the receipt of which is hereby acknowledged, and of the conveyance by the party of the second part hereinafter agreed to be made, hereby agrees to sell, grant and convey to the party of the second part, at a valuation, for the purpose of this contract, of
Twelve Thousand and 00/100 ($12,000) - - - - - - - - - - - - - dollars.

ALL that land with the buildings and improvements thereon, in the Hamlet of Medford, Town of Brookhaven, County of Suffolk, State of New York, as follows:

(here follows complete legal description)

The premises which are to be conveyed by the party of the first part shall be conveyed subject to the following encumbrances: None

The party of the second part, in consideration of one dollar, the receipt of which is hereby acknowledged, and of the conveyance by the party of the first part, hereinbefore agreed to be made, hereby agrees to sell, grant and convey to the party of the first part, at a valuation for the purpose of this contract, of
Fourteen Thousand and 00/100 ($14,000) - - - - - - - - - - - - - dollars,

A Contract of Exchange

ALL that land with buildings and improvements thereon in the Village of Patcnogue, Town of Brookhaven, County of Suffolk, State of New York, as follows:

(here follows a complete legal description)

The premises which are to be conveyed by the party of the second part shall be conveyed subject to the following encumbrances: None

The difference between the values of the respective premises, over and above encumbrances, for the purpose of this contract, shall be deemed to be
Two Thousand and 00/100 ($2,000) - - - - - - - - - - - - - - - - dollars,
and that sum shall be due and payable as follows, by the party of the first part:

Any bond and mortgage to be given hereunder shall be drawn with clauses usually used by, and on forms of, Title Guarantee and Trust Company for bonds and mortgages of like lien; and shall be drawn by the attorney for the seller at the expense of the purchaser, who shall also pay the mortgage recording tax and recording fees.

Said premises are sold and are to be conveyed subject to:

① 1. Building restrictions and regulations in resolution or ordinance adopted by the Board of Estimate and Apportionment of the City of New York, July 25th, 1916, and amendments and additions thereto now in force, or if premises are not situate in the City of New York, to the zoning and building restrictions and regulations, if any, of the village, city or town in which the premises are situate.
2. Encroachments of stoops, areas, cellar steps, trim and cornices, if any, upon any street or highway.
3. Consents by the seller or any former owner of premises for the erection of any structure or structures on, under or above any street or streets on which said premises may abut.

All personal property appurtenant to or used in the operation of said premises is represented to be owned by the respective sellers and is included in this exchange.

This contract covers all right, title and interest of the respective sellers, of, in and to any lands lying in the bed of any street, road or avenue, opened or proposed, in front of or adjoining the premises to be conveyed to the center line thereof, and all right, title and interest of the respective sellers in and to any unpaid awards made or to be made in lieu thereof, and in any unpaid award for damage to said premises by reason of change of grade of any street, and the sellers will execute and deliver to the purchasers, on closing of title, or thereafter, on demand, all proper instruments for the conveyance of such title and the assignment and collection of any such awards.

If there be a mortgage on the premises the seller agrees to deliver to the purchaser at the time of delivery of the deed a proper certificate executed and acknowledged by the holder of such mortgage and in form for recording, certifying as to the amount of the unpaid principal and interest thereon, date of maturity thereof and rate of interest thereon, and the seller shall pay the fees for recording such certificate.

All notes or notices of violations of law or municipal ordinances, orders or requirements noted in or issued by the Department of Housing and Buildings, Fire, Labor, Health, or other State or Municipal Department having jurisdiction, against or affecting the premises, at the date hereof, shall be complied with by the seller and the premises shall be conveyed free of the same, and this provision of this contract shall survive delivery of the deed hereunder. The seller shall furnish the purchaser with an authorization to make the necessary searches therefor.

If, at the time of the delivery of the deed, the premises or any part thereof shall be, or shall have been affected by an assessment or assessments which are or may become payable in annual installments, of which the first installment is then a charge or lien, or has been paid, then for the purposes of this contract all the unpaid installments of any such assessment, including those which are to become due and payable after the delivery of the deed, shall be deemed to be due and payable and to be liens upon the premises affected thereby and shall be paid and discharged by the seller, upon the delivery of the deed. Westchester County Sewer System Taxes and ** shall be excluded from the provisions of this paragraph and the installments thereof not due and payable at the time of the delivery of the deed hereunder shall be assumed by the purchaser without abatement of the purchase price.

The following are to be apportioned to the day of taking title:
1. Rents as and when collected.
2. Interest on mortgages.
3. Premiums on existing policies or renewals of those expiring prior to the delivery of the deed of the following kinds of insurance: fire.
4. Taxes on the basis of the fiscal year for which assessed which, unless otherwise herein provided, shall be the dates set forth on the succeeding page hereof.
5. Water rates on the basis of the calendar year.

If the closing of the title shall occur before the tax rate is fixed, the apportionment of taxes shall be upon the basis of the tax rate for the next preceding year applied to the latest assessed valuation.

If there be a water meter on the premises, the seller shall furnish a reading to a date not more than thirty days prior to the time herein set for closing title, and the unfixed meter charge for the intervening time shall be apportioned on the basis of such last reading.

Each of the parties agrees to convey the property hereinbefore described as sold by such party respectively, free from all encumbrances, except as above specified, and to execute, acknowledge and deliver to the other party, or to the assigns of the other party, a deed in proper statutory short form for record containing the usual full covenants and warranty, so as to convey to the grantee the fee simple of said premises free from all encumbrances except as herein stated.

If there be a tenement erected on the premises and the basement be now occupied for living purposes, the seller thereof represents that a permit authorizing such occupancy has been issued by the Department of Housing and Buildings and not revoked.

A Contract of Exchange (Continued)

The deed shall be the usual * bargain and sale with covenant deed in proper statutory short form for record and shall be duly executed and acknowledged so as to convey to the purchaser the fee simple of the said premises, free of all encumbrances, except as herein stated, and shall also contain the covenant required by sub-division 5 of Section 13 of the Lien Law, as amended.

The seller shall give and the purchaser shall accept a title such as Title Guarantee and Trust Company will approve and insure.

All sums paid on account of this contract, and the reasonable expenses of the examination of the title to said premises are hereby made liens thereon, but such liens shall not continue after default by the purchaser under this contract.

The rights and duties of the parties to this contract, in respect to a material or total destruction of said premises (including destruction by fire) or a material or total taking thereof by condemnation, are now subject to the "Uniform Vendor and Purchaser Risk Act" which became effective May 26th, 1936, and is known as Section 240-a of the Real Property Law, unless said contract expressly provides otherwise.

The deed shall be delivered upon the receipt of said payments at the office of Robert Lawyer, 8 E. Main St., Hometown, N. Y. at 2 p.m. o'clock on March 23, 19—

The parties agree that Donald Wald brought about this exchange and the broker's commission is to be paid as follows: 6% of the contract price of property of party of the second part.

IN WITNESS WHEREOF, this agreement has been duly executed by the parties hereto.

In the presence of:

/s/ Robert Lawyer

/s/ Alfred Kearney
/s/ Albert Brown

* Insert form of deed to be used.
** Insert any other assessments as to which similar agreement is reached between the parties.

Title Guarantee and Trust Company, New York, New York

A Contract of Exchange (Concluded)

① Outside the City of New York, this clause is stricken.

Thus, if the property of the party of the first part is valued at $10,000 and the property of the party of the second part is valued at $8,000, then $2,000 is due to the party of the first part.

The balance of the contract for the exchange then follows the terms of the contract for the sale of real property, along with any special agreement that might be reached.

MISCELLANEOUS PROVISIONS IN REAL ESTATE CONTRACTS

Contingencies

In any contract, whether it be the receipt and agreement to purchase, the contract for the sale, or the contract for the exchange of property, any *contingencies* must be carefully spelled out. If the transaction is to be subject to obtaining FHA approval for a loan in the amount of $10,000, then the contract should state this categorically, not "subject to obtaining an FHA loan," but "subject to obtaining an FHA loan in the amount of $10,000," or whatever the amount may be. If a man is to purchase the property and does not know whether or not his wife will approve the transaction, he might even go so far as to insist on the statement "subject to the approval of my wife, Mary" in the contract.

Provision for Purchase Money Mortgage

Although the purchase money mortgage is discussed in detail in Chapter 6, it merits some mention here. A *purchase money mortgage* is a mortgage that is given by the buyer to the seller as part of the consideration. The seller "takes back" a mortgage as a part of the purchase price. If the seller agrees to do this, the contract should contain a clause stating this willingness.

Assume that the purchase price of a parcel of property is $7,000, $1,000 on the signing of contract, $1,000 at the closing of title, and a purchase money mortgage in the amount of $5,000. The clause spelling out the method of payment in the contract would read:

> The price is Seven Thousand and 00/100 ($7,000.00) Dollars, payable as follows:
>
> One Thousand and 00/100 ($1,000.00) Dollars on the signing of this contract, receipt of which is hereby acknowledged; One Thousand and 00/100 ($1,000.00) Dollars on the delivery of the deed as hereinafter provided, and the balance of Five Thousand and 00/100 ($5,000.00) Dollars, by the purchaser or his assigns executing, acknowledging, and delivering to the seller, his bond (or note) secured by a purchase money mortgage on the above premises, in that amount payable in monthly installments of $100 or more at the option of the owner of the premises, together with interest at the rate of 5½ percent per annum payable with said installments, until four years after the date of the mortgage when the balance shall be due and payable.

Water Rights

Water rights are construed as being appurtenant to real property. *Appurtenant* means incidental to the land when it is a thing used by right with the land for its benefit. Generally, a contract for the sale of real property includes those things that are appurtenant to the land. Because water rights are generally considered to be appurtenances, they are included in a conveyance of the land. However, in many sections of the country, water rights consist of stock held in irrigation companies. If this is the case, special mention should be made of this in the contract. At the closing of title, the stock in the water companies will be assigned to the purchaser. This method of disposition of water rights should be spelled out in detail rather than left to be interpreted.[4]

Acquisition of Plottage

Often a real estate operator will attempt to assemble many small plots of land with the idea of constructing one large building on the entire piece. For example, there are two contiguous parcels of property, owned separately, each with a frontage of 50 feet. *A* decides to construct a building, but needs a frontage of 100 feet. He cannot, without adequate protection, enter into a contract with *X* to purchase his 50-foot frontage without knowing that he can obtain *Z's* property at the same time. In order to protect himself in the event that he is unable to acquire both parcels of property that he needs, *A* will insert a clause into his contract with *X* to the effect that if he is unable to obtain good and marketable title to both parcels of property, he may, at his option, cancel the contract.

Property Under Contract

Property under contract is a special clause that is employed in real property contracts under certain circumstances. For example, *A* enters into a real property contract with *B* to purchase *B*'s property for $10,000. Several days later, prior to his obtaining title to the property from *B*, *A* has the opportunity to sell the property to *X* for a profit. Ordinarily, he will assign his contract from *B* to *X*. However, in some circumstances, his contract may be unassignable, in which case *A* in his contract with *X* inserts a clause stating that he now has property under contract. The clause will be as follows:

[4] This is particularly important in certain areas of Arizona, California, Colorado, Idaho, Montana, Nevada, New Mexico, Oregon, Utah, Washington, and Wyoming.

The seller is not the owner of said premises but represents that he has an interest therein as purchaser under contract dated ......, 19... with ...... which contract the seller herein believes to be valid and binding and which contract was exhibited and read in its entirety by the purchaser herein.

As Is Clause

In some rare instances, a purchaser of property will purchase the property without actually inspecting it. When this is the case, the seller may insist that an "as is" clause be inserted in the real property contract. This declares that the seller has made no warranties or representations as to the conditions of the property, and, further, that the purchaser agrees to accept the property as it is.

Termite Clause

In those parts of the country where termites exist, it is customary to include a termite clause in the real property contract. This is generally worded: "The seller, at his own expense, shall have the premises inspected for termite damage, and if any be found, it is to be repaired at the seller's expense."

ESCROW AND HOW IT IS USED

Escrow may be defined as a scroll, writing, or deed delivered by the grantor into the hands of a third person to be held by the latter until the happening of a contingency or the performance of a condition, and then delivered by him to the grantee.

To understand fully the ordinary workings of escrow, it must be recognized that in many parts of the country sales are made "on contract," as it is commonly called. Thus, when the seller desires to finance a deal himself, instead of taking a purchase money mortgage back as part of the consideration, delivering the deed, and recording the mortgage as a lien against the property, he finances the deal "on contract," or "on a land contract." The seller receives part of the purchase price in cash and the balance of the purchase price later, according to the terms of a contract signed by both the seller and purchaser. This contract names the parties, describes the property, and spells out the purchase price and details of payment. The purchaser is required to keep the premises insured in favor of the seller in the same manner done under a mortgage. The purchaser is entitled to possession as of a time stated in the contract. No deed is delivered to the purchaser; however, for the protection of the purchaser, the contract often will state as follows on page 98:

THIS CONTRACT, Made this 15th *day* March, *19* --, *between* John Seller, residing at 20 "D" St., City of Salem, State of Oregon, *hereinafter called the seller, and* Frank Purchaser, residing at 16 "B" St., City of Salem, State of Oregon, *hereinafter called the buyer,*

WITNESSETH: That in consideration of the mutual covenants and agreements herein contained, the seller agrees to sell unto the buyer and the buyer agrees to purchase from the seller all of the following described lands and premises situated in the County of Marion *and State of* Oregon, *to-wit:*

(here follows complete legal description)

for the sum of Ten Thousand and 00/100 - - - - - - - - - *Dollars ($* 10,000.00 *) hereinafter called the purchase price, in part payment of which the buyer assumes and agrees to pay a mortgage or contract now on said land, described on the reverse hereof, the unpaid principal balance of which is $* 6,000.00, *together with the interest hereafter to accrue on said mortgage or contract according to the terms thereof; the buyer agrees to pay the balance of said purchase price to the order of the seller at the times and in amounts as follows, to-wit:*

1. One Thousand and 00/100 ($1,000) Dollars in cash on signing of this agreement, receipt of which is hereby acknowledged.

2. Three Thousand and 00/100 ($3,000) Dollars at the rate of Fifty and 00/100 ($50) Dollars on the first day of each and every month until paid.

All or any part of said purchase price may be paid at any time; all of the said deferred payments shall bear interest at the rate of 5 *per cent per annum from this date until paid, said interest to be paid* monthly *and* * { in addition to / ~~being included in~~ } *the minimum regular payments above required. Taxes on said premises for the current fiscal year shall be pro-rated between the parties hereto as of the date of this contract.*

The buyer shall be entitled to possession of said lands on March 30, *19* --, *and may retain such possession so long as he is not in default under the terms of this contract. The buyer agrees that at all times he will keep the buildings on said premises, now or hereafter erected, in good condition and repair and will not suffer or permit any waste or strip thereof; that he will keep said premises free from mechanic's and all other liens and save the seller harmless therefrom and reimburse seller for all costs and attorney's fees incurred by him in defending against any such liens; that he will pay all taxes hereafter levied against said property, as well as all water rents, public charges and municipal liens which hereafter lawfully may be imposed upon said premises, all promptly before the same or any part thereof become past due; that at buyer's expense, he will insure and keep insured all buildings now or hereafter erected on said premises against loss or damage by fire (with extended coverage) in an amount not less than $* 10,000.00 *in a company or companies satisfactory to the seller, with loss payable to the seller as his interest may appear and all policies of insurance to be delivered to the seller as soon as insured. Now if the buyer shall fail to pay any such liens, costs, water rents, taxes, or charges or to procure and pay for such insurance, the seller may do so and any payment so made shall be added to and become a part of the debt secured by this contract and shall bear interest at the rate aforesaid, without waiver, however, of any right arising to the seller for buyer's breach of contract.*

The seller agrees that at his expense and within 15 *days from the date hereof, he will furnish unto buyer a title insurance policy insuring (in an amount equal to said purchase price) marketable title in and to said premises in the seller on or subsequent to the date of this agreement, save and except the usual printed exceptions and the building and other restrictions and easements now of record, if any, and the said mortgage or contract. Seller also agrees that when said purchase price is fully paid and upon request and upon surrender of this agreement, he will deliver a good and sufficient deed conveying said premises in fee simple unto the buyer, his heirs and assigns, free and clear of encumbrances as of the date hereof excepting, however, the said easements, restrictions, the said mortgage or contract and the taxes, municipal liens, water rents and public charges so assumed by the buyer and further excepting all liens and encumbrances created by the buyer or assigns.*

And it is understood and agreed between said parties that time is of the essence of this contract, and in case the buyer shall fail to make the payments above required, or any of them, and the payments to become due on said mortgage or contract, principal and interest, or any of them, punctually within ten days of the time limited therefor, or fail to keep any agreement herein contained, then the seller at his option shall have the following rights: (1) to declare this contract null and void, (2) to declare the whole unpaid principal balance of said purchase price with the interest thereon at once due and payable and/or (3) to foreclose this contract by suit in equity, and in any of such cases, all rights and interests created or then existing in favor of the buyer as against the seller hereunder shall utterly cease and determine and the right to the possession of the premises above described and all other rights acquired by the buyer hereunder shall revert to and revest in said seller without any act of re-entry, or any other act of said seller to be performed and without any right of the buyer of return, reclamation or compensation for moneys paid on account of the purchase of said property as absolutely, fully and perfectly as if this contract and such payments had never been made; and in case of such default all payments theretofore made on this contract are to be retained by and belong to said seller as the agreed and reasonable rent of said premises up to the time of such default. And the said seller, in case of such default, shall have the right immediately, or at any time thereafter, to enter upon the land aforesaid, without any process of law, and take immediate possession thereof, together with all the improvements and appurtenances thereon or thereto belonging.

The buyer further agrees that failure by the seller at any time to require performance by the buyer of any provision hereof shall in no way affect his right hereunder to enforce the same, nor shall any waiver by said seller of any breach of any provision hereof be held to be a waiver of any succeeding breach of any such provision, or as a waiver of the provision itself.

In case suit or action is instituted to foreclose this contract or to enforce any of the provisions hereof, the buyer agrees to pay such sum as the court may adjudge reasonable as attorney's fees to be allowed plaintiff in said suit or action.

In construing this contract, it is understood that the seller or the buyer may be more than one person; that if the context so requires, the singular pronoun shall be taken to mean and include the plural, the masculine, the feminine and the neuter, and that generally all grammatical changes shall be made, assumed and implied to make the provisions hereof apply equally to corporations and to individuals.

IN WITNESS WHEREOF, said parties have hereunto set their hands and seals in duplicate on this, the day and year first above written.

/s/ Robert Seller (SEAL)

/s/ Harold Corneilson

/s/ Frank Purchaser (SEAL)

*Strike whichever phrase not applicable.

A Land Contract

This is the general form of contract that is placed in escrow in many states.

ASSIGNMENT BY SELLER-OWNER OF THE CONTRACT ON THE REVERSE HEREOF

Note: Seller's deed should also accompany this assignment.

KNOW ALL MEN BY THESE PRESENTS, That the undersigned, the identical seller named in the contract of sale set forth on the reverse hereof, in consideration of $..................... to the seller paid by..., *hereinafter called assignee, hereby does convey, assign, sell, transfer and set over unto the said assignee all of the seller's right, title and interest in and to the said contract of sale and hereby does grant, bargain, sell and convey unto said assignee the real property described in said contract and all of the seller's right, title and interest therein, subject, however, to the foregoing contract of sale on which there is an unpaid principal balance of not less than $.................................with the interest thereon from ...., 19........ until paid;*

TO HAVE AND TO HOLD the said contract and the said granted premises unto the said assignee and the assignee's heirs and assigns forever.

IN WITNESS WHEREOF, the undersigned seller has hereunto set hand and seal this..................day of...................................., 19..........

....(SEAL)

....(SEAL)

State of Oregon, County of...: ss.

On this......................day of...................................., 19.........., before me, the undersigned, a notary public in and for said county and state, personally appeared the within named...

known to me to be the identical individual...... described in and who executed the within instrument and acknowledged to me that ....executed the same freely and voluntarily.

IN TESTIMONY WHEREOF, I have hereunto set my hand and affixed my official seal the day and year last above written.

[NOTARIAL SEAL]

....
Notary Public for Oregon.

My commission expires..

ASSIGNMENT BY BUYER OF THE CONTRACT ON THE REVERSE HEREOF

KNOW ALL MEN BY THESE PRESENTS, That the undersigned, the identical buyer named in the contract of sale shown on the reverse hereof, in consideration of $..................................... to the buyer paid by.., *hereinafter called assignee, hereby does convey, assign, sell, transfer and set over unto the said assignee, his heirs and assigns, all of the buyer's right, title and interest in and to the said contract of sale and in and to the real estate therein described. Upon full compliance by said assignee of the covenants contained in said contract, the buyer does authorize and direct that conveyance of said real estate be made to said assignee, his heirs and assigns. The buyer does covenant with and warrant unto said assignee that the unpaid principal balance of the purchase price of said real estate does not exceed $.................................with the interest thereon from..., 19........., until paid.*

IN WITNESS WHEREOF, the undersigned buyer has hereunto set hand and seal this..................day of...................................., 19..........

....(SEAL)

....(SEAL)

State of Oregon, County of...: ss.

On this......................day of...................................., 19.........., before me, the undersigned, a notary public in and for said county and state, personally appeared the within named...

known to me to be the identical individual...... described in and who executed the within instrument and acknowledged to me that ....executed the same freely and voluntarily.

IN TESTIMONY WHEREOF, I have hereunto set my hand and affixed my official seal the day and year last above written.

[NOTARIAL SEAL]

....
Notary Public for Oregon.

My commission expires..

CONTRACT

(FORM No. 705)

STEVENS-NESS LAW PUB. CO., PORTLAND, ORE.

BETWEEN

Robert Seller

Address 20 "D" St., Salem

AND

Frank Purchaser

Address 16 "B" St., Salem

Dated March 15, 19--

Lot 16 *Block* 9

Addition Moores

STATE OF OREGON, County of Marion } *ss.*

I certify that the within instrument was received for record on the 24th *day of* April, 19--, *at* 1 *o'clock* P.M., *and recorded in book* 1632 *on page* 47 *Record of Deeds of said County.*

Witness my hand and seal of County affixed.

J. S. Clerk
County Clerk—Recorder.

By Albert Smith *Deputy.*

STATE OF OREGON, County of Marion } *ss.*

On this 15th *day of* March, *19*--, *before me, the undersigned, a notary public in and for said county and state, personally appeared the within named*

Robert Seller and Frank Purchaser

*known to me to be the identical individual*s *described in and who executed the within instrument and acknowledged to me that* they *executed the same freely and voluntarily.*

IN TESTIMONY WHEREOF, I have hereunto set my hand and affixed my official seal the day and year last above written.

/s/ Harold Corneilson
Notary Public for Oregon.

My commission expires December 31, 19--

THE MORTGAGE OR CONTRACT ASSUMED BY THE SAID BUYER ON THE REVERSE HEREOF IS DESCRIBED AS FOLLOWS:

Is it a mortgage or a contract

Mortgage

Mortgagee or seller therein

First Nat. Bank of Salem

Date April 7, *19*--

Where recorded Mortgage *Records*

Marion *County.*

[Neither the contract on the reverse hereof nor either of the above assignments can be recorded in the Deed Records unless acknowledged before a notary public.]

A Land Contract (Concluded)

> The seller within ...... days from the date of this contract will deposit in escrow with ...... (the name of the escrowee is entered here), a good and sufficient deed together with an executed copy of this contract and such other documents including abstract of title or title insurance policy and fire insurance policies which shall pertain to this contract, to be by such escrow agent held in escrow until the terms of this contract shall be completely executed, or until default is made under the same. The terms of such deposit in escrow shall be given by separate escrow agreement to be at the said time executed.

In California, escrow is used quite extensively. There, when the real estate broker has a purchase agreement signed between buyer and seller, the entire transaction is delivered to an escrow agent. He orders a title search made, and then proceeds to close the entire transaction, making the apportionments and performing all of the other details performed by lawyers and brokers in the other states in much the same manner as described in Chapter 23, "Title Closing."

The escrow agent, who is usually an employee of a bank or the escrow department of a brokerage firm or title insurance firm, is paid a fee for holding the instruments in escrow; he then collects the monthly payments on the contract from the purchaser and turns the receipts over to the seller.

In the event of default under the terms of the contract, the seller has a right to foreclose in much the same manner as a mortgagee will foreclose on a mortgage.

Land Contract as a Junior Financing Device

This contract is very often used as a *junior financing device*. For example, when the purchase price of a property is $10,000 and there exists a first mortgage in the amount of $8,500 and the broker has a prospect with only $1,000 in cash, a contract may be used for financing the balance of $500 instead of a second purchase money mortgage. The seller then receives the $1,000 cash, the parties to the transaction enter into a contract for $500, and the purchaser will either "assume" or take the property "subject to" the $8,500 mortgage. This is done where refinancing is not possible.

By discounting the contract, brokers are often able to arrange a sort of "chain reaction" involving a number of transactions. For example, here is an actual situation that was carried through by an astute broker.

Property A:	Selling Price	$12,000.00	
	Mortgage	8,000.00	
		$ 4,000.00	(*A's* Equity)
Property B:	Selling Price	$12,500.00	
	Mortgage	9,000.00	
		$ 3,500.00	(*B's* Equity)
Property C:	Selling Price	$14,500.00	
	Mortgage	11,500.00	
		$ 3,000.00	(*C's* Equity)
Property D:	Selling Price	$21,000.00	
	Mortgage	14,000.00	
		$ 7,000.00	(*D's* Equity)

C, who desired the property of *D*, had $5,000 in cash in addition to his equity of $3,000 in his house; thus, he lacked $2,000 cash with which to purchase *D's* equity. *A* wished to purchase *B's* house, but had no cash; *B* wished to purchase *C's* house, but had no cash. *X* appeared on the scene with $1,000 in cash and wished to purchase *A's* house.

A agreed to sell the home to *X* with $1,000 cash and a contract of $3,000, which he also agreed to sell to an investor discounted to $2,500. An investor was obtained by the broker who purchased the contract between *A* and *X* for $2,500. This gave *A* $3,500 cash with which to purchase *B's* home. *B* upon receiving the $3,500 from *A* used $3,000 of it to purchase *C's* home; *C* then had $2,000 more to add to the $5,000 that he had and was able to purchase the home of *D*. Thus, by finding a purchaser with $1,000 cash, the broker was able to transact $60,000 worth of business.

The same thing can be done by means of the second purchase money mortgage in those areas where the contract is not used.

Also, the same thing can be done with only a single transaction, when the seller is willing to discount the contract or second purchase money mortgage. If, for example, a property is to be sold at $10,000 with an existing mortgage of $7,000, and a prospect has but $1,000 cash and the seller is willing to give a contract for $2,000, the seller might be more than willing to sell for $9,500, discounting the $2,000 contract at, let us say, $1,500.

From an ethical standpoint, it is assumed that all of the parties will at all times be informed of, and be aware of, all the details of the transaction whether it be a single transaction or whether it be of the "chain reaction" type.

In these types of transactions, there is generally inserted in the contract between the buyer and the seller a clause to the effect that the buyer will, when the existing mortgage has been reduced sufficiently, attempt to refinance the property through a bank and pay off the contract. Thus, in the above transaction between *A* and *X* where the contract calls for $3,000 to be paid by *X*, the contract states that *X* will attempt to obtain a new first mortgage when the existing first mortgage of $8,000 has been reduced to $7,000. Or, the statement might say, "when the mortgage has been reduced to that point where the bank will refinance the transaction."

THE INSTALLMENT CONTRACT

The *installment contract* is a device generally employed in the sale of vacant lots. A contract is entered into between the seller and the buyer after the buyer has paid a deposit for the property. The buyer agrees to pay a certain sum monthly on the balance due under the contract; he also agrees to pay the taxes and sometimes part of the development charges. The seller retains the title to the property under such an agreement. However, he agrees to deliver clear title when the balance has been completely paid. In addition, there is generally a provision that, in the event the purchaser defaults, the sums he paid are to be construed as rent and forfeited to the seller.

In some areas the installment contract has been used to finance houses. For example, *A* desires to purchase a home and has insufficient funds for the down payment. The builder or owner may enter into an installment contract with *A* provided that, when he has paid enough on the contract to satisfy lending institutions, he will finance the balance of the purchase price by an FHA loan or other suitable financing. In some cases the buyer is permitted to pay the entire amount in installments, the deed being withheld until full payment has been made.

OPTIONS

An *option* may be defined as a contract to keep an offer open. Previously, it was explained that an offer may be withdrawn at anytime before it is accepted. The option is a device to prevent the seller from withdrawing the offer for a specified time. It has all of the elements of a contract, including a consideration which is paid to the seller for keeping the offer open. When an option is drawn, the practice is usually to prepare a contract for the sale of the property that is complete except for execution. The contract is by custom attached to the option.

Use of Option by Builders

Very often a builder will request an option on a number of lots. He will do this when he is not certain whether the houses will sell readily and when he wishes to remain in a financially liquid position. For example, if there are ten lots in which he is interested, he may purchase one outright and receive an option from the seller on the other nine. After he builds and sells the first house, he may, if the first house was profitable, exercise his option on the other nine lots.

In a situation of this type, the seller should, depending upon his bargaining position, insist that the builder exercise his option on at least two lots at a time. If the lots vary in their price because some are more valuable than others, the owner might examine the possibility of the optionee's exercising his option on a high-priced lot and a low-priced lot at the same time. Otherwise, the builder might just exercise his option on the choice lots, and leave the seller with the poorer lots. This is particularly applicable in a situation where there is a flat price per lot. If the purchaser exercises the option only on the choice lots, the seller would be left in an unprofitable position.

ASSIGNMENT OF CONTRACTS

Although a contract may specifically prohibit the assignment of the instrument, most contracts are freely assignable. Suppose *A* enters into a contract with *B* for the sale of real property. *B*, the purchaser, may arrange to sell the property to *X*. *B* will then assign the contract and thus avoid the possibility of two title closings. If *B* does assign his rights under the contract, instructions for drawing the deed and other instruments should be given to *A*, the seller, as long in advance of the closing date as possible.

The option is also freely assignable. After an assignment has been made, the assignee may exercise the same rights that had been held by his assignor.

The procedure for making an assignment is quite simple. Generally, the following statement is endorsed on the contract:

> For value received, the within contract and all the rights, title and interest of the purchaser hereunder are hereby assigned, transferred, and set over unto . . . and said assignee hereby assumes all of the obligations of the purchaser hereunder.

The assignment is dated and executed by the parties concerned.

SPECIFIC PERFORMANCE

Specific performance has to do with the methods of enforcing the terms of the real property contract. When a contract has been breached by the seller, the buyer may do one of a number of things. He may rescind, that is, declare the contract terminated, recover his deposit, and in effect be in *status quo ante* (in the same position as if there had been no contract). He may choose to sue for damages and, if successful, may obtain a personal judgment against the seller for the difference between the contract price and the market price at the time of the breach. The seller may also rescind or sue for damages in the event of a breach of the contract.

As another alternative, the buyer or the seller may bring an action for specific performance. *Specific performance* is an action brought to compel a party to a contract to perform his contract. This action is brought in a court of equity and generally allowed to be brought in equity by virtue of the fact that real property is unique—there is only one such parcel in existence and a suit for damages will not result in an adequate remedy. If a seller brings an action for specific performance, he will, in effect, compel the buyer to go through with the deal. If the buyer refuses in the face of the court order to tender the purchase price and receive the deed, the buyer stands in contempt of court.

The buyer, too, may bring this remedy, and he will choose this alternative more often than not in a period of rising real estate values.

Right to Rescind Transactions Involving Real Property

Under the Consumer Credit Protection Act of 1968 and Regulation Z (the Truth in Lending Act), it is sometimes possible to rescind a real estate contract. Except where a purchase money security interest in real property is involved, in any consumer credit transaction in which the creditor retains or will acquire or retain a security interest in real property which is the principal residence of the customer, the customer has the right to rescind the transaction until midnight of the third business day following the date of consummation of the transaction or delivery of the disclosures required under Regulation Z, whichever is later.

A purchase money mortgage is a mortgage that is given as part of the consideration for the sale of real property. This will be discussed at length in Chapter 6. Regulation Z, which was adopted by the Board of Governors of the Federal Reserve Board on February 10, 1969, spells out not only the disclosures, including finance charges and annual percentage rates that must be made by creditors, but also the manner in which they must be made.

"The Act does not apply to business loans or commercial loans such as a construction loan to builders, but it will apply when the construction loan is converted to a consumer loan made to the purchaser of the house. The Act will only apply if payment of the loan is made in more than four installments or if a finance charge is or may be made."[5]

Thus, if *A* signs a contract for a residence and financing is arranged through a financial institution, he may rescind the transaction. To do so he may notify the "creditor" of his intention to do so by mail, telegram, or other writing. A creditor is defined by Regulation Z (Sec. 226.2(m)) as "A person who in the ordinary course of business regularly extends or arranges for the extension of consumer credit."

If the customer elects to rescind, he is not liable for any finance or other charge and any security interest becomes void. Within ten days after receipt of notice of rescission, the creditor must return to the customer any money or property given as earnest money or as a down payment.

The customer may modify or waive his right to rescind if:

---

[5] Keith T. Koskie, "Truth-In-Lending" (unpublished paper).

1. The extension of credit is needed in order to meet a good faith, immediate personal financial emergency of the customer;
2. The customer has determined that a delay of 3 days will jeopardize the welfare, health, or safety of natural persons, or endanger property which is his or for which he is responsible; and
3. The customer furnishes the creditor with a separate dated and signed personal statement describing the situation and in which he modifies or waives his right of rescission.

Printed forms may not be used for this purpose. Any waiver must be signed by all joint owners.

QUESTIONS FOR REVIEW

1. Explain the phrase "meeting of the minds."
2. What conditions must be met in a memorandum in writing to comply with the Statute of Frauds?
3. What is a *reduction certificate*? Why may a purchaser be interested in having one delivered to him at the time of title closing?
4. What are *liquidated damages*? Why might a purchaser desire a statement regarding liquidated damages inserted in the contract?
5. What is the distinction between the contract for the exchange of real property and the ordinary contract for its sale?
6. How and why is escrow used when a sale is made "on contract"?
7. When may specific performance be used?

PROBLEMS

1. Suppose a buyer and seller enter into a contract which contains a typical statement in real estate contracts: "Payment at the closing to be paid in United States currency."

   The buyer appears at the closing at the appointed time and place with his personal check for the balance of the purchase price. The seller, having a better offer, wishes to get out of the deal. He refuses to accept the buyer's personal check, stating that it is not United States currency.

   Can the seller escape the contract in this manner? Discuss.

2. Gerald Williams has a house for sale at $10,000. Edward Logan approaches you, a broker, and states that he is willing to purchase the

house at that price, but he has only $1,000 for a down payment. From your past experience as a broker you realize that most banks would be reluctant to lend Logan $9,000 on a mortgage, even though he is a stable person with a fairly good job. You learn from Logan that he is at present living in an apartment and is paying $107.50 a month rent without any undue financial strain.

You believe a bank would readily lend $6,500 on Williams' property; but, of course, a loan of that amount is impossible at present.

You approach your client, Williams, and explain the situation to him. To your surprise (you should have known this when you listed the property), Williams states that he would be willing to help finance the sale himself, but doesn't know how to go about it.

(a) Give a step-by-step explanation of how this can be done.

(b) When you have finished your explanation, Williams says, "That's all very well, but I'd like to get the balance paid off as soon as possible. I can't wait forever for my money." Explain two possible ways by which Williams might obtain the balance of the money due him within four years.

3. Obtain a blank form of binder or receipt and agreement form that is used by brokers in your state. If you are unable to find one, follow the form given in the text. Fill in the blanks from the following:

On December 16, 1973, Howard L. Olsen and his wife, Marie Olsen, gave a listing to John W. Thomas, a registered (in some states called a licensed) broker of Gainesville, Florida. The property listed was lot #26 and the east ½ of lot #25 of the Highland Acres tract recorded July 10, 1950, otherwise described as 1111 N. W. 12th Ave., Gainesville, Florida. Commission to be 6 percent; listing price $17,500. The sellers stated they need at least $5,000 in cash and that they would be willing to accept a note (or bond as used in some states) secured by a first mortgage for the remainder, to be amortized over 15 years in equal semiannual installments, which would include interest at 6½ percent on the unpaid balance. The first installment to become due six months after the closing of title. Possession to be on or after April 1, 1974. Policy of title insurance to be paid for by the sellers.

Thomas received an offer from Cecil Holmes and his wife, Kathy Holmes, residing in Gainesville, subject to the following conditions: occupancy by February 1, 1974; deposit to be returned if the sellers do not agree to the terms and conditions within seven days from the tender of the offer.

On December 26, 1973, John Thomas, broker, agreed to submit the Holmes' offer of $1,000 less than the listing price and he accepted a $500 deposit to bind the offer on the following financial terms: $8,000 cash down including the deposit, remainder by note (or bond) and a first mortgage to be amortized by monthly payments on the unpaid balance at 6 percent. Title policy to be paid for by the sellers.

4. Smith offers Brown a parcel of land for $25,000. The offer is in writing and contains a clause: "This offer is to remain open until January 15, 1975." The offer is dated December 1, 1974. On January 2, 1975, Smith notifies Brown that the offer is withdrawn. On January 8, 1975, Brown writes Smith accepting the offer. Is there a contract for the sale of land?
5. A contract for the sale of real property provided that the seller would convey "subject to any state of facts that an accurate survey would show provided that the same did not render the title unmarketable." The contract also provided that the seller "shall give and the purchaser shall accept a title" such as a named title company "or any reputable title company will approve and insure." The report of the title company excepted from the coverage an encroachment of 2.79 feet uncovered by a survey. The purchaser rejected title at the closing as being unmarketable and uninsurable and sued for his $4,500 down payment. Who wins and why?

SUGGESTED READINGS

Anderson, Ronald A., and Walter A. Kumpf. *Business Law,* 9th ed. Cincinnati: South-Western Publishing Co., 1972. Part II.

Ring, Alfred A. *Real Estate Principles and Practices,* 7th ed. Englewood Cliffs, New Jersey: Prentice-Hall, Inc., 1972. Chapter 5.

Chapter 5

Deeds and Conveyances

The *deed*, which is the second basic real estate instrument used by the real estate practitioner, may be defined as the instrument in writing which conveys an interest in real property. Historically, the deed developed from what was known as *livery of seizin*. A person owning property and desiring to convey his interest in the property to another delivered on the land "in the name of seizin of the land" a piece of turf or a twig and simultaneously made a statement to effect the transfer. The livery of seizin in a later development was usually accompanied by a statement of the transfer in writing. Later the symbolical delivery of the turf or twig was done away with and the written instrument alone was delivered to the grantee.

This writing became what is presently known as the deed. A deed must be signed, sealed (in some states), and delivered.

Because a deed is a contract, it must therefore fill the requirements of the contract as outlined in Chapter 4.

THE PARTS OF A DEED

The Parties

Like most instruments, a deed contains the names of the parties to the transaction. The parties in a deed are called the grantor and the grantee. The *grantor* is the person who is transferring his interest in the property, and the *grantee* is the person to whom the interest is being transferred. In the normal transaction handled by the broker, the seller is commonly the grantor and the purchaser the grantee.

Some state statutes require that the full addresses of both the grantor and the grantee be given in the deed, and it is strongly recommended that they be included in the instrument even when not specifically required by statute. The full address includes the street address, the city or village, the township, the county, and the state.

The Consideration

In all valid contracts a *consideration* is mentioned. Thus, a deed may contain the statement that the grantor "in consideration of Ten and 00/100 Dollars, lawful money of the United States, paid by the grantee. . . ."

The consideration named in the example above is a nominal consideration.[1] The Code of Ethics of the NATIONAL ASSOCIATION OF REALTORS, Article 6, states: "The REALTOR should not be a party to the naming of a false consideration in any document, unless it be the naming of an obviously nominal consideration."

Naming the actual consideration in a deed avoids the possibility of the broker's becoming an innocent party to misleading others about the purchase price of a parcel of property.

Operative Words of Conveyance

Following the statement of the consideration are the so-called *operative words of conveyance* or *granting clause*. The words "grant and release," or "grant and convey," or "grant, bargain, and sell" are operative words of conveyance. These words show the intent on the part of the grantor to transfer the property. Following the words of grant are words of limitation denoting the quantum of the estate granted. In many states the granting clause will read:

---

[1] A few states, Nebraska for example, require that the actual consideration be named in the deed. See *Neb. Rev. Stat.*—Sec. 76-214 (1950). However, where a deed is executed by a grantor acting as a fiduciary, such as guardian or executor, a statement as to the actual purchase price is necessary in all states.

WITNESSETH, that the party of the first part, in consideration of Ten and 00/100 ($10) Dollars lawful money of the United States and other good and valuable consideration paid by the party of the second part, does hereby *grant and release unto the party of the second part, his heirs and assigns forever.* (This is followed by a description of the premises.)

In the statement above the words "heirs and assigns forever" are considered the words denoting the quantum of the estate to be conveyed. In most states the words "heirs and assigns" create the fee simple. In such states the absence of these words creates a life estate in the grantee.

To create a fee simple in a corporation which has no heirs, the deed would read substantially as follows: "To the ABC Corporation, its successors and assigns."

Some states have done away with the necessity of stating "and his heirs" in the deed from *A* to *B* in order to convey a fee simple. Notably, Idaho 55-506 I.C.A. states briefly: "Words of inheritance or succession are not requisite to transfer a fee in real property." Other states having similar statutes are Ohio, Pennsylvania, Tennessee, and Illinois. In such states the deed would read:

Know All Men by These Presents: That Richard Roe, residing at 801 "B" Street, City of Boise, County of Ada, State of Idaho, in consideration of Ten Dollars, does hereby grant, bargain, sell, and convey unto John Doe, the following property in Latah County, State of Idaho, to wit: (and here follows the description of the property). (If it is a life estate, "for life" will appear after "John Doe.")

The Property Description

Following the words of conveyance in a deed, the property to be conveyed is described. The description should be a formal, legal one. The property is described in any one of three methods: by lot and block number, by metes and bounds, or by government survey.

Lot and Block Number. Every map, or *plat,* filed by a subdivider or developer with the clerk of the county in which the property is located contains *lot and block numbers.* Although a street on a map so filed may contain only a name, the law generally requires that these streets be given block numbers and that each lot be given a lot number. Sometimes, only lot numbers are required. After the acceptance of the plat by the proper authorities, the owner of the subdivision may from that time forth describe by lot and block number the property in any conveyance made. For example, if a map is filed under the title "The Map of Smith Acres Development Company," the description may read:

> Lot #3, Block 19, of the Map of Smith Acres Development Company, surveyed by James Jones, Patchogue, July 17, 19— as recorded on page — in Book — of the county of —.

Anyone desiring to know the exact size of the lot can get the information in the office of the county clerk where the plat is filed.

Metes and Bounds. A description by *metes* (measures) and *bounds* (direction) is a second method of defining boundaries of a property. It is often called an "irregular" description. The property is described by beginning at a certain point and measuring and indicating the direction and length of the boundaries of the property until the point of beginning is again reached.

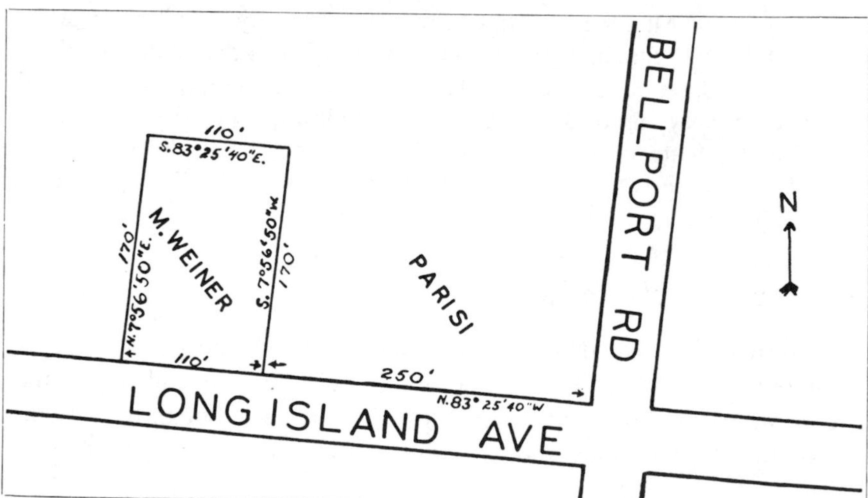

For example, a metes and bounds description of the property mapped above would be as follows:

All that tract or parcel of land, together with the buildings and improvements thereon, situate, lying and being at Medford, in the Town of Brookhaven, County of Suffolk, State of New York, bounded and described as follows:

COMMENCING at a concrete monument set for a bound on the northerly side of Long Island Avenue, distant Two Hundred and Fifty (250) feet westerly from the point of intersection of the Bellport Road; thence running N. 83° 25′ 40″ W. by and with the northerly line of Long Island Avenue, One Hundred and Ten (110) feet to a certain point; thence running N. 7° 56′ 50″ E. by and with other land now or formerly of Michael Weiner, One Hundred Seventy (170) feet to a certain point; thence running S. 83° 25′ 40″ E., by and with other land now or formerly of said Michael Weiner, One Hundred Ten (110) feet to land now or formerly of one Parisi, thence by and with the land now or formerly of one Parisi S. 7° 56′ 50″ W. One Hundred Seventy (170) feet to the point of beginning.

In the event that the land had not been surveyed, the property could still be described by metes and bounds; however, the description would probably not be so accurate.

Government Survey. The *government survey,* or rectangular survey as it is sometimes called, was adopted early in our history by Congress and is used to a large degree outside the original thirteen states. The system refers to a grid of north and south lines and east and west lines which are established in the Land Office in Washington.

The north and south lines are called *meridians,* and the east and west lines are called *parallels.* The distances between those parallels and meridians are twenty-four miles in each direction and are called *checks.*

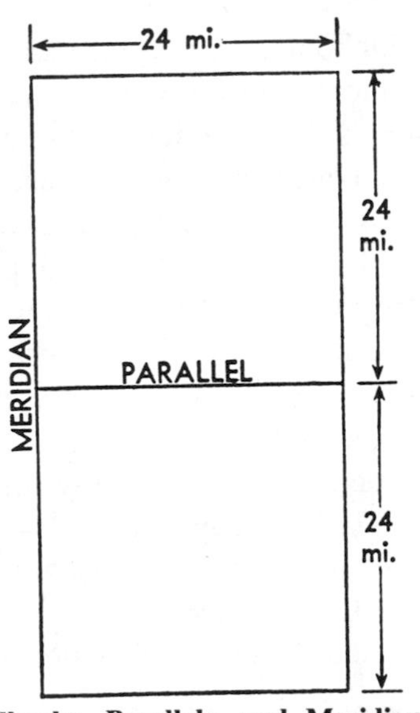

Checks, Parallels, and Meridians

Division of the Check. Each check of twenty-four miles square is divided into sixteen townships of six miles square each as shown below.

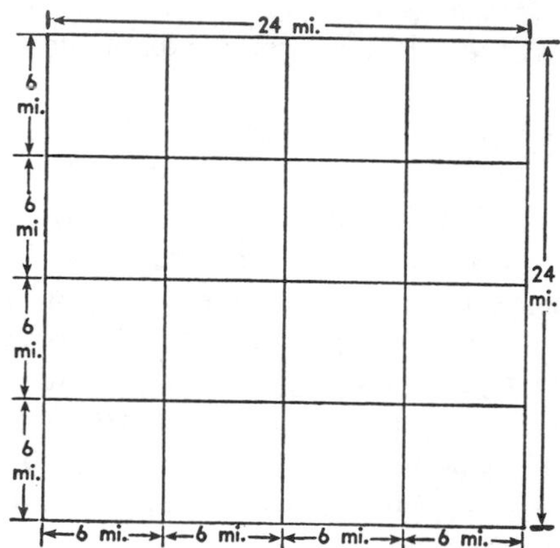

Division of a Check into Sixteen Townships

The Base Line. Certain of the parallels are designated as *base lines*, running east and west. These base lines, running along the parallels, vary among the states; for example, the State of Wisconsin employs a base line which is the southern boundary of the state. Oklahoma, on the other hand, uses a line passing through two towns, Duncan and Sulphur; however, in the "panhandle" section, the base line is the boundary between the Texas and Oklahoma "panhandles."

Townships, or tiers as they are often called, are numbered and designated as being either north or south of the base line.

In the illustration on page 113, the upper right-hand figure is designated as "T. 4 N." which means that this particular township is four tiers or four townships north of the base line. All townships or tiers the same distance north of the base line are numbered the same, that is, "T. 4 N." The same thing is applicable to townships or tiers south of the base line.

The description, "T. 4 N.," is meaningless by itself. The thing that pinpoints the exact township or tier north or south of the base line is the range east or west of a principal meridian along which a particular township or tier is located.

Principal Meridians. Just as certain parallels are designated as base lines, so certain of the meridians are designated as *principal*

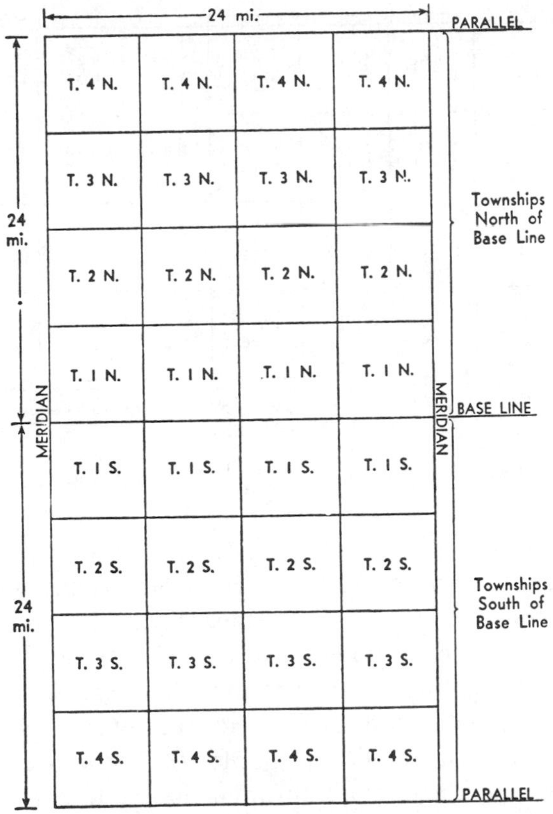

24 mi.

T. 4 N.	T. 4 N.	T. 4 N.	T. 4 N.	PARALLEL
T. 3 N.	T. 3 N.	T. 3 N.	T. 3 N.	Townships North of Base Line
T. 2 N.	T. 2 N.	T. 2 N.	T. 2 N.	
T. 1 N.	T. 1 N.	T. 1 N.	T. 1 N.	BASE LINE
T. 1 S.	T. 1 S.	T. 1 S.	T. 1 S.	
T. 2 S.	T. 2 S.	T. 2 S.	T. 2 S.	Townships South of Base Line
T. 3 S.	T. 3 S.	T. 3 S.	T. 3 S.	
T. 4 S.	T. 4 S.	T. 4 S.	T. 4 S.	PARALLEL

24 mi. 24 mi. MERIDIAN MERIDIAN

Townships or Tiers North and South of the Base Line

meridians. Nebraska and Kansas, for example, use the sixth principal meridian which passes about one mile west of Solomon, Kansas. Washington and Oregon both use the "Willamette" meridian, and Idaho uses the "Boise" meridian. Information in regard to the principal meridians can be obtained from any local surveyor or abstractor.

Just as the tiers or townships are numbered north or south of the base line, they are also numbered east or west of a principal meridian. The township rows east or west of the principal meridian are called *ranges.* Each range in either an easterly or westerly direction from the principal meridian is identified with a number. Thus, a township may be described as being T. 1 N., R. 1 W., which means that it is in the first tier north of the base line and in the first range west of the principal meridian. A diagram of the townships of two checks is shown at the top of the next page.

24 mi. | 24 mi.

T. 4N. R. 4W.	T. 4N. R. 3W.	T. 4N. R. 2W.	T. 4N. R. 1W.	T. 4N. R. 1E.	T. 4N. R. 2E.	T. 4N. R. 3E.	T. 4N. R. 4E.
T. 3N. R. 4W.	T. 3N. R. 3W.	T. 3N. R. 2W.	T. 3N. R. 1W.	T. 3N. R. 1E.	T. 3N. R. 2E.	T. 3N. R. 3E.	T. 3N. R. 4E.
T. 2N. R. 4W.	T. 2N. R. 3W.	T. 2N. R. 2W.	T. 2N. R. 1W.	T. 2N. R. 1E.	T. 2N. R. 2E.	T. 2N. R. 3E.	T. 2N. R. 4E.
T. 1N. R. 4W.	T. 1N. R. 3W.	T. 1N. R. 2W.	T. 1N. R. 1W.	T. 1N. R. 1E.	T. 1N. R. 2E.	T. 1N. R. 3E.	T. 1N. R. 4E.

24 mi.

BASE LINE

North Tiers and West Ranges — PRINCIPAL MERIDIAN — North Tiers and East Ranges

Township Designations by Tiers and Ranges

A frequent and often puzzling question arises with regard to two base lines, one directly above the other. If one begins counting townships north from the southernmost base line, when does one begin to run into townships counted south from the northernmost base line? The answer given by many is that the place where one leaves off counting south or north is by local custom. However, what is behind the local custom? For example, the New Mexico principal meridian runs north and south through that state and is intersected by a base line. Directly north of this New Mexico base line is a base line in Colorado which runs east and west from the border of Missouri to the Utah border and which intersects the sixth principal meridian running north from the northern border of Oklahoma through Kansas and Nebraska to the southern border of South Dakota.

Assuming one is counting north from the base line in New Mexico, when does one meet southern tiers from the base line in Colorado? The answer is that the original surveys laid out sharply defined areas in blocks. These defined areas point out the meeting places of the extreme southern tiers and the extreme northern tiers extending from any base line.

The Township. The township or tier north or south of the base line is numbered in the manner previously shown. If it is the sixth township north of the base line and the first township east of the principal meridian, it will then be designated as T. 6 N., R. 1 E. or Twp. 6 N., R. 1 E. Either "T." or "Twp." is correct for use in a description. A township consists of an area of thirty-six square miles. The thirty-six square miles of each township are divided into square-mile tracts. These tracts are called *sections*, and each section is numbered. Thus T. 6 N., R. 1 E., when divided into sections, would appear as shown below.

6 mi.

6	5	4	3	2	1
7	8	9	10	11	12
18	17	16	15	14	13
19	20	21	22	23	24
30	29	28	27	26	25
31	32	33	34	35	36

6 mi. — 1 mi. — 1 mi.

Division of Township into Sections. Each Township Is Divided into 36 Sections of One Square Mile Each. All Townships Are Numbered in the Same Manner.

The Section. To summarize, the check, an area 24 miles by 24 miles, is broken down into 16 townships each 6 miles by 6 miles, and they in turn are each broken down into 36 sections 1 mile by 1 mile. These sections, containing 640 acres, are each numbered as shown above. Thus, if our description referred to Section 8 of Township 6 N., R. 1 E., it would be designated Sec. 8, T. 6 N., R. 1 E.

The question now arises as to how the section is reduced for descriptive purposes when a parcel of land less than 640 acres is being described. The answer is that the section is halved and then quartered as shown on the next page.

As an example, examine the lower left quarter of the illustration at the top of the next page. It is designated as SW¼ Sec. 8, T. 6 N., R. 1 E. The interpretation of this designation is as follows:

The SW$\frac{1}{4}$ of a section consists of 160 acres, that is, 640 acres divided by 4; Section 8 is of thc Township 6 N., which means a township 6 tiers or 6 townships north of a base line; and R. 1 E. means that this 6th township north of a base line is 1 range east of a principal meridian.

1 mi.
1 mi.
NW¼sec. 8,
T. 6 N., R. 1 E.
160 Acres
NE¼sec. 8,
T. 6 N., R. 1 E.
160 Acres
8
SW¼sec. 8,
T. 6 N., R. 1 E.
160 Acres
SE¼sec. 8,
T. 6 N., R. 1 E.
160 Acres

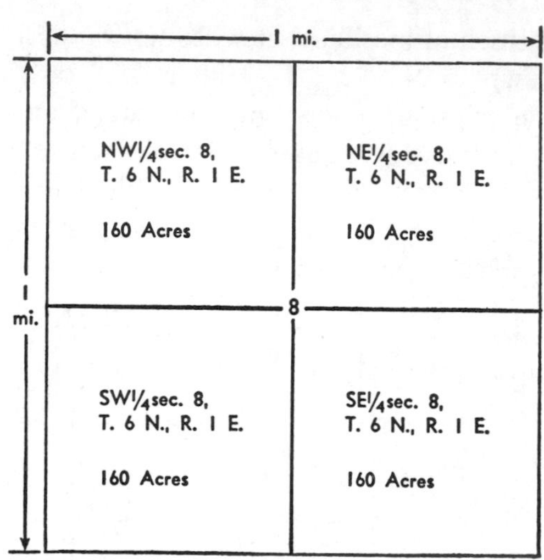

A Section of 640 Acres Divided into Four Quarters

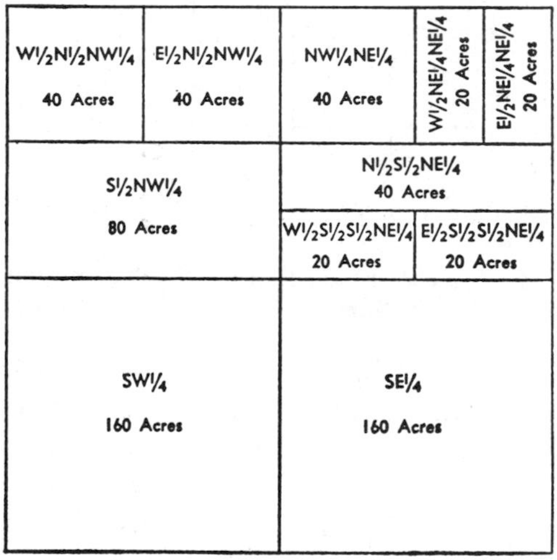

W½N½NW¼
40 Acres
E½N½NW¼
40 Acres
NW¼NE¼
40 Acres
W½NE¼NE¼
20 Acres
E½NE¼NE¼
20 Acres
S½NW¼
80 Acres
N½S½NE¼
40 Acres
W½S½S½NE¼
20 Acres
E½S½S½NE¼
20 Acres
SW¼
160 Acres
SE¼
160 Acres

A Section Divided into Smaller Parcels

The quarter sections of 160 acres can be further broken down as shown at the left.

This illustration shows a section divided into smaller parcels. Assume that it is Section 8, Township 6 North, Range 1 East. The upper left-hand quarter, the northwest quarter, is divided into three parts. The bottom part has been halved, and the upper half has been divided into two equal parts. The south half has been designated as the S½ of the NW¼, an area of 80 acres that is the south half of the northwest quarter of the section. It would be described as the S½ of the NW¼ of Sec. 8, T. 6 N., R. 1 E.

Looking at the north half of the quarter, we find that it has been divided down the middle into two areas: the west one half of the north half of the northwest quarter, and the east one half of the north half of the northwest quarter. The first is designated as W½ of the N½ of the NW¼, and the second as the E½ of the N½ of the NW¼. The westerly half is described as the W½ of the N½ of the NW¼ of Sec. 8, T. 6 N., R. 1 E., while the easterly half is described as the E½ of the N½ of the NW¼ of Sec. 8, T. 6 N., R. 1 E.

TABLE OF LAND MEASURE

Linear Measure	*Square Measure*
1 link—7.92 inches	1 acre—160 sq. rods; 10 sq. chains
1 rod—25 links; 16½ feet; 5½ yards	1 section—640 acres
1 chain—100 links; 66 feet; 4 rods	1 square mile—640 acres
1 mile—5,280 feet; 320 rods; 80 chains	1 township—36 square miles

Appurtenances

After the description of the property there is a clause stating:

> . . . together with the appurtenances and all the estate and rights of the party of the first part in and to said premises.

An *appurtenance* is something that passes with the land, commonly, a right of way or other type of easement. In those areas where water rights for irrigation purposes are important, these water rights are generally held to be appurtenant to the land except when the rights are in a stock company. The broker or attorney handling such a transaction should investigate the exact nature of the water rights.

The Premises

All the essential parts of the deed as outlined thus far—the names of the parties, the consideration, the operative words of conveyance, the property description, and the appurtenance provisions—are called the *premises*.

Habendum

After the premises, there follows the *habendum*. The habendum states:

> To have and to hold the premises herein granted unto the party of the second part . . . (here is limited the estate to be taken by the grantee).

Any reservation or declaration of trust is made at this point in the deed.

There is a possibility of conflict between the limitation of the estate as expressed in the habendum and the limitation of the estate as expressed by the operative words of conveyance in the premises of the deed. Every attempt should be made to draw up an habendum that is consistent with the premises. The general rule is that in the event of a conflict between the habendum and the premises, the premises are construed to indicate the intent of the deed and the habendum is omitted.

Execution and Acknowledgment

Customarily, the deed is executed or signed only by the grantor or grantors. It is only when the grantee is assuming a mortgage, as outlined in Chapter 6, that both the grantor and the grantee sign the deed. In the event that the grantor is unable to write, his mark, properly witnessed, is acceptable in lieu of a written signature.

When the grantor is a corporation, one of the officers is authorized to sign and seal the deed. These words will precede the signature of the officer authorized to sign the instrument:

> In witness whereof, the party of the first part has caused its corporate seal to be hereunto affixed, and these presents to be signed by its duly authorized officer the day and year first above written.

Generally, the signature is attested to by another person.[2]

---

[2] Some states, notably Alaska, Arkansas, Connecticut, Florida, Georgia, Louisiana, Maryland, Michigan, Ohio, South Carolina, and Texas, require that the deed be executed in the presence of, and subscribed by, one, and sometimes two or more, credible witnesses.

In order for a deed to be recordable, it must be acknowledged. This has been defined as the act by which a party who has executed an instrument of conveyance as grantor goes before a competent officer and declares or acknowledges the same as his genuine and voluntary act or deed. The competent officer referred to is generally a notary public. The reason for this is to prevent forged instruments from being recorded. The notary will require identification of those who sign and will require that the instruments be executed in his presence.[3]

The Seal

In some states, in order for there to be a valid conveyance, the deed must be sealed. The *seal* is a formality and is sometimes defined as a particular sign, made to attest in the most formal manner the execution of an instrument. Where required, this is generally done on the line where the grantor affixes his signature and is done by the letters "L.S." (*locus sigilli*), meaning the place of the seal. In many states today, however, the need for the seal has been done away with by statute.

Delivery

In order for the conveyance to be complete, there must not only be a deed drawn and executed in the proper form, but there must also be an actual delivery of the deed. The delivery may be made to the grantee himself, or it may be made in escrow, that is, to a third person for ultimate delivery to the grantee upon the happening of certain stated events.

Between the grantor and the grantee, the conveyance is effected at the time of the delivery of the deed; however, when a deed is delivered in escrow, the time of the conveyance generally relates back to the date of delivery to the escrow agent. For example, on July 1, 1973, a deed is delivered to an escrow agent to be delivered to the grantee upon the final payment of the purchase price on August 14, 1975. When the price has been paid and physical transfer of the

[3] In some states the instrument does not have to be executed in the presence of the notary if the grantor acknowledges his signature. In Arizona and Ohio the deed must be acknowledged to be *valid*.

deed given to the grantee, the date of the conveyance will usually relate back to the day of delivery to the escrow agent.

Recording

Although the delivery of a proper deed from the grantor to the grantee is valid between the grantor and the grantee, it would not ordinarily be valid to third parties. The recording of the deed with the proper official, usually the clerk of the county in which the property is located, gives notice to the world of the conveyance. If there are two successive grantees for value of the same parcel of property, the person recording the property first, in the absence of fraud, has the good title. This is discussed in detail in Chapter 22, "Search, Examination, and Registration of Title."

TYPES OF DEEDS

Quitclaim Deed

The simplest form of deed is the *quitclaim deed*. This deed in effect states that the grantor transfers to the grantee his rights, if any, in the property described. When it is used to convey property, there is no implication that the grantor has good title or any title at all. If he has nothing, then nothing is conveyed. If the grantor has good title, then the grantee can obtain a fee simple by means of the quitclaim deed; however, a transfer by quitclaim deed does not carry with it any implication that the grantee will receive any after acquired title rights.[4]

In general, the quitclaim deed is used when the grantee has, or claims that he has, incomplete or partial title to the premises and the grantor or another person has a possible interest that would otherwise constitute a "cloud on title." Often when there is an heir who might have a right to the property, the quitclaim deed is used.

A very practical use of the quitclaim deed exists when *A*, for example, has purchased a tax deed from a county. In some states he may go through a Torrens proceeding and register the title, but often it is simpler to obtain a quitclaim deed from the person who formerly owned the property.

---

[4] If the sales contract fails to specify that the seller is to convey by warranty deed or a quitclaim deed, the general rule is that it will be a compliance of the contract for the seller to convey by quitclaim deed.

Quitclaim Deed—Individual or Corporation.

THIS INDENTURE, made the 19th day of March nineteen hundred and . . .

BETWEEN Robert Seller, residing at 363 Madison Avenue, Hempstead, County of Nassau, State of New York,

party of the first part, and Francis X. Donovan, 33 Main Street, Floral Park, County of Nassau, State of New York,

party of the second part.

WITNESSETH, that the party of the first part, in consideration of Ten and 00/100 ($10) . . . . dollars, lawful money of the United States, and other good and valuable consideration paid by the party of the second part, does hereby remise, release and quitclaim unto the party of the second part, his heirs and assigns forever.

ALL (Here follows a complete legal description of the property to be conveyed.)

TOGETHER with all right, title and interest, if any, of the party of the first part in and to any streets and roads abutting the above described premises to the center lines thereof.

TOGETHER with the appurtenances and all the estate and rights of the party of the first part in and to said premises.

TO HAVE AND TO HOLD the premises herein granted unto the party of the second part his heirs and assigns forever.

AND the party of the first part, in compliance with Section 13 of the Lien Law, hereby covenants that the party of the first part will receive the consideration for this conveyance and will hold the right to receive such consideration as a trust fund to be applied first for the purpose of paying the cost of the improvement and will apply the same first to the payment of the cost of the improvement before using any part of the total of the same for any other purpose. ①

IN WITNESS WHEREOF, the party of the first part has executed this deed the day and year first above written.

IN PRESENCE OF:

/s/ John Broker /s/ Robert Seller

A Quitclaim Deed

① In those states in which there is no trust created by statute, this clause is omitted.

STATE OF NEW YORK, COUNTY OF Nassau ss.:
On the 19th day of March , nineteen hundred and . . .
before me personally came Robert Seller

to me known to be the individual described in and who executed the foregoing instrument, and acknowledged that he executed the same.

/s/ John Broker
Notary Public, State of New York
Residing in Nassau County
Nassau County Clerk's No. 856
Commission Expires March 31, 19--

STATE OF NEW YORK, COUNTY OF ss.:
On the day of , nineteen hundred and
before me personally came

to me known to be the individual described in and who executed the foregoing instrument, and acknowledged that executed the same.

Title Guarantee and Trust Company, New York, New York

A Quitclaim Deed (Concluded)

The Bargain and Sale Deed

There are two types of bargain and sale deeds in general use: the bargain and sale deed *without covenant* and the bargain and sale deed *with covenant.* A *covenant* may be best described as any agreement or promise. In the case of a deed, it is a promise reduced to writing and contained within the deed.

The operative words in the quitclaim deed state:

> The party of the first part (the grantor) does hereby remise, release and quitclaim unto the party of the second part. . . .

In the bargain and sale deed, either with or without covenant, the operative words are:

> The party of the first part (the grantor) does hereby grant and release unto the party of the second part. . . .

The distinction, then, is this: in either the bargain and sale deed with covenant or the bargain and sale deed without covenant, the grantor asserts by implication that he has the possession of a claim to or interest in the property. This implication is not present in the quitclaim deed.

Bargain and Sale Deed, with Covenant against Grantor's Acts—Individual or Corporation.

THIS INDENTURE, made the 22d day of April nineteen hundred and . . .

BETWEEN Frank Grantor, residing at 63 Franklin Street, White Plains, County of Westchester, State of New York,

party of the first part, and Joseph Massett, residing at 413 "A" Street, White Plains, County of Westchester, State of New York,

party of the second part,

WITNESSETH, that the party of the first part, in consideration of One and 00/100 ($1) . . . . dollars, lawful money of the United States, and other good and valuable consideration paid by the party of the second part, does hereby grant and release unto the party of the second part, his heirs and assigns forever.

ALL (Here follows a complete legal description of the property to be conveyed.)

TOGETHER with all the right, title and interest, if any, of the party of the first part of, in and to any streets and roads abutting the above described premises to the center lines thereof.

TOGETHER with the appurtenances and all the estate and rights of the party of the first part in and to said premises.

TO HAVE AND TO HOLD the premises herein granted unto the party of the second part, his heirs and assigns forever.

AND the party of the first part covenants as follows:
FIRST—That the party of the first part has not done or suffered anything whereby the said premises have been encumbered in any way whatever.
SECOND—That, in compliance with Section 13 of the Lien Law, the party of the first part will receive the consideration for this conveyance and will hold the right to receive such consideration as a trust fund to be applied first for the purpose of paying the cost of the improvement and that the party of the first part will apply the same first to the payment of the cost of the improvement before using any part of the total of the same for any other purpose. (1)

IN WITNESS WHEREOF, the party of the first part has executed this deed the day and year first above written.

IN PRESENCE OF:

/s/ John Broker /s/ Frank Grantor

STATE OF NEW YORK, COUNTY OF Westchester ss.:
On the 22d day of April , nineteen hundred and . . .

A Bargain and Sale Deed

before me personally came Frank Grantor
to me known to be the individual described in and who executed the foregoing instrument, and acknowledged that he executed the same.

/s/ John Broker
Notary Public, State of New York
Residing in Westchester County
Westchester County Clerk's No. 1430
Commission Expires March 31, 19--

STATE OF NEW YORK, COUNTY OF **ss.:**
On the day of , nineteen hundred and
before me personally came

to me known to be the individual described in and who executed the foregoing instrument, and acknowledged that executed the same.

Title Guarantee and Trust Company, New York, New York

A Bargain and Sale Deed (Concluded)

① In those states in which there is no trust created by statute, this clause is omitted.

The bargain and sale deed with covenant, as it is called, goes one step further. There is one covenant inserted in the instrument by the grantor that reads:

> That the party of the first part (the grantor) has not done or suffered anything whereby the said premises have been encumbered in any way.

This means that the grantor during his ownership has not done anything to encumber the land; in short, it means that the grantor has not allowed any liens to be placed against the property.

Warranty Deed

A *warranty deed* is a deed in which the owner of property warrants that he has good and merchantable title to the property he is conveying. It may specify just what interest the owner is conveying and include covenants to protect the grantee in the event that the title should not be as represented. Because the warranty deed gives the grantee the greatest guarantee, it is the best type of deed that can be received.

Warranty Deed with Full Covenants—Individual or Corporation.

THIS INDENTURE, made the 11th day of May nineteen hundred and . . .

BETWEEN Harold Kuhn, residing at 1363 Front Street, Jamaica, County of Queens, State of New York,

party of the first part, and Arthur Grantee, residing at 1433 Johnson Road, Middle Village, County of Queens, State of New York,

party of the second part,

WITNESSETH, that the party of the first part, in consideration of Ten and 00/100 ($10) . . . . dollars, lawful money of the United States, and other good and valuable consideration paid by the party of the second part, does hereby grant and release unto the party of the second part, his heirs and assigns forever.

ALL (Here follows a complete legal description of the property to be conveyed.)

①

TOGETHER with all the right, title and interest, if any, of the party of the first part of, in and to any streets and roads abutting the above described premises to the center lines thereof.

TOGETHER with the appurtenances and all the estate and rights of the party of the first part in and to said premises.

TO HAVE AND TO HOLD the premises herein granted unto the party of the second part, his heirs and assigns forever.

A Warranty Deed with Full Covenants

②
AND the party of the first part, in compliance with Section 13 of the Lien Law, covenants that the party of the first part will receive the consideration for this conveyance and will hold the right to receive such consideration as a trust fund to be applied first for the purpose of paying the cost of the improvement and will apply the same first to the payment of the cost of the improvement before using any part of the total of the same for any other purpose.

AND the party of the first part covenants as follows:

FIRST.—That said party of the first part is seized of the said premises in fee simple, and has good right to convey the same;

SECOND.—That the party of the second part shall quietly enjoy the said premises;

THIRD.—That the said premises are free from encumbrances, except as aforesaid;

FOURTH.—That the party of the first part will execute or procure any further necessary assurance of the title to said premises;

FIFTH.—That said party of the first part will forever warrant the title to said premises.

IN WITNESS WHEREOF, the party of the first part has executed this deed the day and year first above written.

IN PRESENCE OF:

/s/ John Broker /s/ Harold Kuhn

STATE OF NEW YORK, COUNTY OF Queens ss.:
On the 11th day of May , nineteen hundred and . . .
before me personally came Harold Kuhn
to me known to be the individual described in and who executed the foregoing instrument, and acknowledged that he executed the same.

/s/ John Broker
Notary Public, State of New York
Residing in Queens County
Queens County Clerk's No. 2360
Commission Expires March 31, 19--

STATE OF NEW YORK, COUNTY OF ss.:
On the day of , nineteen hundred and
before me personally came
to me known to be the individual described in and who executed the foregoing instrument, and acknowledged that executed the same.

Title Guarantee and Trust Company, New York, New York

A Warranty Deed (Concluded)

① After the description in any type of deed, there is generally included a statement of encumbrances. For example, if there is a mortgage on the premises and the purchaser is taking the property subject to the mortgage, a statement to this effect is included.

② In those states in which there is no trust created by statute, this clause is omitted.

There are five so-called common covenants in a full covenant and warranty deed. They are: (1) Seizin, (2) Quiet Enjoyment, (3) Further Assurance, (4) Encumbrance, and (5) Warranty of Title. New York and several other states include a sixth covenant known as the Trust Covenant.[5]

The Covenant of Seizin. The first covenant in the full covenant and warranty deed is the *covenant of seizin*. This covenant, made by the grantor, is that he is seized or has full possession of the premises in fee simple or any other quantum of estate that he purports to convey. If, for example, the grantor states that he is seized of the premises in fee simple, then his statement amounts to a covenant that he has a fee simple to convey.

The covenant is not broken if there is a lien on the land, but it is broken if the title is in a third person, or if the grantor has not the extent of the estate he purports to convey.

Quiet Enjoyment. The *covenant of quiet enjoyment* states that the grantee shall ". . . quietly enjoy the said premises."

This covenant means that if the grantee is evicted either by the grantor or a third person having a better title than the grantee, then the grantee has a cause of action against his grantor. The meaning goes further than this. In the event that the grantee sells the property and his grantee is evicted by a third person, he may also bring an action against the grantor. For example, *A* conveys to *B* and in the conveyance there is a covenant of quiet enjoyment made by *A*. *B* then conveys to *C*. Then *X*, who has a paramount title, evicts *C*. *C*, in the absence of fraud, then may sue *A* for the damages he has sustained.

The reason *C* may bring the action is that the covenant of quiet enjoyment is a covenant running with the land, the details of which are explained later in the chapter.

Covenant of Further Assurance. This covenant states that ". . . the party of the first part will execute or procure any further necessary assurance of the title to said premises."

[5] California uses a grant deed which contains fewer covenants than the warranty deed. The grantor impliedly warrants that he has not conveyed the same estate, or any right, title, or interest therein, to any person other than the grantee and that at the time of the execution the estate is free from any encumbrances due by the grantor or any person claiming under him.

The *covenant of further assurance*, although omitted in some states from the full covenant and warranty deed, is of some importance. By virtue of this covenant, the grantor may be required to perform such acts as are necessary to perfect title in the grantee. For example, *A* conveys to *B* and it is later discovered that the description on the deed is incorrect. The covenant of further assurance then requires *A* to give *B* a correction deed.

This covenant is enforceable by an equity suit for specific performance and not ordinarily by a suit for damages.

Covenant Against Encumbrances. The *covenant against encumbrances* states that the ". . . premises are free from encumbrances except as aforesaid."

If, for example, there is an encumbrance against the property such as a mortgage, this will have been stated previously in the deed. If, however, any encumbrances do exist against the property and are not excepted, the covenant is violated and the grantee has a cause of action against the grantor.[6]

Covenant of Warranty of Title. This covenant states that the grantor ". . . will forever warrant the title to said premises."

This covenant is important because it guarantees both possession and title to the premises. In the event this covenant is broken by virtue of a third person having a better title, then the grantor will be liable to the grantee for damages sustained by him.

Trust. In New York and several other states a statutory covenant has been created that is placed in all types of deeds. The need for this type of covenant arose because of fraudulent sellers. Suppose, for example, that *A* desires to sell his real property. In order to obtain a better price, he hires a painter to redecorate. *A* does not pay the painter, but immediately sells the property to *B*. The painter then obtains a mechanic's lien against the property as will be explained in Chapter 9. *B*, the new owner, is then placed in a position where he has a lien on his property and thus will become involved in legal process. In order to avoid this, the following is inserted in a deed:

---

[6] "Encumbrance" covers mortgages, tax liens, judgment liens, restrictions, easements, and outstanding dower rights. In California, the term includes taxes, assessments, and *all* liens upon real property. Cal. Civil Code, Sec. 1114.

> That in compliance with Section 13 of the Lien Law, the party of the first part will receive the consideration for the conveyance and will hold the right to receive such consideration as a trust fund to be first applied for the purpose of paying the cost of improvement and that the party of the first part (the grantor) will apply the same first to the payment of the cost of improvement before using any part of the total of the same for any other purpose.

This clause then makes the seller in effect the trustee of the funds that he received from the sale of the property for the benefit of any potential mechanic's lienors. If the seller after having received the purchase price does not pay for the improvements on the property, he has breached his trust and may be held liable under the penal statutes.

Special Warranty Deed

Some states use what is commonly called a *special warranty* deed in which the grantor warrants only against claims asserted by, through, or under him. In brief, the grantor warrants the title against defects arising after he acquired the property and not against defects arising before that time. In the final analysis it is much like the bargain and sale deed with covenant.

OTHER DEEDS

The following pages will discuss a series of special deeds which are used for specific purposes. Because they are special-purpose deeds, they are given specific names; however, they are in reality merely variations of the deeds outlined previously. The fact of the matter is that most of them are a form of quitclaim deed. Most of them are signed by a person other than the "true owner"; consequently, the grantor cannot afford to "stick his neck out" by means of a full covenant and warranty deed, for example.

Deed of Gift

In some states a special deed is used when the grantor conveys the property to the grantee by way of *gift*. The instrument states:

> The grantor (John Doe) for and in consideration of the Love and Affection which he bears unto the grantee herein named does by these presents, grant, alien and confirm unto (Mary Doe) the following described property situated in. . . .

The description is followed by a clause conveying the hereditaments, appurtenances, the reversion or reversions, remainder or remainders, rents, issues, and profits thereof.

In most states, however, it is the custom to convey a gift property either by a quitclaim deed or by a bargain and sale deed.

Referee's Deed in Foreclosure

Normally, when a mortgagee commences a foreclosure action by reason of default of his mortgagor, a referee is appointed by the court to perform certain duties in connection with the foreclosure action. Among other things, it will be his duty to sell the property and to give deed to the purchaser. This deed is entitled the *referee's deed in foreclosure*.

Referee's Deed in Partition

A *referee's deed in partition* is much like the referee's deed in foreclosure. A partition action is usually brought by a joint owner of a parcel of real property to dissolve the concurrent ownership. For example, *A* and *B* own property as tenants in common and *B* brings an action for partition. A referee is appointed and, at the conclusion of the action, the property is sold at auction with the funds being divided according to the respective rights of *A* and *B*. The purchaser at the auction will receive a referee's deed in partition from the referee.

Deed to Mining Claim

In those states of the country where mining is prevalent, the deed to a mining claim is quite common. It is used to transfer the interest in a mine and is similar to a bargain and sale deed with this addition:

> Together with all the dips, spurs and angles, and also all the metals, ores, gold and silver-bearing quartz, rock and earth therein,

and all the rights, privileges and franchises thereunto incident, appendant and appurtenant, or therewith usually had and enjoyed; and also all and singular the tenements, hereditaments and appurtenances thereto belonging or in anywise appertaining, and the rents, issues and profits thereof; and also all the estate, right, title, interest, property, possession, claim and demand whatsoever, as well in law as in equity, of the said party of the first part, of, in and to the said premises, and every part and parcel thereof, with the appurtenances.

Guardian's Deed

The *guardian's deed* is used to convey an interest of a minor (infant) in real property. The deed recites the court order appointing the guardian, the application of the guardian to the court for permission to convey the property, the court order authorizing the sale of the property, the full consideration for the transaction, and this covenant:

> And the said party of the first part, as guardian, covenants with the party of the second part for and in behalf of the said infant that neither party of the first part, as guardian, nor the said infant has done or suffered anything whereby the said premises have been encumbered in any way whatsoever.

Committee's Deed

In many respects the committee's deed is similar to the guardian's deed. Insane persons and idiots are lacking in the requisite capacity to make a valid conveyance just as minors are. When an insane person owns real property, a committee is appointed by the court and, after having obtained the requisite permission, may convey the real property.

Deed by Assignee for Benefit of Creditors

Often a person who becomes insolvent and does not choose to file a petition in bankruptcy will hold a meeting of his creditors. It may be decided that the debtor will pay off the creditors as rapidly as possible. A trust agreement is drawn between the debtor and the creditors and, among other things, the instrument appoints a trustee for the benefit of the creditors. This trustee is often called an assignee for the benefit of the creditors. His job is to gather the assets of the debtor, convert them into cash, and distribute the cash to the creditors according to the terms of the agreement made by them. If the debtor has real property, he conveys it to the assignee by *deed of assignment*. The assignee is then free to convey to a third party and this is done by the *deed by assignee for the benefit of creditors*. This deed recites the conveyance by the debtor to the assignee, and a statement that the assignee conveys:

> . . . all the right, title, and interest that the said (Debtor) had at or immediately before the execution and delivery of said deed of assignment to the party of the first part, and also the right, title, and interest that the party of the first part acquired in, under, and by virtue of said deed of assignment.

Deed of Surrender

The *deed of surrender* is used to merge an estate for life or years with either a reversionary or remainder interest. The same thing can be accomplished by means of a quitclaim deed in which the life tenant, for example, quitclaims to the remainderman.

Correction Deed

A *correction deed*, sometimes called a *deed of confirmation*, is used to correct an error in a deed. For example, if *A* conveys to *B* and there is an error in description, *A* upon request will correct the error. This is usually done by means of a quitclaim deed containing a statement explaining the purpose of the instrument.

If the seller refuses to correct, for example, a description in a deed, a court order can be obtained correcting the error. This is known as a *reformation* of an instrument.

Cession Deed

This is a form of quitclaim deed used to convey the street rights of an abutting owner to a municipality. The purpose of the conveyance is recited in the instrument.

Deed of Release

The *deed of release* is used to release the described premises from a dower interest, a reverter for a breach of condition subsequent, or a remainder interest. It is, however, used mostly in connection with mortgages as described in Chapter 6.

COVENANTS RUNNING WITH THE LAND

Covenants running with the land refer to those covenants within a deed which pass certain rights and duties to subsequent grantees of the land, for example, the covenant of quiet enjoyment mentioned previously.

Restrictive covenants are another type of covenant running with the land. If the owner of a subdivision restricts the size of the buildings on the land, limiting them to two stories, the covenant would be said to be a restrictive covenant and would run with the land. A person buying land in the subdivision would be subject to legal action if he built a three-story building on it.

These restrictions are enforceable in a court of equity unless they are against public policy. The person seeking to enforce a restriction or covenant running with the land can attempt to obtain an injunction against the person violating the covenant.

When a property is subdivided and the deeds from the common grantor contain a statement to the effect that all buildings must be built twenty-five feet back from the street, and if the restriction is commensurate with the quality and character of the land, then it is enforceable by the people whom it was intended to benefit.

The possible existence of covenants running with the land is one of the compelling reasons for making a title search. For example, if *A* conveys property to *B* with the type of restriction that runs with the land, and *B* conveys to *C* without mention of the restriction in the deed, the covenant still runs with the land on the theory that *C*, or any other subsequent grantee for that matter, has constructive notice of the existence of the covenant.

Covenants running with the land generally are limited to a period of time. In any event, a covenant may be ineffective if the neighborhood has changed sufficiently. When this change does take place, a legal action may be necessary to remove the covenant from record.

FRAUDULENT CONVEYANCES

Generally speaking, the courts will not inquire into the consideration in a real property transaction. However, there are some instances when they will. If a grantor conveys property to another without sufficient consideration, and if it can be proved that the conveyance was made with the intent to defraud creditors, then the courts will compel the grantee to reconvey the property to the grantor to satisfy the claims of the creditors.

The situation often arises when property is conveyed to a member of the family for a nominal consideration. If there is an indebtedness to other parties in existence at the time of the conveyance, the conveyance is generally held to be presumptively fraudulent. If the conveyance is made before indebtedness is incurred, however, it becomes necessary to show fraudulent intent to set the conveyance aside.

CONVEYANCE BY WILL

Conveyances of real property described in the previous sections of this chapter are generally called transfers *inter vivos* (among the living). On the average of once every twenty-five years, however, all real property is transferred either by wills or by reason of persons dying without wills.

Wills

A *will* is ordinarily a writing that provides for the distribution of property upon the death of the writer but which confers no rights prior to that time. Prior to his death, the writer may destroy or cancel the will. The person making the will is known as the *testator*, if male; *testatrix*, if female. When a person dies leaving a will, he is said to die *testate*; a person dying without a will is said to die *intestate*.

A gift of land by way of a will is known as a *devise*, and the person receiving the gift is called a *devisee*. A *bequest* or a *legacy* is a gift of personal property, generally money, under a will and the person receiving the gift is called a *legatee*.

Requisites of the Will

A will must satisfy requirements as to both the intention of the testator and the formality of expression of the intention.

Intention. There cannot be a will unless the testator manifests an intention to make a provision that will be effective upon his death. This is called a *testamentary intent*. Ordinarily, this is an intention that certain persons shall become the owners of certain property upon the death of the testator.

Formality. In England prior to 1540, lands could not be devised by will; however, by 1660 lands were fully devisable. In 1667 by act of Parliament, 29 Car. II, it was enacted that "all devises and bequests of any lands or tenements . . . shall be in writing, and signed by the party so devising the same, or by some other person in his presence and by his express directions, and shall be attested and subscribed, in the presence of said devisor by three or four credible witnesses, or else they shall be utterly void and of no effect."

Writing. The above statute declares that there must be a writing to effect a valid will, and with minor variations this rule has been adopted in all of the states of the union.

Signing. The will must be signed. The signature is usually placed at the bottom or at the end of the will.

Attestation and Publication. The act of witnessing the will is known as *attestation*. Generally this includes the signing of the will as a witness after a clause which recites that the witness has observed the signing (execution) of the will. *Publication* is the act of the testator in informing the attesting witnesses that the document which he is signing before them is his will. In some states witnesses are not required; in others two or three are required. When witnesses are required, it is generally specified that they be credible or competent and that they have no interest in the will.

Mental Capacity to Make a Will

To have the mental capacity to make a will one must be of sound mind, though he need not possess superior or even average mentality. One is of sound mind for testamentary purposes only when he can understand and carry in his mind in a general way the nature and extent of his property, the persons who are the natural objects of his bounty, and the disposition which he is making of his property. Furthermore, he must be capable of appreciating the foregoing elements in relation to each other, and he must also be capable of forming an orderly desire as to the disposition of his property.

These requirements have been considered the test of whether or not a person is of sufficiently sound mind as to be regarded competent or incompetent to make a will. The law recognizes two types of insanity: the undeveloped mind and the deranged mind. The first class of persons lack the qualities of mind and memory as to matters which are important in making a will. The minds of persons in the second class are so warped that they are unable to form a rational testamentary plan.

Property Subject to Disposal by Will

Any property that can be transferred by its owner during his lifetime generally can be transferred by will upon his death. The testator by his will may, in addition, exercise any power possessed by him to appoint by will. For example, the testator may have been left a parcel of real property for life with the provision that upon his death it should go to such persons as he specifically names to receive it in his will.

Probate

Upon the death of the testator, the will must be probated. *Probate* by definition means to prove. If the will names an executor, it is his job to go into court and prove the will and carry out its terms. If part of the assets of the decedent's estate consists of real property, the will may authorize the sale of the property or it may declare that the property be transferred to a specific person. In some cases when the will neither authorizes the sale of the property nor devises the real property to a specified person, it may then become necessary to obtain a court order to sell the property. In the case of sale, the property is conveyed by executor's deed.

The Executor's Deed

The *executor's deed* is used to convey real property that was owned by a person who died testate. Basically, it is the same as any other deed, except that it contains a covenant against grantor's acts, the grantor in this case being the executor or executors. In the event that there is more than one executor, they must all join on the deed in order to effectuate a valid conveyance. If the property is sold, the deed recites the full consideration being paid for the property. If the property is being distributed, then it will recite that fact.

TRANSFER BY INTESTACY

If a person does not effectively dispose of his property by will or if he does not leave a will, his property will be distributed to certain persons related to him. Since such persons acquire or succeed to the rights of the decedent and since the circumstances under which they do so are in the absence of an effective will, it is said that they acquire title by *intestate succession.*

The right of intestate succession is not an inherent right, but exists only because the legislature so provides. The legislatures of the individual states have the right to change, modify, or destroy the right to inherit property.

Plan of Intestate Distribution

Actual plans of intestate distribution vary from state to state, but in general they exhibit the following pattern:

Spouses. The surviving spouse, whether husband or wife, will share in the estate. The extent of the share generally depends upon the number of children and other heirs. In the absence of surviving blood relations, the surviving spouse generally takes the entire estate.

Lineals. *Lineals* or *lineal descendants* are blood descendants of the decedent. The portion not distributed to the surviving spouse is generally distributed to lineals.

Parents. If the estate has not been exhausted by this time, the remainder is commonly distributed to the decedent's parents.

Collateral Heirs. These are persons who are not descendants of the decedent but who are related to him through a common ancestor. Generally collateral heirs include brothers and sisters of the decedent.

Administration of Estates

Administration is the means of distributing property of a decedent who has died intestate. When no will is left by the decedent, the court or an officer designated by law appoints one or more persons who are then entitled to administer the estate of the decedent. Generally, the close relatives of the deceased are entitled to *letters of administration* issued by the probate court authorizing the distribution of the assets of the estate. The letters are usually issued to the first relative who applies. In some cases where there are creditors of the deceased and no previous application for letters of administration has been made, the letters may be granted to the creditors. In the absence of creditors or known relatives, letters may be issued by the court to a public administrator. In any event, once the letters have been granted to the administrator, his job becomes much the same as the executor's; that is, he gathers together the assets of the deceased and distributes them in accordance with the pattern of intestate succession established in the states. If there is real property to be sold, then the administrator does this by means of an administrator's deed.

The Administrator's Deed

The *administrator's deed* is in many respects similar to the executor's deed. In order to make a valid conveyance by an administrator's deed, however, an administrator must in all cases obtain specific permission from the court to convey the property. The deed is executed by the administrator and in each case specifically recites the authorization of the court for the sale.

TRANSFER BY ADVERSE POSSESSION

In all states there exists what is known as the *statute of limitations*. When a cause of action exists, the person having the cause of action has a certain time limit within which to proceed with the proper legal action. For example, in many states the statute of limitations bars a lawsuit on a debt after six years. In the final analysis, the law concerning adverse possession of real property is in the nature of a statute of limitations. Thus, a true owner may be unable to assert his true ownership of a parcel of real property against another after a period of years outlined by the statutes or common law.

In order for one person to obtain title to real property by reason of adverse possession, certain requisites must be met. If *A* goes on the property of *B* and the statutory period for adverse possession is 15 years,[7] *A's* possession during the 15-year period must be continuous or uninterrupted in order to ripen into ownership. The possession must also be actual, visible, exclusive, and it must be hostile (holding under a claim inconsistent with the rights of the owner) to the owner. In the situation above, when *A* claims the adverse possession of the property, the statement is made that his possession must be continuous and uninterrupted. This is necessary for *A* to claim the property by adverse possession. But suppose *A* dies and *X*, his son and heir, acquires possession at the end of the seventh year of *A's* possession, and suppose *X* then holds the property continuously and without interruption for another eight years. This succession of possession whereby the time of possession of *A*, the first claimant, is added or tacked to the time of possession of *X*, the second claimant, is called *tacking*. When there is a privity between the persons successively in possession and those persons hold the property for the requisite period, then it is generally held that *X*, the second claimant in adverse possession, will have good title to the property and *B* will be barred from asserting any claim to the property. In some states it is necessary to go into possession of the property under some color of title; that is, claiming under what appears to be a muniment of title. Often the payment of taxes by the person in possession is considered evidence of color of title, and sometimes evidence of being "hostile."

---

[7] The time varies from two years in Arizona (under certain circumstances) to 30 years in Louisiana (under some circumstances). In Colorado it is basically 18 years but only 7 years if the occupant has paid the real property taxes.

QUESTIONS FOR REVIEW

1. Explain how property is described, using the lot and block system; using metes and bounds; using the government survey.
2. What is meant by delivery of a deed? In what ways may delivery be accomplished?
3. Occasionally a TV villain in the current westerns will place a paper before the hero (or heroine) and say: "Sign this bill of sale and then the ranch will be mine." Aside from the fact that duress is used, what, if anything, is wrong with this?
4. What is a *covenant running with the land*?
5. How can real property be conveyed by a will?

PROBLEMS

1. In the material at the end of Chapter 4 you were to prepare a contract for the sale of real property. From this contract prepare a full covenant and warranty deed in the same manner that you prepared the contract.
2. In the case of *Sherwood* v. *Moelle,* how does the court distinguish between a quitclaim deed and the bargain and sale deed?

Sherwood v. Moelle

148 U.S. 21, 37 L.Ed. 350, 13 Sup.Ct. 426 (1892)

Sherwood sued to quiet title to a tract of land obtained from Dosh and his wife through a deed "reciting a consideration of One Hundred Dollars, by which they sold, conveyed, and quitclaimed all their 'right, title and interest' in and to the premises" in controversy. The premises had previously been conveyed to the defendant's predecessor by a deed invalid because of misdescription. Moelle contended that since Sherwood claimed under a quitclaim deed, he could obtain only the title of his vendors; furthermore, that he was not bona fide, since he should have been put on guard by the use of a quitclaim deed and should have investigated.

FIELD, J. . . . The doctrine expressed in many cases that the grantee in a quitclaim deed cannot be treated as a bona fide purchaser does not seem to be of sound principle. It is asserted upon the assumption of the appellant that in the form of the instrument, that the grantor merely releases to the grantee his claim, whatever it may be, without warranty of its value, or only passes whatever interest he may have had at the time, and that this indicates that there may be other and outstanding claims or interests which may possibly affect the title of the property, and therefore, it is said that the grantee, in accepting a conveyance of that kind, cannot be a bona fide purchaser and entitled to protection as such; and that he is in fact thus notified by his grantor that there may be some defect in his title and he must take it at his risk. This assumption we do not think justified by the language of such deeds or the general opinion of conveyancers. There may be many reasons why the holder of property may refuse to accompany his conveyance of it with an express warranty of the soundness of its title or its freedom from the claim of others, or to execute a conveyance in such form as to imply a warranty of any kind even when the title is known to be perfect. He may hold the property only as a trustee or in a corporate or official character, and be unwilling for that reason to assume any personal responsibility as to its title or freedom from liens, or he may be unwilling to do so for notions peculiar to himself; and the purchaser may be unable to secure a conveyance of the property desired in any other form than one of quitclaim or of a simple transfer of the grantor's interest. It would be unreasonable to hold that, for his inability to secure any other form of conveyance, he should be denied the position and character of a bona fide purchaser, however free, in fact, his conduct in the purchase may have been from any imputation of the want of good faith. In many parts of the country a quitclaim or a simple conveyance of the grantor's interest is the common form in which the transfer of real estate is made. A deed in that form is, in such cases, as effectual to divest and transfer a complete title as any other form of conveyance. There is in this country no difference in the efficacy and operative force between conveyances in the form of release and quitclaim and those in the form of grant, bargain and sale. If the grantor in either case at the time of the execution of his deed possesses any claim to or interest in the property, it passes to the grantee. In the one case, that of the bargain and sale, he impliedly asserts the possession of a claim to or interest in the property, for it is the property itself which he sells and undertakes to convey. In the other case, that of the quitclaim, the grantor affirms nothing as to the ownership and undertakes only a release of any claim to or interest in the premises which he may possess without asserting the ownership of either. If in either case the grantee takes the deed with notice of an outstanding conveyance of the premises from the grantor, or of the execution by him of obligations to make such conveyance of the premises, or to create a lien thereon, he takes the property subject to the operation of such outstanding conveyance as a bona fide purchaser. But in either case if the grantee takes the deed without notice of such outstanding conveyance or obligation respecting the property, or notice of facts which, if followed up, would lead to a knowledge of such outstanding conveyance or equity, he is entitled to protection as a bona fide purchaser, upon showing that the consideration stipulated has been paid and that such consideration was a fair price for the claim or interest designated. . . .

3. The diagram below shows a section. Assume it is Sec. 8, T. 4 N., R. 23 W., Cedar County, Kansas.

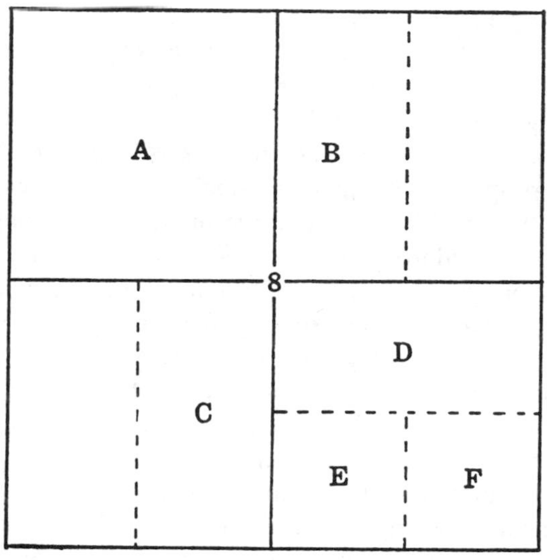

(a) Describe the area marked *A* and determine the number of acres contained therein.

(b) Describe the area marked *B* and determine the number of acres contained therein.

(c) Describe the area marked *C* and determine the number of acres contained therein.

(d) Describe the area marked *D* and determine the number of acres contained therein.

(e) Describe the area marked *E* and determine the number of acres contained therein.

(f) Describe the area marked *F* and determine the number of acres contained therein.

SUGGESTED READINGS

Kratovil, Robert. *Real Estate Law,* 5th ed. Englewood Cliffs, New Jersey: Prentice-Hall, Inc., 1969. Chapter 7.

Ring, Alfred A. *Real Estate Principles and Practices,* 7th ed. Englewood Cliffs, New Jersey: Prentice-Hall, Inc., 1972. Chapter 9.

Chapter 6

Mortgages and Deeds of Trust

The most important cog in nearly every real estate transfer is the financing of the transaction. Generally this is accomplished by using the real property together with its on-site improvements as security for the loan. The total indebtedness secured by real property totaled over $500 billion in 1972.

The idea of using a parcel of real property as the security for a debt can be traced back to Biblical times. However, like many of our legal concepts, the modern basis of our legal theories of employing real property as security for a debt lies with the English law.

In early English law one of the forms of transfer of real property as security for a debt was called *mortuum vadium*. It was so called because under the ancient law the pledgee became entitled to the rents and profits from the land, hence the land was "dead" to the debtor. Another form of pledge was called *vivum vadium*, wherein the profits from the land were applied to the payment of the loan.

Out of these two forms of mortgage there gradually evolved the so-called "common-law mortgage," which, in the last analysis, was a transfer of the property subject to a condition—the condition being that upon the payment of the debt, at a certain time, the estate of the transferee would terminate.

In early law, the condition that the debt had to be paid at a certain time was strictly enforced. The result of this was that the debtor lost the property if he did not pay the sum due by the stated time, even though he may have made partial payment on the debt. To relieve this obvious hardship on the debtor, the courts, about the middle of the seventeenth century, gave the debtor the right to pay off the debt even after it became due. He was given the right to redeem the property, and this right became known as the *equity of redemption*. This concept in turn worked a hardship on the creditor because he might never receive his money. This resulted in placing a time limit on the equity of redemption, by a decree of *foreclosure* issued by a court. By virtue of the decree of foreclosure, the right to redeem was cut off unless the debt was paid by the time named in the decree.

Nearly all modern real property transfers involve the use of the property itself as security for part of the payment of the purchase price. Often, too, real property is used as security for a debt when no transfer takes place. It is a rare occasion when a transfer of real property takes place on the basis of a complete cash payment for the property. In all of these transactions where land is given as security for a debt, there are two instruments involved. Sometimes these instruments are, for brevity's sake, combined into one form, but in the final analysis, they remain two separate and distinct instruments. These instruments are the bond (or promissory note, which in many states is used in place of the bond) and the mortgage. The details of the mortgage will be discussed later in the chapter, but for the moment suffice it to say that a *mortgage* is the creation of an interest in property as security for the payment of a debt or the fulfillment of some obligation.

The *deed of trust*, which will be discussed later in the chapter, is a deed absolute to secure the payment of a debt. There are three parties to the instrument. The borrower transfers the property to a trustee who holds it for the benefit of the lender. On default by the borrower, proper legal steps are taken by the trustee to insure repayment of the loan to the lender. In the following discussion of the mortgage, one should be aware that much of the information relative to the real property mortgage is also applicable to the deed of trust.

THE BOND

In order for there to be a valid mortgage, there must be a debt; and there must also exist evidence of this debt. In most states, the bond is employed almost exclusively as the evidence of the debt; in other states, the promissory note is used as the evidence of the debt. A *bond* is a sealed agreement in writing in which an *obligor* (a borrower) promises to pay under stated terms a sum certain to an *obligee* (a lender). Both parties to a bond must have contractual capacity. In order to be valid, it must embrace the following:

(1) a writing,
(2) an obligor with contractual ability,
(3) an obligee with contractual ability,
(4) a promise or covenant by the obligor to pay a sum certain,
(5) terms of payment,
(6) default clause including mortgage covenants by reference,
(7) proper execution, and
(8) voluntary delivery and acceptance.

It would be well to note here that, as previously mentioned, a mortgage cannot exist without a debt. It follows that the bond which embodies the debt is the primary instrument, while the mortgage is merely a secondary or collateral instrument. Thus, the importance of the bond and its proper execution can be recognized. Of what, then, does the bond consist?

Acknowledgment of Indebtedness

Following the name of the obligor, some bond forms state:

> The obligor is held and firmly bound unto . . . obligee, in the sum of . . . Dollars, lawful money of the United States to be paid to the said . . . (name of obligee), its successors or assigns (if the obligee is a corporation) or its heirs, executors, administrators or assigns (if the obligee is an individual): For which payment . . . I bind myself, my heirs, executors and administrators, jointly and severally, firmly by these presents.

NEW YORK BOND, FULL COVENANT

KNOW ALL MEN BY THESE PRESENTS

That I, James J. Defoe, residing at Long Island Avenue, no street number, Medford, in the Town of Brookhaven, Suffolk County, New York , obligor, am held and firmly bound unto The Peoples National Bank of Patchogue, a national banking corporation, having its banking house and principal place of business at 41 East Main Street, in the village of Patchogue, Town of Brookhaven, Suffolk County, New York , obligee, in the sum of Three Thousand Five Hundred and 00/100 ($3,500) - - - - - - - Dollars, lawful money of the United States of America, to be paid to the said THE PEOPLES NATIONAL BANK OF PATCHOGUE, its ~~executors, administrators,~~ successors or assigns:

FOR WHICH PAYMENT well and truly made I bind myself, my heirs, ~~executors and administrators,~~ jointly and severally, firmly by these presents.

SEALED with my seal, Dated the twenty-eighth day of October, Nineteen Hundred and

THE CONDITION OF THE ABOVE OBLIGATION IS SUCH that if the above bounden James J. Defoe, his heirs, ~~executors or administrators,~~ shall well and truly pay, or cause to be paid, unto the above named THE PEOPLES NATIONAL BANK OF PATCHOGUE, its ~~executors, administrators,~~ successors or assigns the just and full sum of Three Thousand Five Hundred and 00/100 ($3,500.00) Dollars in full on the 28th day of October 19--, as herein provided with interest from date hereof to be computed upon the unpaid principal sum at the rate of Seven and one-half per centum (7½%) per annum, and the said principal sum and interest shall be paid in the manner following: viz: Thirty-seven dollars and ninety-nine cents ($37.99) shall be paid on the 28th day of November, 19--, and a like amount shall be paid on the 28th day of each succeeding calendar month thereafter to and until the 28th day of October, 19--, when the unpaid balance of the principal sum shall be paid together with accrued interest; and each of said monthly payments of $37.99 shall be applied first to the payment of interest upon the unpaid principal sum, and the balance of each of said payments shall be applied to the payment of the principal sum;
without any fraud or other delay, then the above obligation to be void, otherwise to remain in full force and virtue.

AND IT IS HEREBY EXPRESSLY AGREED that the whole of said principal sum shall become due at the option of said obligee, its legal representatives or assigns after default in the payment of any installment of principal for thirty days, or of interest for thirty days, or after default in the payment of any tax, water rate or assessment which may be levied or imposed upon the premises described in the mortgage accompanying this bond for thirty days after notice and demand.

New York Bond, Full Covenant

AND IT IS ALSO AGREED that the said obligor will keep the buildings on the said premises described in the said mortgage insured against loss by fire and will carry extended coverage insurance in an equal amount, for the benefit of the mortgagee therein. All of the covenants and agreements in the mortgage covering premises therein described and collateral hereto, are made part of this instrument.

IN PRESENCE OF

/s/ William Howard

/s/ James J. Defoe (L.S.)

________________ (L.S.)

________________ (L.S.)

STATE OF NEW YORK, COUNTY OF Suffolk ss.:

On this twenty-eighth day of October, Nineteen Hundred and before me, the subscriber, personally appeared James J. Defoe to me personally known and known to me to be the person described in and who executed the within Instrument, and he duly acknowledged to me that he executed the same.

/s/ William Howard
Notary Public, State of New York
Residing in Suffolk County
Suffolk County Clerk's No. 1323
Commission Expires March 31, 19--

Tuttle Law Print, Publishers, Rutland, Vermont

New York Bond, Full Covenant (Concluded)

The phrase "jointly and severally" is added to make it possible for the obligee to collect from the obligors jointly or from any obligor individually.

Some bond forms state that the "obligor does hereby acknowledge himself to be indebted to . . . (name of obligee)."

The Seal

Since a bond is a sealed instrument, a statement to that effect usually appears following the acknowledgment of indebtedness or sometimes at the end of the instrument.

Condition and Promise

At this point there appears in the bond either a bald statement of the obligor containing a promise to pay, in these words: "which sum the obligor does hereby covenant to pay to said obligee," or a condition making the obligation void if payment is made. The condition is generally worded in this manner:

> The condition of the above obligation is such that if the above bounden . . . (name of obligor), his heirs, executors or administrators, shall well and truly pay, or cause to be paid, unto the above named . . . (name of obligee), its successors or assigns (if a corporation) the just and full sum of . . . dollars. . . .

Following this, there appears a statement of the terms of repayment including the rate of interest and the date due. If the debt is to be repaid in installments, the details of the installments are spelled out. After the explanation of the method of payments, there is a statement to the effect that if the payments are made "without any fraud or other delay, then the above obligation to be void, otherwise to remain in full force and virtue."

Default Clause

It is here that reference in the bond is made for the first time to the mortgage. Generally, the first statement in regard to the debt's becoming due in the event of default has to do with the failure of the obligor to make payment of principal or interest, or failure on the part of the obligor to pay taxes of any type. A grace period of thirty days is generally given the obligor to make those payments which he has failed to make. Usually the default clause is expressed in the following manner:

> And it is hereby expressly agreed that the whole of said principal sum shall become due at the option of said obligee, . . . legal representatives or assigns after default in the payment of any installment of principal for thirty days, or of interest for thirty days or after default in the payment of any tax, water rate, or assessment which may be levied or imposed upon the premises described in the mortgage accompanying this bond for thirty days after notice and demand.

The main reason for the inclusion of a clause of this nature is to prevent the impairment of the security (the land) by virtue of unpaid taxes, interest, and principal. It should be noted that the obligee is given the option of taking action to collect the debt of the obligor.

Generally there is added another default clause which requires the obligor to keep the property insured against fire for the benefit of the obligee. It reads as follows:

> And it is also agreed that the said obligor will keep the buildings on the said premises described in said mortgage insured against loss by fire and will carry extended coverage insurance in an equal amount for the benefit of the mortgagee (this is the obligee on the bond) therein.

Following this there is a statement incorporating by reference all of the covenants of the mortgage. To wit:

> All of the covenants and agreements in the mortgage covering premises therein described and collateral hereto are made part of this instrument.

Execution

The bond is generally signed and sealed at the end. The bond is usually sealed because the time limit within which a suit can be brought on a sealed instrument is longer than that upon one that is not sealed.

The bond need not be acknowledged because it is usually not recorded, but, customarily, it is acknowledged.

Collection

Usually, when a bond is given with a mortgage, legal action is brought against the property and on the bond in the event the property brings insufficient funds to cover the debt. However, because the bond is a promise to pay a stated sum, the obligee may bring an action on the bond alone. If he cannot collect the debt due from the obligor, he may then bring a further action against the security for the debt.

It should be remembered that outlawing or extinguishing the bond or note nullifies the mortgage agreement in some states.

THE NOTE

In many of the states the bond is not used with a mortgage or deed of trust as evidence of the debt. Instead, a promissory note is employed—the land being used as collateral security for the note. A *promissory note* is defined as a written promise by one person to pay money to another. It is similar to the bond with the possible exception that it lacks the formality of a seal. A note generally is made in the form shown below.

$ 13,700.00 Gainesville , Florida
March 20 , 19__

FOR VALUE RECEIVED, the undersigned, (jointly and severally, if more than one) promises to pay to Central Florida Mortgage Company , or order, in the manner hereinafter specified, the principal sum of Thirteen Thousand Seven Hundred and 00---------------/100 DOLLARS ($13,700.00) with interest from date at the rate of 7½ per cent. per annum on the balance from time to time remaining unpaid. The said principal and interest shall be payable in lawful money of the United States of America at Gainesville , Florida or at such place as may hereafter be designated by written notice from the holder to the maker hereof, on the date and in the manner following:

in monthly installments of Eighty and 15/100 Dollars ($80.15) commencing on the 20th day of April 1974 and on the first day of each month thereafter until the interest and principal are fully paid except that the final payment of the entire indebtedness evidenced hereby, if not sooner paid, shall be due and payable on the 20th day of March 1999 .

This note with interest is secured by a mortgage on real estate, of even date herewith, made by the maker hereof in favor of the said payee, and shall be construed and enforced according to the laws of the State of Florida. The terms of said mortgage are by this reference made a part hereof.

If default be made in the payment of any of the sums or interest mentioned herein or in said mortgage, or in the performance of any of the agreements contained herein or in said mortgage, then the entire principal sum and accrued interest shall at the option of the holder hereof become at once due and collectible without notice, time being of the essence; and said principal sum and accrued interest shall both bear interest from such time until paid at the highest rate allowable under the laws of the State of Florida. Failure to exercise this option shall not constitute a waiver of the right to exercise the same in the event of any subsequent default.

Each person liable hereon whether maker or endorser, hereby waives presentment, protest, notice, notice of protest and notice of dishonor and agrees to pay all costs, including a reasonable attorney's fee, whether suit be brought or not, if, after maturity of this note or default hereunder, or under said mortgage, counsel shall be employed to collect this note or to protect the security of said mortgage.

Whenever used herein the terms "holder", "maker" and "payee" shall be construed in the singular or plural as the context may require or admit.

Maker's Address

4049 N.W. 12th Avenue
Gainesville, Florida

Robert A. Scales (SEAL)
Mary A. Scales (SEAL)
(SEAL)

A Promissory Mortgage Note

In terms of numbers the note is used in more states than those using the bond. Its use is universal in those states employing the deed of trust as well as many of those using the mortgage.

THE MORTGAGE

As was briefly stated earlier in the chapter, a *mortgage* is the creation of an interest in property as security for the payment of a debt or the fulfillment of an obligation. Property, as was discussed in Chapter 3, is divided into real property and personal property. By implication, our brief definition of the mortgage suggests that real property and personal property may be mortgaged, and so they can. Both types of mortgages are made by an agreement or contract. Thus, an agreement which creates an interest in personal property as security for the payment of a debt or the fulfillment of an obligation might be said to be a *chattel* (personal property) *mortgage*, and an agreement that creates an interest in real property for the payment of a debt or the fulfillment of an obligation might be said to be a *real property mortgage*. Of course, it is the latter in which we are primarily interested.

Essentials of the Mortgage

A mortgage is a contract. Therefore, the instrument creating the mortgage must embrace the elements of a contract, namely:

(1) competent parties,
(2) offer and acceptance,
(3) consideration,
(4) legality of object, and
(5) because it is real property and subject to the Statute of Frauds, it must be in writing and signed.

These elements were discussed in Chapter 4.

The Parties

In general there are two parties to a mortgage: the mortgagor and the mortgagee. The *mortgagor* is the party pledging the property. He is the borrower or obligor on the bond. The *mortgagee* is the party to whom the pledge of the property is made. He is the lender or obligee on the bond.

Theories of Mortgages

There are two principal theories of mortgages used in the United States; namely, the title theory and the lien theory. There are still seventeen states [1] that adhere to the title theory of real property mortgages; the others have adopted the lien theory.

The Title Theory. The basic concept of the *title theory* is that upon making the mortgage, the mortgagor passes title to the property, the subject of the mortgage, to the mortgagee, subject to a condition subsequent. This condition subsequent is the payment of the debt. Upon fulfillment of the condition, title to the property divests (reverts to) to the mortgagor.

For example, *A* (the mortgagor) mortgages real property to *B* (the mortgagee) in a title state. Under the terms of the instrument, title passes to *B*. However, the instrument will state that if *A* complies with the condition (makes payment), then the instrument will be void.[2]

During the period of the mortgage, by virtue of a provision in the mortgage, *A* is generally entitled to remain in possession of the property even though he passed title to his mortgagee.

The Lien Theory. The majority of the states use the *lien theory* of mortgages. Under this theory, title remains with the mortgagor, and the mortgage that is placed on the property is a charge on the title. The mortgage instrument says nothing about title, but states: "The mortgagor does hereby mortgage to. . . ." After the recording of the instrument, it becomes a lien on the property described in the mortgage.

The rule regarding the priority of mortgages whether in *title* or *lien* states is substantially the same rule as that regarding the priority of deeds: the instrument recorded first, in the absence of fraud, is the operative one. For example, *A* mortgages his property to *B* on October 15 with the instrument bearing that date. On the following day *A* mortgages the same property to *C*. *C* records his mortgage before *B*. In the absence of fraud, *C* has a valid enforceable mortgage. To avoid such circumstances, mortgages should be recorded immediately.

---

[1] These are Alabama, Arkansas, Connecticut, Illinois, Maine, Maryland, Massachusetts, Mississippi, New Hampshire, New Jersey, North Carolina, Ohio, Pennsylvania, Rhode Island, Tennessee, Vermont, and West Virginia.

[2] In the strict sense of the word, "void," based on the maxim *ex nihilo nihil fit*, meaning "out of nothing comes nothing," *B* never actually holds title if *A* fulfills the condition.

It is from this idea of having the first lien against the property that the term "first mortgage" was derived. The term "first mortgage" simply means that the party holding such instrument has recorded his mortgage first in point of time and thus has priority over any subsequently recorded mortgages. Second mortgage, third mortgage, and so on, indicates the order of their recording, and by the same token, the priority in case of forcclosure for the private creditors. It should be remembered that in some states, notably California, tax liens, judgment liens, and mechanic's liens can have priority over the first mortgage. This will be discussed more fully in Chapter 9, "Liens."

MORTGAGE

THIS MORTGAGE made the 16th day of April , nineteen hundred and . . .

BETWEEN Walter Hay, residing at 192 Twain Avenue, Town of Taylor, County of Cortland, State of New York , the mortgagor,

and Dennis Barron, residing at 201 Home City Avenue, Town of Taylor, County of Cortland, State of New York , the mortgagee,

WITNESSETH, that to secure the payment of an indebtedness in the sum of Seven Thousand and Five Hundred and 00/100 - - - - - - - - - - - - Dollars, lawful money of the United States, to be paid in the sum of One Hundred and 00/100 ($100) Dollars monthly on the sixteenth day of each and every month, with interest thereon to be computed from 16th day of April . 19 - - , at the rate of 7½ per centum per annum, and to be paid monthly on the sixteenth day of each and every month, according to a certain bond, note or obligation bearing even date herewith, the mortgagor hereby mortgages to the mortgagee

ALL (here follows a complete legal description)

TOGETHER with all right, title and interest, if any, of the mortgagor of, in and to any streets and roads abutting the above-described premises to the center lines thereof.

TOGETHER with all fixtures and articles of personal property now or hereafter attached to or contained in and used in connection with, said premises, including but not limited to all apparatus, machinery, fittings, gas ranges, ice boxes, mechanical refrigerators, awnings, shades, screens, storm sashes, plants and shrubbery.

TOGETHER with any and all awards heretofore and hereafter made to the present and all subsequent owners of the mortgaged premises by any governmental or other lawful authorities for taking by eminent domain the whole or any part of said premises or any easement therein, including any awards for any changes of grade of streets, which said awards are hereby assigned to the holder of this mortgage, who is hereby authorized to collect and receive the proceeds of any such awards from such authorities and to give proper receipts and acquittances therefor, and to apply the same toward the payment of the amount owing on account of this mortgage and its accompanying bond or note, notwithstanding the fact that the amount owing thereon may not then be due and payable; and the said mortgagor hereby covenants and agrees, upon request, to make, execute and deliver any and all assignments and other instruments sufficient for the purpose of assigning the aforesaid awards to the holder of this mortgage, free, clear and discharged of any and all encumbrances of any kind or nature whatsoever.

A Mortgage

AND the mortgagor covenants with the mortgagee as follows:

1. That the mortgagor will pay the indebtedness as hereinbefore provided.

2. That the mortgagor will keep the buildings on the premises insured against loss by fire for the benefit of the mortgagee; that he will assign and deliver the policies to the mortgagee; and that he will reimburse the mortgagee for any premiums paid for insurance made by the mortgagee on the mortgagor's default in so insuring the buildings or in so assigning and delivering the policies.

3. That no building on the premises shall be removed or demolished without the consent of the mortgagee.

4. That the whole of said principal sum and interest shall become due at the option of the mortgagee: after default in the payment of any instalment of principal or of interest for 30 days; or after default in the payment of any tax, water rate, sewer rent or assessment for thirty days after notice and demand; or after default after notice and demand either in assigning and delivering the policies insuring the buildings against loss by fire or in reimbursing the mortgagee for premiums paid on such insurance, as hereinbefore provided; or after default upon request in furnishing a statement of the amount due on the mortgage and whether any offsets or defenses exist against the mortgage debt, as hereinafter provided.

5. That the holder of this mortgage, in any action to foreclose it, shall be entitled to the appointment of a receiver.

6. That the mortgagor will pay all taxes, assessments, sewer rents or water rates, and in default thereof, the mortgagee may pay the same.

7. That the mortgagor within six days upon request in person or within fifteen days upon request by mail will furnish a written statement duly acknowledged of the amount due on this mortgage and whether any offsets or defenses exist against the mortgage debt.

8. That notice and demand or request may be in writing and may be served in person or by mail.

9. That the mortgagor warrants the title to the premises.

10. That fire insurance policies which are required by pargaraph No. 2 above shall contain the usual extended coverage endorsement; in addition thereto the mortgagor, within thirty days after notice and demand, will keep the buildings on the premises insured against loss by other insurable hazards for the benefit of the mortgagee, as may reasonably be required by the mortgagee; that he will assign and deliver the policies to the mortgagee; and that he will reimburse the mortgagee for any premiums paid for insurance made by the mortgagee on the mortgagor's default in so insuring or in so assigning and delivering the policies. The provisions of subdivision 4, of Section 254 of the Real Property Law, with reference to the construction of the fire insurance clause, shall govern the construction of this clause so far as applicable.

11. That the whole of said principal sum shall become due at the option of the mortgagee after default for thirty days after notice and demand, in the payment of any instalment of any assessment for local improvements heretofore or hereafter laid, which is or may become payable in annual instalments and which has affected, now affects or hereafter may affect the said premises, notwithstanding that such instalment be not due and payable at the time of such notice and demand, or upon the failure to exhibit to the mortgagee, within thirty days after demand, receipts showing payment of all taxes, assessments, water rates, sewer rents and any other charges which may have become a prior lien on the mortgaged premises.

12. That the whole of said principal sum shall become due at the option of the mortgagee, if the buildings on said premises are not maintained in reasonably good repair, or upon the failure of any owner of said premises to comply with the requirement of any governmental department claiming jurisdiction within three months after an order making such requirement has been issued by any such department.

13. That in the event of the passage after the date of this mortgage of any law of the State of New York, deducting from the value of land for the purposes of taxation any lien thereon, or changing in any way the laws for the taxation of mortgages or debts secured by mortgage for state or local purposes, or the manner of the collection of any such taxes, so as to affect this mortgage, the holder of this mortgage and of the debt which it secures, shall have the right to give thirty days' written notice to the owner of the mortgaged premises requiring the payment of the mortgage debt. If such notice be given the said debt shall become due, payable and collectible at the expiration of said thirty days.

14. That in case of a sale, said premises, or so much thereof as may be affected by this mortgage, may be sold in one parcel.

15. That the whole of said principal sum shall immediately become due at the option of the mortgagee, if the mortgagor shall assign the rents or any part of the rents of the mortgaged premises without first obtaining the written consent of the mortgagee to such assignment, or upon the actual or threatened demolition or removal of any building erected or to be erected upon said premises.

16. That if any action or proceeding be commenced (except an action to foreclose this mortgage or to collect the debt secured thereby), to which action or proceeding the holder of this mortgage is made a party, or in which it becomes necessary to defend or uphold the lien of this mortgage, all sums paid by the holder of this mortgage for the expense of any litigation to prosecute or defend the rights and lien created by this mortgage (including reasonable counsel fees), shall be paid by the mortgagor together with interest thereon at the rate of six percent, per annum, and any such sum and the interest thereon shall be a lien on said premises, prior to any right, or title to, interest in or claim upon said premises attaching or accruing subsequent to the lien of this mortgage, and shall be deemed to be secured by this mortgage and by the bond or note which it secures. In any action or proceeding to foreclose this mortgage, or to recover or collect the debt secured thereby, the provisions of law respecting the recovering of costs, disbursements and allowances shall prevail unaffected by this covenant.

17. That the whole of said principal sum shall immediately become due at the option of the mortgagee upon any default in keeping the buildings on said premises insured as required by paragraph No. 2 or paragraph No. 10 hereof, or if after application by any holder of this mortgage to two or more fire insurance companies lawfully doing business in the State of New York and issuing policies of fire insurance upon buildings situate in the place where the mortgaged premises are situate, the companies to which such application has been made shall refuse to issue such policies, or upon default in complying with the provisions of paragraph No. 10 hereof, or upon default, for five days after notice and demand, either in assigning and delivering to the

A Mortgage (Continued)

mortgagee the policies of fire insurance or in reimbursing the mortgagee for premiums paid on such fire insurance as hereinbefore provided in paragraph No. 2 hereof.

18. That the mortgagor will, in compliance with Section 13 of the Lien Law, receive the advances secured hereby and will hold the right to receive such advances as a trust fund to be applied first for the purpose of paying the cost of the improvement and will apply the same first to the payment of the cost of the improvement before using any part of the total of the same for any other purpose.

19. That in the event of any default in the performance of any of the terms, covenants or agreements herein contained, it is agreed that the then owner of the mortgaged premises, if he is the occupant of said premises or any part thereof, shall immediately surrender possession of the premises so occupied to the holder of this mortgage, and if such occupant is permitted to remain in possession, the possession shall be as tenant of the holder of this mortgage and such occupant shall, on demand, pay monthly in advance to the holder of this mortgage a reasonable rental for the space so occupied and in default thereof, such occupant may be dispossessed by the usual summary proceedings. In case of foreclosure and the appointment of a receiver of rents, the covenants herein contained may be enforced by such receiver.

This mortgage may not be changed orally, but only by an agreement in writing and signed by the party against whom enforcement of any waiver, change, modification or discharge is sought.

IN WITNESS WHEREOF, this mortgage has been duly executed by the mortgagor.

IN PRESENCE OF:

/s/ Robert Lawyer

/s/ Walter Hay
/s/ Dennis Barron

Title Guarantee and Trust Company, New York, New York

A Mortgage (Concluded)

THE MORTGAGE CLAUSES AND THEIR MEANINGS

In general most of the statutory forms of the mortgage require: (1) a date, (2) the names of the parties, (3) the amount of the debt, and (4) a statement that the "mortgagor hereby mortgages to the mortgagee" certain described property. These elements of a mortgage are discussed in detail on the following pages.

General Clauses

Following the description of the property, the statutory form of mortgage contains this statement:

> And the mortgagor covenants with the mortgagee as follows:

Here follow the general clauses or covenants found in the statutory mortgages in most states. They will vary slightly among the states, but in general they are as described below.

Covenant to Pay Indebtedness. The *covenant to pay indebtedness* states "that the mortgagor will pay the indebtedness as hereinbefore provided." This is self-explanatory.

Covenant of Insurance. The *covenant of insurance* is a promise that the premises shall be covered by fire insurance in a stated amount for the benefit of the mortgagee and that the mortgagor will assign and deliver the policies to the mortgagee. Depending upon the location of the property, a statement should be added to the mortgage in regard to an extended coverage endorsement. The reason for this is that the standard fire policy specifically exempts damage from wind and rain. In hurricane or frequent storm areas, this means that the mortgagee has insufficient protection with the fire policy alone because of the possibility that damage might be done by wind and rain.

Covenant Against Removal. The *covenant against removal* is often included in the statutory form of mortgage and states that the mortgagor will not remove or demolish any building without the consent of the mortgagee. This clause is necessary because the amount generally loaned is based on an appraisal that includes both land and buildings. One case involving this clause arose when a mortgage was given on a farm. The mortgagor, anticipating that he might default and having heard that real property consisted of land and things that were attached to the land, built all of his outbuildings on skids. He did default on the mortgage, and he hauled the buildings on the skids off the land. The court held that despite the fact that the buildings were not physically attached to the land, they were still under the terms of the mortgage. Thus, the mortgagee was entitled to his foreclosure on those buildings.

Covenant to Pay Taxes. The *covenant to pay taxes* is a promise by the mortgagor that he will pay the taxes and assessments that might be levied against the property. Together with this covenant there is generally an acceleration clause stating that if the taxes or assessments are not paid after a certain time has elapsed, the mortgagee at his option may declare the entire amount of principal and interest due. This clause, in effect, gives the mortgagee the right to foreclose after a stated period in the event that the taxes or assessments are not paid.

Acceleration Clause. The mortgage form contains an *acceleration clause*. This clause specifies that, if the mortgagor fails to keep the covenants or if he has a defective title, the entire debt will become due and collectible at the option of the mortgagee.

Warrant of Title. Most statutory forms of mortgage contain a *warrant of title* clause. It states simply that the mortgagor warrants title to the premises. It means in effect that the mortgagor guarantees the title to the property. This will be discussed in detail later in this chapter.

These six clauses are in general use in nearly every type of simple mortgage in all of the states.

Special Clauses

In addition to the general clauses, there are many other clauses that can be and are inserted into the mortgage form to cover special situations. The most common ones are discussed in the following paragraphs.

Covenant to Pay Attorney's Fees. In some states the mortgagor promises under the terms of the mortgage to pay reasonable attorney's fees together with costs and disbursements if the mortgagee finds it necessary to foreclose. Some states do not require a covenant to pay attorney's fees inasmuch as the mortgagee may demand reasonable fees in the event of foreclosure without the statement being included in the instrument.

The After-Acquired Personal Property Clause. There is in some mortgages a clause stating that items of personal property "now or hereafter attached to or contained in and used in connection with said premises" shall come under the lien of the mortgage. Often a list of items that are normally personal property is included together with the statement that the mortgage is not limited to these items. When these items are included in the mortgage, they are sold together with the real property proper in the case of foreclosure.

Suppose, for example, that *A*, as mortgagor, mortgages his property to *B*. At the time *A* mortgages the property, he has no window screens. Suppose further that an after-acquired personal property clause, as outlined above, is included in the mortgage and *A* purchases screens. If *B* finds it necessary to foreclose on the mortgage, he is, by virtue of this clause, entitled to foreclose on the screens even though they were acquired by *A* after the inception of the mortgage.

Receiver Clause. The *receiver clause* states that in any action to foreclose a mortgage the holder of the mortgage shall be entitled to the appointment of a receiver. The *receiver* is one who will collect any rents and profits from the property and maintain the property. This clause is intended to protect the mortgagee during the interval between the commencement of the foreclosure action and the final order of the court. If the receiver, after having satisfied the mortgagee's claim, has a net balance, the mortgagor is credited with that balance.

This clause is especially important when the sale concerns a parcel of real property on which there is a business. For example, suppose *A* sells *B* real property on which there is a shoe store. *B* is really purchasing three things: the land and building, the stock in the store, and the goodwill of the store, this often being regarded by businessmen as having the greatest value. The goodwill is referred to by businessmen as "the key." Suppose that *A* is going to finance the purchase in part by becoming the mortgagee himself for part of the purchase price. Commonly it is said that he "takes back" a mortgage. When a person "takes back" a mortgage as part of the purchase price, he is said to have a purchase money mortgage, as will be discussed in detail later.

Assume that *B* defaults on his payments. *A* has security for the value of the land in the land itself and he has probably been paid for the stock, but what about the goodwill or "key"? This may have given the sale its greatest value. Between the time of default and the time of termination of foreclosure action, *B* might operate the business in such a way as to destroy the value of the goodwill.

With a receiver clause in the mortgage, *A* can readily have a receiver appointed who will run the business in a satisfactory manner and thus preserve the value of the goodwill.

Estoppel Clause. The *estoppel clause* states that upon the request of the mortgagee (lender), the mortgagor (borrower) will furnish a written statement "duly acknowledged of the amount due on this mortgage and whether any offsets or defenses exist against the mortgage debt." In some states this is known as a Certificate of No Defense.

Although it might appear strange for the mortgagee to make a request of the mortgagor of how much the mortgagor owes him on the mortgage, the inclusion of this is extremely important to the mortgagee in the event he desires to sell the mortgage. If the mortgagee decides to sell the mortgage in order to raise capital for a further investment, when he (the mortgagee) approaches a third party to sell the mortgage, the third party will want to know the present value of the mortgage. The third party can demand to see the mortgage, but this will tell him nothing of the present value because part of the face value may have been paid. If the mortgage contains an estoppel clause, the mortgagee can demand an estoppel certificate from the mortgagor indicating the present value of the mortgage. In addition, the mortgagor will certify that there are no defenses up to date in the event of a foreclosure action. After having certified that there are no defenses to a foreclosure, the mortgagor cannot later assert in court that he had a defense as of that time. Technically, he is said to be "estopped."

Good Repair Clause. The *good repair clause* states that if the mortgagor does not keep the premises in "reasonably good repair" or if the owner fails to comply with the requirements of any governmental department within three months, then the mortgagee at his option may foreclose. The test of what is "reasonably good repair" is that the mortgagee is entitled to foreclose if his security is being impaired.

The inclusion of this clause came about as a result of the condemning of buildings by municipalities as being unfit for human habitation. For example, *A* is the mortgagee on an apartment building and *B* the owner and mortgagor. *B* has tenants in the building and allows the building to deteriorate to such a state of disrepair that the municipality feels it necessary to take action. *B* abandons the building, leaving *A* with a worthless, in the sense of untenantable, building on his hands. With a "good repair" clause inserted in the action, *A* could foreclose on his mortgage prior to the time that the municipality takes action and thus protect the security for his debt.

Sale in One Parcel Clause. The *sale in one parcel clause* is generally written as follows: "that in case of a sale, said premises, or as much thereof as may be affected by this mortgage, may be sold in one parcel." This clause is applicable when more than one lot is covered by the terms of the mortgage. In the event of a foreclosure, the mortgagee must offer the lots for sale one at a time until the amount due under the mortgage is paid. If the mortgagor has sold any of the lots "subject to the mortgage," the mortgagee must sell those lots in inverse order of their sale. In short, he must sell those still owned by the mortgagor and then sell those that the mortgagor has already sold, but in inverse order of their sale, last ones first. After they are sold, if this does not bring in enough money, he may sell them in bulk. The sale of the individual lots is tentative until it is ascertained that they have brought sufficient funds to cover the debt.

Owner Rent Clause. The *owner rent clause* creates a landlord-tenant relationship between the mortgagee and the mortgagor in the event of a foreclosure. By means of this clause the owner agrees to pay a reasonable rent for the premises during the time in which he is in possession of the building after the commencement of the foreclosure action. In some states, even if a receiver under the terms of the mortgage has been appointed, the receiver cannot collect any money except that due on property contracts that the owner had. The owner rent clause enables the receiver to collect rent from the owner of the property.

Trust Clause. A *trust clause* is inserted in the deed in some states. In New York State, for example, this clause states:

> The mortgagor will, in compliance with Section 13 of the Lien law, receive the advances secured hereby and will receive the right to such advances as a trust fund to be applied first for the purpose of paying the cost of the improvement and will apply the same, first to the payment of the cost of the improvement before using any part of the total of the same for any other purpose.

The purpose of this is to prevent the owner from improving his property before applying for a loan, and not paying the cost of the improvement. If an owner, for example, hires a painter to paint his house and then obtains a loan without paying the painter, the painter may file a mechanic's lien against the property. A *mechanic's lien* is a species of lien or charge created by statute which exists in favor of persons who have performed work or furnished materials in the erection or repair of a building.

The placing of the lien on the property will involve the mortgagee in legal action. When this clause is included in a mortgage, it puts the burden on the mortgagor to pay for these improvements. If he does not pay, he has breached what amounts to a trust agreement for the benefit of those persons who have improved the property, and he (the mortgagor) will, if he breaches the agreement, become liable under the penal code.

Prepayment Clause. The *prepayment clause* is inserted in the mortgage at the request of the mortgagor. It generally states that the mortgagor may pay the entire or stated amounts on the mortgage principal at anytime he chooses prior to the due date. The mortgagor could not do this without the insertion of the prepayment clause. Some of the prepayment clauses call for the payment of a penalty by the mortgagor for the privilege of prepayment. This penalty may be inserted in the prepayment clause by stating that the entire amount due on the mortgage may be paid upon ninety days' written notice to the mortgagee and upon "the payment of two months' interest." The two months' interest then is the penalty which is in addition to the interest paid between the time of giving of notice and the prepayment. If a bank is the mortgagee, this penalty helps defray some of the bank's costs of making the mortgage.

Effective May 1, 1972, the FHA suspended loan prepayment penalties. The regulation suspends prepayment penalties to borrowers who pay off their loans before the first ten years of the amortization period have passed. The effect is to make the FHA loans more competitive with the VA loans under which no prepayment charges are imposed.

TYPES OF MORTGAGES

There are three types of mortgages and a number of variations of these types which will be subsequently pointed out.

The FHA-Insured Mortgage

The primary feature of the *FHA mortgage* as far as the lender is concerned is that the loan is insured. A loss as a result of failure of the mortgagor to meet his payments will be met by the Federal

Housing Administration, which was instituted under the National Housing Act of 1934. It is now under the jurisdiction of the Department of Housing and Urban Development. This insurance feature enables lending institutions to lend a higher percent of the appraised value than they would under ordinary circumstances.

The VA-Guaranteed Mortgage

The *VA mortgage*, or the so-called *GI mortgage*, is a part of the Servicemen's Readjustment Act of 1944 (amended December 28, 1945). The crux of the law pertaining to real property is that the Veterans Administration will guarantee a certain percentage of a mortgage loan to a veteran up to a maximum amount to qualified lenders who lend money on homes purchased by veterans. The amount of the maximum guarantee, the rate of interest, and the length of the loan can be changed by an act of Congress. They have varied in the past and will probably be changed again.

In some areas, under changes in the law made by Congress, the Veterans Administration has loaned money directly to veterans. For example, from time to time sums of money have been allotted to various counties to be loaned to veterans within that county who have been unable to obtain a VA loan from a bank or other lending institution. In these cases, the veteran obtains a letter from each of two lending institutions who indicate that they will not lend money to the veteran. After having done this, the veteran makes direct application to the Veterans Administration.

The practitioner should keep in mind that when a binder or contract is entered into between a seller and a purchaser who is a veteran and if the veteran intends to obtain a GI loan, the contract or binder should be made "subject to obtaining a GI loan in the amount of $ . . . ." The reason for the caution is readily apparent in the following illustration. Suppose a contract is entered into between a seller and a veteran purchaser for the sale of a house at $15,600. The veteran intends to purchase it under a GI loan, but nothing is said to that effect in the contract which reads: "Subject to obtaining a mortgage." Suppose in the above case the veteran does apply for a GI mortgage and the appraiser from the Veterans Administration appraises the house for only $15,000. This means that he cannot purchase it under a GI mortgage for more than $15,000. In this case, where nothing is said in the contract about "subject to obtaining a GI mortgage," the seller can force the purchaser to seek another mortgage under threat of an action for specific performance. In this case he will apply for a regular mortgage from a bank which will lend him only two thirds of the amount set on the building by its own appraiser, thus forcing him to put up more cash for a down payment. This he may not have. The moral is always to spell out the kind and the amount of a mortgage in a contract.

As will be pointed out in Chapter 15, the number of VA mortgages issued each year depends in part upon the interest rate. As interest rates rise, institutional lenders will move to investments where the rate of interest is not fixed.

The Conventional Mortgage

The term *conventional mortgage* as it is presently used refers to a mortgage that is neither FHA-insured nor VA-guaranteed. In general it can be said that the down payment on the conventional mortgage is higher than either the FHA or VA mortgages. However, in 1972, home buyers could borrow from Savings and Loan Associations up to 95 percent of the value of the home. The loan is guaranteed or insured by a mortgage insurance company which is determined to be "a qualified private insurer" by the Federal Home Loan Mortgage Corporation. The maximum 95 percent conventional loan is $30,000. The private mortgage insurance company will be discussed in detail in Chapter 15.

The capital which flows into the conventional mortgage market remains fairly stable while both FHA and VA mortgage outlays have a tendency to fluctuate because their relatively fixed interest rates make them more sensitive to changes in the interest rate. FHA-insured and VA-guaranteed mortgages account for about 20 percent of the total mortgage market.

VARIATIONS IN THE FORM OF MORTGAGES

Amortizing Mortgage

This is the most common form of mortgage used in FHA, VA, and the conventional-type mortgage. Under the terms of this form, provision is generally made for monthly payments of principal together with interest. The principle of amortization became common as a result of the mortgage foreclosure experience during the depression of the thirties. It enables regular payments to be made on principal and the creation of an equity in the property.

The underlying reason for including an amortization feature in a mortgage is that it will tend to prevent many foreclosures in the event of a depression. This is open to debate. In a study made for the National Bureau of Economic Research in 1956, Dr. J. E. Morton indicated that this might not necessarily be so. He suggested that the poorest risks are not covered by either VA or FHA insurance. This indicates that a downturn in the business cycle might cause a number of these homes to be foreclosed in spite of partial amortization. In addition, the phase of the business cycle in which the loan is initiated is decisive. This means that the closer a loan is made to a major downturn in consumer income and real estate values, the greater the chance that it will end in default.

The Budget Mortgage

The *budget mortgage* is a further development of the self-amortizing mortgage. Although the self-amortizing mortgage provides for monthly payments of part interest and part principal, the budget mortgage includes in the monthly payments one twelfth of the year's taxes, a proportionate amount of the yearly fire insurance premiums, and any other charges which might, if left unpaid, constitute a basis for the foreclosure of the mortgage. Generally, when the mortgagor enters into a budget mortgage, he pays six months' taxes in advance at the title closing in order to provide the lender with a revolving fund. Any surplus in the fund is returnable to the mortgagor when he has made his final payment on the mortgage.

The Package Mortgage

The *package mortgage* is a mortgage of recent innovation that goes a step further than the budget mortgage. Usually, it incorporates all the features of the budget mortgage plus payments for certain mechanical equipment put in the home. In this manner all charges are met in one payment.

The Open Mortgage

The term *open mortgage* is employed to refer to a mortgage that has reached the due date but has not yet been paid. The mortgagee in these cases can demand payment at anytime, but if his security is good and he is receiving a fair return on his investment, he may be content to allow the mortgagor to continue paying interest and leave the mortgage "open."

It should be remembered that there is a statute of limitations on mortgages in most states. Thus, if there is no payment of interest or principal for six years, the mortgagor has a defense in the event of a foreclosure action by the mortgagee.

The Blanket Mortgage

A *blanket mortgage* is briefly defined as a mortgage that covers more than one parcel of real property. It is a type of instrument that is often used by builders to cover construction loans.

The *partial release clause* is generally used in conjunction with the blanket mortgage. It is a clause that is inserted in a mortgage stating that upon partial payment on the mortgage, the mortgagee will issue a partial satisfaction piece that releases a particular parcel or lot from the terms of the mortgage. It would be worded substantially as follows:

> The mortgagee agrees to release any lot from the lien of this mortgage upon payment to him by the mortgagor or his assigns of the sum of $100 per lot upon the lands so released.

The Open-End Mortgage

The *open-end mortgage* is a mortgage in which the borrower is given a limit up to which he may borrow. For example, the loan may be authorized up to $20,000, and the borrower may initially borrow only $15,000; but at a later date he may increase the loan to the maximum authorized, in this case $20,000, without changing the terms of the original agreement.[3]

---

[3] Connecticut, Florida, Kentucky, Louisiana, Maryland, Massachusetts, Missouri, Montana, Nebraska, New Hampshire, New Jersey, North Dakota, Rhode Island, South Dakota, and Vermont have statutes limiting the amount of "future advances" that can be included in a single mortgage.

The open-end mortgage is very often used in connection with corporate loans, for example, the mortgage bonds of the former Northern California Power Company. In that instance a total of $10,000,000 was authorized, but only $5,000,000 was issued. A provision was made in the indenture that the balance could be issued if the net income (after allowing 15 percent of gross income for depreciation and maintenance) was equal to two times the interest on all outstanding bonds.

The Purchase Money Mortgage

A *purchase money mortgage* is a mortgage that is given as part of the consideration for the sale of real property. This type of mortgage typically arises when the seller agrees to "take back," as it is commonly said, a mortgage as part of the purchase price in a transaction. The seller is really financing or partially financing the transaction. For example, *A* wants to sell *B* his property for $5,000 and *B* has only $1,000 cash and is without recourse to any other type of mortgage. In such a case *A* might take the $1,000 from *B* and "take back" a mortgage in the amount of $4,000. It should be remembered that a purchase money mortgage becomes a purchase money mortgage because it is created by spelling it out in the mortgage instrument. In short, a statement that it is a purchase money mortgage is written into the instrument. It is sometimes called colloquially a "P.M." mortgage.[4]

Warrant of Title Clause in the Purchase Money Mortgage. All of the forms of mortgage previously discussed contain a clause warranting title. This states in effect that the mortgagor warrants title to the premises and that he has good title. This means that the property is free from encumbrances according to the mortgagor's declarations. When the seller "takes back" the purchase money mortgage, he signs and delivers the deed to the purchaser, who is the mortgagor. The mortgagor delivers such cash as he is going to pay to the seller and at the same time signs and delivers the purchase money mortgage to the seller, who is the mortgagee. This exchange raises the question of

[4] In California no deficiency judgment is permitted on a purchase money mortgage.

what should be done with the "warrant of title clause" in the mortgage. Conceivably, the mortgagee (who is the seller in this case) may have a defective title which he transfers over to his mortgagor (the purchaser); now the purchaser is placed in the position of the warrantor of title as a result of the clause in the mortgage. To avoid this situation, the warrant of title clause should be supplanted with a clause stating that the mortgagor warrants only such title as has been conveyed to him by the mortgagee. The net effect of this is that the burden of "good title" has been passed back to the seller (mortgagee) who is the logical defender of the title.

Use of the Purchase Money Mortgage by Builders. Although some builders use the option as was outlined in Chapter 4, a combination blanket mortgage containing a partial release clause is perhaps a more favored instrument of the builder who is operating with little cash and who does not want his capital tied up in real property. For example, *A* is a builder and *B* has 100 lots for sale. *A* arranges a transaction with *B* that requires very little cash. After *A* has gone to a bank and has received a tentative commitment for a building loan, he approaches *B* and offers him $100 per lot. He proposes to *B* that he pay $10 cash for each of the lots and that he give *B* a blanket purchase money mortgage covering $90 per lot for the balance of the consideration for the transaction. This is accepted by *B*, and *A* insists that the mortgage contain a partial release clause to the effect that upon the payment of $90, *B* release from the terms of the mortgage any one of the lots that *A* desires. *B* agrees to all of this, and *A* pays out only 10 percent cash at this point, begins building, obtains a commitment from the bank when he has built enough of the house to satisfy the bank appraiser, pays *B* for one lot, receives cash from the bank, finishes up the building, and sells it for a profit.

This hypothetical problem is, of course, an oversimplification, but not completely. The only variations on the figures given would depend upon the bargaining position of the parties. *A*, the builder, might have to put down more than 10 percent cash, but, in the final analysis, it can be done with very little money.

The practitioner will recognize at once that there are "two sides to every coin." If the seller and the builder do make a deal as far as a price is concerned, should the seller draw up the partial release clause releasing one lot for the payment of the balance due on that one lot? It is thought that it might offer more protection to the seller to have *A*, the builder and mortgagee, pay off, let us say, $100 on each lot released, the extra $10 to be applied toward the payment of the principal on the balance of the mortgage. This would mean that the entire balance would be completely paid after which the remainder of the lots would be released from the terms of the mortgage. It might be stated here that the seller should take another precautionary measure in the transaction outlined above. He should insist upon substantially the same protection as that discussed under "Options" in Chapter 4. As all practitioners know, different lots in a block have a different value as a general rule; hence, the partial release clause should be drawn in terms of at least two lots being paid for in full by the purchaser and released at the same time. One lot will be considered to be of greater value than the other. This will effectively avoid the seller's being "stuck" with the poorer lots in the event the builder becomes financially embarrassed before the mortgage has been completely paid.

The Wraparound Mortgage

Strictly speaking, the "wraparound mortgage" is not a mortgage at all. It is a covenant contained within a mortgage used as a "sweetener" to entice sellers of commercial type properties to sell to a buyer with a relatively small down payment, and it is used during periods of high interest rates. For example, suppose a seller has an older apartment house on which there is an existing first mortgage of $20,000 placed some years ago at a rate of 4 percent interest. His property has appreciated and is now worth $100,000. He is approached by a buyer who has only $10,000 for a down payment. The seller agrees to take back a purchase money mortgage in the amount of $70,000, which in reality is a second purchase money mortgage, say at 8 percent, and the buyer is to assume the $20,000 mortgage. The sweetener is this: the buyer agrees not only to assume the $20,000 mortgage and pay the lender 4 percent on the mortgage, but he agrees to pay an *additional* 4 percent on the old $20,000 mortgage to the *seller*. The net effect of this is to increase the effective yield to the seller on his $70,000 mortgage.

It is then said to be a "wraparound" because the new interest rate is being "wrapped around" the old mortgage.

Participations in Mortgages

A participation in a mortgage is used by lenders in very tight money situations and in commercial transactions only when they participate in the income, capital appreciation, or both, of the commercial property. One form of participation is in the income. For example, in order to obtain a loan on an apartment building, an investor may be forced to agree to permit the lender to participate in the gross rent . . . often as high as 15 percent. Another form of participation is where the borrower has to agree to give the lender a percentage of the appreciation if the building is sold. For example, a building is sold for $50,000 over cost. The borrower may have to give the lender as high as 50 percent of his gain. Often the participations combine both forms. Needless to say, there are no prepayment clauses in this type of mortgage because the lender does not want the borrower to refinance in the event mortgage rates drop.

The Mortgage on a Lease

The *mortgage on a lease* usually comes about as an additional security device when the sale of a business opportunity is concerned. For example, *B* has leased a store from *A*, and *B* has permission from his landlord, *A*, to assign and mortgage the lease. *B* has a dry cleaning establishment with fixtures valued at $1,000, but he has built up the business and it is now worth $5,000. Because he needs money in a hurry, he consents to sell the business to *C*, who has only $1,000 in cash. *B* may take the cash and a note and a security agreement as provided for by the Uniform Commercial Code for $1,000 on the fixtures and *C*'s notes with no other security for the balance of the indebtedness. However, in situations of this sort, in order to secure *C's* notes, a mortgage on the lease, or leasehold mortgage as it is sometimes called, would seem to be in order. This mortgage is drawn and designed to give *B* the possession of the business in the event *C* defaults on the payment of the notes. The mortgage on the lease, even in those lien theory states like New York, is drawn in the same manner as the ordinary mortgage in title theory states. *B* assigns the lease to *C*. The lease, under the terms of the mortgage, is transferred back to *B* upon the condition that if *C* pays the notes, then the instrument will be void; and if *C* does not pay, then *B* is entitled to the possession of the premises.[5]

The Crop Mortgage

The *crop mortgage* is a mortgage often given by a farmer, as mortgagor, on growing crops to secure a loan. Usually it is a chattel or personal property mortgage used even in some states where crops are treated as real property. The crop mortgage usually follows the title theory, even in lien theory states. It states that the mortgagor does "grant, bargain and sell" to the mortgagee the crops growing or to be grown in a certain year at a certain described place, and if the mortgagor pays the debt secured by the crops, the mortgage shall be void. It usually contains a clause stating that the mortgagor covenants to take proper care of the crops; and if he fails "to properly harvest, thresh and care for the same in a proper manner and at the proper season," then the mortgagee shall have the right to sell the crops. In addition, there is a clause covering attorney's fees and costs in the event of foreclosure, together with a covenant by the mortgagor that the crops are free and clear from all encumbrances and that he will forever warrant and defend against the lawful claims of any person or persons.

This form of mortgage is employed quite extensively in farm states as security for short-term farm loans.

Junior Mortgage

A *junior mortgage* is a mortgage that is subordinate to any other mortgage of record. This type of mortgage is drawn in the same

[5] For example, *B* is the owner of a small grocery store with $1,000 worth of stock and $1,000 in fixtures. *B's* price is $5,000, plus dollar for dollar for the stock. *C* appears on the scene with $1,000 in cash. *B* may take the $1,000 for the stock, a note and a security agreement on the fixtures for $1,000, and a mortgage on the lease for the balance of the payment on the notes. A better way might be for *B* to take the $1,000 cash for "goodwill," a note and security agreement for $1,000 on the fixtures and notes with the mortgage on the lease in the amount of $3,000. Then, instead of transferring the title of the stock to *C*, *B* might do well to retain the title and consign the stock to *C*, with periodic payments being made to *B* as the stock is sold. In this way, in the event of default by *C*, *B* will have received considerably more cash from the transaction and still have the ownership in the remaining stock.

manner as a first mortgage, with the exception that it should contain two additional appropriate clauses. These are described below.

Default in Prior Mortgage Clause. The *default in prior mortgage clause* states that if the mortgagor defaults in the payment of interest on a prior mortgage, the junior mortgagee may pay the amount, add it to his loan, and immediately institute a foreclosure action.

Subordination Clause. The *subordination clause* states that in the event a prior mortgage is removed, the junior mortgage will not automatically become a first mortgage but will be content to remain in a junior position in case the mortgagor seeks a new mortgage. The clause states also that if the mortgagee receives a new mortgage in a greater amount than is on the premises at the time of execution of the instrument, the excess over the present mortgage will be paid to reduce the principal of the junior mortgage.

Usury

The problem of usury is one that must be met in any discussion of junior mortgages. To begin with, a bank cannot lend money on a second mortgage; therefore, it becomes necessary to approach an individual money lender.[6] The second mortgage involves a greater amount of risk than a first mortgage; therefore, the lender will often ask for a premium or bonus. This bonus in many states will be construed as being in excess of the legal rate of interest, hence usury. Often the lender runs the risk of losing all of the money loaned, plus interest. In order to avoid this risk, many mortgage lenders employ the following device. It should be remembered first that only individuals can raise the defense of usury; a corporation, although a legal entity, cannot in most states.[7] Suppose *A* has a mortgage in the amount of $5,000 on his property and he desires a second mortgage in the amount of $2,000. *B*, a lender, might request that he become

---

[6] In general the lender can collect neither principal nor interest from a borrower if the rate of interest is usurious. However, the National Banking Act (12 U.S.C. 86) protects commercial banks and trust companies from loss of principal if the contract is usurious. Industrial banks can lend on second mortgages.

[7] Section 2401 and Section 2403 of the New York Penal Code states that it is criminal usury if the rate on a corporation is in excess of 25%. In 1973, the state of Virginia removed all state interest rate ceilings on home mortgage loans.

incorporated under the name of "*A*, Inc." *A* conveys his property from *A* to *A*, Inc., and *B* lends the $2,000 to *A*, Inc., in return for a bonus or at a rate of interest over and above the legal rate established for individuals. This transaction will not in any way affect the lien of the first mortgage because the first mortgage will follow the land.

Deeds as Mortgages

Although valid deeds have sometimes been construed as mortgages, they are not used as mortgages customarily, and should, if possible, be avoided. The situation generally arises through ignorance. A loan is made and the lender asks the borrower for a deed for security, stating that upon payment of the loan the deed will be returned to the borrower. When both parties are honest, this arrangement may turn out to the satisfaction of all parties concerned; but when there is dishonesty, or when the lender has died, the heirs might in good faith believe that a valid permanent transfer of title has been made, in which case there will be a lawsuit. If for some reason it is felt that a deed *must* be given, a statement should certainly be inserted in the habendum of the deed stating that the deed was given for the express purpose of securing a loan and that a reconveyance will be made upon payment of the loan by the borrower. This would for practical purposes convert it to a common-law mortgage.

THE DEED OF TRUST

There are a number of states that use a *deed of trust*, a trust deed, or a trust indenture, as it is sometimes called, in the nature of a mortgage.[8] In many of these states the lender is given a choice of using either a mortgage or a deed of trust as the security for a real property loan.

In the ordinary mortgage transaction, as was shown above, there are usually only two parties, the mortgagor and the mortgagee. In the

---

[8] Alabama, Alaska, California, Colorado, Delaware, District of Columbia, Illinois, Mississippi, Missouri, Nevada, New Mexico, Tennessee, Texas, Utah, Virginia, and West Virginia. The Small Tract Financing Act (Sec. 52-401 et seq. Revised Code of Montana) provides for a Deed of Trust, but "only for parcels not exceeding three (3) acres."

deed of trust, however, there are three parties to the transaction. The borrower executes the deed of trust which conveys the property to a third person known as the *trustee* who receives from the conveyance sufficient title to carry out the trust. This trustee holds for the benefit of the owner of the note or bond executed by the borrower at the time of the transaction. The note or the bond is the evidence of the debt. If the borrower defaults, the property is either transferred to the lender, after proper legal proceedings have been completed, or disposed of at a public sale at which the trustee transfers title to the purchaser.

Depending upon state law, the trustee is either a *private trustee* whose only qualification is that he must have contractual capacity, or the trustee is a public trustee. Generally speaking, the *public trustee* is either the county clerk or an individual appointed by the governor of the state. The public trustee in these states is bonded and handles all of the trust deeds recorded in the state.

The deed of trust is also used as security for some corporate bond issues. A corporation, for example, will sell bonds and at the same time deliver a deed of trust to a third person as security for the payment of the money due on the bonds. If the corporation defaults on its payments, the trustee, after proper legal proceedings, will sell the property and pay the proceeds to the bondholders up to the extent of the indebtedness.

Action on Payment of the Indebtedness

Depending on the laws of a particular state, either one of two things happens upon the payment of the indebtedness under the terms of the trust deed. In one case it is done by means of an instrument called a *reconveyance* which releases the security (the land and improvements) from the trust. There are two types of reconveyance. One is a *full reconveyance* which is made by the trustee and evidences satisfaction in full and release of the security. Secondly, there is a *partial reconveyance* which is made by the trustee and evidences satisfaction in part and the release of a portion of the security.[9] Both full

---

[9] Some states use a "marginal release," Tennessee and Maryland, for example. A marginal entry is made on the record in the office where the mortgage is recorded, or a release of mortgage is written on the original and then filed in the office where the mortgage is recorded. C.f. Maryland Code, Art. 21, Secs. 38-44.

and partial reconveyances must describe the deed of trust accurately and in detail, and a partial reconveyance must contain the legal description of the security being released.

The other way the deed of trust is handled upon payment of the indebtedness is as follows. The beneficiary under the trust deed signs an instrument known as a *Request for Release of Deed of Trust*. This is then presented either to the private, or in most cases, to the public, trustee together with the canceled note and the deed of trust. The trustee then signs a Release of Deed of Trust. As in the case of the mortgage, this release may be complete or partial. The Release of Deed of Trust is then recorded in the office of the County Clerk or Recorder of the county in which the property is located.

Deed of Trust [10]

THIS INDENTURE, Made this day of

in the year of our Lord one thousand nine hundred and

between

whose address

part of the first part, and the Public Trustee of

, in the State of Colorado, party of the second part, Witnesseth:

THAT, WHEREAS, The said

ha executed promissory note bearing even date herewith, for the principal sum of

Dollars,

payable to the order of

whose address

after the date thereof, with interest thereon from the date thereof at the rate of percent per annum, payable

Deed of Trust

[10] Although this form is designed for Colorado, basically the same form is used in the other states where deeds of trust are in common use.

AND WHEREAS, The said part of the first part desirous of securing the payment of the principal and interest of said promissory note in whose hands soever the said note or any of them may be.

NOW, THEREFORE, The said part of the first part, in consideration of the premises, and for the purpose aforesaid, do hereby grant, bargain, sell and convey unto the said party of the second part in trust forever, the following described property, situate in the County of , State of Colorado, to-wit:

TO HAVE AND TO HOLD the same, together with all and singular the privileges and appurtenances, thereunto belonging: **In Trust Nevertheless,** That in case of default in the payment of said note or any of them, or any part thereof, or in the payment of the interest thereon, according to the tenor and effect of said note or any of them, or in the payment of any prior encumbrances, principal or interest, if any, or in case default shall be made in or in case of violation or breach of any of the terms, conditions, covenants or agreements herein contained, the beneficiary hereunder or the legal holder of the indebtedness secured hereby may declare a violation of any of the covenants herein contained and elect to advertise said property for sale and demand such sale, then, upon filing notice of such election and demand for sale with the said party of the second part, who shall upon receipt of such notice of election and demand for sale cause a copy of the same to be recorded in the recorder's office of the county in which said estate is situated, it shall and may be lawful for said party of the second part to sell and dispose of the same (en masse or in separate parcels, as said Public Trustee may think best), and all the right, title and interest of said part of the first part, heirs or assigns therein, at public auction at the front door of the Court House, in the County of , State of Colorado, or on said premises, or any part thereof as may be specified in the notice of such sale, for the highest and best price the same will bring in cash, four weeks' public notice having been previously given of the time and place of such sale, by advertisement, weekly, in some newspaper of general circulation at that time published in said County of , a copy of which notice shall be mailed within ten days from the date of the first publication thereof to the said part of the first part at the address herein given and to such person or persons appearing to have acquired a subsequent record interest in said real estate at the address given in the recorded instrument; where only the county and state is given as the address then such notice shall be mailed to the county seat, and to make and give to the purchaser or purchasers of such property at such sale, a certificate or certificates in writing describing such property purchased, and the sum or sums paid therefor, and the time when the purchaser or purchasers (or other person entitled thereto) shall be entitled to a deed or deeds therefor, unless the same shall be redeemed as is provided by law; and said Public Trustee shall, upon demand by the person or persons holding the said certificate or certificates of purchase, when said demand is made, or upon demand by the person entitled to a deed to and for the property purchased, at the time such demand is made, the time for redemption having expired, make and execute to such person or persons a deed or deeds to the said property purchased, when said deed or deeds shall be in the ordinary form of a conveyance, and shall be signed, acknowledged and delivered by said Public Trustee, as grantor, and shall convey and quit-claim to such person or persons entitled to such deed, as grantee, the said property purchased as aforesaid and all the right, title, interest, benefit and equity of redemption of the part of the first part, heirs and assigns therein and shall recite the sum or sums for which the said property was sold and shall refer to the power of sale therein contained, and to the sale or sales made by virtue thereof; and in case of an assignment of such certificate or certificates of purchase, or in case of the redemption of such property, by a subsequent encumbrancer, such assignment or

Deed of Trust (Continued)

redemption shall also be referred to in such deed or deeds; but the notice of sale need not be set out in such deed or deeds; and the said Public Trustee shall, out of the proceeds or avails of such sale, after first paying and retaining all fees, charges and costs of making said sale, pay to the beneficiary hereunder or the legal holder of said note the principal and interest due on said note according to the tenor and effect thereof, and all moneys advanced by such beneficiary or legal holder of said note for insurance, taxes and assessments, with interest thereon at percent per annum, rendering the overplus, if any, unto the said part of the first part, legal representatives or assigns; which sale or sales and said deed or deeds so made shall be a perpetual bar, both in law and equity, against the said part of the first part, heirs and assigns, and all other persons claiming the said property, or any part thereof, by, from, through or under said part of the first part, or any of them. The holder or holders of said note or notes may purchase said property or any part thereof; and it shall not be obligatory upon the purchasers at any such sale to see to the application of the purchase money. If a release deed be required, it is agreed that the part of the first part, heirs or assigns, will pay the expense thereof.

And the said part of the first part, for and for heirs, executors and administrators, covenant and agree to and with the said party of the second part, that at the time of the ensealing of and delivery of these presents well seized of the said lands and tenements in fee simple, and ha good right, full power and lawful authority to grant, bargain, sell and convey the same in manner and form as aforesaid; hereby fully and absolutely waiving and releasing all rights and claims may have in or to said lands, tenements, and property as a Homestead Exemption, or other exemption, under and by virtue of any act of the General Assembly of the State of Colorado, now existing or which may hereafter be passed in relation thereto and that the same are free and clear of all liens and encumbrances whatever,

and the above bargained property in the quiet and peaceable possession of the said party of the second part, his successors and assigns, against all and every person or persons lawfully claiming or to claim the whole or any part thereof, the said part of the first part shall and will **Warrant and Forever Defend.**

And that during the continuance of said indebtedness or any part thereof the said part of the first part will in due season pay all taxes and assessments levied under the laws of the State of Colorado (except income taxes) on the obligation hereby secured; and assessments levied on said property; all amounts due or to become due on account of principal and interest on prior encumbrances, if any; and will keep all buildings that may at any time be on said lands, insured against loss by fire in such company or companies as the holder of said note may from time to time direct, for such sum or sums as such company or companies will insure for, not to exceed the amount of said indebtedness, except at the option of said part of the first part, with loss, if any, payable to the beneficiary hereunder, as interest may appear, and will deliver the policy or policies of insurance to the beneficiary hereunder, as further security for the indebtedness aforesaid. And in case of the failure of said part of the first part to thus insure and deliver the policies of insurance, or to pay such taxes or assessments or amounts due or to become due on any prior encumbrance, if any, then the holder of said note or any of them, may procure such insurance, or pay such taxes or assessments or amounts due upon prior encumbrances, if any, and all moneys thus paid, with interest thereon at per centum per annum, shall become so much additional indebtedness, secured by this Deed of Trust, and shall be paid out of the proceeds of the sale of the property aforesaid, if not otherwise paid by said part of the first part and may for such failure declare a violation of this covenant and agreement.

AND THAT IN CASE OF ANY DEFAULT, Whereby the right of foreclosure occurs hereunder, the said party of the second part or the holder of said note or certificate of purchase, shall at once become entitled to the possession, use and enjoyment of the property aforesaid, and to the rents, issues and profits thereof, from the accruing of such right and during the pendency of foreclosure proceedings and the period of redemption, if any there be; and such possession shall at once be delivered to the said party of the second part or the holder of said note or

Deed of Trust (Continued)

certificate of purchase on request, and on refusal, the delivery of such possession may be enforced by the said party of the second part or the holder of said note or certificate of purchase by any appropriate civil suit or proceeding, and the said party of the second part, or the holder of said note or certificate of purchase, or any thereof, shall be entitled to a Receiver for said property, and of the rents, issues and profits thereof, after such default, including the time covered by foreclosure proceedings and the period of redemption, if any there be, and shall be entitled thereto as a matter of right without regard to the solvency or insolvency of the part of the first part or of the then owner of said property and without regard to the value thereof, and such Receiver may be appointed by any court of competent jurisdiction upon ex parte application and without notice—notice being hereby expressly waived—and all rents, issues and profits, income and revenue therefrom shall be applied by such Receiver to the payment of the indebtedness hereby secured, according to law and the orders and directions of the court.

AND, That in case of default in any of said payments of principal or interest, according to the tenor and effect of said promissory note aforesaid, or any of them, or any part thereof, or of a breach or violation of any of the covenants or agreements herein, by the part of the first part, executors, administrators or assigns, then and in that case the whole of said principal sum hereby secured, and the interest thereon to the time of sale, may at once, at the option of the legal holder thereof, become due and payable, and the said property be sold in the manner and with the same effect as if said indebtedness had matured, and that if foreclosure be made by the Public Trustee, an attorney's fee of the sum of dollars for services in the supervision of said foreclosure proceedings shall be allowed by the Public Trustee as a part of the cost of foreclosure, and if foreclosure be made through the courts a reasonable attorney's fee shall be taxed by the court as a part of the costs of such foreclosure proceedings.

IN WITNESS WHEREOF, The said part of the first part ha hereunto set hand and seal the day and year first above written.

WITNESS:

....(SEAL)

....(SEAL)

....(SEAL)

STATE OF COLORADO } ss. The foregoing instrument was acknowledged before me this day of........, 19....,

County of .... by ....

Witness my hand seal.

My commission expires ....

....

Notary Public.

Deed of Trust (Concluded)

TAXES ON MORTGAGES

As a general rule, corporate mortgagors prefer to use the promissory note in place of a bond. The reason for this is that there is a federal tax on corporate bonds amounting to 11 cents per $100 of the loan.

In some states, New York, for example, there is a tax of 50 cents per $100 or part thereof on the amount loaned on the mortgage. This is commonly stated to be ½ of 1 percent of the amount borrowed. This tax is paid by the borrower.

Some states, notably Florida, have a tax on indebtedness. While this does not apply to mortgages only, it is paid on the mortgage indebtedness. In Florida the rate is 30 cents per $100. It can be anticipated that, as states begin seeking more revenue, some form of tax such as the New York or Florida tax will be adopted.

THE MORTGAGE FORECLOSURE

In the event of default in the payment of principal, interest, or a breach of any of the covenants of the mortgage, the mortgagee may foreclose on the mortgage. A *mortgage foreclosure* means that the mortgagee may institute proceedings to force a sale of the mortgaged property.

The Title Search

One of the first things that the mortgagee does in pursuing his foreclosure action is to have a title search or an abstract of title prepared. The *abstract of title* is a brief history of the particular property with which the action is concerned. The reason for having the abstract prepared is that presumably the mortgagee has the first lien on the property; secondly, it is necessary to bring in all other parties in interest, who generally are lienors junior to his lien. There may be good possibility of the action cutting off the rights of the other lienors, and, consequently, they should have notice of his action. In the event that any surplus monies result from a foreclosure sale, the junior lienors then have the requisite notice to commence a surplus money proceeding in order to establish their rights to whatever surplus monies exist.

Commencing the Action

The summons and the complaint begin the foreclosure action.[11] A copy of the summons and a copy of the complaint are served on the mortgagor and on any of the lienors that were determined from the title search. If the mortgagor has a defense against the foreclosure

[11] In Arizona, California, Florida, Idaho, Illinois, Iowa, Kansas, Montana, New Jersey, New Mexico, North Dakota, Oklahoma, and Oregon, a foreclosure suit is the *only* method of foreclosing on a mortgage.

action, he puts in an answer to the complaint, raising an issue that is triable by jury. In some states a "master in chancery" hears the matter without a jury. In the event that the mortgagor defaults, then the foreclosure proceeds to its conclusion. At the time of the filing of the summons and the complaint, a lis pendens (Notice of Pendency of Action) is filed with the clerk of the county in which the property is located. The *lis pendens* is a warning to anyone concerned with or about to be concerned with the mortgaged property that there is an action pending on it. It is discussed further in Chapter 9.

Completing the Action

After a default is made by the mortgagor, the mortgagee is entitled to a judgment decree which he obtains and files with the court. This judgment directs that the property be sold at public auction, either by a referee appointed by the court or by the sheriff. Notice of the sale is given to all defendants, and it is published in such newspapers as the judge directs and is published for the number of times required by law. At the sale, bids are made on the property; but if the mortgagee does not think the bids are high enough, he may bid on the property himself.

If there is a surplus of monies resulting from the sale, the other defendants in the foreclosure divide it according to the outcome of a surplus money action which establishes their priorities. If there is a deficiency, the mortgagee obtains a judgment for the deficiency on the note or bond against the mortgagor and seeks to collect that amount. In some states, Oregon and California, for example, it is not possible to obtain a deficiency judgment on a purchase money mortgage. Deficiency judgments have been abolished in Nebraska and North Dakota.

There exists in most states a statutory right of redemption. This is the right given mortgagors, judgment creditors, etc., to redeem the land from the foreclosure sale within a certain time by paying the foreclosure sale price.[12] The time limitation varies among the states from two months to two years after the sale.

The foreclosure action is a long and involved proceeding, and as a practical matter in order to avoid additional expenses, especially

---

[12] In some states, Alabama, for example, the entire indebtedness must be paid.

when the prices of real property are deflated, it sometimes is more suitable for all concerned if the mortgagee seeks and obtains a quitclaim deed from the mortgagor.

OTHER REMEDIES OF THE MORTGAGEE

Foreclosure by Advertisement

The *foreclosure by advertisement* is a rarely used means of foreclosing a mortgage. It is employed in some states, however. Upon the default of the mortgagor, under this procedure, notice is given to the owner, public sale of the property is advertised, and the property is sold at such public sale. The purchaser at the public sale is not given possession of the property. To gain possession he may bring an action in ejectment, which is long and costly; therefore, the foreclosure by advertisement is seldom employed.[13]

Foreclosure by Entry and Possession

In several states (Maine, Massachusetts, New Hampshire, and Rhode Island) the mortgagee may foreclose by taking peaceful possession of the mortgaged premises and by remaining in possession for a specified time. The entry is made in the presence of witnesses and a certificate of that fact is filed. The mortgagor has a period in which he may redeem the property. If he does not redeem, then the mortgagee receives good title to the premises.

Foreclosure by Writ of Entry

In some states (Maine, Massachusetts, and New Hampshire) a court proceeding is brought and a writ of entry issued stating the amount due on the mortgage and specifying a time in which the mortgagor has to redeem the property. If no redemption is made within this time, the mortgagee receives good title.

CONVEYANCE OF MORTGAGED PREMISES

If there is an existing mortgage on the property when a buyer and seller enter into a contract for the sale of real property, the

---

[13] Tennessee, North Dakota, and South Dakota do not require an action in ejectment.

purchaser may take the property "subject to" the mortgage, or he may "assume" the mortgage. The distinction between these two terms is subtle, but important. A complete understanding of these two terms is necessary so that loss as a result of their misuse can be avoided.

Subject To

When a parcel of property is purchased subject to a mortgage, there is inserted in the deed the statement:

> This deed is made subject to the following: a certain first mortgage in the amount of $5,000 and interest to date, made by Albert Jones to Arthur Brown on January 2, 1969, recorded January 3, 1969, in the office of the Clerk of the County of Nassau, State of New York, in Liber 2159 of Mortgages at page 5.

This statement means that the purchaser recognizes the existence of a mortgage on the property. For example, Mr. Buyer moves into a house and makes the payments that are due on the property mortgage. At this point things run smoothly; however, what happens if Mr. Buyer fails to meet his payments? Mr. Seller, who had the mortgage placed on the property originally, signed either a note or bond along with the original mortgage. When payments are not met, the mortgagee will commence foreclosure proceedings. The property will be sold and Mr. Buyer will be ousted. Suppose, however, that there is a deficiency of $1,000 due the mortgagee after the foreclosure sale has been completed. The question now is: Who is liable for the deficiency, Mr. Seller, the mortgagor, or Mr. Buyer, who took the property "subject to" the mortgage? Mr. Buyer promised nothing when he took the property "subject to" the mortgage. In effect, he merely recognized the existence of the mortgage. Mr. Seller, however, promised to pay the mortgagee when he signed either the note or the bond. Therefore, the mortgagee will have recourse to the seller for the $1,000 deficiency.

When the seller sells the property "subject to" a mortgage, he may be liable for any deficiency. On the other hand, when the purchaser buys "subject to" the mortgage, he is not liable for any deficiency; and the most that he can lose in the event of foreclosure is any equity that he may have built up in the property.

Assuming the Mortgage

A quite different situation arises when property is sold on which there is a mortgage and the purchaser "assumes" the mortgage. In this event, there generally is inserted in the deed the following clause:

> The conveyance hereunder is subject to a certain mortgage executed by Albert Jones as mortgagor to Arthur Brown as mortgagee, which mortgage is dated January 2, 1969, and was recorded January 3, 1969, in the office of the Clerk of the County of Nassau, in Liber 2159 of Mortgages at page 5, and on which mortgage there is now due the sum of $4,000 with interest thereon at the rate of 6 percent per annum from July 1, 1969, and that the grantee hereby assumes and covenants to pay such mortgage debt and interest as a part of the consideration for this conveyance.

In another situation, Mr. Buyer moves into the property and fails to meet the payments on the mortgage. The mortgagee forecloses and there is a deficiency in the amount of $1,000. Primarily liable for the deficiency is the purchaser, Mr. Buyer, who "assumed" the mortgage.[14]

When a mortgage is "assumed," the purchaser covenants and promises to pay the deficiency. In other words, he has entered into a contract with his seller for the benefit of a third party, the mortgagee. Thus, the mortgagee may collect the deficiency from the purchaser. If the purchaser cannot pay, then the mortgagee seeks payment from the mortgagor on the bond or the note. However, in view of the fact that there is a contract between the mortgagor and the purchaser, the seller (mortgagor) may seek the amount of the deficiency from his purchaser.

In practice, when there is an assumption clause in a deed, both the purchaser and the seller sign the deed as contrasted to the normal situation when the grantor signs the deed alone. The reason for this is that by virtue of the assumption clause the parties are entering into what amounts to a written contract in addition to a deed conveying title to the property.

---

[14] In some states there is no obligation on the part of the mortgagee to seek the payment of the deficiency from the purchaser, unless the mortgagee has previously executed an "assumption and release agreement." In other states he may seek the deficiency from his mortgagor or the purchaser.

In some states where this is not customarily done, the courts have held that the original contract for the sale of real property wherein the purchaser has agreed to "assume" the mortgage may be entered in evidence as proof to that effect against the purchaser.

In about half the states, purchasers customarily buy "subject to" the mortgage, and in the other half, purchasers usually buy "assuming" the mortgage.

The Non-Assumption Clause

In recent years financial institutions have adopted the practice of inserting a non-assumption clause in conventional mortgages. In essence, this clause states that the mortgagor cannot sell his property and have the buyer assume his mortgage without the consent of the lender. The reasoning behind this is quite simple from the point of view of the institutional lenders. For example, suppose a mortgage carries 8 percent interest. Suppose further that the interest rate drops to 7 percent. In this case the institution will readily give permission to the mortgagor to sell the property and have the buyer assume the mortgage (carrying 8 percent instead of the new rate of 7 percent). However, if the rate jumps from 8 percent say to 9 percent, then the institution will refuse permission to the borrower to sell and have the buyer assume at the old rate. They hope, of course, that the property will be refinanced and a new mortgage issued at the 9 percent rate.

It should be noted that the non-assumption clause applies only to conventional mortgages and not to FHA or VA mortgages.

THE FHA MORTGAGE AND FINANCING

The Federal Housing Administration, commonly called the FHA, was organized in 1934 under the authority of the National Housing Act, passed by Congress and signed by the President on June 27, 1934. Reorganization Plan No. 3, effective June 27, 1947, provided that thereafter the FHA would function as a part of the Housing and Home Finance Agency. The Housing Act of 1965 created the cabinet post of a Department of Housing and Urban Development, commonly called "HUD." At this time the FHA was incorporated into HUD.

Many people mistakenly believe that the FHA makes mortgage loans and engages in other types of financing. It does neither, but it does insure approved corporate institutional lenders against loss on approved loans which they either purchase or originate. The main functions of the FHA are to encourage improvement in housing standards, to provide an adequate house financing system, and to aid in the stabilization of the mortgage market.

In general the standards of the FHA are high. It will not insure loans on obsolete homes nor on properties poorly located with respect to transportation and vital community facilities. Nor will it insure properties in areas where essential utilities are lacking. The FHA has adopted the principle of following long-term trends with regard to property value, and in general, its valuation tends to be lower than sales prices. It has also evolved a risk-rating pattern which considers, weighs, and evaluates all the factors affecting each property in which it is interested, including the qualifications of the borrower.

Requisites to Becoming a Lender

In order to become an FHA lender, one must file a simple application form with the FHA for which there is no fee. The prospective lender must be a corporation and have total assets in excess of $100,000.

Originating a Loan

A prospective borrower first finds an FHA-approved mortgagee. The borrower then files statements on approved application forms. The forms include a description of the property, a statement of the prospective borrower's financial condition, and an outline of his personal history. This application is then examined by the lending institution to determine whether or not it should be submitted to the FHA for insurance. It is here that a determination is made as to the type of mortgage that shall be issued and the terms of the proposed loan. The FHA will examine the application received from the lender, value the real estate, and apply its mortgage pattern. If the prospective loan meets all the requirements, the FHA will issue its Commitment for Insurance to the approved lender who will then proceed to lend the money in the ordinary manner.

It should be borne in mind that not all of the FHA investors originate loans, but many acquire their loans by purchase from primary lenders. As a group, the type of investor who buys from primary lenders is often referred to as being in the secondary mortgage market.

When a primary lender sells FHA mortgages to a secondary lender, he very often services the mortgage that he sells. A more complete discussion of the secondary mortgage market will be found in Chapter 16.

Accomplishments of the FHA

Although, as it can be readily observed, there have from time to time been changes in the law, it is felt that the FHA is here to stay. It is further felt that an understanding of the basic features of the FHA as outlined above will enable a ready understanding of future changes in the law.

It is generally believed that had the FHA been in effect during the early 20's and 30's, the losses to mortgage investors would have been considerably lighter. The reasons generally attributed to the success of the FHA are its high standards of construction, land planning, utilization, systematic inspection and appraisal of homes, elimination of high financing costs, low interest rates, and insistence on a gradual repayment through amortization, plus a greater protection to the lender.

As a result of FHA practices, there has been a gradual reduction in junior financing which has in turn reduced the overall cost of home ownership. Perhaps not the least important accomplishment of the Federal Housing Administration has been the development of a wider mortgage market.

Within the past several years, the privately owned mortgage insuring companies have developed rapidly (these will be discussed in detail in Chapter 16). These companies insure the loans to the financial institutions, much like the FHA. The lenders are using them instead of the FHA-type insurance because they are on conventional mortgages at higher rates, and the red tape is not nearly as formidable. The net result is that the total dollar volume of this insurance in 1973 nearly equaled the total dollar volume of FHA insurance.

QUESTIONS FOR REVIEW

1. Define: (a) *bond*; (b) *mortgage*.
2. If *A*, as mortgagor, makes a mortgage to *B* and one to *C* dated one year later on the same property and *C* records his mortgage first, which mortgage, in the absence of fraud, is valid? Why?
3. What is the difference between the lien theory and the title theory of mortgages?
4. Explain the purpose of the receiver clause in a mortgage.
5. How and when is an estoppel certificate used?
6. What is a *prepayment clause* in a mortgage?
7. What is meant by a *budget mortgage*?
8. What is an *open mortgage*?
9. Discuss the use of a partial release clause in a mortgage.
10. What is a *purchase money mortgage*?
11. Explain how a purchase money mortgage is sometimes used by a builder so that he may reduce the amount of cash necessary.
12. Which theory of mortgages does a mortgage on a lease follow?
13. Why must a title search be made in a mortgage foreclosure?
14. How and when is a mortgage on a lease employed?
15. How does a deed of trust differ from a mortgage? In what respects is it the same?
16. What are the advantages, if any, of a deed of trust over a mortgage?
17. Explain the procedure of foreclosing a mortgage.
18. Distinguish between purchasing property "subject to" a mortgage and "assuming" a mortgage.
19. Explain the procedure of securing an FHA loan.

PROBLEMS

1. A broker negotiates a sale of a business opportunity having a contractual value of $18,750. No real property is included in the sale. It is estimated by both the buyer and the seller that the fixtures are worth $3,200 in their present used condition. The inventory is

assessed at $8,000; and "goodwill" is credited with the balance of purchase price.

(a) Assume that the buyer has only $8,500 in cash. Suggest a method of financing the transaction that will give the seller maximum protection.

(b) Assume that the real property is valued at an additional $9,000 and that the buyer has $11,500 in cash. What financing method would you suggest?

2. *A* agrees to purchase a parcel of property from *B* for $10,000; $5,000 is to be paid in cash, the balance by purchase money mortgage. The land is described as Lot #6 of the map of Moore's Addition, your town, your state, your county. Draw a purchase money mortgage to cover the transaction.

3. *A* agrees to purchase Lot #6 of the map of Moore's Addition from *B* for $14,000, on which there is a mortgage of $6,500, which *A* agrees to assume. Draw a deed and insert the proper assumption clause.

4. A mortgagor signed a check to make a payment on his mortgage on which there was an unpaid balance of $31,000. His bookkeeper put the check for the payment in an envelope, then promptly misplaced it. He had a ten-day grace period. One month and eight days after it was due, the holder of the mortgage notified him that the money had not been received and he started foreclosure proceedings. Prior to the foreclosure the mortgagor was never late on a single payment and furthermore had spent $300,000 on improvements on the property. If you were the presiding judge of this matter, how would you rule and why?

5. A mortgagor had paid a mortgage down to a balance of only $6,000. He contacted the mortgagee of record and said that he was ready to pay it off. The mortgagee of record said he couldn't satisfy the mortgage because both the note and the mortgage were in the possession of his brother. The mortgagor then contacted the brother who said that he did have the mortgage papers, but that he had had a fight with his brother and that his brother, because he was angry, refused to sign a satisfaction piece even though he was the mortgagee of record. He said he was sorry, but there was nothing that could be done. The mortgage incidentally contained a prepayment clause. Can anything be done?

SUGGESTED READINGS

Anderson, Ronald A., and Walter A. Kumpf. *Business Law Principles and Cases,* 5th ed. Cincinnati: South-Western Publishing Co., 1971. Chapter 53.

Kratovil, Robert. *Real Estate Law,* 5th ed. Englewood Cliffs, New Jersey: Prentice-Hall, Inc., 1969. Chapter 20.

Ring, Alfred A. *Real Estate Principles and Practices,* 7th ed. Englewood Cliffs, New Jersey: Prentice-Hall, Inc., 1972. Chapter 8.

Chapter 7

Leases and Leasing

A *lease* is a contract creating what is commonly known as a landlord and tenant relationship. The landlord is called the *lessor,* and the tenant, the *lessee.* The contract between the two parties conveys the right of possession of the leased premises to the tenant in return for which the tenant pays the landlord rent. The term *rent* is defined as the compensation, whether money, provisions, chattels, or labor, received by the owner of the soil or buildings from the occupant thereof.

In addition to the covenant upon the part of the landlord agreeing to transfer possession, the agreement contains numerous other covenants defining and limiting the rights of the parties in the leased premises. These covenants are discussed later in the chapter.

A lease may be thought of primarily as a contract; and as a general rule, the parties to a contract may agree to almost anything in a lease.[1] As in any other contract, however, they cannot agree to things which are said to be against public policy.

For example, two people enter into a lease of an apartment. The lease contains a clause stating that the landlord shall not be liable

[1] Actually the lease is *both* a contract and a conveyance.

for his own negligence in regard to that apartment. The landlord hires an incompetent painter who, in painting the apartment, negligently paints the windows in such a manner that they stick. The tenant, in attempting to open the window, slips and pushes his hand through the pane and seriously injures himself. He sues the landlord on the ground that the injury was caused by reason of the negligence of the landlord. The landlord in his defense states that the tenant agreed in the lease to waive any claim of negligence against the landlord, and that the lease is a contract and, as such, is binding upon the parties. In a case such as this, the courts will hold that although it is true that a lease is a contract, it is against public policy to allow the landlord to contract out of liability for his own negligence.

As in all contracts, a lease must be entered into by persons having contractual ability. There must be a consideration, a delivery, and an acceptance. In addition, to validate a lease, there must be a description that locates the premises with reasonable certainty. A lease should contain the term or the duration of the lease. The lease should also have a definite beginning and a certain ending. Study the following case as an example. A written lease stating that the tenant's occupation was for the term of "one year, two years, three years" was sent to the landlord, who was to strike out all except one of the terms mentioned and execute the lease. The landlord, however, executed the lease without striking out any of its terms. The court held there was no meeting of the minds.[2]

A lease must also contain an agreement, technically called "an agreement to let and take," although the words "let and take" rarely appear in the lease. The lease will generally state that the lessor "grants, demises and lets unto the lessee." This is considered to be the agreement to let and take. These words give the tenant the right of possession, and also, in the event that someone appears later who has a better title to the premises than the landlord, give the tenant the right to proceed against the landlord for damages.

Finally, the lease must be executed in accordance with the statute. Some statutes state that the lease must be acknowledged, while others do not contain this provision. As a practical matter, it is a good procedure to have the lease acknowledged in order to enable the lease to be recorded, if the occasion arises.

---

[2] *Sayles* v. *Lienhardt*, 119 Misc. 851, 198 N.Y. Supp. 337.

THE STATUTE OF FRAUDS

The *statute of frauds* is designed to prevent the use of the law courts for the purpose of enforcing certain oral agreements or alleged oral agreements. It specifies which contracts must be in writing in order to be enforced. The fourth section of the English statute upon which the states base their statutes provides that "no action shall be brought unless the agreement upon such action shall be brought, or some memorandum or note thereof, shall be in writing, and signed by the party to be charged therewith, or some person thereunto by him lawfully authorized."

The statute of frauds enters the picture regarding leases much in the same manner as it does in other types of real property contracts. An owner may lease his property for as long a period as he wishes, but in many states only a lease for less than one year's duration may be oral. Leases for over one year in many states under the statute of frauds must be in writing and must contain the requisites described.

If the state law requires a lease to be in writing and the parties have failed to comply with this, or if the lease fails for any reason to meet the statutory requirements, then the lease cannot be enforced. If the lease cannot be enforced and the tenant has not yet gone into possession, the landlord may refuse him the possession. If the tenant is already in possession under a lease that should have been written but was not, the lease may be terminated at anytime by the landlord. On the other hand, the tenant may refuse to take possession, without any liability on his part, under an unenforceable lease. If he has taken possession, however, he will be liable for "use and occupancy" during the period that he has occupancy of the premises.

RECORDING

Under some circumstances, depending upon the term of the lease, the lease may be recorded. In New York, for example, a lease for more than three years may be recorded. This is not to imply that a lease must be recorded; it is merely better practice to record long-term leases. The recording gives notice to the world of the rights of the tenant in the property, although in many cases actual possession of the premises is sufficient to give such notice.

TENANCIES

It will be recalled that in Chapter 3 estates in land were classified as freehold estates (estates of indefinite duration) and estates of less than freehold (estates of definite duration). The types of tenancies with which we are now concerned may be considered as being estates of less than freehold.

Types of Tenancies

There are four kinds of tenancies or leasehold estates: (1) estate for years, (2) tenancy from year to year or periodic tenancy, (3) tenancy at will, (4) tenancy at sufferance.

Estate for Years. An *estate for years* conveys the land for a definite stated period. It has a time of beginning and a certain end. This period is called the *term*. The estate may terminate before the time period by agreement of the parties, under conditions stated in the lease, by application of law,[3] or by merger.[4]

Tenancy from Year to Year. The *tenancy from year to year* or *periodic tenancy* is a tenancy that never exists for more than a year and is commonly from month to month. This type of lease may be either oral or written. It may be terminated by agreement of the parties at the end of any period and by giving proper notice to quit. In most states notice to terminate the tenancy of less than a year requires a notice of equal length to the period of letting.

Tenancy at Will. A *tenancy at will* is a tenancy that may be terminated by either party at anytime. It is distinguishable from the tenancy from month to month by the fact that the term is indefinite. In short, it may be terminated "at the will" of either party. The relationship between the landlord and tenant may be created here either expressly or by implication. Although under the common law no notice was necessary to terminate the landlord and tenant relationship, today most states require that notice be given.

---

[3] For example, a lease calls for a property to be used as a furniture store and the lessee uses it for a garage.

[4] Where the fee simple is conveyed to the lessee.

Problems arise when there are tenancies at will existing on farm properties. For example, a tenant at will on a farm plants a crop; the crop is about ready to be harvested, and the landlord attempts to terminate the tenancy. In cases of this type, the tenant has a right to go on the property to harvest his crops.

Tenancy at Sufferance. A *tenancy at sufferance* is the lowest estate known to law. It exists when a tenant rightfully in possession continues to occupy the property after the expiration of the term. The tenant in this case holds the property merely at the sufferance of the landlord and under the common law is not entitled to notice to quit; however, by statute many states require that even the tenant by sufferance be given notice to quit.

Holding Over

When a tenant stays on at the expiration of the term of the lease, he is said to be a *holdover tenant*. Tenants often "hold over" in either a month-to-month tenancy or a tenancy for years.

If no agreement is made extending the term of the lease, the landlord may bring dispossess proceedings against the tenant; that is, proceedings to oust the tenant from possession and recover the reasonable value for the use and occupancy of the premises during the time that the tenant held over. As an alternative, the landlord may elect to treat the tenancy as renewed for another term upon the same terms and conditions as those of the original lease.

Thus, when a year-to-year tenancy exists, if the tenant pays his rent and the landlord accepts the rent, the tenancy generally continues for a period of another year. During this continuation period, both parties are bound as if a new lease had been drawn and signed.

When the original lease is for a period longer than a year, the holding over is limited for one year. For example, if a tenant holds over at the expiration of a three-year lease, he may remain on the premises for the following year only; in some states on a month-to-month basis.

Long-Term Leases

Leases can range in duration from the tenancy at will to 99 or 999 years. Generally, long-term leases provide for erection of a new building by the lessee and the demolition of the structures on the leased premises at the time of the execution of the lease. Often, too, these long-term leases provide that the tenant shall pay taxes, assessments, and all operating expenses. This provision creates what is sometimes called a "net lease."

TYPES OF LEASES

The Gross Lease

The *gross lease* is a type of lease in which the premises are rented at a fixed rate. The tenant pays his rent to the landlord, and the landlord, in turn, agrees to pay the taxes, insurance, and any other expenses that might be incurred in the operation of the premises. The possible exception to this is that the tenant would pay ordinary repairs if they were called for under the terms of the lease.

The Net Lease

The *net lease* is the type of lease in which the tenant pays the taxes, assessments, and all operating expenses in connection with the use of the premises. The landlord receives a net figure.

Most long-term leases are net leases. The net lease has become increasingly popular with owners of investment properties. Many owners do not wish to sell the property, but wish to obtain a steady income from the property without incurring any of the "headaches" of supervising the premises. The owner may lease the property and receive a flat rental from the lessee. The lease will provide that the lessee pay all of the expenses of maintaining and managing the property. In this type of lease the lessee hopes to make a profit out of the rents that he will receive from the building.

The Percentage Lease

The *percentage lease* is a type of lease in which the rental is based either on a flat fee plus a percentage of the gross or on the net income received by a tenant doing business on the premises.

There are several factors of importance that must be considered in the percentage lease. Suppose, for example, that the rental is based upon a small flat fee plus a percentage of the gross. *A* goes into possession as the tenant, and he does a gross business that by far exceeds his expectations; consequently, his rent is high. Across the street from *A* there is a vacant property that may be rented at a flat or gross rental. *A* then proceeds to open another store across the street from himself. In effect, he enters into competition with himself by drawing some of the patronage away from his original store. This results in a reduction of his gross receipts in the store where the percentage base is in effect. To guard against such a situation, the landlord should insert in the percentage lease a clause to the effect that the tenant may not enter into competition with himself either in the city, if it is a small city, or within a stated number of blocks of the leased premises, if it is a large city.

If the percentage lease is to be based upon a net profit, the definition of net profit must be made clear. Is the flat rental to be a deduction from the gross profit in determining net profit? Are repairs and alterations to be deducted? Who is to pay the taxes? These are but a few of the many questions that must be spelled out in the lease in order to avoid any later misunderstanding.

The lease should contain a clause giving the lessor the right at anytime during the demised term to examine all the books of account and any other records that might reflect the operations of the lessee.

The parties also might consider the feasibility of inserting a *recapture clause*. This clause gives the right to the landlord to take back the demised premises in the event that the tenant's business does not reach a certain gross. The clause may also give the right to the tenant to surrender the premises in the event that business does not reach a stated gross.

The table at the top of the next page illustrates the percentages commonly paid on gross income by certain types of businesses, but it is felt that these figures should be used as guides only and varied in accordance with local conditions.

In the final analysis, the percentages paid will be a matter of bargaining between the parties. This is especially true in the case of shopping centers. Frequently, a shopping center developer will lease to a few large chain operations at an extremely low percentage and on very favorable terms. These large stores attract the smaller ones who do not always receive favorable treatment. There are a number of cases where the smaller operations have received three-year leases

Percentages for Retail Stores Based on Gross Sales[5]

Store	Percentage	Store	Percentage
Army and Navy Stores	10	Groceries, regular	5– 8
Auto Accessories	8–10	Hardware	6– 8
Auto Agencies, new	$1\frac{1}{2}$– 2	Jewelry, installment	5– 8
Barbershops	10–15	Jewelry, regular	8–10
Cafeterias, lunch stands	10–12	Meat Markets, concession	3– 5
Cafeterias, table service	8–10	Meat Markets, regular	5
Candy	8–10	News Dealers	5– 7
Cleaners & Dyers	10–12	Souvenirs	10–15
Department Stores	3– 4	Sporting Goods	6– 8
Drugs, cut-rate	5– 8	Theaters	8–10
Drugs, regular	6–10	Trunks and Leather Goods	10–12
Dry Goods	5– 8	Variety Stores	6– 8
Groceries, cháin	3– 5		

with two-year options, often at a much higher percentage. At the end of the five years the rates are apt to be raised a great deal for the smaller stores. In one case, a nut stand on the mall of a shopping center, occupying very little space, netted $40,000 per year during the first five years and paid a reasonable percentage in rent. At the end of the five-year period, the operator of the stand was given a choice to vacate or sign another five-year lease at 50 percent of net.

It should be added, perhaps, that developers of shopping centers use the lease as a financing device. In brief, leases are obtained from nationally known chains prior to completion of the center. Armed with these leases the developer approaches a financial institution who loans on the basis of the leases. In this manner financing is often obtained to complete the project.

The percentage lease is a device that is beneficial to both the landlord and the tenant during inflationary periods and by the same token is beneficial to both the landlord and the tenant in periods of deflation or depression.

Oil and Gas Leases

In many sections of the United States, real estate brokers are becoming more and more involved in dealings concerning oil and

[5] These figures differ from city to city and from time to time so that it is extremely important to investigate local conditions. Often publications such as *Chain Store Age* can be used as an effective guide.

gas properties. Oil companies lease property which they believe contains oil and/or gas. Generally, the lessee will propose a flat sum as the rental of the land for the purpose of drilling for oil and gas for a stated period of years. The leasing company usually agrees that if oil is discovered, they will pay a stated royalty, often one eighth of a barrel from each barrel of oil, and one eighth of the proceeds from the sale of gas. In the event that drilling operations are not started within one year, the lease generally calls for a flat sum to be paid to the lessor. This payment gives the lessee another year in which to commence his drilling operation.

The lease also calls for the right of either party to assign the lease with all of the covenants of the lease binding on the heirs, assigns, or successors of the parties to the lease.

The right is given to the lessee, in the event that he commences his drilling operation, to continue the drilling operation, and the term of the lease is extended and continued as long as the lessee continues drilling or continues his production operation.

Oil and gas leases are often obtained by individuals who later sell their rights in them to oil companies. Sometimes the leases are assigned to individuals who, in turn, sell them to oil producing companies. An illustration of an oil and gas lease is shown in Appendix C.

The Farm Lease

In rural areas, real estate brokers are often called upon to deal in farm leases. The *farm leases* are drawn for a flat sum of money to be paid to the landlord, or are drawn so that a share of the crops is paid to the landlord in lieu of a flat rent.

In the first instance, the lessee agrees to pay a sum certain as rent. He is given the right to remove timber for the purpose of maintaining the farm and buildings, but not for the purpose of selling the timber as lumber or wood pulp. The lessee also agrees to reside on the premises and personally manage the premises. Generally, the lease contains a clause stating that the lease is unassignable without the written consent of the landlord. The lessee agrees:

1. To manage the soil properly.
2. To conserve straw or manure and use it as a fertilizer.
3. To maintain the premises in good repair, including fences.
4. To maintain existing hayfields.

THIS INDENTURE OF LEASE, Made in duplicate at Seattle, Washington, on this 18th day of March, 19 -- by and between Roger Freeman hereinafter known and referred to as the lessor, (whether singular or plural) and George Roberts, hereinafter known and referred to as the lessee, (whether singular or plural).

WITNESSETH: That in consideration of the covenants, agreements and stipulations herein contained on the part of said lessee to be paid, kept and faithfully performed by said lessee, the said lessor does hereby lease, demise and let unto said lessee that certain premises known as 83 East Main Street, for use as a grocery store only in the City of Seattle, State of Washington

TO HAVE AND TO HOLD said premises hereby leased for a period of two years - from the 1st day of April, 19-- , to and including the 31st day of March, 19 -- , said lessee paying and yielding as rental therefor, during said term, the full sum of Two Thousand Four Hundred 00/100 ($2,400.00) - - - - - - - - Dollars, lawful money of the United States, to be paid as follows: The sum of One Hundred and 00/100 ($100) Dollars to be paid monthly on the first day of each and every month.

That said lessee will make no unlawful, improper or offensive use of the premises; that at the expiration of the said term or upon any sooner termination of this lease, said lessee will quit and deliver up the premises, and all future erection or additions to or upon the same, to the said lessor, or those having their estate therein, peaceably, quietly, in as good order and condition (reasonable use and wearing thereof, fire and other unavoidable casualties excepted) as the same now are or may be put in by the lessor or those having their estate in the premises; that said lessee will not suffer nor commit any strip or waste thereof, nor make nor suffer to be made any alterations or additions to or upon the same, nor assign this lease, nor underlet, or permit any other person or persons to occupy the same, without the consent of the said lessor or those having their estate in the premises, being first obtained in writing, and also that it shall be lawful for the said lessor and those having their estate in the premises, at reasonable times, to enter into and upon the same, to examine the condition thereof.

A Lease

PROVIDED always, and these presents are upon this condition, that if the said rent shall be in arrears for the space of Ten days, or if the said lessee his representatives or assigns, shall neglect or fail to do or perform, and observe any or either of the covenants hereinbefore contained, which on said lessee's part are to be performed, then and in either of the said cases, the said lessor, or those having their estate in the said premises lawfully may, immediately or at any time thereafter, and while said neglect or default continues, and without further notice of demand, enter into and upon the said premises, or any part thereof, in the name of the whole and repossess the same, of their former estate, and expel the said lessee, and those claiming under said lessee, and remove his effects (forcibly if necessary), without being taken or deemed guilty in any manner of trespass, and without prejudice to any remedies which might otherwise be used for arrears of rent, or preceding breach of covenants.

Any waiver of any breach of covenants herein contained to be kept and performed by the lessee shall not be deemed or considered as a continuing waiver, and shall not operate to bar or prevent the lessor from declaring a forfeiture for any succeeding breach, either of the same condition or covenant or otherwise.

Any holding over by the lessee after the expiration of the term of this lease, or any extension thereof, shall be as a tenancy from month to month and not otherwise.

IN WITNESS WHEREOF, the respective parties have executed this instrument the day and year first hereinabove written, in duplicate.

Executed in the presence of: /s/ Roger Freeman (SEAL)

/s/ Alfred Kearney /s/ George Roberts (SEAL)

LEASE

(FORM No. 11)

Roger Freedman

TO

George Roberts

PREMISES

83 East Main Street

Date April 1, 19--

Expires March 31, 19--

STEVENS-NESS LAW PUB. CO., PORTLAND

STATE OF Washington } ss.

County of Kings

BE IT REMEMBERED, That on this 18th day of March, 19-- before me, the undersigned, a Notary Public in and for said County and State, personally appeared the within named Roger Freeman and George Roberts who are known to me to be the identical individuals described in and who executed the within instrument and acknowledged to me that they executed the same freely and voluntarily.

IN TESTIMONY WHEREOF, I have hereunto set my hand and official seal the day and year last above written.

Alfred Kearney
Notary Public for State of Wash.
My Commission expires December 31, 19--

A Lease (Concluded)

In addition, farm leases sometimes call for a basic number of cattle to be maintained by the tenant. The purpose of this is to insure good fertility to the soil by requiring the tenant to put back into the soil organic material.

When a farm lease is drawn on a share basis, the lease contains the provisions listed above and in addition defines the manner in which the crops shall be divided. There may also be a clause inserted in the lease calling for a division of the cost of lime and any commercial fertilizer that might be purchased by the tenant. Leases of this type usually require that an inventory be taken once a year and that books and records be accessible to the lessor at anytime during the term of the lease.

Lease of Roof

In large apartment and office buildings, the tenant who rents either an apartment or an office has no rights to the roof. The landlord reserves this right unto himself. In the case of an office building the landlord generally will rent the roof space for advertising purposes. When this is done, the landlord usually agrees not to rent the roof for any other purpose, nor to allow the advertiser's signs to be obstructed. In addition, he guarantees the tenant free access to the roof.

The type of roof rental that commonly arises in apartment houses usually concerns renting roof space for television antennas. A special agreement is often entered into permitting the erecting of the antenna by the tenant. Sometimes in the larger apartments, the management will erect a single antenna and then rent the tenant the right to hook onto this antenna for a stated rental per month.

FORM OF THE LEASE

A lease need not be in any particular form of language, provided it is clear and definite, showing an intention to transfer possession by way of lease. The written lease usually contains: (1) a date of execution, (2) an identification of the parties, (3) a designation of the term for which the tenancy is to exist, (4) a description of the premises, (5) a statement of the amount of rent to be paid by the tenant and the manner of payment together with any other obligations of the parties, and (6) the signatures of the parties.

The statement of the amount of rent and the method of payment together with any other obligations are termed *covenants*.

COMMON COVENANTS OF LEASES

Rent

The term *rent* has been previously defined as the compensation in money, provisions, chattels, or labor received by the owner of the soil or buildings from the occupant thereof.

Under the common law, rents were due and payable at the end of the term. The concept was that the rent was to be paid out of the profits derived from the use of the premises and that the profits could not be determined until the end of the term. However, most modern leases provide that the rent shall be paid at stated periods, usually the first of each month.

In the discussion of the gross, net, and percentage leases, it was seen that the leases vary mainly in the method of determining the amount of the rent to be paid by the lessee.

The most common type of residential rent is based on a flat scale, or at a stated amount per month. Some rentals are based on a sliding scale with an increase over the term of the lease. Recently there have been some attempts to base rentals on the consumer price index. That is to say, if the cost of living during a certain period rises 5 percent, then the rent is to be increased proportionately. On the other hand, if the cost of living decreases, then the rental paid is to be decreased proportionately. The percentage lease, however, is much more common for business properties and is becoming increasingly more common.

Use of the Premises

When a property is leased, the landlord receives the right to the rent, and the tenant receives the right of possession. In a sense, the tenant is the owner of the premises during the period of the lease. The tenant may use his possession in any legal manner, in the absence of any covenants to the contrary, and the landlord may not prevent him from so doing. There is, however, one restriction by implication on all tenants; that is, that the tenant cannot do anything that will injure or diminish the value of the landlord's interest. Any improper use of the premises by the tenant that does injure or diminish the value of the landlord's reversion is known as *waste*. In the event that the tenant does injure the value of the reversion, the landlord may bring an action for damages, or an injunction which results in a court order restraining the tenant from committing waste, or both. The lease may also provide that such breach by the tenant gives the landlord the right to terminate the lease upon the occasion of such breach.

The parties may agree to limit the use of the premises because the lease is a contract and an enforceable one. It is customary in modern leases to limit the use of the premises. This is done by inserting a covenant in the lease stating what the premises are to be used for and including the words "only" or "no other." For example, the lease will state: "For use as a grocery store and no other (or only)."

The words "only" or "no other" will limit the use of the premises to that specifically stated. In many states in the absence of these words the use of the premises will not be effectively limited.

In many states there are statutes providing that a lease may be terminated if the lessee makes *illegal use of the premises*. The lease under these statutes is declared void.

Covenant to Make Repairs

In the absence of any specific covenant in the lease or of custom or agreement on the point, it is the tenant's duty to make only such repairs as are necessary to prevent any damage which might diminish the value of the landlord's interest in the premises.[6]

Commonly, it is inserted into the lease that "the tenant shall keep the premises in good repair." Under this provision the tenant is required to repair the damage done to the premises, regardless of whether the damage is the tenant's fault or not. However, where

---

[6] Alabama, California, Connecticut, Georgia, Indiana, Iowa, Kentucky, Louisiana, Massachusetts, Michigan, Montana, New Jersey, New York, North Dakota, Oklahoma, Pennsylvania, South Dakota, and Wisconsin have enacted statutes requiring the landlord to keep the rented housing premises in good repair.

damages result to the premises that require rebuilding of the premises or extensive structural changes, the courts generally hold that large expenditures are not within the contemplation of the parties when the lease is drawn.

The terms of some leases limit the amount of money that the tenant is required to pay for repairs. Often, too, a clause will be inserted in the lease requiring the tenant to make all "inside repairs" or "all repairs not requiring structural changes." Phrases of this type are construed in accordance with the ordinary meaning of the words used, taking into consideration the magnitude of the required expenditure in proportion to the rental paid, the length of the term, and all other circumstances to determine whether it was reasonably within the contemplation of the parties that the burden of repair should be put on the tenant.

Generally, the lease not only requires that the premises be kept in good repair, but that if the tenant does not maintain the premises in good repair, the landlord may elect to terminate the lease. In the absence of a provision giving the landlord the option to terminate the lease in the event the tenant fails to make repairs, the only recourse of the landlord is to bring a suit for damages for breach of contract.

Ordinarily, when a tenant leases an entire building, the landlord is liable for repairs only if expressly agreed to by the parties in the lease. However, most states and many cities have statutes or ordinances requiring landlords to repair their property. These statutes are particularly applicable to multiple dwellings.

Covenant Not to Sublet or Assign

In the absence of a provision to the contrary, a tenant has a right to assign his lease or to sublet the premises. An *assignment* is the transfer of the entire term of the lease by the tenant; a *subletting* is, in effect, the making of a new lease in which the original tenant is the lessor and the subtenant the lessee. In the former case, the assignee steps into the shoes of the tenant and is generally liable for the payment of the rent to the original landlord. In the latter case, the subtenant is generally not liable for the rent or other obligations to the original landlord. However, the assignor may also be held for failure of assignee to live up to terms and conditions of the lease.

One distinction between a sublet and an assignment lies in the period of time involved. For example, if a lease was drawn for a term running from January 1 to July 15 and the tenant delivered the premises to another person until July 14, this would be a sublease. However, if the premises were occupied by another person from January 1 to July 15, which is the end of the term, then this would be construed as an assignment regardless of what the transaction was called. A second distinction is that a sublease may convey a portion of the premises.

To prevent the subletting or assignment of leased property, the landlord will usually insist that the lease contain a covenant in which the tenant agrees not to sublet or assign without the written consent of the landlord. The covenant will generally provide that the lease may be terminated if the tenant violates this covenant. Many landlords specifically insert a clause both to keep out undesirable tenants and to receive a bonus from the tenant in the event a tenant desires to sell a business opportunity.

At the time of the drawing of the lease, the tenant should ask to have inserted after the clause preventing assignment these words: ". . . and the landlord shall not unreasonably withhold his consent."

The effect of the insertion of these words is that the landlord *must* grant permission to assign or sublet unless the prospective assignee or sublessee is not financially responsible.

Covenant to Pay Water Charges

Most leases of business properties contain a covenant by the lessee that he will pay for the *water charges*. Often the right is given the lessor to install a meter to measure the amount of water used by the lessee in order to determine the amount to be paid by him.

Recently, some cities have instituted a special tax commonly called a *sewage tax*. The tax is figured on the basis of the amount of water entering the premises. The municipality figures that an equal amount would flow from the building in the form of sewage. Thus, the higher the water charge, the higher the sewage tax. Generally speaking, the covenant for payment of the water rates by the lessee does not mention any charge for sewage tax to be paid by the lessee. This is mainly because, at present, the sewage tax is imposed by only a few municipalities. However, it is felt that this form of taxation will become more and more common as time goes on. In anticipation of such a tax, the lessor, in order to protect himself, should include in the covenant to pay water charges a statement that the lessee will pay any sewage taxes if and when such taxes are imposed and assessed against the property by the municipality.

Fixtures

In the discussion of fixtures in Chapter 3, it was stated that ordinarily trade fixtures are removable by the lessee upon the expiration of the term of the lease. For example, shelving, counters, and similar fixtures can be removed by the tenant upon the expiration of the lease. There are instances, however, when fixtures may become the property of the landlord if so expressed in the lease. There are also instances in which some misunderstanding might arise as to whether or not a particular item installed by a tenant was a trade fixture or became a part of the real property. For example, if the tenant were to install heating equipment in a building, there would be a question of the right of the tenant to remove the equipment upon the expiration of the lease.

In order to prevent misunderstanding concerning the disposition of fixtures, a clause should be inserted in the lease describing the method of disposition of fixtures at the expiration of the lease.

Option to Renew

Often a lease contains an *option to renew* the lease. The option must usually be exercised within a stated time prior to the expiration of the lease. The right to renew may be either for a definite renewal period or for an automatic renewal. There may be included in this covenant granting the option to renew a different amount to be paid as rent for the renewal term.

In the first instance, the option gives a right to the lessee to notify the lessor within a stated time, prior to the end of the term of the lease, that he desires to renew the lease for a stated period under the same terms and conditions as the old lease. The option to renew in the original lease states further that the old lease will be renewed as is, except for the deletion of the clause granting the option to renew.

This suggests, then, that the lease may not be renewed under the option a second time.

The *automatic renewal* is slightly different in that it gives *either* party the right to notify the other within a stated period that he does not choose to renew. In the ordinary option to renew, the right is given only to the lessee, but here both parties have the right to refuse to renew. It is different, too, from the option to renew for a definite period in that the option states that the renewal shall be in accordance with all of the provisions of the old lease "*including this covenant.*" This suggests then that after the first renewal of the lease, the lease may again be renewed at the option of both parties to the original lease.

Option to Purchase

Usually, when a tenant erects a building upon the premises of the landlord, the lease contains an option giving the tenant the right to purchase the improvement and the land at the end of the term. The option may state a price to be paid for the property, or the option may provide that if the lessor and the lessee are unable to negotiate a price, then the lessor and the lessee shall each appoint an appraiser. The appraisers shall then appoint an umpire. Each of the appraisers and the umpire appraise the property. In general, the lease states that the decision of any two appraisers (one of whom is the umpire) as to the price shall be binding on the parties. In the event that the third party then refuses to accept the decision of the other two, it has been held in most states that the proper remedy for the enforcement of the option to purchase at an appraised valuation is by specific performance.[7] This is done in substantially the same manner as was outlined in Chapter 4. When such a clause exists, the proper procedure for its enforcement is by a suit for specific performance in a court of equity.

Distraint

Many leases contain a covenant giving the landlord the right "to distrain for the rent due" or declare the lease terminated if the

---

[7] *Rae Company* v. *Courtney*, 250 N.Y. 71, 165 N.E. 289 (1929).

L E A S E made May 25, 19-- , whereby WE, GLEN OAKS VILLAGE, INC., the landlord, lease and YOU, John Lessee the tenant, take

(Print your name here)

Apartment 26 at 201 Overlook Avenue New York,

for a period of 730 days from June 1 19--, at a rent of $ 2,160.00 and for a period of two years from the first day of the following month, unless cancelled, at a rent of $ 90.00 a month, payable in advance, without demand, on the first day of each month.

WE AGREE TO:

1. Deliver the apartment in good condition;
2. Supply at no extra charge the following:

Gas	A sink and laundry tub
Electricity	Kitchen floor linoleum
Heat as required by law	Window screens
Hot water	*Use of:*
Cold water	Parking areas
Garbage removal	Playgrounds
A refrigerator	Storage & Carriage rooms
A gas range	

YOU AGREE TO:

3. Pay all RENT at our office or other place we specify;
4. Observe each regulation which is part of this lease;
5. Move out when this lease ends;
6. Leave the apartment in good condition when you move out.

BOTH OF US AGREE:

7. We may repair any damage caused by you and charge the cost to you as ADDITIONAL RENT;
8. You will pay full rent pending settlement of any claim you may have for any damage caused by our negligence.

YOU MAY CANCEL THIS LEASE BY DELIVERING TO OUR OFFICE:

9. a. your copy of this lease 3 days before the day you want this lease cancelled, and
   b. your rent in full to the cancellation date you have selected, and
   c. payment for your share of the cost of redecorating the apartment which will be
   $ 15.00 if you cancel in the 1st 6 months;
   $ 20.00 if you cancel in the 2nd 6 months;
   $ 25.00 if you cancel in the 3rd 6 months;
   $ 30.00 if you cancel in the 4th 6 months;

WE MAY CANCEL THIS LEASE BY GIVING YOU:

10. FIVE DAYS' NOTICE if you fail to observe any agreement or regulation which is part of this lease;
11. TEN DAYS' NOTICE if the building is damaged and we decide not to repair it;
12. WHATEVER NOTICE WE RECEIVE if the building, or any part of it, is taken by the government for any reason.

BOTH OF US ALSO AGREE:

13. If you do not move out when this lease ends, we may
    a. start legal action to evict you, or
    b. charge you DOUBLE RENT;
14. If we start legal action to evict you, you will pay as additional rent
    a. the cost of the legal action, including attorneys fees, and
    b. the cost of moving you out.

BOTH OF US SPECIALLY AGREE:

15. You will not assign this lease.
16. You will not sublet your apartment or any part of it.
17. We have made no promises except those in this lease.
18. This lease can be changed in writing only, signed by both of us.
19. This lease is subject to all land leases or mortgages now or hereafter placed on the property.

DEPOSIT AGREEMENT:

20. We have received a deposit of $ 20.00 to guarantee your performance of this lease which we will return when this lease ends, but which you agree we may keep if
    a. we cancel because you fail to observe any agreement or regulation which is part of this lease, or
    b. you do not leave the apartment in good condition when you move out, or
    c. we start legal action to evict you.

GLEN OAKS VILLAGE, INC., (WE)

BY: /s/ Elmer Johns

(X) /s/ John Lessee (YOU)

(Sign your name here)

An Apartment Lease

REGULATIONS

YOU AGREE TO COOPERATE WITH US BY OBSERVING THE FOLLOWING REGULATIONS:

YOU WILL NOT:

1. Leave any personal belongings on lawns, walks, driveways, or stoops, or in public halls;
2. Do anything to disturb your neighbors;
3. Leave garbage outside your apartment except during the periods of collection;
4. Overload the electric system or use the kitchen sink or the toilet for garbage or waste disposal;
5. Erect any window or door signs or private radio and TV aerials;
6. Keep any animals in your apartment;
7. Change the lock on your apartment door;
8. Store furniture, bedding or highly inflammable material in the storeroom;
9. Litter the public halls or grounds;
10. Do anything that will violate any law or increase the insurance rates on the building;
11. Alter the apartment or any part of it without our written permission.

YOU WILL:

12. Place your garbage for disposal as we direct;
13. Use the laundry and drying machines in the manner and at the times we direct;
14. Keep your garage door locked except when leaving and entering;
15. Encourage your children to use the playgrounds instead of the open areas around, and the public halls in the buildings;
16. Use the apartment only as a residence for the persons listed in your application;
17. Take good care of the apartment and the equipment we supply;
18. Permit us to enter the apartment during reasonable hours to
    a. inspect for or make necessary repairs, or
    b. show the apartment to future tenants.

YOU AGREE that we may change these regulations from time to time as may be required to protect the property or add to your enjoyment of it.

I have read the above regulations

Initial { JL } Here

Gross-Morton Company, New York, New York

An Apartment Lease (Concluded)

This is an apartment lease which has met with considerable success. It is an attempt to remove the legal complexities from the lease.

tenant fails to pay his rent. *Distraint* is defined as the right of the landlord to levy upon the tenant's goods and chattels for rent in arrears. This remedy is not available for the collection of any other claim.

Quiet Enjoyment

Ordinarily, a lease contains a covenant of *quiet enjoyment.* It states that if the tenant pays the rent and performs the other conditions of the lease, the tenant "shall and may peaceably and quietly have, hold, and enjoy the leased premises for the term herein mentioned."

Although this covenant may not be written into the lease, the tenant by implication has a right to quiet enjoyment. This covenant, whether it is written into the lease or whether it is by implication, means that the tenant will not lose possession by any act of the landlord, or by failure of the landlord's title, or by the enforcement of any lien superior to the landlord's title. Any breach of the covenant of quiet enjoyment is known technically as an *eviction*.

SALE AND LEASEBACK

A *sale and leaseback* is the sale of a fixed asset which is then leased back to the original owner. The buyer then becomes the lessor, and the seller becomes the lessee.

Although historians have traced this device back to Asia Minor in 200 B.C. and again in 1882 in England, substantial growth of the sale-leaseback did not develop in the United States until shortly after World War II.

Generally, the initial term of the lease is determined by the economic life of the building with a time period left so that the buyer-lessor will have some residual. For example, the estimated economic life of the improvement may be forty years with an initial lease period of thirty years. The residual is then ten years. In practice most of the leases run from twenty to twenty-five years.

Frequently, the lease contains an option to renew and sometimes a purchase option. Periodic rental payments are always included in the lease. The payments are set so that the original investment plus a predetermined rate of return will go to the original investor over the initial term of the lease.

The Pros and Cons of the Sale-Leaseback

Both parties to a transaction of this nature must always analyze the deal in terms of real advantages.

The advantages to the buyer-lessor are:

1. The rate of return should be higher than on a mortgage investment because the buyer-lessor's risk is greater than a mortgage investor.

2. He has direct control over the investment as compared with the purchaser of a mortgage whose control is indirect.

3. If the lease is renewed, his rate of return will be very high because the cost of the property (under a properly drawn lease) will have been returned over the initial period of the lease.

4. Taxable income is reduced. As the owner of what is now a rental property, the lessor may depreciate the building and thus lower his taxable income.

5. Even if the lease is not renewed, there is a potential remainder value. Thus the value will, at a sale, probably exceed the equity.

The disadvantages to the buyer-lessor are:

1. The risk is greater than, say, an investment in a mortgage. The reason is that in a mortgage investment the loan is only a percentage of the property value rather than the whole value.

2. The buyer-lessor is tied into the credit rating and business management ability of the seller-lessee.

3. His income taxes may be high depending upon his tax position.

The advantages to the seller-lessee are:

1. His cash position is improved. For example, instead of tying up $100,000 in a building, the seller-lessee now has the right of possession plus the $100,000 which he presumably will use for working capital purposes.

2. If the seller-lessee had originally sold the property at a profit, it would probably be subject to capital gains tax savings.

3. If the seller-lessee were making mortgage payments, this would not be deductible from his income tax; but the rental payments are. The rental payments are commonly greater than depreciation allowances which the seller would realize by retaining ownership of the property because one can depreciate only the value of the improvements, not the value of the land. After all, the monthly payments by the lessee include a sum for the use of the improvement as well as an additional sum for the use of the land.

The disadvantages to the seller-lessee are:

1. If business declines, the seller-lessee may be in serious financial difficulty resulting from the high fixed rentals.

2. The property will be lost to the seller-lessee at the termination of the lease. This may be undesirable.

3. The costs may be high. Generally, leasebacks run one-fourth of one percent to one percent higher than other types of financing.

4. The mobility of the seller-lessee is restricted under the terms of what amounts to a lease over a long period of time. For example, what is now a good business location may decline as the result of decline of the business area. Yet the seller-lessee is obligated under the terms of his lease to remain in a location or pay the rent without using the premises.[8]

TERMINATION OF LEASES

Breach of Condition

All of the covenants of the lease are generally made conditions of the lease. A breach of any of the covenants is ground for termination of the lease. One of the conditions of the lease is that the tenant shall pay rent to the landlord. If he fails to pay the rent, the lease is breached, and the landlord may then evict the tenant for non-payment of rent.

Eviction. *Eviction* is defined as dispossession of the tenant by the landlord. The eviction may be "actual" whereby the landlord lawfully evicts the tenant, or the "actual" eviction may be unlawfully done by the landlord.

Actual Eviction by Law. Lawful eviction may be had by what is commonly called a "summary proceeding" or "dispossess proceeding."

---

[8] For a complete discussion of the sale-leaseback, see William F. Staats, "Sale-Leaseback of Real Estate as a Financial Device," University of Houston *Business Review,* Volume 9, pp. 1-39; Hyman Adelsberg, "Sale-Leasebacks," *Appraisal and Valuation Manual,* Volume 4, American Society of Appraisers, New York, p. 37; William J. Casey, *Real Estate Investment Planning,* Vol. 1 (1973), Sec. 55, 313.1 *et seq.*

A summary or dispossess proceedings may be brought by a landlord against a tenant for failure to pay rent, or where necessary, for any breach of the covenants of the lease.

In a dispossess proceeding, a statutory notice and the necessary papers are served on the tenant. The tenant is given a time limit in which to appear in court and present his defense. If he fails to appear or if his defense fails, a warrant is issued to a constable or other proper official directing that official to dispossess or evict the tenant from the premises. Generally, at the time of issuing the warrant, the court will grant a judgment against the tenant for any rent that may be in arrears.

When the tenant is dispossessed, the lease is terminated, and ordinarily his obligation to pay rent is terminated. However, most written leases contain a provision that the landlord may retain the right to hold the tenant in damages, measured by the amount thereafter occurring less any amounts the tenant received from reletting the premises.

Actual Eviction (Wrongful). This situation generally occurs where a landlord wrongfully evicts a tenant from part of the premises. In this case the tenant is generally not liable for the rent.

Constructive Eviction. *Constructive eviction* is the term given to acts done by the landlord which so disturb or impair the tenant's possession that he is justified in moving from the premises. If the tenant moves because he has been constructively evicted by a landlord, he is not liable for any monies due under the terms of the lease. The premises must be rendered uninhabitable because of some act or omission on the part of the landlord, and the tenant must have actually moved out. For example, when an apartment is vermin infested to such a degree as to make it uninhabitable, and when the tenant has notified the landlord and has actually moved from the premises, the tenant is said to be constructively evicted. Therefore, he is not liable to the landlord for the unexpired term of the lease.

Surrender and Acceptance

Technically, a *surrender* is the reconveying of the unexpired portion of the lease from the tenant to the landlord. In some cases a surrender may be in writing to conform with the Statute of Frauds. If the surrender is accepted by the landlord, no rent accrues thereafter. If a tenant abandons property he has leased, the landlord need not take possession of the property, nor need he find another tenant for the unexpired portion of the term. The tenant under these conditions is still liable for the rent because the landlord did not under this situation accept the surrender.

However, the situation may arise when the tenant abandons the property and the landlord, in order to protect the property, might inhabit it. This might be construed as an acceptance on the part of the landlord and therefore relieve the tenant for liability of rent for the balance of the term. In order to avoid this, there is generally inserted in the lease a clause to this effect: "If the demised premises are abandoned during the term, the lessor at his option may repossess them as agent of the lessee and relet the premises for the account of the lessee, charging the lessee with any expense, commission, or fee occasioned by such releasing."

In this way the landlord is able properly to care for the property and may proceed to recover from the tenant, if the tenant fails to release the property to the landlord, any rents due and remaining on the lease.

Eminent Domain

Eminent domain is the right of the government to take private property for public use upon making just compensation. The legal proceeding to take property under eminent domain is called a *condemnation proceeding.*

Ordinarily when a leased property is condemned, the tenant has no right to seek any damages that he may have suffered from the landlord.[9] To avoid any possible legal entanglements that might arise on this account, the lease will contain a clause that in the event of condemnation ". . . the lessee shall not be entitled to any part of the award as damages, or otherwise for such condemnation, and the lessor is to receive the full amount of such award. . . ."

Suppose, for example, that *A* rents space in a building for a garage. Over a period of time, he builds up goodwill which gives

[9] Sometimes in extremely rare cases the tenant may seek damages from the firm or political subdivision that condemned the property.

value to the business over and above the fixtures and equipment. Assume that the equipment is worth \$1,000, but that the business, because of the goodwill, is worth \$5,000. *A* sells the business to *B* in return for which *A* receives \$5,000. If the property is then condemned, the landlord will receive compensation for his property, but *B* will be forced to move out of the premises; and all that he will be able to take with him is the \$1,000 worth of equipment. He will thus suffer the loss of the \$4,000 that he had paid *A* for the goodwill of the business. If *A* had not sold the business, he himself would have lost the value of the goodwill that he had developed.

It is therefore important, from the viewpoint of the lessee, to insist upon a clause in the lease stipulating payment to him in the event of condemnation. This clause generally states, in effect, that if the property is condemned before a certain date, the lessee is to receive a stated sum. Other dates are generally inserted with other sums stated, and the clause also contains a final date after which the tenant is not entitled to any part of the condemnation award.

For example, in the event of condemnation, the clause will state:

> The lessee shall receive the following amounts and none other as his agreed share of the award for such condemnation when, as and if it is paid.
>
> If such final order of condemnation is entered before April 1, 1974, the sum of \$6,000; if between April 1, 1974, and April 1, 1977, the sum of \$4,000; if between April 1, 1977, and April 1, 1979, the sum of \$2,000; if thereafter, no award or share whatsoever.

Destruction of the Premises

Under the common law, the tenant was held liable for rent in the event that the premises were destroyed. By statute in the several states, however, a complete destruction of the premises terminates the lease and relieves the tenant from any liability for further rents.[10]

Miscellaneous Ways of Termination

Expiration of the term causes a lease to be terminated. In certain cases, a lease may terminate by mortgage foreclosure.

---

[10] These states are: Arizona, Connecticut, Kentucky, Maryland, Michigan, Minnesota, Mississippi, New Jersey, New York, North Carolina, Ohio, Virginia, West Virginia, and Wisconsin.

Ordinarily it is the duty of the landlord to keep up the payments on a mortgage and comply with the other obligations under the mortgage and protect the tenant. If he fails to do this and the tenant is dispossessed by a mortgagee, then the landlord will be liable to the tenant for any damages that he might have sustained. However, if the lease is subordinate to the mortgage and the tenant has been properly served with the necessary papers by the mortgagee, he may be forced out when the foreclosure sale takes place. A lease is subordinate to a mortgage if it has been recorded prior to the making of the lease.

Most leases, in addition to the above means of termination, will contain a clause that if the lessee becomes bankrupt, the lease will be terminated.

SECURITY FURNISHED THE LANDLORD

Deposits

Very often the tenant is required to give a deposit to the landlord to insure faithful performance of the covenants of the lease. Many states, notably New York, provide by statute that a deposit continues to be the money of the lessee and is to be held in trust by the lessor. The lessor is thus prevented from mingling these funds with his own. The statutes further provide that the parties cannot waive the provisions of the statute requiring that deposits be placed in a trust fund. Ordinarily, the tenant is not entitled to interest on deposits unless there is an expressed agreement to that effect in the lease.

The landlord should place a provision in the lease that in the event the property is sold, he has the right to transfer the deposits to the purchaser after notice to the tenant. If this provision is not written into the lease, the landlord remains personally liable to the tenant even after he has sold the property.

In early 1973, the Pennsylvania legislature amended the Landlord-Tenant Act of 1951 regarding residential property basically as follows: After the *second* year security deposits of more than $100 which cannot amount to more than two months' rent held by a landlord must:

1. Be deposited in an interest-bearing account in an institution regulated by the Federal Reserve Board, The Federal Home

Loan Bank Board, the Comptroller of the Currency, or the Pennsylvania Department of Banking.
2. The tenant must be paid interest earned on the deposit every year.
3. The landlord may deduct a percent of the deposit from the tenant's interest payments for administration of the account.
4. The security deposit may not be increased when the rent has been increased after a tenant has been in possession for five years or more.

With increased interest in consumerism, more and more states will probably adopt similar pro-tenant legislation in the near future.

Guarantors

Very often the landlord will insist that the rents due under the lease shall be guaranteed by someone other than the contracting parties. This situation most often arises when the lease is being signed by a newly formed corporation, and the landlord may have some doubt about its ability to pay rent. In this event, either a separate agreement is entered into between the lessor and a third party, who guarantees payment of the rent, or an endorsement is made on the lease between the lessor and the third party wherein payment is guaranteed by the third party.

Waiver of Right of Redemption

The right of the tenant to redeem the property exists by statute in some states. Briefly, in these states when more than five years remain under the lease and the tenant is dispossessed, the tenant may come in, pay up all arrears, and redeem the property at anytime after the dispossession. This provision by statute is more often than not expressly waived by the tenant in a long-term lease. The landlord does not then have to worry about the tenant's returning after the dispossession proceedings have been completed.

QUESTIONS FOR REVIEW

1. What is a *lease*?
2. What is the difference between a gross lease, a net lease, and a percentage lease?

3. Name and explain two important clauses that should be inserted in a percentage lease.
4. How may one limit the use of certain demised premises?
5. When a lease contains a covenant of repair, what amount of repairs must be made by a tenant?
6. What is the distinction between subletting and an assignment?
7. What may sometimes be inserted in a lease which may effectively enable a tenant to assign or sublet?
8. What is the difference between the usual option to renew a lease and the automatic renewal clause in a lease?
9. What is an *option to purchase* and when is it generally inserted in a lease?
10. List four ways in which a tenancy may be terminated.
11. What should be inserted in a lease to protect the tenant in the event of a condemnation proceeding?
12. Who is a guarantor of a lease?
13. What is meant by redemption in leasing?

PROBLEMS

1. The Hart Corporation has owned a factory for five years and it has a market value of $1,200,000. The value of the land is $200,000 and of the building $1,000,000. The factory has a cost basis of $500,000 after depreciation. The remaining life of the building for depreciation purposes is twenty years. On a straight-line basis the Internal Revenue Service has ruled that it can be depreciated at $25,000 per year (20 × $25,000 = $500,000 remaining depreciable tax life).

   The company sells and leases back the building at a price of $1,200,000 cash. The 25 percent capital gains tax applies. This is $1,200,000 — $500,000 (cost basis). Thus $1,200,000 — $500,000 = $700,000 capital gains taxable income.

   Assume the lease is for twenty years at an annual rental of $100,000. Assume further that the company has to pay 52 percent of its income in taxes.

   (a) How much would be saved, if anything, in taxes per annum as a result of the sale-leaseback? How much is the net cost to the company, if there is a net cost?

   (b) How much would the corporation's cash position be improved after the sale?

   (c) If the company did not sell the building, how much would be the net cost to the company after allowable depreciation?

2. You, a broker, have a vacant store listed with you. It is 45 x 80 feet with a full basement. You feel that because of its location and size, it would be just right for a variety store. You contact the real estate department of a national variety chain, and they send a man out to look at it. He agrees with you and says that his company would be glad to sign a 15-year lease. He also says that his company will pay as rent a sum equal to 1 percent of the gross income for that store, and estimates that in this location they will gross about $500,000 per year.

   You rush to inform your client, but he is not too happy. "I figure I can get about $300 per month on a flat scale from a local businessman," he says. "Maybe there ought to be a minimum of say $200 per month. Besides," he adds, "suppose they don't make $500,000 a year. I figure myself that they will gross only about $200,000. In that case I'll be out money. Moreover, there are other considerations."

   "That's right," you agree, "there are other things, but I think we can work them out."

   (a) What can you suggest to your client regarding his desire for a $200 per month minimum?
   (b) What can you suggest be inserted in the lease to alleviate his worry about the company grossing only $200,000 per year?
   (c) What are the "other things" that must be considered before this lease is signed?

3. You, a realtor, have a business property listed with you for rent at the rate of $250 per month. You are approached by a prospect who states that he is willing to rent the property for a five-year period, provided that at the end of the term, the lessor will renew the lease "as is" at the lessee's option after a written notice thirty days prior to the end of the term.

   He states further that at the end of the second term, if there is a second term, he would like an option to purchase the property. He is quite willing to abide by an umpire's decision as to the price he is to pay at that time, provided that he exercises his option at that time.

   On April 1, your client and the prospect enter into a lease embodying the terms outlined above. Prepare the proper clauses to be inserted in the lease from the information given above.

SUGGESTED READINGS

Anderson, Ronald A., and Walter A. Kumpf. *Business Law,* 9th ed. Cincinnati: South-Western Publishing Co., 1972. Chapter 57.

Ring, Alfred A. *Real Estate Principles and Practices,* 7th ed. Englewood Cliffs, New Jersey: Prentice-Hall, Inc., 1972. Chapter 10.

Chapter 8

Supplementary Real Estate Instruments

In previous chapters the basic real estate instruments were discussed. In this chapter we shall discuss supplementary real estate instruments. The basic instruments are: the contract, the deed, the mortgage, and the lease. The supplementary instruments include: the assignment of mortgage, the estoppel certificate, the satisfaction of mortgage, the partial release, the participation agreement, the subordination agreement, the mortgagee's certificate of reduction, the extension agreement, the consolidation and extension agreement, the spreading agreement, and the building loan agreement. The latter group has to do with mortgages. In addition to these there are other instruments that may be involved in a real estate transaction. Some of them are: the affidavit of title, the power of attorney, the party wall agreement, the beam right agreement, the agreement creating a joint driveway, and the restriction agreement. Other instruments which are peculiar to certain parts of the country, but with which all people interested in real estate ought to be familiar are: the declaration of homestead, the location of a placer claim, and the quartz mining location notice.

A knowledge of the form and content of these supplementary instruments is as necessary as a knowledge of the basic instruments.

Often the completion of a real estate transaction involves the handling of several supplementary instruments, and not infrequently, the successful completion of a transaction depends upon a knowledge and understanding of the uses and possibilities of these instruments.

Many real estate instruments pass across a broker's desk during his career, and if he is to be successful, he should be familiar with all of them.

INSTRUMENTS RELATIVE TO MORTGAGES

Assignment of Mortgage

The *assignment of mortgage* is an instrument used by a mortgagee to transfer his interest in a mortgage to a third party. Since the mortgagee is the maker of the assignment, he is called the *assignor*. The person to whom the assignment is made is called the *assignee*. The instrument names the parties and the consideration and states that the assignor "hereby assigns unto the assignee" his interest in the mortgage being transferred. The mortgage is identified by giving, among other things, the book and the page number in which the mortgage is recorded in the county clerk's office. In some states the assignment makes provision for the description of the property assigned, which should be verified against the premises described in the recorded mortgage. Some assignments may contain a covenant by the assignor to the effect that there are no defenses to the mortgage in case it becomes necessary to foreclose and the assignor verifies the amount due on the mortgage at the time of the assignment.

The signature of the assignor is acknowledged, and the assignment is sent to the office of the county clerk in the county in which the property is located to be recorded. The assignment is there given a book number and a page number, is entered in the book, and a photostatic copy is made. At the same time the county clerk will make a notation on the margin of the photostat of the assigned mortgage indicating the book and page where the assignment has been entered. This enables anyone later searching the records to have notice of the assignment.

A prospective purchaser of a mortgage should have the records searched to determine whether or not a mortgage has been satisfied, has been previously assigned, or whether there are any actions pending on the property described in the mortgage being considered.

ASSIGNMENT OF MORTGAGE WITH COVENANT

KNOW THAT Robert Weathers, residing at 1383 Pacific Street, Borough of Brooklyn, County of Kings, State of New York

, assignor,

in consideration of, Four Thousand and 00/100 ($4,000) - - - - - - dollars, paid by John Murphy, residing at 2301 Atlantic Avenue, Borough of Brooklyn, County of Kings, State of New York , assignee,

hereby assigns unto the assignee,

a certain mortgage made by Floyd Butler, residing at 1863 Ocean Avenue, Borough of Brooklyn, County of Kings, State of New York , given to secure payment of the sum of Six Thousand and 00/100 ($6,000) - dollars and interest, dated the 16th day of April, 19-- recorded on the 19th day of April, 19-- in the office of the Registrar of the County of Kings in Liber 1508 of Mortgages, of Section --- , at page 480 , covering premises (here insert complete legal description)

TOGETHER **with the bond** ~~**or note or obligation**~~ **described in said mortgage , and the moneys due and to grow due thereon with the interest,**

TO HAVE AND TO HOLD the same unto the assignee and to the successors, legal representatives and assigns of the assignee forever.

AND the assignor covenants that there is now owing upon said mortgage , without offset or defense of any kind, the principal sum of Four Thousand Five Hundred and 00/100 ($4,500) - dollars, with interest thereon at 7½ per centum per annum from the 18th day of January , nineteen hundred . . . .

IN WITNESS WHEREOF, the assignor has duly executed this assignment the 23d day of February , 19--.

In presence of:

Richard Roe /s/ Robert Weathers

STATE OF NEW YORK, COUNTY OF Kings **ss.:**
On the 23d day of February , nineteen hundred and . . .
before me personally came Robert Weathers
to me known to be the individual described in and who executed the foregoing instrument, and acknowledged that he executed the same.

/s/ Richard Roe
Notary Public, Kings County
Kings County Clerk's No. 5000
Kings County Register's No. 3000
My commission expires March 31, 19--

Title Guarantee and Trust Company, New York, New York

An Assignment of Mortgage with Covenant

The Estoppel Certificate

An *estoppel certificate* is an instrument executed by a mortgagor showing the amount of the unpaid balance due on a mortgage and stating that the mortgagor has no defenses or offsets at the time of the execution of the certificate, in the event of foreclosure of the mortgage. This is sometimes called a "certificate of no defense" and is used in conjunction with the assignment of the mortgage.

One of the clauses of the mortgage usually states:

> (that) the mortgagor within . . . days upon request in person or within . . . days upon request by mail will furnish a statement of the amount due on this mortgage and whether any offsets or defenses exist against the mortgage debt.

It is this covenant that gives the mortgagee the right to demand that an estoppel certificate be made by mortgagor.

This instrument, which is signed by the mortgagor, is acknowledged. It states the amount due on the mortgage at the time of the execution of the instrument and whether or not the mortgagor has a defense in the event of a foreclosure action. The purpose of the instrument is to enable the prospective assignee of the mortgage to learn from the mortgagor himself the balance due under the mortgage and also whether the mortgagor has a defense in the event of foreclosure. After once having signed and delivered the estoppel certificate, the mortgagor is barred from later asserting that the mortgage was in a lesser amount, or that there was a defense to a foreclosure action. Thus, the courts will not later allow the mortgagor (for he is estopped) to assert in court that he did not owe the amount stated by him in the estoppel certificate.

In practice, mortgages are sometimes sold at a discount (less than the balance due and unpaid).

> *Example: A* may desire to liquidate a mortgage in which he is the mortgagee. At the time the mortgage was made, the amount was for $6,000. At the time *A* wishes to sell, the amount has been reduced to $4,500. *B* is the mortgagor. *A* tells *X* that he is the owner of the $4,500 mortgage but that he will sell it to *X* for $4,000. If *X* examines the record, he will discover that the mortgage states it is for $6,000. Therefore, in order to determine the balance, a request is made by *A* of *B* for an estoppel certificate which can then be shown to *X* verifying *A's* statement that the mortgage is really worth $4,500.

OWNER'S ESTOPPEL CERTIFICATE

THE UNDERSIGNED owning premises situate in the Borough of Brooklyn, County of Kings, State of New York, known as 1863 Ocean Avenue, Borough of Brooklyn, County of Kings, State of New York,

covered by the following mortgage :

Mortgage for $ 6,000.00 dated the 16th day of April , 19-- and recorded in the office of the Register of the County of Kings in Liber 1508 of Section ---- of Mortgages, page 480

which mortgage is about to be assigned by the holder thereof to John Murphy

DOES HEREBY CERTIFY, in consideration of the sum of One Dollar paid, the receipt whereof is hereby acknowledged, and to enable said assignment to be made and accepted, that said mortgage is a valid lien on said premises for the full amount of principal and interest now owing thereon, namely, Four Thousand Five Hundred and 00/100 ($4,500) - - - - - - - - - - - - Dollars, and interest thereon at 7½ per centum from the 18th day of January , 19--, and that there are no defenses or offsets to said mortgage or to the bond ~~or note~~ secured thereby, and that all the other provisions of said bond ~~or note~~ and mortgage are in force and effect.

DATED the 23d day of February , 19--.

IN PRESENCE OF: /s/ Floyd Butler

/s/ Richard Roe

STATE OF NEW YORK, COUNTY OF Kings **ss.:**
On the 23d day of February 19--, before me personally came Floyd Butler to me known to be the individual described in and who executed the foregoing instrument, and acknowledged that he executed the same.

/s/ Richard Roe
Notary Public, Kings County
Kings County Clerk's No. 5000
Kings County Register's No. 3000
My commission expires March 31, 19-

Title Guarantee and Trust Company, New York, New York

Owner's Estoppel Certificate

The Satisfaction of Mortgage

The *satisfaction of mortgage*, or what in some states is called the "release of mortgage," is a receipt signed by the mortgagee stating that the amount due under the mortgage has been paid and may be discharged of record. This means that upon recording, the county clerk will stamp the photostat or typewritten copy of the mortgage as being paid. This instrument is acknowledged and recorded. The effect upon recording is to clear the record of the mortgage.

Many states have statutes imposing criminal penalties upon mortgagees who refuse to deliver the satisfaction when the debt has been paid.

Too much emphasis cannot be placed upon the desirability of immediately recording the satisfaction piece. Without the satisfaction being placed on record, the opportunity presents itself for a fraudulent assignment of the mortgage because a prospective assignee upon examining the record will be led to believe that the mortgage has not been paid and satisfied. Further difficulties are apt to arise if the mortgagor, after having paid a mortgage, fails to record the satisfaction, then attempts to sell his property or to obtain a new mortgage. The record will show the mortgage as not having been paid. In addition, failure to record a satisfaction piece may cause difficulties in the case of death of the mortgagor.

In order to avoid this and to prevent fraudulent assignments, some states require that the mortgage be delivered to the county clerk together with the satisfaction piece in order for the mortgage to be properly discharged of record. The clerk will then efface the original mortgage, which tends to prevent fraudulent negotiation of mortgages which have been paid. To efface the mortgage, the clerk stamps in the margin of a copy of the mortgage filed in his office either "discharged" or "satisfied" and gives also the book and page number where a copy of the satisfaction piece is kept.

Some states, notably New York, prohibit more than one mortgage being discharged by a single satisfaction piece. If there are two mortgages, there must be two satisfaction pieces. In New York, if the mortgage has been assigned, the assignment must be stated in the satisfaction together with the date of each assignment in the chain of title of the persons signing the instrument. The interest assigned and the book and page where each assignment is recorded must be stated. In the event that the mortgage has not been assigned, the satisfaction piece must state it. Furthermore, if the mortgage is held by a fiduciary, including an executor or administrator, the certificate must recite the name of the court and venue [1] of the proceed-

---

[1] *Venue* means the place where the proceedings are held: namely, State of New York; Supreme Court; County of Suffolk.

SATISFACTION OF MORTGAGE

KNOW ALL MEN BY THESE PRESENTS,
that Charles Cox, residing at 53 Wood Street, Village of Hempstead, Town of Hempstead, County of Nassau, State of New York,

DO ES **HEREBY CERTIFY** that a certain indenture of mortgage, bearing date the 14th day of May , 19--, made and executed by Richard Jones

to Charles Cox
to secure payment of the principal sum of Twelve Thousand and 00/100 ($12,000) - Dollars and interest, and duly recorded in the office of the Clerk of the County of Nassau , in Liber 1923 of Mortgages, of Section ----, page 69 on the 16th day of May , 19--.

which mortgage has not been further assigned,

IS PAID, and do es hereby consent that the same be discharged of record.

Dated the 18th day of December , 19--.
IN PRESENCE OF:
/s/ Richard Roe /s/ Charles Cox

NOTICE

Section 321 of the Real Property Law, effective September 1, 1948, expressly provides who must execute the certificate of discharge in specific cases and also provides, among other things, that (1) no certificate shall purport to discharge more than one mortgage; (2) if the mortgage has been assigned, in whole or in part, the certificate shall set forth: (a) the date of each assignment in the chain of title of the person or persons signing the certificate, (b) the names of the assignor and assignee, (c) the interest assigned, and (d) if the assignment has been recorded, the book and page where it has been recorded or the serial number of such record, or (e) if the assignment is being recorded simultaneously with the certificate of discharge, the certificate of discharge shall so state, and (f) if the mortgage has not been assigned, the certificate shall so state; (3) if the mortgage is held by any fiduciary, including an executor or administrator, the certificate of discharge shall recite the name of the court and the venue of the proceedings in which his appointment was made or in which the order or decree vesting him with such title or authority was entered.

STATE OF NEW YORK, COUNTY OF Nassau **ss.:**
On the 18th day of December , 19--, before me personally came Charles Cox to me known to be the individual described in and who executed the foregoing instrument, and acknowledged that he executed the same.

/s/ Richard Roe
Notary Public, Nassau County
Nassau County Clerk's No. 1450
My commission expires March 31, 19--

Title Guarantee and Trust Company, New York, New York

Satisfaction of Mortgage

ings in which his appointment was made or in which the order or decree vesting him with such title or authority was entered.[2]

[2] Section 321, New York Real Property Law.

The Partial Release

In Chapter 6, the need for the insertion of the partial release clause in purchase money mortgages of builders was stressed. The *partial release* is the instrument that is employed to release part of the mortgaged premises from the terms of the mortgage. It simply recites the mortgage, the amount paid for the release, and a description of the part of the mortgaged premises that has been released. The instrument is acknowledged and recorded in the office of the county clerk in the county in which the property is located. The effect of this instrument is that part of the property so released is no longer subject to the mortgage. The owner may then, if he desires, obtain a new mortgage on the parcel so released.

The Participation (Ownership) Agreement

The *participation agreement* is the instrument used to define the ownership or shares that two or more persons may have in the same mortgage. It states the terms upon which the parties to the instrument agree to share in the mortgage. Generally, if both of the parties share equally in a single mortgage, they appear as co-owners on the face of the original mortgage. If they do not share equally in the mortgage, one of the parties will be junior to the other. The participation agreement indicates the extent to which one party is to hold a prior interest and the extent to which the other party is to hold a junior interest in the existing mortgage. It authorizes one of the parties to collect the interest and defines the method of distribution of principal and interest. It also recites the respective rights of the parties in the event of need to foreclose the mortgage.

This instrument is acknowledged but is generally not recorded. It may, however, be recorded in the event that it is subsequently necessary to bring any action under the terms of the instrument.

The participation agreement can sometimes be employed rather effectively in complicated deals involving assemblage. *Assemblage* is the act of bringing together two or more parcels of real estate to form an aggregate whole.[3]

[3] In a few areas "assemblage" is synonymous with "plottage."

RELEASE OF PART OF MORTGAGED PREMISES

WHEREAS, John Mortgagor , by indenture of mortgage, bearing date the 1st day of June , 19--, and recorded in the office of the clerk of the County of Suffolk in Liber 1414 of Mortgages page 567 on the 3d day of June , 19--, for the consideration therein mentioned, and to secure the payment of the money therein specified, did mortgage certain lands and tenements of which the lands hereinafter described are part, unto

Richard Mortgagee,

This indenture made the 16th day of March , nineteen hundred and . . . between Richard Mortgagee party of the first part and John Mortgagor party of the second part,

AND WHEREAS, the party of the first part, at the request of the party of the second part, has agreed to give up and surrender the lands hereinafter described unto the party of the second part, and to hold and retain the residue of the mortgaged lands as security for the money remaining due on said mortgage.

NOW THIS INDENTURE WITNESSETH, that the party of the first part in pursuance of said agreement, and in consideration of One Hundred Fifty and 00/100 ($150) - Dollars, lawful money of the United States, paid by the party of the second part, does grant, release and quitclaim unto the party of the second part, all that part of said mortgaged lands described as follows:

Lots number 1 and number 2, of the Map of Security Acres Development Company, surveyed by James Jones April 3, 1964, and filed in the office of the Clerk of the County of Suffolk August 7, 1964.

Together with the hereditaments and appurtenances thereunto belonging and all the right, title and interest of the party of the first part, of, in and to the same, to the intent that the lands hereby released may be discharged from said mortgage, and that the rest of the land in said mortgage specified may remain mortgaged to the party of the first part as heretofore.

To have and to hold the lands and premises hereby released and quitclaimed to the party of the second part, his heirs and assigns to his and their own proper use, benefit and behoof forever, free, clear and discharged of and from all lien and claim under and by virtue of the indenture of mortgage aforesaid.

IN WITNESS WHEREOF, the party of the first part has signed and sealed these presents the day and year first above written.

IN PRESENCE OF: /s/ Richard Mortgagee

/s/ Richard Roe

STATE OF NEW YORK, COUNTY OF Suffolk **ss.:**

On the 16th day of March , 19--, before me personally came Richard Mortgagee to me known to be the individual described in and who executed the foregoing instrument, and acknowledged that he executed the same.

/s/ Richard Roe
Notary Public, Suffolk County
Suffolk County Clerk's No. 2337
My commission expires March 31, 19--

Release of Part of Mortgaged Premises

It can be used, also, in other complicated transactions:

> *Example:* *X* desires to acquire a number of lots for building purposes. He has $6,000 in cash with which to operate. He approaches *A* who owns 60 lots, and he offers *A* $200 for each of them, a total of $12,000. *A* agrees to sell them to *X* provided *X* can acquire for him from *Y* 10 lots located across the street. *X* approaches *Y* and obtains an option for the 10 lots *A* desires. The price on the 10 lots is also $200 each, a total of $2,000.
>
> Accordingly, *A* will sell 60 lots to *X* at $200 each and receive 10 lots from *Y*. In short, *A* will receive payment for 50 lots, a total of $10,000.
>
> It is agreed that *X* will pay *A* $5,000 in cash and that *A* will "take back" a purchase money mortgage for $5,000. This leaves *X* with only $1,000 cash to purchase from *Y* the lots valued at $2,000, and *A* insists that he wants the 10 lots free and clear.
>
> *Y*, the owner of the 10 lots, is willing to take $1,000 cash and a purchase money mortgage for the balance, *but* if he deeds his 10 lots to *A*, he will have nothing on which to place the mortgage. The parties then agree to use the 60 lots to be deeded from *A* to *X* as the security for the purchase money mortgage, but the mortgage instead of being in the amount of $5,000 is to be in the amount of $6,000 which is the balance due in total to both the parties. *A* is to own $5,000 of the $6,000 mortgage and *Y* is to own $1,000 of the $6,000 mortgage.
>
> At this point *X* and *A* enter into a contract for the exchange of real property. *X* to convey 10 lots to *A*; and *A* to convey 60 lots to *X*.
>
> *X* also simultaneously enters into a contract with *Y* whereby *Y* is to convey 10 lots to *X*.
>
> At the closing, *X* gives *Y* $1,000 in cash, *Y* deeds the 10 lots to *X*, and *X* deeds the 10 lots to *A*. *X* then gives *A* $5,000 in cash and *A* deeds 60 lots to *X*. *X* executes a purchase money mortgage to *A* on the 60 lots. *A* and *Y* then execute an ownership agreement defining their rights in the purchase money mortgage given by *X* to *A*.

In the preceding example, *Y*, having delivered a deed free and clear to *A*, no longer has anything on which to secure the $1,000 indebtedness. Therefore, if he wishes to go through with the deal, he has to rely on *A*'s security. Of course, a transaction of this nature hinges completely upon the amenability of all parties.

OWNERSHIP AGREEMENT

AGREEMENT, made this 29th day of December , one thousand nine hundred and . . . . , between Roger Aiken, residing at 19 Bleecher Street, Borough of Manhattan, City and State of New York, hereinafter designated as the party of the first part and Donald Skidmore, residing at 364 West 160th Street, Borough of Manhattan, City and State of New York,

hereinafter designated as the party of the second part, WITNESSETH that

WHEREAS, the party of the second part holds a certain indenture of mortgage and the bond which it secures made by Ralph Schneider

to Donald Skidmore

to secure the principal sum of Six Thousand and 00/100 ($6,000) - dollars, and interest, dated December 23 19--, and recorded in the office of the Register of the County of New York, December 24, 19--, in Liber 2080 of Mortgages , page 680 covering premises in the Borough of Manhattan , City of New York.

and

WHEREAS, the party of the first part has an interest in said bond and mortgage, to the extent only as hereinafter set forth, and

WHEREAS, the parties hereto desire to declare the terms upon which said bond and mortgage are held by the party of the second part.

NOW, THEREFORE, the parties hereto mutually certify and agree:—

FIRST.—The ownership of the party of the second part in said bond and mortgage is now to the extent of Five Thousand and 00/100 ($5,000) - - - - - - - dollars and interest thereon at the rate of 7½ per centum per annum from December 23, 19--, and the party of the first part is the owner of the balance of said mortgage debt remaining; but the ownership of the party of the second part is superior to that of the party of the first part, as if the party of the second part held a first bond and mortgage for said sum of

Five Thousand and 00/100 ($5,000) - - - - - - - - - - - - - - dollars and interest thereon as aforesaid, and the party of the first part held a second and subordinate and mortgage to secure the interest of the party of the first part in said mortgage debt.

SECOND.—The party of the second part is authorized to collect all the interest which is secured by said bond and mortgage and shall retain therefrom a sum equal to the interest then accrued upon the share of said bond and mortgage owned by the party of the second part, and then remit to the party of the first part any balance of interest remaining.

THIRD.—The party of the second part or any assignee of the interest of the party of the second part in said bond and mortgage is authorized to accept payment of said bond and mortgage and to execute the proper satisfaction therefor, and the holder so satisfying said bond and mortgage shall account to the party of the first part for all money received in excess of the ownership in said bond and mortgage of said party of the second part or such assignee.

FOURTH.—The party of the second part shall have all the rights of any holder of said bond and mortgage including the right to foreclose the same and to receive the proceeds of sale from the referee, but the party of the first part shall in any and every event, have the right to an accounting for all money received by the party of the second part or any assignee of the interest of the party of the second part in said bond and mortgage in excess of the ownership of the party of the second part in said bond and mortgage. In case of foreclosure the party of the second part shall be under no obligation to protect the interests of the party of the first part upon a sale of the mortgaged premises.

FIFTH.—All rights and authority given to the party of the second part under this agreement are irrevocable so long as the party of the second part, or any assignee of the party of the second part has any interest in said bond and mortgage and shall pass to and apply to the party of the second part and to any assignee of the interest of the party of the second part in said bond and mortgage.

An Ownership Agreement

SIXTH.—The interest of the party of the first part under this agreement in said bond or mortgage or mortgage debt is not assignable as against the party of the second part except by an instrument duly executed in the manner required for the execution of a deed of real property and endorsed upon or attached to this instrument; no assignee of the interest of the party of the first part in said bond and mortgage shall have any rights under this agreement, nor be entitled to any payment thereunder until such assignment shall have been exhibited to the party of the second part and a copy thereof shall have been filed with the party of the second part, and the receipt of such copy shall have been noted by the party of the second part on this agreement. Whenever the proceeds of the ownership of the party of the first part in said bond and mortgage shall be paid to the holder thereof, this agreement and all assignments thereof shall be surrendered to the party of the second part. The interest of the party of the second part is assignable to any person or corporation, without liability on the part of the party of the second part, but the interest of any such assignee shall be subject to this agreement.

SEVENTH.—The party of the first part, for himself or itself, and his or its executors, administrators, successors, assigns and successors in interest, hereby expressly waives any and all rights, claims and remedies created or declared by Chapter 921 of the Laws of 1934, and Chapter 838 of the Laws of 1936 and embodied in section 1079-a * of the Civil Practice Act, and any other laws now in existence or hereafter enacted, State or Federal, which in any manner are or shall be inconsistent with the rights and remedies of the party of the second part as set forth in this instrument.

EIGHTH.—This agreement shall be binding upon and inure to the benefit of the successors, legal representatives and assigns of the parties hereto.

* Under Section 1079-a of the New York Civil Practice Act, a junior participant may foreclose the mortgage upon refusal of the senior participant to foreclose after giving notice and demand. Paragraph "Seventh" waives this right.

IN WITNESS WHEREOF, the said parties have signed and sealed these presents, the day and year first above written.

IN PRESENCE OF:

/s/ Richard Roe

/s/ Roger Aiken
/s/ Donald Skidmore

STATE OF NEW YORK, COUNTY OF New York **ss.:**

On the 29th day of December, one thousand nine hundred . . .
before me came Roger Aiken and Donald Skidmore
to be known to be the individual s described in, and who executed, the foregoing instrument, and acknowledged that t he y executed the same.

/s/ Richard Roe
Notary Public, New York County

Title Guarantee and Trust Company, New York, New York

An Ownership Agreement (Concluded)

The Subordination Agreement

The *subordination agreement* is a device by which those with superior rights subordinate those rights in favor of inferior rights. The situation requiring its use often comes about in the following manner. A building, on which *A* for many years held a first mortgage, is worth \$25,000. *A* still owns a first mortgage on the building, but the mortgage has been reduced to \$2,000. As far as *A* is concerned, it is a good investment. There is ample security, and the mortgage does not contain a prepayment clause, which means that the owner cannot pay off the indebtedness before the maturity date of the mortgage. Assume that the owner wishes to sell the property to *B*,

SUBORDINATION AGREEMENT

AGREEMENT, made the 24th day of October nineteen hundred and . . .

BETWEEN William Thomas, residing at 1323 East 116th Street, Borough of Manhattan, City and State of New York, party of the first part, and James Britt, residing at 1450 West 26th Street, Borough of Manhattan, City and State of New York, party of the second part,

WITNESSETH:

WHEREAS, the said party of the first part now owns and holds a certain mortgage and the bond ~~or note~~ secured thereby, which mortgage is dated the 16th day of June , 19-- and made by Robert Calender

to William Thomas

to secure the principal sum of Seven Thousand and 00/100 ($7,000) - dollars and interest and recorded in the office of the Register of the County of New York in Liber 2892 of the Mortgages at page 781 , and covers premises hereinafter mentioned or a part thereof, and

WHEREAS Robert Calendar
the present owner of the premises hereinafter mentioned is about to execute and deliver to said party of the second part, a mortgage to secure the principal sum of Twenty Thousand and 00/100 ($20,000) - dollars and interest, covering premises

(here follows complete legal description)

and more fully described in said mortgage, and

WHEREAS, said party of the second part has refused to accept said mortgage unless said mortgage held by the party of the first part be subordinated in the manner hereinafter mentioned.

NOW THEREFORE, in consideration of the premises and to induce said party of the second part to accept said mortgage and also in consideration of one dollar paid to the party of the first part, the receipt whereof is hereby acknowledged, the said party of the first part hereby covenants and agrees with said party of the second part that said mortgage held by said party of the first part be and shall continue to be subject and subordinate in lien to the lien of said mortgage for Twenty Thousand and 00/100 ($20,000) - - - - - dollars and interest about to be delivered to the party of the second part hereto, and to all advances heretofore made or which hereafter may be made thereon (including but not limited to all sums advanced for the purpose of paying brokerage commissions, mortgage recording tax, documentary stamps, fee for examination of title, surveys, and any other disbursements and charges in connection therewith) to the extent of the last mentioned amount and interest, and all such advances may be made without notice to the party of the first part, and to any extensions, renewals and modifications thereof.

THIS AGREEMENT shall be binding on and enure to the benefit of the respective heirs, personal representatives, successors and assigns of the parties hereto.

IN WITNESS WHEREOF, the said party of the first part has duly executed this agreement.
IN PRESENCE OF:

/s/ Richard Roe

/s/ William Thomas
/s/ James Britt

STATE OF NEW YORK, COUNTY OF New York ss.:
On the 24th day of October , nineteen hundred and . . .
before me personally came William Thomas and James Britt
to me known to be the individual s described in and who executed the foregoing instrument, and acknowledged that they executed the same.

Richard Roe
Notary Public, New York County
My commission expires August 12, 19--

Title Guarantee and Trust Company, New York, New York

Subordination Agreement

and *B* goes to a bank and receives a commitment for a $10,000 loan. The bank or any other lender will discover the existing first mortgage in the amount of $2,000. By law the bank cannot, nor would probably anyone else, lend $10,000 behind an existing first mortgage. The subordination agreement is then put into play. The bank and the first mortgagee agree to place the first mortgage in a secondary position.[4]

The subordination agreement recites the parties. The parties in the above case are *A* and the bank. The subordination agreement recites the existing mortgage by book and page number and describes the premises. It also recites the fact that the present owner is about to deliver to the second party (the bank) a mortgage in the amount of a sum certain. The agreement continues with the statement that the second party refuses to give a mortgage on the property under the circumstances unless the first party (*A*) agrees to become subordinated to any mortgage to be granted. This statement is followed by a covenant binding upon the heirs and assigns of the parties to the effect that the present holder of the first mortgage agrees to allow himself to become subordinated to the mortgage given by the bank.

This instrument is acknowledged and recorded in the county in which the property is located.

Mortgagee's Certificate of Reduction

The *mortgagee's certificate of reduction* is an instrument executed by a mortgagee stating the balance due on a mortgage.

In a sense, it is the counterpart of an estoppel certificate. An estoppel certificate is signed by the mortgagor in order to inform a prospective assignee of the balance remaining due under a mortgage, and also to indicate whether the mortgagor has a defense in the event of a foreclosure. The reduction certificate is used to inform a prospective real property purchaser, who is either assuming the mortgage or taking the property subject to the mortgage, of the amount due on the mortgage. The logical person to certify as to the amount still due on the mortgage is, of course, the mortgagee.

The demand for a reduction certificate usually comes about in this manner. *A* lists with a broker a property having a purchase price

[4] The first mortgagee, as a practical matter, usually relinquishes his position for a slight consideration.

MORTGAGEE'S CERTIFICATE OF REDUCTION

THE UNDERSIGNED, the owner and holder of the following mortgage and of the bond secured thereby:

Mortgage dated the 16th day of January , 19--, made by William Lohr

to Frank Lewis

in the principal sum of $ 8,000.00 and recorded in the Office of the Clerk of the County of Suffolk , in Liber 1400 of Section ---- of Mortgages, page 89 .

covering premises situate in the Hamlet of Medford, Town of Brookhaven, County of Suffolk, State of New York,

in consideration of the sum of one dollar, the receipt of which is hereby acknowledged, **DO ES HEREBY CERTIFY,** that there is now owing and unpaid upon said bond ~~or note~~ and mortgage the principal sum of

Seven Thousand and 00/100 ($7,000) - - - - - - - - - - - - - - Dollars, with interest thereon at the rate of 6½ per centum per annum from the 7th day of August , 19-- ; and that said mortgage is now a lien on the premises covered thereby only to the extent of the said last mentioned principal sum and interest.

DATED, the 28th day of August 19--.

IN PRESENCE OF:

/s/ Richard Roe　　　　/s/ Frank Lewis

STATE OF NEW YORK, COUNTY OF Suffolk **ss.:**

On the 28th day of August 19--, before me personally came Frank Lewis to me known to be the individual described in, and who executed the foregoing instrument, and duly acknowledged that he executed the same.

/s/ Richard Roe
Notary Public, County of Suffolk
Suffolk County Clerk's No. 2735
My commission expires March 31, 19--

Title Guarantee and Trust Company, New York, New York

Mortgagee's Certificate of Reduction

of $10,000 on which there is a $5,000 mortgage. *A* is willing to sell the property for $5,000 over and above the existing mortgage. This means that the buyer must either "assume" or take "subject to" the $5,000 mortgage. The only way the purchaser can make certain that there is only $5,000 due under the mortgage and not a greater sum is to obtain a reduction certificate from the mortgagee.

After the contract for the sale of the property is entered into and prior to the closing date, the owner (who is the mortgagor) requests the reduction certificate from the mortgagee. In the event the mortgage has been assigned, the certificate is obtained from the assignee of the mortgagee.

The certificate recites the date of the mortgage, the principal amount of the mortgage, and the book and page on which the instrument is recorded. It further certifies the balance due on the principal, together with the interest due at the date of the signing of the certificate.

The instrument is acknowledged, but it need not be recorded. The certificate is delivered to the purchaser at the time of closing. In this way the purchaser is certain that the amount of the mortgage he is "assuming" or taking "subject to" is the bona fide amount.

The Extension Agreement

The *extension agreement* is a device employed to extend the due date of the mortgage, and in some cases to modify the original bond or note and mortgage. This modification may take the form of a different interest rate, a different method of amortization, or both.

The situation arises when the mortgage is soon to come due and the mortgagor feels that he cannot, or does not desire to, make the payment. If he does not make the payment, the mortgage will either be foreclosed or remain open. In the latter case, the mortgagee has the right to foreclose at anytime. The mortgagee may, however, be willing to extend the time in which the mortgagor must pay off the mortgage indebtedness.

The instrument recites the parties, the old mortgage, and the amount presently due and payable. It also states that the mortgagor covenants to pay a certain rate of interest, which may or may not be the same rate as that called for by the original mortgage. If the mortgagor cannot make the payment due, this rate will probably be higher than the rate called for in the mortgage instrument itself. All of the covenants of the original mortgage instrument—the covenant to pay taxes, the warrant of title, etc.—are contained in the extension agreement. This instrument should also contain substantially the following clause:

> (The mortgagor) is now the owner and holder of the premises upon which said mortgage is a valid lien for the amount above specified, with interest at the rate above set forth, and that there are no defenses or offsets to said mortgage, or the debt which it secures.

This clause is worded substantially the same as the estoppel certificate and will prevent the mortgagor from later asserting any defenses that he might have had prior to the date of the extension agreement.

The second clause that is inserted in the extension agreement amounts to an assumption clause. In this the mortgagor covenants:

> (that he does) hereby assume, covenant, and agree to pay said principal sum and interest as above set forth—and to comply with the other terms of said bond or note and mortgage as hereby modified.

A question arises as to the position of the original signer of the bond or note in the event that he has sold the property. His liability depends upon what happens to property values. Before the signing of the extension agreement, the original mortgagor on the bond or note can demand that the mortgage be foreclosed. If property values are high, he will know that a foreclosure will result in no deficiency against him. However, after an extension agreement is executed, the

EXTENSION AGREEMENT

AGREEMENT, made the 16th day of July nineteen hundred and . . .

BETWEEN Robert Mortgagee, residing at 423 W. 23d Street, City and State of New York,
hereinafter designated as the party of the first part, and John Mortgagor, residing at 420 Madison Avenue, City and State of New York,
hereinafter designated as the party of the second part.

An Extension Agreement

WITNESSETH, that the party of the first part, the holder of the following mortgage and of the bond ~~or note~~ secured thereby:

Mortgage dated the 12th day of April , 19-- made by John Mortgagor to Robert Mortgagee in the principal sum of $10,000.00 and recorded in the office of the Registrar of the County of New York in Liber 2008 of Section ---- of Mortgages, page 200, which mortgage is now a first lien upon the premises situate in the Borough of Manhattan, City and State of New York, and on which bond ~~or note~~ there is now due the sum of Seven Thousand and 00/100 ($7,000) - - - - - - - - - - - - - - dollars, with interest thereon, in consideration of one dollar paid by said party of the second part, and other valuable consideration, the receipt whereof is hereby acknowledged, does hereby extend the time of payment of the principal indebtedness secured by said bond ~~or note~~ and mortgage so that the same shall be due and payable on the 1st day of April 19--

PROVIDED, the party of the second part meanwhile pays interest on the amount owing on said bond ~~or note~~ from the 16th day of July , 19--, at the rate of 6 per centum per annum on the 16th day of October , 19--, and quarter annually thereafter, and comply with all the other terms of said bond ~~or note~~ and mortgage as hereby modified.

AND the party of the second part, in consideration of the above extension and of one dollar paid by said party of the first part and other valuable consideration, the receipt whereof is hereby acknowledged, does hereby assume, covenant and agree to pay said principal sum and interest as above set forth and not before the maturity thereof as the same is hereby extended, and to comply with the other terms of said bond ~~or note~~ and mortgage as hereby modified.

AND the party of the second part further covenants with the party of the first part as follows:

1. That the party of the second part will pay the indebtedness as hereinbefore provided.
2. That the party of the second part will keep the buildings on the premises insured against loss by fire for the benefit of the party of the first part; that he will assign and deliver the policies to the party of the first part; and that he will reimburse the party of the first part for any premiums paid for insurance made by the party of the first part on default of the party of the second part in so insuring the buildings or in so assigning and delivering the policies.
3. That no building on the premises shall be removed or demolished without the consent of the party of the first part.
4. That the whole of said principal sum and interest shall become due at the option of the party of the first part: after default in the payment of any instalment of principal or of interest for 30 days; or after default in the payment of any tax, water rate, sewer rent or assessment for thirty days after notice and demand; or after default after notice and demand either in assigning and delivering the policies insuring the buildings against loss by fire or in reimbursing the party of the first part for premiums paid on such insurance, as hereinbefore provided; or after default upon request in furnishing a statement of the amount due on the mortgage and whether any offsets or defenses exist against the mortgage debt, as hereinafter provided.
5. That the holder of said mortgage, in any action to foreclose it shall be entitled to the appointment of a receiver.
6. That the party of the second part will pay all taxes, assessments, sewer rents or water rates, and in default thereof, the party of the first part may pay the same.
7. That the party of the second part within six days upon request in person or within fifteen days upon request by mail will furnish a written statement duly acknowledged of the amount due on said mortgage and whether any offsets or defenses exist against the mortgage debt.
8. That notice and demand or request may be in writing and may be served in person or by mail.
9. That the party of the second part warrants the title to the premises.
10. That fire insurance policies which are required by paragraph No. 2 above shall contain the usual extended coverage endorsement; in addition thereto the party of the second part, within thirty days after notice and demand, will keep the buildings on the premises insured against loss by other insurable hazards for the benefit of the party of the first part, as may reasonably be required by the party of the first part; that he will assign and deliver the policies to the party of the first part; and that he will reimburse the party of the first part for any premiums paid for insurance made by the party of the first part on the default of the party of the second part in so insuring or in so assigning and delivering the policies. The provisions of subdivision 4 of Section 254 of the Real Property Law, with reference to the construction of the fire insurance clause, shall govern the construction of this clause so far as applicable.
11. That the whole of said principal sum shall become due at the option of the party of the first part after default for thirty days after notice and demand, in the payment of any instalment of any assessment for local improvements heretofore or hereafter laid, which is or may become payable in annual instalments and which has affected, now affects or hereafter may affect the said premises, notwithstanding that such instalment be not due and payable at the time of such notice and demand, or upon the failure to exhibit to the party of the first part, within thirty days after demand, receipts showing payment of all taxes, assessments, water rates, sewer rents and any other charges which have become a prior lien on the mortgaged premises.
12. That the whole of said principal sum shall become due at the option of the party of the first part, if the buildings on the said premises are not maintained in reasonably good repair, or upon the failure of any owner of said premises to comply with the requirement of any governmental department claiming jurisdiction within three months after an order making such requirement has been issued by any such department.
13. That in the event of the passage after the date of this agreement of any law of the State of New York, deducting from the value of land for the purposes of taxation any lien thereon,

An Extension Agreement (Continued)

or changing in any way the laws for the taxation of mortgages or debts secured by mortgages for state or local purposes, or the manner of the collection of any such taxes, so as to affect said mortgage, the holder of said mortgages and of the debt which it secures, shall have the right to give thirty days' written notice to the owner of the mortgaged premises requiring the payment of the mortgage debt. If such notice be given the said debt shall become due, payable and collectible at the expiration of said thirty days.

14. That in case of a sale, said premises, or so much thereof as may be affected by said mortgage, may be sold in one parcel.

15. That the whole of said principal sum shall immediately become due at the option of the party of the first part, if the party of the second part shall assign the rents or any part of the rents of the mortgaged premises without first obtaining the written consent of the party of the first part to such assignment, or upon the actual or threatened demolition or removal of any building erected or to be erected upon said premises.

16. That if any action or proceeding be commenced (except an action to foreclose said mortgage or to collect the debt secured thereby) to which action or proceeding the holder of said mortgage is made a party, or in which it becomes necessary to defend or uphold the lien of said mortgage, all sums paid by the holder of said mortgage for the expense of any litigation to prosecute or defend the rights and lien created by said mortgage (including reasonable counsel fees), shall be paid by the party of the second part, together with the interest thereon at the rate of six per cent per annum, and any sum and the interest thereon shall be a lien on said premises, prior to any right, or title to, interest in or claim upon said premises attaching or accruing subsequent to the lien of said mortgage, and shall be deemed to be secured by said mortgage and by the bond which it secures. In any action or proceeding to foreclose said mortgage, or to recover or collect the debt secured thereby, the provisions of law respecting the recovery of costs, disbursements and allowances shall prevail unaffected by this covenant.

17. That the whole of said principal sum shall immediately become due at the option of the party of the first part upon any default in keeping the buildings on said premises insured as required by paragraph No. 2 or paragraph No. 10 hereof, or if after application by any holder of said mortgage to two or more fire insurance companies lawfully doing business in the State of New York and issuing policies of fire insurance upon buildings situate in the place where the mortgaged premises are situate, the companies to which such application has been made shall refuse to issue such policies, or upon default in complying with the provisions of paragraph No. 10 hereof, or upon default, for five days after notice and demand, either in assigning and delivering to the party of the first part the policies of fire insurance or in reimbursing the party of the first part for premiums paid on such fire insurance as hereinbefore provided in paragraph No. 2 hereof.

18. That in the event of any default in the performance of any of the terms, covenants or agreements herein or in said bond ~~or note~~ and mortgage contained, it is agreed that the then owner of the mortgaged premises, if he is the occupant of said premises or any part thereof, shall immediately surrender possession of the premises so occupied to the holder of said mortgage, and if such occupant is permitted to remain in possession, the possession shall be as tenant of the holder of said mortgage and such occupant shall, on demand, pay monthly in advance to the holder of said mortgage a reasonable rental for the space so occupied and in default thereof, such occupant may be dispossessed by the usual summary proceedings. In case of foreclosure and the appointment of a receiver of rents, the covenants herein contained may be enforced by such receiver.

19. That the following shall be deemed to be and remain and form part of the realty and are and shall continue to be covered by the lien of said mortgage: all fixtures and articles of personal property now or hereafter attached to, or contained in and used in connection with, said premises, including but not limited to all apparatus, machinery, fittings, gas ranges, ice boxes, mechanical refrigerators, awnings, shades, screens, storm sashes, plants and shrubbery.

20. That any and all awards heretofore and hereafter made to the present and all subsequent owners of the mortgaged premises by any governmental or other lawful authorities for taking by eminent domain the whole or any part of said premises or any easement therein, including any awards for any changes of grade of streets, are hereby assigned to the holder of said mortgage who is hereby authorized to collect and receive the proceeds of any such awards from such authorities and to give proper receipts and acquittances therefor, and to apply the same toward the payment of the amount owing on account of said mortgage and its accompanying bond ~~or note~~ notwithstanding the fact that the amount owing thereon may not then be due and payable; and the said party of the second part hereby covenants and agrees, upon request, to make, execute and deliver any and all assignments and other instruments sufficient for the purpose of assigning the aforesaid awards to the holders of said mortgage, free, clear and discharged of any and all encumbrances of any kind or nature whatsoever.

21. That the party of the second part is now the owner and holder of the premises upon which said mortgage is a valid lien for the amount above specified with interest thereon at the rate above set forth, and that there are no defenses or offsets to said mortgage or to the debt which it secures.

22. That the principal and interest hereby agreed to be paid shall be a lien on the mortgaged premises and be secured by said bond ~~or note~~ and mortgage, and that when the terms and provisions contained in said bond ~~or note~~ and mortgage in any way conflict with the terms and provisions contained in this agreement, the terms and provisions herein contained shall prevail, and that as modified by this agreement the said bond ~~or note~~ and mortgage are hereby ratified and confirmed.

This agreement may not be changed orally, but only by an agreement in writing and signed by the party against whom enforcement of any waiver, change, modification or discharge is sought. This agreement shall bind and apply to the parties hereto, their respective heirs, executors, administrators, successors and assigns.

IN WITNESS WHEREOF, this agreement has been duly executed by the parties hereto the day and year first above written.

IN PRESENCE OF: /s/ Richard Roe

/s/ Richard Mortgagee
/s/ John Mortgagor

Acknowledgment

Title Guarantee and Trust Company, New York, New York

An Extension Agreement (Concluded)

original mortgagor, or maker of the note, is not liable for any value that the property might lose after the signing of the extension agreement because he is no longer a surety.

> *Example: A,* the original owner of the property, obtains a mortgage from *B* in the amount of $15,000 on a parcel of property valued at $20,000. *A* sells the property to *X,* who takes it subject to the mortgage. Later the time for payment becomes due and the mortgage is open. The property has risen in value to $30,000. *A* can demand that *B* foreclose on the mortgage. *B* does not foreclose, but gives *X* an extension. Thus *B* cannot foreclose. Later the value of the property declines to $10,000 and *X* defaults. *B* cannot collect the difference between $10,000 and $15,000 from *A* under the original note or bond signed by *A*.

Consolidation and Extension Agreement

A mortgagee, either by having made a first and second mortgage on a single piece of property or by having purchased two mortgages on one piece of property, may desire to create a single mortgage. This is done by means of a *consolidation and extension agreement.* The mortgagor probably would agree to this arrangement to relieve himself of the burden of high amortization payments because the length of time for payment is usually extended.

The instrument converts both of the mortgages into a single mortgage which becomes a first mortgage. It describes the property and recites the interest and payments to be made, and also the date when the final payment shall become due. The due date is included because, generally speaking, second mortgages have a due date prior to that of first mortgages; and by this means, the monies due under the previously existing mortgages become due and payable at the same time.

The Spreading Agreement

The *spreading agreement* is used by a mortgagee to incorporate other lands owned by the mortgagor under the terms of an existing mortgage. The situation usually arises when the mortgagor requests an extension of a mortgage that is about to become an open mortgage. The mortgagee may feel that he needs additional security in order to

CONSOLIDATION AND EXTENSION AGREEMENT

AGREEMENT, made the 10th day of September nineteen hundred and . . .
BETWEEN Richard Mortgagee, residing at 39 E. 18th Street, Borough of Manhattan, City and State of New York,
the party of the first part, and John Mortgagor, residing at 432 W. 100th Street, Borough of Manhattan, City and State of New York,
party of the second part,

WITNESSETH: whereas, the party of the first part is the holder of the following mortgages and of the bonds ~~or notes~~ secured thereby:

Mortgage dated the 16th day of August, 19-- made by John Mortgagor to Richard Mortgagee in the principal sum of $ 3,000.00 and recorded in the office of the Registrar of the County of New York in Liber 2990 of Section ---- of Mortgages, page 385,

Mortgage dated the 24th day of October, 19-- made by John Mortgagor to Ace Investment Corporation in the principal sum of $ 1,000.00 and recorded in the office of the Registrar of the County of New York in Liber 3030 of Section ---- of Mortgages, page 42,

which mortgages now cover the property hereinafter described, and on which two bonds ~~or notes~~ and mortgages there is now owing the sum of Three Thousand and 00/100 ($3,000) - - - - - - - - - - - - Dollars with interest thereon, and

WHEREAS, the party of the first part, the holder of said bonds ~~or notes~~ and mortgages, and the party of the second part, the owner in fee simple of the property hereinafter described, have mutually agreed to consolidate and co-ordinate the liens of said mortgages and to modify the terms thereof and of the bonds ~~or notes~~ secured thereby in the manner hereinafter appearing.

NOW THEREFORE, in pursuance of said agreement and in consideration of the sum of One dollar and other valuable consideration each to the other in hand paid, receipt of which is hereby acknowledged, the parties hereto mutually covenant and agree as follows:

THAT the liens of the bonds mortgages hereinabove mentioned hereby are consolidated and co-ordinated so that together they shall hereafter constitute in law but one first mortgage, a single lien, securing the principal sum of Three Thousand and 00/100 ($3,000) - - - - - - - - - - - - - - - - - - - Dollars, and interest, upon the property described as follows:

(here follows complete legal description)

That the time of payment of said principal sum secured by said bonds and mortgages, as modified by this agreement, hereby is extended so that the same shall become due and payable as follows: Fifty ($50) Dollars on the 10th day of October 19--, and a like sum on the 10th day of each and every month thereafter until the 10th day of October 19-- when the balance remaining due shall become due and payable.

/s/ Richard Mortgagee
/s/ John Mortgagor

Acknowledgment

Title Guarantee and Trust Company, New York, New York

A Consolidation and Extension Agreement

extend the mortgage. If this is the case, the mortgagee will ask that the mortgagor allow him to cover with the existing mortgage additional lands owned by the mortgagor. This is done by means of the spreading agreement, which is acknowledged and recorded.

The same form used for the consolidation and extension agreement may be quite readily adapted for the spreading agreement.

The Building Loan Agreement

The *building loan agreement* is an agreement entered into between a builder and a lender who agrees to lend the builder money to build on certain described property. The lender agrees to advance the money to the builder at certain stages of construction.

The building loan agreement recites the name of the parties, referring to the builder as the borrower, and the lending institution as the lender. The agreement provides that the borrower will build according to the plans and specifications that have been submitted

---

BUILDING LOAN CONTRACT

THIS AGREEMENT, made the 14th day of March nineteen hundred and . . .

BETWEEN Ace Realty Corporation, Inc., having its place of business at Two Tulip Avenue, Floral Park, County of Nassau, State of New York,

hereinafter referred to as the borrower, and The Fourth National Bank of Mineola, New York, a banking corporation having its banking house at 44 Main Street, Mineola, County of Nassau, State of New York,

hereinafter referred to as the lender.

WHEREAS, the borrower has applied to the lender for a loan of Twelve Thousand and 00/100 ($12,000) - Dollars, to be advanced as hereinafter provided and to be evidenced by the ~~bond or~~ note of the borrower for the payment of said sum, or so much thereof as shall at any time be advanced thereon, on the 14th day of April next ensuing

with interest upon each amount so advanced from the date of such advance at the rate of 6 per centum per annum to be paid on the 14th day of July 19-- and quarter annually thereafter; said ~~bond or~~ note to be secured by a first mortgage on the premises described as follows:

(here follows complete legal description)

TOGETHER with all fixtures and articles of personal property now or hereafter attached to, or contained in and used in connection with said premises, including but not limited to all apparatus, machinery, fittings, gas ranges, ice boxes, mechanical refrigerators, awnings, shades, screens, storm sashes, plants and shrubbery.

WHEREAS, the lender agrees to make said loan upon the terms, covenants and conditions hereinafter set forth and the borrower agrees to take said loan and expressly covenants to comply with and perform all of the terms, covenants and conditions of this agreement,

NOW, THEREFORE, it is agreed between the parties as follows:

1. The borrower expressly covenants to make on said premises the improvement described below in accordance with the plans and specifications therefor which, before the making of the first advance hereunder, the borrower agrees to file with all governmental authorities having jurisdiction and to obtain all necessary approvals of said plans and specifications and all necessary building permits from said authorities. The said plans and specifications shall first be submitted to and approved by the lender in writing; and no changes or amendments thereto shall be made without first obtaining the written approval of the lender. The said improvement to be made shall be as follows:

(here follows a general description and specifications)

A Building Loan Contract

2. Said loan is to be advanced at such times and in such amounts as the lender may approve, but substantially in accordance with the following schedule:

(a schedule of payments follows)

/s/ Ace Realty Corporation, Inc.,
by George Ace, President

(Corporate Seal)

/s/ Fourth National Bank of Mineola, N. Y.
by Frank Jones, Cashier

(Corporate Seal)

Acknowledgment

STATE OF NEW YORK, COUNTY OF Nassau **ss.:**

George Ace being duly sworn, deposes and says:
I am at No. 18 "D" Street, Floral Park, New York
I am the president of Ace Realty Corporation, Inc.
the borrower mentioned in the within building loan contract.
The consideration paid, or to be paid, by the borrower to the lender for the loan described therein is Two Hundred and Forty and 00/100 - - - - - - - - - - - Dollars ($ 240.00), and that all other expenses incurred, or to be incurred, in connection with said loan are as follows:

Broker's commission,	$ none	Sums paid to take by assignment prior existing mortgages which are consolidated with building loan mortgages and also the interest charges on such mortgages,	$ ------
Examination and insurance of title and recording fees,	$ 125.00	Sums paid to discharge or reduce the indebtedness under mortgages and accrued interest thereon and other prior existing encumbrances,	$ ------
Mortgage tax,	$ 60.00	Sums paid to discharge building loan mortgages whenever recorded,	$ ------
Architect's, engineer's and surveyor's fees,	$ ------	Taxes, assessments, water rents and sewer rents paid (existing prior to commencement of improvement),	$ ------
Inspections,	$ ------		
Appraisals,	$ 15.00		
Conveyancing,	$ ------		
Building loan service fees,	$ ------		

and that the net sum available to the said borrower for the improvement is Eleven Thousand Five Hundred Thirty-three and 90/100 - - - - - - - - Dollars, ($ 11,533.90), less such amounts as may become due or payable for insurance premiums, interest on building loan mortgages, ground rent, taxes, assessments, water rents and sewer rents accruing during the making of the improvement.

This statement is made pursuant to Section 22 of the Lien Law of the State of New York. The reason why this statement is made by the deponent and not by the borrower mentioned herein, is that said borrower is a corporation and the deponent is an officer thereof, viz:

The facts herein stated are true to the knowledge of the deponent.

Sworn to before me this 14th day of March 19--.

/s/ Richard Roe
Notary Public, Nassau County, N. Y.
Nassau County Clerk's No. 3015
My commission expires March 31, 19--

/s/ George Ace

Title Guarantee and Trust Company, New York, New York

A Building Loan Contract (Concluded)

to the lender, will file the plans and specifications with the proper government authorities, and will obtain the necessary building permits.

An affidavit is generally included in the building loan agreement. This affidavit shows all of the expenses outside of the actual cost of construction of the building and states the amount available for improvements. Two of these expenses are architect's fees and broker's commissions.

In Chapter 6 the situation in which a builder obtained land by means of a purchase money mortgage was discussed. In practice, before the builder enters into negotiations for the land, he receives a commitment from his lender for the building loan. Often the lender will not commit himself in writing on this, but it should be understood between the builder and the lender that the lender will give him the loan.[5]

Often when the builder reaches the proper stage of construction, he pays to the purchase money mortgagee the amount due on that particular lot and receives a partial release of mortgage from the purchase money mortgagee.

When the building is completed and the money, under the terms of the building loan, has been completely transferred to the builder, the builder may deliver to the lender a "permanent" mortgage on the premises.

The builder will generally place the house on the market when it reaches an advanced stage of construction or completion. When he finds a purchaser, he enters into a contract of sale with that purchaser. The purchaser will ordinarily be financed by the same lending institution as was the builder. The lender will then lend money to the purchaser and obtain a note or bond and a mortgage on the premises. The builder will pay off the building loan, and the difference between that and the purchase price will be his profit.

OTHER REAL ESTATE INSTRUMENTS

The Affidavit of Title

The *affidavit of title* is a sworn statement made by the owner of a parcel of real property stating that he actually is the owner of the

[5] Sometimes written commitments are given to facilitate the purchase of materials by the builder, but only when builders have an outstanding credit rating.

AFFIDAVIT OF TITLE

STATE OF NEW YORK, COUNTY OF Westchester **ss.:**

TITLE No. ....

Robert Smith , being duly sworn, says:
I reside at No. 18 Wood Road, White Plains, State of New York
I am the ①
owner in fee simple of premises known at 18 Wood Road, White Plains, New York, and am the grantee described in a certain deed of said premises recorded in the Register's Office of Westchester County in Liber 1928 of Conveyances, page 83 .

Said premises have been in my ~~its~~ possession since 19--; that my ~~its~~ possession thereof has been peaceable and undisturbed, and the title thereto has never been disputed, questioned or rejected, nor insurance thereof refused, as far as I know. I know of no facts by reason of which said possession or title might be called in question, or by reason of which any claim to any part of said premises or any interest therein adverse to me ~~it~~ might be set up. There are no judgments against me ~~it~~ unpaid or unsatisfied of record entered in any court of this state, or of the United States, and said premises are, as far as I know, free from all leases, mortgages, taxes, assessments, water charges and other liens and encumbrances, except none.

Said premises are now occupied by your deponent

No proceedings in bankruptcy have ever been instituted by or against me ~~it~~ in any court or before any officer of any state, or of the United States, nor have I ~~has it~~ at any time made an assignment for the benefit of creditors, nor an assignment, now in effect, of the rents of said premises or any part thereof.

② I am a citizen of the United States, and am more than 21 years old. I am by occupation a plumber . I am married to Mary Smith who is over the age of 21 years and is competent to convey or mortgage real estate. I was married to her on the 17th day of February, 19--. I have never been married to any other person now living. I have not been known by any other name during the past ten years.

③ That the charter of said corporation is in full force and effect and no proceeding is pending for its dissolution or annulment. That all license and franchise taxes due and payable by said corporation have been paid in full.

There are no actions pending affecting said premises. That no repairs, alterations or improvements have been made to said premises which have not been completed more than four months prior to the date hereof. There are no facts known to me relating to the title to said premises which have not been set forth in this affidavit.

This affidavit is made to induce Arthur Stevens

to accept a conveyance of ~~on~~ said premises, and to induce Title Guarantee and Trust Company to issue its policy of title insurance numbered above covering said premises knowing that they will rely on the statements herein made.

Sworn to before me this 18th day of April , 19-- .

/s/ Robert Smith

Richard Roe
Notary Public, County of Westchester, N. Y.
Westchester County Clerk's No. 2012
My commission expires March 31, 19--

Title Guarantee and Trust Company, New York, New York

An Affidavit of Title

① If owner is a corporation, fill in office held by deponent and name of corporation.
② This paragraph to be omitted if owner is a corporation.
③ This paragraph to be omitted if owner is not a corporation.

property in question. It states further that his possession has never been disturbed, that his title is free and clear of encumbrances, and that no repairs, alterations, or improvements, which have been completed for no longer than the period of filing a mechanic's lien prior to the date of the instrument, have been made to the premises.

A further statement is made to the effect that the affidavit was made to induce the buyer to accept a deed or to induce the mortgagee to give a mortgage on the premises. This statement is inserted in the instrument in order to allow the admission of the affidavit in evidence and to establish proof of fraud in the event that the affiant (one who makes an affidavit) has made false statements.

The instrument establishes the identity of the person offering the deed at a closing to be the same person as appears from the record. Suppose that the judgment roll shows that John Smith has a judgment entered against him. John Smith, the grantor, states that the judgment is against another John Smith and that he is willing to sign the affidavit because it is in fact another John Smith against whom the judgment is recorded. In this case, the affidavit of title will state: "That there are no judgments against me unpaid or unsatisfied of record entered in any court of this state or of the United States. . . ."

This instrument might be used effectively in those states where the lien laws are lax, or where there is a fear that the seller might have unpaid bills for improvements on the premises. As previously mentioned, in New York State the warranty deed provides that the seller of a parcel of real property is required to hold the proceeds from the sale as a trust fund to apply toward the cost of any improvements that were made to the property, and that he will do so before using any part of the monies for any other purpose. Most states do not have such a provision either in the statutes or in the warranty deed. The occasion arises many times in those states when the broker or attorney checking title is suspicious of the seller. For example, he may believe that the seller has caused improvements to be made on the premises without having paid for them. In this case the broker, or attorney, at the closing, might obtain an affidavit of title from the seller. This affidavit should contain the statement, "That there are no actions pending affecting said premises. That no repairs, alterations, or improvements have been made to said premises, which have not been completed more than (insert here the time limit for the filing of a mechanic's lien in the state) prior to the date hereof."

Power of Attorney

The *power of attorney* authorizes an agent to perform certain acts in the place and stead of a principal. For the purposes of real estate, it enables the agent to convey property, mortgage the property of the principal, or do any other acts that might be done concerning real property if the principal were present. The power of attorney is acknowledged and recorded in the county in which the real property in question is located. For example, if someone is leaving a state and turns his real property over to a broker to be disposed of, he may execute the proper form of power of attorney and record it. If the broker makes a sale, he is empowered to sign the deed. He signs it in the name of the owner, and under the signature signs his own name as attorney-in-fact. If the owner has died prior to the time of the signing of the deed, then the transaction is invalid because death of the principal terminates the agency. If the grantor of the power becomes insane, the agency also terminates.

The general rule that an agency may be terminated by the principal at anytime applies here, too. However, it is slightly more difficult than in the case of the ordinary agency. If the owner wishes to terminate the agency when a power of attorney has been given and recorded, the owner must, in most states, prepare a revocation and record it in the office of the clerk of the county in which the original power of attorney was recorded. More than one person may be named to act as attorney-in-fact for a principal. In this case, it is necessary only to name the parties in the power of attorney and to state that they have been authorized to act jointly.

Party Wall Agreements

A *party wall* is a dividing wall between two buildings to be used equally for all the purposes of an exterior wall by both parties, that is, by the respective owners of both houses.[6]

In highly developed urban areas where property values are high, the owners of property frequently take advantage of the full width of their lots by building to the boundary line. Both owners of adjoining properties have this right. Economically, it is better to

[6] *Harber* v. *Evans*, 101 Mo. 661, 665; 14 S.W. 750.

GENERAL POWER OF ATTORNEY

Notice: The powers granted by this document are broad and sweeping. They are defined in New York General Business Law, Article 13, sections 222-234, which expressly permits the use of any other or different form of power of attorney desired by the parties concerned.

KNOW ALL MEN BY THESE PRESENTS, which are intended to constitute a **GENERAL POWER OF ATTORNEY** pursuant to Article 13 of the New York General Business Law:

That I, Albert Smith

residing at No. 36 Ocean Avenue, Village of Patchogue, Town of Brookhaven, County of Suffolk, State of New York,

do hereby appoint Fred Skinner

residing at No. 16 Jennings Avenue, Village of Patchogue, Town of Brookhaven, County of Suffolk, State of New York,

my attorney(s)-in-fact TO ACT (a)

FIRST: in my name, place and stead in any way which I myself could do, if I were personally present, with respect to the following matters as each of them is defined in Article 13 of the New York General Business Law to the extent that I am permitted by law to act through an agent:

[Strike out and initial in the opposite box any one or more of the subdivisions as to which the principal does NOT desire to give the agent authority. Such elimination of any one or more of subdivisions (A) to (K), inclusive, shall automatically constitute an elimination also of subdivision (L).]

To strike out any subdivision the principal must draw a line through the text of that subdivision AND write his initials in the box opposite.

(A)	real estate transactions;	[ ]
(B)	chattel and goods transactions;	[ ]
(C)	bond, share and commodity transactions;	[ ]
(D)	banking transactions;	[ ]
(E)	business operating transactions;	[ ]
(F)	insurance transactions;	[ ]
(G)	estate transactions;	[ ]
(H)	claims and litigation;	[ ]
(I)	personal relationships and affairs;	[ ]
(J)	benefits from military service;	[ ]
(K)	records, reports and statements;	[ ]
(L)	all other matters;	[ ]

(b)

SECOND: with full and unqualified authority to delegate any or all of the foregoing powers to any person or persons whom my attorney(s)-in-fact shall select.

I will not question the sufficiency of any instrument executed by my said attorney(s)-in-fact pursuant to this power notwithstanding that the instrument fails to recite the consideration therefor or recites merely a nominal consideration; any person dealing with the subject matter of such instrument may do so as if full consideration thereof had been expressed therein.

IN WITNESS WHEREOF I have hereunto signed my name and affixed my seal this 12th day of March 19--.

/s/ Albert Smith , (Seal)
(Signature of Principal)

(a) *If more than one agent is designated and the principal wishes each agent alone to be able to exercise the power conferred, insert in this blank the word "severally." Failure to make any insertion or the insertion of the word "jointly" will require the agents to act jointly.*

(b) *Special provisions and limitations may be included in the statutory short form power of attorney only if they conform to the requirements of section two hundred thirty-four of Article 13 of the New York General Business Law.*

Acknowledgment

Title Guarantee and Trust Company, New York, New York

A Power of Attorney

have a common wall between the two buildings. This common wall is called the party wall.

The building of the party wall is preceded by an agreement between the two parties called the *party wall agreement*. Several situations are likely to develop. For example, assume lot number 1 is owned by *A* and lot number 2 is owned by *B*. *A* desires to build, but *B* does not wish to build at that time. *A* and *B* may enter into an agreement which provides that *B* may use the wall if he at anytime decides to build on his lot, and when he does decide to build, that he pay *A* one half the cost of the wall. The agreement will also usually provide that one half the wall is to be constructed on the land of *A* and one half is to be constructed on the land of *B*. There will also be included any specifications as to the construction of the wall.

Another situation that commonly arises is when *A* owns two lots and builds two buildings, but with one common wall between. If *A* then sells one of the buildings to *B*, the courts will presume that the buyer has the right to support from the remaining building and that *A* also has a right to support from the building that he has sold. This does not infer the right to support for new construction but merely the right to support between the existing buildings.

An illustration of a party wall agreement is on page 248.

The Beam Right Agreement

The *beam right agreement* is an agreement between two adjoining landowners granting permission for one of the parties to use the wall of another as a party wall and to set his beams into it. Ordinarily, the wall so used does not stand on the dividing line between the adjoining lots, and therefore, technically speaking, is not a party wall. The beam right agreement is used in order to avoid the expense of building a wall when the wall of the neighbor can be used with the same degree of efficiency as a new wall. An illustration of a beam right agreement appears on page 249.

Restriction Agreement

A *restriction agreement* is an agreement between property owners limiting the use of occupancy of real estate. Restrictions are placed upon land by a "restrictive covenant" in a deed.

PARTY WALL AGREEMENT

AGREEMENT made the 10th day of July 19-- between Louis Owens, residing at 1423 East 53d Street, Borough of Manhattan, City and State of New York, party of the first part, and Frank Lowey residing at 121 West 49th Street, Borough of Manhattan, City and State of New York, party of the second part,

WITNESSETH

WHEREAS, the party of the first part is the owner of the premises located and described as follows:

(here follows a complete legal description of the property of the party of the first part)

and

WHEREAS, the party of the second part is the owner of the premises described as follows:

(here follows a complete legal description of the property of the party of the second part)

which said premises adjoin the aforesaid premises of the party of the first part; and

WHEREAS, the party of the first part is about to erect a building upon the said premises owned by him and it is desired that the south wall of said contemplated building be located on the dividing line between the said premises of the parties and that said wall should be a party wall and constructed for one-half its thickness on each side of the line dividing said premises of each party,

NOW, THEREFORE, in consideration of One and 00/100 ($1) Dollars and other good and valuable consideration and the mutual covenants herein the parties mutually covenant and agree for themselves, their respective heirs and assigns as follows:

FIRST: That the said contemplated wall shall be used and maintained as a party wall forever and that the party of the first part shall be licensed and permitted to enter upon the premises of the party of the second part to make necessary excavations for the erection of the said wall and for the construction thereof.

SECOND: The said wall shall be built as follows: (here is inserted a complete description of the wall and where it is to be located)

THIRD: The cost and expense of construction of the said wall shall be borne solely by the party of the first part and the party of the first part agrees to indemnify and hold the party of the second part harmless from any cost, expense or liability by reason of the construction of said party wall.

FOURTH: The party of the second part shall have the full right to use the said party wall for the insertion of beams or otherwise up to the point where it shall have been built.

FIFTH: If the said wall is at any time extended after the original construction, the cost of such extension shall be paid by the party making such extension.

SIXTH: If it shall become necessary to repair or rebuild the wall or any portion of the wall as constructed or extended, the cost of repairing and/or such rebuilding, as to such portions of the wall at the time used by both the parties, shall be borne equally by both parties; as to the remaining portions, such repairing and/or rebuilding shall be wholly at the expense of the party who shall exclusively use that portion.

SEVENTH: If and when the said wall is rebuilt, it shall stand upon the same place and be of the same or similar materials and of the same proportions as the contemplated wall described.

EIGHTH: This agreement shall be perpetual and shall be a covenant running with the land, provided, however, that nothing herein shall be construed as a conveyance by either party of his respective rights in the fee of the land upon which the said party wall shall stand.

IN WITNESS WHEREOF, the parties hereto have signed and sealed this Agreement the day and year first above written.

IN THE PRESENCE OF:

/s/ Richard Roe

/s/ Louis Owens L.S.
/s/ Frank Lowey L.S.

STATE OF NEW YORK, COUNTY OF New York **ss.:**

On the 10th day of June , one thousand nine hundred and . . . before me came Louis Owens and Frank Lowey to be known to be the individuals described in, and who executed the foregoing instrument, and acknowledged that they executed the same.

/s/ Richard Roe
Notary Public, County of New York

A Party Wall Agreement

BEAM RIGHT AGREEMENT

This indenture made this 4th day of December, 19--, between Franklin Johnson of 30 Main Street, Poughkeepsie, New York, party of the first part and William Phillips of 28 Main Street, Poughkeepsie, New York, party of the second part:

WITNESSETH:

WHEREAS, the party of the first part is the owner in fee of the lot known as number 18 Brown Street, Poughkeepsie, New York, and the party of the second part is the owner in fee of the lot known as number 20 Brown Street, Poughkeepsie, New York, immediately adjoining to and on the north side of said lot, on which lots respectively the parties are about to erect brick buildings; and

WHEREAS, it has been agreed between them that the party of the first part shall be entitled to the use of a wall, upon the terms, conditions, and considerations, hereinafter mentioned, the wall to be used as a party wall, standing and being entirely on said lot of the party of the first part,

NOW, THEREFORE, THIS AGREEMENT WITNESSETH, that the party of the first part in consideration of the sum of One Thousand and 00/100 ($1,000) dollars to him in hand paid by the party of the second part receipt of which is hereby acknowledged, agrees immediately to build and erect a wall on the north side of said lot number 18 Brown Street so that the north side of said wall shall join the south side of said lot of the party of the second part to be built 15 feet westerly from the westerly side of Brown Street, and 48 feet high above the sidewalk; and the party of the first part hereby grants and conveys to the party of the second part, his heirs and assigns, the right to use said wall as a party, in the erection of a building on said lot number 18 Brown Street, and for that purpose to insert the beams of the building on the said lot into the wall so to be built by the party of the first part, to the extent of six inches, and for the same purpose, to insert or tie the courses of the front and rear walls into said party wall as may be necessary, and to keep and maintain such use of said party wall so long as said wall shall stand.

The parties mutually covenant and agree, that if it shall hereafter become necessary to repair or rebuild the whole, or any portion of said party wall, the expense of such repairing or rebuilding shall be borne equally by them, their respective heirs and assigns and that whenever said party wall, or any portion thereof, shall be rebuilt, it shall be erected on the same spot where it is now to stand, and shall be of the same size, and the same or similar materials, and of like quality, and that this agreement shall be perpetual and all times be construed as a covenant running with the land; but that no part of the fee of the soil upon which the wall of the party of the first part, above described is to stand, shall pass to or be vested in the party of the second part or his heirs or assigns, by virtue of this agreement.

IN WITNESS WHEREOF, the parties have signed and sealed this agreement the day and year first above written.

In the presence of:
/s/ Richard Roe

/s/ Franklin Johnson L.S.
/s/ William Phillips L.S.

Acknowledgment

A Beam Right Agreement

These restrictive covenants are usually placed in the deed by a developer. For example, when a large tract of land is divided into lots, the subdivider may feel that it will be advantageous to place restrictive covenants in the deed. He may therefore provide that all houses placed on the property be of a certain size, of a certain value, or a certain distance from the street. In a sense these restrictive covenants are an attempt on the part of an individual through private agreement to accomplish much the same ends as is done by municipalities through the enactment of zoning ordinances (which are limitations placed upon the land by municipalities).

The courts will generally uphold only those restrictions which are reasonable in character and will not enforce them if the character of a neighborhood has so changed that the original beneficial purpose for which the restrictions were imposed can no longer be achieved.

A typical restrictive covenant in a deed might be worded as follows:

> This conveyance is made upon the express condition, and the party of the second part covenants that the premises shall be used for residential purposes only, and the premises to be used for no other purpose than those herein specified.

These restrictive covenants are covenants running with the land and are binding upon the heirs and assigns of the parties.

Joint Driveway Easement Agreement

An agreement between two parties permitting each of them to use a part of the other's land as a driveway is a *joint driveway easement*.

This so-called "right-of-way" can be created either by a builder or by an agreement between adjoining landowners. When it is created by a builder, a clause is usually inserted into a deed, after the description of the property being conveyed, as follows:

> Together with an easement for a right-of-way for ingress and egress of pleasure automobiles over the easterly six feet of the premises adjoining the above described premises on the west.

If the right-of-way or joint driveway is to be created by agreement, the agreement is signed by the parties, acknowledged, and

JOINT DRIVEWAY AGREEMENT

THIS INDENTURE made and entered into this 3d day of April, 19-- between Robert Bell, residing at 365 Clinton Street, Village of Bay Shore, Town of Islip, County of Suffolk, State of New York, , party of the first part,

and Franklin Page, residing at 363 Clinton Avenue, Village of Bay Shore, Town of Islip, County of Suffolk, State of New York, , party of the second part,

WITNESSETH: That the party of the first part in consideration of the sum of One and 00/100 ($1) Dollars and other good and valuable consideration, lawful money of the United States, to him in hand paid by the party of the second part, does hereby remise, release and forever quitclaim unto the party of the second part his heirs and assigns a right to use a driveway jointly with the party of the first part his heirs and assigns, for all ordinary purposes of ingress and egress, over the same, leading from Main Street on the east side of the premises of the party of the first part, far enough to allow the party of the second part to enter upon his premises from the south.

IN WITNESS WHEREOF, the party of the first part has hereunto set his hand and seal; the day and year first above written.

/s/ Robert Bell (L.S.)

STATE OF NEW YORK, COUNTY OF Suffolk **ss.:**

On the 3d day of April, 19--, before me personally came Robert Bell, to me known to be the individual described in and who executed the foregoing instrument and that he executed the same.

/s/ Richard Roe
Notary Public, Suffolk County, N. Y.

A Joint Driveway Agreement

recorded. This instrument merely recites the names of the parties, a consideration, and a description of the easement.

Release of Easement

A *release of easement* is an agreement between the dominant tenement and servient tenement removing an easement.

The release of the easement recites the instrument, if any, by which the dominant tenement received the easement, the names of the parties, and a statement substantially as follows:

> ". . . in consideration of $10 and other good and valuable consideration, I do hereby release, remit, and quitclaim to the said

John Doe his heirs and assigns forever, the said right-of-way and easement described as follows: . . . ."

Then follows the description of the easement as contained in the original grant. The instrument should be recorded in the office of clerk of the county in which the property is located.

Declaration of Homestead

The *declaration of homestead* is used in the states having homestead laws. In those states where the family owns and occupies a tract of land as their home, the declaration of homestead may be filed. This instrument is filed by the husband.[7] It states that the filer is married; it describes the land briefly; and it declares an estimated value of the homestead. After it is acknowledged, it is filed in the office of the clerk of the county in which the property is located.

In some states, homestead rights attach only to a certain area; in others, homestead rights attach only in terms of a limited value. In most states homestead rights do not attach unless the declaration is completed and properly filed.

Once the homestead has been created, it cannot be sold at a forced sale for the payment of debts. It cannot be mortgaged during the lifetime of the husband and the wife without the consent of both. At the death of the husband, the property may be occupied by the widow and the children during the life of the widow and the minority of the children. The latter is a special provision not generally applicable to all homesteads.

Location Notice of a Placer Claim

In those states where mining is prevalent, there are a number of instruments concerning mining properties of which the broker should be aware. The *location notice of a placer claim* is one which describes the placer claim by metes and bounds beginning with a stake not less than four inches in diameter and not less than four feet high. This instrument is acknowledged by the discoverer of the claim as locater

[7] In California and some other states the declaration may be filed by a head of a family, in addition to the husband. In Florida the effect of a homestead declaration by the head of the family will exempt the first $5,000 of the assessed value from the real property tax.

DECLARATION OF HOMESTEAD

KNOW ALL MEN BY THESE PRESENTS: That I do hereby certify and declare that I am married, and that I am the head of a family and that I do now, at the time of making this declaration, actually reside with my family on the land and premises hereinafter described. That my family consists of Mary Smith and my son, John Smith . That the land and premises on which I reside are situated in Moscow , County of Latah , State of Idaho and bounded and described as follows, to-wit:

(here follows complete legal description)

That it is my intention to use and claim the said lot of land and premises above described, together with the dwelling house and all appurtenances thereon, as a Homestead, and I do hereby select and claim the same as a Homestead for the joint benefit of myself and my wife, Mary Smith, and my son, John Smith , and that I have not heretofore claimed the same as a Homestead. That the actual cash value of said property, I estimate to be Six Thousand and 00/100 ($6,000) - - - - - - - - Dollars.

IN WITNESS WHEREOF we have hereunto set our hands and seals this 23d day of September , A. D., 19--.

Signed and sealed in presence of

/s/ Roger Jones

/s/ Frank Smith (Seal)
/s/ Mary Smith (Seal)

Declaration of Homestead

and is filed in the office of the clerk of the county in which the claim is located. The county clerk records the document in a book (liber) of placer claims.

Quartz Mining Location Notice

The *quartz mining location notice* varies slightly from the notice of location of a placer claim. It states that the person making the claim is a citizen of the United States,

> . . . conforming to the mining laws thereof and of the state of . . . and the local rules, regulations, and customs of miners.

There follows a description of the property and the location of the discovery monument. It names the adjoining claims, if any, and then states:

> All the monuments aforesaid are marked upon the side facing toward the discovery with the name of the claim on the corner or

end center, which each of said monuments represents, and all of said monuments are at least four inches in diameter and at least four feet high above the ground.

The instrument is acknowledged and recorded in the office of the clerk of the county in which the property is located; there it is entered in the book of mining claims.[8]

QUESTIONS FOR REVIEW

1. What is a *partial release* and how is it used?
2. The reduction certificate is sometimes thought of as being the counterpart of an estoppel certificate. Explain.
3. What is a *participation agreement*? How could the participation agreement be used to finance the purchase of a high-priced parcel of real property?
4. What function does the satisfaction or release of mortgage perform?
5. What situation may give rise to the use of an extension agreement?
6. Suppose you were going abroad for an extended trip. You list a house at a firm price with a realtor. You tell him that if he obtains a good offer, he should close the deal and deposit the funds in your bank account. How can he do this if you are abroad?
7. How can an affidavit of title be used as protection against mechanic's liens?

PROBLEMS

1. Assume that you are the mortgagee on Lot #9 of the map of the Security Acres Development Company located in your city and state. Ralph Shepherd, who also lives in your city and state, is the mortgagor. He pays you the full amount of the mortgage. Prepare the necessary papers for him.
2. Assume that you are a builder and that a bank in your city and state agrees to lend you $10,000 while you are building on Lot #56 of the map of Security Acres Development Company located in your city

[8] A broker operating in territory where there is mining activity should also be familiar with the need for filing annually a Proof of Labor, a Notice of Intention to Hold Mining Claims, and especially the deed to a mining claim as was discussed in detail in Chapter 5.

and state. You have purchased Lots 1-60 on a purchase money mortgage from Robert Slater, and he has agreed to release them to you upon the payment of $500 on each lot. You begin to build and finally complete the building and enter into a contract for $12,000 for the sale of the property with Howard Maxwell also of your city and state. The bank which has given you the building loan agrees to give Maxwell a twenty-year, self-amortizing mortgage in the amount of $9,000. Draw all of the necessary papers.

3. Some brokers spend part of their time in what is sometimes called "mortgage brokerage." This means that for a commission they negotiate the sale of mortgages. Frequently, these mortgages with which they deal are second mortgages. They are frequently sold at a percentage of face value called a discount. This will be detailed later in the text. Assume, then, a second mortgage with a face value of $1,250 and a discount of 23 percent. The broker's commission is 2.5 percent. An investor is willing to buy the mortgage.
   (a) How much cash does the investor pay?
   (b) What is the net to the seller?
   (c) What should the investor do to protect himself against possible fraud on the part of the seller?
   (d) What instrument(s) should the investor require?
   (e) If the mortgage is due in two years and calls for 7 percent interest, what is the effective rate of return?

4. Mr. Rogers owns a vacant parcel of land in an area rapidly being "built up" by commercial buildings. He thought of constructing an office building but decided the time was not appropriate. The adjoining lot is owned by Mr. Speculator who decides to build. He feels cramped for space and approaches Mr. Rogers to "make a deal" but does not wish to buy any additional land.
   (a) What can Mr. Speculator propose to Mr. Rogers?
   (b) Mr. Speculator discovers Mr. Rogers' lot is encumbered by an extremely high mortgage. What may be done to remove this obstacle?

5. You are a developer of an office building. Ace Federal Savings and Loan Association writes you a letter saying that upon completion of building they will give you a permanent loan of $100,000 at 8¾ percent. Prepare this necessary instrument assuming that the Friendly National Bank will give you $85,000 interim financing.

SUGGESTED READINGS

Lusk, Harold F. *Law of the Real Estate Business,* Rev. ed. Homewood, Illinois: Richard D. Irwin, Inc., 1965. Ch. XV.

Ring, Alfred A. *Real Estate Principles and Practices,* 7th ed. Englewood Cliffs, New Jersey: Prentice-Hall, Inc., 1972. Chapter 11.

Chapter 9

Liens

A *lien* is a hold or claim which one person has upon the property of another as security for a debt or charge against the property of another. There are two parties involved in the lien, the lienor and the lienee. The *lienor* is the person who owns or holds a lien, and the *lienee* is the person whose property is subject to a lien.

The ownership of a lien is capable of being transferred, and this is done by means of an assignment. For example, a mortgage may be a lien; and the ownership of the mortgage (lien) is transferred, as we saw in Chapter 8, by means of the assignment of mortgage.

The various types of liens exist either by virtue of an appropriate statute or by virtue of the common law. The former is best illustrated by the mechanic's lien, which is discussed below, and the latter by the innkeeper's lien, which gives the owner of an inn the right to seize the luggage of a lodger who has not paid for his board and room.

There are two types of real property liens: statutory and equitable liens. *Statutory liens* are created by statute. *Equitable liens* are not rights in the land itself but personal obligations or rights against the owner or the grantor of the land, which the courts will enforce under their equitable jurisdiction. An equitable lien arises when the owner makes a written agreement that his land shall be security for some obligation (a mortgage, for example). In the final analysis, the courts will declare the existence of equitable liens mainly because considerations of right and justice under the circumstances seem to require such action. All of the liens with which we are concerned are statutory liens, with the possible exception of the vendor's and vendee's lien. In most states this, too, is a statutory lien, but in some jurisdictions it is an equitable lien by means of which the unpaid vendor has an equitable lien upon the land for the remainder of the purchase price.

The liens against real property with which we are concerned may be further classified as specific liens and general liens. The *specific lien* affects only a specified piece or pieces of real property; the *general lien* affects all of the property of a debtor.

THE MECHANIC'S LIEN

The *mechanic's lien*, created solely by statute, gives the right of lien to those persons who have furnished work or materials for the improvement of real property. The persons who are entitled to the lien include contractors, subcontractors, laborers, materialmen, engineers, and architects.

The underlying basis of the right of lien lies in the fact that as a result of the work done, or materials furnished a property, the property is improved. *Improvement* means generally the erection, alteration, or repair of any structure upon, connected with, or beneath the surface of any real property. Some state laws define improvement as follows:

> (Improvement) . . . shall also include any work done or materials furnished for its (the structure's) permanent improvement, and shall also include any work done or materials furnished in equipping any such structure with any chandeliers, brackets or other fixtures or apparatus for supplying gas or electric light, and shall also include the drawing by any architect or engineer or surveyor of any plans or specifications or survey, which are prepared for or used in connection with such improvements, and

shall also include the value of materials manufactured for but not delivered to the property.[1]

Because the lien is based on the idea of improvement, it can be placed against only the improved property. For example, *A* owns two parcels of property. *B* works on one of them and is not paid. His right to a lien exists against only the property on which he has actually worked. The right of lien does not exist against both parcels of property.

Because the mechanic's lien is created by statute, all of the requirements must be strictly complied with. If they are not, the lien may prove ineffective.

Consent or Contract of Owner to Improvement

Although the lien laws are different among the states, they may be generally classified as either contract statutes or consent statutes. In states having the *contract statutes*, the lienor must show that the improvement was made at the *request* of the owner or his agent. This is to prevent the owner from having a lien placed on his property where he has not requested the improvement. For example, when a tenant orders work done on the landlord's house without the request of the landlord, the person ordinarily entitled to the lien cannot place a lien on the landlord's property. In other states it is enough to show that the owner or his agent *consented* to the improvement. These statutes are called *consent statutes.*

Notice of Mechanic's Lien

The first step in the establishment of the mechanic's lien is the filing of a notice of mechanic's lien. After the notice is prepared, the original is generally filed with the clerk of the county in which the property is located, and a copy of the notice is mailed by registered mail to the owner of the property against which the lien is being placed, although in some states a mailed notice is not required.

Because the lien is created by statute, there must be strict compliance with the statute. Therefore, the notice of lien must be properly drawn. The notice gives the name of the lienor, the name of the

[1] New York Lien Law (Section 2).

NOTICE OF MECHANIC'S LIEN (New York Form)

To the clerk of the County of Westchester and to all others whom it may concern:
PLEASE TAKE NOTICE THAT ① John Lienor
residing at ② 2675 East Hardy Way
City of Jamaica County of Westchester
has and claims a lien for principal and interest for the value and the agreed price of the labor and materials hereinafter mentioned upon the real property hereinafter described and upon the improvements, pursuant to the provisions of the Lien Law of the State of New York and all the acts and laws amendatory thereof, as follows:

1. The name of the owner of the real property against whose interest therein a lien is claimed and the interest of the owner, as far as known to the lienor, is as follows:

③ Walter Owner
and his interest in the said property is that of the owner in fee.

2. The name of the person by whom the lienor was employed and to whom he furnished materials is ④ Jerry Contractor

3. The labor performed and the materials furnished and the agreed price thereof are as follows:

All of the electrical work including wiring, electrical fixtures and all other articles necessary to complete the building on the premises hereinafter described and all the work and labor in installing said materials in said building, and the agreed price and the value of such materials was Two Thousand Five Hundred and 00/100 ($2,500) - - - - - - - - - - - - - - - - - - dollars and the reasonable value of certain extra work, included in the materials and labor above enumerated, was the sum of Two Hundred and 00/100 ($200) - - - - - - - - dollars, which work and materials were directed to be performed and furnished by the person with whom the lienor made the contract above stated.

4. The amount unpaid to the lienor for such labor and material is the sum of
One Thousand and 00/100 ($1,000) - - - - - - - - - - - - - - - - dollars.

5. The time when the first item of said work was performed was the ⑤ 12th day of April , 19--, and the first item of materials was furnished on the ⑤ 12th day of April , 19--, and the time when the last item or work was performed was the ⑤ 31st day of May , 19--.

6. The property subject to this lien is known as ⑥ (legal description)

dated the 28th day of July , 19--.

/s/ John Lienor

____
Acknowledgment

A Notice of Mechanic's Lien

The filing of the above notice with the county clerk creates the mechanic's lien against the property therein described.

① The name of the lienor.
② The address of the lienor.
③ The name of the owner.
④ If the lienor is a contractor or subcontractor, the name of the person with whom the contract was made is inserted here.
⑤ The reason for inserting these dates is to ascertain that the lien is filed within the statutory period.
⑥ Here is inserted a description of the property; the more complete, the better.

party with whom the lienor entered into the contract, a description of the labor performed, and the materials furnished for the job. In addition, the notice states the contract price, the amount paid under the contract, and the balance remaining due and unpaid. The notice states, too, the date of commencing the work, the date when the first items of materials were furnished, and the date of completing the work, or furnishing the last items of materials. The property is also described and the description must sufficiently identify the property. The notice is verified by the lienor or his agent.

Time in Which to File

In most states, the notice of lien also contains a statement regarding the time in which to file. Generally, it states:

> that four months have not elapsed dating from the last item of work performed, and dating from the last items of materials furnished. . . .

The purpose of this statement is to show compliance with the statute when, for example, the statute states that the notice must be filed within four months after the last work or last items of materials are furnished. Although most state statutes require that the lien be filed within four months, other states vary. They may vary, too, the time in which the materialman has a right to file and the time in which the laborer has a right to file. For example, in Idaho and Oregon, the materialman must file within sixty days after the last items of materials are furnished; the laborer must file within ninety days after he has performed his last work.

The time in which to file varies greatly among the states. In Colorado, for example, a laborer has only 30 days within which to file, while contractors and subcontractors have 90 days within which to file. To be on the safe side, one should examine the laws of each state.

Priority

The problem concerning the priority of liens may be divided into two parts: first, between various mechanic's liens; second, between the mechanic's lien and the mortgage.

The priority that establishes the rights between the various mechanic's liens that may be placed against a property is fixed by the time of recording. When the notice of lien reaches the county clerk's office, the date and time of the recording are stamped on the notice of lien; and a note indicating the time of recording is entered in the proper index. This establishes the priority. The first notice of mechanic's lien filed has the prior right over subsequently filed notices of liens.

In some states, the lien of the mechanic is attached when he begins his work. The date of priority is not dependent upon the actual filing of the notice; although without any filing within the requisite period, the lien may be lost. In these states, a number of situations can arise. For example, the owner has a mortgage on the property and *A* commences work. In this case, the rights of the mortgagee are superior to *A*. But if *A* begins work and then the owner mortgages the property, *A's* lien will be superior to the mortgage even though he has not yet filed the notice. The third situation that can arise in these states is when there is no mortgage and *A* commences work. The owner then mortgages the property, and hires *B*. In this case, the right of *A* is superior to the mortgagee, but the right of the mortgagee is superior to *B* who began working after the mortgage was recorded.

The situation varies among the states as to the rights of the mechanic's lien over the rights of a mortgagee. In New York, for example, if the mechanic's lien is filed before the mortgage is recorded, the rights of the lienor are superior to the rights of the mortgagee. On the other hand, if the mortgage is recorded prior to the filing of the lien, the mortgagee's rights are superior. The reason for this is that the lien does not attach until it is actually filed. The states following this rule are said to operate under the "New York System" of mechanic's liens.

In most states, the lien will date back to the day of the beginning of the job by the prime contractor. For example, a prime contractor begins a job on July 1. On August 1, the owner obtains a mortgage on the premises. On August 15, the prime contractor hires a painter as a subcontractor to finish up the job. In these states, the painter will have a lien against the premises superior to that of the mortgagee, his time relating back to the commencement of the job by the prime contractor, which was July 1.

In still other states, it is the date of the contract that controls, even though work has not commenced. For example, on July 1 a contract is entered into between an owner and a prime contractor; a mortgage is placed on the property on August 1; and work is actually commenced on August 15. The lien in this case relates back to the agreement between the owner and the prime contractor. Therefore, the lien takes priority over the mortgage.[2]

Length of the Lien

The mere filing of the lien does not in itself entitle the lienor to his money. The lienor may have one to three years to commence his action to enforce his lien.[3] The enforcement of the lien is by a foreclosure action handled in much the same manner as the foreclosure of a mortgage that has been defaulted.

Lis Pendens

The *lis pendens* is a notice of a pendency of action. (See page 264.) It is, in effect, constructive notice to a prospective purchaser, or any party in interest, that an action is pending involving a particular parcel of property. In view of the time limits set by the several states for the commencement of an action to foreclose a mechanic's lien, the lis pendens takes on an additional importance. The filing of the lis pendens prevents the lapsing of the lien within the time limit after the filing of the notice of mechanic's lien. In other words, when the time limit of the lien is one year, and a lis pendens or notice of action to foreclose the mechanic's lien is filed, then the mere passage of one year does not in itself cause the lien to lapse.[4]

---

[2] In Arizona, Arkansas, California, Connecticut, Delaware, District of Columbia, Georgia, Idaho, Iowa, Kansas, Louisiana, Michigan, Minnesota, Montana, Nebraska, Nevada, New Hampshire, New Mexico, Ohio, Oklahoma, Rhode Island, Tennessee, Utah, Washington, West Virginia, and Wisconsin mechanic's liens growing out of a particular job relate back to the beginning of the job. In Illinois and Maine a mechanic's lien attaches to the land on the date on which the owner contracted for improvements.

[3] In Colorado and Oregon the lienor must begin his action within six months.

[4] In the few remaining common law states a lis pendens need not be filed. In those states the suit itself is notice.

① NOTICE OF PENDENCY OF ACTION

Supreme Court of the State of New York,
County of Suffolk

Franklin P. Smith
Plaintiff

—against—

John Jones, HoHum Construction Co., Inc., and Irving Ware
② Defendant s

NOTICE IS HEREBY GIVEN that an action has been commenced and is pending in this Court upon the complaint of the above-named plaintiff against the above-named defendant s for foreclosure of a certain mortgage bearing date the 15th day of June , 19--, executed by the defendant John Jones to the plaintiff to secure the payment of the sum of Four Thousand and 00/100 ($4,000) - - - - - - - - - - - - - - - Dollars with interest which mortgage was recorded in the Office of the Clerk of the County of Suffolk on the 16th day of June , 19--, in Liber 2350 of Mortgages, page 342 .
AND NOTICE IS FURTHER GIVEN that the premises affected by said foreclosure action are, at the time of the filing of this notice, situated in the Town of Brookhaven , County of Suffolk , State of New York and are described in the said mortgage as follows:

③ (here follows a complete legal description)

Date the 20th day of July , 19--.

/s/ John Apple
Attorney for the Plaintiff
(P.O. Address)

The Clerk of the County of Suffolk is hereby directed to index this notice to the names of all the defendants.

/s/ John Apple
Attorney for the Plaintiff
(P.O. Address)

A Notice of Pendency of Action

① The Notice of Pendency of Action is the *lis pendens* referred to in the text. It is filed in a mortgage foreclosure as shown here, a partition action to foreclose a mechanic's lien, and a tax lien, to mention only some. It is usually filed at the time of filing a verified summons and complaint with the county clerk.

② The fact that there are a number of defendants here indicates that they are parties in interest to the action. Conceivably, HoHum Construction Co., Inc., may have a mechanic's lien against the property. They are all made parties to the action.

③ The exact description of the property as it appears on the mortgage is entered here.

Contractors and Subcontractors

In regard to *contractors* and *subcontractors*, the laws of the states divide themselves generally into one of two classes: those using the "New York System" and those using the "Pennsylvania System."

In defining the rights of lienors, it is necessary to distinguish between the contractor and the subcontractor. A *prime contractor* is a person who is hired directly by the owner; a *subcontractor* is hired by the contractor.

New York System. Under the "New York System," a subcontractor is limited in the amount he can collect by the amount due the contractor from the owner. For example, an owner enters into a contract with a builder for $10,000, and the contractor hires a subcontractor to do work in the amount of $2,000. If the subcontractor gives the owner notice as to the amount of monies that will become due on his contract with the contractor, then the owner is entitled to withhold that sum from any payments to the contractor. Notice to the owner is imperative. If no notice has been given from the subcontractor to the owner and the owner pays the entire contract price of $10,000 to the contractor, the subcontractor cannot collect his $2,000 from the owner but must look to the contractor.

In many of the states following the "New York System," the law contains very strict provisions governing the actions of the contractor. For example, a prime contractor makes a contract with an owner for $15,000, and then hires a subcontractor. The owner pays the contractor in full, but the prime contractor fails to pay his subcontractor; the subcontractor may then make a demand upon the contractor for the books and records concerning that particular job. If the contractor fails to produce such books and records within a specified time, there is a presumption of grand larceny on the part of the contractor. In the event that the contractor produces his books and they show that he has "diverted" any part of the $15,000 that he received under the contract, he may also be held for grand larceny. The term "diverting funds" means either that the contractor employed the monies for his own personal use, or that he used the money for another job. For example, if the contractor was working two jobs at one time and used part of the $15,000 to pay a lumber bill on the second job, then he is guilty of diverting funds; and there is a subsequent presumption of grand larceny.

Pennsylvania System. Under the "Pennsylvania System," the subcontractor has the right to file a mechanic's lien for his labor even though the entire contract price has been paid by the owner to the contractor. In short, there need be no indebtedness from the owner to the contractor. Under this system, a hardship is often placed upon the owner because the subcontractor is entitled to collect from him even though he has honestly and in good faith paid his entire contract price to the contractor.

Protection Against Liens

Most states are concerned with a serious question which is continually being raised by prospective mortgagors and owners about the methods by which they might have protection against liens that are placed against their properties. In some states, New York, for example, there is no serious question as far as mortgagees are concerned. As was stated above, if the mortgage is filed prior to a lien, then it has priority over the lien. However, what can be done in the other states? In some states there is the so-called "no lien contract." This is a contract between the owner and the prime contractor wherein the prime contractor agrees that no liens can be placed against the property. This contract is then recorded. By virtue of the recording, there is constructive notice to the world. Therefore, subcontractors become bound by the terms of the contract and cannot file effective liens against the property.

Waiver of Lien. This instrument waives the right of the contractor to file any liens against the premises of the owner. Sometimes this is signed by the contractor when final payment is made and sometimes the instrument is executed prior to beginning work on the premises. In the event the contractor enters into this type of agreement, he is bound by its terms not to file liens. However, in some states, although he cannot file a lien in the event that he has not been paid, he may still obtain a personal judgment against the owner.

Completion Bond. Another means of protection against liens is to have the contractor obtain a *completion bond*, a type of surety bond, prior to commencing a job. In the event that any parties remain unpaid, they will be taken care of under the terms of the bond and no liens will be attached to the property of the owner.

Holding Funds. Very often when a business opportunity is sold, the purchaser will hold back part of the purchase price for payment to any possible creditors. *Holding funds* can be utilized effectively to thwart mechanic's liens. The owner merely holds back part of the contract price until the period for the filing of the mechanic's liens has passed. After this period, the balance due the contractor is paid.

In those states where the lien relates back to the commencement of the job, another method of holding back funds is employed. A mortgage is executed by the owner and mortgagor of the property and this is recorded. After the recording, the contractor starts his job. In this case, no actual cash is delivered to the mortgagor at the time of execution of the mortgage, but it is turned over to him for payment to the contractor as the job progresses. The mortgage is recorded prior to the beginning of the job and, therefore, is prior in right to any subsequent mechanic's liens. This method is used mainly on new construction.

Disputes Between Contractor and Subcontractor

Very often disputes arise between the contractor and the subcontractor. For example, a general contractor enters into a contract with a mason subcontractor to erect the foundation for a building. When the foundation is completed, the general contractor refuses to pay the subcontractor on the grounds that the foundation was not built according to specifications. In all probability, the subcontractor will attempt to file a mechanic's lien. If he does so, the contractor should deposit the amount in dispute with the county clerk. This amount will subsequently be distributed by the county clerk after final decision of the court.

The great temptation on the part of the contractors is the feeling that they are justified in their refusal to pay the subcontractor, and they do not deposit the money. Instead they employ the money for other jobs and, as a result, in many states, end up in the position where they have been charged with diversion of funds, for which they may become criminally liable.

Assignment of Lien

A lien is a cause of action and an asset. It may be assigned, therefore, much like any other cause of action. In the *assignment of the lien*, the lienor in reality creates an irrevocable power of attorney in the assignee, giving the assignee the right to act in his place and stead. The assignment, in addition to giving the assignee the right to act in the place of the lienor, contains a statement by the assignor that he has done nothing to encumber or to impair the lien in any way. Armed with this, the assignee may then proceed to foreclose on the lien.

The Satisfaction of Lien

When a lien has been paid, the lienor signs and acknowledges the *satisfaction of lien*. This instrument is then recorded and effectively discharges the lien of record.

Liens Discharged by Court

After the time for the prosecution of the lien has passed, the lien appears open on the records of the county clerk. This may be objectionable to a title company from whom title insurance is being sought, or it may be objectionable to an attorney who is passing on the abstract of title. In any event, the lien should be removed from the record. This is done by an order of the court to vacate or cancel the lien for failure to prosecute. In this case, the court will issue an order discharging the lien. This order is filed with the county clerk and has the effect of removing the lien from the record. On the record of the lien is written "Discharged by Order of the Court."

Partial Release of Lien

Just as there may be a partial release of mortgaged premises, so there may be a *partial release of a mechanic's lien*. For example, a contractor obtains a lien against two adjoining lots. If the owner pays him a sufficient amount on account, the contractor may, if he desires, partially release the lien. The important thing to be remembered here is that the description must be accurate and describe *only* that part of the premises to be released from the mechanic's lien.

SATISFACTION OF MECHANIC'S LIEN

State of New York }
County of Suffolk } ss.:

I, John Lienor , residing at number 14 Maiden Lane , in the Village of Bellport , Town of Brookhaven , County of Suffolk , State of New York, DO HEREBY CERTIFY, that a certain Mechanic's Lien, filed in the office of the Clerk of the County of Suffolk , on the 12th day of April , 19--, at 10 o'clock in the forenoon , in favor of John Lienor , claimant, against the building and lot with the improvements thereon situated on the northerly side of Main Street , being more particularly described as follows:

(here follows a complete legal description of property)

for the sum of One Thousand Eight Hundred and 00/100 ($1,800) Dollars, claimed against Richard Lienee as owner, is paid and satisfied, and I do hereby consent that the same be discharged of record.

Witness my hand this 29th day of September , 19--.

/s/ John Lienor

State of New York }
County of Suffolk } ss.:

On this 29th day of September , 19--, personally appeared before me John Lienor , known to me, and to be known to be the person described in and who executed the foregoing instrument and he acknowledged to me that he executed the same.

/s/ Edward Roe
Notary Public, Suffolk County, N. Y.

A Satisfaction of Mechanic's Lien

OTHER SPECIFIC LIENS

Vendor's and Vendee's Liens

In any real property contract, the seller is commonly known as the *vendor* and the purchaser as the *vendee*. Under certain circumstances, each of them may obtain a lien against the property involved in the contract of sale. The vendor's lien comes about when he has conveyed title to a parcel of real property, but has not received the entire purchase price. He then has a lien to the extent of the unpaid balance and may foreclose against the property much in the nature of a mortgage foreclosure.

The vendee's lien comes about when the purchaser has placed a deposit on a parcel of property, and he seeks the return of the down payment when the seller has defaulted. For example, a purchaser places a deposit on a parcel of property and the seller is unable to deliver marketable title and refuses to return the down payment. In this case, the vendee impresses a vendee's lien against the property.

The vendee's lien does not ordinarily extend to damages for loss of bargain, nor will the vendee's lien extend to attorney's fees or cost of title examination. However, if the contract of sale provides that in the event of any legal action the seller is to pay the attorney's fees and the cost of title examination, the vendee may impress a lien for attorney's fees and cost of title examination in addition to the amount of the down payment.

Both the vendor's and the vendee's liens are equitable liens and enforceable by foreclosure. The equitable liens in general may be said to be liens so declared by the courts to prevent injustice, or an unjust enrichment of a party at fault.

Bail Bond Lien

Very often after a person is arrested on a criminal charge, bail is set for that person. The bail may be arranged either by placing an equal amount in cash, by a bond placed with the court by a professional bondsman, or by offering real property in lieu of cash or bond. Usually when real property is used for bail, the equity of the owner must be at least twice the amount of the bail. For example, if the bail is $1,000, and the property is worth $7,000 with a $5,000 mortgage, the property will be acceptable because the equity of the owner is twice the amount of the bail. When property is offered as bail, notice is filed in the office of the county clerk in the county where the property is located, and it constitutes a *bail bond lien* against the property. The lien is discharged by a certificate of discharge obtained from the district attorney and recorded after the person held on bail is discharged from bail.

Real Property Taxes and Assessments

Municipal governments generally raise the money necessary for their operation by means of *real property taxes.* The property is assessed and the amount of the tax entered on the tax rolls. In the event that the tax is not paid within a stated time, the property is "sold for taxes." A tax certificate is delivered to the purchaser, and the owner has the right to redeem the property usually within three years. That is, if the taxpayer pays the purchaser of the tax certificate the back taxes, together with interest on his money (in some localities 18 percent), he then has a right to the property. If the taxpayer does not redeem within the period, the county will give the purchaser a quitclaim deed; or the county may foreclose and deliver marketable title to the purchaser.

When a quitclaim deed is delivered to the purchaser at a tax sale, lending institutions will usually refuse to lend money on that property for further improvement, unless either the period for adverse possession passes or the title is registered by means of a Torrens proceeding as will be explained in Chapter 22, or as provided in some states an individual institutes a tax foreclosure proceeding. In the first instance, for example, if there is a five-year statutory period for adverse possession, the individual purchasing the tax deed must wait the five-year period before banks or other lending institutions feel safe to lend money on the property. As an alternative, if the state statutes so provide, the individual may institute a Torrens proceeding. The *Torrens proceeding* is a system of land registration which provides a permanent method of title registration with an insurance fund out of which losses due to title defects are paid. The third alternative is possible where the statutes provide for the institution of a tax foreclosure proceeding. This is done much in the same manner as a mortgage foreclosure. The main purpose is to bring into the action all the parties in interest, such as lienors. The effect of the tax foreclosure is to cut off all prior liens. This gives the lending institutions a clear title upon which to lend funds.[5]

Assessments

An *assessment* is a charge against real estate made by some unit of government to cover the proportionate cost of an improvement. For example, if a municipality were to construct curbs along the side of the road, all of the property owners would be assessed for their proportionate amount of the cost of building the curbs. After a stated lapse of time, the assessment may become a lien against the property so assessed, and in most cases the property assessed is sold at public auction to the highest bidder. The former owner, however, has the right of redeeming the property after payment of the taxes, penalties, and interest within a certain time.[6]

Attachments

Generally, *attachments* are liens placed against the property of a defendant in a lawsuit for money damages prior to the commencement of an action. For example, if *A* is going to sue *B*, he may in some instances obtain an attachment against *B's* property. In order to obtain the attachment, he must file a bond to compensate *B* for any loss in the event that *A* does not win the action.

Most states will allow the filing of an attachment only under special circumstances, such as when it is believed that the defendant is about to flee the state with his property, or when the defendant is a nonresident of the state where the action is being brought.

Brokers should be especially wary of certain types of attachments when the plaintiff attempts, by virtue of an attachment, to impound the funds of the defendant. For example, a purchaser has deposited money with a broker. The plaintiff, in an action against the seller, claims that the money in the hands of the broker belongs to the seller, and, therefore, that it is subject to being impounded. Any monies received by the broker are in the nature of trust funds. It should be recalled by the broker that the monies in his possession do not belong to the seller until the closing of title. This, therefore, suggests

[5] In a few states the resulting title will be only as good as the taxpayer had.
[6] In some states the lien against the property is sold.

that if one seeks to impound monies in the hands of a broker, the broker should adopt a strictly neutral attitude and not disburse any of the monies until specifically ordered by the court. Otherwise, the broker could be in a position where he would be liable to the purchaser for any monies so disbursed.

GENERAL LIENS

Judgments

When an action at law is commenced, there are two or more parties to the action: the *plaintiff*, the party who brings the action, and the *defendant*, the party against whom the action is brought. At the conclusion of the action, if the plaintiff is successful, he is more often than not awarded a money judgment. The *judgment* is then recorded in the office of the clerk of the county in which the judgment has been rendered. The clerk indexes the judgment alphabetically, with the name of the defendant as the judgment debtor and the name of the plaintiff as the judgment creditor. At this point the judgment creditor may levy against the goods and chattels of the judgment debtor. However, prior to levying against the property of the judgment debtor, it becomes necessary for the judgment creditor to determine whether or not the judgment debtor has any assets. This determination is usually done by a supplementary proceeding whereby a *subpoena duces tecum*, meaning in Latin, "thou shalt bring with thee," is served upon the judgment debtor. The *subpoena duces tecum* orders the judgment debtor into court to be examined, and it further orders him to bring his books and records of account. The judgment debtor is examined to determine his assets. If any are found, an order is made to the sheriff to seize them and sell them for the account of the judgment creditor. If the assets sold cover the amount of the judgment, the county clerk is notified to mark the judgment as satisfied. In some states, tax liens and judgments have priority over other liens, but not as a general rule.

As soon as the judgment is entered, it becomes a lien against the real property of the judgment debtor. The duration of the lien usually varies according to the statutes of the individual states, for example, from one year in Tennessee to five years in Idaho to ten years in California, New York, and most other states. In the third instance, although the judgment is good for twenty years, it is only a lien against real property for a period of ten years unless renewed.

When a title search is made and a judgment against an individual has been entered, this constitutes a "cloud on the title" of the judgment debtor. For example, the judgment creditor examines the judgment debtor in supplementary proceedings as explained above and finds that the judgment debtor has no assets except real property that is already encumbered with a mortgage. The judgment creditor may take a chance and sell the property, after first paying off the prior existing lien of mortgage, but more often than not, he prefers to wait. If the judgment debtor attempts to sell the real property at anytime prior to the time when the lien against the property lapses, then the judgment debtor must satisfy the lien. If he fails to do so, the property is sold subject to the lien. This he does by paying the judgment creditor and receiving from him the satisfaction of judgment, which is filed by the purchaser. On the surface it would appear as if the seller (judgment debtor) would file the satisfaction piece himself, but by custom, when a sale takes place, he gives the satisfaction piece to the purchaser to be filed at the title closing. The reason for this is that after the sale, the seller would have no real interest in filing the satisfaction piece, and in order to make certain that this is actually done, the purchaser does it himself.

In the event that *A* owns a parcel of property with a judgment filed against it, and he sells the property to *B* without satisfying the judgment, the lien follows the property. That is, the new owner will have a cloud on his title. If a judgment is entered in Suffolk County, and the judgment debtor has property in Nassau County, the judgment may also be filed in Nassau County and it becomes a lien against the property in Nassau County.

Federal Court Judgments

Title 28, Section 812, of the United States Code provides that a judgment rendered in a federal court in any state shall become a lien on property in the state in the same manner as if it were rendered in a state court of general jurisdiction. Thus, if a judgment is obtained in a federal court and is docketed in the proper county clerk's office, it becomes a lien on the debtor's property. If the state fails to provide a statute for the docketing of federal judgments, the

JUDGMENT FOR PLAINTIFF AFTER TRIAL BEFORE A JURY

Supreme Court of the State of New York,

County of Suffolk

Richard Roe

Plaintiff

—against—

John Doe

Defendant

The above-entitled action having been duly tried before Mr. Justice D. Ormonde Ritchie and a jury, at Part I of the New York Supreme Court, held in and for the County of Suffolk, at the County Courthouse therein on the 14th day of October, 19--, and the jury having duly rendered a verdict in favor of the plaintiff and against the defendant, in the sum of Three Thousand and 00/100 ($3,000) - - - - - - - - Dollars, and the costs of the plaintiff having been duly taxed in the sum of Twenty-seven and 00/100 ($27) - Dollars, now on motion of John Lawyer, attorney for the plaintiff, it is

ADJUDGED, that the plaintiff, Richard Roe, does recover of the defendant, John Doe the sum of Three Thousand and 00/100 ($3,000) - - - - - - Dollars, together with the sum of Twenty-seven and 00/100 ($27) - - - - - - Dollars, costs as taxed making in all the sum of Three Thousand Twenty-seven and 00/100 ($3,027) - Dollars and that the plaintiff have execution therefor.

Dated the 20th day of October, 19--.

/s/ R. Ford Hughes
Clerk

A Judgment for Plaintiff after Trial before a Jury

federal judgment is automatically made a lien on the debtor's property in the state.

Federal Tax Liens

Federal tax liens attach either because of transfer of the property upon death or because of violation of the income tax laws. In the first instance, the "inheritance" tax, if not paid, becomes a lien upon the estate of the decedent.

In the second case, if a person is delinquent in his income tax payments, the government may issue a tax warrant which is filed in the county in which property of the delinquent taxpayer is located, and it becomes a lien upon that property.

State Inheritance Tax

The *state inheritance tax* is a tax imposed by most states upon the property of deceased persons. The amount of the tax becomes a lien against the estate. The discovery of this type of lien is an important step in the search and examination of title.

Corporation Franchise Tax

Most states impose a *corporation franchise tax* upon the right of the corporation to do business within the state. There is generally a minimum tax, for instance $25 per year, and graduated rates, depending upon the amount of net income. In the event this tax is not paid by the corporation, the state may file a lien against the property belonging to the corporation.

Liens for Debts of Decedent

When a person dies, his property passes either to his heirs or devisees. Creditors' rights are superior to the rights of heirs or devisees and the latter, therefore, take the property subject to the debts of the deceased. Debts are first paid out of the personal property of the estate, using, first, the property not specifically bequeathed, and second, the property disposed of by legacies. If there are still debts outstanding after this, the real property may be sold. When real property is being sold, it is therefore necessary to ascertain that there are no liens outstanding in favor of creditors of the decedent.

MISCELLANEOUS LIENS

Liens Against Homesteads

In Chapter 8 the filing of the declaration of homestead was discussed. The filing of the declaration exempts the property from execution up to certain limits. However, there are special limitations with regard to liens against homesteads in those states having the homestead laws. In most of those states, the homestead is subject to judgment liens if the judgment was entered on the record prior to the filing of the homestead declaration. It is subject to the lien of a mortgage if the mortgage was recorded prior to the filing of the declaration of homestead. It is also subject to the lien of mortgage after the filing of the declaration of homestead, provided that both the husband and the wife execute the mortgage as the mortgagors. The homestead is also usually subject to mechanic's liens.

Old-Age Assistance

In many states where old-age assistance or welfare assistance is given an individual, the amount given may become a lien on real property of the recipient of the assistance. For example, a person who owns real property receives welfare assistance. In some states, the recipient and the commissioner of welfare enter into a contract whereby the recipient promises to repay the commissioner. This contract is filed and becomes a lien against the property.

In other states, a person owning real property transfers his property title to the commissioner of welfare, who advertises the property, sells it by bid, and offsets any money paid to the recipient of the welfare out of the sale price.

QUESTIONS FOR REVIEW

1. Explain the operation of a "no lien" contract.
2. What effect does a judgment have on a real property title after the judgment is entered?

3. What is the purpose of a supplementary proceeding?
4. In a state using the "Pennsylvania System" of mechanic's liens, how can a prospective mortgagee protect himself against liens on new construction?
5. What is a *lis pendens?*
6. Assume a mechanic's lien is filed against a home and that it is not paid. What is the next step that must be taken in order to collect on the lien?
7. If a tax lien is foreclosed, what sort of title does the purchaser at the foreclosure sale receive?
8. What must be shown before property can be attached?

PROBLEMS

1. In the case of *Mochon* v. *Sullivan,* the court discusses the theory of the mechanic's lien. How does the court distinguish between the common-law lien and the mechanic's lien?

Mochon v. Sullivan
1 Mont. 470 (1871)

This was a suit against Sullivan and others to enforce a mechanic's lien. The trial court decreed a foreclosure thereof and also awarded a personal judgment against the owner. It is contended that the court could not combine both suits in one.

MURPHY, J. . . . The mechanic's lien is derived from the principle of the lien on personal property at common law, and is based upon statutory enactment in the different states and territories. It is remedial in its character, and rests upon the broad foundation of natural equity and commercial necessity. It is not a common-law right, but simply a creature of the statute, and differs in some respects from all other liens known to the law.

Under the common law, a lien exists only while the party continues in possession of the property upon which he has bestowed his labor, for by parting with possession he shows that he thereafter trusts to the personal credit of the debtor. But to the validity of his lien no possession is necessary, for it is a charge upon the property in the hands of the owner, and once it attaches, it relates back to and takes effect from the commencement of the labor or appropriation. It continues with or without notice, for a certain period according to the statute, and then is kept alive by the act of the party and judicial process.

It is not a general but a particular lien, and is in its nature peculiar and of equitable character. The doctrine upon which it is founded is upon the consideration of natural justice that the party who has enhanced the value of property, by incorporating therein his labor or materials, shall have a preferred claim on said property for the value of his said labor and materials. The foundation of the suit to enforce it arises only by virtue of an express or implied contract with the owner. . . .

The theory of the lien is that the party by whom the labor is performed or materials furnished for the erection or repair of buildings, on credit, retains his claim to them after they have entered into the structure and become inseparably connected with it. The object of the statute is to create and preserve ample security to the laborer or materialman, and, therefore, to charge the estate with a lien, or encumbrance, independent of any personal remedy he may have. The artificer or businessman acquires a qualified property in the thing upon which he has bestowed his time and labor, or into which he has incorporated his materials. The very principle upon which the right is grounded comes from the increased value of the property he has brought about and by the accession of his labor or materials and is purely an equitable one.

And the owner thus benefited holds his property subject to and liable for this equitable claim, which grows out of and depends upon this enhanced value of his interest. We are of the opinion that this lien, being an equitable right, or in the nature of an equitable right, must be enforced in conformity to the established rules and principles governing proceedings in chancery. We hold, therefore, that insofar as the mechanic's lien law of this territory authorizes the rendering of a personal judgment as at law, it blends law and equity together in the same proceeding, as in contravention of the organic act . . . and is void and of no effect.

The case is remanded, and the judgment is modified in conformity with the order made at the last term. It is ordered that the decree of the court below in this case be so modified as to make void the personal judgment against the defendant Sullivan, and in favor of Mochon, for the amount of the mechanic's lien on the premises, and that after sale of the premises judgment be rendered in favor of the plaintiff and against the defendant Sullivan for any deficiency, after such sale, and that the decree provide that the sheriff be appointed special master commissioner to make sale of said premises, and that the decree, when modified as herein specified, be and the same is hereby confirmed.

2. A lumber and coal company placed a lien against a property for lumber purchased for use in the construction of a building and for coal which was used to heat the building during the course of construction. A hardware company also placed a lien against the property for the following items: stovepipe, saw files, buckets, brooms, mopsticks, ice picks, saw blades, and push brooms.

   In a lawsuit that followed, the defendant argued that certain of the items of lumber were used in the erection of sheds, latrines, and forms for concrete and not consumed in such use and that the stovepipe, etc., "did not enter the construction of the building and are not lienable." [7]

   (a) As a general rule, what is the test as to whether an item delivered to a job by a materialman is subject to a mechanic's lien?

   (b) What would your decision be in the above case if you were the judge?

3. In the case of *Bank of Italy* v. *MacGill et al.,* what argument did the plaintiff make in order to try to sustain the priority of his mortgage? Why was the argument unsuccessful? When does the lien attach in California?

Bank of Italy v. MacGill et al.
93 Cal. App. 228, 269 Pac. 566 (1928)

The plaintiff sued to foreclose certain mortgages. This is an appeal from a judgment awarding priority to mechanic's lien claimants.

PLUMMER, J. . . . The findings of the court are to the effect that the defendant C. B. Kahl had begun work upon the lots in question, and that there were visible evidences upon the lots in question of the work being performed by C. B. Kahl prior to the time when the mortgages in question were recorded by the plaintiff's assignor. The court also found that the Hammond Lumber Company had begun the delivery of building materials for the erection of buildings upon the lots in question prior to the date of the recording of the mortgages now held by the plaintiff. The point made by the (plaintiff) as to the delivery of materials is that materials delivered by the Hammond Lumber Company were not actually placed or delivered upon the lots on which the buildings were erected, but that the lumber and other building material was piled or placed upon an adjoining lot, and

[7] See *Walker* v. *Collin's Construction Co.,* 121 Neb. 157, 236 N.W. 334 (1931).

therefore that the plaintiff's mortgages should be given priority. The (plaintiff's) argument in this behalf is interesting but not very convincing. Section 1186 of the Code of Civil Procedure, which gives a materialman a mechanic's lien, does not provide that a lumber company shall pile the lumber actually delivered for the building upon the lot where the building is to be erected. That section reads:

"Thc licns provided for in this chapter are preferred to any lien, mortgage, or other encumbrance which may have attached subsequent to the time when the building, improvement, or structure was commenced, work done, or materials were commenced to be furnished; also, to any lien, mortgage, or other encumbrance of which the lienholder had no notice, and which was unrecorded at the time the building, improvement, or structure was commenced, work done, or the materials were commenced to be furnished."

By this section, the lien attaches as soon as the work is begun or as soon as materials are commenced to be furnished. In the case at bar, the findings show that work had begun upon the premises on which the buildings were to be erected. It is true that the work begun upon the lots in question was work being done by the defendant C. B. Kahl, but the work, as found by the court, being upon the lots adjoining, on which the lumber was piled, gave visible evidence and information to everyone as to the lots upon which the buildings were to be erected, and for which buildings the material was being delivered. We cannot shut our eyes to what is common knowledge to everyone who lives in a city, that building materials are not piled upon the lot where the building is to be erected or is being erected, but are ordinarily and commonly delivered upon and piled upon the streets. We can see no logical distinction between delivering materials upon the streets and upon adjoining lots. If work is being done upon the lots, indicating, as found in this case, where the buildings are to be erected, all persons having to do with the lots are immediately placed upon notice.

The court having found that labor was being performed by the defendant C. B. Kahl and materials also being furnished by him, and also that materials were being furnished by the defendant Hammond Lumber Company prior to and at the time of the recording of the mortgages upon which the plaintiff bases its actions, it becomes wholly unnecessary for us to review the argument based upon the case of *McClain* v. *Hutton,* 131 Cal. 132, and Sections 1186 and 1183 of the Code of Civil Procedure as they read at the time of the decision of the case of *McClain* v. *Hutton* and the subsequent amendments thereto, for the simple reason that whether there was or was not any contract between the owner of the lots and the contractor is wholly immaterial.

The court has found that the priority of the mechanic's liens asserted by the lumber company and by C. B. Kahl rests upon the fact of the delivery of the materials. Under Section 1186, Code of Civil Procedure, that is all that is necessary to give priority. . . .

4. Assume that you are a builder and have constructed a house valued at $14,000 on which there is still due $4,000 from the owner, Richard Roe. The house is built on Lot #9 of the map of the Security Acres Development Company in your city and your state. Within 79 days after the completion of the job you decide to file a notice of mechanic's lien. Prepare the notice. After you have filed the notice, what is done next?

SUGGESTED READINGS

Anderson, Ronald A., and Walter A. Kumpf. *Business Law Principles and Cases,* 5th ed. Cincinnati: South-Western Publishing Co., 1971. Chapter 26.

Ring, Alfred A. *Real Estate Principles and Practices,* 7th ed. Englewood Cliffs, New Jersey: Prentice-Hall, Inc., 1972. Chapter 16.

Chapter 10 Home Ownership

Between 1890 and 1950, the number of owner-occupied units increased from 47.8 percent to 55 percent, and in 1970 this figure just shaded 63 percent. What is perhaps more startling is that the total owner-occupied units jumped from about 6.6 million in 1890 to about 40 million in 1970. All of this suggests, of course, that not only has population increased, but more and more people are interested in home ownership.

However, with increasing costs, one noted land economist does not paint a very happy picture of the future of home ownership, at least for many. He states, "Assuming that current building, zoning, and housing codes reflect what is regarded as minimum housing standards, the lowest-cost lot and new house today sells for $21,200. Then the monthly principal, interest, property taxes, and insurance payments (PITI) for a loan of $21,000 comes to $214 per month."

"In this example it is necessary to use a low down-payment requirement because 26 percent of all families have liquid assets of less than $500 and 14 percent have no liquid assets to meet the $200 down payment required. Returning to the $214 monthly PITI and using the rule that it should be about 25 percent of income, the income required to purchase this home is $10,300 per year. Unfortunately only 26,300,000 of the country's 64,300,000 households, or 41 percent, have the income to afford owning this minimum new house. Put another way, 59 percent of the country's households cannot afford to own this home."[1]

Recently the concept of home ownership and the type of ownership has changed. A survey by the National Association of Home Builders revealed that of the builders surveyed in 1971, 15.8 percent built townhouses and condominiums, and this figure in 1972 was expected to be 27.3 percent. Furthermore, "The typical unit built in the decade following World War II was small—800-1,000 square feet, a three-bedroom, one-bath ranch or Cape Cod, on a slab or with a basement. By 1968 the average square footage of new houses approached 1,700 square feet. Since then, the average floor area has declined—to 1,640 square feet in 1969, to 1,500 in 1970, and 1,450 in 1971."[2]

Historically, the concept of *free men* was related to the ownership of land. Even though this is no longer true, many immigrants came to the United States picturing a way of life which would enable them to own their own land. To many, home ownership is still a way of life.

REASONS FOR OWNING A HOME

The reason for owning a home may be thought of as being either sociological or personal. Though some of us may try to avoid our social responsibilities, they do exist. Each of us owes certain duties and has certain responsibilities to the community in which we live.

Sociological Reasons

A strong sense of civic responsibility is one of the results of home ownership. The homeowner's civic participation appears to be greater than the nonhomeowner's. In other words, the degree to which

---

[1] Clyde Richey, "Bankruptcy of Subsidized Housing" (Boulder, Colorado: Center for Real Estate and Land Use Studies, Graduate School of Business Administration, May, 1973), pp. 1 and 3.

[2] Michael Sumechrest, "Home Building Continues to Change," *Director's Digest,* Vol. 31, No. 19 (October, 1972), p. 7.

an individual actually engages in the organized activities of his community in terms of membership, attendance at functions that affect the community, contributions, and offices in which he is willing to serve seems to correlate with his home investment.

Home ownership in standard housing areas of a community increases the general health of the community, reduces the number of crimes, and reduces the costs to the community for various kinds of assistance. Poor housing seems to be a breeding place for crime and disease.

Personal Reasons

In addition to the sociological reasons for home ownership as outlined above, there are personal reasons for owning one's home. Although one might include such reasons as peace of mind, pride, and credit, perhaps the basic reasons for owning one's home are security and savings.

Security. Owning a home gives a person a certain feeling of security and independence. When a home has been paid for, wide fluctuations of the business cycle will always find the homeowner with a "roof over his head." Even in a period of full employment and rising prices, the homeowner is more secure than the renter. If prices rise, the value of the home will rise accordingly.

It is a deep feeling of satisfaction to a man with a family to know that if he predeceases his wife and children, they are provided with a home. To encroach upon the domain of the philosopher, the "future" of most men lies in their children; and in a sense home ownership protects the children and thus protects the future of man.

A study indicated that 32 percent of people who buy a home do so because they enjoy and appreciate the security in ownership.[3]

Savings. The purchase of a home with its attendant obligations is a form of forced saving. The average person encounters difficulty in establishing a concrete and systematic savings program for himself. A person who must meet various payments, such as principal,

[3] Eugene P. Conser, "Why Do People Buy?" (Editorial), *Realtor's Headlines*, Vol. 34, No. 44 (October 30, 1967), p. 2.

interest, and taxes, at fixed times must learn to set aside money to meet these obligations. The house often constitutes the major or only savings of medium to low income groups.

Although there are other arguments for and against home ownership as opposed to renting, financially both are probably equally expensive methods of providing housing in terms of gross outlay. There are those who argue that the homeowner pays taxes and interest in addition to his mortgage payments and also loses the interest that his investment in some other commodity might provide. While this is true, a tenant must pay these to the landlord when he pays rent. In other words, a landlord not only receives a return on his initial investment, but he must charge rent sufficient to cover interest, taxes, and utilities payments as well.

Since this is true, why shouldn't rent be paid to oneself? This is essentially what happens in home ownership. Finally, when a house is completely free of debt, there will be an equity of the owner in the property no matter how bad business conditions become.

The fact of the matter is that 10 percent of the persons in the study referred to above buy because they feel that rents are too high.[4] Much of this is borne out in a study conducted by the United States Savings and Loan League. Ten percent of the respondents replied that when you pay rent you have nothing to show for it but receipts from your landlord; and 6 percent stated that buying is cheaper than renting; while 22 percent of the respondents said buying enables one to build an equity in real estate.[5]

DISADVANTAGES OF HOME OWNERSHIP

Maintenance

This is sometimes regarded as a disadvantage to home ownership. It has been estimated that maintenance will run about 1½ percent of the cost of the house per year. For example, if a house cost $20,000, it is estimated that the cost of maintenance will be about $300 annually. This is the average cost and, of course, in some years the cost will be considerably higher than in other years.

---

[4] *Ibid.*, p. 2.

[5] *Savings and Loan Fact Book*, United States Savings and Loan League, 1972, p. 44.

As an Investment

Whether this is a real disadvantage depends upon circumstances. Several things can take place which might impair the investment. If a person loses his job, has to move in a hurry, or is unable to meet fixed mortgage payments in his later years, his investment may be impaired. More often than not, if this latter situation occurs, the owner might think in terms of refinancing and thus lower his monthly payments.

METHODS OF ACQUIRING A HOME

Basically, there are four ways to start on the road to home ownership.

1. Buy a lot and build a home. This method involves the purchase of a lot and the building of his own home *by the individual.* With the rising cost of homes in recent years, this method has become more and more popular even with people who know little about home construction. If this method is decided upon, care must be taken not to incorporate any objectionable features in the building that might injure the resale value. Much of the future value depends upon the plan of the home; therefore, in planning a home, the home builder should either (a) obtain an architect's plans, or (b) make use of plan services. In the first case, an architect will prepare plans in conformity with the individual's ideas, the cost of construction, and the site. After the preliminary sketches have been agreed upon, the architect will then prepare working drawings.

There are throughout the country many plan services that furnish complete working drawings and specifications for homes for a relatively nominal fee. An important thing to remember here is that if any changes are to be made in these plans obtained from a plan service, these changes should be made by a competent person.

2. Select a home from plans and let out a contract. This second method of acquiring a home is often used. There may be in this method the danger that the plans selected will not fit the site, but the greatest danger in using this method is in the selection of a competent contractor. Care must be taken to find a contractor who is both a reliable workman and reliable financially. If either of these requisites is lacking, the contractor is apt to skimp on materials.

3. Buy an already erected home. This method of acquiring a home has certain advantages over the two methods previously discussed. First, the purchaser is able to know to a certain degree what he is getting. Second, homes of this type are usually in developments where the character of the neighborhood has been created to conform with the homes in them. In short, the neighborhood is generally a new one; and the purchaser need not worry for some time about economic obsolescence. Third, where the home to be purchased is in a development, the house can usually be purchased for less than if the individual had the home constructed from plans. Developers, because they are building a number of homes at one time, usually can effect savings that are passed on to the purchasers.

When an already erected home is to be purchased, it should be examined carefully to determine whether material has been skimped on and then hidden by the builder in the cost of construction.

Some of the things that should be examined are: (a) Is the concrete work in the foundation crude? (b) Is the cutting and fitting of corner bracings, bridgings, and similar items expertly done? (c) Are the nails of the right type and size? (d) Are there hammer marks, unset nails, or crushed edges on the trim and millwork? (e) Do the doors stick because of poor fitting? (f) Are holes and other imperfections in the woodwork puttied? (g) Is the house wired for adequate power, and are there sufficient outlets in each room?

4. Buy an older home and remodel if necessary. Many older homes are excellent buys and can be purchased with the idea of making them over into comfortable modern living quarters. The great danger in purchasing an older home with the idea of remodeling is the neighborhood. This cannot be too strongly emphasized. All properties are interdependent, that is, their value tends to be either raised or lowered as a result of the value of adjacent properties. For example, it is possible to overimprove, in which case the sale value of the property is decreased by the less desirable character of the neighborhood. Thus, one might spend $2,000 on modernization and discover that it enhanced the value of the house only $1,500. On the other hand, an expenditure of $1,000 might enhance the value of the property $1,200.

In the final analysis, the method of acquisition depends to a large extent upon the individual, his financial condition, and his preferences. There are, however, important basic considerations when buying a home, regardless of individual preferences.

BASIC CONSIDERATIONS OF HOME SELECTION

There are several factors that must be given important consideration in the selection of a home. It is believed that a knowledge of these factors is important, not only to the prospective homeowner, but to the practicing broker who desires to make the sale. By stressing these things in presenting a property, the broker can show his prospect that the home being shown him is fitted to his needs.

Trend of the Neighborhood

With the growth of a city or even a fairly small town, there are created neighborhoods or districts. These neighborhoods result from economic pressures; and these pressures cause neighborhoods to be in a constant state of flux. As a result of neighborhood changes, more often than not from a higher to a lower level of use, there develops what is known as economic obsolescence. *Economic obsolescence* is defined as the impairment of desirability or usefulness of property brought about by economic and environmental changes of a neighborhood. In all probability houses decline in value more from economic obsolescence than from any other cause. It becomes obvious, then, that one of the prime considerations in the selection of a home is the trend of the neighborhood.

In general, older sections of a city begin their decline soon after newer sections begin to make a strong appeal with home buyers. A prospective purchaser of a home should look for a neighborhood containing a high percentage of owner-occupied homes. Neighborhoods with owner-occupied homes as distinguished from tenant-occupied homes tend to be relatively stable in value. Further, one should look for a neighborhood that contains well-planned and well-located homes of the same physical characteristics. This is discussed in more detail in Chapter 27.

Some studies have indicated that changes in the physical characteristics of a neighborhood alone will not cause people to move. Apparently people will move more readily if the social characteristics of the neighbors become different from their own, even if they like their homes. The rule seems to be, the higher the socioeconomic status of the individual, "the more likely he is to be content with the characteristics of the neighbors."[6] Furthermore if a person

[6] Martin Meyerson, Barbara Terrett, and William L. C. Wheaton, *Housing, People, and Cities* (New York: McGraw-Hill Book Company, 1962), p. 88.

believes his dwelling is temporary, the social characteristics of the neighborhood are relatively meaningless.

Site

In selecting the site, whether it be a vacant lot or an already built home, great care must be taken to avoid such things as a site located in the prevailing wind carrying noxious odors from factories and railroads. When the site is located near water, one should determine whether or not rivers will flood or if the nearby area will become swampy. The soil should be tested to determine whether or not the quality of the soil is such that it will bear the weight of the house. Often piles must be driven into the ground, thus adding materially to the cost of the house. In the final analysis, the site should afford privacy, and if possible, a pleasant view together with enough space for family recreation.

Utilities

This is an important consideration when selecting a building site. *Utilities* generally means the existence of electricity, telephone, water, and sewage disposal. Of course, when a house is already erected, the presence or absence of these things is obvious. Still, this factor is an equally important consideration when selecting a building lot. Without water or sewage disposal, there will be the necessity of digging a well and the construction of septic tanks which will add substantially to the real cost of the lot.

Family Needs

Probably the most important consideration in the selection of a home is family needs. A home must be geared to the needs of the individual family. A good house design or plan should incorporate within it rooms and areas designed to accommodate these needs. When examining a house, one should ask three major questions:

1. Does the house have the necessary "housework space"? This means that one must examine the building in terms of kitchen space, laundry (where is it?), housecleaning (that is, storage space

for housecleaning tools), maintenance space (that is, basement workshop), and possible space for domestic help, if that is a consideration of the family.

2. Does the house have the necessary and properly laid-out space to fulfill the needs of family group life? Does it have the proper dining space (that is, a separate dining room, living room-dining room, or part of the kitchen)? Is the living room large enough? Does it have a space for recreation (that is, basement game room)? Does it have the requisite space for small children's activities, if that is a factor? Is there a playroom? If not, will the living room fulfill this need?

3. Does the house have the necessary space to fulfill the needs for family private life? This means that the bedrooms must be adequate, in terms of numbers and size, there must be sufficient space to insure proper clothes storage, and there must be a sufficient number of baths. In addition, one might consider whether the house has a study area. If there is to be entertaining of overnight guests, one must raise the question as to the size and type of guest accommodation.

Convenience

Convenience means convenience of the location for the family unit. What may be convenient for one family may not be convenient for another. One family may need a home located near schools; another may not be interested in location with regard to schools. In selecting a house, however, the family must give consideration to its location in terms of convenience to the various members of the household. Convenience of transportation will always be important to the breadwinner of the family, while nearness to stores or shopping centers is important to the shopping member of the family. Nearness to churches, recreational areas, etc., must also be considered.

Exterior Appearance

Exterior appearance is an important consideration in home selection. Architectural styles and designs vary with climate, customs, location, and economic conditions of the time in which the homes were built. The person contemplating purchasing an older home should ask himself whether or not the exterior appearance of the home under consideration conforms with the neighborhood. And he should also give serious consideration to the question of whether or not the established landscaping is in harmony with the exterior appearance of the home.

In a study done for the United States Savings and Loan League by the research and design firm of Raymond Loewy/William Snaith, Inc., the motivations toward homes and housing were examined. Information was gleaned from 2,514 respondents in various age and socioeconomic strata. Among the many things examined was the rating of comparative importance of housing appeals shown below.

How study respondents rated "comparative importances" of housing appeals

	EXTREMELY IMPORTANT	VERY IMPORTANT	SOMEWHAT IMPORTANT	NOT TOO IMPORTANT
Good workmanship	61.7%	35.7%	2.1%	.6%
Builder's reputation	53.2	36.2	7.3	3.2
Good neighborhood	50.5	43.5	5.1	.9
Interior styling	27.1	43.9	21.7	7.2
Established community	26.1	43.5	21.3	9.1
Nationally branded materials	25.8	42.0	22.1	10.1
Landscaping	17.0	45.3	28.3	9.4

Source: *Savings and Loan News*, March, 1967, Vol. LXXXVIII, No. 11, p. 39.

THE EXPENSE OF HOME OWNERSHIP

What should one pay for a home? The old rule of thumb was that the price of a home should be about two and one half times one's annual income. This is no longer the case. It has been found that the amount paid for housing varies with one's income. Schwabe's Law with regard to rent states that rent expenditures increase with increases in income but at a slower rate. In short, lower income groups pay a greater percentage of their income for housing. Higher income groups pay more rent in dollars than do lower income groups, but it is a lower percentage of their total income. In general low income groups spend between 25 and 30 percent of their income for housing, and higher income groups spend between 15 and 20 percent of their income for housing. In reality, there is considerable dispersion within an income group for the following reasons:

1. Size of the family. Within any income group large families tend to spend less for housing than smaller families.

2. Scales of preference. Some families prefer to spend more out of their family budget for housing than do others within the same income group for social and ethnic reasons.

3. The wealth position of the family. Some families within an income group can spend more for housing than others can spend because of their ability to draw from savings and other assets.

4. Length of time that families have been in any income group. There is a time lag of adjustment of housing expenditures as a percentage of income to changes in income.

5. Locational influences. There is a variation in housing expenditures within any income class due to differences in cities, number and types of utilities, and other factors.

Population concentration in metropolitan areas may also affect the costs of home ownership. A study [7] of 77 metropolitan areas involving almost 123,000 mortgages shows essentially that the cost of owning houses is higher in areas with large populations than in areas with relatively small populations.

Home Ownership and Age

By the end of the 1950's, population was rising at the rate of about three million persons per year. However, the population of the 25-44 age group—which accounts for most purchasers of single-family residences—remained virtually stable.[8] The stability of number in this age group is generally regarded as a legacy from the depression of the thirties. These people have been for the most part demanders of single-family residences as has already been indicated. Consequently, if this group remains relatively stable, it would appear that residential housing may also remain stable.

Those below the 30-40-year-old group seem to be demanders of rental housing, and it appears as if persons in this age group will

---

[7] *Insured Mortgage Portfolio,* Federal Housing Administration, Vol. III, No. 2 (Winter, 1953-54), p. 18.

[8] *Federal Reserve Bulletin* (December, 1962), cf., United States Savings and Loan League *Digest,* Vol. 22, No. 1 (January, 1963), pp. 8-11.

increase, suggesting a concomitant demand for rental units. At the same time persons 65 years or older are continuing to increase. In the 1920's persons 65 or older accounted for 5 percent of the population. In the early 1950's this group accounted for 8 percent of the population, and in 1971 they represented nearly 10 percent of the population.

In the early 1920's retirement income and other factors were unfavorable to separate living. The fact of the matter is that it was not uncommon for three generations to share the same household.

Between 1920 and 1930 home ownership rose, but during the Great Depression fell drastically. However, from 1940 to 1950 the rate rose from 43.6 percent to 55 percent. From 1950 to 1960 the rate rose 6.9 percentage points. There was an increase of 7.1 million homeowners between 1960 and 1970, yet only a 1 percent gain.

One area where "home ownerships" has shown and probably will continue to show marked gains is in the area of the "second" home. The last census revealed that 1.7 million of the 58.8 million households owned a second home which they used as a vacation home. About 21 percent of the persons owning a second home are 65 years or over.

It is not entirely inconceivable that if family incomes rise, the demand will increase rapidly in this market, particularly the condominium market.

FINANCING HOME OWNERSHIP

Generally, the ownership of real property is financed by either land contracts or mortgages. In essence, a land contract is used when the seller finances the property himself. This was the situation discussed when the seller and the purchaser enter into a contract for the sale of real property; usually, the purchaser makes a down payment. The contract is placed in escrow, monthly payments of principal and interest are made on the contract, and the deed is delivered when the payments have been completed. This method is often employed as a junior financing device. It would be well for the broker to keep this method of financing in mind.

The purchase money mortgage, as outlined in Chapter 6, is the second method by which the seller finances the sale.

Cash sales amount to such a small percentage of the total home sales that they are insignificant.

However, most sales of real property are financed by means of the mortgage. Mortgages are divided by characteristics into three forms: the FHA-insured mortgage, the VA-guaranteed mortgage, and the conventional mortgage.

The FHA-Insured Mortgage

An *FHA-insured mortgage* is a mortgage which is insured by the Federal Housing Administration. The FHA is actually an insuring corporation; and in event of default on a mortgage, the lending institution receives its money after foreclosure and FHA procedure. The FHA sets standards and procedures for accepting or rejecting the loan application sent it by a lending institution. In order to obtain insurance, the applicant must meet three standards:

a. The property must meet certain minimum standards as to quality of material and workmanship, room planning, lot size, etc.
b. The location must be acceptable.
c. The individual seeking the loan must have earning power and income that will enable him to pay off the loan according to the terms of the mortgage.

In arriving at a proper balance between prospective housing expense and net effective income, the FHA considers various factors, including the relationship of housing expense to the person's income and his use of installment credit as reflected in items on the family budget. No handy formula is used to relate housing expense or purchase price to a prospective homeowner's income. "FHA considers both the borrower's income and age, but only as they relate to other factors that affect his ability to pay." [9]

VA-Guaranteed Mortgage

The *VA-guaranteed loan* is commonly called the GI mortgage because it makes veterans of World War II, the Korean conflict,

[9] "Financing Home Purchases and Home Improvements," *HUD IP-31* (July, 1967), pp. 6-7.

and the Vietnam conflict eligible for loans under its terms. Originally, the veteran had from 10 to 20 years from the date of his discharge to make application for a loan. However, an amendment to the Housing Act of 1970 removed all termination dates for applying for a VA-guaranteed loan.

It is guaranteed because the Veterans Administration will (currently) guarantee the lending institution 60 percent of the loan or $12,500, whichever is the lesser. For example, on a $10,000 loan the government will guarantee up to a maximum of $6,000, while on a $25,000 loan the government will guarantee $12,500 in the event of default of the borrower.

Under the terms of the law, the selling price of the home to a veteran cannot be higher than it is appraised by a VA appraiser. For example, a seller might desire $17,000 for a home which appraises out at only $16,000. This would mean a veteran could not pay more than $16,000 for the home. Naturally, the seller can, if he wishes, sell it to other buyers for as much as he can get.

Together the FHA-insured and the VA-guaranteed loans account for about 20 percent of the total mortgage loans; conventional mortgages account for the rest.

The Conventional Mortgage

A *conventional mortgage* is a mortgage that is neither government insured nor government guaranteed. Typically, in a conventional mortgage the interest rate is higher than the rates on both FHA and VA mortgages. This interest rate fluctuates with the government "tight" or "easy" money policy as outlined in Chapter 15.

Closing Costs

Advertisements for a home often read: "$500 down plus Closing Costs," or "No down payment plus Closing Costs." What comprises closing costs? The total amount will vary whether there is a VA-guaranteed loan, a conventional mortgage, or an FHA-insured mortgage involved, but in general they amount to the same items which will also vary with the location of the property. The amount shown at the top of the next page is fairly typical of a privately insured conventional loan on a $20,000 home, with the loan of say $18,000.

Closing Costs

Finders fee 1 percent of the loan	$180.00
Title Insurance (varies with area)	95.00
Fire Insurance (varies with area)	42.00
Survey (varies with area)	50.00
Credit Report (varies with area)	10.00
Appraisal fee	40.00
Mortgage Insurance (first year in advance)	58.00
Recording of Deed (varies with area)	4.00
Recording of Mortgage (varies with area)	4.00
Attorney's fee for drawing mortgage (varies with area)	25.00
Taxes one year in advance (varies with area)	125.00
	$633.00

A study done for the United States Savings and Loan League indicated that the greatest number of conventional borrowers are between 35 and 54. This might suggest that the majority of FHA and VA borrowers are probably below 40 years of age. The study also showed that most of the homeowners are in the 35-54 years of age group, and, what is perhaps more important in terms of predictions of future home ownership, that as incomes rise so does home ownership. This suggests that the proportion of home ownership in any group varies directly with income. Thus, if incomes continue to rise, it can be safely predicted that the percentages of home ownership will also rise, which means additional prosperity for the broker. This was pointed out in Chapter 1, but it merits additional emphasis.

LARGE OR SMALL DOWN PAYMENTS?

The question of whether or not an individual should put as large a down payment on his house as he can afford or place the maximum mortgage on the house is a question open to debate and can be resolved only by the individual. In general the arguments take the following form:

1. A large down payment is a form of investment because it reduces the total interest payments. Some argue against this, saying interest is not great enough when figured in terms of yield possibilities of other investments. In addition, it is argued that this form of investment is nonliquid and that it is tied up, at least until the owner is able to sell the house for what he paid for it.

2. A small down payment is better, some say, because the interest payments are deductible from the individual income tax, which offsets the interest payment on the mortgage.

3. In an inflation period it is good to have money in a house as distinguished from holding cash because, as there is a general rise in the price level, the value of the home will have a tendency to increase with it.

4. Where there is a possibility that the homeowner may have to move, it is better to make a small down payment because it is easier to sell to a person "assuming" or "taking subject to" the existing mortgage.

TAXES AND ASSESSMENTS

Although real property taxes and assessments are applicable to all types of real property, because of the greater numbers of homeowners involved, the topic will be dealt with here.

The personal income tax is largely the province of the federal government, but the property tax, both real and personal, lies within the taxing power of local and state government. Approximately 80 percent of tax revenue collected by local governments is from property taxes.

At the moment there is considerable doubt as to whether the real property tax can continue to be used to finance elementary and secondary public school education. The courts in three states, California, Minnesota, and New Jersey, have already said this cannot be done. It should be emphasized that the real property tax has *not* been outlawed in these states. The ruling is simply that expenditures for public education cannot be permitted because different school districts have different amounts of wealth, hence some school districts have more money to spend on public education than other districts. The result of this has been held to be discriminatory.

The Need for Local Income and the Budget

Local government, like any other governmental unit, must pay its debts. About 40 percent of its income goes for schools; 20 percent for highways; 13 percent for health, hospitals, and sanitation; some 9 percent for welfare; and the balance is distributed to pay for other goods and services. Therefore, to arrive at the amount of real property tax, a budget is prepared and an estimate is made of income from all sources and the probable expenditures that will be necessary during the ensuing fiscal year. An estimate is made of sources of income other than from real property taxation, and this amount is deducted from the budget. These sources may be a local sales tax and special license taxes, for example.

Assessed Valuations

In practice, as a part of the budget-making process, the proper city officials will have an idea as to the assessed valuation of all taxable real property. The total assessed valuation of property is determined by an appraisal by the tax assessors of all taxable property. In most areas assessors do assess at fair market value, which is defined as the price, estimated in terms of money, which a property will bring if exposed for sale in the open market, allowing a reasonable time to find a purchaser who buys with knowledge of all uses to which it is adapted.

Determining the Tax

Once a budget has been prepared and once the total assessed valuation of properties is known, the tax rates can be determined. For example, suppose the budget is $100,000. Assume $25,000 income is estimated from sources other than the real property tax. The balance of $75,000 is to be raised by real property taxation. Assume that the tax roll shows an assessed valuation of $1,000,000. To determine the rate, the $1,000,000 is divided into the needed $75,000 which is a rate of .075 per $1 or $7.50 per $100 of assessed valuation.

This may be subject to several local variations. In some states, the state government may set a maximum rate per $100 that the municipality can tax, for example, $2.50 per $100 of assessed valuation. In these areas assessors frequently have deliberately assessed properties at a percentage of fair market value and then have entered the properties on the rolls as that of their fair market value. For example, a $10,000 home may be assessed and the tax applied to 50 percent of value. Thus, if the local rate has to go above the state limitation of $2.50 per $100 of value, the assessors can, the following year, assess at 55 percent of value to increase the local tax revenue.

Assessments

Assessments are charges placed against a parcel of property to pay for a specific improvement. For example, curbs may be placed along a street. The theory is that those living along that particular street will be benefited from the curbs. Furthermore, the assumption is that the land will benefit; consequently, buildings are not considered in the assessment process. The charges for the curb in this instance are apportioned among the property owners whose land is benefited. Frequently, property owners will be able to spread out the assessment over a number of years in order to make payments. This is true even though assessments are not recurring as are real property taxes. For example, a parcel may be assessed $1,000 for an improvement. Rather than force the property owner into the position of assuming this heavy burden in one year, the owner may be billed for $200 per year over a five-year period.

It should be noted that courts will refuse to permit special assessments unless it can be demonstrated that the property will be benefited. This has been interpreted in most cases to mean that the value of the property must be enhanced by the proposed improvement.

Tax Sales

If the property taxes are not paid within a specified time, the taxing authority has a lien against the property. This lien is enforced by means of a tax sale. The lienor advertises the property for sale, and the sale is held in one of two ways, depending upon the state statute.

1. Bidding "On Interest." This is the most common way of holding the sale. Assume that the tax due is $100, and that the penalty for unpaid taxes provided by statute is 18 percent for the first six months the taxes are in arrears, 12 percent for the second six months, 6 percent for the entire second year, and 6 percent for the entire third year. (These rates may vary from state to state or, in some cases, even between counties within a state.) Assume, for purposes of simplification, there are only two bidders, *A* and *X*. When the parcel is put up for sale, *A* may shout, "Twelve, first six months." At this point, it is necessary to be aware of the fact that a successful bidder will receive a "Tax Certificate." If he then pays the taxes for three more years (two in some states), he will receive a quitclaim deed from the county treasurer, and the property will be his. However, if the taxpayer pays the taxes which are in arrears plus penalties during this period, the bidder must assign the tax certificate to the taxpayer. The net effect of this is to remove the claim, and the property is again held free and clear by the taxpayer. Thus, when the bidding is "on interest," the bidders are setting the penalties within the statutory limits. Therefore, *A's* bid is interpreted as follows: he is willing to pay the tax of $100 per year for the next three years, and if the taxpayer wants to redeem at anytime during the first six months, he must repay *A* $100 plus 12 percent interest for that time period. Furthermore, if the taxpayer does not redeem until the last day of the three-year period, he must pay *A* interest on taxes that have been paid by *A* during the period as follows: 12 percent for the first six months, 12 percent for the second six months, and 6 percent for the balance of the time.

In the situation above, *X* may follow *A* by putting in a bid, "First six months off." This means that he is willing to pay the tax and take no interest during the first six months. Thus, if the taxpayer redeems during the first six months, *X* will merely receive the $100 he paid in taxes, but will receive no interest. However, if the taxpayer redeems after the first six months, then he will have to pay *X* the taxes he paid plus the statutory rate of interest.

After *X* has bid the first six months off, *A* can bid the second six months off, or even "All off." The "all off" bid means that *A* is willing to pay the taxes for three years; and if the property is redeemed at any time during that period, the taxpayer pays no interest to *A*. *A* is taking a chance that the taxpayer will fail to redeem and that he will receive the property at the end of the three-year period. In addition, *A* is assuming that if he does receive the property, then the value of the property will be greater than the amount of taxes that he has paid during that three-year period.

2. Bidding on Property. In some states where a tax lien exists, the property is put up for public auction. The highest bidder receives the tax certificate. The taxpayer may redeem his property by paying the bidder the *taxes* (not necessarily his bid), plus the statutory interest for the statutory period (usually a maximum of three years).

In many of the states where the bidding is on the property, the successful bidder at the end of the statutory time either receives a quitclaim deed from the county treasurer or he may foreclose on the tax lien much in the nature of a mortgage foreclosure.

MOBILE HOMES

The fastest growing segment of the single-family housing industry is the mobile home. At the time of this writing about a half million mobile homes are being built and sold annually. This type of residence accounts for about a third of the single-family residences being built each year. More important perhaps, mobile homes account for about 96 percent of *all* the single-family homes costing less than $15,000. According to L. Joseph Salm, United States Savings and Loan League assistant vice president: "Mobile homes, after all, are inexpensive housing, and they fill a void found in most communities." [10]

With the increased popularity of the mobile home, the design has changed. In 1961, 98 percent of all mobile homes were 10 feet wide by 50 or 60 feet long. Today most of the units are 12 feet wide and 60 to 65 feet long. The prices range from $5,000 to $25,000 with an average cost of $6,000. And recently in St. Paul, Minnesota, the Mobile American Corporation constructed a mobile home park in which the units are placed in a concrete structure stacked three high. This marks the beginning of the high-rise mobile park, with another in the planning stage of seven stories high.

Financing

The rapid rise in mobile homes sales can be directly attributed to the Housing Act of 1968. The Act provides that mobile homes can be FHA insured on a consumer-type loan. The "consumer-type" loan referred to is an "add-on" interest loan. *Add-on* refers to

[10] "Mobile Homes: On a Clear Day You Can See Some Clouds," *Savings and Loan News,* Vol. XCII, No. 11 (November, 1971), p. 46.

the technique in which interest on the entire principal over the life of the loan is added on at the start when the installment payments are computed. Thus a 10-year, $6,000 mobile home loan written at a 7 percent add-on rate carries an effective yield of 11.69 percent.

Currently the longest allowable maturity on a savings and loan association mobile home loan is 12 years, and the experience of lenders indicates that many loans are repaid in six years.

Advantages and Disadvantages

Like any type of shelter, the mobile home has its advantages and disadvantages.

Advantages. One of the biggest advantages in favor of the mobile home is that it does offer housing to people who could not otherwise afford to buy a home. It has helped to fill the void left by the relatively high cost of conventional housing. For young couples it offers a complete housing package, including furnishings, at a relatively low cost. For the elderly, it also offers relatively inexpensive housing and often a retirement life-style similar to that offered in condominium complexes. In many instances this is true because it is easier to qualify for a mobile home mortgage than for an FHA, VA, or conventional mortgage on the conventional single-family house.

Disadvantages. One of the biggest arguments against the mobile home is that many of them are substandard because of lack of code enforcement. This has resulted from the very nature of the mobile home. The lack of enforcement logic moves in a big circle. First, it is argued that because mobiles have wheels, they are treated as vehicles and taxed as vehicles. Second, because they lack engines, they don't come under motor vehicle safety codes. Finally, since they are not affixed to foundations, they are not subject to building codes. All of this contributes to substandard construction in many of the inexpensive homes.

Directly related to the substandard construction is the danger from fire. Due to the fact that much of the paneling has a lacquered finish, they are likely to burn at a much more rapid rate than do more conventional homes.

Another argument against the mobile home is the high interest rate that was previously indicated. The rate is high because the loan is treated as a consumer loan rather than as a real property loan.

Mobile homes have a tendency to depreciate in value rather than appreciate, as do conventional homes during periods of rising prices. The highest rate of depreciation comes in the early years of the mobile home. It has been estimated that after 6½ years the mobile has a market value of only about half its original life. After 15 years, it will sell at a price somewhere between 20 percent and 35 percent of its original cost.

Future Trends

Recently nearly one out of three families moving into single-family units moved into mobile homes. This suggests that the mobile home is becoming a substitute for the conventional home. Furthermore, the high cost of construction is aiding in the growth and acceptance of the mobile home. In addition, mobile home parks are becoming more attractive, which should contribute to the growth of this industry. There is no reason to believe that the popularity of mobile homes will not continue in the future. In fact they should account for from 25 to 30 percent of the new single-family dwelling units in the next few years.

QUESTIONS FOR REVIEW

1. List and explain three reasons for owning a house.
2. What are the four methods of acquiring a home?
3. Discuss two advantages of home ownership and two disadvantages.
4. Discuss the biggest advantage and the biggest disadvantage to owning a mobile home.
5. What generalization can be drawn with regard to the relationship between income and housing expense?
6. What are the basic FHA standards that must be met on a property before the FHA will insure a loan?
7. The following statement appeared in the *New York Times* in an article entitled "Equity v. Mortgage"—"Another question to be considered is that of inflation. Money tied up in the home's equity is

subject to the same inflationary reactions as funds that are immobile in life insurance accounts." Point out and explain the fallacy.

8. Distinguish between a real property tax and a real property assessment.
9. Comment on the possible future of the real property tax.

PROBLEMS

1. Frank and May Smith rent an apartment for $250 per month. Some of their friends are trying to get them to buy a home to obtain tax advantages.
   (a) What are the advantages of home ownership?
   (b) The Smiths both hate yard work, but they do want the tax advantages. What should they do?
2. David and Eloise Shaw would like to buy a home for $25,000. They have two children, and David earns $7,500 annually. They have $2,000 in cash and could assume two mortgages of $23,000 consisting of a first mortgage with monthly payments of $144.10 (including principal, interest, insurance, and taxes) and a second mortgage of $67.06.

   Can they afford this home? Why, or why not?

SUGGESTED READINGS

Ring, Alfred A. *Real Estate Principles and Practices,* 7th ed. Englewood Cliffs, New Jersey: Prentice-Hall, Inc., 1972. Chapter 29.

Weimer, Arthur M., Homer Hoyt, and George F. Bloom. *Real Estate,* 6th ed. New York: The Ronald Press Company, 1972. Chapter 21.

Chapter 11

Real Property Insurance

The broad subject of real property insurance has a definite place in the study of real estate and real estate principles. One of the reasons is that the real estate practitioner often engages in the insurance business. A more important reason, perhaps, is the fact that any businessman dealing with property of any type must, of necessity, become involved with a certain amount of risk. Over some of these risks, such as economic, political, or social, the individual has little or no control. However, the businessman should be aware of those risks involving possible property loss over which he has no control and those risks which he can shift to others. All property owners face the risk of loss by fire, but this is a risk type that can be shifted to someone else in the form of fire insurance.

FUNDAMENTAL PRINCIPLES

Insurance Defined

Insurance is a device by means of which one party through a contract, called a *policy,* and for a consideration, called a *premium,* undertakes to assume for another party certain types of risk of loss.

Insurance is basically social in nature in that it represents cooperation for mutual protection. Through the payment of premiums by many assureds, the few who suffer losses are indemnified.

Statistically, insurance is based on large numbers of individual risks, for what is unpredictable for the individual becomes predictable for a large number of individuals. It would be a gamble for an individual *not* to insure his real property against fire, but it is not a gamble for an insurance company to sell security against fire loss. This is true because it is possible for the company to predict the probable number of losses that will be suffered out of a known large number of risks. There is also the assurance that the small contributions of the individual policyholders will more than compensate for any loss claims that may be made against the company.

To make insurance feasible, therefore, large numbers of individual risks must be combined with a relative independence of events. For example, a fire insurance company will not insure too many homes in any one location for fear that the uncertain events will be dependent. A major fire in one section of a city might produce an undue number of claims against an insurance company that unwisely provided insurance for large numbers of contiguous properties.

Insurable Interest

An *insurance policy* is a contract whereby the insured pays the insurance company a premium, and the company agrees to pay the insured for any loss that he might suffer to his property, provided that the loss actually occurs. It must be remembered that the insurance contract is not a gambling contract. Historically, many insurance contracts were in reality gambling contracts. This was especially true of marine insurance. Early in England during the development of marine insurance, people who neither owned the ship nor the cargo took out insurance on either a ship or its cargo and hoped that the ship would be lost. They were, in fact, betting that the ship would go down, and in many instances they collected the value of the cargo or ship from the insurance company. This was soon discouraged by an act of Parliament, and from this there developed our modern concept of "insurable interest."

Today, in order for one to collect under an insurance policy, one must have an insurable interest in the subject matter of the insurance. What then is an insurable interest? For there to be an *insurable interest*, there must exist a relationship between the insured and the event insured against so that the happenings of the event will cause the insured some injury or loss. The interest of the insured may be legal or equitable, but he does not have to have legal or equitable title in the property. The insured must, however, in some way be actually interested in the subject matter of the insurance at the time of loss.

THE STANDARD FIRE INSURANCE POLICY

Like any other insurance policy, a fire policy is designed basically to indemnify. It should be noted at the very beginning that the policy does not call for the assured's making a profit from a fire loss. He is reimbursed his full loss under certain conditions and no more.

The fire insurance contract went through a number of forms until, in 1943, through the work of the National Association of Insurance Commissioners, the New York standard fire insurance policy was developed. This standard policy has since been adopted by the District of Columbia and all the states, except Maine, Minnesota, Massachusetts, and Texas, where the variation is very slight.

The Parties

The insurance policy is a contract; and, like any other contract, it contains the names of the parties. This is important because the contract does not follow the property; it is a contract with a particular person—a contract to indemnify that particular person in the event of a loss. Thus, it becomes obvious that this is the real reason for the care that must be exercised by the broker or attorney upon title closing to transfer the insurance or to have a new policy issued to the purchaser. Because, having transferred the property, a seller no longer has an insurable interest in the property and also because this is a "personal contract," a new policy must be made between the company and the new owner as the parties to the contract.

It will be recalled that in the discussion of mortgages it was stated that one of the common clauses of the mortgage is the insurance clause stating that insurance will be carried by the mortgagor for the benefit of the mortgagee. Therefore, where such a situation exists, the mortgagee is named as one of the parties to the insurance contract, and the amount of the loss to the extent of the interest of the mortgagee in the property will be paid to the mortgagee. Any loss over and above the interest of the mortgagee will be paid to the owner or mortgagor.

Consideration

Like any other contract, the insurance contract has a consideration commonly called the *premium*. Here is mentioned the amount of the policy, and the consideration is given as so much per $100 of the coverage of the policy. It should be remembered at this point that the face value of the policy merely measures the maximum liability on the part of the company, and not necessarily its actual liability on any particular loss, except in those states which have valued policy laws.

Description of the Property

The description of the property is an important part of the insurance contract. The description is given by means of a "form" that is attached to the policy and describes not only what is insured but also the location of the insured property. Because the insurance rates vary with the location and the use of the premises, various forms are employed to cover different situations. For example, if the property insured is a private home, the form will specifically state that the coverage is for a private dwelling. If a manufacturing concern is being covered, the form will describe the building, machinery, stock, etc., because the various items mentioned may carry different rates of insurance.

In the final analysis, the form is a device to aid brokers and agents. Through its use the brokers and the agents have a ready instrument to cover all situations without the necessity on their part of drawing up the contract, using their own language, which would more often than not prove inadequate and a source of later trouble. Thus, the many types of coverage are readily available for the brokers and agents in the forms; i.e., dwelling house forms, apartment forms, mercantile forms, and forms for churches, garages, and so on.

Extent of Protection

The standard fire policy clearly delineates the extent of the protection given under the policy. The policy insures against *direct* loss, "by fire, lightning, and by removal from premises endangered by the perils insured against in this policy, except as herein provided." The words "direct loss" have been interpreted so as to exclude any loss engendered as a result of business interruption and the like. Other policies, which will be discussed later in this chapter, cover those situations.

There must, of course, be a loss by fire. This means that there must be a loss from a "hostile" fire. This suggests then that there are "friendly" fires, and further suggests that the policy does not cover damages resulting from such fires.

The fire in a stove is a friendly fire. Assume for the purpose of illustration that the household furniture in a home is covered by a policy, and that a piece of furniture is accidentally thrown into the fire, then loss would not be covered by the policy. By the same token any damage to the home, as a result of smoke from a damaged chimney, would not result in a recoverable loss. However, if the house catches on fire as a result of a defective chimney, then it is said to be a hostile fire and the company is liable for loss under the terms of the policy.

In general, any damages caused by war, rebellion, civil war, usurped power, and the like, are specifically excluded from the policy. Evidences of debt (the note or bond on a mortgage, for example), along with loss of manuscripts and currency are also excluded from the coverage of the standard policy. The policy also specifically excludes damage from windstorm, hail, riot and civil commotion, explosion, aircraft and motor vehicle damage, and smoke. Damages resulting from these causes are taken care of by an extended coverage endorsement attached to the standard policy.

The Extended Coverage Endorsement

The standard fire policy contains a clause which states:

> Any other peril to be insured against or subject of insurance to be covered in this policy shall be by endorsement in writing hereon or added hereto.

This is the clause granting permission to extend the policy to include those things that have been excluded from coverage, that is, for damage from windstorm, hail, riot and civil commotion, explosion, aircraft and motor vehicle damage, and smoke. Extended coverage endorsement will cover loss from these factors.

The extended coverage endorsement is extremely important as far as giving full protection to both the owner of property and any mortgagees. Many lending institutions throughout the country not only insist that the mortgagor procure fire insurance, but also require that there be an extended coverage endorsement on the policy in order to insure full protection to the security for the loan.

Cash Value

The policy states that the company "does insure to the extent of the actual cash value at the time of the loss." Thus, there may be complete destruction of a building and there may not necessarily be a payment to the insured of the full face value of the policy. Recall again that the face value of the policy defines the maximum. In the final analysis, this means that the company will usually pay the *replacement* value of the property. Thus, the clause above is construed to mean reproduction cost less depreciation.

Arbitration

The standard policy contains a provision for arbitration in the event the contracting parties cannot agree as to the extent of the loss. Ordinarily when a loss occurs, the insured obtains estimates of the cost of replacing the loss and any differences are amicably adjusted between the insured and the adjuster for the insurance company. However, in some instances where the parties cannot agree as to the extent of the loss, the policy provides that each of the parties may select an appraiser to estimate the damage. Between them they select an umpire, and the findings of the appraisers are submitted to the umpire for his consideration. If the parties cannot agree upon the umpire, then the judge of a court of record may be asked by either party to select an umpire. The award arrived at is considered to be the actual cash value of the property at the time of the loss, and this then is the amount that is paid to the insured.

Pro Rata Liability

In addition to the clauses above, the standard fire policy contains the statement:

> This company shall not be liable for a greater portion of any loss than the amount hereby insured against shall bear to the whole insurance covering the property against the peril involved, whether collectible or not.

This clause is inserted to provide for the situation in which the insured may have placed his insurance with several companies. This is done particularly when large policies are involved. For example, let us assume that one policy is placed with company *A* in the amount of $30,000, and a second policy is placed with company *B* in the amount of $10,000, totaling $40,000 in all. Under these circumstances, if a loss occurs, then company *A* is liable to the extent of three quarters of the loss under the pro rata liability clause, and company *B* will be liable in the amount of one quarter of the loss.

Diminution by Loss

An important feature for fire policyholders to remember is that the face value of the fire policy decreases when the loss occurs.[1] For example, if the face value of a policy is $10,000, and a loss in the amount of $3,000 occurs, then the policy will continue for only $7,000. In order to bring the policy up to the original amount of $10,000, it is necessary to reinstate the policy in the original amount. This is done by the payment of an additional premium.

Cancellation

The policy contains a clause which states:

> This policy may be canceled at anytime at the request of the insured, in which case, this company shall, upon demand and

[1] This differs in Missouri. The uniform standard Missouri form states: "Any loss hereunder shall not reduce the amount of this policy." This is also true in a few other midwestern states. Another exception may be if the house is under-insured and a partial loss occurs but no repair is made and the house is still worth the face of the policy; then the policy may be left at face value. Under this policy, the face would be paid if loss occurred again and if the loss equaled the face.

surrender of this policy, refund the excess of paid premium above the customary short rates for the expired time.

The important thing to be remembered about this clause is that upon cancellation by the insured, the "short rates" are applicable to the policy for the period of time it was in effect. This means a higher premium rate than a strict mathematically pro rata amount for the period covered by the policy. It should be remembered that in order for the policy to be canceled, there must be actual notice given to the company. This notice may be either oral or written.

Subrogation

The insurance contract contains this clause:

> This company may require from the insured an assignment of all right of recovery against any party for loss to the extent that payment therefor is made by this company.

Although the insured may collect from the company even though the loss is due to his own negligence, the subrogation clause is added to enable the company to collect any sums that it may have paid out to the insured as a result of the negligence of third persons. For example, suppose that a house is situated near a farm and that the farmer on the adjoining premises burns weeds at the edge of his farm in such a negligent manner that the house of the insured catches fire and is destroyed. The insurance company pays the insured and from the insured may, if it desires, have any rights assigned to it that the insured might have had against the farmer for his tort. The company may then bring an action against the farmer for negligence for the amount it has paid out to the insured.

Coinsurance

This clause states, in effect, that the company shall be liable in the event of loss only in the proportion that the amount of insurance bears to the insurance required. The purpose of the coinsurance clause is to adjust the rates equitably between the various policyholders. The fact is that in most fires there is not total loss. Thus, if one were to insure his property for far less than its real worth and there was a fire, without the coinsurance clause he would be able to collect the full amount without paying much in the way of a premium. This would be unfair to the person whose property was insured in the proper amount and who had been paying a higher premium.

The most common coinsurance clause is known as the "80 percent clause," although there may be a 70 percent or 90 percent clause. Under this type of clause, it would not be economical for a person to carry either too little or too much insurance. The question then becomes "How much is enough?" Someone once remarked that anything that made sense could be reduced to a formula, and so it is with the problem of coinsurance. The coinsurance clause states:

> This company shall not be liable for a greater proportion of any loss or damage to the property described herein than the sum hereby insured bears to 80 percent of the actual cash value of said property at the time such loss shall happen, nor for more than the proportion which this policy bears to the total insurance thereon.

Converting this statement into a formula, the result is this:

$$\frac{\text{Amount carried}}{\text{Amount should carry}} \times \text{Actual loss} = \text{Recovery}$$

Assume that the actual cash value of a building is \$20,000 and that an 80 percent clause is in effect; assume further that *A* carries insurance in the amount of \$16,000, and that there is a loss in the amount of \$5,000. Will *A* be able to collect the full \$5,000? Applying the formula given above we get this result:

$$\frac{\text{Amount carried, \$16,000}}{\text{Amount should carry, } (.80 \times 20{,}000)\text{, \$16,000}} \times \$5{,}000 \text{ (loss)} = \$5{,}000$$

Assume the same situation as above, except that *A* carries \$20,000 in insurance instead of \$16,000. Apply the following formula:

$$\frac{\$20{,}000}{\$16{,}000} \times \$5{,}000 = \$6{,}250 \text{ (recovery)}$$

Will this mean that the insured will be able to collect $6,250 when there has been a $5,000 loss? The answer is obviously in the negative. No one makes a profit from a loss; therefore, the insured, *A* in our case, will collect only the $5,000 loss. The inference from this is that *A* is carrying more insurance than he should carry, and is wasting his money on the extra $4,000 worth of insurance.

Assume that the same situation exists, except that *A* is carrying only $10,000 in insurance. Then:

$$\frac{\$10{,}000}{\$16{,}000} \times \$5{,}000 = \$3{,}125$$

In this third situation, the insured did not carry the amount that he was required to carry, and so with the 80 percent clause he was able to collect only $3,125.

The important thing, as far as the homeowner and the broker are concerned, is to be aware of the amount that is required and to carry no less. Extreme care must be taken, however, in periods of rising prices to ascertain the proper amount to carry; otherwise, the insured may discover that he has an insufficient amount of insurance.

LIABILITY INSURANCE

There are many types of liability insurance, but the basic purpose of all the various types of liability policies is to protect the insured from any acts of negligence that he may have committed against the public. For there to be negligence, the insured must have acted without exercising reasonable care. For example, a landlord may fail to repair carpeting on the stairs of his apartment building after he has been notified that it is defective. Someone falls as a result of the defective carpeting and is injured. The landlord is sued—the allegations being that the injury was caused by reason of the negligence of the landlord and that the injured person was in no way contributorily negligent.

Without insurance to cover this type of situation, the owner of the property may suffer the loss of his property. Hence, the property owner must be covered for any number of situations, some of which will be discussed below. In general, the types of liability insurance carried by property owners covers either bodily injury, property damage, or both.

Owners', Landlords', and Tenants' Liability Policy

This type of policy covers liability arising from ownership, maintenance, or use of the premises described in the policy. *Use*, in this case, is interpreted as meaning, among other things, pickups and deliveries, installation, servicing, or removal. The policy also covers injury resulting from uninstalled equipment and abandoned or unused materials.

This type of policy covers the premises and accidents that occur away from the premises in connection with the insured's business.

The so-called "fall down" cases are covered by this type of policy. For example, the floor of a bank is wet after a rainstorm, the bank has failed to wipe the floor, and a customer falls and is injured.

In general, the policy does not cover accidents resulting from defective elevators or hoists of any kind without extra premium being paid for that protection; nor does it cover any situation that should be covered by workmen's compensation insurance, products liability insurance, or a contractor's policy.

Elevator Liability Policy

This is a special policy designed to give protection for the specific exemption in the owners', landlords', and tenants' liability policy. The basis here is that insurance is given against liability arising out of the ownership, maintenance, or use of elevators, hoists, shafts, and so forth. As a practical matter, the amount of the policy should be higher on this type of policy than on any other type of liability policy purchased in connection with real property. The reason for this is that the more serious accidents and, consequently, the greater damages in terms of money loss to owners usually result from accidents of this nature.

A genuine accomplishment resulting from this type of insurance is that even in cities where the city elevator inspection is poor, the owners of buildings with elevators are subject to frequent inspection on the part of the insurance inspectors, with consequent increase in the safety of this type of equipment.

Water Damage Liability Policy

This policy is designed to cover damage to commercial and private properties resulting from water escaping from proper receptacles and conduits. Thus, any leakage from plumbing systems, heating systems, air conditioning systems, or refrigerating systems may be covered. Rain or snow entering through a broken skylight or defective roof and causing damage to the premises and water entering through an open door and causing damage are covered by this type of policy. If a water tank on a roof collapses, with consequent damages, this also is covered by a water damage policy.

Like most policies, the water damage liability policy contains some exceptions. Among them are damages from sprinkler systems, floods, rising tides, and blocked sewers. It also does not cover seepage through the floors of the basement or the building walls.

Sprinkler Leakage Insurance

Most of the modern industrial buildings are equipped with automatic sprinkler systems for protection from fire. With the installation of a sprinkler system, the fire insurance rates are lowered. However, with the installation of the system, it is necessary to obtain sprinkler leakage insurance.

The policy covers damage from three causes: leakage, accidental discharge, and accidents to the tank that furnishes water to the system. In general, any damages to stock, furniture, and fixtures are covered under the policy. It follows from this that the rates are different, depending upon the type of merchandise that is most likely to be found in stock, in the particular type of property insured.

Steam Boiler Insurance

Steam boiler insurance is the common name given to boiler and machinery insurance, often called *power plant insurance*. In essence it is insurance against explosion or breakdown of boilers, engines, machinery, and electrical apparatus, such as motors and generators. The policy includes not only an agreement by the company to pay for loss of the insured's property damaged by an accident, the extra cost of repairing the property as expeditiously as possible, bodily injury, and loss to another person's property, but also for indirect losses if provided for by endorsements. The endorsements cover use and occupancy; that is, a certain sum per day for total suspension of business and a pro rata sum for partial suspension of business. In addition, consequential damages may be covered by an endorsement; that is, damage to property other than the insured object. By endorsement "outage" may also be covered; that is, a sum per hour for each hour that the object named in the schedule is "out."

Glass Insurance

In this type of policy, a schedule is attached to the policy listing all of the glass to be covered under the terms of the insurance. The company promises to pay for any damage to glass, excluding coverage from damage by fire. The rates are determined by the size, cost, kind and use, location, type of occupancy, and territory in which the glass is located.

The Comprehensive General Liability Policy

This type of policy is designed to offer comprehensive coverage so that the client does not have to purchase individual policies covering plate glass, elevator, and the other individual policies described above. A "survey of exposures" is made by an insurance company who by means of this survey notes the kinds of coverage needed by the insured. The types of operations of the insured are described, together with other features of the buildings to be insured; for example, the types and conditions of the elevators. Property damage from any hazard is not included in the basic contract, but may be added to apply to all types of property damage.

Insuring Consequential Losses

This type of insurance insures the policyholder against losses from a fire other than the direct loss to the property of the insured. It is important for the real estate broker to be aware of this type of insurance because the damages resulting from these consequential losses may oftentimes be greater than the loss suffered from the damage by fire to the property itself. The important forms of loss to remember are rent, leasehold, and demolition insurance.

Rent Insurance. This type of insurance covers the loss of future rents or rental value of the premises. This is in the nature of an endorsement to a fire policy and protects the insured from the loss of rents or rental value if the property is made untenantable by fire or other physical damage. The time during which payments are made is limited by the policy; but in no case is the insured entitled to more than the net income that he would have received had the property not been damaged.

Leasehold Insurance. This type of insurance covers loss of the leasehold value. In other words, it protects a tenant when he has leased property with a use value greater than the contract value in the lease. The use value may be greater because of the tenant's having made a profitable lease, improvement in business conditions, improvement in the building or neighborhood, or because of his subletting the premises for more than his contract price. The loss falls on the tenant in this case, either as a result of the termination of the lease or as a result of the loss of use of the premises during the period of repair in the event the lease is not terminated.

Demolition Insurance. By the demolition endorsement to the fire policy, the company assumes liability for any increased cost of repair to the building if such increase is due to legal requirements regulating modes of construction.

Workmen's Compensation Insurance

The key to workmen's compensation insurance coverage are the words "arising out of his employ." Thus, an employee who suffers an accident or contracts a disease arising out of his employ is entitled to workmen's compensation.

In all of the states of the Union, employees are covered by workmen's compensation laws. These laws came about as the result of dissatisfaction with existing laws prior to the advent of the compensation laws. The laws were hard on the workingman—the burden of proof was on him. He had to prove his lack of contributory negligence in order to collect for an injury. He had to overcome the assumption-of-risk rule whereby he was presumed to be paid for any ordinary risks of the employment. In addition, the employer was not liable for any injury caused by the negligence of a fellow employee, and in some states, the right of action against the employer ceased with the death of the injured.

Under the workmen's compensation laws, the theory of negligence is done away with, and the laws provide for compensation for injuries arising out of the injured workman's employment. Therefore, to protect themselves against loss by reason of injury to their employees, employers obtain workmen's compensation policies. If an employee is injured, limits of payments are set up in terms of percentages of weekly salaries. Terms of payment are set up for permanent disabilities, permanent partial disabilities, and death.

The rates paid by the employer are based on an estimate of the payroll of the employer. This estimated payroll, however, is subject to an audit which is usually made about the time that the policy is to expire. After the audit is completed, adjustments of the rate are made to the actual payroll. The amounts of the premiums vary according to the types of hazards encountered by reason of the employment.

QUESTIONS FOR REVIEW

1. What is meant by *insurable interest*?
2. Distinguish between a "hostile" fire and a "friendly" fire. What is the importance of the distinction?
3. Explain the term "cash value" as it is found in a fire insurance policy.
4. If the face value of a fire policy is $15,000 and there is a $5,000 loss which is paid to the assured as a result of the loss, and there later is a $12,000 loss, what is the maximum the company will pay in most states?
5. What is meant by the 80 percent coinsurance clause in a fire policy?
6. Explain the difference between rent insurance and leasehold insurance.
7. What are rates in workmen's compensation based on?

PROBLEMS

1. A mortgagee has a mortgage on a parcel of real property in the amount of $6,000. The building is valued at $15,000 and the land is valued at $5,000. How much fire insurance does the mortgagor have to carry in order to satisfy the mortgagee? Assume that there is an 80 percent coinsurance clause in the policy.
2. *A* owns a building valued at $50,000 without the land. There is an 80 percent coinsurance clause in his insurance contract. *A* insures the property with company *X* for $10,000 and with company *B* for $20,000. The building burns and damages the property to the extent of $30,000. What is the liability of each company?
3. Joe Smith has a building with an appraised value of $100,000. There is a fire causing damage of $25,000. He has one policy of $25,000 with company A, one of $35,000 with company B, another $35,000 with company C, and one of $5,000 with company D. How much is each company liable for?
4. A person living in the country has a kerosene lamp; he left the house unattended.
   (a) The lamp caused soot damage. Can the owner collect under his fire policy?
   (b) A curtain blew over the flame of the kerosene lamp and the house was destroyed by fire. Can he collect under his fire policy?
5. An insurance contract is said to be a personal contract. How does the case of *Porobenski* v. *American Alliance Ins. Co., of New York,* bear out this statement?

Porobenski v. American Alliance Ins. Co., of New York
Supreme Court of Pennsylvania, 317 Pa. 410, 176 A. 205

DREW, J. This is an action on a policy of fire insurance upon a barn and its contents issued by the defendant to the plaintiff. The policy contained the usual provision that "this entire policy shall be void . . . if the interest of the insured be other than unconditional and sole ownership." At the trial, plaintiff admitted that the property was held by himself and his wife as tenants by the entirety, under a deed made to them jointly by the plaintiff after their marriage. There was no proof that the plaintiff had the entire beneficial ownership or that the defendant or his agent had any notice as to how the property was held. On motion, the trial judge entered a compulsory nonsuit at the close of the plaintiff's case on the ground, *inter alia* (among others), that the plaintiff was not the unconditional and sole owner of the property insured. The court refused to take off the nonsuit and the plaintiff appealed.

It is true that a tenant by the entirety is regarded as seized of the whole estate, and not of an undivided interest . . . and that the right of the survivor to the whole is considered as arising not from a new estate but from a continuation of the old. . . . But the husband is not the sole and unconditional owner, as the plaintiff contends. If he predeceases his wife, the entire estate continues in her, to the exclusion of his heirs, his judgment creditors, and purchasers under judgments against him. . . . He is not the sole owner because his wife has rights as great as his; he is not the unconditional owner because his interest will cease and determine if he predeceases her. . . .

It follows that the nonsuit was properly entered, for the reason that the plaintiff was not the unconditional and sole owner of the property insured. In this state of the case it is unnecessary to pass on the other questions argued by the parties.

SUGGESTED READINGS

Athearn, James L. *Risk and Insurance.* New York: Appleton-Century-Crofts, 1962. Chapters 5, 13, and 25.

Greene, Mark R. *Risk and Insurance,* 3d ed. Cincinnati: South-Western Publishing Co., 1973. Chapters 8, 9, and 10.

Ring, Alfred A. *Real Estate Principles and Practices,* 7th ed. Englewood Cliffs, New Jersey: Prentice-Hall, Inc., 1972. Chapter 22.

Chapter 12

Industrial and Commercial Property

Broadly speaking, industrial and commercial property is classed by government statisticians as nonresidential construction. This includes such things as highways and sewer and water systems as well as our major interest here, namely, industrial buildings and commercial buildings, including office buildings and retail stores and excluding apartment buildings. Although industrial-commercial activity is but a part of nonresidential construction, it is, by any standards, big business. For example, in 1972 the dollar volume of nonresidential private construction topped $36 billion and will probably approach this for some years to come.

THE DEMAND FOR INDUSTRIAL AND COMMERCIAL PROPERTY

The demand for land and for industrial and commercial property is said to be a derived demand. The thought underlying this is that there are four things which a producer has to employ in combination in order to produce a good. These four items are: land, labor, capital, and enterprise or management. In combination these items are called the production function.

The demand by profit-seeking firms for these factors arises because consumers are willing to pay for the produced good now or in the future. Consequently, the demand for the factors is ultimately derived from effective consumer demand. Thus, if there is a demand for men's shirts, there will then be a demand for land upon which to construct the factories to produce men's shirts. By the same token, if there is a population (consumer) movement from the central city to outlying areas, there will be derived from that a demand for retail space to serve these consumers.

LOCATION OF INDUSTRIAL ACTIVITY

Industry and manufacturing follow the growth of trade. However, there are additional factors determining the location of industry. Most important is the availability of adequate and economical transportation. Historically, the most economical transportation was both water and rail.

Heavy industry locates close to sources of raw materials so that the hauls will be relatively short and transportation charges will be relatively low. Conversely, location of industries near the markets assures shorter hauls and lower transportation charges on the finished products.

There are a number of patterns of industry location relating to transportation. The petroleum refining industry frequently locates close to the source of crude oil from which refined oil can be economically transported by pipeline. Forest product processing, which results in reduction of weights, is frequently located near areas producing timber because of transportation charges. Mineral smelting is conducted near industrial cities to which ore can be economically transported from the mines. In short, freight rates are used as a device for promoting or concentrating industry or for its dispersion. It cannot be overemphasized that transportation facilities and rates are tremendous factors in the location of the cities.

According to Hoover, the principal factors in the location of industry are:

1. Available labor supply, number of skills represented, wage rates, degree of unionization, history of labor-management relations.
2. Location of markets to be served.

3. Accessibility to raw materials used in the industrial process.

4. Community acceptance of the industry, degree of cooperation to be expected from governmental officials in granting permits, equitable tax rates, and similar terms.

5. Costs of operation in the location, including utilities, labor, and materials.

6. Living conditions for employees.

7. Existence of competing and supplementary industries.[1]

An analysis of a number of studies evaluating industrial location factors pretty well bears out Hoover's basic assumptions.[2] The results are compiled in Table I (pages 326 and 327) and summarized in Table II (page 328), with markets being the primary factor for plant location and taxes and financial inducements being of little significance.

Location from the Viewpoint of the Firm

Although Hoover's principal factors of location listed above are theoretical, firms do locate with many of these factors in mind. Some firms approach the problem mathematically. For example, Walter Kidde Constructors, a consulting firm, will rate both tangible and intangible factors. They use 1000 points as the top grade, with minimum and maximum points for each factor after careful analysis of alternative sites as well as careful analysis of the firm itself. Analysis of the firm includes examination of operating statements, sales records, and the like.

Table III on page 328 compares alternative sites A and B for a light-metal fabricating company.

It should be noted that each factor is broken down and analyzed. For example, the site factor has a minimum of 50 and a maximum of 70 points. This range is based on level site requirements with good soil-bearing characteristics. In this case A was given 70 points (the perfect score for site), while B was awarded only 60 points. Although both met the maximum (70 points) standard, it was

---

[1] Edgar M. Hoover, Part One, "Locational Preferences and Patterns." *The Location of Economic Activity* (New York: McGraw-Hill Book Company, 1948).

[2] William E. Morgan, *Taxes and the Location of Industry* (Boulder, Colorado: University of Colorado Press, January, 1967).

TABLE I

Evaluation of Industrial Location Factors [a]

AREA	STUDY	PERIOD OF STUDY [b]	NUMBER OF RESPONSES	LOCATION FACTORS					
				MARKETS	LABOR (AVAIL-ABILITY OR COST)	RAW MATERIALS	TRANSPOR-TATION	TAXES	FINANCIAL INDUCEMENTS
Colorado	Crampon and DeGood	1948-1957	253	3	2	3	2	1	1
Florida	Greenhut	1956-1957	752	3	2	2	2	1	1
Georgia	Cobb	1954-1956	130	3	2	2	2	1	1
Maryland	Maryland State Planning Commission	1946-1951	118	3	3	3	3	1	1
Minnesota	Business Executive's Research Com.	[c]	215	3	3	2	3	2	1
New Jersey	Flink	1954-1956	242	2	2	[d]	3	2	1
New York City Area	Griffin	[c]	309	3	2	2	2	1	1
Oregon	Ballaine	1948-1958	166	3	2	3	2	1	[d]
South	Bergin & Eagan	1956-1960	1,800	3	3	3	2	1	1
South	Cella	1945-1954	[e]	3	3	3	3	1	1
Texas	Escott	1952-1954	122	3	2	2	2	1	[d]
Texas	Paine	[c]	350	3	3	3	2	1	[d]
West Virginia	Thompson and Isaack	1945-1956	93	3	3	3	3	1	1
Wisconsin	Business Research Council, Univ. of Wisconsin	[c]	463	3	3	3	2	3	[d]

TABLE I (Concluded)

United States & Canada [f]	Metro. Life Ins. Co. & Nat'l. Elec. Light Assoc.	[c]	10,267	3	3	3	2	1	1	
Nineteen Cities [f]	Business Week	[c]	283	3	3	3	3	2	[d]	
[f]	Dun's Review	[c]	107	3	3	2	3	1	1	
Total Responses			15,670							
Total and Percent Distribution of the Coded Values of the Location Factors										TOTAL
Unweighted Total				50 (23.6%)	44 (20.8%)	42 (19.8%)	41 (19.3%)	22 (10.4%)	13 (6.1%)	212 (100.0%)
Weighted Total Based on the Sample Size of Each Survey (Excludes U.S. and Canada Survey)				15,967 (23.7%)	14,235 (21.1%)	13,848 (20.6%)	11,867 (17.6%)	7,069 (10.5%)	4,369 (6.5%)	67,355 (100.0%)
Weighted Total Based on the Sample Size of Each Survey (Includes all Surveys)				46,768 (23.3%)	45,036 (22.4%)	44,649 (22.2%)	32,398 (16.1%)	17,336 (8.6%)	14,636 (7.3%)	200,823 (100.0%)

[a] Code: 3—Primary location factor.
2—Of some importance.
1—Of little or no importance.

[b] Period of time during which the firms sampled located in the area.

[c] Sample was not selected on the basis of the time period in which the plants located in the area.

[d] Factor was not included on the questionnaire.

[e] Number of responses not indicated.

[f] Area not indicated.

Sources: Based on the findings of the seventeen surveys listed above.

TABLE II

Significance of Location Factors According to Business Opinion, as Revealed by 17 Questionnaire Surveys

FACTOR	NUMBER OF SURVEYS		
	PRIMARY SIGNIFICANCE	SOME SIGNIFICANCE	LITTLE SIGNIFICANCE
Markets	16	1	—
Labor	10	7	—
Raw Materials	10	6	—
Transportation	7	10	—
Taxes	1	3	13
Financial Inducements	—	—	13

Source: Based on Table I.

TABLE III

Comparison of Alternative Sites

	MIN-MAX	LOCATION A	LOCATION B
Sites	50-70	70	60
Shipping and Transportation	35-61	29	59
Labor	300-553	538	316
Utilities	30-52	35	47
Community Factors	90-129	102	106
Taxes	49-75	65	55
Inducements	20-60	50	44
Total	565-1000	909	687

Source: *Factory,* December, 1962, p. 58.

discovered that there was a history of flooding at extreme conditions. Therefore, B was given only 60 points.

Table IV at the top of the next page has more subdivisions, again each with a minimum and maximum; A's total and B's total from this separate analysis are incorporated into Table III, which is sort of a master sheet.

TABLE IV

Shipping and Transportation Point-Rating Breakdown

CLASSIFICATION	MIN-MAX	LOCATION A	LOCATION B
Freight In and Out	15-20	17	20
Railroad Service	5-10	5	10
Commercial Supply			
Houses Nearby	3-5	3	5
Airport Service	1-2	1	2
Trucking Service	5-15	5	15
Post Office, First Class	3	3	3
Travel Distance from:			
Corporate Headquarters	0-1	1	0
Main Highway System	2-3	3	3
Water Transportation	1-2	1	1
Total	35-61	39	59

Source: *Factory,* December, 1962, p. 58.

In the table above Freight In and Out was the most important factor. Because it was determined that location A would cost $265,000 for this factor while B would cost $245,000, A was given 17 points and B, 20. Thus each item is scored and totals carried to the master sheet.[3]

Location from the Viewpoint of the Community

Most communities feel that industry is an asset to the community. Some specific reasons are given in Chapter 27. Basically the reason for the desire for additional industry in an area is economic; however, there are other reasons. In smaller cities young people frequently leave the community because of lack of employment opportunities. One school of thought holds that the community has fostered loyalty to the community in early life, by guidance and through education, and "this sense of loyalty should not be disillusioned by economic difficulties when the time comes for young people to enter the job market on a full-time basis . . ." [4]

---

[3] "Plant Location," *Factory* (December, 1962), pp. 56-59.

[4] Richard B. Andrews, *Urban Growth and Development* (New York: Simmons-Boardman Publishing Corporation, 1962), p. 14.

Furthermore, having invested much money in the education of youth, their leaving is an economic waste. Their leaving also reduces the pool of industrial labor resulting in possible demands for increased wages by remaining labor. This, in turn, may force local industry into other areas.

Another argument for having industry in the community has been termed the "Tax Profit" aspects of manufacturing.[5] Briefly this means that industrial and commercial property on a per property basis has a high value; and community services, for example, fire protection, are less expensive to the community as a result. For example, it is cheaper to protect one $2,000,000 industrial building than 100 homes of $20,000 each which are spread out over a relatively large area. Hence, the idea of "tax profits."

Of course, from the community viewpoint, it behooves city fathers to tax industry equitably rather than make it the "tax goat" as some cities have done.

When seeking industry, many communities seek industry that is considered "clean." In short some community leaders argue that industry must not be offensive to "sight, sound, or smell." This implies "light" manufacturing in most cases. As a general rule, this attitude is reduced in proportion to city growth. The idea of "clean" versus "unclean" industry is highly controversial and will continue to be for some time to come. It might be well for some city fathers to recognize that as a general rule "clean" industry is "light" industry, frequently renting space rather than purchasing space. This implies, of course, that "light" industry can move its operations to another community more readily than "heavy" industry.

The Location of Commercial Space

It would seem desirable for analytical purposes to examine commercial space in terms of (a) retail space, and (b) other commercial property.

Retail Space. Like the demand for industrial property, the demand for retail property is said to be a derived demand. Put more succinctly, retail trade follows the consumer. As a general rule, retail

[5] *Ibid.*, p. 10.

trade, hence the demand for retail space, seems to be moving along with suburbia to areas outside the central business district. For example, in 1960, the number of citizens living in the suburbs had grown to equal the number residing in the large cities. By 1970 their proportion had diminished to 45 percent, while the suburban share of the population rose to 50 percent. At the same time as the consumer spending power in the cities rose by about a fifth, the spending power in the suburbs rose two thirds.[6]

With the movement of population to suburban areas, shopping centers have developed. A *shopping center* is an area in which a large number of stores and shops of various types are located and in which the large majority of consumer wants may be satisfied. It has been said that the modern shopping center is really an initial development in the ecological adjustment of commercial enterprise. In short, it is change in the economic structure of the central city.

There are five commonly identified retail areas: (1) central shopping districts, (2) secondary shopping centers, (3) local neighborhood shopping areas, (4) the ribbon-type business development along streets zoned for commercial use, and (5) the modern, planned, integrated center. Centers are divided into four main categories:

(a) The regional shopping center with a major department store of 100,000 square feet and a total store area of 250.000 to 1,000,000 square feet on a 50-100-acre tract. This type center can be supported only in a trade area with a population of 200,000 persons or more.

(b) A community center with a junior department store of 25,000 to 90,000 square feet, and a total store area of 100,000 to 400,000 square feet on a site of 15 to 40 acres, supported by a population of 100,000 or less.

(c) A large neighborhood center with a variety or clothing store of 10,000 to 20,000 square feet as the largest unit with a total store area of 50,000 to 100,000 square feet on a site of 10 to 20 acres.

(d) Small neighborhood centers with a supermarket of 20,000 to 30,000 square feet as the largest unit and a total of not over 50,000 square feet including a drugstore, hardware

[6] "A Decade of Suburban Growth," *The Conference Board Record,* U.S. Department of Commerce, Vol. VIII, No. 9 (September, 1971), pp. 38-39.

store, and other local convenience shops on a site of five to ten acres. These centers need between 5,000 to 10,000 population.[7]

(e) The superregional shopping center consisting of two, three, or four major department stores with an aggregate store area of 500,000 square feet; specialty apparel stores with 200,000 square feet; and other stores with 300,000 square feet. There must be a minimum of 100 acres, with additional space for office buildings and apartment buildings adjacent to or in the center. There must be at least 100,000 families with an estimated annual income of at least one billion dollars to support such a center.

The important point here is that all of these retail structures are the result of a derived demand from population. In the development of a shopping center both prospective tenants and financial institutions demand an economic feasibility study to determine whether or not a shopping center is likely to succeed. These studies usually consist of six parts: (1) population, (2) income of the population, (3) buying power (attempting to break down dollars available to population in relation to expenditures by proposed store types and price lines), (4) competitive facilities, (5) accessibility of the proposed site, and (6) other related considerations, for example, shoppers' buying habits.

OTHER COMMERCIAL PROPERTY

Other commercial property includes such things as office buildings, wholesale buying and selling offices, warehouses, and loft-type buildings housing light industry. Office buildings are typically located in the central city core, devoted to financial institutions, lawyers, and others rendering service to other businessmen and industrialists. The warehouses and light industry are frequently located on the periphery of the central business district.

While much retail activity has been moving to the suburbs, so has much industrial activity. Manufacturing firms whose plants have

[7] Homer Hoyt, "Land Values in Shopping Centers," *The Appraisal Journal*, Volume XXXVII (July, 1969), pp. 345-359.

become obsolete have often been unable to expand because of ancient zoning regulations. Furthermore, farmland around big cities has frequently been sold to industry for $2,500 to $5,000 per acre, while acreage in industrial areas of the cities has gone for as much as $150,000 per acre. Central business districts have been left to office buildings and their satellites: a stationer to supply the offices would fall into this category.

Two major reasons seem to have prevented offices with their financial activities from fleeing as rapidly to suburbia. (1) Information is the stock-in-trade of security dealers and bankers, i.e., information on credit standings. (2) Face-to-face negotiations are often crucial in financial transactions.

INDUSTRIAL ZONING

Although zoning will be detailed in Chapter 28, "City Planning and Zoning," it seems appropriate to make mention of industrial zoning here. As the name falsely implies, an industrial zone is an area set aside for industrial use. In most areas the false implication which breeds trouble arises as a result of what some regard as an improper approach to industrial zoning. The point is that frequently residences are permitted in industrial areas. The latter has merit; the former has not. Historically, the industrial zone was the low man on the zoning totem pole. Land is set aside for industry, but residences are permitted to encroach upon the industrial zone. No thought is given to the *detrimental* effects residences may have in locating in the industrial zone. This may be a loss in efficiency of operation, a loss of "tax profits," previously mentioned, or even "complaints" by homeowners in the industrial area.

More and more citizens and city planners have come to realize that manufacturing is an asset to a community. Not only are residences being excluded from industrial zones, but in many areas the industrial park, both privately and community owned, has grown. In both cases the zoning regulations frequently prohibit more than 50 percent of the land being covered by buildings. Urban industry in dingy buildings generally downgrades the quality of adjoining residential zones. Living near an industrial park surrounded by acres of woods and meadow often proves the reverse.

INDUSTRIAL PARKS

In recent years there has been a rapid growth of the so-called modern industrial park. It has been said that the industrial park is the twin of the residential subdivision. In most cases industrial parks are located in suburban areas and are spacious and beautifully landscaped, and as such are very attractive, so much so, it has been noted that urban dwellers lacking sufficient city park space often are observed on a Sunday afternoon driving around industrial parks just to get out into the wide-open spaces.

What Is an Industrial Park?

One of the best definitions of the *industrial park* is that of the California State Chamber of Commerce, who has defined it as: A planned industrial park in a special or exclusive type of industrial subdivision developed according to a comprehensive plan to provide serviced sites for a community of compatible industries. The industrial park, under continuing management, provides for adequate control of the tract and buildings through restrictive covenants and/or adequate zoning, with a view to maintaining aesthetic value throughout the development.

Types of Industrial Parks

There are basically three types of industrial parks classified according to improvements and facilities:

1. *The Industrial Tract.* This is simply an improved tract of land including provisions for streets, access roads, and utilities. There are no buildings provided.
2. *The Industrial Subdivision.* This is an improved tract of land with industrial buildings. No special services or facilities provided.
3. *The Fully Packaged Estate.* This is an improved tract with buildings with a large enough area to provide sufficient economies of scale and to offer special facilities to industrial occupants.

Benefits to Industry

There are a number of reasons why it may be desirable for industry to locate in an industrial park. The following are a few:

1. Site development costs are reduced. As a rule of thumb, industrial development costs, such as putting in streets, sewers, railroad spurs, etc., will run from three to eight times the cost of the raw land. In the park, the economies of scale by the developer permit cheaper per acre development costs.

2. Smaller plants may have the advantages of large-scale operations (e.g., a common sewer plant).

3. The site is ready. The time lag between the decision to locate and the beginning of production is reduced.

4. "Package plans" are often available. In short, often industry need not get involved much in local negotiations for such things as a zoning change. Furthermore, many industrial parks can offer engineering services and often actual financing of both the land and proposed buildings.

5. Investment protection. Industry doesn't have to buy excess land to insulate itself from deterioration of nearby properties if the industrial park is well conceived.

Benefits to the Community

The community may gain from:

1. Diversification of industry. In short, the economic base of the community may be broadened by diversification and hence become economically more stable rather than become a "one-industry" town.

2. Increased payroll and hence income to the community as a whole.

3. Lower community costs. Duplication of streets, utilities, etc., are often avoided.

4. Compatibility and sound relationship of land use.

Limitations of the Industrial Park

Like most ideas the industrial park does have limitations.

1. Industrial parks are not suitable for all industries, for example, operations with large land and utility requirements, such as a steel plant.

2. Industry expansion problems. A firm will have difficulty expanding if there is no more land available within the park.

3. Developmental restrictions. Times change and restrictions which once seemed reasonable may become burdensome as production processes change with the introduction of such things as new product lines.

4. A young firm may not be able to afford to locate in the park.

Financing the Industrial Park

While many industrial parks are sponsored by private community groups (generally a group of interested businessmen, railroads, joint municipal government and private community groups, or by government) still many are sponsored by private real estate developers. When the private real estate developer is involved, he generally finances the development with the assistance of a financial institution. This is done in two ways: the mortgage plan and the purchase-lease plan.

Under the mortgage plan:

1. The developer erects the buildings, leases the property, and then applies for a mortgage loan.

2. The developer sells the site; the purchaser applies for a loan and erects his own buildings.

In connection with this, it is interesting to note a recent development; namely, lease guarantee insurance. For example, Knickerbocker Enterprises, Inc. of Moonachie, New Jersey, recently constructed two industrial plants which they tentatively leased. However, two lending institutions requested that lease guarantee insurance be obtained in view of the fact that the prospective tenants carried less than AAA credit ratings.

New York Guaranty Corporation, a wholly owned subsidiary of MGIC Investment Corporation, insured more than $2,500,000 in lease payments due over 15 years.[8]

Under the purchase-lease plan:

1. The developer can erect a building, lease the property, and then offer it for sale to an institutional investor.

2. The developer sells the site; the purchaser erects a building. The purchaser sells the property to an institutional investor and

[8] *The MGIC Newsletter* (September, 1972), p. 4.

leases it back, or he may sell the property to a private investor and lease it back.

OPPORTUNITIES IN INDUSTRIAL REAL ESTATE

As was previously discussed, industry and much commerce are moving from central business districts and more will probably move in the future. The main reason for this is due to decay and obsolescence in the declining area of the central city. In spite of the higher cost of moving, there has been a shift in industrial employment from the "traditional concentrations in the Northeastern, and North Central United States, to the South, South West, South Central, and Pacific Regions. This has required many new industrial states in the expanding areas."[9] Consequently, this should suggest two business opportunities for the real estate practitioner: (a) a marketing opportunity, and (b) an opportunity for rehabilitation.

It is suggested that practitioners may conduct their own surveys to discover firms desiring new plant locations and attempt to fit their listings to their needs.

As older properties in the central business district become available, there exist possibilities of rehabilitation. Typically, the older buildings are located in a mixed area of industrial, commercial, and residential zones. Typically, too, these buildings are multiple-storied buildings. The nearness to residences enables some industries to locate in rehabilitated space because of a good labor supply for apparel manufacturing, for assembly of electrical components, and for clerical work. The central location has also encouraged rehabilitation for discount houses, warehouses oriented to the central business districts. Thus the location, poorly situated for intensive industries, is often adaptable to other industries.

All floors are rented and frequently to different smaller firms. To do this, Shenkel suggests that the purchase price must be low enough, the property tax assessments must not be discriminatory, and the physical features must be such as to encourage rents high enough to justify rehabilitation. This includes such things as on-site parking and building accessibility.

---

[9] Kennard, William N., *Industrial Real Estate*, Society of Industrial Realtors, 1967, p. 29.

QUESTIONS FOR REVIEW

1. What is included in the term "nonresidential property"?
2. The demand for industrial property is a derived demand. Explain.
3. List the principal factors in the location of industry.
4. Discuss light versus heavy industry from the viewpoint of the community.
5. Why has retail trade been moving from the central business district in recent years?
6. What are the five commonly identified retail areas?
7. What is an *economic feasibility study?*
8. In recent years the concept of industrial zoning has changed. Comment.
9. List and discuss the limitations of the industrial park.

PROBLEM

1. Tax discrimination is frequent against industrial property by some communities. Too often assessors have failed to realize that the older type buildings have become functionally obsolete. Assume you wish to prepare a study for purposes of pointing out this form of tax discrimination. You search the county clerk's records and find 15 sales of industrial property at a total of $17,000,000. You also find that during the same period 32 sales of commercial properties with total sales prices of $22,000,000 were consummated. All property sales of 38,500 parcels during that time period totaled an even $516,000,000. An examination of records in the assessor's office shows that: (a) the 15 industrial sales were assessed at $5,610,000, (b) the commercial properties were assessed at $8,360,000, and (c) all properties were assessed at $154,800,000.

   From this information prepare an argument for purposes of seeking reassessment of the industrial properties.

SUGGESTED READINGS

Shenkel, William M. "Rehabilitation of Industrial Buildings." *Journal of Property Management,* Volume 28, No. 2, (Winter, 1962).

Weimer, Arthur M., Homer Hoyt, and George F. Bloom. *Real Estate,* 6th ed. New York: The Ronald Press Company, 1972. Chapter 22.

Chapter 13

Tax Factors in Real Estate

In 1969 Congress passed the Tax Reform Act making several basic changes relating to real estate investments. At the time of its passage it was immediately dubbed the Lawyers' and Accountants' Relief Act—happily, however, it is not quite that complex.

In spite of the Act, one of the big advantages of owning real property still lies in its tax advantages. As to the tax problems to be examined here, we can logically divide the problem into residential property and income-producing property.

RESIDENTIAL PROPERTY

Any profit made on the sale of a residence is tax exempt if the seller within one year of the sale of the property applies the profit to the purchase of a new home at the same price or at a higher price. If the taxpayer builds a new house, he can also apply the proceeds against the new building if it is built within 18 months of the prior sale.

For example, *A* buys a home in 1950 for $10,000 and sells it in 1975 for $15,000. Within a year *A* buys a new home for $19,000. The $5,000 profit that he made on the 1950 purchase is not taxable.

However, the cost of the new home is figured *not* at $19,000, the purchase price, but at $14,000 ($19,000 — $5,000). In short the profit is figured in determining what is called the "base" of the new home. If house No. 2 sells for $17,000, the gain is figured at $3,000 ($17,000 — $14,000 = $3,000).

One question that arises is: How many times may a homeowner defer the tax? The answer is that tax deferment may occur any number of times *provided:* (a) that he makes not more than one transaction per year, and (b) that the new residence is not purchased and resold before the older home is sold.

Adjustments in the Base

In determining the amount of gain on which the homeowner may postpone paying taxes, there are basically three things that may change the base or the cost of the older home. These are: (a) cost of improvements added by him to the property; (b) "fixing up" expenses; and (c) selling expenses.

Cost of improvements means improvements of a substantial and permanent nature; for example, adding a new porch or garage as distinguished from repairing a light fixture.

"Fixing up" expenses means expenses involved in assisting the sale of the older home. In order to qualify under this category, the expenses must have been made for work during a 90-day period immediately prior to the sale, and they must have been paid for on or before 30 days after the sale. This type of expense would include such things as redecorating and the like.

Selling expenses include such things as brokerage commissions and legal fees.

For example, suppose *A* purchases a home for $15,000 and sells it for $20,000. Assume further that he added a porch for $2,000; fixing up expenses, $500; and his selling expenses totaled $1,000. For tax purposes the base of his home is to be calculated as $15,000 + $2,000 + $500 + $1,000 or $18,500; consequently, his gain would be determined to be $1,500 ($20,000 — $18,500 = $1,500).

Sales on Installment Plan

When real property is sold on the installment plan, the profit is proportioned; thus, the tax on the profit can be spread out. The question is, what is meant by "installment plan"? Sales on the *installment plan* include all sales in which the initial payments do not exceed 30 percent of the selling price. *Initial payments* means payments made or received in cash or property other than purchase money obligations during the taxable year in which the sale is made. This includes all payments, not just the down payment.

For example, *A* sells property for $10,000. $1,000 is paid on signing the contract, $2,000 is paid on closing, $7,000 is paid on a purchase money mortgage taken back by the seller, and an additional $700 is paid during the taxable year. Here, the initial payment is $3,700, which is more than the maximum 30 percent:

On contract	$1,000
On closing	2,000
Payment on mtge.	700
	$3,700

The Tax Advantage in Residential Ownership

The tax advantage in residential ownership is twofold. First, the real property tax is a deduction from ordinary income on one's personal income tax return, thus reducing the tax to be paid.

Secondly, interest paid on one's mortgage is also deductible on one's income tax return. In these times of high interest rates, this sort of deduction actually reduces the effective rate of interest paid on a mortgage loan.

Converting Residence to Income Property

Although the advantages of income-producing property will be explained later in the chapter, sometimes a residence is converted to rental property, and thus the advantages of income-producing property will take effect. However, in order for this "conversion" to take place, certain rules must be followed. The point is that the Internal Revenue Service is not going to permit any type of bogus lease agreement. The test is whether one "intends" to convert the property into business or rental property. In all legal matters involving "intent," the facts and circumstances of the particular case are examined. Actual renting is one manifestation of intent. Merely listing the property for rent may not be a manifestation of intent. One case held that listing a property for rent followed by a sale within a year did not convert the property to rental property.

On the other hand, it has been held that listing of property for rent without an intent to sell has converted the property into rental property, even though it was never rented.

Generally, actual renting of the property has been considered sufficient to convert the property from a residence to income-producing property. But even here there may be some doubts. For example, rental of part of the property, such as the garage, has been held to be insufficient to convert the property.

The only real conclusion that can be reached is the point that was made above; namely, that each situation must stand on its own merits and be able to bear scrutiny by the Internal Revenue Service.

INCOME-PRODUCING PROPERTY

One question that should arise at this point is: Why, aside from income, should one become involved with income-producing property? The answer is that it is a means whereby one can reduce the burden of an already high income tax. This can be done in one of two ways. First, through the sale of real estate at a profit and being able to take advantage of the long-term capital gains tax; and secondly, by being able to depreciate income property against any flow of income.

Long-Term Capital Gain or Loss

It is necessary to discuss the concept of the long-term capital gain or loss because under certain circumstances property held for more than six months may be treated as a long-term capital gain or loss. In short, it is not treated as ordinary income and may result in a lower tax bill. For example, assume that *A* is in a tax bracket whereby 60 percent of his ordinary income is taxable. Thus, if he earns an extra $1,000, the tax would amount to $600. However, if he realizes $1,000 on the sale of property held for six months or more, his income is a long-term capital gain and may be taxable at 25 percent or $250. Whether it may be taxable at 25 percent depends on his income. Under the Act of 1969 the rate is 35 percent after 1972, but the 25 percent rate still applies in the first $50,000 of long-term capital gains or ($25,000 for a married person filing separately). The rate to corporations is 30 percent after 1971.

Offsetting Gains and Losses

Under the 1969 Act \$2 of long-term capital loss can be used to offset \$1 in ordinary income. For example, suppose *A* has a short-term capital gain (ordinary income) of \$1,000. He has a second piece of property held longer than six months on which he is fairly certain to lose \$2,000. He can sell the property, take the loss, and offset the \$2,000 loss against the \$1,000 ordinary income and pay no tax on the \$1,000.

Suppose the individual has a long-term capital gain on one transaction of \$2,000 and a long-term loss of \$5,000. Can he carry over the net loss of \$3,000 (\$5,000 loss — \$2,000 gain = \$3,000) and substract it from other income? No. He can deduct only \$1,000 from other income in the year of the loss and then carry the balance of the loss forward to future years and offset the excess loss at the rate of \$1,000 per year.

Capital Gains on Sales of Residences

A long-term capital gain on the sale of a residence normally arises when a person sells his older home with the exception that if a taxpayer is over 65, in which case other provisions are made, the gain on the sale of a residence is not taxed where the adjusted sales price is \$20,000 or less.

Depreciable Property

For tax purposes certain types of property are considered "depreciable" property. The first prerequisite is that there must be an income flow from the property against which to depreciate. For example, assume that *A*'s sole income is from an apartment house from which he has gross rentals of \$10,000 per year and that depreciation is \$9,000. This leaves him a net of \$1,000 on which to pay income taxes.

More commonly, individuals have several sources of income other than apartment houses. For example, suppose *A* has income from his job of \$12,000 per year and gross income from an apartment house of \$10,000 per year, totaling \$22,000. Assume his depreciation amounts to \$11,000 per year. He pays a tax on \$11,000.

In essence, the remaining $11,000 is tax free. If this same individual had invested the same amount in some financial institution and received interest income of $10,000 per year, his tax base would be the $22,000. However, like all situations all is not black or white. In order to take advantage of various tax situations, one must play by the rules which will be detailed later in the chapter.

THE CLASSIFICATION OF "INCOME" PROPERTY

There are four types of income-producing property, and the tax regulations are quite different depending upon the category in which it falls. They are: (1) real property held for sale to customers; (2) real property held for use in a trade or business; (3) real property held for investment; and (4) real property held for the production of income.

Strictly speaking then, only the last one is considered "income" producing, although the holders of real estate in the other three categories generally hope for some sort of gain.

Real Property Held for Sale to Customers

If a person holds real estate for sale as a dealer, he is treated as any other dealer of merchandise. In short, the tax treatment of both is the same. A gain is ordinary income, and a loss is an ordinary loss. A dealer in TV sets is treated the same. If he fails to sell his merchandise within six months, he is not entitled to take a long-term capital loss, and so it is with a dealer in real estate. A dealer may, however, deduct any real property taxes or interest paid on his "stock in trade." He is also entitled to deduct for casualty loss, maintenance, repairs, and other expenses in connection with the conservation of the property. In the event he converts the property into income-producing property, he may deduct depreciation as well as current expenses.

Real Property Held for Use in a Trade or Business

This would cover such property held by a manufacturer or retailer. If he sells the property at a gain, he may treat the profit as a long-term capital gain. He may also deduct his expenses and depreciation against his income.

In the event of a loss he is given special treatment not found in the other categories. If he sells the property at a loss, he may deduct the loss as an ordinary loss against current income. If the loss is greater than current income, he may carry forward or carry back. This means he may choose to offset the loss against income received during the previous three years and thus make himself eligible for a tax refund. Or he may carry forward for five years, thereby reducing his net taxable income for five years in the future.

Real Property Held for Investment

Basically, this is the situation where one purchases a parcel of property hoping for appreciation. In this case, gains and losses are treated as capital gains and losses. However, one may deduct management costs such as taxes, maintenance costs, and repair costs, as well as any interest payments on loans against the property. Depreciation allowances are not deductible because the property presumably is not producing income.

Real Property Held for the Production of Income

Strictly speaking, this is the only category of property against which one may take depreciation allowances. In order to fall into this type of classification, the property must be held for the purpose of producing current income.

Generally, land is not depreciable. Consequently, only the improvements are depreciable. Improvements include such things as buildings, fences in the case of farm or ranch property, gutters, and private streets.

At this point the Tax Reform Act of 1969 has made several basic changes relating to real estate investment. These will be noted in the discussion of depreciation.

Depreciation on Real Estate Investments

There are four approved methods of depreciation, each of which is described in detail beginning on the next page.

1. *Straight-Line Method:* $\frac{\text{Unrecovered costs}}{\text{Remaining economic life of building}} = \text{Rate of depreciation}$

Example: A $50,000 building with a remaining economic life of 20 years:

$\frac{\$50{,}000}{20} = \$2{,}500$ depreciable sum of 5 percent per year

For purposes of illustration the example given is slightly oversimplified. The primary reason for this is that most properties whether real or personal have some scrap value at the end of their remaining economic life. Thus, to be more realistic, the estimated scrap value has to be taken into account. Assume that there is a $50,000 building with a remaining economic life of 20 years and that it has a scrap value of $10,000. Then: $50,000 — $10,000 (scrap value) = $40,000 amount to be depreciated. Therefore, $\frac{\$40{,}000}{20} = \$2{,}000$ the permissible deduction against the current income flow.

Three other so-called "fast write-off" methods are permitted. The decision whether or not to use them depends upon an individual situation. For example, *A* may decide to use it if he anticipates a sharp decline in future income compared to his present income. He may also decide to use it if he anticipates "trading" the property for a like property in the future. The benefits of a "trade" or exchange will be discussed below.

These "fast write-offs" are (a) the 200 percent declining balance, (b) the 150 percent declining balance, and (c) the sum-of-digits.

2. *The 200 Percent Declining Balance:* With this method the unrecovered cost each year is twice the straight-line rate. Actually, the law states that the rate is not to exceed "twice the approximate straight-line rate computed *without* (etabis mini) adjustment for salvage." This odd twist means that salvage value is not taken into account as with the straight-line method, *except* the property cannot be depreciated below the scrap value.

Assume the same problem as above: a $50,000 building with a remaining economic life of 20 years and a scrap value of $10,000. Under the straight-line method, the rate of depreciation is 5 percent. The declining rate is 10 percent (2 × .05). Thus, the first year's deduction is $5,000 (.10 × $50,000). The second year's deduction is \$4,500 (.10 × \$45,000). The third year's deduction is \$4,050 (\$40,500 × .10), and so on. The 200 percent declining balance can be used *only* if the property is new; thus it is available to the first owner only.

3. *The 150 Percent Declining Balance:* This is used by the owners other than the first owner. Thus, if the rate is 5 percent, the declining rate is (1.5 × 5) or 7.5 the first year, and so on.

4. *The Sum-of-the-Digits Method:* Here the cost minus salvage is depreciated at a steadily diminishing rate per annum. The rate is determined by a fraction which according to the law "the numerator (of which) changes each year to a number which corresponds to the remaining useful life of the assets (including the year for which the allowance is being computed), and the denominator which remains constant is the sum of all the years' digits corresponding to the estimated useful life of the asset."

Reduced to a formula this means:

$$\frac{\text{The remaining economic life}}{\text{The sum of the years of useful life at acquisition}}$$

Again assume a \$50,000 building with a remaining economic life of 20 years and a scrap value of \$10,000. Then the denominator is the sum of the digits or $1 + 2 + 3 \ldots . + 20 = 210$

$$\frac{20 \text{ (remaining economic life)}}{210 \text{ (sum of the digits)}} = \frac{2}{21}$$

$$\$50{,}000 - \$10{,}000 \text{ (scrap value)} = \$40{,}000$$

First year depreciation $2/21 \times \$40{,}000 = \$3{,}809.52$
Second year $19/210 \times \$40{,}000 = \$3{,}619.04$, and so on.

The net effect of the fast write-off is to give high deductions in the early years of ownership and smaller deductions in the later years.

Effects of the 1969 Act on Depreciation

The depreciation "rules of the game" were changed by the 1969 Act. The Act divides real property into: (a) nonresidential and (b) residential, with different rules applying to each category.

1. Nonresidential Property. Nonresidential property is said to be commercial, industrial, and such things as bowling alleys. Thus on *new* nonresidential property bought or constructed or under a binding contract on or after July 24, 1969, the maximum "fast" write-off or depreciation allowable is the 150 percent declining balance. Also permitted is any other consistent method which will not producc depreciation greater than the 150 percent method during the first two thirds of the property's life. Thus, the 200 percent declining balance and the sum-of-the-digits method is not allowed on nonresidential property.

Secondly, the Act provides that second and subsequent owners of nonresidential property can use only the straight-line method or a comparable method approved by the Commissioner of Internal Revenue.

Rules of Recapture. Recapture can be defined as depreciation which is recouped on the sale of the property. Thus, under the Act all depreciation in excess of straight-line depreciation which is recovered after 1969 in the sale of nonresidential property is taxable as ordinary income. For example, assume a property is depreciated at the allowable 150 percent rate to the extent of $82,000. Assume that if one had depreciated on a straight-line basis, the amount would have been $42,000. The excess depreciation is $40,000 ($82,000 — $42,000 = $40,000), and is taxable as ordinary income.

2. Residential Property. The rules regarding depreciation on residential property depend on whether the property is (a) new construction or (b) used residential property.

The Act defines residential property as any building whose gross income is at least 80 percent derived from the rental of dwelling units. This excludes transient units such as hotels and motels.

(a) New Construction: On new construction only the first owner may, if he wishes, use the 200 percent declining balance method, the 150 percent declining method, or the sum-of-the-digits method.

Under the Act, if the owner sells the property, the "excess" depreciation (excess meaning that amount over the straight-line method) is taxable as ordinary income up to 100 months. In short, if the "excess" depreciation is $40,000 and the owner sells at any time from the first month he owned it up to the 100th month of ownership, the $40,000 is taxed as ordinary income. However, the "excess" depreciation subject to tax as ordinary income is reduced one percent per month beginning with the 101st month. Suppose the excess depreciation is $25,000 and the sale is made in the 101st month; then one percent of $25,000, or $250, is taxed as a long-term capital gain; and $24,750 is taxed as ordinary income. If the property is held 200 months or 16⅔ years and is then sold, all of the recouped excess depreciation can be treated as a capital gain.

(b) Used Residential Property: Second and subsequent owners of residential property are strictly limited in their "fast" write-off. Provided the property has a remaining economic life of 20 years or more, then they may elect to write it off at the rate of 125 percent declining balance. If the remaining economic life of the property is less than 20 years, they must use the straight-line method.

The same rules regarding the recovery of excess depreciation apply to used property as to new property.

Residential Rehabilitation Expense

To encourage rehabilitation for low and moderate income families, Congress provided for a "fast" write-off on capital improvements.

Under the 1969 Act, Congress provided that improvements could be written off under the straight-line method in five years, disregarding any salvage value. However, to qualify for the fast write-off, the rehabilitation cost must exceed $3,000 per unit, but it cannot be greater than $15,000 per unit.

If the property is sold within 12 months after the rehabilitation, all the write-off is subject to recapture as "excess" depreciation. If the property is held 12 months, but less than 100 months, all excess write-off over straight-line depreciation is recaptured. After 100 months the amount subject to recapture decreases by one percent per month.

For example, suppose a rehabilitation expense of $10,000 is incurred on a unit with a remaining economic life of ten years. Ordinarily, under "pure" straight-line depreciation it would depreciate at $1,000 per year. But under the five-year rule the owner can take $2,000 per year. Suppose he keeps the property seven years and then sells it. He would have taken $2,000 per year over the first five years, or the full $10,000. Because the sale was made in seven years (84 months) rather than after 100 months, the "excess" depreciation over "pure" straight line is recaptured, which in this case would be $3,000 ($10,000 fast depreciation — $7,000 "pure depreciation" = $3,000 recapture). The $3,000 "recapture" is taxed as ordinary income.

Tax-Free Exchanges

When properties are exchanged, they are often called *tax-free* exchanges. This is one of the most misunderstood problems in taxation. In reality there is no such thing as a tax-free exchange; it is a tax deferment. If the taxpayer exchanges a capital asset held for investment purposes for a capital asset held for like purposes and the asset is a piece of real property, the taxable gain on the exchange is deferred until the sale of the parcel being acquired by the taxpayer. For example, *A* owns investment property on First Street for which he paid $8,000 but which is now worth $12,000. *B* owns a $15,000 piece of property on Second Street that is now worth $12,000. They make an even trade. But *A* holds the property on Second Street with an adjusted basis of $8,000 (the price he paid for the property on First Street) and *B* holds the property on First Street with an adjusted basis of $12,000.

Mortgages in Exchange

The problem in a so-called tax-free exchange may be somewhat complicated when there is a mortgage against the property. The general rule is that the amount of the mortgage debt is treated as the equivalent of cash. However, if the owner either assumes a mortgage or takes subject to a mortgage on the property received by him in the exchange, the mortgage will not affect his tax position.

To illustrate the situation, suppose *A* owns an apartment now valued at $75,000 which cost him $50,000; he trades for an apartment with *B* valued at $200,000 on which there is a $100,000 mortgage. The basis of the new apartment will be $150,000. Thus:

Value of old apartment (basis)	$ 50,000
Mortgage assumed	100,000
Basis of new apartment	$150,000

At this point there is no taxable gain against *A*.

For the other party, (*B*), assume that *B* has an adjusted basis on the $200,000 apartment that he traded with *A* for $155,000, then:

Value of apartment received from *A*	$ 75,000
Plus mortgage assumed by *A* of	100,000
Total	$175,000
Minus adjusted basis of the apartment he transferred to *A*	155,000
Taxable gain	$ 20,000

The Effect of "Boot"

More often than not on an exchange there is money paid to one of the parties "to boot." "Boot" may be either cash or "unlike" property. Consequently, the gain is figured as actual cash or the fair market value of the "unlike" property.

For example, *A* has an apartment building valued at $100,000 which he trades for one valued at $50,000. He receives $25,000 in cash and a note secured by a mortgage of $25,000. The depreciated value of his $100,000 apartment is $30,000.

The value of apartment received	$ 50,000
Cash	25,000
Note & Mortgage	25,000
	$100,000
Depreciated basis of apartment transferred ..	— 30,000
Gain on the exchange	$ 70,000

But the gain recognized immediately is:

Boot:	
Cash	$ 25,000
Note	$ 25,000
	$ 50,000

Gain recognized to extent of "boot":

Cash & Notes	$ 50,000
	$ 20,000

Here the gain is postponed. The tax will be paid on the sale of the second apartment. The new property takes the basis of the old one, $30,000, minus the cash and unlike property, here $50,000, leaving

$20,000 which will be recognized for tax purposes when he sells the new property.

Taxes and Leases

If a landlord-tenant relationship is created, as has already been indicated, the landlord reports his rental income and deducts his expenses, real property taxes, and depreciation. The tenant deducts his rent as an expense if it is commercial or business property. This is all cut and dried, but often special situations arise which require different handling in lease situations.

1. Lessee's Improvements. Suppose an owner of vacant land rents it to a tenant who agrees to build on it. The land is valued at $25,000 and the tenant agrees to build a $100,000 gas station. Further, it is agreed that at the end of the term the landlord is to receive the land and building. Assume that at the end of the term the land is worth $30,000 and the building $25,000. He sells it for $55,000. The basis is $25,000 cost of the land, and tax is figured as a long-term capital gain, $55,000 — $25,000 (cost) = $30,000 taxable gain.

Had the landlord built the $100,000 gas station, he would have had to charge more rent as the rent minus depreciation would have been taxable as ordinary income. Depending on circumstances, the lessor may be better off with the tenant building the station.

2. Bonus Paid by Lessee. Frequently, a tenant pays a bonus to obtain a favorable lease. This is reportable as ordinary income when received by the landlord. However, it is *not* immediately deductible by the tenant, but must be written off during the life of the lease.

3. Security Deposits. Technically, a security deposit paid by a tenant should be deposited in a special account by the landlord and used only to cover a cost as outlined in the written agreement. However, legally or illegally, depending on the state, lessors in practice frequently use security deposits either as working capital or as income.

As far as the Internal Revenue Service is concerned, if the security deposit is actually held as a deposit, it is not taxable. By the same token, as long as it is held as a deposit the lessee *cannot* deduct this amount as an expense.

At the time the deposit is used, it then becomes income to the lessor and a deduction to the lessee.

USING A MORTGAGE TO DEFER TAXES

The use of a mortgage may be a handy device to defer taxes where capital appreciation has taken place. Suppose *A* purchased a small apartment house years previously for $100,000. He has depreciated it as much as possible. It has appreciated in value to $150,000. During the period in which *A* held the property, he dutifully paid off the mortgage. For purpose of illustration, say his depreciation has brought his adjusted basis down to $25,000. If he sells it now, he would realize a long-term taxable gain of $125,000 ($150,000 — $25,000 adjusted basis = $125,000 taxable gain).

The logical thing would be to refinance the building, say at 60 percent of $150,000 of appreciated current value = $90,000 cash in hand. True, *A* would be paying from 6 percent to 7¼ percent on the $90,000, but this is deductible; and depending on his income tax bracket, his *effective* interest payment may be as low as 5 percent. *A* may then spend the $90,000; or, better still, invest it in a second income-producing property against which he may take a "fast write-off," resulting in some tax-free income.

QUESTIONS FOR REVIEW

1. What is the general rule for deferring the tax on a gain resulting from the sale of a residential property?
2. What are the restrictions on the number of times an individual may defer the tax on a gain in a sale of residential property?
3. Explain how a residence may be converted into income property.
4. What is a *long-term capital gain*? What tax advantage is there, if any, in labeling a gain "a long-term capital gain?"
5. Distinguish between a "dealer" in real property and a "holder of property for production of income." How is each treated with regard to income taxes?
6. Explain the mechanics of depreciating a piece of real property by the "200 percent declining balance" and the "sum-of-the-digits" methods.
7. What is a *tax-free exchange,* and how is it used to defer income taxes?

8. What is *boot*? How is it treated?

9. How is a bonus paid by a tenant treated for tax purposes? (a) by the lessor? (b) by the lessee?

PROBLEMS

1. *A* buys a residence for $14,000. He sells it for $20,000 in seven months. The commission is $1,200 and legal expenses are $100. What is his gain or loss? How is it treated, *i.e.*, long-term capital gain or what?

2. *A* sells an income-producing property that he paid $10,000 for after holding it a year. He sells it for $25,000. His selling expenses are $1,000. He receives $5,000 the first year, the balance of $20,000 to be paid off in 10 years. What is his gain on the sale? What is the reportable gain the first year?

SUGGESTED READINGS

Current Tax Services.

Cerf, Alan R. *Real Estate and the Federal Income Tax*. Englewood Cliffs, New Jersey: Prentice-Hall, Inc., 1965. Chapters 1, 4, 5, 6, 7, and 9.

Smith, Dan Throop. *Tax Factors in Business Decisions*. Englewood Cliffs, New Jersey: Prentice-Hall, Inc., 1968. Chapters 4 and 5.

Chapter 14

Real Estate Investment

There are many types of real estate investment opportunities. These include vacant land, single-family tracts, apartment houses, office buildings, shopping centers, industrial properties, and other special-purpose properties.

No one can say except in general terms which investment is good for a particular individual. Thus an investment in an apartment house may be good or bad depending on location. In short, a market analysis such as suggested in Chapter 2 may be in order. Or a particular individual in a high tax bracket may need a specific tax shelter as outlined in Chapter 13.

WHY INVEST IN REAL ESTATE?

There are two main reasons for investing in real estate. The first is the tax shelter it provides as suggested previously. The second is that it appears to be a near-perfect hedge against inflation. *Inflation* can be thought of as a persistent rise in prices, which means that the dollar purchases less and less during an inflationary period.

The results of inflation on the individual can be devastating. Inflation favors debtors at the expense of creditors and fixed-income receivers. If you lend a man $1,000 today to be paid back a year from now, and if during the year prices have doubled, you will be paid back in *real purchasing power* only about one half as much purchasing power as you lent him. In the German inflation of 1920-1923 when prices increased a trillionfold, creditors were completely wiped out. Bondholders were financially destroyed, and the assets of all life insurance companies were completely wiped out. In the United States, government savings bonds bought for $75 in 1961, paid off $100 in 1971. But the dollars in 1971 bought less than $75 did in 1961 and today less than that.

The avowed governmental policy has been to hold the rate of inflation to an annual rise of 3 percent or less—if possible. The fact of the matter is that the Consumer Price Index is going up at the rate of about 4.6 percent per annum and the Wholesale Price Index at about 3.58 percent. Both threaten to rise even faster.

The Consumer Price Index is a barometer of inflation and is an index of the cost of some 400 goods and services gathered in fifty-six cities. It is a barometer of inflation because if one's income does not keep up with a rise in the index, then the individual is falling behind in terms of what his money will buy. If the index rises 30 percent and the individual's income fails to rise, his dollars in terms of real purchasing power fall somewhat less than 30 percent.[1]

What has all this to do with real estate investment? Simply that all things *do not* inflate at the same rate. There is general inflation and specific inflation. General inflation is reflected in the Consumer Price Index, while specific inflation is reflected in a particular commodity, such as real estate. For example, between 1970 and 1971

---

[1] It is somewhat less than 30 percent because when prices rise, the dollar falls by less. The value of the dollar falls reciprocally. Thus, if prices rise by 100 percent from a base of 100 to 200, the value of money cannot fall 100 percent to zero. The formula is

$$\frac{\text{Base Year Prices}}{\text{Current Year Prices}} = \frac{\text{Value of Dollars in Current Year}}{\text{Value of Money in Base Year}}$$

Thus

$$\frac{100}{130} = \frac{x}{100} \quad \text{or} \quad 130x = 10{,}000 = 76.9^{+}$$

Then $100 - 76.9 = 23.1$ percent (The decline in the value of money.)

the Consumer Price Index rose 4.61 percent; at the same time construction costs, based on an average of 30 cities and reflected in the American Appraisal Construction Index, rose 14.53 percent. This means that while purchasing power of cash dollars lost 4.61 percent, persons holding real estate *gained* as a result of inflation 14.53 percent, a *net* gain of 9.92 percent (14.53 − 4.61). Thus, investments in real estate are not only an excellent hedge against inflation, but they may also be a way of making inflation work for you.

THE RISKS OF ANY INVESTMENT

Every investment by its very nature has a certain amount of risk—some more than others. One of the risks is the purchasing power risk.

Purchasing Power Risk

Essentially, the previous discussion concerned itself with the purchasing power risk. In short, in an inflationary period the yield on an investment may be wiped out by a loss of real purchasing power. As a matter of fact, inflation combined with income taxes may even cause a loss. For example, suppose an individual has a savings account earning 5 percent. If inflation is at the rate of 4.5 percent a year, it might be assumed that there is a net gain of approximately .5 percent (5 − 4.5 = .5). Conceivably, however, this may turn into a loss as a result of income taxes depending on the tax bracket of the individual. The reason is that the tax is paid on the full 5 percent earnings, which, of course, doesn't take the inflation into account.

The Market Risk

The market risk arises from fluctuations in market prices of securities over time. This can come about from many causes; and the individual investor has no control over any of them. For example, an individual may invest in a cotton mill and then public taste may shift to synthetics. Earnings in a particular firm may decline due to a recession. Even fraud may cause a decline in the market price of a security. For example, a few years ago a firm that looked good on the surface issued stock which rose rapidly to $122 per share. When its weaknesses were discovered, it fell as rapidly to $2 per share and can now be bought for a few cents.

The Interest Rate Risk

This is a risk of loss in certain securities due to fluctuations in the interest rates. It is particularly applicable to bonds and preferred stock.

It simply amounts to the fact that when interest rates rise, the value of bonds falls. Although this will be detailed in Chapter 15, a short explanation is in order here. When a person buys a bond for $1,000, say at 6 percent, it amounts to a contract on the part of the seller to pay the buyer his $1,000 at a future date plus $60 per year. If rates go up to 12 percent on a *new* bond issue, then depending on the length of maturity the old bond will fall to $500. It still pays $60 per year; but if *A* buys it at $500, the yield is 12 percent, the same as the new issue. The reason it falls is simply that the holders of the old bonds will attempt to sell them to take advantage of the new rates. The reasoning is that if *A* holds an old bond and can sell it for $1,000, he will take that $1,000 and buy the new issue which earns $120 instead of $60. Unfortunately for *A*, all the bondholders think the same way and all try to sell at the same time; hence the fall in the price.

The Earning Power Risk or Risk of Business Failures

The risk of business failure either through poor management or the vagaries of the marketplace is connected with any form of business enterprise. Stockholders who have invested "equity" capital may find themselves wiped out. Bondholders who have lent money to a corporation may find themselves in a better position if the bonds are secured by corporate assets. And even they may be wiped out if the bonds are unsecured.

The Liquidity Risk

This is the risk of losing money as the result of a need to convert an asset into cash quickly. The more liquid the asset, the less sacrifice upon conversion into cash. Obviously, cash is the most liquid of all assets. Real estate is the least liquid of assets. Thus, it is necessary to sacrifice liquidity in a real estate investment to gain its numerous benefits.

The table below shows the various risks and rates of return on various investments.

Investment Evaluation Matrix

Investment Media	Gross Before Tax Rate of Return	Net Before Tax Rate of Return[a]	Primary Risk Types
Cash	Nonearning asset	—3.0%	1. Purchasing Power
Savings Accounts	4-5¼ %	1-2¼ %	1. Purchasing Power
Savings Certificates of Deposit	4½-6%	1½-3%	1. Purchasing Power
U.S. Government Bonds, Notes, and Certificates	3-6%	0-3%	1. Interest Rate 2. Purchasing Power
Corporate Bonds	6½-7½ %	3½-4½ %	1. Interest Rate 2. Purchasing Power 3. Market
Preferred Stocks	5-8%	2-5%	1. Interest Rate 2. Market 3. Purchasing Power
Common Stocks	Historically 9%	6%	1. Market 2. Earning Power 3. Purchasing Power
Real Estate	Normal Range 10-15%	7-12%	1. Liquidity

[a] Net before tax rate of return is obtained after deducting an average rate of inflation, for illustration purposes, of 3% rounded off.

Source: Karvel, George R., and Donald A. Rogers, *Real Estate and the Competition for Investment Dollars,* Center for Real Estate and Land Use Studies, Business Research Division, Graduate School of Business Administration, University of Colorado, May, 1972, p. 6.

LEVERAGE

One of the advantages, and sometimes one of the disadvantages, of a real estate investment is leverage. *Leverage* is using borrowed money to increase gains. The assumption is that the borrower can earn more on the borrowed money than the cost of the borrowed money. For example, if *A* borrows at 5 percent and then earns 10 percent, he is obviously using leverage advantageously. This can, of course, work in reverse. If *A* borrows at 5 percent but earns only 3 percent for a loss of 2 percent, he is courting disaster.

Leverage works in the following manner. Suppose an individual has $50,000 to invest in real estate. Several alternatives are open to him. One alternative is that he can simply buy an income-producing property for $50,000. Assume that he can earn 10 percent on his investment; then his income is $5,000.

Suppose he can borrow an additional $50,000 at 8 percent and purchase a $100,000 property. Assume further that he can make 10 percent on the total $100,000 investment:

Borrow	$50,000	Earn on	$100,000
At 8%	.08	At 10%	.10
Cost	$ 4,000		$ 10,000

Effect of leverage:

Earned on $100,000	$10,000
Cost of borrowing on $50,000	4,000
Net earnings	$ 6,000

Ratio of earnings to equity $\frac{\$\ 6{,}000}{\$50{,}000} = 12\%$ on the $50,000

The example above is borrowing on a one-to-one ratio, or $50,000 equity to $50,000 borrowed.

Suppose the borrowing is done on a one-to-two ratio:

Borrow	$100,000	Earn on	$150,000
At 8%	.08	At 10%	.10
Cost	$ 8,000		$ 15,000

Effect of leverage:

Earned on $150,000	$15,000
Cost of borrowing	8,000
Net earnings	$ 7,000

Ratio of earnings to equity $\frac{\$\ 7{,}000}{\$50{,}000} = 14\%$ on the $50,000

As previously suggested, this can work in reverse. Suppose instead of 10 percent, the net earning are only 7 percent on the money:

Borrow	$50,000	Earn on	$100,000
At 8%	.08	At 7%	.07
Cost	$ 4,000		$ 7,000

Thus: Earned on	$100,000	$7,000
Cost of borrowing on	$ 50,000	4,000
Net earnings		$3,000

Thus the investor would have been better off if he had invested his $50,000 alone, even though it would have earned only 7 percent.

CASH FLOWS AND TAX FLOWS

Cash flow is the cash that is left over to the investor after all operating expenses, interest, and payment on the principal are made. It is *not* the same as taxable income, earnings, yield, or profit. It is fairly obvious, for example, that the higher the mortgage principal payments, the lower the cash flow. Also, an unusual number of vacancies in an apartment will reduce cash flow. Furthermore, unusually high operating expenses will reduce cash flow.

A typical cash flow situation is illustrated below:

Gross income	$19,200		
Less vacancy allowance	576		
Effective gross income			$18,624
Expenses:			
Real property taxes	2,000		
Insurance	500		
Utilities	1,000		
Maintenance and replacement	1,000		
Management	1,150		
Miscellaneous expenses	1,000		
Total operating expense		$ 6,650	
Interest payments		4,000	
Payments on principal *		750	
			11,400
Cash Flow			$ 7,224

* Although the "debt service" annual payments of principal and interest total $4,750 in this example, they are split here because they need to be in determining tax flow. The interest is regarded as an expense.

From the example above, it can be seen that the cash flow can change; e.g., if the debt service is greater. It could even be that with increased vacancies the cash flow can be negative. Generally, the smaller the down payment, the smaller the cash flow.

The *tax flow* is the amount on which taxes are paid. Thus the formula for tax flow is:

Cash Flow + Payments on Principal — Depreciation = Taxable Income (Tax Flow)

The payments on principal are included because part of the rental income is building up the individual's equity. In short, they reduce the amount of the mortgage debt and hence are income. Thus, tax flow, using the example above, is:

Cash Flow $7,224 + Payment on Principal $750 = $7,974 — Depreciation assumed here to be $4,000 = Tax Flow $3,974

As discussed in the previous chapter, the depreciation would vary depending on the method used. Thus, in the case above "spendable income" would be $7,224 (cash flow); but because of the "tax shelter," only $3,974 is subject to tax.

REAL ESTATE SYNDICATES

One of the more popular forms of real estate investment, particularly for the small investor, is the syndicate or limited partnership. This consists of a general partner and limited partners who are the equity investors. The purchases and/or operations of the partnership can take many forms. For example, a broker may form a limited partnership for the purpose of buying and holding a piece of land for future resale. In this case he may form a limited partnership with contributions ranging from $1,000 up. Generally, the agreement incorporates a stipulation that the general partner will share any capital appreciation with the limited partners. This may be as high as 50 percent.

Often the limited partnership takes place where a builder-developer is involved. He acts as the general partner, agreeing to sell the land to the partnership, build at a predetermined price, and manage the property. The agreement provides for sharing of profits, losses, and cash flow. In this case, the general partner usually receives 5 percent and the limited partners share 95 percent. There is also a provision for the sharing of any capital appreciation if the property is resold. Often the percentage of the capital appreciation is on a 50-50 basis after the limited partners have received the return of their equity investment. In most cases, if the project is an apartment house, or even a shopping center, the limited partners contribute one third on the signing of the agreement, one third on completion of construction, and one third when occupancy reaches 95 percent. This form of payment may vary with the agreement.

The Tax Shelter to the Limited Partners

The tax advantage to the limited partners is the same as if they had been individual investors. They share pro rata in any tax loss that can be written off against other income. In case of resale, their pro rata shares are subject to long-term capital gains.

The Regulation of Limited Partnerships

The offerings to limited partners have been ruled as security offerings and subject to federal and state regulations. Unless the offering is "private," it must be registered under the Securities Act of 1933. Although never statutorily defined, a private offering has been presumed to be a sale to fewer than 25 persons. It should be noted, however, that even a private offering does not exempt the seller from the fraud provisions of the Act. There must be a full disclosure to proposed investors of all facts, circumstances, and risks involved in the investment. Furthermore, state laws have recently tightened up, which may affect the offering of limited partnership shares.

Risks of the Limited Partnership

As in any investment, there are risks in the limited partnership:

1. Under the Tax Act of 1969, as discussed in the previous chapter, the investor may have to recognize ordinary income if the property is sold within the first few years.
2. Rents may be lower than projected and operating expenses may be higher.
3. A partnership interest is not readily salable; consequently, there is a high degree of liquidity risk.
4. It is conceivable that a future Congress may reduce or even repeal liberal depreciation.

Is It a Limited Partnership or a Corporation?

Not only is the Securities and Exchange Commission interested in the "limited partnership," but the Internal Revenue Service also looks over the shoulder of the investors. The point is that unless the agreement is properly drawn, the IRS will construe the limited partnership as a corporation. In this case, losses and other tax advantages *cannot* flow through to the investor. The IRS Code Section 7701 and its regulations provide that a partnership shall be classified as an association taxable as a corporation if its major characteristics *more* closely resemble those of a corporation than those of any other type of business organization.

There are six tests of a corporation:

1. Is it an association?
2. Is there an intention to do business for a profit?
3. Does it have continuity of life?
4. Is there centralization of management?
5. Does it have free transferability of interests?
6. Is there limitation to the organization's property of liability for the organization debts?

Because the first two are common to all business organizations, they are excluded. There must exist *more* than two of the remaining four characteristics for the limited partnership to be ruled as a corporation. As to number 3, under the Uniform Partnership Act the general partner can dissolve the partnership at any time. Or, in the alternative, the partnership agreement contains a terminal date. As to centralization of management, most limited partnerships have that. As to free transferability of interests, a properly drawn agreement would contain a clause requiring permission of the general partner or other partners before an interest could be transferred. Since the IRS regulations state that this interferes with free transferability, this test is eliminated. As to limitation to the organization's property of liability for the organization's debts: since the general partner has unlimited liability for the partnership debts, this point is eliminated.

This leaves only four which fit into the corporate category. Remember that the agreement can be more loosely drawn and even permit free transfers, for example, without losing the advantage of the limited partnership.

Real Estate Investment Trusts

The real estate investment trust, or "Reits" as it is called, was set up by Congress in 1960, effective January 1, 1961. The intention of Congress was to give the "little man" an opportunity for tax-sheltered investment. In essence the trust is not taxed first as a corporation but is treated as a conduit with respect to income distributed to the beneficiaries of the trust.

Very few trusts were organized until 1968 when stock was sold in quantity by over 200 Reits which commercial banks and insurance companies began to sponsor.

To qualify as a real estate investment trust, the following tests must be met: [2]

1. A Reit must be managed by one or more trustees.
2. A Reit beneficial ownership must be evidenced by transferable shares of beneficial interest.
3. A Reit would (except for those provisions of Sec. 856-858 of the Internal Revenue Code) be taxable as a domestic corporation.
4. A Reit must not hold property primarily for sale to customers in the ordinary course of its trade or business.
5. The Reit shares must be held by 100 or more beneficial owners.
6. The Reit must elect to be treated as a real estate investment trust.
7. At least 90 percent of the Reits' gross income must be derived from dividends, interest, rents on real property, or gains from the sale of real estate securities.
8. Seventy-five percent of the Reits' gross income must be derived from rents from real property, interest on mortgages, or interests in real property.
9. Less than 30 percent of the Reits' gross income may be from the sale or other disposition of stock or securities held for less than six months and real property held for less than four years.

Types of Trusts

There are three types of real estate investment trusts. These are:

---

[2] Robert B. Klein, "Tax Problems of Mortgage Investment Trusts," *The Arthur Young Journal* (Summer, 1971), pp. 18 and 21.

1. *Equity Trusts.* These are trusts which invest in equity interests in real property in return for rental income. An example of this would be an equity investment in an apartment house.

2. *Mortgage Trusts.* Here the investment is in real property mortgages in return for interest income.

3. *Combination Trusts.* These are the most popular type of Reits. The investment combines some equity investment and some mortgage investment.

QUESTIONS FOR REVIEW

1. What is the difference between general inflation and specific inflation?
2. Explain the interest rate risk in a real estate investment.
3. What is *leverage*?
4. How can leverage work in reverse?
5. What is the biggest risk one takes when investing in real estate?
6. How must a limited partnership be organized to avoid classification as a corporation?
7. Explain the organization of the real estate investment trust.

PROBLEMS

1. You are analyzing an apartment house and see the following figures:

Effective gross income	$120,000
Operating expenses & taxes	92,000
Net income	$ 28,000

   (a) You discover a 10 percent error in the effective gross income. How many percentage points does this change your net income?

   (b) You discover an error of 10 percent in the fuel expenses. The fuel item is $5,000. Assuming the effective gross to be $120,000, less the error, how many percentage points does this change your net income?

2. (a) You have $100,000 cash, and purchase an income property producing a net of $11,500 before depreciation. What is your yield on cash down?

   (b) You get a $50,000 first mortgage on the property. The debt service is $4,750 per year, including interest. What is the return on cash down?

(c) You get a second mortgage of $15,000 and pay $1,750 per annum, including interest. What is your return in cash down?
(d) The items above are examples of what?

SUGGESTED READINGS

Hoagland, Henry E., and Leo D. Stone. *Real Estate Finance,* 5th ed. Homewood, Illinois: Richard D. Irwin, Inc., 1973. Chapter 7.

Ring, Alfred A. *Real Estate Principles and Practices,* 7th ed. Englewood Cliffs, New Jersey: Prentice-Hall, Inc., 1972. Chapter 14.

Seldin, Maury, and Richard H. Swesnik. *Real Estate Investment Strategy.* New York: Wiley-Interscience, 1970. Chapters 2, 3.

Chapter 15

The Interest Rate and Sources of Funds

Frequently, in recent years, funds available for mortgage loans have suddenly seemed to disappear. In a few short months, the supply of money has become scarce. The scarcity of money slowed down construction, made loans for older homes difficult and sometimes impossible to obtain, and, consequently, reduced the income of individual brokers.

What caused the supply of money to become scarce? The answer is directly tied to shifts in the interest rate and the monetary policies of the Federal Reserve System.

THE FEDERAL RESERVE SYSTEM AND THE INTEREST RATE

The Federal Reserve System

In 1913, the Federal Reserve Act was passed by Congress and signed by President Wilson. The Act divided the country up into 12 federal reserve districts, with a federal reserve bank in each district. The initial capital was obtained by stock subscriptions of commercial banks within the districts. The subscribers are the "member banks."

Technically, the federal reserve banks are owned by the member banks although, in practice, the Federal Reserve works closely with the President and the Treasury. They work so closely that the Federal Reserve is in reality a central banking authority. One of the functions of this central bank is to influence the cost, the availability, and the supply of money and, consequently, the rate of interest. By making money scarcc, interest rates are raised. This rise in rates is often called a "tight" money policy.

The Interest Rate

The *interest rate* is thought of as being the price paid for the use of money. Some define it as the "rent" paid for the use of money. Money is a commodity like other goods in the sense that the price, or interest rate, will tend to fluctuate with shifts in the supply and demand. For example, if the supply of money becomes scarce and the demand for money is high, the price, or interest rate, rises. This suggests that if the interest rate is allowed to move up and down according to the "law of supply and demand," those persons willing to pay the higher interest rates will be the ones who will receive the mortgage loans. Suppose that the interest rate rises to 10 percent. Those persons willing to pay 10 percent for mortgage money would be able to get the money. Those unwilling to pay would be unable to borrow money.

In real life, however, there are legal restrictions on the amount persons can pay for the use of money. Most states provide for a maximum contract rate of interest, which is the highest rate that can be charged in that state. Consequently, if the rate did go up to 10 percent, investors faced with alternative investment opportunities would tend to move away from mortgages and into another kind of investment to take advantage of the higher rate. The net result of this shift would be a shrinkage of the funds available for mortgage financing.

Why Is the Interest Rate Controlled?

The interest rate is raised and lowered by the Federal Reserve because it is thought to have a direct effect on inflation and deflation. *Inflation* occurs when there is an increase in the volume of money or in the rate of money turnover in relation to the supply of goods and services for sale. In short, when an excess in the supply of money begins chasing scarce goods and services, the prices of the goods and services will rise.

Deflation arises from an increase in the supply of goods and services in relation to the money available for buying them. For example, if production were suddenly to double throughout the nation, and if people did not have the money or credit with which to purchase this increased production, then prices would drop and deflation would result.

Briefly, the thinking of the Federal Reserve in raising the interest rates to avoid or reduce inflationary pressures goes something like this. Suppose a businessman desires to build an irrigation ditch to furnish water to farmers in an arid area of the West. He estimates that his return will be 10 percent per year; consequently, the project will pay for itself in 10 years. He knows that he can borrow money at 8 percent. If this is so, it would pay him to proceed with the project because he will net 2 percent. His actions combined with many other businessmen working on similar projects will put inflationary pressures on the price of cement, machinery, and other commodities that might happen to be relatively scarce.

The Federal Reserve thinks that when they raise the interest rate to 9 percent, this businessman, and many others, will not proceed with their projects. The businessmen will figure they cannot earn enough money. The net result will be no inflationary pressure on cement, machinery, and the other commodities.

If the Federal Reserve is worried about the possibility of deflation, they will reverse the process. In short, they will reduce the interest rate to make the building of projects more profitable. For example, they might reduce the interest rate as low as 6 percent to make proposed projects more tempting from a profit viewpoint.

How Are Interest Rates Shifted?

To raise interest rates and fight inflation, there are five steps open to the Federal Reserve System: (1) adopt a restrictive open market policy; (2) increase the discount rate; (3) increase reserve requirements, thereby reducing the reserve base for credit expansion;

(4) when authorized by Congress, impose selective controls; (5) moral suasion.

Restrictive Open Market Policy. The Federal Reserve has the right, through its open market committee, to buy and sell government bonds. By making the interest rate attractive, government bonds are sold to banks. As the banks purchase these bonds, dollars are exchanged for them. This reduces the amount of dollars available in banks for loan purposes. Money is now scarce. Bankers are more selective regarding individuals to whom they are willing to lend money; and, because they are faced with the opportunity of buying more government bonds with no risk and little handling cost, they will begin raising the rate of interest on the money they have left. Suppose, for example, the government issues a 6 percent bond. It costs the average banker 1.25 percent to handle a mortgage; therefore, to break even, the average banker must receive at least 7.25 percent on a mortgage loan. Consequently, unless he can get over 7.25 percent on a mortgage loan, he will move away from mortgage loans and into more government bonds or other investments where he is able to earn a greater return. Thus, the interest rate is raised by making money scarce, with the result that some proposed projects will be abandoned and inflationary pressures will be reduced.

Increase the Discount Rate. The *discount rate* is the rate of interest a bank must pay when it borrows from its federal reserve bank. Member banks may take certain promissory notes that they have received from customers and discount these notes with the Federal Reserve. In short, they discount notes to their district federal reserve bank and with the funds received make further loans. To do this, they must pay the Federal Reserve a sum of money. The amount they must pay is called the discount rate. When this rate is raised, it sometimes means that it no longer pays to discount the notes. More often, however, it exerts a significant influence on credit psychology, inducing the banking system to reexamine its lending policies, and other lenders to reappraise credit conditions.

The result, of course, leads to a scarcity in the supply of money. Money is no longer borrowed from the Federal Reserve. This scarcity leads to the raising of the interest rate.

Increase Reserve Requirements. The banking system in the United States operates as a *fractional* reserve system. This means that banks are legally prohibited from lending out 100 percent of their deposits. For example, if a bank receives a deposit of $1,000, it cannot lend out all of this sum—only part of it. The balance must be deposited in the federal reserve bank in its district. This deposit is called a "legal minimum-reserve balance" and must be equal to a stipulated percentage of demand deposits (checking accounts) and a smaller, but stipulated, percentage of time deposits (savings accounts). The percentages that must be held in reserve are set by Congress which, from time to time, sets a minimum and a maximum reserve requirement. The Board of Governors of the Federal Reserve System is permitted to change the reserve requirements of member banks within this set minimum and maximum.

For example, suppose that $1,000 is deposited with a member bank and suppose the reserve requirement is 20 percent. This means that the member bank must deposit 20 percent of the $1,000 with the Federal Reserve. This leaves only $800 available for loans. If the Board of Governors decides to raise the reserve requirement to 25 percent, then a member bank will be permitted to lend out only $750, the balance of $250 being deposited with the federal reserve bank.

It can readily be seen that if the Federal Reserve wishes to raise interest rates by making scarce the money available for loans, it can do so by raising the minimum reserve requirements, thereby taking additional sums out of circulation.

Selective Controls. *Selective controls* are authorized from time to time by Congress and provide specific terms under which credit may be used. One example of this was Regulation X. The Defense Production Act of 1950 empowered the President to regulate certain aspects of real estate financing. Under this act the Federal Reserve Board from time to time increased down payments on homes and reduced the time of maturity on mortgages. The authority for this act ceased in 1953, but the act is an example of a type of restrictive control.

Increased down payments under this act, coupled with reduced maturity of mortgages, forced certain buyers from the market. This, too, tended to reduce inflationary pressure.

Moral Suasion. *Moral suasion* is sometimes called "jawbone" policy. In an inflationary period, the federal reserve banks sometimes try to discourage banks from extending undue amounts of credit for speculative purposes which are inconsistent with the maintenance of sound credit conditions. This may cause bankers to restrict credit.

THE SECONDARY EFFECTS OF A "TIGHT MONEY" POLICY

Effect on Institutional Investors

A secondary effect of a tight money policy takes place with life insurance companies and some of the other financial institutions. About 34 percent of the total assets of United States life insurance companies are currently in mortgages. With an increase in the interest rates, some companies are often forced into a position in which they are unable to lend as much money on mortgages as they would like. This results directly from the effects of the higher interest rate on the bond market.

Higher Interest Rates and the Bond Market

With increased interest rates, the bond market is affected. This, in turn, is a disruptive influence on the mortgage money market. For example, suppose there is an existing government bond with a face value of \$100 that pays 4 percent or \$4.00 per year. If the Federal Reserve desires to raise interest rates, they may issue a \$100 bond at 8 percent paying \$8.00 per year. The net result will be that existing bonds begin to drop. Theoretically, the 4 percent bond will drop to \$50 because those individuals holding the 4 percent bonds would sell them for \$100, and buy a \$100 bond of the new issue which will earn them 8 percent on the same investment of \$100. In real life, however, the investors in bonds are fully aware of what is taking place; therefore, if *A*, a prospective investor, has \$100 to invest in bonds, he is certainly not going to pay \$100 for a bond paying only \$4.00 when he can take the same amount of principal and, by buying a \$100 bond of the new issue, earn \$8.00 per year. Thus, when old bondholders offer bonds for sale, they are offered only \$50 earning \$4.00 per year, or 8 percent, the equivalent of the new issue, i.e., $\$50 \times .08 = \$4.00$.

In practice, the old bond will not drop $50 unless the date of maturity approximates the new issue. The drop is related to the date of maturity on the old bond. Obviously, if the due date on the old bond is next year, no one will sell it for $50 when he has to wait only one year before the government pays him the $100 or full face value of the bond.

Thus, with the increase in interest rate, federal, state, local, and corporate bonds begin to drop. This has two effects on institutional lenders, particularly life insurance companies. These companies often hold government bonds because they are highly liquid. They may intend to sell some of their bonds and invest that money in real estate mortgages. When the bond market drops, they cannot afford to sell and thereby take a capital loss. They must hold onto those bonds. As a direct result of this they are unable to liquidate, thereby adding to the scarcity of mortgage money.

When government bonds drop, high-grade corporates also decline in price. With relatively fixed interest rates on mortgages, the insurance companies often find it profitable to purchase these corporate bonds rather than invest in real estate mortgages. This, too, adds to the shortage of mortgage money.

Effect on Existing Mortgages

In addition to the effects of a tight money policy on institutional investors, there are also repercussions in the secondary market for existing mortgages. Existing mortgages are purchased, not only by the Federal National Mortgage Association, as will be detailed in Chapter 16, but by mortgage companies and correspondents of life insurance companies and mutual savings banks. For example, a mortgage in Dallas, Texas, may be purchased by a mutual savings bank in Springfield, Massachusetts. The money moves from Springfield to Dallas. The effect of this is to release more money for mortgages in Dallas. However, mortgages fluctuate in price like anything else. A mortgage may sell at a premium or at a discount, *again depending on the interest rate*. When the interest rate goes up, mortgage prices go down.

Suppose that the interest rate rises to 8 percent and a mortgage is yielding 7 percent. If an investor has $10,000 to invest, he would be unwise to invest in a mortgage yielding 7 percent when he could be earning 8 percent on his money, assuming that the risks are equivalent. Therefore, the secondary market purchasers of mortgages will not pay $10,000 for a mortgage bearing a face value of $10,000. They will purchase the mortgage only if it can be had at a discount.

Effects of Tight Money on Junior Financing Devices

A tight money policy affects junior financing devices in several ways. First, it has a tendency to increase the numbers of second mortgages and contracts in use. In some parts of the country, where new construction is heavy, bank refinancing of older homes comes to a virtual standstill. If a seller desires to sell his home for $10,000, a prospective buyer is unable to go to a bank and obtain a new mortgage. Suppose there is a $5,000 mortgage on the property and a prospective buyer has only $3,000 in cash. Without new bank financing, the seller has little choice but to finance the remaining $2,000 himself. The seller will receive $3,000 in cash, and the buyer will either assume or take the property subject to the $5,000 mortgage, and give the seller a contract or a second mortgage for the remaining $2,000. The contract or second mortgage will be used depending upon the section of the country where the transaction takes place.

A second effect on junior financing takes place in the market for contracts and second mortgages. Investors trade in second mortgages and in junior contracts. During times when mortgage money is relatively plentiful these junior liens sell at discounts anywhere between 8 and 15 percent. A $2,000 second mortgage, for example, sold to an investor at a 10 percent discount will bring the seller $1,800. However, when money is tight, the number of junior liens increases. This makes investors more selective. Coupled with an increase in the supply of junior liens *and* the higher interest rate, the discount rate for junior liens will jump as high as 30 percent in some instances. This means, of course, that a seller who takes back a junior lien for $2,000 can get only $1,400 for it instead of $1,800 where it is discounted at 10 percent.

When sellers are aware of this, they sometimes attempt to pass all or part of this increased discount on to the buyer. Where the buyer in the case above lacks $2,000 on a $10,000 purchase price, sellers will try to raise the purchase price. For example, they might point out to the buyer that they will have to discount the junior lien 30 percent, in which case they may insist that the buyer sign the second mortgage or contract for roughly $2,600 instead of $2,000.

Summary of Some General Effects of Monetary Management

TIGHT MONEY	EASY MONEY
(1) Marginal borrowers are forced out of credit market.	(1) Converse true—more marginal borrowers.
(2) Some potential borrowers will defer projects, expecting rates to decline.	(2) Converse true—less deferment of projects.
(3) Bond prices decline, reducing the supply of loan money. Institutions holding bonds are reluctant to sell and take capital losses in order to make other loans.	(3) Converse true—institutions will sell bonds at capital gain to make other loans.
(4) Credit standards are raised by financial institutions.	(4) Converse true—credit standards slackened.
(5) Attempts made to liquidate marginal credit.	(5) Converse true—little attempt to liquidate marginal credit.

THE HYPERSENSITIVITY OF MORTGAGE FUND TO MONETARY MANAGEMENT

The two major classes of borrowers for residential construction funds are home purchasers and home builders.

Home Purchasers

In the past the home purchaser borrowers have been relatively unaffected by higher or lower interest rates. There are three primary reasons for this:

1. The higher ratio of mortgage loans to property values. This means that smaller down payments are required. This brings marginal purchasers into the market.

2. Maturities extended, for example, increasing maturity time of FHA loans from 25 to 30 years. This means smaller monthly payments over longer periods of time. Because of this, more lower income groups are able to become purchasers.

3. Rising personal incomes. This means that possible higher monthly payments will drive fewer demanders of residences out of the market. Furthermore, it makes it easier for more people to save enough for down payments.

Whether or not home purchasers are unaffected by higher interest rates in the future is open to considerable doubt, depending on the price of the home. An analysis of the effects of interest rate rises or declines on a $35,000 home has been done by the U. S. Savings and Loan League.[1]

In this analysis the measure of mortgage-carrying capacity and home-buying ability was made by assuming that families allocate one quarter of their monthly income to monthly payments for principal, interest, taxes, and insurance. Table I below shows the impact of interest rates on mortgage-paying capacity.

TABLE I

Impact of Interest Rates on Mortgage-Paying Capability

Interest rate	Monthly mortgage payment(1)	Number of qualifying families(2)	Increase in qualifying families	
			Actual	Cumulative
8.25%	$260	13,322,000	—	—
8.00	256	13,783,000	461,000	461,000
7.75	251	14,398,000	615,000	1,076,000
7.50	247	14,859,000	461,000	1,537,000
7.25	243	15,371,000	512,000	2,049,000
7.00	239	15,832,000	461,000	2,510,000
6.75	234	16,447,000	615,000	3,125,000
6.50	230	17,011,000	564,000	3,689,000

(1) Monthly mortgage payments assume the purchase of a $35,000 new home which is the average cost of a conventionally financed home in recent months. Payments are based on a 75% loan-to-value ratio and a loan maturity of 25 years. Monthly property taxes and insurance are based on FHA estimates.

(2) "Qualifying families" means the number who could make the required payment assuming one quarter of their income was devoted to interest, principal, real estate taxes, and insurance. Data on family income are based on "Consumer Income," U. S. Department of Commerce, Bureau of the Census, 1970. Income distribution is essentially as of March, 1970.

Source: *Savings and Loan News,* February, 1971.

[1] John Stafford, Research Director, U. S. League and Diana Cheseldine, Research Assistant, *Savings and Loan News* (February, 1971), pp. 60-62.

The table on page 377 indicates, among other things, that if interest rates moved down from 8.25 percent to say 7.25 percent, an additional 2,049,000 families could qualify for mortgages on a $35,000 home. If it moved from 8.25 percent to 6.50 percent, an additional 3,689,000 families would qualify.

As is well known, house buyers tend to be segregated by age groups, the largest group of house buyers being in the 35- to 44-year-old group. Mortgage paying by age groups can also be analyzed as shown by Table II below:

TABLE II

Mortgage-Paying Capacity by Age Group

Interest rate	Number of qualifying families	Increase in qualifying families	
		Actual	Cumulative
	Families headed by 25-34 year old		
8.25%	2,200,000	—	—
8.00	2,317,000	117,000	117,000
7.75	2,452,000	135,000	252,000
7.50	2,570,000	118,000	370,000
7.25	2,676,000	106,000	476,000
7.00	2,784,000	108,000	584,000
6.75	2,930,000	146,000	730,000
6.50	3,056,000	126,000	856,000
	Families headed by 35-44 year old		
8.25%	3,576,000	—	—
8.00	3,717,000	141,000	141,000
7.75	3,877,000	160,000	301,000
7.50	4,018,000	141,000	442,000
7.25	4,147,000	129,000	571,000
7.00	4,278,000	131,000	702,000
6.75	4,448,000	170,000	872,000
6.50	4,588,000	140,000	1,012,000

Source: *Savings and Loan News,* February, 1971.

The table above suggests, for example, that if interest rates merely moved from 8.25 percent to 8.00 percent, an additional 117,000 buyers in the 25- to 34-year-old group could move into the market for $35,000 homes. A reduction from 8.25 percent to 7.25 percent would potentially bring in nearly a half million buyers, and so forth.

In the 35- to 44-year-old age group, a quarter percent drop from 8.25 percent to 8.00 percent would move 141,000 potential buyers into the $35,000 home market and a full percentage point drop from 8.25 to 7.25 percent would bring 571,000 potential buyers into the market, and so forth.

While interest rate charges on a $35,000 home show increases, price changes appear to affect the market potential even more drastically, as shown in Table III below:

TABLE III

Impact of House Prices on Mortgage-Paying Capability

Cost of	Number of qualifying families	Increase in qualifying families	
		Actual	Cumulative
$35,000	13,322,000	—	—
34,000	14,141,000	819,000	819,000
33,000	15,115,000	974,000	1,793,000
32,000	15,986,000	871,000	2,664,000
31,000	17,011,000	1,025,000	3,689,000
30,000	18,189,000	1,178,000	4,867,000
25,000	24,696,000	6,507,000	11,374,000
20,000	32,023,000	7,327,000	18,701,000
15,000	38,428,000	6,405,000	25,106,000

Note: Assumptions regarding mortgage terms and income allocated to payments are identical with those used in preceding tables. However, the mortgage rate is held constant at 8.25%.

Source: *Savings and Loan News,* February, 1971.

This table suggests that even if the mortgage interest rate is 8.25 percent, a drop in the price of a $35,000 home of only $1,000 would bring an additional potential into the market of 819,000 families. A drop of $5,000 from $35,000 to $30,000 would result in a whopping 4,867,000 potential increase in the home market.

Builder Borrowers

With rising interest rates, builder borrowers are adversely affected. The question is not whether the higher rates *per se* affect them adversely, but they are affected because available mortgage money declines.[2]

It has been suggested that demands for mortgage funds are apt to be more sensitive to interest rate changes than, for example, consumer installment loans. There are a number of reasons for this extreme sensitivity, as indicated previously. To these might be added the fact that mortgage borrowers have a distinct disadvantage in the competition for funds with corporate borrowers. Assuming a pool of funds being sought often by both types of borrowers, then:

1. Mortgage borrowers, in the final analysis, seek financial institutions as lenders. These are savings and loan associations, life insurance companies, commercial banks, and mutual savings banks, as will be discussed later. Once these funds are exhausted in a tight money situation, mortgage borrowers, for all practical purposes, have no place to go. Corporate borrowers not only go to the institutions for money but can turn to individual investors as purchasers of bonds. This group is relatively untapped and is generally unavailable as a source of funds to mortgage borrowers.

2. In a completely free market, interest rates would move just as would the prices of any other product. However, both FHA-insured and VA-guaranteed mortgages have an artificial ceiling. This prevents as wide a movement of interest rates as the market might dictate. Hence, the competition for funds is not on an equal basis.[3]

Although large discounts might come into being during a period of tight money, some institutional investors will not acquire the government underwritten mortgages at these large discounts. This is particularly true of insurance company investors. The reason for this is that it might be poor public relations with a resulting loss of insurance sales. In addition, most states have usury laws limiting rates to be charged. This means lenders will move to alternative investment opportunities where yields may be greater.

---

[2] cf. Jules I. Bogan and Paul S. Nadler, "The Causes and Effects of Higher Interest Rates," The Graduate School of Business Administration, New York University, 1960.

[3] On November 28, 1968, Senate Bill S. 2700 was reported out of committee to permit HUD to establish the rate on FHA and VA loans "at not to exceed such per centum . . . as the Secretary (of HUD) finds necessary to meet the mortgage market."

As of January, 1973, this bill had not been enacted. Although rates on FHA's and VA's would be permitted to rise, some argue that an increase of even 1 percent would raise the monthly payments on some mortgages as much as $25-40 per month and would drive many buyers out of the market.

The Variable Interest Rate

A highly controversial concept being pushed in some quarters is the variable interest rate. Basically the idea is simple. A home buyer signs his mortgage and instead of agreeing to pay, say 7 percent interest, agrees to pay the *going rate,* whatever it is.[4] The going rate is tied to a "reference rate." One thought is that the "reference rate" might be the prime rate of a large commercial bank. The *prime rate* is the rate charged on loans to its best customers by the bank. For example, *A* agrees to pay so many points over the reference rate, say two percentage points. Assume that when he signs, the reference rate is the prime rate, e.g., 5.50 percent. This plus the two points would mean 7.5 percent to be paid by the borrower. If the "reference rate" goes to 6 percent, then he pays 8 percent interest. On the other hand, if the reference rate declines, say to 4.75 percent, this plus the 2 percent equals 6.75 percent paid in interest.[5]

Why The Controversy?

There are currently two ideas regarding monthly payment. One: the borrower's monthly payments would vary with the interest rate, but the number of payments would remain the same. For example, assume a 15-year mortgage with say 10 years or 120 payments left. If the rate moves from 7 percent to 7.5 percent, then the borrower's monthly payments would go from say $239 to $247, and he would still have 120 payments left.

All well and good, the argument goes, but what if the owner is transferred and wants to sell his house? It will be more difficult to sell. The study mentioned earlier on the $35,000 home indicates that 973,000 potential buyers have suddenly moved out of the market. Furthermore, assuming that $239 per month is stretching an owner's budget, then the additional rise in payments might hurt him financially.

The second idea is to leave the monthly payments constant even if the rate does change. For example, if you are paying $239 per month now, even if the increased rate causes your interest payments

---

[4] Alan J. Krupneck, "Variable-Rate Mortgages—Boon or Bane," *Business Review 1972,* Federal Reserve Bank of Philadelphia, pp. 16-22.

[5] It has also been suggested that the "reference rate" be the treasury bill rate.

to rise, the increase comes out of the $239 and you still pay only $239. This can be done by automatically extending the life of the mortgage say from 120 months to 150 months in order to accommodate the interest payment change. In this situation, it has been argued that in some instances if interest rates rise quickly enough while monthly payments remain constant, all of the monthly payment would be needed to cover the interest cost, leaving nothing for payment on principal. In short, the buyer could never pay off his mortgage. To guard against this, it has been suggested that provision be made to increase monthly payments temporarily until rates fall. This brings the argument back full circle: namely, the same problems as in the first instance outlined above. In the final analysis, it would cause a probable increase in mortgage foreclosures.

SAVINGS AND AVAILABILITY OF MORTGAGE MONEY

Homes are durable goods. Home building plays a significant role in the nation's economy because it adds to the nation's stock of real capital resources. And any investment in capital assets, whether it be by groups or individuals, is very closely related to savings, for mortgage money comes from savings.

The processes of savings and investment are often independent acts made by different groups or individuals. It is obvious that saving—that is, not consuming all of one's current income—is necessary in order to permit someone else to invest in *excess* of his current resources. For example, *A* may save by depositing $10,000 in a savings and loan association, and that same $10,000 may be loaned to *B* on a mortgage for the construction of his home. More often than not, however, it takes many savers depositing a total of $10,000 in order to provide money that would be loaned to finance *B's* investment in his home.

In some cases, the savings and investment process takes place with the same person. *A*, for example, may decide to invest the $10,000 in his own home, in which case he is both saving and investing.

Competition for Saving

In 1971 the production of goods and services in the United States reached an all-time high of over one trillion ($1,046.8) dollars. This brought personal disposable income up to $741.3 billion, and there was left after consumption expenditures a residue of savings amounting to $60.5 billion. This was more than triple the amount of personal savings in 1960.

This constitutes part of the pool of money for which builders, home buyers, and other users of funds compete. It should be understood that annual savings is only part of the pool of funds. The balance consists of paybacks from outstanding mortgages and other types of past savings.

One type of competition for funds that must be met by builders and home buyers comes from local authorities selling tax exempt bonds. Corporations also need additional funds and often go to the market to obtain these. The United States Treasury is one of the largest users of borrowed funds and is very active in the money market. Consumers, too, are demanders of part of the nation's savings with which to finance installment purchases. Farmers, along with small unincorporated businesses, also dip into the pool of savings for necessary funds.

Of the aggregate amount of past savings, mortgage borrowers were able to get their share. By the end of 1971 the mortgage debt on 1- to 4-family nonfarm homes reached almost $308 billion—representing an increase during the year of about $28 billion.

The question remains: Where do savers save, so that their savings may be a source of funds for home builders and buyers?

Most individuals save their excess of current resources over current expenditures with various financial institutions. These institutions act as financial intermediaries and channel the mortgage loans to the borrowers. A second group from which individuals borrow money are the noninstitutional lenders.

INSTITUTIONAL LENDERS AS A SOURCE OF FUNDS

There are four major types of financial institutions currently active in the home mortgage market. They are savings and loan associations, insurance companies, mutual savings banks, and commercial banks.

Savings and Loan Associations

Savings and loan associations are state or federally chartered and of a mutual or stock type operation. In Massachusetts they are called "cooperative banks," and in Louisiana, "homestead associations." Of the 5,544 associations in the country, about 2,049 operate under federal charters and are known as "federal savings and loan associations."

The policies of the institutions are directed by a board of directors who are local business or professional men and who are elected at the annual meeting of the shareholders, those having deposits or shares in the association over a certain sum.

Historically, the first savings and loan association began with 40 members in 1831 with the founding of the Oxford Provident Building Association in Frankford, Pennsylvania, now a part of Philadelphia. The idea was that each member was to save a certain sum each week; and, as soon as the accumulated sums were large enough, the money would be loaned to one of the members of the group for home building purposes. Because savings were limited, some members had to postpone home purchases; thus, they began inviting savings accounts from others.

From the very beginning, then, the savings and loan associations specialized in home financing. The only other types of investments generally permitted the associations are in United States government bonds, home improvement loans, and, in most states, in bonds of their states and municipalities.

By the end of 1971 the combined mortgage portfolio of the associations exceeded $174.4 billion, representing nearly one third of all recorded home mortgages. In 1971 they placed about 35 percent of all mortgage debt. As specialists in home mortgage lending, they accounted for 46.4 percent of all 1- to 4-family mortgages by the end of 1971.

Most of the savings and loan association mortgage loans are made on conventional mortgages, which yield a higher rate of interest than either the FHA-insured or VA-guaranteed mortgage. The savings and loan association is permitted to lend up to 95 percent of the appraised valuation of the property on a conventional mortgage provided it is insured by a private mortgage company. In 1971, 85.9 percent of the savings and loan association mortgage loans made were conventional loans, 7.9 percent were FHA loans, and 6.2 percent were VA loans.

The Federal Home Loan Bank System. The Federal Home Loan Bank System is so closely connected with most savings and loan associations that it must be discussed in relation to the latter.

In 1932 Congress established the Federal Home Loan Bank System. It was to serve somewhat the same purpose with respect to savings and loan associations as the Federal Reserve System was originally intended to perform for commercial banks.[6] It was to serve as a central reservoir for thrift and home-financing institutions.

The country is presently divided into 12 federal home loan bank districts with an FHL bank in each district. Originally, most of the capital stock was purchased by the government. By 1951, however, the capital stock of the federal home loan banks had been purchased from the government by their members. There are three types of institutions eligible for membership in the system. They are savings and loan associations, savings banks, and insurance companies. On December 31, 1966, 48 of the 5,031 members were savings banks, two were life insurance companies, and the rest savings and loan associations.

Those savings and loan associations which are *federally* chartered—some 2,049 in 1971—are required to be members of the Federal Savings and Loan Insurance Corporation. This performs a function somewhat similar to that of the Federal Deposit Insurance Corporation in that it insures deposits up to $40,000 in federal savings and loan associations.

As was mentioned previously, the FHL banks constitute a permanent pool of credit to maintain liquidity of members or to provide means for mortgage lending when local funds are insufficient. Three sources of funds are available for the operation of the FHL banks: capital stock, deposits of member institutions, and consolidated obligations sold on the market.

---

[6] Gordon W. McKinley, "The Federal Home Loan Bank System and the Control of Credit," *The Journal of Finance,* Vol. XII, No. 3 (September, 1957), p. 319.

When members need funds, they obtain the money by borrowing from their district banks on their own notes. When necessary, the FHL bank consolidates these obligations and in turn obtains the necessary money in the investment market by borrowing on their own notes from commercial banks throughout the country.

As the interest rate rises and money becomes more scarce, greater demands are made upon the savings and loan associations for mortgage loans. To obtain these funds, they borrow from the FHL banks. Also, in recent years, as money became scarce, some savings and loan associations found themselves in an embarrassing position with regard to withdrawals. After having loaned money on long-term mortgages, some of the associations were faced with the problem of paying out unexpected withdrawals. They had expected depositors to keep their money on deposit, but some depositors began withdrawing deposits, most of them using their savings to buy autos, refrigerators, and the like. It became necessary for these savings and loan associations to go to the FHL banks for loans; consequently, they had to refuse additional mortgage loans until they received more money from paybacks and new deposits.

In addition, it should be noted that the FHL banks, when entering the investment market in a period of scarce money, are no better off than any other borrower. In short, they, too, are forced to pay the higher interest rate for funds borrowed by them. They, too, will therefore raise the interest rates on advances made to members. This somewhat restricts both the desire and ability of some members to borrow, thus adding to the shortage of mortgage money.

Life Insurance Companies

At the end of 1971, life insurance companies reduced their residential loans about $1 billion over the previous year. This brought the total life insurance companies' investments in home mortgage loans to a total of 26.3 billion. At the close of 1971, these companies held about 15.1 percent of the nation's mortgage debt.

Unlike the savings and loan associations who specialize in home mortgages, the life insurance companies lend on farms, commercial properties, and industrial properties as well as homes.

In the aggregate, about 20 percent of life insurance company mortgage holdings were either VA-guaranteed or FHA-insured loans by the end of 1971. Conventional loans made up the balance of the mortgage holdings by life insurance companies. The conventional loans of life insurance companies usually amount to two thirds of the appraisal value of the residence.

Most of the lending done by life insurance companies on residential mortgages is handled through mortgage companies and mortgage bankers. This will be discussed further in Chapter 16.

Although the life insurance companies are of great importance in mortgage lending, their participation in direct ownership of real estate must be stressed also. Although only 3.1 percent of their assets was directly invested in real estate ownership by the end of 1971, the amount in dollars is nevertheless significant. The total real estate ownership of United States life insurance companies by the end of 1971 reached $6.9 billion.

Many of the properties purchased by the life insurance companies are bought on a leaseback basis. In short, a company will purchase a commercial building and lease it back to the seller on a long-term lease. In the past, some of these direct purchases, or ownership by the life insurance companies, have been in apartment houses and projects. Some of the past projects were built with government aid and some entirely out of their own resources. On the whole, the yield experience from housing projects acquired by the companies has not been favorable. For this reason, it can be assumed that this sort of investment by life insurance companies will be relatively small.

Mutual Savings Banks

The *mutual savings banks* are the oldest type of savings institution in the United States. They have no stockholders; their objectives are for the mutual benefit of depositors. Historically, these institutions were formed for the purpose of encouraging savings to help relieve the distress of the poor. They are located in eighteen states and the Virgin Islands, the greatest number being concentrated in the Middle Atlantic and New England States, with Massachusetts having the greatest number, followed by New York. All earnings after payment of operating expenses and taxes and setting aside of necessary reserves for the protection of depositors are distributed to the depositors in the form of interest.

About 69 percent of the assets of the mutual savings banks are invested in mortgages. Of the total mortgage indebtedness in the country they hold 12.4 percent. They tend to invest more heavily in government underwritten mortgages than do either the savings and loan associations or the life insurance companies.

Commercial Banks

Commercial banks are private enterprises organized under federal or state charters for the benefit of their stockholders. They receive funds from time deposits and demand deposits. The funds from time deposits of commercial banks are invested in corporate bonds, state and municipal securities, consumer installment loans, business loans, purchases of federal securities, and mortgages.

Most of the lending is of the conventional type, followed by FHA-insured and VA-guaranteed. At the end of 1971, the commercial banks held 16.5 percent of the total mortgage debt.

Because only 13 percent of the commercial bank's total assets are in mortgage loans, some are apt to relegate the commercial bank to an inferior position as a source of mortgage funds. The indirect influence of this type of institution must be stressed. First, in a tight money market, as was previously pointed out, the savings and loan associations are forced to call on the Federal Home Loan Bank Board for additional funds. To do this, the savings and loan association signs a note. These notes are consolidated and sold upon the open market. More often than not, the commercial banks are the purchasers of the consolidated obligations of the Federal Home Loan Bank Board. It can be readily seen then that this is an indirect source of mortgage money.

In addition to the purchase of these consolidated obligations, the commercial banks are a further indirect source of funds for mortgage loans by reason of their mortgage warehousing operations. Mortgage warehousing will be fully described in Chapter 16. For the present, *mortgage warehousing* can be thought of as a relatively short-term loan for builders. For example, a builder might need two million dollars for a project. The builder approaches a mortgage banker to arrange the financing. The mortgage banker makes contact with a life insurance company with whom he has been doing business. He is informed by the insurance company that they have already committed their available funds and that no new funds (from premiums and loan paybacks) will be available until 1976. The builder wants the money now. A deal is arranged between the mortgage banker, the insurance company, and the commercial bank. The bank agrees to put out the two million now, and the insurance company agrees to take over the mortgages on the homes in 1976. This permits present construction, with the commercial banks holding the mortgages until the time the insurance companies have agreed to take them over. Thus, indirectly, the commercial banks again are a source of mortgage money.

NONINSTITUTIONAL SOURCES OF MORTGAGE FUNDS

There are five basic noninstitutional sources of funds for mortgage loans. These are mortgage companies, trust funds, the Federal National Mortgage Association, individuals, and pension funds. The major difference in types of loans between those from an institution and those from a noninstitutional source lies with the fact that legally and from a policy viewpoint the noninstitutional sources are more apt to lend funds on properties where a greater risk is involved. At present, the aggregate share of the mortgage loans held by the noninstitutional lenders including Federal Agencies is about 21 percent of the total.

Mortgage Companies

A *mortgage company*, according to the constitution of the Mortgage Bankers Association of America, is: "Any person, firm or corporation . . . engaged in the business of lending money on the security of improved real estate in the United States. . . ."

Approximately 2 percent of the total mortgage indebtedness in the country is held by mortgage companies. As a direct source of funds they are limited by the amount of their own available investment capital. Their major function, however, is to represent institutional lenders.

Trust Funds

Trust funds are monies placed with a trustee for the benefit of a third person or the person who places these funds in trust. For example, *A* may deposit money either while living or by will with an individual or the trust department of a bank in trust for the benefit of *C*. Sometimes, if the creator of the trust is living, the trustee will hold the funds for the benefit of *A* himself. It is up to the trustee to invest these sums as a reasonably prudent man would invest money. For the most part, trustees have wider discretion with regard to investing than do financial institutions. Often, therefore, they will lend money on commercial buildings, university buildings, and other such structures for which some financial institutions are reluctant to lend or prohibited by law from lending money.

In the overall mortgage financing picture, their percentage of the total mortgage market is less than one percent.

Federal National Mortgage Association

The Federal National Mortgage Association was provided for in the terms of the National Housing Act of 1934. In 1938 the association was organized with original financing by the Reconstruction Finance Corporation. The details of "Fanny May," as it is sometimes called, will be thoroughly discussed in Chapter 16. However, it should be noted that in recent years it has become somewhat a direct source of home mortgage lending. By the end of 1971 it accounted for over 3.5 percent of the total home mortgage debt outstanding.

Individuals

Individuals are a source of both first and second mortgage loans. For the most part, they are professional men of the community with surplus funds which they are willing to invest in mortgages. As a general rule, when individuals lend money on first mortgages, the term of the loan is less than when money is loaned by the institutional lenders. Generally, a ten-year period appears to be the maximum term on which individuals will make a loan. It is individuals, too, who can be most readily approached for second mortgage money; in most cases, second mortgage loans from individuals can be had only when the seller of the mortgage will market the mortgage at a discount.

Pension Funds

Only in recent years have pension funds become active in the mortgage market, and then only to a small extent. The real question is whether or not these growing funds will be able to be tapped as a source of mortgage money. Aside from the legal difficulties, problems of pension funds being used across state lines, etc., there are other problems. The evidence seems to point to the fact that in relative amounts the increase in pension funds will have little or no effect on the mortgage market. The noninsured funds have traditionally sought equities such as stocks and bonds as an investment medium.[7] It is believed that the trend toward this will continue due to past equity earnings of the funds and threats of inflation. Even if there is no inflation, yields on equities will remain at levels high enough to be an attractive investment for the noninsured pension funds. In the past as the size of the funds increased, there has been a tendency to shift from government bonds to corporate bonds and stocks as a means of investing the increased funds. Furthermore, the greatest money volume (90 percent of the funds) is controlled by commercial bankers whose thinking and training are geared to the equities market rather than the residential mortgage market.

It is also felt that the insured pension funds will be a minute influence on the residential mortgage market. There will probably be a shift to term insurance policies as pensions are increased. This will provide the life insurance companies with less money to invest in the residential mortgage market. Because of competition between the insured and the noninsured funds, the life insurance companies are attempting to have legislation passed to permit the segregation of pension fund assets from other company assets in order that these assets may be invested in equities. All of this suggests that pension funds will play a relatively small part in the residential mortgage market.

The Organization of the Mortgage Market [8]

The general organization of the mortgage market is shown at the top of the next page.

---

[7] The principal feature distinguishing the insured pension funds from the noninsured funds is that once a pension plan is arranged with a life insurance company and the costs have been determined, the insurance company undertakes to guarantee a certain level of benefits for the covered employee upon retirement. In the case of the noninsured funds, however, the level of benefit will depend upon the amount of money in the fund or trust when the benefits become due upon retirement.

[8] J. A. Cacy, "Specialized Mortgage Marketing Facilities," *Monthly Review*, Federal Reserve Bank of Kansas City (July-August, 1967), pp. 3-13.

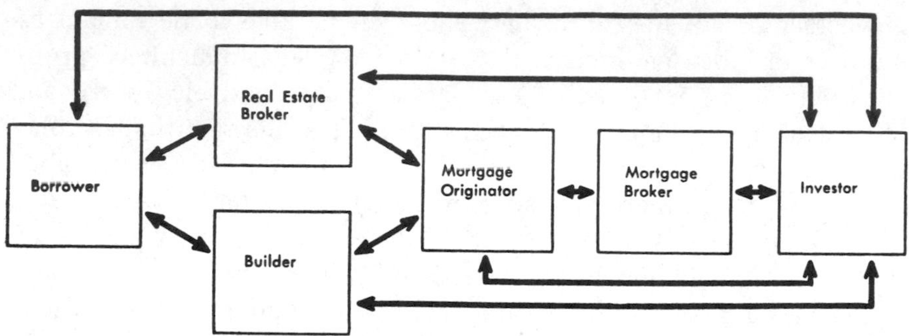

The Organization of the Mortgage Market

Source: *Monthly Review,* July-August, 1967, Federal Reserve Bank of Kansas City.

The chart suggests that there may be a direct flow from borrower to investor (e.g., savings and loan association) or through one or more intermediaries. For example, the borrower may contact a broker who in turn contacts an originator. Again it may be a savings and loan who originates the loan creating a negotiable, financial asset which could be sold later to an investor (e.g., life insurance company) by the savings and loan association.

QUESTIONS FOR REVIEW

1. The upper level of interest rates is limited by the usury laws of the states; hence any action by the Federal Reserve to raise interest rates may be stopped by legal limitations. Discuss.
2. Discuss the present actions available to the Federal Reserve Board to raise or lower interest rates.
3. Mortgage bankers perform a useful function in that they tend to cause interest rates to equalize in various parts of the nation. Discuss.
4. Pension funds are unlikely to play an important part as a source of mortgage funds in the coming decade. Discuss.

PROBLEMS

1. Examine the table on page 393 and answer the following questions:
   (a) What is meant by *points*?
   (b) Why are there no "points" on conventional loans?
   (c) What do "points" effectively accomplish from the viewpoint of the lender?

Five Ways to Finance a Home

A 30-YEAR LOAN ON A $25,000 HOME	Conventional Loans			Loan Backed by Federal Housing Administration	Loan Backed by Veterans Administration
	80%	90%	95%		
DOWN PAYMENT	$5,000	$3,500	$1,250	$1,200 †	0 †
MORTGAGE	20,000 at 7¼%	22,500 at 7¾%	23,750 at 7¾%	23,800 at 7%	25,000 at 7%
MONTHLY PAYMENT (principle & interest)	136.44	161.20	170.16	158.51	166.33
MORTGAGE INSURANCE	0	0	1% first yr* ¼% thereafter to 80%	9.87 per mo.*	0

† plus an extra charge—"points"—in most instances, based on size of loan
* insurance payment decreases gradually as amount of loan outstanding declines

Source: *Realtor,* April 12, 1973, p. 8.

2. Analyze the following in terms of the chapter discussion:

"Although happenings in the money market sometimes defy comprehension, one thing is certain: There is no credibility gap as to the direction of national policy. Both the Federal Reserve and the administration are determined to slow not only the rate of inflation but inflationary expectations; and what's more, they evidence their determination by deeds as well as words. Beating this message into the heads of the disbelievers may give rise to a few migraines, but, nevertheless, the policy makers give every indication of their intent to pound away.

"Assistance in the war against inflation also will be forthcoming from the Treasury. By using debt management techniques that tap the longer-term market to the largest extent possible, the Treasury avoids the increases in the money supply that occur when the Treasury relies excessively on short-term borrowing. Look for pressure to mount in lifting the . . . maximum rate on government bonds, including savings bonds.

" 'Better late than never' might be the attitude of economists as they view the economic statistics. After six months of patient and impatient waiting, the numbers are beginning to show some slowdown in business activity. Because every effort will be made to avoid sacrificing these hard-won gains on the altar of political expediency, both the Fed and the administration will be slow to back away from the policies of restraint. Tight money is no short-term phenomenon.

"Even though bond prices may appear to be at a bargain basement level, any substantial and sustainable recovery as based on a change in the fundamentals should not be forthcoming in the immediate future. Psychologically, however, the money market may be ripe for an upward move if the 'right' event occurred to provide the necessary push. For the moment, the preferred course of action by most portfolio managers is to sit cautiously on the sidelines, even though they risk getting in after the bottom has been reached. Because the policy makers still have not fired all the shots that may be necessary to subdue exuberance in the money market, there is the distinct possibility of some further retreat in prices.

"For the longer run, the downside risk should be less than the upside potential, and, therefore, portfolio managers appropriately should begin to review their holdings, liquidity requirements and anticipated money flows with an eye for making some switches that have profit potential. With the prospect of more balanced conditions in the credit market in the last half of the year, interest rates should be near their peaks; but they more likely will remain on a high plateau rather than decline precipitously. Demands for money from government—particularly state and local—and from business and consumers continue high. Any decrease in rates would be offset by borrowers rushing to the market to raise funds."

James A. Hollensteiner, Staff Vice President, United States Savings and Loan League, p. 11, Vol. XC, No. 3, March, 1969, *Savings and Loan News*.

3. The Smiths own a home with an FHA appraised value of $16,500. The maximum loan-to-value ratio is 97 percent on the first $15,000 of value or less; 90 percent beyond $15,000 to $20,000. At present their existing mortgage balance is $12,250. They have a conventional mortgage at 6 percent on the unpaid balance. The mortgage has eleven years to run. The mortgage has a prepayment penalty clause of 1.25 percent of the unpaid balance. They consider refinancing and obtaining an FHA-insured mortgage. The manager of the financial institution informed them that a 7½ percent FHA mortgage is possible, but the current money market in their area calls for 4.5 points discount.
   (a) What is the maximum FHA loan they may obtain?
   (b) How much of a prepayment penalty would they have to pay?
   (c) How much cash would they receive above the present mortgage?

SUGGESTED READINGS

Hoagland, Henry E., and Leo D. Stone. *Real Estate Finance,* 4th ed. Homewood, Ill.: Richard D. Irwin, Inc., 1969.

Savings and Loan Fact Book, Current Issue, United States Savings and Loan League, Chicago.

Chapter 16

The Secondary Mortgage Market and Mortgage Banking

Since the end of World War II, mortgage financing has grown more sophisticated and, at the same time, more complex. Many will argue that the recent rapid development of this area of finance has to a large degree been merely a process of "catching up" with other forms of financing. Whether one agrees with this or not, the fact remains that many of the advances in mortgage financing have taken place due to advances in the secondary mortgage market type of financing.

SECONDARY MORTGAGE MARKET

A *secondary mortgage market* is a market for the purchase of existing mortgages with the idea of providing more liquidity for mortgages. The concept arose out of the success of the Federal Reserve System in providing liquidity for certain types of paper held by commercial banks, and of the Federal Home Loan Bank Board in providing similar liquidity for mortgage loans held by savings and loan associations. For example, a small-town commercial bank which is a member of the Federal Reserve System may discount (or sell) some of its notes to the federal reserve bank in its district.

Suppose a commercial bank holds an acceptable note for $5,000 with interest at 7 percent. Under some circumstances it might desire to discount the paper with the Federal Reserve. The Federal Reserve might have a rediscount rate of 6 percent. This means that, for practical purposes, the bank can receive $5,000 for the note, pay the Federal Reserve 6 percent interest, receive 7 percent, and then lend out the $5,000 it received at whatever rate is obtainable.

The purpose of the secondary mortgage market is to provide a similar mechanism. For example, if there is a secondary market, then conceivably a financial institution might lend out $10,000 on a mortgage which is FHA-insured at 8½ percent (including ½ percent for insurance) [1] and then sell the mortgage on the secondary market. After having done this, the financial institution will presumably have $10,000 more cash in hand with which to be able to make a new mortgage loan.

The National Housing Act of 1934 and the Secondary Mortgage Market

The National Housing Act of 1934 establishing the Federal Housing Administration provided for the establishment of *privately* owned mortgage associations to operate a secondary mortgage market on a national scale. However, there was no attempt under the 1934 Act to form such associations.

In 1935 the Reconstruction Finance Corporation began buying some mortgages on urban commercial properties, but it exercised no direct influence on the residential mortgage market.

In 1938 legislation was enacted to provide for a government-sponsored secondary mortgage market for residential mortgages. The RFC in that year provided the necessary capital for the Federal National Mortgage Association which was to operate as a secondary market. For ten years, the Federal National Mortgage Association, called "Fanny May," did relatively little buying of mortgages. In 1950 FNMA was transferred from the jurisdiction of the Reconstruction Finance Corporation to the Housing and Home Finance Agency which had been created in 1942.

[1] Interest rates on all types of mortgage loans have been fluctuating rapidly in recent years. This includes FHA and VA loan rates. The present rate may be obtained from recent government publications or from your local real estate offices.

The Interest Rate and the Growth of "Fanny May"

To fully understand present-day FNMA operations, it is necessary to take a brief historical glance at its development. After World War II, financial institutions were able to make VA-guaranteed loans and FHA-insured loans profitably. In the heyday of VA loans (1946) the loans were being made at 4 percent, while at the same time, FHA loans were made at 4.25 percent. During this year, yields on government bonds were at an all-time low of 2.15 percent. It has been estimated that in 1946 the cost to financial institutions for servicing loans, office expenses, and risks ranged between 1.25 and 1.50 percentage points. This means that when the financial institutions were faced with the alternative of investing in a relatively costless government bond at 2.15 percent yield and a VA loan netting them 2.5 percent, they chose the VA loan. In other words, they figured the difference between 4 percent of the VA loan less 1.50 percent cost, or a net yield of 2.50 percent on the VA loan. This meant an increase of .35 percent (2.50 − 2.15 = .35) if they invested in the VA loans. Therefore, money for both VA and FHA loans was plentiful in 1946.

In 1947 under the influence of monetary policy, as was explained in Chapter 15, the interest rates began to rise. Financial institutions began to invest in alternative investment opportunities because of the chance to make greater profits in the face of the then fixed rate of 4 percent on VA loans and the FHA fixed rate of 4.25 percent. The supply of money for VA loans began to dry up. However, beginning in July, 1948, "Fanny May" was authorized to buy VA mortgages for the first time, as well as FHA mortgages. At first, under the law, FNMA was allowed to purchase only 25 percent of the eligible mortgages in a lender's portfolio, eligible mortgages being only the FHA and VA mortgages. By August, 1948, this limit was raised to 50 percent of the eligible mortgages and by October, 1949, FNMA was authorized to purchase 100 percent of the eligible mortgages in the lender's portfolio.

The Commitment Concept

Before proceeding further, it is important to understand the term "commitment" as it relates to FNMA. As will be pointed out later, the term is slightly varied when used by the mortgage banker. A *commitment,* as used by FNMA prior to 1968, was an agreement between FNMA and a mortgage lender whereby FNMA agreed to purchase the mortgage from the lender at par. For example, suppose a project builder who needed $10,000 secured by an FHA mortgage approached a lender. Recall from Chapter 15 that when the interest rate rises, the value of bonds and mortgages goes down. For practical purposes, this means that lenders when faced with rising interest rates, or the prospect of rising interest rates, will hestitate in making a loan because, conceivably, as soon as they have loaned the $10,000, the value of the "paper" will fall. The reluctance to make loans as a result of this fear will cause the supply of funds for residential construction to diminish. However, if someone or some corporation or government-sponsored organization will agree to take the mortgages off their hands at par, then the lending institutions will no longer hesitate in making the loans because they cannot lose any money on the transaction. *Par* means at the face value, in this case $10,000.

Until the end of March, 1950, FNMA was authorized to make advance commitments to lenders, agreeing to take their mortgage loans where readily available. This action by FNMA offset rising interest rates and what would ordinarily be its effect on the supply of mortgage funds—namely, a reduction in supply of money for mortgage lending purposes. This meant that FNMA, during this period, was in reality a *primary* supplier of funds.

The Role of FNMA Between 1950-1953 [2]

After March, 1951, yields on long-term government securities became firm. This meant that for a time, at least, the interest rate did not fluctuate. At the same time, because of statutory limitations, FNMA was unable to purchase many mortgages. With the firming of government bond rates, this meant that the market price of *old* government bonds held by such financial institutions as life insurance companies began to fall. As was pointed out in Chapter 15, this meant that if the companies were to sell these bonds, they would take a capital loss. As a result, the companies did not sell the bonds and

[2] Ross M. Robertson, "Federal Influence on Urban Residential Mortgage Markets," *Monthly Review*, Federal Reserve Bank of St. Louis, Vol. 35, No. 9 (September, 1953), p. 8.

had no immediate funds to lend out on mortgages. Money began to dry up as far as the mortgage market was concerned. FNMA still bought a few mortgages, not by advance commitments, but on an over-the-counter basis and only from originating lenders. *Over-the-counter* means on a noncommitment basis or on the open market. Without the advance commitment, as had been done in previous years, lending institutions again became reluctant to put out money on mortgages.

By the spring of 1952, interest rates again were on the rise. This meant that both FHA and VA mortgages began to fall in price in the secondary markets. FHA's went as low as 97, that is, $97 for each $100 of face value; and VA's fell as low as 90. Funds for both the FHA and VA loans became scarce by early 1953.

By administrative action during the first week of May, 1953, the interest rates on VA loans were raised from 4 to 4.50 percent and on FHA loans from 4.25 to 4.50 percent. It was thought that this action would bring the yields on these types of mortgage loans in line with the yields on both government bonds and corporate bonds. If this had been so, then a plentiful supply of money would again have probably been available for mortgage loans. However, interest rates in general continued to rise, and in September, 1953, FHA and VA mortgages carrying the new rates of interest were selling at discounts of 2 and 3 points. This meant $98 or $97 on every $100 of face value.

Discounts

The problem of a discount arises from having a contractually fixed rate of interest on some paper being offered to investors in a market where the interest rate is rising or falling as the result of federally managed monetary policy, and/or competition for money affecting the supply of funds. For example, a mortgage at 4.50 percent is being offered for sale by the holder in a market where the interest rate has been raised to 3.25 percent by monetary policy, and/or the result of other factors is reducing the money supply. If the cost of servicing a mortgage is 1.50 percent, then the net return on the mortgage will be 4.50-1.50 for a net of 3 percent. Naturally, an investor will move out of mortgages to the 3.25 percent bond, especially if it is a riskless government bond. This means a shortage of mortgage money and an inability on the part of the holder of the 4.50 percent mortgage to sell it at face value. It will have to be sold at less than face value. The difference between the face value and the market price of the mortgage is the discount.

Builders, in 1952 and early 1953, began to guarantee *par* paper to lenders in order to obtain financing. In effect, they were stating that, regardless of the discount, they would absorb the discount. They began passing on these costs to buyers. This was done by increasing the closing costs by enough to cover any discount that they might have to pay. However, the Veterans Administration, by a regulation issued on May 18, 1953, sought to prevent this sort of guarantee by builders. Under the terms of the regulation, builders were required to certify that they had not paid or absorbed any closing fees and charges other than those authorized by the Veterans Administration. This regulation resulted in protest, confusion, and a slowdown in residential building and to amendments to the National Housing Act of June 30, 1953.

The Amendments of June 30, 1953

The amendments to the National Housing Act of June 30, 1953, attempted to cover the major problems resulting from discounts. The law permitted the originating lender to get as many points as necessary from a builder or seller to offset the discount at which the mortgage would sell. Briefly, this meant that if the discount was 3 points (or if the mortgage would bring only 97 on the secondary market), then the originating lender could charge the builder or seller $3 per hundred of face value for the loan. *Originating lender* means the financial institution making the loan, for example, bank to mortgagor. It was specifically provided in the Act that the charges could not be passed on to the buyer.

The Housing Act of 1954 and FNMA

Because FNMA was a wholly owned government corporation borrowing money from the Treasury and because FNMA often acted as a primary source of funds rather than a true secondary market, as was pointed out above, Congress rechartered FNMA under the Act of 1954. On November 1, 1954, FNMA began a new operation.

It was rechartered as an agency of the Housing and Home Finance Agency. The HHFA administrator is the chairman of the board of directors of FNMA with the power to appoint the other four directors. Under the 1954 Act, FNMA was to become divorced from government ownership and become *privately* owned. The method by which FNMA was to proceed to private ownership is as follows: (1) The capital, surplus, and earnings of the old FNMA, which in 1954 was about $70 million, was to be used as working capital. In payment of this $70 million, preferred stock was issued in that amount and delivered to the Treasury. Dividends on the preferred stock are cumulative. The rate of the dividend was to be fixed by the Treasury, based on the current average interest rate on outstanding government obligations. *Cumulative preferred stock* means that if there have not been sufficient earnings to pay the dividends in any one or a number of years when there are earnings, the "cumulated" amount of unpaid dividends must be paid before any dividends can be made available to common stockholders. (2) The lenders doing business with FNMA were, and are, under the Act, those who are to become the common stockholders and eventually the private owners of the secondary market facility. Originally, the lenders were required to invest 3 percent of the amount of the mortgages they sold to FNMA in nonrefundable capital contributions which were exchanged for common stock. This meant that, originally, if a lender wanted to sell a $10,000 mortgage to FNMA, it would in effect have to purchase $300 worth of common stock. By administrative action, the percentage of the loan that had to be used by the lenders to buy common stock in FNMA had been lowered and then raised. At one time, the amount was only 1 percent of the loan (this amount being the minimum under the 1954 Act); it was then raised to 2 percent of the loan. This amount can be expected to fluctuate depending on whether or not FNMA has funds readily available. If money was short or tight, the percentage could be raised. If money was plentiful, the percentage could be lowered.

The Housing Act of 1957 amended this requirement. The amendment established that the *maximum* stock purchase requirement be at 2 percent and the minimum at 1 percent.

In 1958 the situation was changed. The nation dipped into a recession; and, in order to stimulate the building industry, Congress poured money into FNMA with which to purchase mortgages and further removed service charges and the requirement that sellers of mortgages to FNMA were required to purchase stock. As soon as FNMA retired the preferred stock held by the Treasury out of its earnings and surplus, it would be privately owned.

In addition to having FNMA move toward private ownership, the Act provided for three other things:

1. Secondary Market Operation. "Fanny May" was to continue its secondary market operation. It could buy and sell any mortgage insured or guaranteed after August 2, 1954. These mortgages, however, had to be of such quality that they could meet the purchase standards required by private investors. In order to prevent excessive use of the FNMA facilities, a purchase and marketing fee of one half percent of the unpaid principal balance was to be charged in connection with the purchase of eligible mortgages, and a fee of one percent was charged in connection with the purchase of mortgages of lesser marketability. The prices paid by FNMA for these mortgages varied according to the area and market terms. In short, prices varied with the geographical area. In reality, this meant a variance in price which, in the final analysis, was determined by the supply of mortgage funds within a given area.

2. The Special Assistance Function. Under the terms of the Act, the President has the authority to authorize advance commitments and purchases of mortgages by FNMA to support special types of housing programs. These special types of housing programs are urban renewal or relocation housing programs under the urban renewal program, covered in detail in Chapter 29. In addition, the President also had the special authority to order FNMA to buy mortgages generally in the event such purchases were necessary to stop or retard a decline in home building activities. Under the Act such purchases could not exceed $300 million at any one time.

3. The Management and Liquidation Function. The new FNMA charter required that FNMA manage and liquidate its portfolio of mortgages acquired prior to November 1, 1954. FNMA began selling the $2.4 billion dollars worth of mortgages it held at the time. The prices varied according to the type of mortgage offered, and all prices were subject to change without notice.

Operating Capital

Under the 1954 Act, FNMA needed operating capital to carry out its secondary market activities. It was provided in the Act that after obtaining the consent of the Treasury, FNMA could sell its obligations up to 10 times its capital, surplus, reserves, and undistributed earnings. The Treasury could invest in these obligations up to $500 million plus an amount equal to the reduction in FNMA's mortgage portfolio, but not more than $1 billion, until the Treasury's investment in FNMA was retired.

In 1957, the Act of 1954 was amended with regard to operating capital for FNMA's secondary market function. The amendment provided that the amount of preferred stock of FNMA which could be held by the Treasury was increased by $65 million. Because FNMA could borrow $10 for every $1 of its capital and surplus, this $65 million increase in its capitalization enabled it to borrow an additional $650 million.

The New Look of "Fanny May"

Beginning on May 6, 1968, FNMA took on a completely new look. FNMA had previously quoted a price that it would pay on FHA and VA mortgages, less ½ of 1 percent as a servicing charge. For example, a quote of 99 on a VA mortgage meant that a holder of VA mortgages would then sell it at 99 in order to replenish his money supply for further lending in the mortgage market. However, as of May 6, 1968, all of that changed. Currently, each week Fanny May announces the amount of money it has for the purchase of mortgages, and mortgage lenders bid for the money—at a large discount if money is tight, and a smaller one if money is easy.

In reality this amounts to an auction. Roughly 1,500 persons, mostly mortgage bankers, name the dollar amount of mortgages they want to sell to FNMA and the yield they will accept on mortgages they will deliver within four months. For example, *A* wants to sell FNMA $1 million in FHA mortgages in four months, say at 98. This means *A* will receive $980,000. A competitor may bid 95, meaning he will deliver $1 million in mortgages for $950,000, in which case *A* doesn't get the money. The auctions take place on

Mondays, alternating between FHA and VA loans one week and conventionals the next.

Once the bid has been accepted, the mortgage banker pays a nonrefundable fee of ¼ of one percent. The individual winning the bid is not required to deliver the mortgages; but if he doesn't, he loses the fee. A mortgage banker would naturally not take the money if rates were to drop during the four-month interim and he could get the money cheaper elsewhere.

The Private Fanny May

As of May, 1968, Fanny May was established as a privately owned corporation rather than a combination government/private corporation as it had been. The $142 million of FNMA stock held by the Treasury was retired; and the common stockholders, who accounted for $139 million of the agency's capital (as of May, 1968), had the sole equity interest in the portfolio of mortgages valued at $5.5 billion (as of May, 1968). The new Fanny May is run by a 15-man board of directors. Ten members of the board are to be elected by the stockholders; and five, representing real estate, mortgage banking, and home building, are appointed by HUD. In 1970, FNMA was authorized to buy conventional mortgages as well as FHA and VA mortgages.

To raise money FNMA sells securities backed by its pool of mortgages. Furthermore, because it is said to be a private corporation with a public purpose, the Secretary of the Treasury has authority to buy up to $2.25 billion of Fanny May obligations at any time.

The Government National Mortgage Association

A newcomer on the mortgage financing scene is to be the Government National Mortgage Association. This cannot help but have the nickname of Ginny May or, as some prefer, Mae. Ginny May is to hold the old, and still existing, Reconstruction Finance Corporation paper. It is to underwrite special-assistance loans, such as those on low-income housing projects, and operate liquidation and management functions.

GNMA and the Tandem Plan. As part of its special-assistance function, GNMA is involved in low-cost housing and hence the so-called Tandem Plan. For example, if a low-cost housing development is sponsored by a non-profit corporation and interest rates rise, financial institutions will not lend except at market rates. Thus Ginny May insures a commitment to the lender or seller of the loan at a fixed price at *par,* then it sells it to FNMA at the prevailing market price and absorbs the loss. For example, and for purposes of illustration: suppose the project costs $1 million, then GNMA pays the seller $1 million, but if rates have risen and the $1 million is discounted to $950,000, then GNMA sells the loan to FNMA for $950,000 and absorbs the $500,000 loss, which usually shows up in the federal deficit.

In August, 1971, the "Super Tandem" plan was created. This included the purchase of unsubsidized FHA and VA loans. This program was initiated to keep FHA loans attractive when their interest rates were below the prevailing market rates.

How GNMA Raises Funds. Basically, GNMA raises funds by selling a variety of securities all fully guaranteed by the U. S. government bearing the full faith and credit of the federal government. In addition, all the various types are backed by an underlying pool of mortgages as security. The funds raised are, of course, used to purchase additional mortgages. These securities are:

The Straight Pass-Through Security. Here, monthly payments of principal and interest are paid to the investor from payments *actually* collected on the pooled loans in an amount proportionate to the investor's share in the pool.

The Modified Pass-Through Security. Here, investors are paid monthly principal installments and a *fixed* rate of interest on unpaid mortgage principal balances. Both principal and interest payments must be made whether collected or not by the issuer.

The Bond-Type Security. Here, a specified rate of interest is paid to the investor semiannually. The principal is returned at the end of the term.

Freddie Mac. In 1970 the Federal Home Loan Mortgage Corporation was formed and immediately dubbed "Freddie Mac." This secondary market for conventional loans was sought after primarily by savings and loan associations and is an "arm" of the Federal

Home Loan Bank Board whose chief officers are three members of the Bank Board.

It is authorized to hold, deal, or sell mortgages or part interest in loans. In short, it can do for conventional mortgages everything that FNMA has been doing for FHA and VA loans. However, where FNMA does not require delivery of the loans committed for, FHLMC does.

The original $100 million in capital was subscribed to by the 12 district Federal Home Loan Banks. Additional funds are raised by the sale of Freddie Mac certificates. The principal and interest are guaranteed by the Federal Home Loan Mortgage Corporation, backed by mortgages. Interest is paid by FHLMC on the amount outstanding whether or not collected. The principal passes through as collected. If the mortgage is delinquent, the principal is paid as collected. If there is a loss of principal due to a foreclosure, such loss is not passed through to the investor, but paid by Freddie Mac.

Maggy May. Maggy May is a *private* secondary market; it is a subsidiary of MGIC Investment Corporation of Milwaukee. The true name of Maggy May is the MGIC Mortgage Corporation, the largest of nine such private corporations. They do three things:

1. Insure conventional residential loans. For example, savings and loan associations can issue 95 percent conventional loans if they are insured. MGIC has about 6,800 lenders for which they write mortgage insurance.

2. Insure leases. For example, New York Guaranty Corporation, a subsidiary of MGIC, recently insured lease payments to a lessor of over $2,500,000 over a 15-year period. This arises when a financial institution will not lend on a project where the prospective tenants do not have AAA credit rating. However, when the rent payments are insured, then the financial institution will make the loan for the project, being assured that the loan will be paid off if necessary from the insurance.

3. Purchase mortgages as a secondary market. To this end they started with a capital base of $10 million and have a revolving line of credit with New York banks of $100 million. In short, they borrow on the line of credit by mortgages and with the paybacks on the mortgages pay the bank.

Other Secondary Markets

Although FNMA is the major secondary market, there are others which cannot be overlooked. Sometimes, for purposes of adjusting their portfolios, one type of institutional investor who is a permanent investor might sell the mortgages to another type of institutional investor. For example, an insurance company owning a block of mortgages in a particular area might sell the mortgages to a savings and loan association which desires to put its funds to work. In this sense, the savings and loan association constitutes a secondary market.

Individuals, estates, and trustees often constitute a secondary market, although, for the most part, individuals, estates, and trustees purchasing directly from mortgage bankers are thought of as primary lenders. In the sense that they assume the position of the permanent lender in the chain much like the institutional investor who has made a commitment to the mortgage banker, they can be regarded as a secondary market.

MORTGAGE BANKING

A *mortgage banker* has been defined as: "Any person, firm, or corporation . . . engaged in the business of lending money on the security of improved real estate in the United States and who publicly offers such securities, or certificates, bonds, or debentures based thereon, for sale as a dealer therein, or who is an investor in real estate securities, or is the recognized agent of an insurance company or other direct purchaser of first mortgage real estate securities for investment only."[3]

In residential financing, the mortgage banker has a place of great significance and influence. In a recent year, for example, these firms originated over two fifths of all home mortgages containing FHA-insured or VA-guaranteed provisions. Without the assistance of these firms the average project builder would be out of business. Because of their great influence in real estate finance, we shall examine their modes of operation.

---

[3] Constitution of the Mortgage Bankers Association of America (1946).

BUILDER-MORTGAGE BANKER RELATIONSHIP

Basically, the mortgage banker operates in two broad areas. These might be called the builder-mortgage banker operation and the correspondent operation.

Builder-Mortgage Banker Operation

This situation arises when a project builder approaches a mortgage banker for financing. Assume the builder desires FHA-insured financing and local banks cannot or will not deal directly with the project builder. Assume, further, the builder needs $1 million. The problem actually breaks down into two parts: (a) the need for a short-term loan in the nature of a construction or building loan; and (b) the long-term mortgage that is to be placed on the property as buyers move in and buy the homes with the FHA mortgage loans.

The problem of the short-term building loan needed by the builder for construction purposes is generally solved either by the mortgage banker employing his own funds to finance the builder or by the use of his credit with a commercial bank. In the latter instance, the mortgage banker obtains a short-term loan from his commercial bank on the strength of his own credit plus the credit of the builder, using the property owned by the builder as additional security for the loan.

The problem of the long-term FHA-insured mortgage to be placed on the property is generally taken care of well in advance of the actual construction. If it is not taken care of in advance, the chances of the mortgage banker's obtaining the construction loan from a commercial bank are slim from the beginning. Hence, there is, in reality, a close relationship between (a) obtaining the construction loan, and (b) providing for the long-term mortgage loan.

In practice, therefore, the mortgage banker has to make certain that he can obtain the long-term mortgages on the project before his local commercial bank is even approached with the idea of lending for the short-term construction loan. The mortgage banker first obtains from the permanent investor what is known as an advance commitment.

Advance Commitment. The *advance commitment*, or *forward commitment* as it is often called, is the all-important first step in the process of the mortgage banker's obtaining funds for a builder. The mortgage banker approaches the permanent investor, generally an insurance company or a mutual savings bank, with the statement that a builder is *going* to build a group of homes on which there is to be $1 million worth of mortgages. The permanent investor then agrees (makes a firm commitment) to purchase the government-underwritten mortgages which will be placed on the property. The mortgage banker agrees to deliver these mortgages at a future date. In reality, it is a purchase order given *in advance* of construction. The delivery date is determined by the time required for construction, plus time for selling, plus time for processing and transmitting the documents. Or delivery may be set *at a time convenient* for the purchaser of the mortgages.[4]

After having obtained the advance commitment, the mortgage banker then goes through step (a); namely, obtaining the short-term construction loan through his local commercial bank or one willing to deal with him. In practice, most commercial banks will not make the short-term loan without the advance commitment from the permanent investor.

In the simple situation, the permanent investor takes up the long-term mortgages from the mortgage banker when the house is sold, the construction loans are paid off, and the papers are processed.

The Take-Out Letter. The agreement for the advance commitment is called a *take-out letter*. This lists in detail the time of delivery of the mortgages, the amount of loans that will be granted, and the fees that will have to be paid.

Armed with the take-out letter, the mortgage banker's ability to obtain a construction loan is facilitated. The reason for this, of course, is that the commercial bankers have greater assurance that the loans will be paid. It should be added that frequently these construction loans are placed with more than one commercial bank due to limitations as to the size of loan that commercial banks are permitted to make under state laws.

Standby Commitment. The situation bringing about the *standby commitment* arises when the mortgage banker is unable to obtain an

[4] Mortimer Caplin, *Recent Institutional Arrangements in Mortgage Lending*, a paper presented at the annual meeting of the American Finance Association, December 28, 1957, Philadelphia, Pennsylvania.

immediate advance commitment from a permanent investor. This arises most typically in a period of high or rising interest rates. If for some reason money is tight, the insurance companies and other investors may not be able to see their way clear to make an immediate advance commitment. In this case, the commercial bank makes a standby commitment. In essence, the agreement between the mortgage banker and the commercial banker is that the *commercial bank itself* makes a firm commitment to buy the mortgages at a future date in the event the mortgage banker is unable to find a permanent investor by a specified date. The price that the commercial bank will pay the mortgage banker in the event a permanent investor is not found in time is known as the *forfeiture price*. Suppose, for example, that a mortgage banker is able to obtain an advance commitment for a $10,000 mortgage from a permanent investor. Assume the service charge is 1½ percent (this amount will vary with "easy" or "tight" money market conditions). This means that the mortgage banker will be charged $150 on the $10,000 mortgage. In practice, this sum is passed on to the builder. Suppose, further, that the mortgage banker is unable to obtain an advance commitment and then gets a standby commitment from a commercial bank. The fee charged for the standby commitment is larger than the fee charged by the permanent investor for the advance commitment, in this case, say 2 percent or $200. In addition, the price at which the commercial bank agrees to take over the mortgage in the event that the mortgage banker is unable to obtain a permanent investor within the stated time may be $9,500; this price, then, is the forfeiture price.

Conditions Affecting Ability to Obtain Advance Commitments

The question often arises as to why mortgage bankers are sometimes able to obtain advance commitments with ease and why at other times it becomes difficult or almost impossible for them to obtain the advance commitments. In the final analysis, the advance commitment is a handy device for those financial institutions who put their money in mortgages through mortgage bankers. For example, an insurance company can figure fairly closely the amount of money it will have on hand 18 months hence. It figures it will receive money from "paybacks" on outstanding mortgages, savings in the form of premium payments, the sale of government securities, and other securities currently held in its portfolio. By issuing an advance commitment for mortgages ready for it to take over in 18 months, it is able to determine ahead of time just what its investment portfolios are going to be. In addition, there is no need for last-minute buying to have the sort of mortgage investments it desires. There may also be a certain amount of profit from the advance commitment. In periods of low or stable interest rates, there is no real problem.

The difficulty appears, however, when interest rates begin to rise. When this happens, bond prices begin to fall. Government bonds and other bonds held by the permanent investors decrease in value. They cannot dispose of these securities because of the large losses they might sustain. This obstruction to rapid liquidation is commonly called a *freeze-in.*

At this point not only are the institutions unable to grant new advance commitments to mortgage bankers, but they may have difficulty in "taking-out" mortgages under prior advance commitments. As a result of this inability to obtain the normal advance commitment, the mortgage brokers are led to the standby commitment at a higher cost.

As far as previous commitments are concerned, institutional investors who are "frozen-in" look to the commercial banks for temporary loans. They do this by using the mortgages coming in from the previous commitments as security for the loans from the commercial banks. This is, of course, costly and has a tendency to reduce the overall profit of the transaction. When financial institutions are caught in situations of this type, they are commonly said to be *over-committed.*

Mortgage Warehousing

Mortgage warehousing is an interim loan by a commercial bank between the time a mortgage is closed by a mortgage banker and the time it is taken up by a permanent investor. It has also been defined as the granting of interim loans by commercial banks to nonbank real estate lenders.[5]

[5] Jack Guttenberg, "Mortgage Warehousing," *Journal of Finance,* Vol. XII, No. 4 (December, 1957), pp. 438-450.

There are three types of mortgage warehousing with which the mortgage banker may become involved. Each is discussed in detail in the following sections.

Committed-Technical Warehousing. This is the most prevalent and easily understandable type of warehousing. For example, suppose a mortgage banker is dealing with a builder engaged in constructing 100 homes. He has received an advance commitment from an insurance company. When a home is completed and sold, the purchaser signs the mortgage or deed of trust as mortgagor or trustor, and the mortgage banker is the mortgagee, or beneficiary if a deed of trust is used. There is now a time lapse before the mortgage banker is able to deliver the instruments and other necessary papers to the permanent investor (the insurance company, in this case). The time lapse arises for various reasons, one being that it takes time to record the mortgage. It must be sent to the county clerk who records it and sends it back. Fire insurance policies must be put in final form. Depending on the real estate activity in a particular area, this may take from five to six months. In the interim, because the average mortgage banker operates with relatively limited capital, the commercial bank lends the amount of the mortgage to the mortgage banker. The mortgage itself is the collateral for this relatively short-term loan. Details completed, the mortgage is taken over by the permanent investor.

The flow for committed-technical warehousing appears as follows: home buyer (mortgagor) to mortgage banker (originating lender) to commercial bank (the warehouse) to permanent investor (insurance company or other institutional investor).

Uncommitted-Technical Warehousing.[6] This type of warehousing may be with recourse or without recourse against the mortgage banker. This situation arises when the mortgage banker has been unable to obtain an advance commitment with a permanent lender. Here, the mortgage banker is given a time limit within which to find a permanent investor. The mortgage is closed with the mortgage banker as mortgagee. The bank advances money to the mortgage banker with the mortgage as collateral.

---

[6] *Ibid.*

If the warehousing is made *with* recourse, the mortgage banker *must* take up the mortgage by the end of a stated time. If he is unable to find a permanent investor, he must take the mortgage back from the commercial bank. Presumably the mortgage banker will attempt to find a permanent investor at a later date. The flow of the uncommitted-technical warehousing transaction will therefore be the same as the flow of the committed-technical warehousing as outlined previously. If, however, the mortgage banker is unable to find a permanent investor in time, the flow of the uncommitted-technical warehousing *with* recourse will be as follows: home buyer (mortgagor) to mortgage banker (originating lender) to commercial bank (the warehouse for the time allotted) to mortgage banker (originating lender) to the permanent investor (an institutional lender or anyone else that can be found later).

Uncommitted-technical warehousing *without* recourse varies only in small detail. Again this is the situation where the mortgage banker obtains a standby commitment from a commercial bank, and again the commercial bank advances funds to the mortgage banker with the mortgage as the collateral for the loan. The mortgage banker is given a time limit within which to find a permanent investor. However, in the event the mortgage banker fails to find a permanent investor within the time allotted, the commercial bank takes up the mortgage. This they do at the forfeiture price as was outlined above. In this case the flow for an uncommitted-technical warehousing transaction *without* recourse is as follows: home buyer (mortgagor) to mortgage banker (originating lender) to commercial bank (the warehouse taking at the forfeiture price and, if possible, later selling to another financial institution).

Committed Institutional Warehousing. This situation typically arises when the permanent lender makes an advance commitment and then has suffered a "freeze-in" or his net inflow of funds is less than anticipated. For example, a permanent investor gives an advance commitment to a mortgage banker in anticipation of selling government bonds a year hence, at which time it is felt that the home will be built and sold to the mortgagor home buyers. In the interim, the interest rate rises and the market price of the government securities consequently falls. The investor is unable to liquidate the securities because he would have to take large capital losses. However, because of the advance commitment contained in his takeout letter, he is bound to take up the mortgages on delivery; the present investor is overcommitted. In this case, the institutional lender borrows from the commercial bank with the mortgages being used as security for the loan.

These loans are generally paid in one or two years; the mortgages are then delivered by the commercial bank to the permanent investor.

A situation leading to committed institutional warehousing may also arise when paybacks on previously held mortgages are not as great as was anticipated or if any other factor reduces the net inflow of cash below that which was anticipated.

It can readily be seen that when the permanent investor is thus overcommitted and is in the position where he has to borrow from the commercial bank, he refrains for a time in making further advance commitments to mortgage bankers.

The flow for the committed institutional warehousing is as follows: home buyer (mortgagor) to mortgage banker (originating lender) to commercial bank (committed-technical warehouse) to permanent investor to commercial bank (committed institutional warehouse) to permanent investor (after time lapse when net cash flow has increased sufficiently to enable permanent investor to take out mortgage).

Economic Effects of Commitments and Warehousing. When interest rates are low and advance commitments are readily available, the flow of funds via the mortgage banker operates smoothly and with very little risk of loss. Savings in one part of the nation may be tapped and distributed to another part of the nation where savings may be in short supply. In this way excessive fees (which in the final analysis is excessive effective interest to either builder or buyer) are prevented. Effective interest payments tend to stabilize, or reach an equilibrium position. For example, in New England savings and, consequently, the supply of funds may be plentiful; in Dallas, Texas, there might be a building boom which has dried up the supply of local funds. Through the operations of the mortgage banker in Dallas, the funds from New England can be fed into the area where they can be put to work to better advantage.

The more important economic effects of the commitment in its various forms and of warehousing take place during a period of rising interest rates. The committed institutional warehousing prevents serious loss on the part of the institutional lenders during a "freeze-in." If it were not for warehousing, financial institutions that had made advance commitments prior to the rise in the interest rates might be forced to sell depreciated government bonds or other depreciated securities in order to abide by the terms of their agreement with the mortgage bankers.

If money gets tight, the result is a slowdown in construction activity. Mortgage bankers may then be forced into standby agreements. If so, in order to avoid losses as the result of forfeitures, they will tend to seek different types of investments—pension funds, for example. This means tapping new savings and bringing those savings into the mortgage money market. In addition, this sort of activity slows down declines in construction and other real estate activity; for example, land sales, during periods of tight money. However, mortgage warehousing may lead to inflationary pressures if productive capacities in the nation are in short supply. It might be added that any type of credit expansion under the same conditions in any segment of the economy will also increase inflationary pressures.

Without the commitment and the warehousing devices, the mortgage bankers would, for the most part, be out of business. The construction industry would suffer, for without an advance commitment it is virtually impossible to get construction loans for large projects. This would result in a more serious shortage of housing than already exists. It is entirely conceivable that this, in turn, would cause much more serious inflationary pressures as the result of a short supply of houses than would the increased credit expansion resulting from commitments and mortgage warehousing.

The Risks of Mortgage Banking

So far it appears that mortgage bankers are in the happy position of doing business without possibility of loss. Unfortunately, this is not so. As in any other business, the mortgage banker is subject to risks.

The major risk in mortgage banking evolves directly as the result of shifting interest rates. In periods of tight money they often have to rely on using the standby without recourse. This means they may find themselves subject to paying a forfeiture price due to inability to find a permanent investor.

Another risk of loss comes about in the standby agreement with recourse. Here they must take the mortgage from the commercial bank within a stated time, and the loss may be even greater if the interest rate rises more rapidly than anticipated. For example, suppose in the uncommitted technical warehousing without recourse, par is 100 and the forfeiture price is 95. If the bank takes up the mortgage, the mortgage banker stands to lose 5 points plus the cost of a fee to the bank for agreeing to take them up in the first place. Hence, in the uncommitted technical warehousing without recourse, part of the risk is placed on the bank. How? If the market price of the mortgage falls below 95, the loss is borne by the bank.

In the uncommitted technical warehousing with recourse, the mortgage banker *must* take up the mortgage. The fee is smaller, but the mortgage banker assumes more risk—that is, the risk of a drop below 95. If the mortgage dropped to 90, he would lose 10 points plus a fee.

Servicing the Mortgage

Generally, when a mortgage banker is involved in the financing of a project, the mortgage instrument or deed of trust in the nature of a mortgage, as the case may be, is made with the mortgage banker as mortgagee or beneficiary. This means that the monthly payments are made to the mortgage banker by the home buyer (borrower). These payments are made to the mortgage banker even though the mortgage has been purchased by a permanent investor. The mortgage banker receives the monthly payment which usually includes a proportion of the yearly taxes and insurance premiums. The amount of the taxes and insurance is deducted and placed in an escrow fund until such time as it is necessary to pay the taxes and the insurance on the property. The mortgage banker deducts his servicing fee which is generally one half of one percent of the unpaid balance of the loan and sends the balance of the monthly payment to the permanent investor.

At the proper time, the mortgage banker pays the taxes and insurance on the property. In the event either taxes or insurance premiums or both have risen during the year, he sees to it that the difference is paid by the mortgagor.

From time to time, the mortgage banker inspects the property to ascertain if the buyer is wasting the property or has done other things which might be in violation of the covenants contained in the mortgage.

If the mortgagor is delinquent in the payment of the monthly amounts due, the mortgage banker must take immediate steps to bring the payments up to date. The mortgage banker, with the consent of the permanent investor, will begin mortgage foreclosure proceedings if it is necessary to protect the permanent investor. In the case of FHA-insured loans, this must be done in accordance with current FHA regulations.

QUESTIONS FOR REVIEW

1. What is a *secondary mortgage market?*
2. How do shifts in the interest rate affect the volume of VA-guaranteed loans in any one year?
3. Explain the term "commitment" as it relates to FNMA.
4. How is it possible that an FHA-insured mortgage or a VA-guaranteed mortgage can be sold for less than face value?
5. What is meant by the term "originating lender"?
6. Define *mortgage banker.*
7. How does the mortgage banker help a builder?
8. Explain the term "advance commitment."
9. What is a *take-out letter?*
10. What is a *standby commitment?*
11. Define *mortgage warehousing.*
12. Distinguish between committed-technical warehousing and uncommitted-technical warehousing.
13. What are the economic effects of commitments and warehousing?
14. Explain how mortgages are "serviced" by a mortgage banker.

PROBLEMS

1. Economists often refer to credit situations as being "easy," "taut," or "tight." The term "taut" seems to be used to indicate an area between easy and tight and moving in the direction of tight.

Assume you are a mortgage banker with an opportunity of placing $300,000 worth of mortgages. You have a large life insurance company to whom you can look as a permanent investor for this money.

Indicate by means of a diagram the probable flow of funds in each of the above three situations suggesting the various type commitments, warehousing, etc., that would logically be necessary. You might also assume that you can deliver your "package" (the entire lot of mortgages) in about 18 months.

2. The following excerpt is from an issue of *Realtor's Headlines:*

"Secondary market purchase prices for government-backed 4½ percent mortgages were cut, and advance commitments to buy them were discontinued last week by the Federal National Mortgage Association.

"FNMA, which buys FHA-insured and VA-guaranteed mortgages from lenders, thus renewing their cash resources, said that effective October 22 its prices for FHA and VA 4½ percent mortgages would range from 90 to 92, depending upon the area and amount of mortgagor's equity. The previous price range was 92 to 94.

". . . unaffected by the order were FHA mortgages bearing interest rates of 5 and 5¼ percent. Their price schedules have not been changed, and they will continue to be eligible for standby commitments."

(a) Explain the terms "advance commitments" and "standby commitments" as used above.

(b) Why should the price of mortgages vary with the "area" or geographical location of the mortgage?

(c) Can any conclusion be drawn from this with regard to the direction in which the interest rate is moving?

3. The following statement is made by Jones.[7] "Providing a market for existing mortgages will, for example, increase the appetite for mortgage investments. A more liquid mortgage would reduce the likelihood of their being frozen in. Thus the volume of highly liquid non-mortgage assets held for portfolio adjustment purposes could be reduced in favor of higher-yielding mortgages."

(a) What is meant by "being frozen in"?

(b) Can a secondary market guarantee that mortgages will always be liquidated without a loss? Discuss.

---

[7] Oliver Jones, "The Development of an Effective Secondary Mortgage Market," *Journal of Finance,* Vol. XVII (May, 1962), p. 313.

4.

> The White House has announced the Government National Mortgage Association will begin purchasing a wide variety of unsubsidized FHA and VA mortgages, using $2 billion in special assistance funds. Included in the program is a slight bias against existing housing in favor of new construction.
>
> The new program was instigated as an attempt at keeping the FHA-VA rate at its current 7 percent. To do this, GNMA will buy FHA-VA mortgages at a fixed price of $95 per $100 of mortgage for existing homes or $96 for new homes, thus giving new housing a 1-point advantage over existing housing.
>
> Once GNMA buys the mortgages, it will then attempt to resell them to private investors, such as the Federal National Mortgage Association. If the market price for the mortgages falls below $95 or $96, which at present is almost certain to happen, GNMA will absorb the difference . . . .

Source: *Realtor's Headline,* Vol 38, No. 33, August 16, 1971, p. 1.

(a) Read the above and explain its meaning in terms of the discussion of this in the text.

(b) If GNMA is to absorb the difference, where do the funds come from?

SUGGESTED READINGS

Case, Frederick E. *Real Estate,* Rev. ed. Boston: Allyn and Bacon, Inc., 1962. Chapter 15.

Hoagland, Henry E., and Leo D. Stone. *Real Estate Finance,* 4th ed. Homewood, Illinois: Richard D. Irwin, Inc., 1969.

Ring, Alfred A. *Real Estate Principles and Practices,* 7th ed. New York: Prentice-Hall, Inc., 1972. Chapter 13.

Weimer, Arthur M., Homer Hoyt, and George F. Bloom. *Real Estate,* 6th ed. New York: The Ronald Press Company, 1972. Chapter 18.

Chapter 17

Brokerage

Strictly speaking most real estate brokerage firms perform a number of functions in addition to sales. Some engage in construction, finance, appraising, counseling, and insurance. Our concern here is, for the most part, with the sales function. In so occupying himself, the broker acts as a middleman. He takes neither title nor possession, except in the case of trades, which will be discussed later.

At least one study has indicated that most real estate firms are made up of fewer than five employees, and those with twenty or more employees are about 5 percent of the total. This study also suggests that the small firms have been in business an average of about fifteen years, and the smaller firms operate under the proprietorship form of business.[1]

The real estate broker operates in a more complex environment than most individuals engaged in other types of brokerage. A stockbroker, for example, operates within the framework of an organized market. In the sale of real estate, the brokers have a much more

[1] Warren R. Seyfried, "Characteristics of Real Estate Sales Firms in Seattle, Washington, 1962," *Business Review*, Vol. XXII, No. 5 (Seattle: June, 1963), p. 16.

difficult problem; the unit price of the commodity is often higher than in ordinary manufactured goods, the buyers are ill-defined, and more often than not the real estate broker must become involved in financing the sale of his product. However, the most important complication with a real estate transaction lies in the fact that the real estate market is relatively disorganized, as was pointed out in Chapter 2. With this in mind, it is necessary to examine what the real estate broker does and how he manages to survive in a highly competitive world.

THE REAL ESTATE BROKER

In the business sense a *real estate broker* is a person or corporation engaged primarily in the marketing of one or more of the various rights in real property. His basic function is that of a negotiator. His success or failure lies in his ability to bring together a buyer and a seller who are "ready, willing, and able."

In the legal sense, a *real estate broker* is defined as:

> . . . any person, association, copartnership, or corporation, who for a compensation or valuable consideration sells or offers for sale, buys or offers to buy, or negotiates the purchase or sale or exchange of real estate, or who leases or offers to lease or rents or offers to rent, any real estate or the improvements thereon for others.

Primarily, the practicing broker's business consists of selling or leasing property or space in a building, placing a mortgage or collecting rents, or performing other services for a certain percentage of the money value of the transaction.

The broker operates under a contract of employment. In many states this contract of employment need not be in writing nor need it be in any particular form. However, in fifteen states the employment contract must be in writing. The contract under which the broker operates, whether it be oral or in writing, is known as a *listing contract*. These listing contracts give the broker the right to sell or lease the property and to classify and file descriptions of the property. Because the broker works under a contract of employment for either the buyer or the seller (or sometimes both by consent of the parties), he is governed by the law of agency.

THE AGENT AND AGENCY

An *agent* is one who acts for another known as the *principal* in dealing with third persons on behalf of the principal. A contract of agency is established in an agreement between the parties, or it may be created by appointment. The agency right is most often expressly granted by the principal in written or oral form, but sometimes agency is created by the implied act or acts of the principal. Literally, the term "agent" is of broader scope than the term "broker." A person is an agent or a broker depending upon the extent of the authority given to him. For example, when a real estate broker is given the authority to enter into a written contract on behalf of his principal, he is a true agent; when this authority is absent, he is a broker only in the legal sense.

There are three parties involved in every contract the agent negotiates: the principal (the seller in real estate), the agent (the broker), and the buyer.

Purpose of an Agency

Generally, an agency can be established for any lawful purpose. This means merely that the objects of the agency may not be contrary to public policy or criminal in nature.

Who May Be a Principal or an Agent

Anyone who is legally competent to enter into a contract may be a principal or an agent. A person capable of acting for himself is capable of acting for another provided that he is properly authorized to do so. Also, a person capable of acting for himself can appoint another capable person to act in his stead.

This normally excludes the insane and minors. Most of the states having real estate licensing laws specifically exclude minors from holding a real estate broker's license. However, in many of these states, for example, New York, a minor may be a real estate salesman. In other states, Florida, for example, a minor may be a real estate salesman if his "disability" has been removed by a court order.

Kinds of Agents

Sometimes agents have been classified as ostensible and actual. An *ostensible agency* occurs when the authority for the agency arises from the fact that a third person has relied upon the express or implied representations of the principal to the effect that the relationship existed. The *actual agency* relationship is one in which the authority to act has been delegated by the principal. Another method of classification of agents is in terms of the business to be transacted by them as general, special, or universal.

A *general agent* is authorized by the principal to transact all of his affairs in connection with a particular kind of business or trade, or to transact all of his business at a certain place.

A *special agent* is authorized by the principal to transact a business affair or to do a special act. In real estate, for example, when a broker is authorized to purchase a particular house, the broker is designated as the special agent of the principal.

The *universal agent* is authorized to do all acts that can be lawfully delegated to a representative.

Termination of the Agency

Ordinarily the agency is terminated when the purpose for which the principal and agent relationship was established has been completed, but it may be terminated at anytime by the principal. The agency may also be terminated by the death or insanity of either party or by bankruptcy of the principal. In this latter instance the agency is said to have been terminated by "operation of law." Destruction of the subject matter of the agency will also terminate the relationship. For example, if a house is listed with a broker for sale and the house is destroyed by fire, then the principal and agent relationship is terminated.

There is one exception to the general rule that an agency may be terminated by the principal at anytime; that is, when the agency is said to be "coupled with an interest." In order for the agency to be coupled with an interest, the agent must have an interest in the authority granted to him or an interest in the subject matter of the agency. In the first instance, the agent has an interest in the authority when he has given a consideration or has paid for the right to exercise the authority granted him. In the second instance, an agent has a property interest in the subject matter with which he is dealing.

As far as real property is concerned, to be coupled with an interest, the agency must in some way concern the land itself and not merely the proceeds from the sale of the property. Division of the proceeds with the owner does not give the selling agent an interest in the land sold, nor does a commission on the sale make the agent's authority irrevocable.[2]

Consider the following example in which the agency is said to be "coupled with an interest" because there is an interest in the authority when money is borrowed to purchase real property.

A approaches *B*, a real estate broker engaged in management, and tells *B* that he desires to purchase an office building. *A* asks *B* to lend him money on a mortgage on the premises. *B* is willing to lend the money to *A* provided that he has a right to manage the building. *B's* real purpose in managing the building is to obtain additional security for his loan. Assume that *A* agrees to allow *B* to manage the property. Sometime later *A* attempts to dismiss *B* as the management agent of the building. In a situation of this type the courts generally hold that the agency of *B* cannot be terminated at the will of *A* because *B's* agency is of such a nature as to be "coupled with an interest." He has, in effect, an interest in the authority.

Broker's Protection Against Termination

Although it is the general rule that an agency may be terminated at anytime, there are a number of exceptions to the rule that have particular application to real estate brokers. The most obvious situation in which the agency cannot be terminated at the will of the owner occurs when the broker has procured a purchaser and the owner then states that the agency is terminated. In this case, the broker is entitled to a commission. If no time for the duration of the agency is included in the broker's contract of employment, and the broker is negotiating with a prospect, the owner (principal) cannot terminate the agency and finish the transaction himself without paying the broker.

For example, an exclusive real estate agency contract specifies the duration of the contract. On the basis of this agreement the

[2] *W. M. Martin & Son* v. *Lamkin,* 188 Ill. App. 431 (1914).

broker spends money advertising and showing the property; the owner then terminates the contract before the expiration of the time called for in the contract. In a case of this nature, the owner may be liable to the broker for the money and time spent seeking a purchaser for the property.

Duties of the Broker as Agent

Just as the principal has certain obligations to the agent, the agent has certain obligations to the principal.

Loyalty. Foremost among these obligations is loyalty. The broker must be loyal to his principal. He is given a position of trust and confidence, and he is not permitted to make a secret profit as a result of this position of trust. He cannot secretly purchase for himself either directly or indirectly a property listed with him, nor can he attempt to make a secret profit therefrom. For example, *A* lists a property with a broker for $7,000. The broker later states that he has an offer for $5,000, and *A* accepts the offer. At the closing, *A* transfers a deed to a woman and later discovers that the woman is the wife of the broker and is using her maiden name. *A*, meanwhile, has paid the broker $250 in commissions. *A* may recover the $2,000 and the commission paid. In New York State *A* is entitled to recover the commission that he has paid, and, in case of deception, is entitled to recover four times the amount of the commission paid.

Must Account for Money and Property. A real estate broker handling funds or property belonging to a principal must account for the money or property upon demand from the principal. In some states the broker is required by law to submit a closing statement to the interested parties in a sales transaction. This, in effect, requires an accounting in writing by the broker of those funds handled by him. In other states the principal can force the accounting by order of the courts.

The theory behind this is that when a broker receives money or property for a client, he is placed in the position of a trustee. Thus, he becomes liable not only under the brokerage laws of the states, but in the event that he breaches his trust, he may become liable under the penal laws of the states as well. As trustee, he holds the money for the benefit of the client, and he must exercise care with any funds held by him. He must not under any circumstances commingle the money that he holds for a client with his own funds. It is a nearly universal provision of the brokerage license laws that the mere commingling of the broker's own funds with those of his clients is a basis for the revocation or suspension of his broker's license. To avoid this situation, the broker upon entering business should immediately open a special account in the place where he is banking, and this special account should be reserved exclusively as a depository for the funds belonging to his clients.

An Agent Cannot Delegate His Authority. The agent is selected by the principal because the principal places trust and confidence in him and him alone. A broker may, however, delegate to another ministerial or mechanical duties involving the agency. In order to avoid complications of this nature, most of the broker's contracts of employment contain a statement substantially to this effect:

> You may, if desired, secure the cooperation of any other broker, or group of brokers, in procuring a sale of said property.

In the absence of a statement of this nature, the broker takes the risk of a refusal on the part of the owner to consent to such employment when he employs a subagent. However, the owner may consent either expressly or by implication. If the owner keeps silent, the broker's employment of a subagent will be construed by the courts to be an implication of consent on the part of the owner.

A broker is generally held liable for the acts of a subagent employed to handle the sale of a property. For example, a property is listed with a broker at $25 per acre. The broker hires another broker, *X*, to help him transact the deal. *X*, the subagent, receives an offer of $45 per acre but reports only an offer of $25 per acre to the broker. The owner accepts the offer and the property is deeded over to a person conspiring with the subagent. The subagent later sells the property to the original offeror. The owner may sue the broker under these circumstances, and the broker will be held personally liable for the actions of his subagent even though he had no actual knowledge of the deceptive phase of the transaction.

Duty to Obey Instructions. When a property is listed with a broker, the listing contains instructions to the broker that he must obey. In addition, the owner may impose limitations on the broker by special instructions, which he is also bound to obey. If a broker deviates from the instructions given him by his principal, he may find himself liable to his principal for damages resulting from such deviations.

Must Not Be Negligent. The general rule of agency regarding negligence is applicable to brokers. The agent is bound to exercise the same skill as other brokers operating in the same capacity. If the agent is negligent in the pursuance of his duties, then he is liable for any resulting loss that might be sustained by his principal.

The Fiduciary Concept. It is commonly stated that the agent acts in a fiduciary capacity with his principal. At all times, then, the broker is required to act completely "above board" with his principal. He must reveal to his principal all information and all material facts concerning a transaction. If he knows that his purchaser is acting for someone else, he must reveal that fact to his principal.

May Not Act for Both Parties. It has been written that "no man may serve two masters," and so it is with regard to real estate brokers. No broker may ordinarily serve both parties to a transaction because the interests of the buyer and the seller are diametrically opposed. The seller desires to obtain the highest price possible for the property, and the purchaser wants to buy it at the lowest price possible. The broker obviously cannot serve both the seller of the property and the prospective buyer equally well in this regard.

A broker may serve the interests of both parties when he obtains the consent of both the buyer and the seller. This consent should be obtained in writing from both of the parties and should be kept in the files of the broker. In some states the real estate license laws specifically require that this consent be obtained in writing and filed "in the deal envelope." In these states, the law goes on further to declare that the state real estate board may, at anytime, demand to see the consent. In the absence of such written consent, a broker may lose his license.

May Not Misrepresent the Facts. A broker must not make any statements misrepresenting material facts. If the broker misrepresents the facts, he will not only lose his commission, but he will be liable to the purchaser for resulting damages. For example, a parcel of property described as having a frontage of 100 feet is listed with a broker. The broker brings his prospect out to see the property, which is bordered on one side by a hedge. The broker assumes that the property line begins with the hedge. The purchaser asks the broker if the property includes the hedge, and the broker answers in the affirmative. On the basis of this statement, the property is purchased. Later it is discovered that the property line is actually about 14 feet inside the hedge. The purchaser sues the broker and collects damages as a result of this misrepresentation even though it was not deliberate on the broker's part.

Extravagant Statements. The broker is not ordinarily liable for extraordinary and extravagant statements made in the course of selling a parcel of property. The attitude of the courts is that a buyer, as a reasonable man, should not believe such statements implicitly, and therefore he cannot hold the seller to them should they prove false. For example, if a broker takes a prospect to a piece of property and tells him that the property has the "best view in the world," the purchaser cannot later bring an action against the broker claiming that the property actually did not contain the "best view in the world." The purchaser either knew or should have known that the broker was making an obviously extravagant statement about the property.

Acting for an Undisclosed Principal

Very often real estate brokers are called upon to negotiate for a principal without disclosing his identity. The broker has two alternatives: he may proceed as if he were buying the property himself; or he may state that he is acting for a principal who prefers to remain anonymous.

In either situation, the agent can sue or be sued upon any contract that he executes. By the same token, upon discovery the principal can either sue or be sued on any contract that has been executed on his behalf by the agent. If the agent states that he is working for a principal, the agent may clearly indicate in the contract that he assumes no personal liability under the contract.

Ratification

Agents are generally authorized to do a specific act, and the agents are bound to obey the instructions given them by the principal. However, if the agent performs an authorized act, this act may be ratified by the principal. Ratification has been defined as:

> the express or implied adoption and confirmation by one person of an act or contract performed or entered into on his behalf by another who at the time assumed to act as his agent in doing or making the contract, without the authority to do so.[3]

For there to be ratification, the person acting must have done the act as the agent and not on his own behalf. In addition, the person ratifying must have full knowledge of all of the material facts or have sufficient facts to enable him to choose to assume full responsibility for the act.

It should be especially noted that the principal cannot ratify part of the transaction and disaffirm the remainder of the transaction. If he seeks to ratify the act of his agent, he must ratify the entire act. He will then be bound by the entire act of his agent in the same manner as if he had given the agent the authority to carry out the act.

Honest Mistake

The broker cannot be held liable for an honest mistake unless it can be shown that the honest mistake was the result of gross negligence. For example, a seller tells a broker that the size of his property is 160 acres and shows the broker a survey showing the property to be 160 acres. After having acquired a purchaser, it is shown that the property is only 150 acres in size. The broker cannot be held liable in a situation of this type; his mistake was an honest mistake.

[3] 2 Corpus Juris, Sec. 77.

Fraudulent Representations

The penalty for fraudulent representations made by a broker is serious. For example, a broker subdivides a parcel of property and represents to prospective purchasers that he has arranged for water and sewage disposal. The prospect purchases the property, then discovers that no such arrangements have been made, nor was there any attempt on the part of the broker to arrange for sewage and water disposal for the subdivision. In a case of this kind, not only is the broker liable for damages to the purchaser for fraud, but his license will be removed either on the grounds of misrepresentation or on the grounds that he had indicated that he was untrustworthy.

THE BROKER'S EMPLOYMENT CONTRACT

Many states provide that the contract of employment, or listing contract as it is commonly called, between the broker and his client must be in writing.[4] In these states a written agreement is a prerequisite to the collection of a commission. In the other states the contract of employment may be oral. Even in these states, however, it is desirable that employment contracts be in writing, especially those contracts containing an exclusive right or an exclusive agency agreement. The advantage of a written agreement is that it avoids later misunderstanding about the true contents of the listing and avoids misunderstanding about the rights of brokers under the contract of employment.

The ordinary real estate broker's listing contract contains the names and addresses of the seller and the broker, the selling price, and any encumbrances against the property. The contract describes the property and states the manner in which the property is to be conveyed. There is a statement of the percentage of the selling price that is to be paid to the broker as a commission. The contract also lists the personal property that is included in the deal, such as shades, venetian blinds, and door screens, and a declaration by the seller that he shall deliver to the buyer a bill of sale to cover the transfer of such personal property. If it is an exclusive contract, the instrument will contain an expiration date. In some states, such as Oregon,

[4] Arizona, California, Idaho, Indiana, Iowa, Kentucky, Michigan, Montana, Nebraska, New Jersey, Ohio, Oregon, Texas, Utah, Washington, and Wisconsin.

all listing contracts must have a definite expiration date. The contract is signed and a copy is kept by the broker. In some states, the brokerage laws require that the broker deliver a copy of the listing contract to the seller. At this point it would be a good idea to study the broker's employment contract form on pages 432 and 433.

Automatic Renewal Clauses

Most states have outlawed the inclusion of an automatic renewal clause in the listing contract. A clause of this type can cause endless trouble between seller and broker, and furthermore, it is basically unfair to the seller. In contracts containing an automatic renewal clause, the contract includes an expiration date for the contract and states substantially as follows:

> After the date last mentioned, this contract will continue in force as a nonexclusive listing in every respect as above set forth until canceled by me in writing, or until the property is sold.

In states where the automatic renewal clause is prohibited, brokers should be certain that it is not included in their contracts, because its inclusion in a broker's contract of employment may lead to the loss of his license.

TYPES OF CONTRACTS OF EMPLOYMENT

Open Listing

The *open listing* is a listing that is given by an owner to many brokers. In giving an open listing the owner hopes that one of the brokers will be able to produce a purchaser for the property. In the event broker *A* enters into negotiations with a prospect and obtains a signed binder, or contract, broker *A* is not entitled to a commission if another broker has succeeded in obtaining a signed binder or contract prior to completion of the transaction by broker *A*.

In many respects an open listing is bad not only from the broker's viewpoint, but it is also bad from the owner's viewpoint. Brokers are naturally reluctant to spend a great deal of money advertising a property when they know it may very well be all in vain; hence, owners who give open listings often receive no action on their properties.

No. 674 © Rev. TL
Stevens-Ness L.P.Co.
Portland, Or. 97204

REAL ESTATE BROKER'S EMPLOYMENT CONTRACT

RESIDENCE PROPERTY

DESCRIPTION: ______________________________

____

(If said property is incorrectly described, owner hereby expressly authorizes broker subsequently to write in hereon or attach hereto, the correct legal description thereof.)

City of ______________, County of ______________, State of ______________; for better description see owner's title deed on record, now made a part hereof. For personal property, if any to be included in property offered for sale for price next mentioned, see below or see signed inventory, to be attached.

Selling price, free of encumbrances: $ ______________; Terms ______________

____

Is signed inventory attached as part hereof? Yes_____; No _____; to be attached as part hereof? Yes_____; No_____.

To ______________ (REAL ESTATE BROKER) ______________ (CITY) ______________ (STATE) ______________ (DATE), 19_____

FOR VALUE RECEIVED, you hereby are employed to sell or exchange the property described hereon at the selling price and on the terms noted. You hereby are authorized to accept a deposit on the purchase price. You may, if desired, secure the cooperation of any other broker, or group of brokers, in procuring a sale of said property. In the event that you, or any other brokers cooperating with you, shall find a buyer ready and willing to enter into a deal for said price and terms, or such other terms and price as I may accept, or that during your employment you place me in contact with a buyer to or through whom at any time within 90 days after the termination of said employment I may sell or convey said property, I

hereby agree to pay you in cash for your services a commission equal in amount to__________% of the above stated selling price. I agree to convey said real estate to the purchaser by a good and sufficient deed, to transfer and deliver said personal property, if any, by good and sufficient bill of sale and to furnish title insurance insuring marketable title to said real estate and good right to convey. I hereby warrant that the information shown hereon below is true, that I am the owner of said property, that my title thereto is a good and marketable title, that the same is free of encumbrances except as shown hereafter under "Financial Details" and except taxes levied on said property for the current tax year which are to be pro rated between the seller and buyer. In case of an exchange, I have no objection to your representing and accepting compensation from the other party to the exchange as well as myself. I hereby authorize you and your customers to enter any part of said property at any reasonable time to show same. Also, I authorize you, at any time, to fill in and complete all or any part of the "Informative Data" below, except financial details. The following items are to be left upon the premises as part of the property purchased: All irrigation, plumbing, ventilating, cooling and heating fixtures and equipment (including stoker and oil tanks but excluding fire place fixtures and equipment), water heaters, attached electric light and bath room fixtures, light bulbs and fluorescent lamps, venetian blinds, wall-to-wall carpeting, awnings, window and door screens, storm doors and windows, attached floor coverings, attached television antenna, all plants, shrubs and trees and all fixtures except______________
The following personal property is also included as a part of the property to be offered for sale for said price: ______________

______________(or see signed inventory, if any, attached). This agreement expires at midnight on______________, 19_____, but I further allow you a reasonable time thereafter to close any deal on which earnest money is then deposited. In case of suit or action on this contract, I agree to pay such additional sum as the court, both trial and appellate, may adjudge reasonable as plaintiff's attorneys fees. It is further agreed that my signature affixed to the renewal clause below shall have the effect of renewing and extending your employment to a new date to be fixed by me on the same terms and all with the same effect as if the said new date had been fixed above as the expiration date of your employment.

*THIS LISTING IS AN EXCLUSIVE LISTING and you hereby are granted the absolute, sole and exclusive right to sell or exchange the said described property. In the event of any sale, by me or any other person, or of exchange or conveyance of said property, or any part thereof, during the term of your exclusive employment, or in case I withdraw the authority hereby given prior to said expiration date, I agree to pay you the said commission just the same as if a sale had actually been consummated by you.

I HEREBY CERTIFY THAT I HAVE READ AND RECEIVED A CARBON COPY OF THIS CONTRACT.

Accepted: ______________, 19_____ Owner ______________

Broker ______________ Owner ______________

Owner's Address ______________ City ______________ State ______________ Phone ______________

FOR VALUE RECEIVED, the above broker's employment hereby is renewed and extended to and including ______________, 19_____

Accepted: ______________, 19_____ Owner ______________

Broker ______________ Owner ______________

FINANCIAL DETAILS

Selling price (free of encumbrances)

$ ____ Terms: ____

Payments include: Prin. ____ Int. ____ Taxes ____ Ins. ____
(Check items to be included in payments)

Interest on deferred payments ____ %

Fire ins. $ ____ Ann'l prem. $ ____

Taxes last fiscal year $ ____

F.H.A. commitment $ ____

ENCUMBRANCES Payable

1st mtg. $ ____ Int. ____ % ____

2nd mtg. $ ____ Int. ____ % ____

Mtg. held by ____

Contr. bal. $ ____ Int. ____ % ____

Delinquent taxes $ ____

Municipal liens $ ____

	B	1F	2F	A	Comment
Living rm.					
Dining rm.					
Family rm.					
Kitchen					
Brkft. nk.					
Bedrms.					
Slpng. pch.					
Bath					
Den					
Party rm.					
Utility rm.					
Hallway					
Attic:	Fin.		Unfin.		

RESIDENCE PROPERTY INFORMATIVE DATA

Off ce
Listing No. ____

Address ____ Bet. ____ & ____ District ____

Lot ____ Block ____ Addition ____ Facing N ____ S ____ E ____ W ____

Dimension of lot ____ x ____ Dimension of house ____ x ____ No. rooms ____ No. stories ____ Attic ____

Owner has: Abstract ____ Title Insurance ____ Cert. of Title ____ Contract ____ Deed ____

Occupied by: Owner ____ Vacant ____ Renter ____ Renter's name ____ Tel. ____ Rent $ ____

Owner's name ____ Te. ____

May we use pass key ____ Key at ____

Possession may be had ____

Type of house ____

Type of construction ____ Type of roof ____

Condition: roof ____ paint exterior ____ paint interior ____

Utilities: Electricity ____ Gas ____ Phone ____ Water ____ Garbage service ____

For details as to chattels included in sale: See employment contract ____ See signed inventory ____

FEATURES & FINISH	HEATING & COOLING	OUTSIDE	DISTANCE TO
Sink ____	House ____	Garage: Sgle. Dbl. ____	Bus ____
Dishwasher ____	____	Carport ____	Name of line ____
Disposal ____	____	Lawn ____	Grade School ____
L. trays ____	____	Garden ____	High School ____
Shower ____	____	Shrubbery ____	Pub. Park ____
Hdwd. floor ____	____	Sprinkler ____	Grocery store ____
Fir floor ____	____	____	MISCELLANEOUS
W/W Carpeting ____	Water ____	____	Sewer ____
Vinyl floors ____	____	STREETS	Cesspool ____ Sep. tank ____
Plaster ceil. ____	BASEMENT	Paved ____	Outdoor frplce. ____
Beam ceil. ____	Full ____ Part ____	Macadam ____	Walks ____
Rms. papered ____	Fin. ____ Unfin. ____	Graded ____	Weatherstripping ____
Rms. tinted ____	Floor Drain ____	Ungraded ____	Insulation: Ceil. ____ Wall ____
Enam. finish ____	____	Sidewalk ____	Blt. in Rng. ____ Oven ____
Nat. finish ____	____	Alley ____	Wired elect. stove ____

Remarks: ____

Listed by ____

Signs permitted ____

Inspected by ____

Will consider exchange for ____

BROKER'S COPY

* TO MAKE NON-EXCLUSIVE—Strike complete paragraph following asterisk (*) in Employment Contract and have owner initial deletion.

A Real Estate Broker's Employment Contract Form

Exclusive Agency

The *exclusive agency* gives a broker the right to sell a property exclusive of all other brokers. If broker *A* receives an exclusive agency, he is entitled to a commission from the owner even though the property is sold by broker *B*. However, in the exclusive agency, the owner may sell the property himself and not be liable for payment of a commission to the broker.

The Exclusive Right to Sell

The *exclusive right to sell* differs from the exclusive agency only in one respect; the broker is entitled to receive his commission no matter who sells the property. When the exclusive right is given, although the owner sells the property, the broker is entitled to a commission from the owner.

Although some brokers favor open listings and exclusive agency listings, most brokers favor the exclusive right. The problems facing the broker are similar in many respects to the problems facing the marketeer of any other commodity. To market a commodity properly, the marketeer must have confidence in his ability to deliver his product to the purchaser. A real estate broker selling under an open listing cannot be sure of his ability to deliver, for at anytime another broker may tender the seller a bona fide offer ahead of him. It is difficult for a broker to represent his client properly when his "stock in trade" is of a nebulous character.

Some of the advantages of the exclusive listing to the owner are that the broker holding exclusive sales rights can afford to spend time and money promoting a sale because he is assured of compensation if he succeeds. By giving the listing his close attention, he is likely to effect a sale at a better price; confidence placed in one broker helps to insure action in the best interests of the owner; cooperation with other brokers is still possible; and an exclusive broker saves the owner time which the owner would otherwise spend in talking with many agents and their prospects. The broker cannot in good conscience, nor does he, devote the same amount of time and energy to a client who has listed a property with him as an open listing as he can to other clients with whom he has an exclusive listing. The broker seeking exclusive listings should point out to his

VAN SCHAACK & COMPANY

REAL ESTATE SALES
MANAGEMENT
LOANS
INSURANCE

EXCLUSIVE RIGHT TO SELL LISTING CONTRACT
(RESIDENTIAL)

________________________________, Colorado ___________________________________, 19 __________

In consideration of the services of the hereinafter named real estate broker, I hereby list with said broker, from __________________________ 19 _____, to __________________________ 19 _____, inclusive, the property described below and I hereby grant said broker the exlusive and irrevocable right to sell the same within said time at the price and on the terms herein stated, or at such other price and terms which may be accepted by me, and to accept deposits thereon and retain same until the closing of, or defeat of, the transaction. I further authorize said broker to list the property with any multiple listing service in which he is a participant, at the broker's expense, and to accept the assistance and cooperation of other brokers. I hereby agree to pay said broker _____ % of the selling price for his services (1) in case of any sale or exchange of same within said listing period by the undersigned owner, the said broker, or by any person, or (2) upon the said broker finding a purchaser who is ready, willing and able to complete the purchase as proposed by the owner, or (3) in case of any such sale or exchange of the said property within the 120 days subsequent to the expiration of this agreement to any party with whom the said broker negotiated and whose name was disclosed to the owner by the broker during the listing period.

Address: ____
(Street) (City)

Legal Description:

Price$ __________________________________Terms:

Subject to general taxes and ____
for year of closing, building and zoning regulations, easements and restrictive covenants of record, and the following encumbrances:

I authorize the holder of any note secured by the above listed encumbrances to disclose to the broker the amount owing on said encumbrances and the terms thereof.

Price to include any of the following items currently on the premises: Lighting, heating and plumbing fixtures; all outdoor plants, window and porch shades, venetian blinds, storm windows, storm doors, screens, curtain rods, drapery rods, central air conditioning, ventilating fixtures, attached TV antennas, attached mirrors, linoleum, awnings, water softener (if owned by seller), fireplace screen and grate, built-in kitchen appliances, wall to wall carpeting and ____
____
all in their present condition, free and clear of all taxes, liens and encumbrances; provided, however, that the following fixtures of a permanent nature are to be excluded from the sale: ____
____

In case of sale or exchange I agree to furnish, at my option and expense, an abstract of title to said property, certified to date, or a current commitment for title insurance policy in an amount equal to the purchase price, showing merchantable title in the owner. If the title insurance commitment is selected, I agree to deliver the title insurance policy to purchaser after closing and pay the premium thereon.

In case of sale or exchange I agree to execute and deliver a good and sufficient ____________________ warranty deed to the purchaser conveying said property free and clear of all taxes, liens, encumbrances and easements, except as listed above.

General taxes for year of closing, prepaid rents, water rents, sewer rents, FHA mortgage insurance premiums and interest on encumbrances, if any, and ____
____,
shall be apportioned to date of delivery of deed.

Taxes for all special improvements now installed, whether assessed or not, shall be paid by owners.

Possession of premises shall be delivered to purchaser on ______________________________ 19 _____, subject to the following leases and tenancies:

The owner agrees to refer to the broker all inquires from other brokers, salesmen and prospective purchasers received during the term of this listing.

The owner agrees that the broker shall not be responsible for maintenance of the premises nor shall the broker be liable for damages of any kind occurring to the premises, unless such damage shall be caused by the negligence of the broker.

The undersigned owner and broker, by their respective signatures hereon, agree that they will not discriminate against any prospective purchaser because of the race, creed, color or national origin of such person.

Additional Provisions:

This agreement executed in multiple copies and my signature hereon acknowledges that I have received a signed copy.

Accepted **VAN SCHAACK & COMPANY** ____________________________________
Broker Owner

By: ____ ____________________________________
Owner

Phone ______________________________________ Address ______________________________

Phone ____________________

The printed portions of this form approved by the Colorado Real Estate Commission (LC 10-7-71)
#0199-6558

An Exclusive Right Listing Form

clients these facts. There are strong arguments in favor of the exclusive listing, and the client should be made aware of them so that he may appreciate the values of exclusive listing.

The main disadvantage of the exclusive listing to the owner is that no matter how capable the broker may be and no matter how hard he may work, his circle of contacts could not possibly include all of the buyers in a city.

Multiple Listings

A *multiple listing* is defined as an arrangement among real estate board or exchange members whereby each broker brings his listings to the attention of other members so that if a sale results, the commission is divided between the broker bringing the listing and the broker making the sale, with a small percentage going to the real estate board.

In practice, a broker upon entering business joins the multiple listing bureau. For the privilege of joining the bureau, he pays a fee. These fees vary with the size of the city and the length of time that the bureau has been in existence. When the broker obtains an exclusive listing, he is bound by the rules of the bureau to transmit the listing to the bureau after a stated number of days. Within the stated period the broker is privileged to attempt to sell the property on his own account. If he fails to sell the property within this period, he transmits the information to the bureau who sends out the listing to all of the members. In this way the seller has both the advantages of the exclusive listing and the open listing in that all the members of the bureau now attempt to sell the property. When the property is sold, the commission is divided between the listing broker and the selling broker. If the listing broker himself makes the sale, he is entitled to the entire commission on the transaction, less whatever percentage may be due the listing bureau.

Often, the multiple-listing bureau will have an appraisal committee. These men appraise the properties coming into the bureau mainly to determine if the listing is excessively high. If they find that it is, they attempt to persuade the owner to relist the property at a reasonable figure. Not all buyers are aware that they are using a multiple-listing service.

On November 15, 1971, the multiple-listing policy of NAR (then NAREB) was adopted by its board of directors.

The MLS policy represents NAR's firm determination that Realtor multiple-listing services shall be organized and operated to serve the basic purpose for which they are established: "to make possible the orderly dissemination and correlation of listing information to its members so that Realtors may better serve the buying and selling public." [5]

The 14-point policy is as follows:

1. A multiple-listing service shall not: "Fix, control, recommend, suggest, or maintain commission rates or fees for services to be rendered by members."
2. A multiple-listing service shall not: "Fix, control, recommend, suggest, or maintain any percentage division of commission or fees between cooperating members or non-members."
3. A multiple-listing service shall not: "Require financial support of multiple-listing service operations by any formula based on commission or sales prices."
4. A multiple-listing service shall not: "Require or use any form which establishes or implies the existence of any contractual relationship between the multiple-listing service and the client (buyer or seller)."
5. A multiple-listing service shall not: "Make any rule relating to the posting or use of signs."
6. A multiple-listing service shall not: "Make any rule prohibiting or discouraging cooperation with non-members."
7. A multiple-listing service shall not: "Limit or interfere with the terms of the relationship between a member and his salesmen (Interpretations 16 and 17)."
8. A multiple-listing service shall not: "Prohibit or discourage any members from political participation or activity."
9. A multiple-listing service shall not: "Make any rule granting blanket consent to a selling member to negotiate directly with the seller (owner) (Interpretation 10)."
10. A multiple-listing service shall not: "Make any rule regulating the advertising or promotion of any listings."
11. A multiple-listing service shall not: "Prohibit or discourage a member from accepting a listing from a seller (owner) preferring to give 'office exclusive.' "

[5] *Realtor's Headlines*, Quarterly Magazine Section (October 2, 1972).

M. S. L.

UNIFORM SALES AGENCY CONTRACT   MLS Listing No.

TO______________________________ DATE__________________, 19____

Listing Realtor

In consideration of your agreement to use your efforts to find a purchaser, and to list with the members of the MULTIPLE LISTING SERVICE COMMITTEE of the Gainesville Board of Realtors, property described herein, I hereby grant to you and the other members of MULTIPLE LISTING SERVICE COMMITTEE, the exclusive right for the term of SIX________months from the date hereof to sell the property described as:

Legal Description

House Number   Street   City of   County

for the sum of $__________ cash or $__________ payable $__________ down and $__________ per month, including interest at ______% or upon any other price, terms or exchange to which I (we) may hereafter consent.

If, during said period, the property is sold by you or me or anyone else (including non-member brokers and salesmen), or if you or any member of the MULTIPLE LISTING SERVICE COMMITTEE produce a purchaser ready, willing and able to purchase the property; or if it shall be sold within three months after the expiration to any persons with whom you or any member of Multiple Listing Service Committee has had negotiations for sale thereof I (we) agree to pay you, out of the first monies received from any sale, a commission of ______% upon the purchase price procured for said property. The commission will be in accord with the suggested rates of the Gainesville Board of Realtors.

I represent the title to said property to be a good merchantable title and I will execute and deliver a deed, or land contract, or land contract assignment as shall be required with full covenants or warranty, free of all encumbrances except__________

and furnish abstract and tax history certified down to date, or a Title Insurance policy in a recognized responsible Title Insurance Company doing business through an established agency in this County.

You are authorized to place a "For Sale" sign on said property and to remove all other "For Sale" signs and to have access to the building or buildings on the property for the purpose of showing the same at reasonable hours. I acknowledge I have received a copy of this listing. I agree to refer to the listing Realtor all inquiries received concerning said property during the period of this listing.

Accepted by ________________ Realtor   ________________ L. S

________________ Salesman   ________________ L. S

A Typical Multiple Listing Form

12. A multiple-listing service shall not: "Adopt any rule denying a listing member from controlling the posting of 'sold signs.' "

13. A multiple-listing service shall not: "Refuse any exclusive listing submitted by a member on the basis of the quality or price of the listing."

14. A multiple-listing service shall not: "Adopt rules authorizing the modification or change of any listing without the express, written permission of the listing member."

Net Listings

The *net listing* results when an owner lists a property with a broker and says in effect: "I want $10,000 for the property. Anything over that amount is your commission." When this is done, the listing may be made with the broker as an open listing, an exclusive right, or the exclusive agency type of listing.

This type of listing is considered by most brokers to be bad business. Some states prohibit the net listing under its license law, and the broker runs the risk of losing his license. Rule 6 of the Michigan Corporation and Securities Commission, for example, states:

> A broker shall not become a party to any net listing agreement for an owner or seller as a means of securing a real estate commission.

Even in those states where net listings are not specifically prohibited, the astute broker will avoid securing listings in this manner. They are a constant source of trouble for the broker and make for extremely poor public relations. No matter what the broker receives as a commission under this type of listing, he is bound to be criticized by either the buyer or the seller, and more often by both.

Relationship Between Listings and Sales

Many practitioners are firmly convinced that sales are made or broken at the time listings are made. One prominent practitioner states: "Closing the sale begins with the listing of a property." [6] Sutton strongly suggests that the individual listing of the property

[6] Eugene C. Sutton, "You Lose or Make Sales When Listing," *Realtor's Headlines*, Quarterly Magazine Section, Vol. 29, No. 28 (July 9, 1962), p. 1.

should analyze the seller's problems and motivations. In addition, he suggests that the seller should be informed of the fair market value, regardless of what the seller-owner thinks, because frequently the asking price is based on rumors and incorrect information.

COMMISSIONS

Employment

In order for a real estate broker to establish a claim for a commission, he must show that he was actually employed by the principal. In states where the employment contract must be in writing, the broker must produce the written contract authorizing him to act as the agent for the seller. In those states where the contract is not in writing, a suit for a commission becomes a question of proof to be submitted to the jury. The broker testifies at the trial that he was employed by the seller. If there are no witnesses to corroborate his statement, the broker is apt to discover that he has lost the action.

Be Licensed

A second requisite in establishing a claim for a commission is that the broker must be licensed. In those states that require a license, if the broker is suing for a commission, he must allege in his complaint:

> . . . that at all times hereinafter mentioned, the plaintiff was, and still is, legally engaged as a real estate broker duly licensed to carry on business under the laws of the state of. . . .

At the trial he must prove such allegation. The broker proves that he is licensed by submitting his license in evidence. Generally, in practice, the pocket card is admitted in evidence at the trial for this purpose.

Not only must the broker be licensed, but he must be licensed at the time that he has rendered his service. The courts have held that the broker renders his service when he brings together two people "ready, willing, and able," or when there is a meeting of the minds between the seller and the purchaser.

Purchaser Ready, Willing, and Able

The broker must find a purchaser who is ready, willing, and able to purchase the property. *Ready and willing* means that the broker has produced a purchaser who is prepared to accept the terms offered by the owner and who has indicated his willingness to enter into a written contract with the owner. The best evidence of the readiness and willingness of the purchaser to purchase is a signed binder or receipt and agreement to purchase. However, the readiness and willingness of the purchaser can also be established when there is an oral agreement between the purchaser and the seller.

In the final analysis, when a binder or a receipt and agreement to purchase have been entered into by the parties, they are considered contracts for the sale of real property. A binder signed by a prospect and drawn according to the terms of the listing contract establishes a meeting of the minds between the buyer and the seller.

Even though there is no written contract between the buyer and the seller, if the buyer has indicated that he is ready, willing, and able, and the seller refuses to go through with the sale, the broker is entitled to his commission.

In addition to producing a purchaser who is ready and willing, the broker must produce a purchaser who is *able*, meaning that the purchaser must be financially able to go through with the transaction, or the seller is not liable to the broker for a commission. In the event of legal action, the broker has the burden of establishing proof of the financial ability of the prospect. He must show that the purchaser actually possesses, or has the ability to raise, the amount of cash necessary for the signing of the contract and the closing of title. When part of the purchase price is to be in the form of a purchase money mortgage, the broker need not show that the purchaser has sufficient cash or other assets to pay off the mortgage in order to succeed in his suit.

Deferring or Waiving Commissions

A commission becomes due to the broker when he produces to his principal a party ready, willing, and able to purchase on the terms of sale authorized or accepted by his principal. However, in many brokerage offices, it is considered good policy to defer or to waive the commission if the title to the property for some reason does not pass.

The contract for the sale of the property usually contains a clause stated substantially as given below.

> The parties agree that (the broker's name) brought about this sale and the seller agrees to pay the commission at the rates established or adopted by the Board of Real Estate Brokers in the locality where the property is situated.

If the broker wishes to waive or defer his commission, there is inserted in the contract an additional statement:

> It is understood and agreed by the undersigned that the seller shall incur no obligation or liability for said brokerage commissions, except only when, as, if, and in the event title actually closes, at which time the said brokerage commissions shall become due and payable.

The contract is then initialed in the margin by the parties and by the salesman. It is important that the salesman initial the clause in order that the broker be relieved of liability to the salesman in the event the title is not conveyed.

For example, a person makes application for a broker's license and takes the examination on June 27. On June 30 he produces a purchaser for a seller and the purchaser and seller enter into a contract for the sale of real property, title to close one month later, July 30. On July 15 the person receives his broker's license and proceeds to the closing on July 30. There arises a question here as to whether or not the broker is entitled to his commission on July 30. The broker is not entitled to the commission because he was not duly licensed at the time he rendered his service, that is, when he brought together two people who were "ready, willing, and able."

Procuring Cause

The broker must be the efficient or procuring cause of the sale in order to enable him to become entitled to a commission. For example, a broker has an open listing and brings a prospect to the property. The owner is not at home and the prospect states that he does not wish to buy, but he later returns to the owner and concludes a private deal with the owner. The broker is entitled to the commission because the law would hold that he was the procuring or efficient cause of the sale.

It has been held that the broker is the procuring cause of the sale if his action indirectly procures a buyer. For example, a broker introduces a prospect to a seller. The prospect does not purchase the property, but his cousin does. In a case of this sort, the broker is entitled to his commission.

One device commonly employed by brokers to avoid possible trouble when owners are not at home and property is shown to prospects is to use a postal card. The card is printed as follows:

May 10, 19--

Dear Mr. Owner

This is to inform you that we have this date shown your property at 2519 Eastbourne Ave. to John J. Prospect

We regret that you were not at home at the time, and if anything further develops, we shall let you know immediately.

Sincerely yours

John Doe

John Doe, Broker

Postal Card Notice of Showing of Home

At the very least, this device may prove a moral deterrent on the part of the seller from making a private sale to the prospect. It also indicates to the seller that the broker is working on his property. Further, this card can be used as a legal weapon if a copy is made and a postal receipt is requested from the post office at the time of mailing. If the owner makes a private sale despite the card and the broker sues for a commission, the postal receipt will indicate that the card was mailed. If the seller is served with a notice to produce the card at the trial and fails to do so, the copy may be offered as evidence without violating the "best evidence" rule.

Sale on Terms of Employer

The broker must bring about the sale on the terms that have been authorized by the client. If a broker brings an offer to his client for an amount less than that included in the listing contract, the broker is not entitled to a commission. However, if the seller accepts the offer, the sale is on the terms of the employer, and the broker is entitled to his commission.

If the owner lists a parcel of property with a broker at $10,000 and the broker finds a purchaser ready, willing, and able, the broker is entitled to a commission even if the seller refuses to sell at that price because he has found a purchaser on the terms authorized by the seller. The salesman may sue the broker for his share of the commission arguing that the broker can waive if he wishes, but that this does not relieve the broker of the commission due the salesman. The courts agree and the broker is forced to pay the salesman his half of the amount due, although the broker has actually received no fee himself.

Co-Brokerage

Co-brokerage occurs when the broker, either by consent of the owner in writing or by implication, hires another broker to assist him in the sale of property. Generally, the listing broker agrees to pay the co-broker half of his commission in those cases in which the co-broker brings about the sale. More often than not, large investment properties are sold in this manner.

Some Factors Buyers Appreciate

As in any other service, clients dealing with brokers appreciate good service on the part of brokers. Foremost would be honesty, patience, and courtesy. Little things done by brokers are also appreciated, such as assistance in getting utilities or refrigerators installed as well as aid in obtaining financing.

QUESTIONS FOR REVIEW

1. Discuss the expression "ready, willing, and able."
2. What is meant by co-brokerage, and what must a listing broker do to be certain he is not violating the law of agency when he enters into a co-brokerage agreement?
3. Explain the open listing, the exclusive agency, the exclusive right, and the net listing.
4. When may a broker act for both the buyer and the seller?
5. Who may be an agent?
6. What are the advantages to multiple listings?
7. List and explain four requisites to the broker's earning of a commission.
8. Discuss the advantages to a seller in giving the broker the "exclusive" right to sell.

PROBLEMS

1. Seller employed Broker to sell four lots on an open listing contract. Broker sold three of the lots to Frank Smith who informed his cousin that the fourth lot was still for sale. The cousin approached Mr. Seller directly and purchased the fourth lot. Mr. Broker then claimed Mr. Seller owed him a commission on all four lots. Discuss.
2. In states where employment contracts are required to be in writing, many brokers feel that this is an unjust discrimination against brokers. Prepare a statement for a real estate board in which you argue that this type of law should be required in all states.
3. Mr. Jones hired Mr. Broker to sell a parcel of land. Shortly thereafter, Mr. Smith hired Mr. Broker to buy land of that nature. Mr. Broker then promptly brought Mr. Smith to Mr. Jones, and they entered into a contract which finally consummated in a sale. Mr. Broker then charged Mr. Jones a full commission. He also charged Mr. Smith a full commission. Which one, if any, is liable to Mr. Broker for the commission?
4. Mr. Broker without any request from Mr. Sullivan, an owner of land, brought Sullivan an offer of $9,000. Sullivan told him the land was worth $10,000 whereupon Mr. Broker brought him in an offer from another person for $10,000, but Sullivan refused to sell. Mr. Broker sues Sullivan for a commission. Is he entitled to a commission? Why or why not?

SUGGESTED READINGS

Brown, Robert K. *Essentials of Real Estate*. Englewood Cliffs, New Jersey: Prentice-Hall, Inc., 1970. Chapters 4 and 12.

Case, Frederick E. *Real Estate Brokerage*. Englewood Cliffs, New Jersey: Prentice-Hall, Inc., 1965. Chapters 3 and 4.

Ring, Alfred A. *Real Estate Principles and Practices,* 7th ed. Englewood Cliffs, New Jersey: Prentice-Hall, Inc., 1972. Chapter 18.

Weimer, Arthur M., Homer Hoyt, and George F. Bloom. *Principles of Real Estate,* 6th ed. New York: The Ronald Press Company, 1972. Chapter 16.

Chapter 18

Operating a Real Estate Office

Although a real estate firm performs a variety of functions, much of the operation is concerned with the marketing function, which includes such things as sales of property and negotiation of leases. At the moment there are about 440,000 licensed brokers in the nation and about 615,000 real estate salesmen. Most of the brokers own their own offices and many of the salesmen have ambitions in that direction. Like any other form of free enterprise, this involves an investment of capital and labor—to be successful, much labor. In addition, for the protection of the public as well as the broker himself, all of the fifty states and the District of Columbia have licensing laws. California leads the list with the largest number of brokers. Massachusetts is second, and New York is third. Alaska, the largest state in the Union, has the fewest licensees per square mile.

LICENSING OF REAL ESTATE BROKERS AND SALESMEN

Only a few of the states permit a novice to take the broker's license examination without prior experience. Most of the states require that an individual must be employed as a salesman until he has acquired sufficient experience to become a broker. The time period ranges from six months to two years. In New York, for example, a person must have two years of practical experience, must have served as a salesman for a minimum of two years, or after September 1, 1971, must have served one year and successfully completed at least a 45-hour real estate course in an approved school. The state of Nevada requires 96 hours of real estate schooling prior to taking an examination.

The revised Ohio licensing law, which became effective on January 2, 1972, permits a person to take his exam and be issued a license. However, within two years from the date such license is issued, the licensee shall successfully complete, at an institution of higher learning, 30 hours of classroom instruction in both real estate practice and real estate law. If the instruction is not successfully completed within two years, his license shall lapse. In the future more and more states will move in that direction.

Ordinarily, the examination for the real estate salesman is not as difficult as the examination for the real estate broker. The examination for the salesman usually requires one to three hours for completion, but for the broker it often takes a full day.

Typical License Laws

Although the license laws of the various states differ, there are a number of things in common to all licensing laws. Basically, the purpose of all licensing laws is to protect the public from incompetent and unscrupulous brokers. Fundamentally, these laws are generally divided into several parts: the statutes, as enacted by the several state legislatures; the administrative orders, as promulgated by the body governing the licensing laws; and very often the Code of Ethics of the NATIONAL ASSOCIATION OF REALTORS, which is incorporated into these laws by administrative order.

The statutes of all states define the broker in more or less the same manner:

> (A broker is) a person who, for compensation or promise thereof, sells or offers for sale, lists or offers to list, buys or offers to buy, negotiates or offers to negotiate, either directly or indirectly, the purchase, sale, exchange, lease, or the rental of real estate or any interest therein.

Some states include the sale of a business opportunity under the jurisdiction of the real estate broker. In these states the law defines a business opportunity as a "business, an established business, a business opportunity, or goodwill of an established or existing business, or any interest therein."

Other states divorcc the sale of business opportunities from the real estate broker so that the seller of a business opportunity requires no license. In such states, for example, New York, when a seller of a business opportunity sells the real property along with the business opportunity, he does not need a real estate license if he can show that the real estate was a part of the going concern.

The statutes of the various states all provide exceptions to the requirement of being licensed; for example, the Washington state law provides:

> This chapter shall not apply to (1) any person who purchases property and/or a business opportunity for his own account, or who, as the owner of property, and/or a business opportunity, in any wise disposes of the same; nor (2) any duly authorized attorney in fact, or an attorney at law in the performance of his duties; nor (3) any receiver, trustee in bankruptcy, executor, administrator, guardian, or any person acting under the order of any court, or selling under a deed of trust; nor (4) any escrow agent.

The New York brokerage law specifically exempts attorneys at law who may, by virtue of this exemption, act as real estate brokers and receive commissions without being licensed. However, if they hire real estatc salesmen, they must become licensed.

The statutes usually provide further for examinations for brokers and salesmen, and for penalties in the event there has been a violation of the law. Also, there is provided in all of these laws procedures for hearings on possible suspensions or revocations of licenses by the administrative bodies who enforce the laws, together with the right of appeal from a decision of the administrative body.

In addition to criminal penalties, some states provide for civil damages by a party aggrieved. For example, the New York law provides for damages in the amount of four times the commission when a broker is charged and subsequently convicted of defrauding a client.

The second part of the license laws typically consists of rules and regulations promulgated by the Real Estate Brokers Board, the Division of Licenses, or whatever the administrative body administering the license laws may be called. Until these rules and regulations have been declared void by a court of competent jurisdiction, they have the full effect of the law in the same manner as if they had been made a part of the statute by the state legislature.

These rules are more or less similar among the several states. They provide, among other things, that the real estate broker must not insert "blind" advertisements in any advertising media. This means that the broker must give his name as a broker or make it clear that it is an advertisement submitted by a broker, rather than make it appear as if the advertisement were placed by an individual.

They also generally provide that there shall be no automatic renewal clauses incorporated in listings. They provide that monies received by the broker on behalf of a client shall not be commingled with his own monies and that the broker shall not purchase property listed with him on his own behalf either directly or indirectly without first making his true position known to the client. Some rules provide that a broker shall not purchase property listed with him on his own behalf either directly or indirectly without first making his true position known to the client. Some rules provide that a broker shall not place a sign on a parcel of property without first obtaining the consent of the owner.

Often the governing body will incorporate into the state's licensing law the Code of Ethics of the NATIONAL ASSOCIATION OF REALTORS, which is found in Appendix A. The Code of Ethics contains a preamble and is divided into three parts: Part I, dealing with relations to the public; Part II, with relations to clients; and Part III, with relations to fellow-REALTORS. Every person interested in real estate and real estate transactions not only should be familiar with the Code, but should adhere completely to its tenets.

Advantages to Licensing

Prior to the advent of real estate licensing laws, many sharp practices flourished. The "free lot" racket was practiced with many variations in form. For example, a person might purchase some relatively useless land and send deeds to several lots to an individual on one pretext or another. Thereafter, the real estate racketeer might send that individual a letter on fancy stationery informing him that a corporation desires to build a factory on the land owned by that individual and inquiring as to the number of lots held by that person. When the recipient of the free lots stated that he owned Lots #1 and #2, the racketeer would write back and state that they were interested in purchasing Lots #1 and #2, only if they could get Lots #3 and #4 along with it. The idea was to get the owner of Lots #1 and #2 to purchase Lots #3 and #4 which would be sold to him at an excessively high price. When this was done, the corporation writing the letter was no longer in existence.

It was to protect the public against people like this and other sharp practitioners that the licensing laws were originally enacted.[1] License laws have also operated to the advantage of the legitimate broker because they have protected him from the unfair competition of the opportunist broker.

Another advantage of the license regulations is that they have eliminated the curbstone broker. All state laws require that each broker maintain a definite place of business where his license must be displayed. In many states, a broker may maintain an office in his home. In states where this is permitted, it is generally required that the broker display his license in that part of his home used for an office, and that he display the proper real estate office sign.

It is clearly evident that with the passage of time the license laws have brought about great improvements in the real estate business which have benefited both the public and the real estate profession. The mere presence of the laws on the statute books has served in a large measure to discourage dishonest dealings.

Typical Real Estate Examinations

Because the laws are designed in part to protect the public from incompetent brokers, most states require proof of competency by examination. Typically, the real estate broker's examinations are divided into four parts:

1. True-false questions on real estate laws and practices.
2. Questions testing mathematical knowledge in regard to figuring commissions, interest, and closing statements (in some states).

---

[1] To protect the public from "free lot" schemes and other forms of fraud, New Mexico in 1963 enacted a law providing for fines up to $100,000, five years in prison, or both.

3. Fill-in or multiple-choice questions testing the applicant's knowledge of real estate law and practices and the licensing laws of his own state.

4. Questions designed to test the applicant's knowledge of property descriptions.

Generally, 75 percent is the passing grade on these examinations, and if the applicant fails the examination, he must reapply and take the examination again. Some states have prepared real estate primers or guides containing some of the information that will be asked of the applicant on an examination. In other states, it is necessary for the applicant to study general texts on real estate to acquire the necessary information to pass the examination.

In many states the applicant for a broker's license must be recommended by several responsible property owners or citizens who certify that the applicant has a good reputation for honesty and fair dealing. The numbers and qualifications of the sponsors vary in different states. In those states where a broker must be licensed and can be licensed without passing a formal examination, this is one of the most important requisites to the granting of the license.

In most states an applicant for a salesman's license must be sponsored. This sponsor is generally a broker or brokerage firm who has agreed to hire the salesman in the event he successfully obtains a license. In other states, a salesman after having been employed is granted a temporary license enabling him to be gainfully employed until the time of the examination.

Brokers' Bonds

In states where the law makes no specific provision for a money penalty or no provision for returning money fraudulently obtained, the licensee is required to post a bond. The amount of the bond varies generally from $1,000 to $2,500. This protects the customer because revocation of the broker's license will not compensate a defrauded individual, and in most instances brokers who engage in sharp practices have no tangible assets. The bond is especially desirable because it not only protects the broker's client, but it also tends to insure that the broker will faithfully perform his duties.

In 1963 the state of Arizona took what may prove to be a leading step toward further protection of the public. A bill initiated and backed by the Arizona Association of Realtors was passed by the Arizona legislature. In essence the bill provides for a real estate recovery fund from which damages could be paid to any person "aggrieved" by an act of a real estate broker or salesman and unable to collect damages from them. The fund is financed through the collection of additional fees from the licensees of that state. Since that time California, Colorado, and Idaho have adopted similar statutes. At this writing a number of other states have bills of this nature pending before their legislatures.

Nonresident Brokers

Many states have entered into reciprocal agreements with neighboring states providing that if a broker is licensed in one state, he may be licensed in the neighboring state and practice there without actually residing there. This is done to require the nonresident broker to meet the same qualifications as the resident broker.

When state laws regulate nonresident brokers, they require an irrevocable consent to the service of process which must be filed, generally with the Secretary of State. An *irrevocable consent* is a written statement that (1) actions and suits at law may be started against such nonresident broker in any county of the state wherein a cause of action may arise, (2) service of summons in any such action may be served upon a designated officer of the state real estate commission (or secretary of state) for and on behalf of such nonresident broker, and (3) such service shall be held sufficient to give the courts jurisdiction over such nonresident broker and the broker's salesmen.

CHOOSING THE FORM OF OWNERSHIP

When one has the requisite experience as a salesman and has taken and passed the broker's examination, the next step is to open an office. This office can be established as an individual proprietorship, a partnership, or a corporation.

The Individual Proprietorship

The great majority of American business enterprises are operated in the form of the individual proprietorship. This form of business organization is usual where the scope of the enterprise is small enough for one person to manage and when the proprietor owns all the required capital and needs no outside financing.

The individual proprietorship has certain obvious advantages including those of ease of organization, absolute control, flexibility, ownership of all profits, and the intangible reward (sometimes called *psychic income*) that comes to the owner in the feeling of independence. On the other hand, the operations of the owner are limited to the extent of his capital and experience, and the success of the enterprise depends upon his continuous personal attention to the business.

The individual may operate under his own name, or he may operate under an assumed or trade name. In the latter case the proprietor gives his business a name and carries out his operations under the assumed name.

When a person operates under an assumed name, he must register the assumed name with a recording office, generally the office of the county clerk. This is done by filing a certificate of doing business under an assumed name. The certificate contains both the assumed name and the true name of the person filing. The proprietor will be addressed in legal papers as "Frank Smith doing business under the name and style of Lake City Realty" or "Frank Smith d/b/a Lake City Realty."

The purpose of requiring persons doing business under an assumed name to file the certificate of doing business under an assumed name is to prevent the individual from defrauding creditors. Whether an individual operates under an assumed name or under his own name, he does not reduce his liability to creditors. All of the individual's property, both the business property and all other property owned by the proprietor, is subject to the payment of the business debts.

In many states the law prevents the individual who files the certificate of doing business under an assumed name from using "and Company" or "& Co." unless there actually are other owners in addition to the one or more named in the title. The name or names included in the "Company" must be identified in the certificate of doing business under the assumed name. Similarly, words in the title which imply, contrary to the fact, that the business is incorporated or authorized to do a banking or trust company business are prohibited.

In the event that a real estate broker does business under an assumed name, he must take his license out under the assumed name; and in the event that he changes his business name, he must notify the board enforcing the licensing laws.

The Partnership

A *partnership* or *copartnership*, as it is sometimes called, is a legal relationship created by the voluntary association of two or more persons to carry on a business for profit as co-owners. The rights and duties of the partners toward each other and toward the public are regulated by a partnership agreement and by the state partnership laws. The agreement between the individuals comprising the partnership may be either oral or written. In most instances the agreement is written, and in most states the law requires that a certificate of doing business under a partnership name must be filed in the same manner as a certificate of doing business under an assumed name.

The partnership agreement is a contract, and any business that a person may lawfully operate may be conducted in the partnership form. The contract or articles of agreement between the partners set forth the capital and service that each of the partners is to contribute, the share of the profits and losses to which each may be entitled, and other details concerning their relationship and the operation of the business.

Ordinary partnerships are classified as *general* and *special* partnerships. A *general partnership* is created for the conduct of a particular kind of business or several kinds of business. For example, if two or more persons enter into a partnership for the purpose of carrying on a real estate business, the partnership is general.

A *special partnership* is formed for a single transaction. If two or more persons enter into a partnership for the purchase and resale of a certain type of building, there is a special partnership. There are other types of partnerships, but they need not be discussed here.

Advantages of the Partnership. The chief advantage of the partnership is that it permits the pooling of the capital, skill, experience, and business contacts of the co-owners, thereby increasing the scope of the business and enhancing its prestige.

Freedom from federal taxation is regarded as another of the advantages of the partnership form of business enterprise. Although the individuals are taxed on their share of the income, the partnership entity as such is not taxed.

Disadvantages of the Partnership. Under the partnership laws of most states, there is a presumption that each partner has an equal voice in the operation of the partnership, that each of the partners is the agent of the other, and that, unless the partnership agreement provides otherwise, each partner is bound by the other when acting within the scope of the business. The laws of some states afford protection by providing that persons outside the firm who make certain types of contracts with a partner, such as a contract to sell all of the partnership assets of the firm, must ascertain whether he has been authorized to so act by the other partners.

A further disadvantage is that the personal assets of each of the partners may be looked to by the creditors. In short, there is an unlimited liability feature that is a major disadvantage.

The licensing laws of the majority of the states provide that when a partnership exists between two or more persons for the purpose of conducting a real estate business, all of the partners must be licensed as brokers. Thus, one partner cannot be a broker and the other partner a salesman.

Corporation

The third form of business enterprise is the corporation. Some understanding of the nature of the corporation is necessary when considering this form for the brokerage business. First, a *corporation* is an instrument for the ownership and the management of a business enterprise. Second, it is a device whereby a person may invest a sum of money in the enterprise without becoming personally liable for its indebtedness beyond the amount invested. A characteristic peculiar to the corporation is its status as an artificial being or entity separate and apart from its stockholders, officers, or directors—to such a degree that it may sue or be sued by any one of them on a matter affecting the relationship between them.

A corporation may come into existence when a certificate of incorporation or charter, signed by three or more incorporators or prospective stockholders, is accepted for filing by the proper state authority who is generally the Secretary of State. Thereafter, it is authorized to hold property and conduct the type of business specified in its charter. In exchange for such property or money capital it issues shares of stock to the stockholders. Such shares, representing the stockholder's ownership interest in the corporation, are readily transferable.

As a practical matter, two persons may become the sole owners of a corporation. For example, if *A* and *B* desire to form a corporation for the purpose of engaging in the real estate business, they must ask *C* to be one of the incorporators in order to comply with the law that three persons are necessary to form the corporation.[2] *C* along with *A* and *B* signs the certificate of incorporation and then at the first meeting of the stockholders, *C* assigns his interest in the enterprise to *A* and *B* and thus is no longer an interested party.

Advantages of the Corporation. A major advantage of the corporate form of business enterprise is the limited liability feature which is often the first thought of anyone or any small group of people considering a business enterprise. A second advantage is the ease with which capital can be obtained for the initial organization or for its expansion. A corporation often is given a perpetual life which is a further advantage of the corporate form of doing business.

The deciding factor in incorporating small business units seems to be, first, a feeling among the parties that they understand the law under which a corporation operates, since it seems to be more clear-cut than the law governing partnerships, and second, the fact that one person often contributes the lion's share of the capital and feels that he can retain control by holding a majority stock interest.

Disadvantages of the Corporation. One disadvantage of the corporate form of business enterprise is the cost. This includes the cost of incorporating and often stock transfer taxes.

Another drawback the small corporation may encounter is the difficulty of obtaining credit, since the potential creditor knows that he cannot proceed against the stockholders to satisfy a debt that is beyond the ability of the corporation to pay from its own assets. He knows that he can sue an individual or partnership and get a

[2] Most states require that three or more persons are necessary to form a corporation; some state statutes say that a corporation may be formed by any number of persons, and this is held to mean more than one person.

judgment against their personal assets. As a practical matter, the prospective creditor of a corporation will often demand that the owners of the corporation sign a note pledging their personal assets in addition to the individual executing the note as an officer of the corporation. When this is done, the major advantage of the corporation is negated.

One of the major disadvantages of the corporate form of business is the federal tax. The income of the corporation is taxed, and the amounts distributed to the stockholders are taxed again in the nature of a personal income tax. This is often referred to as "double taxation."

When a corporation is formed for the purpose of engaging in the real estate business, most state laws require that at least one of the officers of the corporation be a licensed real estate broker. Some state laws require that only one of the officers be a licensed broker. This means that the other owners may be only licensed real estate salesmen. In states having laws of this type, where only one of the officers of the corporation may be licensed and both of the incorporating parties have brokers' licenses, one of them gives up the license while he remains an officer of the corporation. He is given a salesman's license with the stipulation that if he disengages himself from the corporation and desires to practice as an individual, his broker's license will be returned to him.

SELECTING A LOCATION AND EQUIPPING AN OFFICE

Assuming that a person desires to practice as an individual, the first problem is selecting and equipping an office. Before any consideration is given to this, the novice must ask himself the question of the type of brokerage in which he is going to engage. Will it be selling houses, leasing, specializing in industrial sales, or one of the numerous other facets of the real estate business? The answer to this question is more important in determining the location of an office in large cities than it is in the smaller towns and villages. If a broker is in a city and he decides that he is going to handle the selling of homes, he should investigate the possibility of establishing himself in a neighborhood rather than in a downtown section of the city. He should make certain that the neighborhood is progressing and not in an advanced stage of decay. If he decides that he is going to specialize in store leases, the new broker might do better to locate himself in a downtown section of the city rather than in a surburban area.

The broker who is establishing an office in a country town should recognize the necessity of establishing himself in a "live" section of town. Anyone with experience in a city and knowledge of that city will encounter no difficulty in establishing himself in a desirable area.

The problem of furnishing an office is so elementary it needs but brief mention in passing. Whether an office is extensively or simply furnished depends to a large extent on the amount of funds available to the individual. The important thing is that it be furnished in good taste.

Capital Requirements

Too many potentially good brokers fall by the wayside for lack of sufficient capital. At the start of operations the beginning broker should have a certain minimum amount of capital for furniture and other initial expenses. It is felt, too, that the new broker ought to have enough capital to cover his estimated operating expenses and living expenses for at least six months. Unless the person embarking on a brokerage career has several commissions in sight, the question of ready capital must be given the proper attention, otherwise the venture may result in tragic failure for the broker—and what is worse, for his family.

To a large degree, the question of sufficient or insufficient capital may be a deciding factor of whether the new broker will enter business as an individual proprietor or seek partners either in the partnership or corporate form of enterprise.

Borrowing Money

The desirable thing, if possible, is to enter business debt free. When lack of capital stands between the broker entering business and success, however, it is often desirable to borrow. There are several sources of funds open to the beginning broker. The simplest way of arranging a personal loan to start a business may be to obtain the money from some near relative who might be satisfied with getting a return of a certain percent on the money loaned.

If one goes outside the family for financial assistance, the viewpoint is apt to be different. A friend needs more incentive than a relative. The friend is apt to be interested in the proposition from the investment viewpoint. He may not care to risk his money in a new venture unless he receives a percentage of the profits in addition to his interest, and an arrangement to this effect might be made.

A future possibility of venture capital is a loan from a bank, although this is highly improbable in a new venture. The bank may be induced to lend money on a personal note if the person entering business has a good credit standing in the community. If the new broker has any assets, such as an automobile, that might be pledged with the bank as security for a loan, the problem of obtaining the loan is that much simpler. If the new broker is a veteran of World War II, the Korean War, or the Vietnam conflict, he might investigate the possibility of obtaining a business loan under the "G. I." bill.

In any situation when one desires to obtain a loan, it is a good idea to prepare a financial statement to submit to the source of the loan, be it relative, friend, or bank. The financial statement should show the assets, liabilities, and the net worth of the individual.

Operating Expenses and Taxes

In all businesses there are certain operating expenses, such as advertising, entertainment of prospects, monthly rental, telephone bills and other utilities, salaries, and incidentals. The most important operating expense in the real estate office at first is advertising and entertainment of prospects.

Taxwise the broker will have to pay for his license, his social security, and his income taxes. In calculating profits and income taxes to be paid, the broker is entitled to deduct from gross operating income reasonable amounts for entertainment, transportation of customers, and depreciation of furniture and equipment. In cases where the broker practices from his own home, he may deduct a reasonable value for the use of the premises in the nature of an operating expense. It is felt that a good policy when possible is to establish charge accounts. For example, establish an account with a gas station in order to more accurately deduct the amount allowed for transporting prospects.

OBTAINING LISTINGS

Listings are the stock in trade of any broker. Without listings, the broker has nothing to sell. Therefore, after having established himself in business, the broker should go out and solicit listings.

Canvassing

There are several ways in which brokers canvass for listings. Many brokers habitually scan the classified sections of their local newspapers looking for advertisements placed by owners. These brokers telephone the owners and try to persuade the owners to list the property with them. Some brokers write letters to these owners requesting the listing. However, this method generally produces poor results because it is human nature to follow the path of least resistance, and owners are reluctant to answer letters.

Door-to-door canvassing or "punching doorbells" is an effective means of obtaining listings for some brokers. The beginner should determine the attitude of the local real estate board prior to seeking listings in this manner as the boards in some localities are opposed to this method of obtaining listings. However, when there is no opposition, neighborhoods can easily be canvassed and listings obtained. The difficulty with this method is that many owners will list their property, but at prices that the broker knows are too high.

One effective device used by some brokers who canvass door to door is to have an attractive card printed that can be easily affixed to the doorknob when the owners are not at home (see page 462).

In some areas, financial institutions often have properties for sale. A letter to them requesting a list of their properties and permission to offer them for sale may result in a satisfactory number of listings.

Another good way of obtaining listings is by watching for "For Sale" and "To Let" signs in a neighborhood, then locating the owner and obtaining from him the authority to sell or lease the property.

News items are frequently a source of leads to properties that might be for sale. Items often appear stating that certain owners are moving from the city. If such persons are property owners, they will probably want to sell or rent their homes immediately. Property often is sold upon the death of the owner, and listings can be obtained by contacting the attorney acting for a decedent's estate.

XYZ REALTY COMPANY

We called on you today to find out if you wish to sell your home. Our office has had several inquiries about homes in this neighborhood. If you are interested, please telephone 621-1234 and ask for Frank Smith.

Frank Smith

A Broker's Door Card

A letter to real estate operators will often result in listings, but more often than not, these listings are open listings or in the nature of co-brokerage. An *operator* in real estate is a person who buys and sells on his own account, hoping to make a profit on the change of the market. Often, too, he will buy "sleepers" (bargains) and attempt later to sell the properties for their true market value. Even though many of the listings from operators are open listings or invitations for co-brokerage, they are good to have, for they add to the broker's listings and to his possibility of satisfying buyers. Also, it will give the broker an opportunity to determine the types of properties in which the various operators are interested. If the broker then has this type of property among his other listings wanted by the operators, he may offer them for sale to the operators. They make good prospects because they know what they want; and, if the right property is available, they will purchase it with little or no effort on the part of the broker.

Advertising

Advertising is probably the least effective way of obtaining listings. The listings obtained by this method are mainly of the co-brokerage type of listing. However, advertising for listings in newspapers is a method of presenting the firm name to the public and thus may be said to have some value. In addition to newspaper advertising, letters to selected prospects may bring good results.

Personal Contacts

Business and social contacts are probably the most fertile source of listings for brokers. The broker who establishes a reputation for rendering service to the community, either through his business relationships with the rest of the community or through memberships in service organizations, will never lack for listings.

Selling the Listing Service

Some people persist in attempting to sell their property without the services of the real estate broker. Often it is no easy matter to persuade people to allow the broker to handle the sale of the property; therefore, the broker must be prepared to sell his service to owners. The owner's confidence and respect must be won. Some of the arguments used to convince owners to list property with a broker are:

1. The real estate broker is in a much better position than the average owner to sell a property at a fair price. He has a knowledge of the current market and knows where favorable prospects may be found.

2. Because the broker has no interest other than as a middleman, he is able to negotiate with a better chance of reaching an agreement than if two interested persons sat face to face across the same table.

3. The average buyer is timid about talking things over frankly with an owner. He may dislike discussing his financial situation, or he may ask for terms that make the deal an impossibility.

4. The real estate broker knows how to advertise properties to the best advantage.

5. The owner of the property is inclined to be sensitive. He resents criticism and his interview with a prospect may end in an argument instead of a sale.

6. The commissions charged by the broker are small compared with the advantages of having the sale in the hands of an expert.

SALES MANAGEMENT PROBLEMS

Inspecting the Premises

While obtaining a listing or immediately after obtaining a listing, the property must be inspected. All listings should be personally inspected either by the broker or his salesman. He must know his product before he can sell it. The property should be inspected regardless of whether it was listed in the same office at some previous time. One broker, for example, had a rambling old house listed with him. He thought he was familiar with the house, having played in it when he was a child. But it had passed through many hands. He took a prospect out to see it and things went smoothly until he reached the second floor which was faced with a long row of bedrooms. He showed the prospect the first bedroom and then happily flung open the door of the second bedroom. To his utter amazement, he and the prospect were greeted by the peeping of a thousand baby chicks which the owner was brooding in the bedroom. Needless to say, he lost the sale. Had he inspected the property, he certainly would not have brought the prospect to the property.

When inspecting a property, one of the best procedures is to start with the listing form, filling in all of the blanks in detail. In addition to increasing the broker's knowledge of the product he is selling, this will increase the confidence of the seller in the broker, because it will impress him with the broker's thoroughness.

The advantages of the property should be noted. They will be the strong selling points to be pointed out to the prospect when selling the property. Familiarity with the property enables it to be discussed intelligently and hence more quickly sold.

In the course of inspection the broker may also note physical changes that are needed to effect an early sale. He may see fit to suggest these changes before making an offer.

Setting the Price

One of the most difficult problems that confronts the broker in obtaining listings is the establishment of a selling price. Owners have a tendency to overestimate the value of their homes, which is a distinct disadvantage to both the owner and the broker when a sale can result only from a modification of terms and after a considerable delay.

After a careful inspection and evaluation, the owner should be told what the broker thinks the property will bring at the prevailing market price. This should be done tactfully. Informing the owner of an opinion as to fair market value is in accordance with the Code of Ethics of the NATIONAL ASSOCIATION OF REALTORS which states:

> It is the duty of the REALTOR to be well informed on current conditions in order to be in a position to advise his clients as to the fair market price.

It may be better to refuse the listing unless the owner will agree to a reasonable and fair price for the property. Many owners do not realize that a listing that is too high receives little attention. Frequently brokers resort to the bad practice of accepting a listing that is too high and merely filing it in the office. It is regarded as better practice to reject a listing that is unfairly priced by the owner. By doing this, the broker will actually perform a service for the owner and at the same time build up a better reputation for himself.

The Property Brief

The *property brief* is, in essence, an information folder concerning a particular property. It should contain a sketched map showing the relationship between the property and schools, shopping districts, and transportation. The sketched map may, for example, show the property, including dimensions of the lot, located in the center of Thomas Street, and may bear the notations: bus line one block, grammar school two blocks, shopping four blocks, with arrows indicating the direction of each from the house.

In addition, the brief should contain a photograph of the building, a diagram showing the floor plan, and a notation regarding the taxes and insurance rates on the building. In the event that the property is an income property, all of the pertinent information concerning income and expenses should be included in the property brief, together with information about the balance of the mortgage due and the rate of amortization. See examples on pages 466 and 467.

The property brief is a timesaver when it comes to selling the property. Many trips to the property can be eliminated by showing the prospect the brief prior to leaving the office.

The Sales Kit

The *sales kit* is one of the most inexpensive, yet most effective means that the broker has at his command to aid him in the sale of real property. The kit provides answers to many of the questions

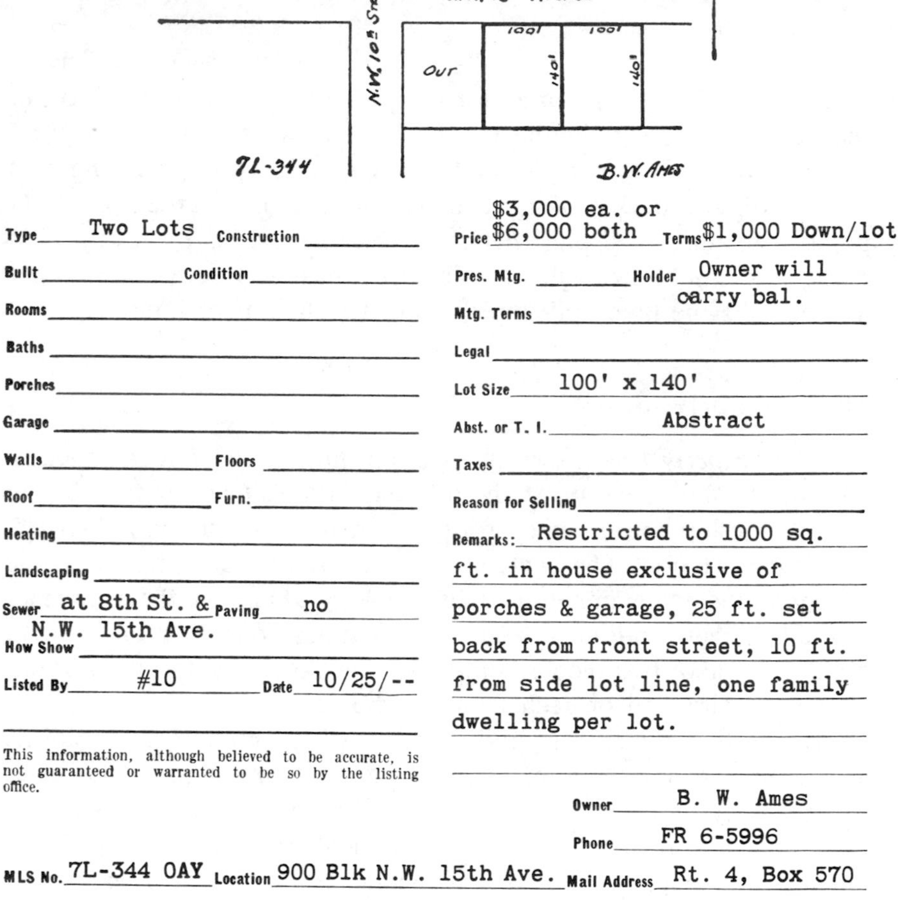

Type Two Lots Construction
Built Condition
Rooms
Baths
Porches
Garage
Walls Floors
Roof Furn.
Heating
Landscaping
Sewer at 8th St. & N.W. 15th Ave. Paving no
How Show
Listed By #10 Date 10/25/--

This information, although believed to be accurate, is not guaranteed or warranted to be so by the listing office.

Price $3,000 ea. or $6,000 both Terms $1,000 Down/lot
Pres. Mtg. Holder Owner will carry bal.
Mtg. Terms
Legal
Lot Size 100' x 140'
Abst. or T. I. Abstract
Taxes
Reason for Selling
Remarks: Restricted to 1000 sq. ft. in house exclusive of porches & garage, 25 ft. set back from front street, 10 ft. from side lot line, one family dwelling per lot.

Owner B. W. Ames
Phone FR 6-5996

MLS No. 7L-344 OAY Location 900 Blk N.W. 15th Ave. Mail Address Rt. 4, Box 570

A Portion of a Property Brief Showing Lots for Sale

that will be put to the broker by the prospect and often is the thing that causes the prospect finally to make up his mind.

The contents of the kit are varied and should be changed from time to time. A map of the city together with a zoning map is essential. It is also wise to have tax rates, data on insurance rates, amortization tables, and a table showing the various amounts tenants pay in rent over certain periods of years and at different monthly rents. Newspaper clippings containing pertinent information about the city should be included; for example, the government is going to

2 BEDROOM NEAR JEFFERSON SCHOOL
3RD BEDROOM STARTED. FINE YARD -- PATIO

FIRST FLOOR 4 rms.
Living rm. YES
Dining rm. NO
Finish PAPERED-LIGHT WOODWORK
Fireplace YES
Features
Kitchen
Builtins FAIR nook YES
Cooking ELEC ref.
Features
Bedrooms 2 floors HDWD
Bath YES floor LINO
Tub YES basin YES toilet YES
Porch NO linen YES

SECOND FLOOR NONE rms.
Floors attic
Bath floors
Tub basin toilet

BASEMENT size FULL
Floor CONC Laundry YES
Room BEDROOM

Lot 14 Blk 2
Add. ALAMO PARK
Size 50 x 125

Grade YES pave YES walk YES
Sewer YES
Grounds IMPROVED
View

Blks. bus. 1/2
Blks. school 7 JEFFERSON

Garage YES floor CONC
Drive FROM 38TH
Occupant NEVILLE
Phone 741 7595 key
Age 36
Rent
Condition GOOD
HEAT HA STOKER

PRICE $18,500
Cash $3,000
Bal. $75
Including 7½%
Mortgage CLEAR
Payable

Contract

Taxes $81.86
List RMG
38 1007 E

F. S. Barrett & Co., Realtors

A Portion of a Property Brief Showing a House for Sale

spend a large sum on a dam or atomic energy plant in the locale, or a large corporation is going to build a plant in the city. These data should be kept in the sales kit to show to prospects who are strangers to the city, or to prospects who are interested in purchasing investment properties or business opportunities in the city.

Reports of the local chamber of commerce on population trends and reports of bank deposits showing increases over a period of years are other items that might be included in the kit. All of these things provide information that will assist the salesman in making the sale. The zoning map, for example, may even prevent the salesman from inadvertently offering a lot in a residential zone for sale as a business property.

FORMS AND RECORDS

Listing Forms

The real estate broker who opens his own office should obtain a number of forms in addition to the various types of contracts of employment. The most important of these is the *listing form.* This contains all of the pertinent details of a property, such as its location, price, the amount of the mortgage, the number of bedrooms, baths, and so forth. Copies of these forms are made so that each salesman has a copy from which he can obtain this information prior to showing the property to a prospect.

Listing File

The contents of the listing file should be arranged in some definite and logical order—according to the various types of properties. For example, residential properties and industrial properties are kept separate. The file should be subdivided into sections. Some brokers do this by neighborhood and others by price classes.

Usually when a prospect makes an inquiry for a property, he is interested in location, type of house, and price. He will be limited by a price range, but will desire a particular type of house and will have a preference as to location. Thus, in addition to indexing listings by location and price, properties may also be indexed by type of house.

A systematic filing system is essential and will prove to be a great timesaver. The material should always be as complete as possible, and active and inactive listings should be separated.

Binder Agreements

In those states where the broker does not prepare the earnest money receipt and agreement to purchase, the broker should have a suitable binder agreement in his office that will comply with the Statute of Frauds. This simple form contains a place for a date and a brief description of the property. It also contains the terms of the sale and a place for the signature of the parties. It contains, too, a statement that the parties agree as to the broker who brought about the sale and that the parties will enter into a more formal contract within a specified number of days.

After the binder has been signed by both of the parties, a copy is usually turned over to the attorney for the seller who prepares the contract for the sale of real property. Then a date for closing of title is set.

The binder, despite its simplicity, is a valid contract for the sale of real property provided that all of its details have been completed, and provided that there really is nothing further for the parties to do but enter into the more formal contract as called for by the binder agreement. The binder agreement is illustrated on page 77.

The Earnest Money Receipt and Agreement to Purchase

In many states the broker actually prepares the *contract for sale*, which is a combination receipt for the earnest money and a contract of sale. It is more complete than the binder agreement in that the property description is more detailed; it contains a closing date and the type of deed that is to be transferred by the seller, a description of any personal property that is included in the transaction, and a statement that such personal property will be transferred by a bill of sale.

In the final analysis, it is an offer to be transmitted by the broker to the seller. However, it is more than that because it contains a time limit for the seller to accept the offer. Once the seller has accepted the offer, no other contract must be prepared, as is the case when a binder agreement is used. An illustration of a receipt and agreement to purchase is given on page 88.

Prospect Cards

Everyone who comes into the broker's office, as the result of an advertisement or for any other reason, is a potential customer. If the needs of the customer cannot be satisfied with the listings that the broker has at the moment, his needs might be satisfied at some future date. This suggests that the potential prospect should not be allowed to leave the broker's office without the broker's having first obtained some information from the prospect. Once having obtained this information, the broker ought to make a record of it on a prospect card. The *prospect card* contains the name, address, and telephone number of the prospect. It also contains the price range in which the prospect is interested, and the amount of down payment he has available. The card might also be used to test the effectiveness of advertising by asking the prospect the cause of his coming to the office.

After having obtained the above information, the card should be filed; and when new listings are obtained that might satisfy the

Type of Property Wanted	Price Range	Size and Use	Location	Sale ☐ Exchange ☐ Lease ☐ Rental ☐

Prospect .... | Prospect particularly interested in
Price Range
Address.................... City.................... Phone.................... | $.............. to $..............
Source of Inquiry....................
Wants....................
Size and Use....................
Remarks....................
Location....................

FORM No. 792
PROSPECT CARD
STEVENS-NESS LAW PUBLISHING CO
PORTLAND, OREGON 837

A Prospect Card

needs of the prospect, the prospect should be notified personally, by telephone, or by mail.

RELATIONSHIP WITH SALESMEN

Hiring Salesmen

Every broker that hires salesmen wants good salesmen. The problem is to determine if a man is going to be good before hiring.

One state study did attempt to determine tests for real estate salesmen.[3] A study was made of 650 real estate salesmen who were rated by their employers as "good," "poor," and "average" salespersons. Ninety were eliminated from the study for various reasons, leaving 560 individuals to be tested. Four psychological tests were given these persons and their scores compared with their brokers' reactions to them, that is, good, poor, and average.

Curtis established that under present hiring practices, a realtor must hire eight salesmen to get four good ones. The study indicated that it is possible to predict success or failure as a real estate salesman if the applicant's interests are compared with those of good real estate salespersons. To do this, minimum scores are established in the four tests.

It is suggested that the broker involved with hiring relatively large numbers of salespersons consider such tests to assure himself of satisfactory employees.

Compensation

The usual arrangement for compensating salesmen is on a commission basis. One study revealed that 95 percent of the firms relied on straight commissions. Commissions and drawing accounts were used in 4 percent of the firms. The smaller firms are the most frequent users of straight commissions, while only 1 percent of the firms employing over fifty employees used straight commissions.[4]

---

[3] Clayton C. Curtis, Project Director, Florida Association of Realtors Project No. 3 (October, 1962).

[4] Clyde Richey and H. L. Fusilier, *Real Estate Sales Career Opportunities versus Student Expectations—Is There a Gap?* (Boulder, Colorado: University of Colorado, Center for Real Estate and Land Use Studies, December, 1971), p. 3.

Where commissions are used, the rate to the broker is generally 6 percent of the selling price, although this percent may vary with the selling price of the property. Of the 6 percent the salesman generally receives one half and the broker receives one half.

If a salesman obtains a listing and the property is sold by another salesman, the listing salesman usually receives 10 percent of the commission; the selling salesman, 45 percent; and the broker, 45 percent. This policy is followed to encourage the salesmen to obtain listings for the office.

Because the rates of commission vary considerably, especially in areas where multiple listings are used, the rates of commissions and any other duties of salesmen should be made clear to the salesman when he is hired in order to avoid occasions for any future misunderstanding between the salesman and the broker.

The Stick

In offices having large sales forces, trouble sometimes arises concerning which salesman is to handle a prospect who calls at the office. Many of the larger offices attempt to solve this problem by means of what is commonly called "the stick." It is simply a board on which the names of the salesmen are listed. The salesman whose name is on the bottom of the list handles the first prospect entering the office and the salesman's name is then placed at the top of the list. The next salesman's name in order falls into the bottom position and he handles the next prospect. In this way, each salesman gets a turn at the prospects as they come into the office.

Another method used by brokers is to assign customers for one day to one salesman and the following day to another salesman who "takes the floor."

Agreement with Salesmen

Generally speaking, the salesmen in most offices pay gas and oil expenses on their automobiles out of their own pockets. Naturally, for income tax purposes, the salesmen take these expenses as deductions. However, in a few instances these deductions have been disallowed by the Internal Revenue Service because the salesmen had no written agreement with their brokers. IRS contended, due to the lack of a written agreement, this expenditure was a gratuity on the part of the salesmen. IRS was upheld in its contention. It is, therefore, extremely important for the salesmen to enter into a written agreement with their brokers. The agreement should state, among other things, that the salesman himself is to pay for gas, oil, and maintenance of his automobile. In this way, a deduction will be allowed the salesman for income tax purposes.

Furthermore, because oral instructions are often vague and forgotten, it is suggested that salesmen will be more aware of what is expected of them if given the following suggestions in writing:

1. Consider your employment to be as it would be in any other business or profession as an accountant, store owner, doctor, or lawyer.
2. Take a full day off each week.
3. Keep your appearance neat.
4. Show your appreciation for referrals.
5. Follow up prospects.
6. Be proud of the work you are in and talk and show it whenever the opportunity arises.
7. Selling is creative. Keep your mind active; imagination is your friend.

QUESTIONS FOR REVIEW

1. What is the purpose of the brokerage licensing laws?
2. In general, who are the persons exempted in most states from taking the brokerage examinations?
3. List and explain the advantages of the licensing laws.
4. What is the purpose of requiring brokers to be bonded in many states?
5. What is meant by an *irrevocable consent* to the service of process?
6. What are the three types of business organization by which a broker may enter business?
7. Compare the advantages and disadvantages of the partnership form of business enterprise to the corporate form of business enterprise.
8. What are the common sources of capital funds available to the beginning broker?
9. Name and explain three ways of obtaining listings.

10. List and explain 5 advantages to an owner of having property handled through a brokerage office instead of attempting to sell the property himself.
11. Why should a broker inspect the premises that he has listed or is about to list?
12. Why is setting a price on a property sometimes difficult, and what should be done if the owner persists in demanding an unreasonable price for his property?
13. Explain the use and the makeup of a property brief.
14. What is a *sales kit,* and in general of what is it composed?
15. What is a *prospect card* and how is it used?
16. What is the usual arrangement between brokers and salesmen in regard to commissions?
17. Explain the advantages of having a written agreement with the salesman.

PROBLEM

1. The following is a partial quotation from Section 475.43 of the Florida Real Estate License Law:

   "An option contract may sometimes amount only to an exclusive listing. This will occur where it is understood that the optionee has no intention of buying the property himself, but intends to sell it to someone else for a sum sufficient to net a compensation for his efforts. A contract of this character is frequently given as a means of expediting a brokerage transaction. Thus, the owner may live at a distance, and a quick sale may result. In this way the broker may bind the principal to sell, and the broker's authority to do so may be exhibited to the prospect. It does not change the essential relations of the parties and cannot be considered as a true option. . . ."

   (a) Why is it not a true option?

   (b) Suggest another way of accomplishing the same thing given in the illustration above.

SUGGESTED READINGS

Case, Frederick E. *Real Estate,* Rev. ed. Boston: Allyn and Bacon, 1962. Chapter 21.

Ring, Alfred A. *Real Estate Principles and Practices,* 7th ed. Englewood Cliffs, New Jersey: Prentice-Hall, Inc., 1972. Chapter 18.

Chapter 19

Selling

For most real estate brokers, selling is the heart of their entire operation. Because he is an intermediary between seller and buyer, the sale is vital to the broker's very existence.

At the outset, it should be recognized that selling is hard but interesting work. More important to recognize, perhaps, is the very competitive nature of the work. In selling anything, the salesman must compete. He competes with other salesmen in his own firm, and he competes with the salesmen of competitors. In the final analysis, the salesman must also compete with himself ". . . against his past performances. He wants each year to be better than the last, and every order from each customer to be larger than previous orders. His own best records can be a salesman's fiercest competition." [1]

SELLING RESIDENTIAL PROPERTY

Real estate is a fundamental commodity; people need it, and people want it. The novice should realize that psychologically people

[1] C. A. Kirkpatrick, *Salesmanship* (5th ed.; Cincinnati: South-Western Publishing Co., 1971), p. 114.

want to buy. To be able to buy something flatters the ego, and the very act of buying itself gives the purchaser a feeling of pleasure. The salesman ought to realize that the purchaser contemplating the purchase of a home is in fact anticipating the pleasure of enjoyment in the owning of *his* home, and the person purchasing commercial property is anticipating the possibility of profits from *his* purchase.

At this point, the logical question might be: If people really want to buy, why is it so difficult to sell them something—especially real estate? It is ordinarily true that people are not ready buyers. Sales resistance by a prospect is often built up consciously and sometimes unconsciously. Most buyers have only a limited amount of funds with which to make purchases. Doubts may be built up by conflicting claims that are making demands upon these sums. The prospect may fear being sold something that he does not need; he may be cautious because he desires to be certain of making a good bargain. He may not want to feel that he is being pushed into making a decision. The reasons for the resistance to buying are endless, and the attempt to sell real estate may increase the psychological effect of these deterrents to an even higher degree because for the average person the purchase of a parcel of real property is probably the largest investment he will make during his lifetime.

Preparation for the Sale

The successful broker is the one who has prepared himself to sell. He is the man who has imbued himself with a full knowledge of real estate and all of its phases. In the field of marketing it is an axiom that any sound marketing program begins with the ultimate consumer. It is important for the broker to have a knowledge of the buyers in the area in which he is operating. What does the market consist of? Who are the available buyers? As a first step, the broker should contact his state employment and security agency and obtain figures of average monthly employment by industry in his county of his state. In this way he will be able to determine the average income of his potential purchasers and thereby know where his mass market lies. For example, if the majority of wage earners in a county average $9,000 per year, it should be recognized that in all probability the greatest mass market lies within this group. Thus, the more listings the broker has in his files that lie in the price range of the $9,000 per annum purchasers, the more opportunity the broker has for potential sales. Perhaps this appears impractical, but the proof lies in the actions of the largest of our corporate enterprises. They know where the potential market lies, and they act to exploit that market. Their marketing programs are geared to the buyer. The broker should also have a knowledge of the market and should always be aware of general business conditions, price trends, the actions of his competitors, and the many other market factors.

Knowledge of Buying Motives

Motives tend to explain *why* things are done or not done. Buying motives tend to explain *why* people buy. Buying motives are either emotional or rational. That is, if the decision to buy is made as a result of an emotional rather than a rational mental state, the motive is characterized as emotional. By recognizing the buying motives of their potential purchasers, the real estate brokers or salesmen can "help their prospects buy" instead of "selling" them. It is only when the broker helps his prospects buy that he has really satisfied customers.

These motives or desires of prospective purchasers are not too unlike the motives that are appealed to in advertising—economy in use, expectation of profit, comfort, love of children, pride of possession—to mention only a few. If a salesman has a prospect who is interested in the purchase of a home because of his love for children, the salesman should know that this is one of the strongest motives for his prospect's purchase of a home. As a result of the knowledge of this motive, when the salesman comes to the street on which the property is located, he points out to the prospect those things which make the street safe for children. It is not a through street; there are signs warning drivers to slow down; the street has a jog in it which naturally slows down the drivers. He makes the prospect see then that this is the neighborhood for him. He has assisted the prospect in satisfying his buying motive.

On the other hand, if the prospect is looking at a commercial property with the idea of making a profit from the property, the salesman can go over the income and expense figures with him, show him where the profit lies and how much he will earn from the property. That is what he wants—expectation of profit is his buying motive. The salesman should be frank and honest with his prospect, who will then respect his judgment. If he does not try to conceal anything from the prospect, he will have gained the prospect's confidence.

The ability to recognize the motives of the prospect is, in the final analysis, a very important part of the preparation for selling.

Knowledge of the Product

Although a broker must have a knowledge of the product that he is selling, many brokers are sadly lacking in really knowing anything about their listings. There is a saying among people in real estate that "a house well listed is half sold." In the chapter on brokerage, much space was devoted to the listing of the home and the inspection of the home. This does not mean there is nothing beyond the mechanics of taking a listing. When a property is listed, the broker must be sure, first, that it is a salable listing; that is, that it is not listed at a price which is too high. Secondly, inspecting the listing must involve more than just the mechanics of going over the property. Inspecting the property means obtaining a thorough knowledge of the product that is going to be sold. Mental photographs of the property, both inside and out, are taken by the person inspecting the property.

In addition to losing a sale, ignorance of the product may have serious legal consequences for the broker. For example, one broker listed a home, noting a fireplace on his listing card. After having placed a great deal of emphasis on the comforts to be derived from the fireplace, he sold the property to his prospect. The first night in his new home, the prospect gathered his family about him while he lighted the fire. It nearly exploded in his face, filling the room with soot and burning an expensive rug. The fireplace had no flue. It was for decorative purposes only. The resulting lawsuit cost the broker $1,800, not to mention immeasurable damages to his reputation. He had little knowledge of his product.

The broker should know everything there is to know about the product, and especially have at his fingertips the reason that the seller wants to sell. Every prospect will raise this question because he feels that the seller is trying to make a profit from the deal.

Sources of Prospects

The sources of prospects are almost limitless. One important source may be the neighbors of the listing owner. Upon obtaining a listing, the broker might stop at the home of the next door neighbor and tell him that he has just listed the home and that it is the broker's desire to bring into the neighborhood people who will be amiable. This sort of approach will reap rewards. The neighbor may suggest a friend who might be interested in the house or the neighbor might be interested in listing his own home for sale. At any rate, this sort of approach cannot help but promote goodwill and good public relations for the broker. The neighbors will realize that the broker is trying to serve them by informing them of his actions. The entire block might be worked in this manner. It will be surprising the number of listings and the number of prospects that will be brought forth in this way. It will, in effect, create a situation whereby everyone in the block will be thinking of prospects for the broker, if for no other reason than to protect his own interests in the neighborhood. The neighbor might even want to purchase the property.

Former Customers. Previous customers of the broker are always good prospects. Generally, the broker will find that he can build one sale into two if he employs the lists of his previous clients.

Owners of Listed Properties. The broker knows or should know the reason why every person who has listed property with him desires to sell the property. Many of these people want to sell because they desire to move to a new neighborhood. Some of the older people who have listed their homes for sale have done so because their families have grown to adulthood and left home. Perhaps they no longer have a need for a large home and want to move to a smaller home. They may be prospects for a sale.

Investors and Operators. Brokers who deal in investment properties should have a list of investors handy. This list can easily be built up by the beginner from advertisements in newspapers and in real estate journals. As a routine matter, all listings of investment properties that might be of interest to the operator or investor should be submitted to them, preferably personally, although in large cities this might not prove to be practicable.

Recent Sellers. Recent sellers are a particularly rich source of prospects. The chances are that they are qualified, at least from a monetary point of view, as prospective purchasers. Current lists of sellers can be made from the real estate pages of newspapers or from the records in the county clerk's office. It is important to keep these lists up to date and to use them as rapidly as possible. This source of prospects is especially good in a rising market because the chances are that these sellers have made a profit from the sale of their previously held property and believe that they can do it again, in which case they will be susceptible to sales overtures.

The Open House. About 2 percent of sales result from the "open house." Usually a well-furnished listing in a moderate price bracket is selected for the "open house." An advertisement is run stating that the home will be open for inspection, giving the time and the date. Generally, the open house is handled by two salesmen—one who is stationed at the front door, and another at the back door or in the kitchen. When prospects come in, they are treated as guests and shown the house. If the "open house" is run properly, the salesmen are able to obtain a list of prospects, not only for the house shown, but for other listings if the house shown does not happen to meet the needs and requirements of the prospects.

Tenants. The real estate broker who combines a management department with his selling department becomes known to a great many people. At least once a month the tenants call at the management office, and most of these tenants sincerely desire to own their own homes one day. The property manager, if he does his job well, is acquainted with the financial status of his tenants. Tenants often discuss their personal problems with the property manager, and the manager may have a listing that is suitable for a particular tenant who desires a home of his own.

Often tenants will become prospects for investment or commercial type properties. By promoting good public relations with the tenants, the broker will have a ready source of prospects.

Personal Contacts. There is no question but that in order to be successful the broker, especially in a small town, must sacrifice a certain amount of his family life. He must keep up his contacts, and must take part in civic affairs. Although these contacts are time-consuming, it is through them that the broker finds many prospects.

The sources of prospects are infinite, and the successful broker is quick to recognize situations that lead to purchasers. He should neither forget that he is a real estate broker nor let other people forget it. As a broker, he has a service to perform; therefore, he should become acquainted with as many people as he can. It is a good policy for him to try to inform at least four people a day that he is in real estate. It is surprising the number of additional prospects that can be developed from these new contacts.

The Housing of Current Buyers

One question answered in a 1967 study is significant with regard to prospecting for buyers: What is the housing status of current buyers? [2] The report found that 54 percent of the buyers of existing homes were renters; 39 percent current owners; and 7 percent newlyweds. But for buyers of new homes the proportions were quite different: 49 percent were renters; 32 percent current owners; and 19 percent newlyweds. From this a broker can conclude that a large untapped market lies both in renters and in newlyweds.

Qualifying Prospects

The essence of qualifying a prospect is to determine his needs and to match those needs with the listings in the office. It must first be determined, however, if the prospect is a real prospect, or if he is a "shopper." The latter type of person is quickly found out and no time is wasted on him.

Qualifying a prospect is akin to diplomacy. People resent others prying into their personal affairs, but the broker must do this without seeming to and without offending the prospect.

The obvious things to determine are his name, his address, the business in which he is engaged, whether he is married and has children, and the number of children in the family.

Does he have the money with which to purchase a home? This is one of the most difficult answers to obtain from a prospect. As

---

[2] Eugene P. Conser, Editorial, *Realtor's Headlines,* Vol. 34, No. 44 (October, 1967).

Samuelson expresses it: "Even where income is known within the family, there is a quite natural reticence to reveal it to outsiders; thus investigators who made a survey of the birth-control habits of native white Protestants of Indianapolis often found it harder to get financial data than intimate personal information." [3]

This, in essence, is one of the problems with which the broker is faced in qualifying his prospects. But it must be done; otherwise much time will be wasted before the prospect is shown a house that fits his income.

Where would the prospect like to live? What is his church preference? These and many other questions of a personal nature are important to the broker in qualifying the prospect. This information should be noted and later copied on a prospect card in the event that the prospect does not buy at the moment. With this information, the broker can proceed with the sale. He has an idea of the neighborhood in which the prospect wishes to live, an idea of the price he can afford to pay, and the size of the house he needs. If he has children, it will have to be near a school or close to an available school bus. From the qualifications of the prospect, the broker has partially determined his needs—unless the prospect has misrepresented facts.

There still remains, however, the problem of fitting these needs to the broker's listings. This is basically an analytical problem. For example, the prospect has $4,000 cash, a boy and a girl of school age, and a wife who is unable to drive an automobile. To take this prospect out and show him homes at random would be a sheer waste of time. At this point, the broker must raise the question in his mind as to the needs of the prospect. To show him a one- or a two-bedroom house would be futile. He needs at least a three-bedroom house. Where must it be located? With two children of school age, it must be within a reasonable distance of a school. It may have to be near some mode of transportation in order for the wife to travel conveniently to a shopping district, and it should be priced somewhere between $20,000 and $23,000. How, then, does the broker match listings and needs?

The broker should have at his fingertips the listings in his files that fit these requirements. He should think over these listings in terms

---

[3] Paul A. Samuelson, *Economics* (8th ed.; McGraw-Hill Book Company, 1970), p. 108.

again of the *needs* of his prospect and decide which of the listings best fits the bill. He should categorize them in the best order possible. Perhaps the broker has found out from the prospect that he prefers a brick house to a frame house. In this case, he should first show the brick house that best fits the prospect's needs in relation to the other factors. After having thus analyzed the prospect's needs, the time has come for the broker actually to show the property.

If a prospect has come into the office in response to a specific advertisement, the broker should show him the property even though he doesn't think the prospect is able to make the purchase. However, this does not mean that the broker should not qualify the prospect in terms of the property advertised. Perhaps it will not comply at all with the prospect's needs. The broker, recognizing this, should have listings available that will comply with the needs of the prospect. In this way, the broker may still be able to make a sale even though the property is not the one in which the prospect was first interested.

Showing the Property

Prospects should be shown property under the most favorable circumstances. If the property is occupied, it would be well to make sure that the present occupants are ready to receive visitors. If possible, the prospect and his family should be shown the property together; otherwise, it may necessitate several useless trips to the property.

One of the important factors in making a sale is appearance. Not only is the appearance of the salesman important, but in the mind of the prospect, so is the salesman's car. It should be clean and uncluttered; otherwise, a bad impression will be created. A bad impression causes the prospect to lose confidence in the broker who is showing the property.

There is an easier and more efficient way of making sales than merely to drive the prospect around at random. The broker has determined the needs of the prospect; the only remaining problem is to allow the prospect to convince *himself* that the property being shown supplies these needs. The broker must think in terms of his client's problems. He must adapt himself to individual cases and concentrate on the finer points of the listing. By doing this, the broker wipes away the deterrents that were mentioned in the beginning of the chapter. For example, the prospect may normally hesitate for fear of being pushed into making a decision. If he has been properly qualified, he is not being pushed into anything. It is what he needs, and his fear is wiped away if the broker shows the proper listing.

On the way out to the property, the broker should refrain from discussing the property unless the prospect has asked specific questions in regard to the property itself. Presumably, the broker has prepared himself thoroughly, having imbued himself with a knowledge of the product (listing) that he is selling. If the prospect should ask questions concerning the property, the broker is prepared to answer these questions in detail. If the prospect is a stranger to the city, he can talk about the city, the cultural advantages, the beautiful scenery, the good fishing that may be had nearby, and any other thing that will point up the city advantageously. If the prospect is familiar with the city, then he can discuss the neighborhood in which the listing is located. If the prospect has children, the broker can drive past the school in order to show its location in relation to the home that he is about to show him.

After arriving at the home to be shown, the broker should not park his car directly in front of the property. He should park a few doors away and let the prospect walk to the house and up the front walk. In this way, the prospect is given the feel of the neighborhood—a feeling of belonging.

Once in the house, the broker or salesman should talk very little. Too many sales are ruined by salesmen who talk themselves out of a sale. If the prospect asks questions, the salesman should answer them thoroughly and intelligently. One important thing to remember is that real estate, like anything else, develops a jargon of its own. For example, the salesman is apt to think in terms of dry wall construction, poured concrete, and so forth. In answering questions of prospects, the salesman should avoid this jargon. Its usage is perfectly valid among other people in real estate, but never the prospects. Prospects may not understand what the salesman is speaking about and will not ask for an explanation for fear of showing what he may think to be his "ignorance." Some prospects may even feel that the jargon is being used in an attempt to "put something over" on them.

If the prospect seems dissatisfied with the property that has been shown him, then the prospect should be shown another property that will perhaps more closely fit his needs. If at all possible, the prospect should not be shown more than two or three homes at one time, or there will be too much possibility of confusion arising in the mind of the prospect. The good salesman will be able to sense the one property out of the three that have been shown that appeals most to the prospect. This ability to sense the right property, and consequently, the one to concentrate on, is done not by some mystic sixth sense, but by getting the prospect to talk. Generally, he will reveal his likes or dislikes about a certain property. If the prospect says that he wants to wait and think it over, the salesman should be sure to follow up on the prospect and give him a call as soon as possible after he has had a chance to make up his mind.

If the prospect is being shown an older house, the salesman should be familiar with its defects and try not to avoid them. If the house needs redecorating, for instance, he should keep in mind a fairly firm figure of the cost of redecoration. If the prospect objects on the ground that the house needs redecorating, the salesman should be informed of the cost.

Handling Objections

Objections to a sale must be met and overcome. Experience is the best teacher here, but there are some elementary rules that can be learned. The tendency on the part of the novice salesman is to try to argue the prospect out of the objection. This is a mistake that is fatal more often than not. As a basic rule, never argue with a prospect. Agree with him with a, "Yes, but. . . ."

Cheaper to Rent. A prospect may state that it is cheaper to pay rent than to buy, for example. The answer is, "Yes, but if you pay $100 per month rent, at the end of ten years you will have paid $12,000 out in rent, and you will have nothing to show for your money except a handful of rent receipts." This information should be in your sales kit so that you can actually show the prospect the cost of renting over a period of time.

Price Too High. Another objection is often that the price is too high. The prospect feels that the price of real estate will come down. You might point out to the prospect that, in general, real property values have increased over the past 50 years. You might also add that with our growing population there will be an ever-increasing demand for houses. This will have a tendency to force future prices up.

Often the objections will be trivial. In this case, the best thing to do is to brush over them lightly and then ignore them. Agree with the prospect and then proceed to more important features of the house. Generally, the prospect will not bring up the objection again. People have a great fear of being "sold" something; therefore, they will on occasion think of the trivial, which is usually just a defense mechanism.

Key Actions for Successful Selling

As reported in *Realtor's Headlines* [4] Dr. Charles L. Lapp, Professor of Marketing at the Washington (St. Louis) University School of Business suggests six key actions for someone to become successful during what he considers the "salesmen's decade." These are:

1. Have the proper viewpoint toward selling. Consider yourself a professional salesman and sell like a professional. Also have the proper viewpoint toward your superiors. Selling is a real art and being an art, salespeople should perfect their persuasive know-how through more practice.
2. Be organized to utilize your time and talents most effectively. Put some time on pre-call planning and specific pre-approach analysis to improve your face-to-face selling.
3. Conduct your sales interviews professionally. Sell your product properly and then ask the person to buy. Improve each phase of your sales interview from approach through follow-up activities.
4. Use tested selling strategies such as eye control, hesitating, and questioning. Dr. Lapp also believes that the "yes, but" technique should be replaced by the "I know how you feel, others have felt the same way, and now our customers have found thus and thus," technique.
5. Follow some fine lines in your face-to-face selling such as: being effectively persuasive and ineffectively high pressure; being effectively persistent and ineffectively a pest; and being effectively creative and ineffectively accused of trickery.

[4] *Realtor's Headlines,* Vol. 39 No. 2 (January 10, 1972).

6. Set up a program of self-analysis and self-improvement. He suggests you might, during a six-week period, learn at least five selling points; set up a work pattern for more efficiently covering existing clients; make a pre-call analysis of prospects; and read one book on selling or real estate every six weeks.

Dr. Lapp concluded by suggesting that salesmen make a point "to professionalize your selling by practice . . . practice . . . and more practice."

Closing the Sale

Closing the sale is the logical conclusion of all that has gone before. The proper listing, the proper qualification of the prospect, the proper showing of the property are all concluded in the closing. It is difficult to determine when the psychological moment has arrived. Most buyers have a fearful moment before they are ready to sign the sales agreement. The broker might ask the prospect when he would like possession of the property. By this means, he will be prodded into action. The broker should be calm and unafraid of the prospect or his reaction to the gentle prodding.

The prospect may not be willing to offer the listed price. If he offers a price lower than the listed price, accept it and explain that you will communicate his offer to the seller. Try to obtain as large a down payment as possible, especially if the offer is less than the listed price. The larger the down payment, the easier it will be to convince the seller of the sincerity of the offer and the more difficult it will be for the buyer to back out of the deal. Too many transactions are lost after a contract has been signed because only a small deposit has been made.

When the time comes for the signing of the earnest money receipt and purchase agreement (the binder as it is called in some states), explain the agreement in detail in order to prevent later discussion and misunderstanding of detail. In those states where the broker does not fill in the sales agreement, tell the purchaser that the binder will be delivered to the attorney for the seller who will draw the contract. Explain, too, that this formal contract can be read by the attorney for the purchaser and that his attorney will see that the transaction is carried through smoothly to completion.

SALES BY MEANS OF TRADES

A comparatively recent innovation is selling real estate by means of trades. In this respect the automobile industry is far ahead of the real estate industry. For many years auto dealcrs have been taking used cars in on trade. In most cases, the equity of the owner of the used car is used as a down payment on the new car. In the real estate business, however, most of the individuals owning an older home first find it necessary to sell the older home and then, with the cash equity received, make a down payment on a new or more expensive home. Trading in homes is an attempt to use the older home as the down payment much in the same manner as the auto dealers employ the used car in making a deal for the sale of a new car. In using trades in the sale of homes, however, it should be recognized that the sums involved are far greater than in the automobile transaction and the legal requirements make the transaction far more complex.

Basically there are three types of trades:

1. The simple trade. This is generally done with a builder and a prospect. For example, the builder has a house that he's selling for $20,000, and the prospect has a house worth $10,000 with a $5,000 mortgage. The builder agrees to take title to the $10,000 house and assume the $5,000 mortgage. The builder further agrees to allow the prospect his $5,000 equity in the older home as a down payment on the new $20,000 home.

2. The time allowance trade. Here a broker or builder agrees to sell a prospective buyer a certain home, provided the older home is sold within a stipulated time. If it isn't sold, the deal is off. For example, a broker with an exclusive listing on the home of *A* takes a contract from purchaser *B*, contingent upon his selling *B's* home within a stated time period. If the broker fails to sell *B's* home within the time, then *B* will not be held to the contract with *A*. Of course, all parties must be amenable to the transaction.

3. The trade-in guarantee. In this case, the broker agrees with a prospective buyer that if he fails to sell the older home within a certain specified period of time, he will take the old home at an agreed price.[5] Usually, and in order to protect himself, the broker guarantees

[5] On a national average, the broker exercises the guarantee in 3 out of 20 house sales, or in 15 percent of the cases.

the prospect between 80 and 90 percent of the appraised value of the home. For example, an older home appraised at $10,000 has a $6,000 mortgage, and the seller desiring a new home needs $2,000 for the down payment on the new home. The broker then agrees to take over the old home at $8,000 if he fails to sell the place within a stipulated time. This means that at the cnd of the time the broker can assume the $6,000 mortgage and pay $2,000 to the seller to enable him to purchase a newer home.

Often the broker can obtain refinancing on the older home with FHA help which enables him to make the deal without any cash out of pocket. Suppose the house has a $10,000 FHA appraised value. Suppose, too, that the broker has guaranteed $9,000 on the home which has a $6,000 mortgage. Under these circumstances, the broker hypothetically gets an $8,500 FHA loan on the older home, assuming a loan-to-value ratio of 85 percent to value. Out of the $9,000 he pays off the $6,000 existing mortgage and gives his seller $3,000 in cash, $500 of which is out of pocket. The seller uses this as the down payment on the newer home.

As a word of caution, this is a fairly complex type of business because of constant variations of FHA regulations, and the practitioner should regularly consult with local FHA officials on the amount that FHA will lend on such transactions.

In terms of homes traded, there has been a gradual growth of trading. It appears, however, that many lenders in FHA do not understand the workings of trade-in. Furthermore, too many lenders do not base their loan on their own appraised value. Frequently, they cut down the size of the loan because the trader has a lesser investment than the appraised value. In addition, where corporations are involved in trading because employees are transferred, they tend to use appraisers who are not familiar with the market where property is located.

When well organized and operated in an ethical manner, trade-in programs can be quite beneficial to both owners and brokers. Properly operated, they do play an important part in the whole real estate industry.

QUESTIONS FOR REVIEW

1. List the deterrents to buying as outlined in the text.
2. Why should the real estate broker be interested in learning the status of his mass market?
3. What are buying motives and how are they generally classified?
4. List four buying motives and explain whether they are rational or emotional motives.
5. Why is a knowledge of the listing (product) important in selling real estate?
6. List and explain the seven sources of prospects as outlined in the text.
7. What is meant by *qualifying a prospect*?
8. Why should the broker be interested in determining the needs of a prospect?
9. Distinguish between "helping a prospect buy" and "selling" a prospect. How does one help a prospect buy?
10. Why should a salesman avoid real estate jargon in the process of selling property?
11. How does a salesman avoid arguing with a prospect when the salesman and the prospect are in basic disagreement?
12. Why should a salesman attempt to obtain as large a down payment as possible when closing a sale?

PROBLEMS

1. Listed below are some of the factors a broker should analyze in terms of his prospect's needs in qualifying a prospect for a particular property. Study the list, then add to it other factors which should be included.

   (a) What kind of construction does the prospect desire? Brick .... Frame .... Other .....
   (b) One story or two story? .... (Maybe the prospect is ill and cannot, on doctor's orders, climb stairs.)
   (c) Can the husband drive? .... Can the wife drive? .... (Silly? But suppose the wife cannot drive and they have to be near transportation.)

(d) Children? No? .... Boys .... Girls .... Ages ..... (This is important because the prospect may want to be reasonably near schools or a school bus. It may also determine the number of rooms necessary.)
(e) If the prospect rents, how much rent does he pay? .... (You are trying to get an idea of the amount of monthly payment the prospect can afford. This, of course, doesn't tell the whole story.)
(f) Amount of maximum down payment available? ...... (This is the question that can often make or break a deal.)
(g) His church? .... (He would probably prefer a location near his church.)
(h) Any preferred location? .... (His friends might be located in one section of town and this may be most desirable for him.)

2. In selling real property, the prospect is apt to offer objections. Some will be serious and some can be ignored by the salesman. Below are several common objections to buying. Examine them and offer counter-arguments or suggestions to overcome the objections.
   (a) Prospect looks at a home, shakes his head sadly. "I like it," he says, "but I'm afraid of business conditions. I think the market is going to drop. If I wait, I won't lose any money."
   (b) "It's a good home," the prospect declares, "but the price is too high."
   (c) "I rather like the property," the prospect says, "but I'd like to talk it over with a friend and see what he says about it."

3. This problem involves a trade. A homeowner desires to purchase a home selling for $15,800, using an FHA-insured mortgage loan. This person now owns a home with an estimated value of $10,000 to $10,500. He owes $6,100 on the mortgage of his present home. Assume the FHA appraised valuation of the new home is $15,000, the FHA mortgage commitment is $14,350, the closing costs are $430, and prepayments are $140.

   Assume further that the FHA appraised valuation of the older home is $10,000, the seller's loan costs (discounts) are $400. How much cash is required on the new home? How much cash would be due the owners of the old home upon completion of the trade? [6]

[6] This problem was suggested by S. C. Bluh, President of the S. C. Bluh Company, mortgage bankers, Coral Gables, Florida.

SUGGESTED READINGS

Kirkpatrick, C. A. *Salesmanship,* 5th ed. Cincinnati: South-Western Publishing Co., 1971. Chapters 4 and 7.

McMichael, Stanley L. *How to Operate a Real Estate Business,* Rev. ed. Englewood Cliffs, New Jersey: Prentice-Hall, Inc., 1967.

Ring, Alfred A. *Real Estate Principles and Practices,* 7th ed. Englewood Cliffs, New Jersey: Prentice-Hall, Inc., 1972. Chapter 18.

The Real Estate Salesman's Handbook. Chicago: National Institute of Real Estate Boards, 1969. Sections 4-11.

Weimer, Arthur M., Homer Hoyt, and George F. Bloom. *Real Estate,* 6th ed. New York: The Ronald Press Company, 1972. Chapter 16.

Chapter 20

Advertising

Webster defines *advertising* as "The action of calling something (as a commodity for sale, a service offered or desired) to the attention of the public especially by paid announcements." In 1932, *Advertising Age* sponsored a contest to define advertising, and the winning definition was "The dissemination of information concerning an idea, service, or product to compel action in accordance with the intent of the advertiser."

THE FUNCTIONS OF ADVERTISING IN REAL ESTATE

Many brokers are apt to forget that advertising should be looked upon as an "assist" to selling. An advertisement can only *aid* in bringing about a sale; it cannot, in and of itself, create a sale. The question that must be raised by the broker is: How can I most effectively bring myself to the attention of a prospect?

In the real estate business the broker is faced primarily with a marketing problem. The sooner he realizes this, the greater will be his chance of success. Once he recognizes this truth, the broker should look upon advertising as having the functions of: (1) introducing the product to the market and (2) preparing the way for the sale of property.

To introduce the product to the market properly, it is necessary that the broker determine the market to be reached. In short, he must answer the question: Who will purchase the property? He should know the condition of the local real estate market and the prices that people can afford to pay for the property. He should prepare a market analysis (discussed in detail in Chapter 2). In other words, he should attempt to determine what price the greatest number of people in a given area can afford to pay for a home. Even a rough market survey may reveal that the earnings of the largest number of wage earners in an area are in the $8,500 per year income bracket. This would suggest that the mass market is in the $19,000-$21,000 home; consequently, the broker's advertising efforts might be directed toward this market.

The practical broker will not spend too much time and effort advertising a $60,000 home in an area having potential purchasers in the $18,000 home bracket. The experienced broker who gets a listing for a $60,000 home usually advertises it in the newspapers of the largest nearby city rather than in the local papers which go to residents in an $18,000 selling area.

The second major function of real estate advertising is that it prepares the way for the sale. In other words, the advertisement creates the contact between the broker and the potential buyer. It brings prospects into the broker's office, and, having done that, it has served its purpose. The rest depends on the quality of the product and the selling ability of the broker.

Here is a word of warning. The novice in real estate often expects too much from advertising. Advertising has a cumulative effect. Its favorable results have a tendency to build up over a long period of time. It not only brings people into the office to purchase, but the constant presentation of one's name to the public may bring tangible results in the form of listings and intangible results in the form of goodwill. In this sense, the goodwill lies in being known to the public.

TYPES OF REAL ESTATE ADVERTISING

Real estate advertising generally falls into three broad categories: goodwill, institutional, and specific advertising. All three types have definite purposes and are by their very nature limited in their scope and appeal.

The Goodwill Advertisement

The so-called *goodwill advertisement* is sometimes referred to as general advertising. The primary purpose of this type of advertising is to present and keep the broker's name before the public. Its effectiveness in terms of specific results is difficult, if not impossible, to evaluate. For example, if an advertisement is inserted in a program of a church benefit, it is generally done to present one's name to the public and not with the idea of promoting a specific piece of real estate. Any suburban broker will speak eloquently on the unproductiveness of this type of advertising, but it is just one of those things that *has* to be done by brokers in small communities.

Goodwill advertising may exist in the form of a name card inserted in the classified columns of a newspaper, for example, "KENNETH BROWN—INVESTMENT PROPERTIES." On page 496 is an example of goodwill advertising.

A card advertisement in a real estate trade journal circulated among investment property owners is an effective means of advertising for the broker interested in obtaining management properties. An insertion in this type of journal having a wide circulation among brokers, operators, and landlords is not only a goodwill advertisement but a general invitation to operators to investigate your investment properties. It is also an invitation for a co-brokerage participation in your listings.

This type of advertising may work in a dual capacity; namely, promoting goodwill and promoting *immediate* productive results.

The Institutional Advertisement

The *institutional advertisement* as it is employed in the field of real estate may best be thought of as a joint advertisement done by a board or group. The primary purpose of the advertisement is to promote confidence in the board or group, or it may be used by the group to promote confidence in a particular community.

An example of the institutional type of advertising was employed by a Long Island real estate group to instill the idea of the value to

the individual in owning his home. "If you rent," the advertisement read in part, "you will have nothing but a handful of rent receipts to show for your money at the end of twenty years."

It then went on to explain the price home that could be purchased by paying off at different rates on a mortgage instead of paying the equivalent amount in rent. This advertisement proved very effective in terms of sales among the group who ran the advertisement.

This type of advertising has been criticized by some who say that the figure taken as the mortgage payments does not take into account the maintenance, real property taxes, and insurance necessary to carry the building. On the other hand, this argument may be countered by the fact that at least part of the monthly payments on the property builds an equity in the property and is in the nature of forced savings, while the interest and the real property tax paid is deductible from the homeowner's income tax.

The Specific Advertisement

The *specific advertisement* is written and designed to sell a particular parcel of property. In most cases it is inserted in the classified columns of the local newspapers. This type of advertising may be considered as best illustrating the two functions of advertising: namely, introducing the product to the market and assisting the salesmen to contact the prospect.

ADVERTISING MEDIA

Advertising media may be defined as the means by which an advertisement is presented to the public. The most common forms of advertising media are newspapers, magazines, radio, and television.

Newspapers

The most important advertising medium for the real estate broker is the newspaper. About 80 percent of the average broker's advertising budget is spent on this medium. One study revealed that between 30 and 45 percent of the actual number of contacts and subsequently produced sales come from newspaper ads.[1]

When to Run Classified Advertising

Most classified advertising is done on Sundays, brokers feeling that this will result in more sales. However, research done at the University of Arizona by Professors Draper, Hansen, and Scott

[1] *National Real Estate and Building Journal.*

suggest that classified advertising on Sundays does not bring about the best results.[2] The purpose of the study was to measure the relative effectiveness of four different time periods within the week—Monday and Tuesday, Wednesday and Thursday, Friday and Saturday, and Sunday only.

"The results of the experiments suggest that weekdays rather than weekends afford greater response to classified advertisements on residential properties," they reported.

"Moreover, the pattern of response shows that the early part of the week is superior to midweek, which, in turn, is superior to the weekend for producing inquiries in the advertised properties," the researchers stated.

It appears that there are fewer advertisements run in the early part of the week and that these have less competition for readership on the part of prospective buyers than advertisements run on Sundays and the latter part of the week.

A recent study of media selection has indicated that national or even regional patterns do not exist for the most effective media.[3] The authors of the study tried to determine how Colorado home buyers select a particular real estate firm contrasted to similar findings in California and Connecticut. The results are summarized in the table below.

Effectiveness of Advertising Media

Media	Colo.	Conn.	Calif. 1	Calif. 2
"For Sale" signs	33.4%	10%	27.7%	50%
Newspaper ads	21.0	38	32.0	14
Referrals	19.1	26	30.0	16
Misc.	26.5	26	10.3	20

The California #2 study referred to above applies only to *new* homes which show a surprising 50 percent effectiveness from "For Sale" signs.

Fusilier and Richey concluded, among other things: "The effect of local factors on the real estate market carries important implica-

[2] As reported in *Realtor's Headlines*, Vol. 38, No. 7 (February 15, 1971).

[3] H. L. Fusilier and Clyde W. Richey, *What Is Effective Residential Real Estate Advertising*? Boulder, Colorado: Center for Real Estate and Land Use Studies, Business Research Division, University of Colorado, January, 1972.

tions for the broker's advertising program. The broker must accumulate accurate data as to the effectiveness of his advertisements, according to the type of property offered. His expenditures are too substantial to approach the problem haphazardly. (We found that the average firm spent approximately 20 percent of the total operating expenses, excluding commissions, for advertising.)

"Each broker must determine which advertising media is best for the specific types of property according to the characteristics of the market in his locality. Only by accumulating fairly extensive records on the responses received from his advertising program will the broker be able to make effective, and money-saving, decisions on advertising media." [4]

Buying Space. The term "buying space" is given to the purchasing of rights to advertise in newspapers. In most papers, space is purchased by the agate line. However, in most small towns advertising rates are usually quoted by the column inch. There are 14 lines to the column inch regardless of the size of the type that is employed, or how wide the column of the newspaper may be. An advertisement 2 inches deep and 1 column wide is 28 lines ($2 \times 14 \times 1$).

Rates. Generally, rates are set at so much per line, or as was previously mentioned, so much per column inch. For example, *The New York Times* charges by the line, and might quote a rate of $3.70 per line for a classified or display advertisement on the real estate page. In this case it would cost $51.80 an inch regardless of the size of the type employed. On the other hand, a small town paper might quote 4 cents per word or $3 per inch for a display advertisement.

Each newspaper has different rates which are set by the publisher. The rates of papers within a city are usually proportionate to their circulation. Thus, the larger the circulation of the paper, the higher the rate. Generally, newspapers have three rates that they offer prospective advertisers: the open rate, the quantity discount, and the time or frequency discount. The *open rate* is quoted to the occasional advertiser and generally is the highest rate. The *quantity discount* refers to a discount given an advertiser because of the number of lines he may use during a stated period of time. The *time*

---

[4] *Op. cit.*, p. 11.

or *frequency discount* refers to the number of times an advertisement is inserted. For example, the table below shows the difference between open rate and quantity and time discount charges.

QUANTITY DISCOUNTS	PER LINE	TIME DISCOUNTS	PER LINE
Open rate	$ .42	Open rate	$ .42
2,500 lines within one year	.39	13 times within one year	.39
5,000 lines within one year	.37	26 times within one year	.37
10,000 lines within one year	.33	52 times within one year	.33
20,000 lines within one year	.29		

Ordering Newspaper Space. The ordering of space is generally done in two steps. The first step involves entering into a *space contract*, which is an agreement as to the rate and the amount of advertising to be used by the advertiser. The second step is the actual insertion of the advertisement, which is called an *insertion order*.

Magazines and Real Estate Journals

Magazines and real estate journals are rarely used for advertising specific properties but are used to invite co-brokerage. They are excellent media for offering properties that might be purchased by operators or syndicate buyers. They are also good media for those brokers who are seeking to increase their management properties.

Every broker should be aware of the various trade journals and the groups by whom they are read. For example, many of the farm journals are excellent sources of farm sales, and the cost is not much greater in some instances than the cost of an advertisement in a local newspaper. Another example of the use of a trade journal is the trade journal circulated among people in the motel business. Many brokers having motels for sale find it profitable to advertise in this type of magazine. It is read by people interested in motels, and, in addition, it is employed by brokers all over the country with whom co-brokerage deals can very often be arranged.

Although strictly speaking a paper like *The Wall Street Journal* cannot be considered a trade journal, recognition should be given it in terms of advertising the higher-priced business and industrial properties. In addition, West Coast brokers have found it a profitable medium for the sale of high-priced ranch and farm properties. As it circulates throughout the country, although there is an East Coast and a West Coast edition, buyers may be obtained from without the locale of the property being advertised.

Window Display

Although most brokers in the country or suburban areas have the opportunity to use window displays with great effectiveness, this is probably the most poorly used of all the advertising tools that the broker has at hand. It costs virtually nothing to prepare an attractive window, but dusty and fly-specked windows seem to be the rule rather than the exception.

Pictures, for example, should be used to dress up a window, but they should not be allowed to remain there until dirty and yellow with age. Aside from the unattractiveness that will be brought about by old pictures, potential clients will receive the impression that the house is a "lemon" if the picture is allowed to remain in the window for any great length of time. As a general rule, a few attractive pictures seem to serve better than many. A small spotlight at night focusing attention on one particular photo has helped some brokers with their sales. Above everything else, the display should be changed frequently, and an attempt should be made to make the display as interesting and as attractive as possible.

Direct Mail

Direct mail, although an expensive form of advertising, has many uses for the real estate broker. This form of advertising is used to a large degree by country farm brokers who live near urban areas. Generally an advertisement is prepared and inserted in the classified column of a nearby city newspaper. The advertisement states that a free catalog or list of farm properties will be mailed by the broker on request. These brokers generally have their listings prepared in a form ranging from mimeographed material to a well-planned and well-printed catalog. Once the broker has received requests for a catalog, he has a ready-made mailing list to which further listings can be sent. As in the case of all mailing lists, care should be taken to prevent the list from becoming inactive. If a list brings only a few results in the form of inquiries, then the persons who fail to respond after several mailings should be weeded out. The names of any persons whose mail is returned for lack of forwarding address should also be eliminated.

Methods of Obtaining Lists. In addition to obtaining mailing lists as described above, one of the most effective, but sadly neglected, ways is by obtaining the names and addresses of any prospects that call at the office. These names should be classified in terms of price bracket interest. For example, a prospect calls at the office in answer to a newspaper advertisement for a $20,000 home, but he does not like the particular listing offered. The prospect's name and address should be obtained, and an attempt should be made to obtain a listing in the $20,000 bracket that might be satisfactory. As soon as this is done, a letter should be written to the prospect informing him of the new listing together with all pertinent details. After all, the secret of success in real estate is the matching of the available listings with the wants and desires of the prospects.

Presumably the broker will have studied the advertisements of his competitors, and presumably he will know other local brokers who might have the listing the client desires. If this is true, then the thing to do is to contact the fellow broker and work out a co-brokerage deal with him. "Half a loaf is better than none."

Another method of obtaining a mailing list, especially for brokers in small towns, is to watch the newspaper announcement of weddings. A courteous letter should be sent to the newlyweds suggesting that in the event they desire a new home, you might be able to help them. Although this may not bring too many immediate results, it may pay off in the long run. Your name as a broker will be uppermost in their minds; and if they ever want a house in the future, they may come to you for help.

Various Uses for Direct Mail. Direct mail has other uses for the alert broker. It is used to a very large degree to invite co-brokerage. Usually a listing is run off on a mimeograph machine or is printed by means of the photo-offset process and mailed to a number of brokers. The list is generally obtained from the classified section of the telephone directory.

A list of operators will be obtained by the alert broker. These are people who buy and sell investment properties hoping to make a profit on a change of price, or often they will keep a property for investment purposes if the percentage of return is high enough. The names of operators are obtained either by word of mouth or from the advertisements of the operators themselves. Listings that might appeal to this type of purchaser should be prepared and mailed to them.

By far the largest users of direct mail are those brokers involved in the sale of industrial real estate. For example, if a broker decides he has an industrial listing suitable as a manufacturing plant for plumbing supplies, then he will prepare a brochure describing the property and use direct mail as a means of contacting plumbing supply manufacturers. Generally, his list will be prepared from either a trade organization directory or *Thomas' Register*, a directory of manufacturers.

Radio and Television

In recent years radio and television as media for advertising have been used with increasing effectiveness by real estate brokers. Most of the advertising is used to keep the broker's name before the public rather than to sell a specific property. In general, brokers successfully use station break announcements, one-minute announcements, or special features.

The Federal Communications Commission requires that all stations identify themselves every half hour. This has led to the practice of shaving off 20 to 30 seconds from 15-minute shows. Thus, in addition to providing time for the station to identify itself, the station sells the remaining time for brief announcements.

The one-minute announcements which are also sold by stations enable the advertiser to employ a commercial of about 125 words in length, and they have been employed by some brokers for the purpose of selling specific properties. This usage has, for the most part, been limited to rural areas.

The special features used by real estate brokers are usually news reports, weather forecasts, and market reports.

It might be added that most of the use of the radio by real estate brokers is typically done in rural areas. It is in the cities that television has found most of its use among brokers. Usually, the brokers who employ television are developers or subdividers. In these cases, pictures of model houses or of the subdivision are flashed on the screen with a brief announcement stressing their desirable features.

Outdoor Advertising

The outdoor or billboard type of advertising is generally an institutional advertisement in the real estate field. A local broker's board will pay the cost of advertising for the town or city with the purpose in mind of building confidence in the city, or the board of brokers may advertise a Red Cross drive as a public service. However, this type of advertising is often used by an individual in the nature of a specific advertisement. Developers of country and summer homes often use billboard advertising. The billboards are strategically located along main arteries of travel leading toward the development. The billboards contain pictures of the development along with a statement as to the distance of the development.

Broadly speaking, the "For Sale" sign may be classified as outdoor advertising. With the results related to cost, this is probably the most effective type of advertising.

It is suggested that when a property is sold, a "Sold" sign be placed over the "For Sale" sign. This sort of thing will make for more effective public relations for the selling broker.

GENERAL ADVERTISING RULES

Attract Attention

The advertisement must attract attention before it will be read; it must be eye-catching. However, a broker must use discretion in choosing eye-catching pictures so that they will be in good taste. There must be a close kinship between the picture or illustration and the text of the ad.

Hold Attention

It is all very well for the broker to attract attention in his advertising copy, but it is perhaps even more important for him to *hold* the attention of the reader. To hold attention and arouse the interest of the reader, the advertisement should:

1. Be written in the present tense whenever possible. This makes the reader experience the act as he reads the copy.

2. Use pictorial nouns and descriptive adjectives. Create a picture in the reader's mind so that he can identify himself with the story that is being told.

3. Use short, simple-sentence construction. Punctuation should be adequate and carefully done.

4. Use a vigorous, flowing style.

Repetition

As a general rule most advertising is repetitious; however, real estate advertising is peculiar in this respect. If the same advertisement for the same house is repeated in the same form too many times, the reader will receive the impression that the house is difficult to sell and that there will eventually be a reduction in price. In other words, repetition of the advertisement may defeat its purpose. One should try not to keep the same form more than twice running; he should change it, break up the copy, and reword it or even create entirely new copy.

Honesty

Is the advertisement honest? Every broker should raise this question to himself before submitting an advertisement for publication. Dishonesty in advertising is not only unsound ethically, but it may prove to be an economic catastrophe. Real estate brokers have had a difficult time living down the dishonest and misleading advertisements written in the past by some of their colleagues. Nothing can cause the loss of a sale faster than a dishonest advertisement. It may bring people into the office filled with great expectations, but it will only cause them to leave filled with great apprehension.

A California study revealed something even more serious resulting from what prospects considered misleading advertising. In cases where the prospect *thought* the ad was misleading, 40 percent of the prospects absolutely eliminated the offending broker from any future transactions.

The Buyer's Viewpoint

It is axiomatic in the marketing of any product that the advertising of the product must be approached from the viewpoint of the potential buyer. What the broker thinks regarding the property is of little importance. More corporations have failed in their selling campaigns because of the sales egotism of the management than from any other cause. An agent should not become so enthusiastic over the house that he fails to see it through the eyes of the potential buyer. And he should not take the opposite view of looking at a house and say to himself, "I wouldn't pay a dollar for that shack." Nobody cares what you, as an individual, would do. That shack might look like a palace in the eyes of a buyer.

It should not be taken for granted that a buyer can see the merits in a house as well as the agent. The merits of the property should be made known in the advertisement and should be instilled in the buyer's mind even before he sees the building.

ADVERTISING APPEALS

Basically, advertising is designed to appeal to two broad classes of motives or reasons why people buy. The motives upon which the advertiser seeks to play are emotional motives or rational motives, generally a combination of both.

Jackson points out that research by television and radio advertisers suggests that the twelve most "selling words" are: "you, money, save, new, results, health, easy, safety, love, discovery, proven, guarantee." [5]

Emotional Motives

Emotional motives are those that lead a person to react in a certain way in response to a specific set of stimuli without consciously bringing into play logical analysis of the situation. A photograph of a pretty girl in a bathing suit to advertise summer cottages, for instance, is a common type of advertising presenting an emotional appeal. To choose the most effective emotional appeal for a specific purpose, one must exercise great care. There are many of these emotional appeals, the most common of which are discussed below.

---

[5] Herbert T. Jackson, "Every Word Counts in Ads That Pay," *Realtor's Headlines,* Quarterly Magazine Section, Vol. 30, No. 1 (January 7, 1963), p. 1.

Pride. One of the basic human needs is the need for shelter. It might be said then that any building that will keep us warm and dry should be sufficient to supply our housing needs. But this is not the case. *Pride* is one of our strongest emotions and makes us want something more than we actually require. The practicing real estate broker knows that when he has a house listed in an outstanding neighborhood, he has the house almost sold, provided the price is right. If the broker has an "exclusive" on such a property, he should not hesitate to advertise the neighborhood. The words "good neighborhood" or "high class" neighborhood in the advertisement are not enough. Play up the neighborhood. It appeals to the pride of the prospect to live in the best area that he can afford. Use such words as "High Street Section" or "Roe Park" in the advertisement. This pinpoints the property in the mind of the reader and enables him to imagine the delights and benefits of living in a so-called "high class" neighborhood.

Emulation. *Emulation* may best be described as "keeping up with the Joneses." It is somewhat connected with pride. It seems to be human nature to want to conform to the actions of the leaders of the "crowd." In presenting an advertisement designed to appeal to the desire to emulate, the advertiser should stress modern up-to-date features. For example, nationally advertised kitchen fixtures should be emphasized in presenting a home, the implication being that this is the kind of kitchen the "Joneses have."

Comfort. People want a home instead of a shack in which to live because of their desire for comfort. A man visualizes himself toasting his toes before a fireplace, his pipe stuck in his mouth, and his thoughts at peace with the world. If a listing has any of the features that might appeal to comfort, the broker should stress them. A fireplace, gas heat, air conditioning, or other things in a modern home that make living easier should be featured in the advertising.

Love for Children. Parental love is one of the strongest of all the human emotions. Everyone wants his children to have the best. Many city dwellers believe that the country is the best place to raise children. Every married man wants his family to enjoy good health. The real estate broker should take a tip from this and advertise his properties accordingly.

A broker might advertise a summer cottage in a city newspaper with the headline: "Is your family's health worth $500? Only $500 down and $25 a month insures healthful summer living for you and your family."

Parents want their children to have good schooling and religious upbringing. A broker will stress in his advertising the nearness of schools along with the availability of churches and shopping centers.

It should be proved to the reader of the advertisement that the home being offered will make a child happier, healthier, and more efficient. The broker who can do this has the house half sold. A lesson might be learned from the typical approach of the encyclopedia salesman. If there are children in the home, the approach is through them by pointing out to the proud parent that books of the type he is offering will help educate the children.

Security. The desire for security is present in each of us. Most of the advertisements promoting the "family farm" play upon the desire for security. The idea is that no matter what happens to the economy, inflation or depression, the owner of the farm can be sufficient unto himself. The headline of this type of advertising generally reads "Compact Security Farm" or "Ideal Retirement Farm." It is to fulfill this desire for security that one finds more and more city dwellers migrating to the country with ever-increasing opportunities for the broker who handles any sort of agricultural properties.

Fear. Although advertisements instilling fear have no true place in the advertising of real estate, they have been used rather effectively in some parts of the country and are, therefore, important enough to bear mention here, if only to discourage their use.

Rational Motives

Rational motives are those motives for buying that involve a form of conscious reasoning. The prime use of rational motives in real estate advertising is found in the promotion of investment properties. However, it should be remembered that the rational advertisement can also be employed in advertising residential properties. When effectively combined with emotional appeals, rational appeals can aid greatly in selling real estate. A discussion of some of the more common rational motives follows.

Economy. Businessmen or investors in property are vitally interested in the answer to one major question; namely, how much will this property net? They are, therefore, interested in economy of purchase and economy in use. In an investment property, therefore, the amount of cash needed to close the deal should be advertised. Investors are interested in net returns on cash invested; they are not so interested in the purchase price of the property. Advertise the net return, or if you have the proper listing, use an eye-catching headline that would appeal to the investor, such as, FOUR TIMES RENT. This means that there will be a return of 25 percent on the money invested and that the buyer's cash investment will be returned to him in four years.

The idea of economy in use is employed both in advertising designed to promote investment properties and in advertising to sell residential properties. For example, when a broker mentions that a house is insulated, he is trying to put forth the idea that the insulation not only makes the house warmer but also reduces the cost of fuel.

Convenience. Convenience as a motive is used to a large degree in the sale of homes, and also in the rental of apartments and lofts, or buildings to be used for factory purposes. An advertisement reading, "One Minute to School, One Minute to Churches, and Three Minutes to a Bus Stop," might be the deciding factor in the sale of a home.

Nearness to transportation can very well be a decisive factor in the rental of an apartment. The breadwinner of the family wants to live in a place where he can get to his job quickly. He wants to do it without changing his mode of transportation. A recent advertisement emphasizing this was very successful in renting apartments in suburban New York. In order to reach many of the apartment houses in that area it is necessary to take first the subway and then the bus. One clever display advertisement pictured men waiting in the rain while making the changeover from the subway to the bus. It pointed out that there were no changes in transportation necessary to reach the apartment advertised.

The question of transportation is of vital importance to renters of lofts and factory space. Factory help is easier to obtain if the loft is located near suitable transportation. The ease of transportation should be emphasized in this type of advertising because experienced factory managers will shun property not located near suitable transportation.

Enhancement of Earnings. Enhancement of earnings is another type of rational appeal. If the property is an investment property in the nature of an apartment house, or if it is a business opportunity like a grocery store and if the present owner is not receiving as much in net returns as he should, then this should be pointed out in the advertisement. Perhaps a new landlord could get higher rentals with the installation of certain improvements, or perhaps the owner of the grocery store has been ill so that the earnings as shown on the books do not reflect the true potential of the business. In cases such as these the information as to the causes of the low earnings should be emphasized in the advertisement.

Special Appeals to Women

Truer words were never spoken: "Never underestimate the power of a woman." Women are interested in social status and "high class" neighborhoods. If a listing has any special features at all, advertise them. A kitchen with built-in appliances, a bath with lavatory, a dishwasher and disposal, wall-to-wall carpeting are the things that attract women buyers, and these, then, are the things that should be advertised. This may make the difference between an advertisement that pulls and one that fails.

Novelties

Novelties have their place in the advertising of real estate. The forms of these are numerous, ranging from calendars to record books. Some brokers employ them to promote goodwill after a sale has been made. A gift of a wallet with "Thanks—Paul B. Larsen, Real Estate" inscribed on it will bring both the buyer and the seller into the office for aid in any of their future needs. The important thing in employing novelties is that they must be in good taste.

COPY AND LAYOUT

Copy consists primarily of plotting out and writing the advertisement. A decision on the appeals to be used and the approach to be followed is made; then these are put into words. *Layout* refers to the form in which the final advertisement will appear.

Paragraphs

The paragraphs in an advertisement should be short and to the point. Each paragraph should be indented and not kept flush with the preceding paragraph. In order to make the advertisement more readable, it should be double leaded between paragraphs. In essence this means that there should be more space between the paragraphs than between the lines within the paragraphs. The amount of space left between lines will depend upon the type size, the legibility of the type face, and the length of line used.

Copy Blocks

The *copy block* refers to the width of the copy. It should not be too wide in relation to type size. As a general rule, larger type sizes are used at the beginning of the advertisement and gradually drop to the smaller type size.

Subheads

Subheads or subheadlines are used to break up copy and to lend better appearance to the body of the advertisement.

Type Size

The size of type should be as large as is consistent with the copy length. More important than the size of the type is the question of whether the copy holds interest. If it does hold interest, then a smaller type size can be used than is ordinarily indicated.

White Space

White space when used effectively can arrest the attention of the reader. The copywriter should not employ white space unnecessarily, however, for every unnecessary line of white space prevents the addition of copy that might be considerably more effective than the white space itself.

Artwork

Because the real estate broker employs classified advertising more often than display advertising, he does not often use artwork to illustrate his ad. However, when artwork is used, the broker should keep in mind that it is not used for decoration; it is used fundamentally to illustrate and substantiate the story that is being told in the advertisement.

Headlines

Headlines designed to attract attention seem to be the most difficult part of the advertisement to write. They must be eye-catching, have punch, and at the same time must not be too trite. The approach should be different, but not too different. Only a very few of us can get away with advertisements that are too unusual or too far out of the ordinary.

It should be noted that even a headline having punch and eye appeal will lose its effectiveness if it is too crowded. Use plenty of white space as a device for making the headline stand out. The following portions of advertisements are some examples of effective and attractive headlines.

JONES PARK
an
INVITATION
to
LUXURY

If you appreciate finer living, this is your opportunity to realize your finest dreams. . . .

Appeal of Luxury

Economy of Purchase

> IT'S MAGIC: LIKE A RABBIT
> OUT OF A HAT!
>
> Try to Duplicate This:
>
> (A description of the property follows.)

The above headline is not only eye-catching, but also makes a subtle appeal to economy of purchase.

a. *Durability.*	SOLID BRICK HOME
b. *Convenience.*	Convenient to Everything
	! We Dare You !
c. *Economy of Purchase.*	We dare you to compare this home with any other in this price class in Coeur d'Alene. Check this list and see it for yourself.
d. *Durability.*	1. All-brick ranch type.
e. *Possible Appeal to Women.*	2. Beautifully landscaped.
f. *Easier Housekeeping.*	3. Six rooms, all on one floor.
g. *Love of Comfort.*	4. Log-burning fireplace.
h. *Convenience.*	5. Three bedrooms.
i. *Love of Luxury.*	6. Two modern tiled baths.
j. *Love of Recreation.*	7. Finished recreation room in basement.
k. *Economy in Use.*	8. Completely insulated.
l. *Easy Credit.*	9. Check this price; not $60,000, not $45,000, but only $39,500, terms.

Remember that business property advertisements should be designed to improve the pocketbook of the prospective purchaser. The following headline is an example.

Enhancement of Earnings

> "KEY TO SUCCESS"
> The right location at the right price
> —4 stores on busy corner.

Completeness in the Advertisement

Advertising, like anything else, if done at all, should be done properly. Too many brokers are penny-wise and pound-foolish in this regard. The broker should put into his advertising copy whatever is necessary to help effect the sale. A nickel or a dime saved here and there by unintelligible abbreviations may very well lose a sale. Too little copy is often a mistake.

As an example, compare the two advertisements shown below which advertise the same property. The advertisement by Mr. Willsey won first prize in a contest of the New York Realtors. The first line is eye-catching; there are no hackneyed phrases and abbreviations. The advertisement is complete and attractive.

THE MOST PRICELESS
thing in America today is privacy for family living. Situated on 100 x 120 lot on the crest of a hill and framed by 47 big white pines is this gorgeous 7-room brick and frame split-level home. Gas heat, attached garage. An appealing place for $37,500. Call 421-8701 today for appointment.

REALTOR
CARL A. WILLSEY
225 W. Church St., Elmira, N. Y.

7-rm. brick & frame house, gas heat, att. gar. 100 x 120 lot. $37,500. Call 421-8701 for appt.

Carl A. Willsey, Elmira, New York

The idea of completeness in the advertisement is illustrated below.[6]

Say something descriptive like this:	*Instead of saying these cut-and-dried things:*
White picket fence surrounds yard studded with palm trees	Landscaped lot
Furniture fits comfortably in 20 × 24 living room	Large living room
Compact one-car garage	Garage
White clapboard house	Frame house

[6] *St. Petersburg Times,* St. Petersburg, Florida.

Cream brick, 6-apartment
building .... Good 6 flat

For practice the reader might rewrite some of the cut-and-dried classified ads that constantly appear in our daily newspapers with the above sort of thing in mind, eliminating such surplus verbiage as "must be seen to be appreciated."

THE MUSTS AND THE MUST NOTS

There are certain things that an effectively written ad should contain, and there are certain factors surveys suggest should not be contained in a real estate ad. The factors that should be included are location, price, financing, and physical characteristics. It is therefore suggested that ads be built around these factors.

In general, ads have been criticized as being too flowery, deceptive, and lacking sufficient information. It has also been found that copy place abbreviations are particularly offensive to buyers. Prospects are entitled to ads that provide precise information on location, facilities, physical characteristics, price, and financing. Advertisements should be designed to be helpful, not confusing.

The Follow-up Card

It is good business practice for the real estate broker to use the follow-up card when running an advertisement. This type of card, printed on an ordinary postal card, is illustrated on page 516. It has a good psychological effect on the seller and indicates an interest in his property. In addition, there is a possibility of obtaining additional listings as a result of the satisfied client showing the card.

PUBLICITY

Successful publicity campaigns are possible because of that queer quirk of human nature that makes all of us want to be "in on the know." Paid advertising is publicity in the strict sense of the word; however, we have reference here specifically to what is commonly called a "reading notice." This type of publicity is not paid for and in some ways is even better than paid advertising.

YES! Your Property Is Being Advertised

Here Is A Copy of Some Current Advertising

You can rest assured that consistent advertising and recommendation of your Real Estate is being made at all times to consummate a quick, satisfactory sale.

ARNOLD REALTY CO.

Fred B. Arnold, Realtor — Phone 376-6679

Brokers have a specialized knowledge of which the public as a whole is unaware. A broker should not hide his talent, for modesty does not often become the broker. Therefore, the up-to-date broker will not hesitate in sending to newspapers articles concerning the property transactions in which he has recently been engaged. The following sections present some basic ideas on publicity.

Releases

A *release* is the name given to the information sent to the newspapers. The word "release" should be written in the upper right-hand corner of the news story. In the event that it is desirable to have the story published as soon as possible, then under the word "release" the statement "For immediate release" should be written. If for some reason a delay in the release is necessary, then the words "Not to be released before January 5" should be typed under the word "release." This is important especially if the story has been sent to a number of papers, and it is desired that they all be given an equal chance at the feature.

Contents. The difficult problem involved in any press release is creating a story that will be newsworthy. It is a relatively simple matter to get publicity regarding a new development in a small community, but it is difficult to receive mention of an event so prosaic as the sale of a single house. Make the release newsworthy; the editor of a newspaper attempts to fill the paper with news and not with the mere mention of the broker's name. Try, for example, to find out some historical event concerning the building that is sold; or if it is a new property, perhaps the land was once a part of the farm belonging to a noted personage of the village; or perhaps some historic event of local interest occurred in the vicinity. Anything that will attract it to the eye of the editor who is receiving the release is important. Perhaps the seller might have an unusual reason for selling the property; if so, be sure to point up the unusual reason in the copy for the story.

The Form. The form of the news release is extremely important. A release has more chance of publication if it is brief and to the point than if it is long and rambling. The lead paragraph is the important paragraph in any newspaper story. The first paragraph should contain the essence of the entire story so that if the editor desires, he may cut the rest of the release without losing the "meat" of the story. The remainder of the release contains the details designed to complement the first paragraph. Be sure to mention your name in this first paragraph because, after all, this is what you really want the public to see and notice. Study the example below.

Release

For Immediate Release

The home of Mr. and Mrs. James Johnson, 289 Ocean Avenue, located near the site of the city's first grist mill, has been sold to Frank Smith, it was announced today by James Jones, real estate broker.

(A story about the mill follows this.)

If the releases are not always printed, do not become discouraged. Keep sending them to the papers and sooner or later one of them will be printed, if for no other reason than that the editor just happens to need something to fill up the space in his paper.

ADVERTISING CHECKLIST

1. Is it eye-catching? ______
2. Is it honest? ______
3. Has it been repeated too many times in the same form? ______
4. Does it appeal to:
   a. Pride? ______
   b. Desire to emulate? ______
   c. Comfort? ______
   d. Love for children? ______
   e. Security? ______
   f. Fear? ______
   g. Economy of use? ______
      (1) Economy of purchase? ______
      (2) Enhancement of earnings (investment)? ______
5. Is it written from the buyer's viewpoint? ______
6. Does it have special appeals to women? ______
   a. Modern kitchen? ______
   b. Modern bath? ______
   c. Automatic washer? ______
   d. Garbage disposal unit? ______
   e. Automatic dishwasher? ______
   f. Other love of luxury? ______

QUESTIONS FOR REVIEW

1. What are the two functions of real estate advertising?
2. What is meant by the *cumulative effect* of advertising?
3. Describe the three types of advertising.
4. Distinguish between rational and emotional motives of advertising.
5. Give three examples each of emotional motives and rational motives in advertising.
6. List and discuss three types of advertising media.
7. Why should the advertising of investment properties be of the rational type?
8. Explain two methods of building up lists for direct mail.
9. Discuss the general rules of advertising.
10. How is outdoor advertising usually used by a real estate broker?
11. What is meant by *layout* and *copy*?
12. What is meant by the *buyer's viewpoint?*
13. Why is it important that a publicity release be newsworthy?

14. Is there any relationship between a paid advertisement and so-called publicity; if so, what is it?
15. How should enhancement of earnings be used in real estate advertising?

PROBLEMS

1. Listed below are several typical lines of copy from real estate ads. For each line of copy identify the market segment you feel the copy would be most likely to reach; identify the appeal which makes the copy effective; or rewrite the copy to make it more effective.
   (a) $99 total closing costs with VA financing.
   (b) If you're handy with tools, here's an older home you can have fun with.
   (c) Economy plus luxury. An excellent buy at only $42,500.
   (d) Five bedrooms. Close to schools and parks. Excellent home for a growing family.
   (e) If you really want to get the maximum square footage for the money, you must see this two-story beauty.
   (f) At the end of a dead-end street.
2. On this page and the next are advertisements from the real estate section of various papers and journals. Analyze them in terms of their appeals, using the checklist given on page 518.

SHARONVILLE PISGAH

WHY WAIT? YOU CAN BUY NOW!

FOR A LIMITED TIME WE CAN OFFER THE FOLLOWING FINANCING ON THESE NEW HOMES IN

WESTCHESTER GLEN

- **20% Down, 25 Years**
- **8% Annual Percentage Rate**
- **No Closing Cost** • **No Pre-Payment Penalty**

Three and four bedroom homes of superior quality and workmanship . . . priced from high $40's. Example: $50,000 purchase price; $10,000 down; 300 monthly payments of $308.73 (principal and interest). No closing costs!

OPEN TODAY 1-6

DIRECTIONS: From 275 take Mason-Sharonville exit North (Route 42) to Pisgah; left on Westchester Road to Westchester Glen.

777-5166 NORV ROBERTS 777-2184

the WALTON co

7

UNBELIEVABLE

52 beautiful level-to-rolling grass acres in El Paso's lower valley. $11,750 total. $100 down, $60 month, no interest, no other costs. **Call owner, Harlan O'Leary (915) 565-1428; evenings, (915) 751-8576. 3233 N. Piedras, El Paso, Texas 79930.**

8

PLEASANT RIDGE #930

LOOKING FOR FIRST HOME?

Darling two bedroom all brick home on dead end street. Full size dining room, eat-in kitchen, beautiful private rear yard. Don't miss this one at $18,900. Call now for private showing 793-2121.

9

HYDE PARK

Charm & Location

An attractive, well maintained and tastefully decorated older home on one of Hyde Park's most desirable streets. Living room with woodburning fireplace, formal dining room, modern, appealing and fully equipped kitchen, breakfast room, large pleasant porch, carpeting downstairs. Four bedrooms, paneled basement recreation room.

RUTH HALL

561-4140 561-5800

Comev & Shepherd

12

MOBILE HOME PARK

Under construction in prime location. Present gross $2000 mo. Estimated $7500 per mo. when completed. Will sell for part interest.

BY OWNERS 831-6616 IF NO ANSWER 683-1411 or 831-7831

10

APT. COMPLEX — West Palm Beach, near ocean and intercoastal. $170,000. Net income $26,000. Financing arranged. Send replies to Box E-238, The Enquirer.

11

SUGGESTED READINGS

Case, Frederick E. *Real Estate,* Rev. ed. Boston: Allyn and Bacon, 1962. Chapter 23.

Ring, Alfred A. *Real Estate Principles and Practices,* 7th ed. Englewood Cliffs, New Jersey: Prentice-Hall, Inc., 1972. Chapter 20.

Weimer, Arthur M., Homer Hoyt, and George F. Bloom. *Real Estate,* 6th ed. New York: The Ronald Press Company, 1972. Chapter 16.

Chapter 21

Real Property Management

Real property management, like other areas of management, involves a great deal of decision making. When property is entrusted to the professional manager, he is on his own in the sense that he must make a profit for his principal or he will fail to survive in the highly competitive world. To this end, many feel that the management specialist must often employ a greater combination of skills than in most other areas of the real estate business. Recognizing the need for specialists, in addition to awarding the CPM (Certified Property Manager) designation to those qualified, the Institute of Real Estate Management of the NATIONAL ASSOCIATION OF REALTORS has broadened its educational program to prepare better qualified men for this ever-expanding field.

THE BACKGROUND OF REAL PROPERTY MANAGEMENT

Although of comparatively recent origin, the management of real property has assumed a tremendous role in the real estate business. The property manager must have a vast background in real estate and business to enable him to do the job properly. He must be many things in one: he must be able to sell and to negotiate; he must have a knowledge of advertising; he must possess a wealth of information concerning the fundamentals of engineering. He must, in addition, be a practical economist, with the ability to forecast the value of rental space and to convert these forecasts into leases that will afford the greatest return to his principal.

The Development of Management

The field of real property management has developed as a result of three major factors. First, the increase of absentee ownership resulting from the real estate investor has caused an increased interest in management. Although many property owners operate and manage their own properties, there are many more who own property as an investment and cannot or do not desire to be burdened with the problems of management. Consequently, these burdens have been passed on to those who specialize in management, often with the result that these specialists are able to operate the property more efficiently, thus increasing the earnings of the owners.

A second reason for the increase in management is the result of the increase in corporate and syndicate ownership in investment-type properties that lend themselves to management. Here again the individual members of the corporation or the syndicate would find it difficult, if not impossible, to run the properties themselves.

A third reason for the increase in management has resulted as an indirect outgrowth of the depression of the thirties. Banks and other financial institutions found themselves with more and more properties on their hands as a result of mortgage foreclosures. At first, one of the members of the bank staff was generally appointed to take care of these properties. The concept was, of course, that management was limited to the collection of rents. These special appointees of the financial institutions in many cases soon found, however, that the management of property was outside their scope, and more and more specialists were sought to handle this type of business.

The Scope of Management

Approximately 2.74 percent of our national income consists of rentals from real estate. Indirectly these rental properties furnish a substantial portion of our national income in the form of expenditures for maintenance and wages. In addition, large sums are paid by property owners to municipalities for the operation of municipal governments. In what ways, then, do real property managers become involved in this vast and varied economic activity?

Residential Buildings. To a very small degree management is involved in caring for and making available a fair return to the owners of single-family units. However, management's major function in the residential field is concerned with the operation of multiple dwellings whether they be individually owned, partnership owned, or corporate or syndicate owned. Recently, more institutions seeking a fair return on their money have turned to real estate investment in the form of institutionally owned residential properties which are turned over to management concerns or sometimes operated by their own specialists in the field of real property management.

Although much controversy rages about the Housing Act of 1949, the fact remains that since its enactment, there has been an increase in the number of public housing units in the United States. These public housing units have employed the aid of property managers and provide a source of employment of professional managers seeking government jobs.

Commercial Property. Primarily, *commercial property* may be categorized as store property and office buildings. It is within these categories that we find one of the most active aspects of property management.

Store Property. Generally, *store properties* are considered as buildings of one or two stories in height. The ground floor is usually occupied by retail establishments; the second story is devoted to office space.

Typically, the retail-office type of store is an outgrowth of the so-called "taxpayers" which were first built during the waning years of the depression. Although this type of property has always been important to managers of real property, it is felt that it will become increasingly more important with the present trend toward controlled shopping centers and other types of shopping centers being constructed in suburban areas.

Office Buildings. Although most office buildings have their ground floors devoted to store space and many store properties have their second stories devoted to office space, the *office building* is distinguished by the fact that it has many stories, that it is generally located in downtown sections of cities, and that its primary purpose is the rental of space for office use.

Many of the larger office buildings are operated under the supervision of the owner who, besides having a building manager, may also have a legal staff to prepare leases and handle other pertinent legal details. There remains, however, a large segment of existing office buildings operated by management concerns.

Industrial Property. As was stated previously, office buildings in the larger cities usually are in the downtown sections. When this is true, the office building section is usually surrounded by an industrial section. Although many of the larger industrial establishments are operated by their owners, most of the smaller establishments are rented and provide a fertile field for the property manager.

These industrial properties often take the form of storage buildings, warehouses, and the so-called "loft" buildings tenanted by manufacturers engaged in light industry. For the most part, those real estate concerns engaged in industrial management of this type specialize also in the rental of these types of properties.

Is Management Justified?

The question often arises in the minds of some as to the justification of the management process. This is the same question that frequently arises in connection with the function of the middleman in the field of marketing. Many people feel that the existence of the middleman is not justified; and, by the same token, they feel that the existence of the professional real property manager is not justified. The critics of the middleman are reminded of the axiom that "you can get rid of the middleman, but you cannot get rid of his functions." It is felt that this is equally true concerning the professional manager. In most cases he is able to operate more efficiently than the individual owner. For example, he is able to buy maintenance supplies in larger quantities than the individual and thus take advantage of quantity discounts that can be passed on to the owner. He very often is able to employ his labor more efficiently than the individual owner. He may have one man working in a number of different buildings rather than have the employee waste his time which he might very well do while working for an individual with a comparatively small investment property.

Management is a highly specialized field and can more often than not operate buildings more efficiently than can individual owners. Efficient operation appears to be the keystone of management justification. When the operation is done efficiently, the critics of management seem to have no more valid argument than do the critics of the middleman.

The efficiency of the professional manager may be demonstrated by the Institute of Real Estate Management's annual listings that show net vacancy rates. While the rates are averages, they show that professionally managed apartment buildings do have vacancy rates that are lower than the national average.

MANAGEMENT PROBLEMS

The Office Budget

A *budget* is a financial plan of future operations. In its simplest form it is an estimate of future receipts and disbursements. It would be well, therefore, prior to commencing management operations, to prepare an office budget showing estimated receipts and disbursements of the office. A survey should be made of prospective business, and an estimate should be made of disbursements required to operate the estimated volume of business.

It is suggested that the raw figures be tempered with good judgment. An accountant discovering a loss from the operation of a ribbon counter in a department store or a fountain in a drugstore might suggest its removal, but the question arises as to the amount of business attracted to the store by the ribbon counter or by the fountain. Tenants are a source of prospects for making sales. Owners are a source of listings. Though the budget of the management department might show a slight loss, it would be well to raise the question of the possibility of added sales resulting from the activities of a management department.

The Individual Property Budget

A budget should be prepared by the management office for each property managed. In an older building, the basis of this is, of course, previous experience with that building. In a new building, the income is estimated after determining the estimated income of the property based on present pricing policies. The expenses will, for the most part, be based on experience with similar buildings.

The expenses fall into three categories: operating expenses, maintenance expenses, and fixed charges. The operating expenses include cleaning supplies and labor; electricity, which includes repairs and labor; heating, including repairs, labor, and fuel; air-conditioning costs, if any; plumbing, including repairs; elevators, including repairs and labor; and administrative expense. The maintenance expenses include tenant alterations, tenant decorating, and general repairs. The fixed charges include insurance, real property taxes, and depreciation on the building and equipment.

In the older building, leases must be examined for dates of expiration and current rentals. Assuming a lease is near its end, a determination of future rental income must be made in terms of a possible new lease. Should the period of the new lease be long or short? Should the rents for new leases be high or low? The owner naturally desires to maximize his profits. To accomplish this, the period of the lease and the rent very often are determined by the position of the business cycle. If there is a depression or threat of business contraction, the manager might be wise to suggest a short-term lease with rent commensurate with business conditions. The reason for this is that with improving business conditions a new lease for a longer term may be written with a higher rent. In a period of business expansion, the lease may be written for a longer period.

The budget to be complete must include estimated disbursements, together with an allowance for the customary 10 percent deduction from income for vacancies and repairs.

One suggestion for budget preparation is that the manager prepare an annual budget, including therein such large items as annual taxes and insurance. The estimates are made on the basis of past experience or experience with similar properties. Included in the budget also are large items such as anticipated major repairs. The annual budget is divided by twelve to create the monthly budget.

Automatically, then, reserves are included for the large tax items and repair items. A rigid comparison is made with the monthly items as actual operating expenses are incurred. An analysis is made of any deviation from the norm. For example, if a gas or electric bill is unusually high, a check is made to determine the reason. From such investigation, leakages or other problems may be found.

The article cited also points out that thc building in of reserves into the budget generally avoids feast or famine type situations. This is satisfactory to the owner because it provides him with a steady flow of income and he can thereby estimate monthly income.

Alternate Budgets

The astute property manager will, when feasible, prepare an alternate budget for his client. This must be prepared with a great deal of care. The purpose is to point out to the owner the possible increase in income as a result of improving the property. The gross income of the building as it stands may not be as high as it could be if improvements were made. The life of the building may, for example, be lengthened with certain improvements, or modernization might increase net income. The estimates of the cost of improvements are accurately computed together with estimated increases in income as a result of these improvements. Any final decision must lie with the owner, but a service of this nature accurately computed will be of help to the owner and ultimately tend to build the reputation of the management firm.

Obtaining Management Business

Although most of the smaller real estate concerns engage themselves in management either as a convenience to an old client or with the hope of increasing their income from sales, the firm with a complete management department must be active in obtaining management business. In order for the management firm to employ its resources to the highest degree of efficiency, it is necessary to obtain a large volume of management business.

Owners of property—whether they own individually, as a syndicate, or in the corporate form—are the main sources of business for the management firm. A careful and complete list of these types of owners must be maintained and kept current. A daily list of transfers of ownership should be obtained from the recorder's office and contact made with new owners. This can be done by approaching the new owner directly or by direct mail solicitation. Each transfer of ownership involves a possible source of new business. In large cities lists of this type can often be purchased from abstract companies. In the City of New York, for example, a list of 5,000 properties can be purchased for as little as $100. This type of service includes monthly supplements.

Contacts should be made with attorneys, especially those who handle large estates and whose main source of income in many instances is from real estate. In the larger cities most of the savings banks have real estate departments. The managers of these departments should be contacted with the idea of obtaining future management business. The chain stores, too, have real estate departments and are a good potential source of business.

Many of the investments held by insurance companies are in the form of real property. For the most part, the employees of a company manage the larger rental projects that their company owns; however, in many instances, when the company owns smaller properties, it is more economical for it to hire an outside management firm. Therefore, the company should be contacted and shown how the job of property management can be done more efficiently by employing the service of a management firm.

Another method of building a management portfolio is to approach owners having vacant properties. The owner is asked to turn over the management of the property if a good tenant is obtained on a lease basis.

Merchandising of Space. Most successful management firms combine space merchandising with their management activities. The problems of merchandising residential property are somewhat different from those involved in merchandising space.

In already existing buildings, listings for rentals must be obtained. In general, they are obtained either by advertising or by direct solicitation from the owners.

When new multiple-unit residential properties are being constructed, the job of renting the apartments is generally let out on bid. The active renting agent will seek out the owner or builder early in order to obtain the necessary information for bidding on the job. It is suggested that concerns interested in securing this type of renting business obtain information from the city building department as to permits issued for this type of construction. Thus, if practicable, the owner can be approached even before construction has begun.

One word of warning here: a definite agreement should be reached between the renting agent and the owner as to the payment for advertising, the number of lines of advertising, and the media to be used.

Time is an important element at this point. The bid is often given at a flat rate, so much for renting all of the units; therefore, the faster the units are rented, the greater the profit. Needless to say, this type of renting often leads to a permanent owner-management relationship.

Like any other type of selling, the prospective tenant must be qualified in terms of his *needs*. The prospect is shown vacancies in terms of his needs. He should never be shown too many places at one time, for this may only confuse him. It should, of course, be made clear to the tenant that his application will be investigated prior to his acceptance as a tenant. In any event, no concessions should be promised other than those specifically agreed upon by the landlord. Those salesmen of the firm who in their eagerness to rent space do promise any other type of concessions should be immediately discouraged from such practice. It is at this point that bad tenant relations often start.

Commercial Space Renting. The renting of commercial space presents many different aspects from the renting of residential space. The main thing, however, is to supply the needs of the prospect. A person seeking a loft for purposes of light manufacturing should not be shown a property suitable for heavy industry. On the other hand, where loft space is listed, prospects who would be interested in loft space should be contacted, not prospects who are interested in heavy industrial space. Analyze the property; then attempt to find those prospects who are best suited for the property.

One important method of obtaining future management business is to keep, insofar as possible, a complete record of existing leases and their termination dates. Obtain the dates of expiration of store leases. The merchants who have to vacate their space are a source of prospects for other suitable space, and the space being vacated is a source of listings that can be sold to still other prospects.

Chain stores constitute a source of prospects that is often overlooked by firms engaged in renting commercial space in larger cities. In most large cities there are many types of chains comprised of numerous small units, such as dry cleaning establishments and food shops. These chains are constantly on the lookout for new locations. Most chain stores have real estate managers who are only too willing to supply the broker with a precise list of their requirements in terms of the number of locations needed, the floor space required, the most desirable locations within the city, and any other pertinent details that the broker requests. Their requirements should always be kept in mind and kept up to date by frequent contact with their real estate departments. Supply their needs, and a deal is assured.

In the final analysis, when a commercial property is listed for rent, the question should arise: Who is best suited for its occupancy? After having answered this question, the broker's next step is to contact all of those persons for whom it is best suited.

Rent Schedules

In connection with the preparation of the budget for operating a property, there is a need for the management firm to think in terms of rental schedules for new buildings. These schedules are prepared prior to the construction of the building and often prior to the commencement of construction. The object of the rent schedule is to secure a fair return on the investment in the building.

To determine the investment from which a fair return is to be received, the following items must be considered:

1. The cost of construction of the completed building.
2. The value of the land.
3. The cost of taxes and insurance incurred during the construction of the building.
4. The interest lost during construction.
5. Promotion costs, unless they have already been included in the cost of the building.

The total of the items above equals the investment from which a return must be received. However, the income to be received on the property can never be estimated as being more than that of like accommodations in a like location. Essentially, this means that the person estimating the return on a property must look to the returns from other properties that are similar. It does not necessarily mean that just because a certain sum is invested in a property that rentals can be established which will provide a fair return on the investment in the property.

Concessions

A *concession* is a special service rendered by an owner to a tenant for the purpose of creating a difference between the named rent and the real rent paid or to be paid by a tenant. For example, in order to get a tenant into a building, the landlord may pay the cost of moving expenses. If the moving expenses cost $60 and the rent to be paid by the tenant is $100 per month, then the effect of paying for the moving expenses is to reduce the rent $5 per month. Often a concession is given by offering the first month's rent free to a tenant. The purpose behind this is actually to induce prospective tenants to rent a property without reducing the rental figure. Thus, if market conditions warrant the raising of the rent, the owner can do this without changing the rent schedule by merely refusing to offer concessions to new incoming tenants. The important thing for the management firm to keep in mind is that the problem of concessions should be ironed out with the owner at the time the firm takes over the management of the building.

Selecting Residential Tenants

One of the criteria for selecting a tenant for residential property is his capacity to pay. For the average tenant, capacity to pay depends to a large degree upon his income from employment. This suggests that the prudent property manager will investigate the source of his prospective tenant's income. Not only should he be interested in the source of the income, but more so in the type of employment. The best risks generally are those tenants whose employers are least affected by any downward swings in the business cycle. For example, the earnings of a carpenter or bricklayer are generally high during periods of prosperity; but during a depression or sometimes even during a slight recession, their earnings are likely to be reduced or, what is even more likely, these people will be unemployed. On the other hand, the earnings of a governmental or institutional employee do not rise as rapidly during periods of prosperity; neither do they fall as much in a depression. In other words, in terms of future earnings, a government or institutional employee might make a better tenant than would an employee in a trade or firm.

Selecting Commercial Tenants

It goes almost without saying that the financially strong, long-established commercial firms and the various government agencies make the best-paying tenants. Unfortunately, however, there are not enough financially sound firms to go around. It is incumbent upon the renting agent, therefore, to select commercial tenants with care. For example, if a newly formed, financially weak corporation leases a commercial property, the manager should try to obtain the signature of one of the corporate owners as an individual on the lease. The owner signs this as surety for the payment of the rent. If practicable, it is sometimes well to obtain the signature of a third party as a guarantor. In this way the property manager is able to overcome the limited liability feature of the corporate entity, at least insofar as the corporate owners are personally responsible financially.

Credit Standing

Prior to selecting any type of tenant, the property manager should obtain a credit report on the prospective tenant. The credit report will, of course, reflect upon the tenant's capacity to pay. The report will show or should show whether the prospect has any notes, chattel mortgages, judgments, or any other debts outstanding, together with life insurance purchases or any time payments he must make.

In the final analysis, the property manager should carefully consider the following factors when he is evaluating the credit rating of residential or commercial tenants of any type:

1. Their ability to pay.
2. Their character.
3. Their paying habits. (This will show proof of their intent to pay.)

4. Their identification.

5. The security. (An attempt should be made to see if the tenant has any collateral. This is especially applicable to commercial tenants.)

Collections

The cornerstone of the success of any management organization is that it must be prompt in collecting the rent. Rent must never be permitted to remain in arrears. It is, therefore, necessary for the property manager to send due bills to the tenants in advance of the due date.[1] In the event payment is not immediately forthcoming, a letter reminding the tenant of his delinquency is in order. The letter should be carefully worded in order to avoid the possibility of antagonizing the tenant. If payment still is not made, a more strongly worded letter follows, and then a notice that legal action will be taken to collect the rent. If, then, the rent is not promptly paid, the legal action is begun. The time allowance for payment of delinquent rent varies from state to state; however, the time allotted the delinquent tenant for the payment is generally from three to five days. If the debt is not paid within the allotted time, the action is carried through to the point where the tenant is evicted and a judgment is entered against the tenant for the amount of rent that is overdue.

Tact on the part of the manager is the key to all collections. The manager must be firm with the tenants without arousing antagonism. Each person within the management firm should be constantly kept aware that he must build the goodwill of the firm and that with the proper tact this can be done even while enforcing a firm collection policy.

Relations with Tenants and Owners

The manager acts, to a large degree, as a buffer between owner and tenant. Part of the manager's job is to make sure that both parties receive just and equitable treatment. Among other things, one might say the role of the manager has a close kinship with that of the diplomat. The manager must strive constantly to maintain the

[1] Some firms dispense with the rent notice in order to reduce expenses.

goodwill of the tenant toward his client. In essence, then, there is a constant public relations job to be done.

Tenant Relations. All complaints concerning the property will be directed toward the property manager. These complaints must be investigated and given proper attention. It is relatively easy for the slipshod manager to brush complaints aside, either by ignoring them completely or by making a flat statement that they will be corrected. At the beginning of the relationship with the tenant, an understanding must be reached between the manager and the tenant. This understanding should result in a mutual acceptance of what will or what will not be done for the tenant by the management firm. Once this understanding has been reached, the tenant will know that certain things are not his for the asking.

Good tenants are a valuable asset to the management. If a good relationship is established and maintained, the manager need not fear more than the normal number of vacancies. In addition, with good tenant relationships the property will be well advertised to the friends and acquaintances of the tenants, and this is the best type of advertising a firm can have.

Owner Relations. The owner is the client of the property manager and the avoidance of misunderstanding begins with a clear, written contract defining the respective rights and duties of owner and agent. The second step toward a good owner-manager relationship is in the monthly statement of receipts and disbursements. The owner knows or should know what to expect in terms of income from his investment. An accurate monthly statement that meets his expectations will keep the relationship on an even keel. However, all too frequently the owner's expectations, as a result of an unusual expense, may not be met. When this occurs, a reasonable and logical explanation of the failure to live up to the owner's expectations becomes important. Preferably, this should be done by personal contact with the owner or, if personal contact is not feasible, then a detailed letter of explanation must accompany the monthly receipt and disbursement statement to the owner. Under no circumstances should any extraordinary expense be made without proper explanation. In the final analysis, a good owner-manager relationship depends fundamentally on the honesty and efficiency of the property manager.

Most property owners, being businessmen, can readily recognize these attributes and know whether their expectations will be met.

Accounts and Records

The management contract calls for a monthly statement of "receipts, expenses, and charges," and the management is to remit receipts less disbursements.

This means, then, that each month a complete statement must be remitted to the owner. How then are these records to be kept? The basis of the management accounting system lies in an accounts receivable ledger. Each page contains the name of the tenant, a description of the space, a brief statement as to the terms of the lease and a debit column, the debit column consisting of the total rent and any other charges which the tenant might incur. A credit column and a debit balance column are shown. Basically, the record shows the amount billed each month, the amount collected each month, and any balance remaining due at the end of the month.

The information from the tenant's accounts receivable ledger is posted to a master sheet called a *transcript*. The transcript is divided into columns, containing: (1) the apartment number, (2) the number of rooms, (3) the expiration date of the lease, (4) charges for the current month, (5) debit balance carried over from the previous month, (6) total debits, (7) less credits, and (8) an ending balance.

The transcript is submitted to the owner together with a summary receipt and disbursement statement. The summary shows the income in the manner shown at the top of the next page.

INCOME	BILLED	COLLECTED
Rentals	$1,250	$1,000
Others	500	500
Total Income	$1,750	$1,500

From this the operating expenses are deducted, leaving the net operating receipts. To the net operating receipts is added Other Income, such as receipts of withholding taxes, all of which is in accord with good accounting practice. Other disbursements are deducted from this figure, leaving a balance of net receipts remitted.

The gross figures for the operating expenses are substantiated by a statement of Operating Expenses Paid which shows in detail the expenses paid. For example, the Receipts and Disbursements Statement may concern such an item as Repairs and Maintenance, $300.

The detailed statement of operating expenses may show this as:

Ace Contracting Co.	$150
Rogers Electric Co.	150
	$300

Records are, of course, kept for all expenses in connection with a property. Invoices are recorded in the proper records of account, and all payments should be made by check.

As previously stated, no money of the client must be commingled with any money of the manager. It is permissible, however, to place all of the clients' money in a single, special account.

Compensation

The property manager usually receives a percentage of the gross income from the building with a minimum amount per month. In some areas these commissions are paid on a sliding scale, for example, 6 percent on the first 100,000 of gross income, 3 percent on the second $100,000, and so forth.

In addition to the commission of the gross income from the property, the manager receives a commission on the renting of space. This, too, is generally on a sliding scale and based on the type of lease. In most parts of the nation local or state boards of realtors have established the fees. For example, in Colorado the fee on a month-to-month tenancy is one half the first month's rent; on leases the commission is 5 percent to 6 percent of the face value of the lease, but not less than one half the first month's rent; nor shall the commission be greater than the commission would have been had there been a sale of the fee.

Condominium Management

The management of condominiums is a relatively new field and presents a new opportunity for professional managers. Basically, condominiums are divided into two types with managers functioning somewhat differently in each area. These types are: (1) The permanent resident-type condominium and (2) the recreational-type condominium.

In connection with the residential-type condominium, the management problems are not too unlike those of the ordinary apartment house except that the manager collects no rent. Payments are made by the owner to the financial institution holding the loan. However, there are assessments collected which are included as costs in the operating budget. These generally are:

1. Real estate taxes, where not included in the owner's monthly payments; in any event, a share of taxes on common spaces.
2. Fire insurance, again where not included in owner's monthly payments.
3. A share in the cost of landscaping.
4. Comprehensive liability insurance.[2]

In connection with the recreational-type condominium, the manager determines the time during which the owner desires to rent the condominium. He may rent it then on a daily, weekly, or monthly basis, providing maid service much like a motel. From the rents he deducts a fee, pays the additional expenses, and remits the balance to the owner. Other than this, he operates in the same manner as the manager of a residential condominium.

The Management Agreement

The *management agreement*, like any other contract, defines the rights and obligations of the contracting parties.

The agreement creates an exclusive agency in the named agent and is binding upon the heirs and assigns of both the owner and the agent. Briefly, the agent agrees to manage the premises, to investigate prospective tenants, to place and supervise tenants, to insure the property in accordance with the owner's instructions, and to render monthly statements of receipts and disbursements.

The agent is generally given the authority to advertise and make leases, collect rents, and make all repairs. However, a limitation on the amount that the agent can spend for repairs is usually included. Any sums over the specified amount may be disbursed only after the owner's consent has been received.

---

[2] Lloyd D. Hanford, Sr., C.P.M., *The Property Management Process* (Chicago: Institute of Real Estate Management, 1972).

CONTRACT for MANAGEMENT

In consideration of the covenants herein contained, Hans C. Jensen (hereinafter called "OWNER") and Economy Real Estate Corporation, Inc. (hereinafter called "Agent"), agree as follows:

1. The OWNER hereby employs the AGENT exclusively to rent and manage the property known as: 121 W. 49th Street, New York, New York

upon the terms hereinafter set forth for the period of two years beginning on the 1st day of January 19--, and ending on the 31st day of December 19--, and thereafter for like periods from time to time, subject to termination of this agreement as outlined below.

2. The AGENT agrees:

   A. To accept and does hereby accept the management of the said premises for the period and upon the terms herein provided, and agrees to furnish the services of his/its organization for the renting, operating and managing of said premises.

   B. To investigate carefully all references of prospective tenants.

   C. To aid, assist and co-operate in the matter of real property taxes and insurance loss adjustments, and to perform such duties in connection therewith as may be requested by the OWNER.

   D. To care for, place and supervise, subject to OWNER'S instructions, all insurance coverage.

   E. To render monthly statements of receipts, expenses and charges and to remit receipts less disbursements. In case the disbursements shall be in excess of the rents collected by the AGENT, the OWNER agrees to pay such excess promptly upon demand.

   F. ______________________________

Contract for Management

3. The OWNER hereby gives the AGENT the following authority and powers, and agrees to assume all expense incurred in connection therewith:

A. To advertise the premises or any part thereof for rent, to display signs thereon, and to rent the same; to sign, renew and/or cancel leases for premises or any part thereof, with express authority in the AGENT to sign leases for terms not in excess of_______years; to institute and prosecute actions to oust tenants and recover possession; to sue for and recover rent and other sums due; and, when expedient, to settle, compromise and release such actions or suits.

B. To collect rents due or to become due and give receipts therefor.

C. To make or cause to be made and supervise repairs and alterations and to do decorating on the premises; to purchase supplies and pay all bills. The AGENT agrees to secure the approval of the OWNER on all expenditures in excess of $__________for any one item, except monthly or recurring operating charges, and/or emergency repairs in excess of the maximum, if in the opinion of the AGENT, such repairs are necessary to protect the property from damage or to maintain services to the tenants as called for by their tenancy.

D. To hire, discharge and supervise all labor and employees required for the operation and maintenance of the premises; it being agreed that all employees shall be deemed the employees of the OWNER and not the AGENT, and that the AGENT may perform any of its duties through its attorneys, agents or employees and shall not be responsible for their acts, defaults or negligence if reasonable care has been exercised in its appointment and retention. The AGENT shall not be liable for any error of judgment or for any mistake of fact of law, or for anything which it may do or refrain from doing hereunder, except in cases of willful misconduct or gross negligence.

E. To make contracts for electricity, gas, fuel, water, telephone, window cleaning, ash hauling, vermin extermination and other services or such of them as the AGENT shall deem advisable; the OWNER to assume the obligation of any contract so entered into at the termination of this agreement.

F. ____

____

____

____

4. The OWNER further agrees:

A. To save the AGENT harmless from all damage suits and costs incurred therefrom in connection with the management of the premises and from liability from injuries suffered by any employee or other person whomsoever and to carry, at his own expense, necessary liability and compensation insurance adequate to protect the interest of the parties hereto, which policies shall be so written as to protect the AGENT in the same manner and to the same extent as the OWNER.

B. To advise the AGENT in writing if payment of mortgage indebtedness, property or employee taxes, special assessments or the placing of fire, liability, steam boiler or any other insurance is desired.

Contract for Management (Continued)

C. To pay the AGENT each month:

(a) FOR MANAGEMENT: 3 per cent of the gross amount of money received from the operation of said premises during the period herein provided.

(b) FOR LEASING: The regular New York City Real Estate Board leasing rates for all new tenants secured, and one-half of such rates for renewals of leases during the period herein provided for.

(c) FOR SUPERVISION OF REPAIRS: The regular New York City Real Estate Board supervision fees shall apply.

(d) FOR SELLING: The regular New York City Real Estate Board rates shall apply.

(e) Special clauses

5. The OWNER reserves and has the right for any reason whatsoever at any time subsequent to the 18th day of June 19-- to terminate this agreement upon 30 days written notice to the AGENT, subject to the rules and regulations of the Real Estate Board of New York City as to commissions due the AGENT under the unexpired portion of any and all leases of the whole or any part of said premises in existence at the time of the termination of this agreement as above mentioned.

6. This agreement is entered into by and between the OWNER and AGENT, subject to any and all provisions, when properly signed, on the reverse side; and shall be binding upon the successors and assigns of the AGENT, and the heirs, executors, administrators, successors and assigns of the OWNER.

IN WITNESS WHEREOF the parties hereto have affixed or caused to be affixed their respective signatures this 15th day of December 19--.

WITNESS:

/s/ Eugene H. Bigelow

/s/ Hans C. Jensen

OWNER.

Economy Real Estate Corporation, Inc.
By James T. Austin

AGENT.

Contract for Management (Continued)

The following provisions when signed by the OWNER and the AGENT shall become a part of the foregoing Management Agreement for the premises designated and shall be binding on both parties for the term therein:

1. The Owner hereby gives the AGENT the authority, and agrees to assume the expense incurred in connection therewith, to provide, equip and maintain suitable office in the premises, if deemed advisable by the AGENT.

Economy Real Estate Corp., Inc. — **AGENT**

Hans C. Jensen — **OWNER** — Date 12/15/--

2. The OWNER hereby makes, constitutes and appoints the AGENT as his true and lawful attorney and agent, (said AGENT to be subject to the direction of the OWNER, when such directions are given in writing concerning the policy or policies pertaining to the management of these premises), for him in the name, place and stead of the OWNER, for the purpose of carrying out the intents and purposes of this instrument to do and perform all and every act and thing whatsoever requisite and necessary to be done in and about the premises; as fully and to all intents and purposes as the OWNER might or would do if personally present, with full power to substitution and revocation, hereby ratifying and confirming all that said attorney shall lawfully do or cause to be done by virtue hereof.

Economy Real Estate Corp., Inc. — **AGENT**

Hans C. Jensen — **OWNER** — Date 12/15/--

3. The OWNER hereby instructs the AGENT to pay, out of the rents collected from the premises, the following items of expense other than normal operation expense:________________

____

____

____

Hans C. Jensen — **OWNER**

Economy Real Estate Corp., Inc. — **AGENT** — Date 12/15/--

CONTRACT FOR MANAGEMENT

between

Owner Hans C. Jensen

and

Agent Economy Real Estate Corp., Inc.

For property located at

121 W. 49th Street

New York, New York

Beginning January 1, 19 --

Ending December 31, 19 --

Contract for Management (Concluded)

One of the most important clauses in the contract from the viewpoint of the agent is that the agent has the right to hire and to fire all labor or employees used in connection with the maintenance of the premises. These employees, according to the terms of the contract, are deemed employees of the owner. It will be recalled that in our discussion of the laws of agency, one general rule of law is that the act of the agent is construed as being the act of the principal. Therefore, the management firm includes a clause of this type to protect itself from any negligent acts of persons whom they employ.

An indemnity clause is also generally inserted in the contract whereby the owner agrees to indemnify the agent in the event of any lawsuits arising from the management of the premises and from liability from injuries suffered by any employee. The owner also agrees to carry, at his own expense, compensation insurance.

The contract, of course, spells out in detail the method of payment and the rates of compensation of the agent for management, renting of the space, and the sale of the premises by the agent.

QUESTIONS FOR REVIEW

1. Discuss in detail the scope of management.
2. Explain the importance of determining the *needs* of a prospect before attempting to merchandise space.
3. What should be done in order to obtain greater security for an owner when a newly formed corporation or a financially weak firm seeks to lease a property?
4. What is a *transcript*?
5. Discuss in detail the typical owner-management contract.

PROBLEMS

1. You have listed in your office a number of store properties rented on a flat rental basis. You have determined from your reading and study that a downswing in the business cycle is anticipated. The leases on these store properties are about to terminate. Prepare and substantiate suggestions you might give your principal with regard to renewing these leases.
2. As the owner of XYZ REALTY CO., you are about to enter into a contract with the Paradise Realty Co., Inc., who owns an apartment

building containing 100 apartments. The gross rental from these apartments amounts to $12,250 per month. From information obtained from the local real estate board, and using the management contract illustrated in the text, prepare a contract to extend over a two-year period.

3. You are suddenly deluged with listings of store rental properties. They range in size from the small "hole in the wall" to large spaces suitable for supermarkets. Prepare a list of prospects for these spaces. How would you make contact with the prospects?

SUGGESTED READINGS

Case, Frederick E. *Real Estate,* Rev. ed. Boston: Allyn and Bacon, 1962. Chapter 24.

Hanford, Lloyd D., Sr. *The Property Management Process.* Chicago: The Institute of Real Estate Management, 1972.

Ring, Alfred A. *Real Estate Principles and Practices,* 7th ed. Englewood Cliffs, New Jersey: Prentice-Hall, Inc., 1972. Chapter 21.

Weimer, Arthur M., Homer Hoyt, and George F. Bloom. *Real Estate,* 6th ed. New York: The Ronald Press Company, 1972. Chapter 17.

Chapter 22

Search, Examination, and Registration of Title

Although the average person in the real estate industry will never be called upon to prepare an abstract of title, it is nevertheless extremely important that the technical aspects of title searching be understood. For example, appraisers should be aware of the existence of records from which comparable sales data may be obtained. A knowledge of abstracts and title insurance is important to facilitate the selling of property. Clients will frequently raise questions regarding their distinction. A knowledge of title searching is important in market analysis. In short, title searching and its ramifications serve as the capstone of the more technical aspects of real estate.

OBJECT OF THE SEARCH

There are numerous instances in real property transactions when a title search is needed. The scope of a search varies according to the purpose for which the search is made.

When a contract for the sale of real property is executed, the purchaser will want an abstract of title.[1] The *abstract of title* is a

[1] In some states where title insurance is used exclusively, the purchaser will never see an abstract of title although the title companies may have one for their own use.

condensed history of the title to land. It consists of a summary of the operative parts of all instruments of conveyance affecting the land, or the title or any interest therein, together with a statement of all liens, charges, and encumbrances thereon, or liabilities to which the land may be subject, and of which it is in any way material for the purchaser to be apprised (given notice of). In the usual transaction, the abstract of title will be ordered either at the request of a buyer or of a seller according to the terms of the sales contract. The purpose of the search will be to determine if there are any flaws in the title. A *flaw* is an apparent gap or break in the chain of title (the history of the previous ownership of the property). In addition, the purpose of the search is to disclose any possible *cloud* on title (an outstanding claim or encumbrance) which, if valid, would affect or impair the owner's title. For example, a mortgage or judgment or even an imperfect description of the property might be a cloud on a title. In a real sense, the cloud does not reach the merits of the title, but will tend to obscure it.

When a prospective mortgagee orders a search made, he has a different purpose in mind than a purchaser has. His main object in making the search is to determine: first, whether or not the person making the application for the loan actually owns the property; second, whether or not any liens exist against the property that might be superior to his lien. A bank may lend money only on first mortgages; hence, it must make certain that no mortgages are outstanding against the property under consideration as security. The bank's main object in ordering a search is to determine its position relative to other possible lienors in the event that the loan is granted.

A mortgagee and the holder of a mechanic's lien always have a title search made prior to a foreclosure action. They, too, are interested in the possibility of prior existing rights against property defaulted. They are interested in any liens that might exist against the property, for to complete properly their foreclosure action, it is necessary to bring into the action any parties having interests in the property which is the subject of the action. This must be done even though the interests of the parties may be inferior to their own. Not to bring in all parties having interests would be to render the foreclosure action defective.

For example, a mortgage foreclosure action is initiated that involves property on which there exists a mechanic's lien. The mechanic's lien is inferior to the mortgage because it was placed against the property after the inception of the mortgage. The mortgagee brings his foreclosure action against the property in the amount of $5,000, and the property brings $10,000 at the foreclosure sale. The overplus of $5,000 is paid to the mortgagor. The lienor's rights would be severed if it were not for the fact that the law requires that all parties having interests in the property be notified. In our hypothesis this notification was not made. Thus, the mortgagee's purpose in making a search is to identify any parties having interests in the property in order that proper notice might be given them.

The Chain of Title

An abstract of title is a history of all the instruments affecting a particular parcel of land. A chain of title is a part of that history. The *chain of title* shows the ownership of the property over a period of time, depending on the length of the search. It can be run back to the original title. Thus, it may show that *A* received the property as a grant from the King of England in prerevolutionary days; *A* then conveyed to *B*, *B* to *C*, and so forth until the present date.

The Recording Acts

The *recording acts*, which are similar in all the states, are statutes of registration and provide generally for the recording of every instrument in writing by which any estate or instrument in land is created, transferred, mortgaged, or assigned, or by which the title to land may be affected either in law or in equity.[2]

The purpose of the recording acts, which exist in substantially the same form in all of the states, is to give notice to anyone concerned with a title about the status of that title. By virtue of the recording acts, persons can be prevented from selling the same land twice. Notice can be *actual notice* of the fact that *A* owns a certain parcel of real property. The notice may be actual because *A* has informed *B* that he owns the property; therefore, it may be said that *B* has actual notice of the ownership of the property.

[2] Some acts use the term "filing." Generally, filing and recording are synonymous.

The recording acts, however, are designed to go a step further in the giving of notice. They are designed to give notice to the world of the fact that *A* owns a certain parcel. This concept of "notice to the world" is figurative, for not many people actually *know* the status of property in a certain locale. This notice to the world is called *constructive notice.* However, in order for there to be constructive notice concerning a particular parcel of property, it is necessary to comply with the recording statutes.

Basically, the recording acts state that conveyances may be recorded in the office of the county clerk, county recorder, or county registrar depending upon the particular state involved. Conveyances in this sense are generally taken to mean:

> (written instruments by which) any estate or interest in real property is created, transferred, mortgaged or assigned, or by which the title to any real property may be affected, including an instrument in execution of a power, although the power be one of revocation only, and an instrument postponing or subordinating a mortgage lien; except a will, a lease for a term not exceeding three years, an executory contract for the sale or purchase of lands, and an instrument containing a power to convey real property as the agency or the attorney for the owner of such property.[3]

The recording, then, is the entry in detail upon the proper records of the clerk of the county in which the property is located of a written instrument meeting certain qualifications. The recording may be done by copying or by photography. Most counties now use photography. After the instrument is reproduced, it is indexed so that it may be easily found. In most states, the recording acts provide that separate sets of indexes be made for the various types of instruments; for example, one for conveyances, one for mortgages, and so forth.

Each set of indexes consists of two indexes, one for each party to the instrument. When a deed is presented to the clerk to be recorded, it is indexed in a grantor index and at the same time in a grantee index. A mortgage is indexed in a mortgagee index and in a mortgagor index.

These sets of indexes are lists that are kept in alphabetical and chronological order. They are generally alphabetized according to the

---

[3] Sec. 290-3. New York Real Property Law. The laws of the several states are substantially the same.

last and first names. For example, the name of a present property owner is Frank Johnson and someone desires to determine from whom he had received the property. The basic assumption then is that Frank Johnson is the grantee of somebody. The question is of whom? The searcher will proceed to the grantee index marked "J," which indicates that those grantees whose last names begin with "J" will be found there. The first page in the index will contain a list of those persons whose last names begin with the letter "J" and whose first names begin with the letter "A." Thus, the first name in the list might be Jamison, Abe; followed by Jones, Albert; Jurgens, Arthur, and so forth. To find Frank Johnson, then, the searcher would turn to the page where the last names begin with the letter "J" and the first names with the letter "F." The exact procedure is discussed in detail later in the chapter.

In some counties where conveyances are relatively infrequent, indexes are prepared by last name only. In some states, however, where there are many conveyances, the indexes are broken down to a finer degree. For example, in the County of Suffolk, State of New York, the conveyances are indexed alphabetically both by beginning letters of the last and first names and also by townships. There is a grantor and grantee index in which lands in the town of Brookhaven are indexed. This index is alphabetized according to first letters of the last and first names.

As previously mentioned, the indexes are kept in alphabetical and chronological order. It can now be recognized that the names are not listed in strict alphabetical order, but only by the beginning letters of the first and last names. The real reason for this is that the entries are made in the indexes as the instruments are received for the purpose of recording. Assume that the recorder starts with a blank page in his index. On September 1 a deed comes into the office to be recorded. This deed is analyzed and is entered on line "1" of the index according to the beginning letters of the last and first names. On September 2 another deed is to be recorded in which the beginning letter of the first and last name is the same as the instrument recorded on September 1. The second instrument is entered on line "2" of the index, even though from a strict alphabetical point of view it comes ahead of the September 1 instrument.

Acknowledgments. The county clerk, recorder, or some other designated person is required to record and index certain instruments as provided by the statute. He is not required, however, to record these instruments until they have been properly acknowledged. An *acknowledgment* is a formal declaration made before some public officer, usually a notary public, by a person who has signed a deed, mortgage, or other instrument stating that the instrument is his act and deed. The instrument to be recorded is usually signed in the presence of a notary or other public officer with the acknowledgment attached substantially in the following form:

State of Idaho
County of Ada } **ss:**

On this 18th **day of** June**, 19––, before me came**
James Overton
known to me and to me known to be James Overton **the individual described in, and who executed the foregoing instrument, and duly acknowledged to me that he executed the same.**

Franklin Slade**, Notary Public**

(SEAL)

An Acknowledgment

Authentication of Acknowledgment. Although the county clerk may not record an instrument unless it has been properly acknowledged, he may sometimes not record an instrument even when it has been acknowledged. Most states require that if the acknowledgment is made in a state other than the one in which the property described in the instrument is located, the acknowledgment must be authenticated. In other words, the county clerk in *Y* county of state *B* needs proof that the notary before whom an acknowledgment was made in county *X* of state *A* actually was a notary.

This proof is furnished by the clerk of the county where the notary or other public officer who took the acknowledgment resides or has filed. The proof consists of a certificate commonly called a "flag." When a notary receives his commission or warrant, he signs his signature on a card in the office of the county clerk of each county in his state in which he desires to act as a notary. The cards contain the name of the notary, the expiration date of his commission, his residence, and other pertinent information. When a "flag" or certificate is desired, the county clerk checks his file of signed cards to determine if the person named is a commissioned notary. If he locates a card for the person named, he certifies that the person is actually a notary. The certificate is attached to the instrument to be recorded, and with the certificate the instrument will be accepted for recording.

In some states, notably New York, a certificate is required between counties. Thus, if an acknowledgment is taken in Queens County before a Queens County notary who has not filed in Suffolk County, the clerk of the County of Suffolk will refuse to record the instrument unless a certificate is attached.

Time of Recording. When an instrument is presented to the county clerk to be recorded, the date and time are stamped on the instrument together with the book and page where it is recorded. In law, the general rule is that an instrument is considered to be recorded when it is delivered to the clerk.

Subsequent Purchasers. In most states, the statutes provide that a conveyance that is not recorded is void against subsequent purchasers in good faith. For example, *A* executes and delivers a deed to *B* on July 1. *A* then executes and delivers a deed to *C* dated July 2. If *C* is a bona fide purchaser and records the instrument before *B*, then the conveyance will be deemed to have been made to *C*.

But, if *C* had actual notice of the transaction between *A* and *B*, *C* would not have made the purchase in "good faith." Hence, even though *C's* deed was recorded prior to *B's* deed, *B* would have defensible title to the property.

Recording Fees. The recording fees vary between the various states and counties. Generally speaking, the fee is determined by the number of pages of the instrument to be recorded. It is charged at a rate of so much per page.

THE MECHANICS OF TITLE SEARCHING

The Grantor-Grantee System of Indexing

Assume that a search is to be made to determine whether Frank Johnson owns free and clear of any encumbrances Lot #1 Block #3 of the map of Greenacres Development Company. Frank Johnson makes available a copy of his deed so that his title can be traced. (Ordinarily a search begins with the deed showing title in the present owner.) Assuming that his deed shows that on July 1, 1964, Frank Johnson was the grantee of John Huff, the following procedure would be followed in making a title search.

Running the Chain of Title. The first step in the process is to run the chain of title in order to find the ownership of the property for a number of years past. John Huff conveyed the property to Frank Johnson and, hence, must have been a grantee himself. Since he conveyed title on July 1, he must have received title sometime before July 1, 1964. The searcher examines the grantee index beginning in the "H" index at the *end* of the list of names of persons whose first names began with "J" and which were recorded on July 1, 1964. Thus, he proceeds backward, searching from the last entry on July 1 back to June 30, June 29, and as far back as necessary. Suppose that Huff received the property on June 25. The page in the index might appear something like this:

GRANTEE	GRANTOR	DATE	LIBER [4]	PAGE
1. Hendrickson, James	Schmidt, Lincoln	June 24	348	99
2. Hartley, Joseph	Weiner, Mike	June 24	348	187
3. Hundson, Junior	Felice, John	June 25	359	52
4. *Huff, John*	Kelly, Francis P.	June 25	360	14
5. Heathcliff, James	Schneider, Donald	June 26	362	89
6. Hobart, Jansen	Leavandowsky, Frank	June 27	366	673
7. Hester, Junior	Karakas, William	June 28	370	19
8. Hooten, Joseph	Dyer, Carlos	June 29	372	345
9. Herd, Jones	Steiner, Hyman	June 30	377	65
10. Hanson, Jan	Corelle, Sam	July 1	379	90

In tracing the conveyances of title to Huff, the searcher looks first at the date column, reasoning that the conveyance to Huff must have been made prior to July 1. Thus, he begins with the conveyance from Sam Corelle to Jan Hanson and works back up the list of grantees until he comes to the conveyance from Francis P. Kelly to John Huff dated June 25. Part of the entry reads "Liber (book) 360, page 14." This notation indicates the location of the recorded deed. The searcher finds Liber 360 and turns to page 14 to check the photostat of the deed from Kelly to Huff against the property description on the deed being searched. The reason for this check is that

[4] *Liber* means book, and in some states this column will be entitled "Book."

the conveyance quite conceivably may be an entirely different parcel from the one being searched. If the property in Liber 360 on page 14 turns out to be different from the one being traced, the searcher continues his search, examining each deed in the name of John Huff until he finds a property conveyed to Huff that answers the correct description.

Assume that the deed from Kelly to Huff in Liber 360, page 14, checks with the property that is being searched. After having determined that, the next step is to ascertain if it is a quitclaim, bargain and sale, full covenant and warranty, or other type of deed. The searcher then examines the deed to determine if internal revenue stamps are affixed (on deeds after April 1, 1932), whether or not the deed was acknowledged, the date of acknowledgment, the date of recording, and the date of execution. The deed is then read to determine whether or not it contains any restrictive covenants, easements, or any other unusual features that might introduce a flaw in the title. Notations of all these items are made so that they might later be incorporated into the abstract of title. Assume that Francis P. Kelly transferred the deed to the property to John Huff on June 7, 1964. The notations made might appear like this:

Francis P. Kelly to John Huff	warranty deed (Liber 360, p. 14) dated June 4, 1964 ack. June 4, 1964 recorded June 25, 1964 revenue stamps $2.20

Conveys premises at head of search.[5]

The next step in the chain of title is to determine the source from which Francis P. Kelly obtained the property. Although Francis P. Kelly was the grantor to John Huff, he, himself, was the grantee of someone. Thus, the grantee index will be examined to determine Kelly's grantor. The searching process is repeated until the chain of title has been run back to the date of the beginning of the search.

Checking the Grantors. After having completed the chain of title, the next step is to check the grantors. The question to be answered is:

[5] The premises mentioned in the illustration refer to the property being searched, which is fully described at the beginning of the completed abstract.

Did any of the grantors in the chain of title convey the same property twice? It is known that Frank Johnson recorded a deed to the property from John Huff on July 1, 1964. It is also known that John Huff received the property from Francis P. Kelly on June 25, 1964. What happened between June 25 and July 1 during the ownership of Huff? Conceivably, Huff may have made a conveyance to someone other than Johnson in the interim. In order to determine this, the searcher must check the grantor index. The grantor index is set up in almost the same manner as the grantee index except that the grantee and grantor columns are reversed. The searcher looks now for John Huff as grantor between the date he recorded the property he received from Francis P. Kelly and the date he conveyed the property to Frank Johnson.

If John Huff is a builder or real estate operator, there may be a number of conveyances between those dates. Each one of those conveyances must be examined and the description checked against the premises being searched. Somewhere, the index will list John Huff as grantor and Frank Johnson as grantee together with the liber and page number of the deed. If Huff did not convey the property to any other grantee, Johnson may be assumed to have good title as far as ownership is concerned. The same process is repeated with each person named in the chain of title for that period of time during which he owned the property.

In community property states or where dower or homestead still exists, it is important that one check for husband and wife relationships. Where real property is sold under these circumstances, the signature of the wife must be on the deed.

Mortgages. When all of the persons in the chain have been "grantored," the next step in the search is to examine the mortgagor index to check whether or not any of these persons in the chain of title have had a mortgage on the property and whether these mortgages are still in force. Beginning with the last person in the chain of title (Frank Johnson), and checking backwards, a search for mortgages is made against each person in the chain during that period of time during which he held the property.

Assume that James R. Skinner owned the property being searched from August 1, 1932, to September 22, 1938. By checking the mortgagor index, it is determined that he made a mortgage to the First

National Bank of Patchogue, New York, recorded November 15, 1932. The entry in the index appears as follows:

MORTGAGOR	MORTGAGEE	DATE	LIBER	PAGE
James R. Skinner	The First National Bank of Patchogue	Nov. 15	89	365

A notation is made of this entry, and Liber 89 of mortgages, page 365, is checked. If the mortgage remains unpaid, a copy of the mortgage will appear on page 365 and that is all. Assume, however, that the mortgage has been satisfied. In this case there will be a notation on the margin of the recorded mortgage in this manner: "Sat. Liber 2010, page 34."

Liber 2010, page 34, will then be examined to determine whether the satisfaction was made properly. A notation is made of the findings for later incorporation into the abstract of title.

If the mortgage has been assigned by the bank, a notation will appear on the margin of the copy of the mortgage to this effect: "Assignment Liber 2389, page 56."

The assignment will then be examined to determine its validity and the ownership of the mortgage.

Lis Pendens. In Chapter 9 it was explained that the *lis pendens* is a notice of pendency of action. Whenever a legal action is begun concerning a particular parcel of property, the notice of pendency of action is filed in the office of the clerk of the county in which the property is located. This lis pendens index is set up alphabetically according to plaintiffs and defendants. The index is examined for all people in the chain of title as possible defendants.

Each time a lawsuit is filed, the case is assigned a file number by the county clerk. An envelope or a folder with the file number is set up by the clerk; and all papers concerning that suit, including any record of disposition made, are filed therein.

The *lis pendens index*, in addition to containing the names of plaintiffs and defendants, contains the date of the filing of the lis pendens and a column for file numbers. If someone in the chain of title has been sued, his name will appear in the index as a defendant. The file number of the action is also recorded. The searcher upon discovering this will examine the file to determine the disposition of the suit.

Judgments. When a judgment is entered, it becomes a lien on the real property of the judgment debtor within the jurisdiction of that court. The length of the lien varies among the several states. If the judgment remains a lien against the property for ten years (as it is in many states), then it becomes necessary to search back for ten years. In other words, those persons who had title to the property under consideration for the past ten years may have had a judgment lien against the property that followed the property to the date of the search. The judgments are entered alphabetically on the judgment rolls in the county clerk's office in the county in which the property is located.

In the case here, the judgment roll would be searched from July 1, 1964, back to July 1, 1954. The searcher checks back in the judgment debtor column for those who had title for the past ten years. The judgment roll contains the names of the judgment creditor, the judgment debtor, and generally the name of the attorney for the judgment creditor, the time and date of the entry of the judgment, and the file number of the case. In addition it indicates whether or not the judgment was satisfied and the time and date of satisfaction, if any. In the event that a judgment is found, the file is investigated to determine the disposition of the case.

Minor Liens. A search is made for the so-called minor liens. Each type of lien has a separate index which must be examined. Included among these are mechanic's liens, criminal surety bonds, federal tax and building loan agreements, and warrants. In addition, it is the custom to search for financing statements of sale on the assumption that one might be filed affecting the real property in some manner.

In several states when a person is the recipient of public welfare, the recipient enters into a written agreement with the Commissioner of Public Welfare. This agreement becomes a lien on the property to the extent of the amount of money received from the commissioner as public assistance. In those areas a search must be made for that type of instrument in addition to the minor liens.

Tax Search. Taxes on real property are due and payable at a stated time each year; and when the date of the search is made after this time, and before the time fixed for the sale of lands for delinquent taxes, a search must be made to ascertain the fact of payment or nonpayment. In the final analysis, this means that as a practical matter tax rolls are always searched. The tax rolls are generally located in the county treasurer's office in the county in which the property is located, or in the tax assessor's office in the city in which the property is located. Usually, the tax rolls are indexed according to property description.

City Taxes. In most sections of the country, there is no way to determine from an examination of the county records if city taxes have been paid. To protect himself, therefore, the buyer will often require that the seller sign a statement certifying that there are no city taxes due on the property.

Surrogate or Probate Court Records. Very often when the searcher is running a chain of title, there will be a break in the chain, or he may run across an administrator's or executor's deed in the chain. In either of these situations, it becomes necessary to examine the records of the surrogate or probate court.

In the first instance, suppose that one finds a deed conveyed by Mary Reynolds. Upon searching the grantee records for Mary Reynolds, he finds no deed conveyed to her. The probate court records will be searched for the death of a Reynolds to determine finally whether the deceased "Reynolds" is the husband of Mary. If one is found, the files of the probate court are examined to determine whether Mary Reynolds was actually entitled to the property and therefore entitled to execute a deed herself, as grantor, to someone else as grantee.

In those states where there is a state inheritance tax, it also becomes necessary to determine whether the tax was paid. Or, if the value of the property was low enough to be exempted from tax, there should be a tax waiver in the files of the probate court to indicate that the tax had been waived. If there is no record of the tax payment, the tax department must be queried to determine whether or not any tax is due. If there is none due, a tax waiver is obtained from the state tax department.

The files of the surrogate or probate court are also to be examined when there is an administrator's or executor's deed in the chain of title. This is done to determine whether or not the property was distributed to the proper persons.

Dower. In the third chapter *dower rights* were described as the rights which a wife has in her husband's estate at his death. In those states where common-law dower rights still exist, the wife must join the husband on a deed in order to transfer real property effectively. If the wife does not execute the deed, at the death of her husband she may have an interest in the property, although it may long since have been in the possession of another person under a deed executed by the husband.

Although dower has been abolished by statute in most states, it still raises a perplexing problem to the title searcher. For example, in New York dower was abolished unless the parties were married prior to September 1, 1930, and even then dower applied only to real property owned by the husband prior to that date. The net result of this causes a problem in this way: If the husband held an estate of inheritance prior to September 1, 1930, and *after* that date conveyed the property without having his wife join him on the deed, it appears that after his death the widow is still entitled to her dower right; and she could attack the title of the present owner.

The Lot and Block System of Indexing

In some areas, New York City for example, a lot and block system of indexing has been created and is employed in place of the grantor and grantee index. This system is relatively simple and can be used without difficulty. The use of this system is described below.

The Maps. The entire city is mapped and divided into lots and blocks. Each block is given a number and each lot on the block is given a number. For example, a block may be numbered 2700. In this block there may be 30 lots numbered from 1 to 30. The dimensions of each lot and the dimensions of the building occupying the lot are also shown on the map. This may or may not be accurate, depending on how many new constructions have taken place in the particular block. In addition, the blocks have corresponding street numbers. Thus, the searcher may have no other information on a property other than the street number of the building and property on which he desires to make the search and, yet, may easily find it.

For example, a searcher is interested in 119 West 49th Street in Manhattan, New York City. In this case he finds the map containing 49th Street, finds number 119 West 49th, and corresponding with the street number he will find the lot number. On the same map is printed the block number. He has then found the lot and block number of the property in which he is interested. Thus armed, the searcher proceeds to the index. The index is laid off in block numbers. The property in question is located on block number 2700. Block number 2700 is then found in the index. Contained therein will be a list of all the conveyance and mortgage transactions of all the lots in block number 2700. The searcher merely has to search for transactions concerning the lot he is searching. The numbers and pages of the conveyance and mortgage libers are given and examined in the same manner as outlined under the grantor-grantee system of indexing.

At this point, the search is made in substantially the same manner as it is made in the grantor-grantee method of searching.

Preparation of the Abstract of Title. During the search, the searcher makes notes concerning all of the transactions regarding the property. After the search is completed, he organizes the notes into the form of an abstract or brief history of the property. An abstract of title is shown below.

ABSTRACT OF THE TITLE OF

FRANK JOHNSON

Premises: Lot #1, Block #3 of the Map of Security Acres Development Company.

James Jones and wife to Michael Felice and wife	Warranty Deed dated March 4, 1912 ack. March 4, 1912 rec. April 16, 1912 Liber 46, p. 89

Conveys premises at the head of the search.

Michael Felice and wife to Vincent D'Angelo and wife	Warranty Deed dated May 2, 1919 ack. May 2, 1919 rec. May 16, 1919 Liber 158, p. 453

Conveys premises at head of search. Restrictive covenant against abators.

Vincent D'Angelo and wife to James R. Skinner	Bargain and Sale Deed dated July 14, 1929 ack. July 14, 1929 rec. July 23, 1929 Liber 235, p. 67

Conveys premises at head of search.

James R. Skinner to First Nat. Bank of Patchogue	Mortgage dated November 10, 1932 ack. November 10, 1932 rec. November 15, 1932 Liber 89, p. 365

Mortgages premises at head of search. $1,500 mortgage at 5½ per cent interest payable quarterly.

First Nat. Bank of Patchogue to James R. Skinner	Satisfaction of Mortgage dated October 5, 1934 ack. October 5, 1934 rec. October 8, 1934 Liber 108, p. 87

Satisfaction of mortgage recorded Liber 89, p. 365 on November 15, 1932.

James R. Skinner to Francis P. Kelly	Warranty Deed dated September 23, 1947 ack. September 23, 1947 rec. September 24, 1947 Liber 64, p. 120 Revenue stamps $3.30

Conveys premises at head of search.

Francis P. Kelly to John Huff	Warranty Deed dated June 14, 1952 ack. June 14, 1952 rec. June 25, 1952 Liber 360, p. 14 Revenue stamps $4.40

Conveys premises at head of search.

John Huff to Frank Johnson	Warranty Deed dated June 30, 1952 ack. June 30, 1952 rec. July 1, 1952 Liber 380, p. 35 Revenue stamps $6.60

Conveys premises at head of search.

The abstract contains also a certification and exceptions, substantially as follows:

> This is to certify that I have searched the records in the office of the clerk of the County of Suffolk, State of New York, for deeds, mortgages, judgments and any other liens that might affect the premises at the head of the search and find nothing; except what any records of the federal courts might show and any other exception that might be made.

EXAMINATION OF TITLE

Although the real estate broker plays no direct part in the examination of title, he should be aware of what the title examiner is doing. Examinations of titles, because of the highly technical nature of real property law, are generally made by an attorney or an examiner of title employed by a title insurance company. Those states having real estate brokers' license laws specifically prohibit the broker from giving an opinion of title, and for the broker to give an opinion of title is tantamount to the practice of law without a license.

The question is, then, what takes place when the title is examined? Technically, an attorney who is to pass upon the title is given a state of facts upon which to base his opinion. This state of facts is presented to him by the abstract of title. Technically, too, the attorney is not presumed or supposed to extend his investigations beyond what is directly or inferentially disclosed by the abstract of title. Where links in the chain of title are missing, the examiner must make inquiries regarding these missing links, but the existence of unrecorded evidence or of equities not apparent or fairly deducible does not properly come within the province of the examiner.

However, many examiners of title feel that they should go beyond what is technically required of them. In many cases, the examiner feels it is necessary to inquire into the present possession of the property. The feeling is that, although the purchaser of the land under examination is protected by the records, it should be determined that the actual state of title corresponds with what appears of record. For example, the record may show *A* as the owner, but actual inspection of the premises may show *B* in possession of the premises; and from actual inspection and inquiry concerning the premises, it may be shown that *B* is the true owner of the property under examination.

Certain types of easements that do not appear in the record may be shown by actual inspection of the property, easements by implication, for example. This is the reason why so many lending institutions and title companies require a survey in addition to the abstract of title. The thought is that the survey will reveal easements and encroachments that the record does not reveal.

The Opinion of Title

The *opinion of title* is contained in the *certification of title* which is annexed to the abstract as outlined above. In essence, this certification of title is based on the assumption of title in a particular person at a certain date, and the examiner certifies the title from his examination of the records from that date. This raises the question as to how far back a title search should be made. To some degree this depends upon the purpose for which the search is being made. Most examiners feel reasonably certain in searching back forty years. This figure seems appropriate because of various statutes of limitations that have been passed in the several states prohibiting actions after the passage of certain specified lengths of time. Some states have statutes defining the length of time of the search for specific purposes. For example, when one registers a title under a Torrens proceeding (see page 566), some states require that an abstract of title be filed going back forty years. Some states require that an abstract be filed with a map of the subdivision and that the abstract go back twenty years.

When a title is being certified, the examiner looks for defects in the title. If any are found, steps are taken to remedy them. However, if the client is willing to accept the title with the defects, they are listed as exceptions to the title.

Title Insurance

Historically, abstracts of title were, and in many suburban areas still are, made by attorneys. With the advent of abstract companies, abstracts of title were prepared by them, and the abstracts were examined for legal defalcations by attorneys. In many ways both the abstract companies and the certifications of title by attorneys are imperfect and open to objection. An attorney, for example, may make an honest mistake against which the owner of a real property has no recourse. The honest mistake may be due to a forged deed or any number of other types of false statements that are impossible to detect. If an attorney makes a negligent mistake or if an abstract company is guilty of negligence, the property owner may be indemnified. However, although the property owner may have recourse against an attorney who is negligent, it does not necessarily mean that he may be compensated for his loss. To provide this protection, title insurance is available.

When a title policy enters the picture, the homeowner will be compensated not only if the company is negligent, but for any of the unknown defects in title, subject to any exceptions in the title policy, for which an attorney is not ordinarily liable.

In short, when a title policy is issued, the title to the property is guaranteed. Upon the payment of a flat fee as the premium, the policy insures for any undisclosed defects in the title, subject to any exceptions in the title policy. As far as an owner is concerned, the policy should be for the full value of the property; however, the situation is a little different as far as a mortgagee is concerned as will be seen later.

The Owner's Title Policy. Like any other contract of insurance, the policy contains the names of the parties and a consideration, which in this case is the premium paid for the policy. The maximum loss for which the company may be liable is stated in the policy as being so many dollars as follows:

> . . . which the Insured may sustain by reason of any defect in the Insured's title to all of the estate or interest in the premises specified and hereinafter described or by reason of liens or encumbrances charging the same at the date of the policy, saving and excepting, and this policy does not insure against loss or damage by reason of any estate or interest, defect, lien, encumbrance or objection hereinafter set forth in the written or printed exceptions contained in this policy.

This is followed by "Schedule *A*." Schedule *A* describes the estate or interest covered by the policy and then describes the property that is insured by the policy.

"Schedule B" in the owner's title policy contains exceptions, substantially as follows:

This policy does not insure against:

1. Any state of facts an accurate survey and inspection would show; the existence of roads, easements or ways not established of record, or existence of public roads; water locations; water rights, mining rights; exceptions and reservations in United States patents.

2. Rights or claims of persons in possession or claiming to be in possession, not shown of record; rights claimed under instruments of which no notice is of record but of which the Insured has notice; material or labor liens of which no notice is of record.

3. Matters relating to special assessments and special levies, if any, preceding the same becoming fixed and shown as a lien; taxes not yet payable; matters relating to vacating, opening or other changing of streets or highways preceding the final termination of the same.

4. Regulations and restrictions imposed by building and zoning ordinances or by a planning authority; any governmental action based on the claim that any part of the insured premises is within or under navigable waters.

The policy, of course, contains certain conditions. Ordinarily a policy reserves the right of the company to defend suits. It contains several other conditions which must be met for payment to be made; for example, when there has been a final determination in a court of competent jurisdiction under which the insured may be dispossessed. The policy also contains a statement that the policy is not assignable.

The Purchaser's Policy. The *purchaser's policy* insures the interest of the purchaser of real property. The main distinction between the owner's policy and the purchaser's policy is that in the former case the owner's title itself is insured, while in the latter case the title of the seller is insured. By means of this the purchaser knows that the title being delivered to him is free and clear from all encumbrances. This policy is most common in those states where the purchaser is responsible for having his own title search made. The owner's policy is most common in those states where it is the responsibility of the owner to furnish the purchaser with either an abstract of title or a title insurance policy.

The Mortgagee's Policy. The *mortgagee's policy* insures the interest of the mortgagee in the property under consideration. It covers any loss of the mortgagee arising from a defect in the mortgagor's title or by reason of any lien or encumbrance impairing the security of the mortgage with the exceptions basically outlined in the discussion of the owner's title policy.

The mortgagee's policy is used most often by banks to insure the security for the loan. It is paid for by the mortgagor, and in general when a title company has already issued a policy to the mortgagor, the fee is very reasonable. Unlike the owner's policy, the mortgagee's policy is assignable by the lender.

The ATA Policy. The *American Title Association Loan Policy*, which is an additional coverage policy, goes a step further in its coverage in that it includes the exceptions listed on page 563. For example, the ATA Mortgagee's Policy states, among other things, that the insured shall be insured for ". . . any statutory lien for labor or material . . . which now have gained or hereafter may gain priority over the lien upon said land of said mortgage."

This clause gives a measure of security otherwise not available in those states following the "Pennsylvania System" of mechanic's liens as outlined in Chapter 9. Under the "Pennsylvania System" of mechanic's liens, a mechanic's lien filed within the statutory period relates back to the date of the completion of the contract or the last delivery of materials to the job. Thus, under the ATA mortgagee's policy, a mortgagee knows that he is protected even if a mechanic's lien is filed after his mortgage has been recorded.

The title companies protect themselves from the possibility of a later lien being filed by a rather tight inspection system. A representative of the company visits the property to be insured and examines it for any recent improvements that have been made upon the property. They look also for any materials or tools that might have been recently delivered to the land, and for any excavation work or grading done on the land.

The title policies of the various states have minor variations, but they are essentially uniform.

TITLE REGISTRATION

Development of Methods of Supporting Titles

From very early times, it has been the custom and the law of every civilized nation to establish rules of evidence in support of land titles. During the time of the Roman Empire, deeds were required to be in writing and to be executed formally in the presence of numerous witnesses. In feudal England, title was transferred by livery of seizin. The livery of seizin was superseded by the written conveyance which is employed in all enlightened nations of the world today.

The requirement that conveyances of real property be in writing was an advance toward securing a degree of proof in support of titles. However, it was soon recognized that even though conveyances were in writing, something was lacking. The instruments were drawn with a great deal of care, and they themselves were not at fault. The delivery of the deed to the vendee became the symbolic delivery of the land in the same manner as the former livery of seizin. However, unless the vendor upon the delivery of the deed surrendered the possession of the land to the vendee, the deed could in no way protect the vendee against fraud or error. Unless the vendee went into immediate possession, nothing could prevent the vendor from making a second conveyance. The deed thus fell short of accomplishing the desired end—that of preventing fraud and error. It became obvious that the defect lay in the lack of publicity. Conveyances were private transactions cloaked with secrecy. The logical result was uncertainty of titles.

To provide what was thought to be a final remedy for removing uncertainty, various recording laws were enacted. They impose upon the recipient of a conveyance the duty to make the transaction a matter of public record. By these recording laws, certain legal effect is given to all records publicly filed. The first secures ownership of a bona fide instrument first filed. Secondly, priority of liens among creditors was secured where land was made the basis of credit. Secret titles and secret liens were no longer recognized. Creditors recognized for the first time that land afforded them the safest security for their claims. Sales of real property were stimulated.

Thus, at present, publicity concerning titles to land prevails, and the laws charge all persons with notice of that which the public record reveals. With the frequent changes of ownership of land and the passage of time, the title to land grows more and more complex. With this increasing complexity, purchasers and prospective lenders demand a careful examination of the records. Such examinations involve the expenditure of time and money and the ever-increasing possibility of error. To meet the needs of the times, there have been developed systems of title registration employed at present in 19 states and a number of foreign countries. These systems of title registrations, which are fundamentally the same, originated with the Australian law known as the Torrens Law, which is described below.

The Torrens Law

In 1857, Sir Robert Torrens, a British businessman, worked out a system of title registration which was first adopted in South Australia in 1858. The Torrens Law, where it has been adopted, seeks to provide that any landowner who has been issued a Torrens certificate of title shall in law conclusively be presumed to be the owner of the land described in the certificate. Under the Torrens system the law reaches out to the title itself to set it at rest against the rest of the world. One should be aware of the great distinction between the deed and the Torrens title. Under the system of recording deeds, the deed is always open to contest and is thus an object of possible future controversy. A deed is not conclusive evidence of title. Under the recording system a deed is registered, but under the Torrens system the *title* to real property is registered, and this is the great distinction. In the remaining sections of this chapter, detailed attention is given to a number of aspects of the Torrens system.

Procedure for Registering Title. In the states where the Torrens system has been adopted, the procedure for registering title varies, but only to a minor degree. Basically the procedure is the same:

1. The owner of the property must himself seek to have the title registered. He does this by petition under oath in a court designated for that purpose.
2. The application or petition usually contains the name, age, residence, and domestic condition of the applicant (that is, whether or not the applicant is married, divorced, widowed, and so forth); the land is described and the nature of the interest of the owner is mentioned. For example, "The estate interest or right claimed by the petitioner in the property the title to which is sought to be registered is as follows: fee simple absolute."
3. If the land is occupied by anyone else other than the petitioner, their names and addresses and their interest in the property are mentioned.
4. A statement is made of the liens against the land, if any, together with the names and addresses of the lienors.

5. The names and addresses of any person (including any corporation) having or claiming any interest in or lien upon the property, or any part thereof, the title to which is sought to be registered, and whether or not any of them are minors or otherwise incompetent are included in the petition to register title.

6. The application is addressed to the court having the proper jurisdiction in the county in which the land is located and power is given to that court to inquire into the condition of the title and to make all necessary orders, judgments, and decrees, including removal of clouds on title, the establishing and declaring of the title or interest against all persons known or unknown, and to declare the order of preference of all liens and encumbrances.

7. As soon as the application is filed, an order is entered referring the application to one of the examiners of title appointed by the Registrar of Title (he is usually the county clerk).

The examiner then examines into the title and the truth of the facts recited in the petition. He is given the full power to administer oaths and to examine witnesses, and may if he finds it necessary, apply to the court for directions. After his examination, the examiner reports to the court his findings and conclusions from these findings.

8. The court may then either (a) reject the application *in toto,* (b) defer entering a decree until such future time as may be deemed according to the justice in the case, or (c) enter an order that the registrar issue a certificate of title to the petitioner or to such other person as may be entitled to a certificate of title.

Conveyances and Liens after Registration. For there to be any force and effect of future dealings after the title to the land has been registered, it is necessary that all instruments pass through the registrar's office and be noted on the registered land. For example, if a registered owner wishes to convey the land, he makes out a deed and transfers the deed together with his certificate of title. The deed and the certificate of title are filed with the registrar. The registrar cancels the old certificate of title and makes out a new one to the grantee. Each certificate issued contains a statement of all liens and the order of their priority.

If the registered owner desires to mortgage the property, the mortgage is made out in the usual way and filed with the registrar who notes upon the certificate of the owner the facts of the lien of mortgage. If no notation is made by the registrar, then, as a general rule, the mortgage is of no effect. In the same manner, all other dealings affecting the registered lands, such as mechanic's liens, lis pendens, judgments, levies, and decrees are noted by the registrar of title.

The Insurance Fund. The question arises as to what will happen in the event of error in these somewhat complicated proceedings. In some states indemnity for errors or fraud is provided for by requiring that the registrar of title, as well as the examiner of title, execute indemnity bonds in favor of the people of the state. In addition to this, all states require the establishment of an indemnity fund. In some states a small fraction of the value of the property is charged at the time the land is registered, while in others a portion of the fees collected is set aside. For example, assume the enactment of a registration system where a $50 fee is established for the cost of registering the title. Thus, after the completion of the action, there exists $50 in the indemnity fund. The second action increases the fund to $100, and so on.

Arguments for the Torrens System. The proponents of the Torrens system feel that both the owners of property and the public will be benefited by the system.

The owner benefits because:

1. He knows that his title, after having been registered, is safe beyond question.
2. He can easily and accurately and without expense exhibit his title to any prospective purchaser or to any person to whom application for credit is being made.
3. No abstracts or examinations of title are necessary after title is registered, thus eliminating this expense.
4. There will be no loss of sales through delay in securing abstracts or from frequent and technical objections of examining attorneys.

The public at large benefits because:

1. A prospective mortgagee can learn within a few minutes the nature of his security; and a loan can be closed within a few hours after application, thus speeding up commercial transactions.
2. A prospective buyer can at no expense and in a few moments ascertain from the registrar of title the status of the title of the property that he desires to purchase.

3. A judgment creditor can ascertain easily and without expense whether or not the judgment debtor has lands subject to execution.

4. Unskilled abstractors and conveyancers will be unable to bungle transactions leading to later doubts of the status of title.

Arguments Against the Torrens System. The opponents of the Torrens system offer a number of arguments, the chief ones being:

1. In many states the indemnity funds are applicable only in the county in which previous fees have created the fund. For example, the funds paid to the registrar in Suffolk County, New York, do not provide an indemnity for property registered in New York County. Thus, the opponents of the Torrens system say that it would be almost useless to bring valuable property under the provisions of the law.

2. Some opponents of the Torrens system argue that the cost of title registration is much greater than the cost of title insurance, even after due allowance is made for the cost of the survey (which in most instances must be filed with the petition in a registration proceeding and which in many instances is a prerequisite for obtaining title insurance). In addition, the registration proceeding takes time and is sometimes exceedingly complex.

3. Although "memorials" (notations) are made on the certificate of title of mortgages, liens, etc., they are only warnings; and the original instruments creating these memorials must be carefully and methodically examined as to nature and extent of such interest.

4. Property once registered cannot be removed from the system except by permission of the court.

5. It may deprive a person of property without due process of law and thus be repugnant to the constitution. This argument is based on the fact that notice is published naming the parties to the action. Some parties having an interest in the property may not have been named in the publication of the notice because their names might have been overlooked in preparing the abstract. It is argued that such an omission does, in a very real way, deprive them of their property without due process of law.

Conclusions. The Torrens system has been used effectively in some areas, but in other areas abstracts and title insurance are preferred. In some areas, the Torrens system has been used effectively in very special cases. For example, in the County of Suffolk, State of New York, there are probably more subdivisions than in any single county of the United States. Many of the lots in these subdivisions have been lost to the county for nonpayment of taxes. When these lots are purchased from the county by individuals, the banks refuse to lend money for improvements on these lands on the strength of the tax title. Many individuals, therefore, have resorted to the title registration proceeding in order to "clear" the title. The use of the registration system has built up the fund to a respectable amount.

It is believed that the Torrens system will have a more widespread use particularly in suburban areas where property has been sold by tax deed and, further, when and if the public demands a more simplified method of supporting the evidence of title.

QUESTIONS FOR REVIEW

1. Distinguish between actual notice and constructive notice.
2. Briefly explain the Torrens system.
3. Explain how the grantor and grantee indexes are set up.
4. When running a chain of title, why does the searcher commonly work backwards?
5. What are the advantages of a title insurance policy over an abstract?
6. What is the purpose of the recording act?

PROBLEMS

1. Obtain a list of rates from your local title company and compare them with the fees charged either by a local abstract company or local lawyer's fees for preparing an abstract.
2. Select a lot in your town, your county, and your state and prepare an abstract going back 10 years. Use the materials located in the county clerk's office or the county recorder's office.
3. The First National Bank is going to lend Baker $10,000 on a purchase he is about to make from Simon. At the closing the bank is presented with the following abstract. Examine the abstract, and suggest what, if anything, the bank should do before making the loan.

ABSTRACT OF TITLE

The Old National Bank, a National Banking Association, grantor to F. L. Kenny, grantee	Warranty Deed dated October 28, 1939 rec. November 21, 1939 Liber 98, p. 345 Cons. $2,350

Does hereby grant, bargain, sell, and convey the following property in Latah County, State of Idaho, to wit:

Commencing at the Northeast corner of Lot Five (5) of Russell's Addition to Moscow, running thence West sixty-four (64) feet; thence South at right angles eighty (80) feet; thence East at right angles sixty-four (64) feet; thence North at right angles eighty (80) feet to the place of beginning.

SUBJECT TO an easement for an under surface pipe executed by Henry Brody to Alfred Burns dated June 7, 1926, and recorded in Book 4 of Leases and Agreements at page 393.

F. L. Kenny and Mary Kenny,
his wife, grantors
to
H. J. Meal and Jean Meal,
his wife, grantees

Warranty Deed
dated July 9, 1945
rec. April 2, 1946
Liber 109, p. 70
Cons. $1.00
Revenue stamps $3.85

Conveys premises at head of search subject to easements, covenants, and restrictions of record.

H. J. Meal, grantor
to
Walter G. Teal, grantee

Warranty Deed
dated March 25, 1946
rec. April 2, 1946
Liber 109, p. 80
Cons. $10.00
Revenue stamps $8.80

Conveys premises at head of search subject to easements, covenants, and restrictions of record.

Walter G. Teal and Isadora
F. Teal, his wife, mortgagors
to
Rockport First National Bank,
mortgagee

Mortgage
dated April 1, 1946
rec. April 2, 1946
Liber 67, p. 81

The premises under consideration are mortgaged to secure payment of $8,000 with interest at the rate of 4 percent per annum, payable in monthly payments of $59.18 per month commencing May 1, 1946. Said payment to include interest.

Isadora F. Teal, grantor to Walter G. Teal, her husband, grantee	Deed to Gift dated January 29, 1947 rec. February 2, 1948 Liber 114, p. 270 Cons. love and affection

Conveys premises at head of search subject to easements, covenants, and restrictions of record.

Walter G. Teal, granting his sole and separate property, to I. M. Simon, grantee	Warranty Deed dated January 26, 1948 rec. February 2, 1948 Liber 114, p. 272 Cons. $1.00 Revenue stamps $4.40

Conveys premises at head of search subject to easements, covenants, and restrictions of record.

Subject to the balance of principal and interest on that certain mortgage and note therein described, recorded in Book 67 of Mortgages at page 81 of the official records of Latah County.

4. When running claims of title, one may find the estate of *A* showing distribution to heirs *B* and *C* and a court order discharging the administrator. Later *B* and *C* sell their interest to *D*. Is the estate of *A* entirely eliminated from consideration in the title in the future? Discuss.

SUGGESTED READINGS

Case, Frederick E. *Real Estate,* Rev. ed. Boston: Allyn and Bacon, 1962. Chapter 13.

Lusk, Harold F. *Law of the Real Estate Business,* Rev. ed. Homewood, Illinois: Richard D. Irwin, Inc., 1965. Chapter XI.

Ring, Alfred A. *Real Estate Principles and Practices,* 7th ed. Englewood Cliffs, New Jersey: Prentice-Hall, Inc., 1972. Chapter 7.

Chapter 23

Title Closing

For most real estate practitioners, the *title closing* marks the completion of a transaction. At the closing the necessary documents change hands, computations are made to determine amounts due all the parties connected with that transaction, and the necessary monies are paid to the parties involved. Most closings move along without a hitch, yet some present problems that cause much difficulty.

Title closing in those many southern, western, and midwestern states where the broker himself closes title is an important phase of a real estate transaction whereby an error or uncertainty on the part of the broker may cause the transaction to collapse. In the states where title is closed by attorneys, the closing of title is important to brokers, too, because with a little knowledge they can often avoid losing a hard-earned commission.

METHODS OF CLOSING

At the closing of title, either one of two things will happen:

1. A deed may be delivered in escrow. *Escrow* may be defined as follows:

> A scroll, writing, or deed delivered by the grantor into the hands of a third person to be held by the latter until the happening of a contingency or the performance of a condition and then delivered by him to the grantee.

2. A deed may be delivered to the purchaser. This is the more common procedure.

Delivery of Deed

In the latter situation, the deed is actually delivered, and a mortgage is taken by a bank or other lending institution to cover part of the purchase price of the property. This is the consummation of the terms of the ordinary contract for the sale of real property. At the closing the deed is executed and delivered by the seller to the purchaser; the mortgage is executed and delivered by the purchaser (mortgagor) to the lending institution (the mortgagee); and the funds are paid over to the seller.

Assuming the closing is being handled by attorneys, the closing will be handled in the following manner. The purchase price of a particular parcel of property is $22,000; $1,000 was paid as earnest money on the signing of contract, $3,400 is to be paid by the purchaser at the closing of title, and a $17,600 mortgage is to be taken by a bank. At the closing, both the seller and the purchaser will be present, together with their respective attorneys. The attorney for the bank will be there, and, assuming that title insurance is being taken on the property by the purchaser, a representative of the title company will also be present. The closing will take place either at the office of one of the attorneys or at the bank. If a real estate broker is in the picture, he will also be present at the closing in order to collect his commission from the seller.

Upon arriving at the closing, both of the attorneys will make a note of the persons present at the closing. If a broker is handling the closing, he, too, should make a notation of the persons present at the closing. This is an important record to make in the event that any later question arises, for if there is any dispute, the names of the witnesses are available for consultation.

After this has been completed, the attorney for the seller delivers a prepared deed to the attorney for the purchaser who examines it for proper description and so forth. The attorney representing the bank will also examine the deed. The title policy will be examined by both attorneys—the attorney for the purchaser and the attorney for the bank.

A bond and mortgage, or a note and mortgage, are usually prepared by the attorney for the bank and are examined by the attorney for the purchaser for description, prepayment clauses, or any other pertinent details. This, together with the bond or note, is then signed by the purchaser. The bank representative gives a check in the amount of $17,600, in our case here, payable to the purchaser. The purchaser endorses the check and delivers it to the seller together with the $3,400 due to the seller, and he receives from the seller a properly executed deed, which is then promptly recorded by the attorney for the purchaser. The attorney for the bank records the mortgage.

Closing Through Escrow

In some states it is customary to sell real estate "on contract," as it is commonly stated, rather than for the seller to take back a purchase money mortgage. When the sale is on a land contract, escrow is used. A formal contract for the sale of property is drawn, defining the rights of the parties, the amount to be paid on closing, and the interest to be paid. A deed is prepared and executed by the seller, and an abstract or title insurance is generally obtained by the seller. The abstract or insurance may be obtained by the purchaser, however, depending on local custom. In those states where it is the custom for the seller to deliver the abstract or title insurance policy (which will have been spelled out in the contract of sale) and where title insurance is a relatively new thing, most sellers who have received abstracts of title themselves will deliver an abstract rather than a title policy. When the purchaser desires a title policy in these states, he might make an arrangement with the seller for a title policy, agreeing, if necessary, to pay any additional costs.

The purchaser pays the down payment to the seller. The deed, the insurance policies, and the contract are then delivered to an escrow agent. The escrow agent is often a real estate broker or a bank with an escrow department. The escrow agents charge a small fee in return for which they collect the monthly payments and deliver the sums collected to the seller.

A carefully drawn list of instructions which defines the duties of the escrow agent are included in addition to the instruments listed above. These instructions are signed by both the purchaser and the seller.

When a deed is delivered in escrow, title is transferred to the grantee only upon performance of the conditions of the contract. Usually, however, the purchaser, by terms of the agreement, is entitled to the possession of the property, and the grantor retains the right to foreclose in the event of default upon the part of the purchaser.

These in gross are the ways in which title is closed. However, there are numerous details that must be examined from the point of view of both the seller and the purchaser.

Escrow can also be used when large sums of money are involved. The deposit is often placed with an escrow agent (often an attorney) on the signing of the contract of sale. At the closing, this sum is transferred to the seller and applied on the purchase price.

THE CLOSING FROM THE SELLER'S VIEWPOINT

Taxes and Liens

The seller will be required to bring to the closing the latest tax receipts that have been received by him from the treasurer of the county in which his property is located. The receipts indicate that his real property taxes have been paid. Although the purchaser will know either from the abstract of title or from the title policy whether or not the seller has paid his taxes, it is quite conceivable that an error might have been made by the tax collector's office, and the receipts will indicate that the seller has truly paid the taxes. If the seller has paid his taxes in advance, an appointment, which is explained later in the chapter, will be made with the seller receiving credit for that part of the taxes which he has paid in advance.

Great care must be taken by the person closing title to determine the tax regulations of the locale in which the property is situated. In some localities, although tax bills are not presented to the taxpayer until the middle of the year, they nevertheless become a lien against the property from the first of the year. In these places it is customary to prorate the taxes on the basis of the previous year's tax bill.

The seller knows, or should know, before appearing at the closing, whether or not there are any liens against his property. He must take care of these prior to the closing; otherwise the deal will not succeed. If, for example, he has a judgment against him in the amount of $100, then the seller will appear at the closing with a satisfaction piece. The satisfaction piece, together with the recording fee, will be delivered to the attorney for the purchaser; or, if there is a bank involved, to the attorney for the bank who will record the satisfaction piece at the same time that he records the mortgage.

The seller must, at this time, be prepared to remove any other liens or clouds that he may have on his title. If there is a preexisting mortgage, for example, either the seller must appear with a satisfaction of mortgage indicating that the mortgage has been paid, or he must notify the mortgagee who will then appear at the closing with a properly executed satisfaction that he will deliver to the seller upon receiving payment at the closing.

Possibility of Reduction Certificate

If the contract for the sale of the property calls for a statement of the amount due on existing mortgages that are being "assumed" or taken "subject to" by the purchaser, then the seller must obtain and bring to the closing the mortgagee's certificate of reduction filled out in the manner set forth in Chapter 8. The certificate shows the amount of the unpaid principal, the interest thereon, the rate of interest, and the date of maturity of the mortgage.

Insurance Policies

At this point the subject of insurance becomes of paramount importance to the purchaser or to the mortgagee. The seller, therefore, brings his insurance policies to the closing. He does this for several reasons, one being: if a question arises about the amount of apportionment to be made, a ready answer as to the amount of premium paid will be available. In some instances the purchaser will want to accept the existing policies. The seller should obtain a letter from the insurance company in which the insurance company agrees to the transfer of the policies to the purchaser. In this case the policies themselves are assigned to the purchaser.

Leases

In the event the purchaser is buying investment property and there are tenants in the property, it is incumbent upon the seller to deliver the original leases to the new purchaser, together with a prepared schedule of rents being paid by the tenants in the building. Any tenant's deposits are turned over to the purchaser who gives a receipt and indemnifies the seller from any subsequent claim of the tenants.

Bill of Sale

When personal property is involved in the deal, the seller should appear at the closing with a bill of sale covering it. Whereas the deed conveys title to the real property, the *bill of sale* conveys title to personal property.

The bill of sale names the parties to the transaction together with the statement that the seller conveys title to the chattels contained in a schedule, which is made a part of the instrument. This is followed by a covenant whereby the seller warrants to defend the sale of the goods and chattels. A schedule of the items sold is then made up and attached to the bill of sale and made a part of it. The instrument is executed by the seller and an acknowledgment is usually made.

Sometimes a statement is contained in the bill of sale to the effect that it was made to induce the purchaser to purchase the chattels. This statement provides an easy way of proving one of the necessary elements of fraud should the seller's title to the chattels later prove defective. Technically, it shows that there was an intent on the part of the seller to defraud.

Internal Revenue Stamps

Until January 1, 1968, a provision of the Internal Revenue Code provided that a stamp tax amounting to 55 cents for every $500 or part thereof over $99 be placed on deeds in the form of a stamp. This was abolished in 1968. Most states have enacted legislation providing for a nominal tax on deeds based on the selling price. The purpose of this is to enable county assessors to determine actual selling prices for tax purposes and to aid appraisers to ascertain selling prices to determine comparative market values of homes under appraisement.

THE CLOSING FROM THE PURCHASER'S VIEWPOINT

The Title Search

Whether the abstract of title or title insurance is to be furnished by seller or purchaser, a search must be made. This is done substantially as outlined in Chapter 22.

In those states where the broker, rather than an attorney, customarily closes title, he must not render a judgment or an opinion concerning the validity of the title as shown by the abstract. To do this would be to encroach upon the province of the attorney and in all cases is a violation of the broker's law.

The attorney will examine the title report and pass upon any encumbrances or liens that are shown therein. It is at this point that the title may be rejected on the grounds that it is not "good and marketable," as called for in the contract. It may be that the contract for the sale of the property called for the title to be an "insurable title." If there are encumbrances that cannot be cleared up within a reasonable time, the title will be rejected. The deposit will be returned to the purchaser and, in some instances, the seller may find himself liable to the purchaser for his out-of-pocket expenses and also to the broker for commissions due.

Survey

In many parts of the country, a survey is required by lending institutions before they will lend money on a particular parcel of property. It is from the survey that one may determine some things that are not of record, for example, encroachments. The eaves of a roof overlapping the property of a neighbor, or a building on an adjoining property wrongly built upon the land which is the subject of the transaction are examples of *encroachments*.

The survey may also show a zoning violation that would be of interest to a lending institution. For example, a municipality passes a zoning ordinance stating in effect that no building shall be built less than fifteen feet from either side of the property line. A survey will show the relation of the building to the property line. If the building has been built after the ordinance is passed and is less than fifteen feet from either line, this is a clear violation of the ordinance, and a lending institution may refuse the loan.

Examination of Existing Leases

If the building is an income property and there are existing leases at the time of the sale, the attorney for the purchaser must examine the leases in detail. The leases are examined in conjunction with statements made by the seller in the contract. For example, the purchaser wishes to purchase a parcel of property with the idea of demolishing the existing building and constructing a parking lot on the land. In the contract for the sale of the property, there should be a statement about the length of existing leases and the amounts of rent received from each of the tenants. It is quite conceivable that the termination date of the leases might have been misrepresented in the contract, in which case it might be impossible for the new purchaser to proceed with the demolition of the building at that time.

If the property is being purchased for income purposes, the attorney will examine the leases to see whether or not the income is as represented by the contract.

In connection with this, the brokers, when obtaining listings of this type, attempt to ascertain the income from rents as accurately as possible, and in those areas having rent control to determine whether or not the rents are at ceiling or above.

If there are leases in conjunction with a closing, the mere examination of the leases in and of itself is not enough. The purchaser must be protected from the possibility that the rents have been paid to the seller in advance. Therefore, to protect the purchaser, the attorney for the purchaser should insist that the seller make an affidavit to the effect that no rents have been paid in advance by the tenants to the seller.

Corporate Franchise Taxes

If there are state and corporate franchise taxes in the chain of title that are unpaid, they should be cleared up at the time of the closing. Some states and the federal government place a tax on a corporation for the privilege of doing business. This tax is not based on income, but must be paid regardless of whether or not any business is actually done by the corporation. The franchise tax is not customarily apportioned, but is paid by the seller unless by special agreement to the contrary.

Certificate of Occupancy

In some instances, especially when a new building is being purchased, a certificate of occupancy is one of the items required to be delivered by the seller to the purchaser. Many municipalities have enacted ordinances requiring that certain standards be met, especially with regard to the plumbing and the electrical wiring. When a building is constructed, it is inspected to determine whether or not these standards have been met; if they have been met, a certificate of occupancy attesting to the fact is delivered to the builder. This certificate should be obtained from the seller at the closing when it is necessary.

Violations of Municipal Departments

Any violations of municipal departments must be removed by the seller at the time of the closing. For example, there may be a fire violation against the premises. In the event that the seller has not removed the violation at the time of closing of title, it is customary to deposit in escrow a sum sufficient to clear the violation. The seller is then given a certain time after the closing to remove the violations. In the event that the violations are not removed by the time stated in the escrow instructions, then the purchaser may himself proceed to remove the violations. The seller authorizes the escrow agent to apply the deposit against any cost of removing the violations and further agrees that in the event of deficiency, he will pay the difference. If there is any balance in escrow after the violations have been removed, it is paid to the seller.

Apportionments

At the closing certain charges must be apportioned between the parties. The items commonly apportioned are taxes, water charges, electric charges, gas, rents, certain services that have been paid in advance like burglary protection, and sometimes even the value of growing crops.

The problem of apportionment boils down to a problem of simple arithmetic. The main difficulties that arise are that first the local customs with regard to apportionment must be determined and, second, these customs must be followed down to the letter.

The customs with respect to title closing adopted by the Real Estate Board of New York state in part:

> I. All adjustments of interest, rents, taxes, water rates, and insurance premiums shall be made as of the day immediately preceding the day on which title is closed.
>
> II. Interest, taxes, water rates, and insurance shall be computed by the 360-day method, each month representing 1/12 of the annual charge and each day 1/30 of the monthly charge.

For example, a closing occurs on July 1. Taxes in the amount of $144 for the full year have been paid in advance by the seller; therefore, the seller must receive something back. The question is, how much?

Following New York Rules I and II given above, the adjustment would be figured in this manner:

$144 ÷ 12 mos. = $12 per month
$ 12 × 6 mos. = $72 (paid in advance by the seller, and to be returned to him)

This return is made by crediting the seller with the prepaid taxes on the closing statement as is discussed later.

Other customs adopted by the Real Estate Board of New York state that:

> III. Rent shall be computed on the basis of the days in the particular month in which title is closed.
>
> IV. Where the period for which the computation of interest, taxes, water rates, and insurance is to be made is more than one month, the elapsed time shall be computed by full months and by the actual number of days in excess of such full months.
>
> V. When the period for which the computation of interest, taxes, water rates, and insurance is to be made is less than one

month, the actual number of days shall be counted, excluding the first day and including the last.

These rules mean that the seller shall be charged with interest, taxes, water rates, and insurance to and including the day immediately preceding the day on which title is closed and that the purchaser shall bear these items from the day on which title is closed and receive rent for that day. This has always been the practice when title is closed on the first day of the month, and the purpose of these rules is to apply the same practice to closings occurring during the month.

For example: A title closes on June 4. Mortgage interest was paid to but not including March 15. The first half of the taxes has been paid. Insurance has been paid to June 15. Rents have been collected for the month of June. The computation would be:

Allow the purchaser interest from March 15 to June 3 both inclusive—2 months and 20 days—and rent from June 3 to June 30—27 days.

Allow the seller insurance premium from June 3 to June 15—12 days—and taxes from June 3 to June 30—27 days.

For example, a purchase price of a property in the amount of $10,000 and a $5,000 mortgage with interest at 5 percent payable quarterly is to be "assumed" by the purchaser. A tenant in the building pays $50 per month for rent on the first of each month, and $144 per year for taxes payable semiannually. What are the amounts to be allowed the purchaser and seller, ignoring for the moment any sums to be paid on the purchase price? Assume that the closing is to be on June 4 as stated above. The adjustments would then be figured as follows:

1. Allow the purchaser interest from March 15 to June 3 both inclusive—2 months and 20 days.

$5,000 (mtge.) × .05 (int.) = $250 per annum
$250 ÷ 12 = $20.83 per month
$20.83 × 2 = $41.66
20/30 × $20.83 = $13.89
$41.66 + $13.89 = $55.55 interest allowed purchaser

This is *allowed* to the purchaser because when the next quarterly payment becomes due, he will have to pay the entire amount from

March 15 to the due date. Thus he will have to pay to the mortgagee a sum of interest, part of which accumulated during the ownership of the property by the seller.

2. Allow the purchaser rent from June 3 to June 30—27 days.

Because June is a 30-day month, each day's rent shall be figured at 1/30 of the rental in accordance with Rule III.

1/30 of \$50 = \$1.67 per day
\$1.67 × 27 = \$45.09 allowed the purchaser

This is *allowed* the purchaser because the rents in this hypothetical problem have been paid in advance and the ownership of the property will be in the name of the purchaser during those 27 days.

3. Allow the seller taxes from June 3 to June 30—27 days.

Taxes are paid semiannually at \$144 per year. Thus the seller paid in advance \$72 through July 1.

1/12 of \$144 = \$12 per month
27/30 of 12 = \$10.80

This is *allowed* the seller because he paid the tax in advance including the 27 days after which he will have transferred ownership of the property; therefore the purchaser must pay the taxes for the period of his ownership.

ADJOURNMENT OF CLOSING

Unless the contract for the sale of the property states that "time is of the essence," the closing may, if necessary, be adjourned for a reasonable time. The occasion may arise when a bank, for example, has not yet completed the processing of a loan, or the abstractor has not yet completed the title search. In such instances as these, the closing will be adjourned until a later date.

Generally, a stipulation for adjourning the closing is entered into between the attorney for the seller and the attorney for the purchaser. Under the terms of the adjournment, a new closing date is set. The stipulation may either make specific provisions for adjustments or omit any specific terms concerning adjustments. The rules of the New York Real Estate Board take this into consideration in this way:

> VI. When the time for closing a title is adjourned without any specific provisions as to the adjustments, all adjustments shall be

made as of the day prior to the adjourned date, and the seller shall not be entitled to interest from the original date either on the unpaid balance of the purchase price or on any purchase money mortgages.

VII. When the time for closing a title is adjourned under a stipulation that all adjustments are to be made as of the original date, the seller shall be entitled to interest at the legal rate on the unpaid balance of the purchase price and on any purchase money mortgages from the original date set for closing title.

THE CLOSING STATEMENT

The *closing statement* is a report on the closing of the title. The statement varies according to whether the closing is handled by an attorney or whether it is handled by a real estate broker. In eastern seaboard states title is usually closed by an attorney; whereas in many western states the broker closes title.

Where closings are customarily handled by real estate brokers, the brokerage laws generally state that a closing statement shall be given to the seller and to the purchaser upon the closing of title.

Assume a broker is closing title. The purchase price is $41,500. The buyer has given the broker $1,000 as a deposit upon signing of the contract. The closing is May 23. The buyer is assuming a mortgage in the amount of $24,766.96. From the bank holding the mortgage the broker learns that accrued interest from May 1 to the date of closing will be due at 6¾ percent interest or $4.644 per day. Taxes for the previous year are $780.80. There was a shortage in the escrow account due the mortgage company in the amount of $38.64 later to be paid by the buyer. The tax reserves in the mortgage company account is $132.18. The mortgage company is charging the buyer a loan transfer fee of $35. A loan payment of $248 is due June 1. Typically, when the closing is so close to the first of the month, it is collected at the closing.

A documentary fee (charged by the state and varying from state to state) is ⅒th of 1 percent of the purchase price and is payable by the buyer. The recording fee for the deed is $2, payable by the buyer. A certificate of taxes due obtained from the county treasurer, and also payable by the buyer, is $3.

The house is located in an area where some of the surrounding land is held "in common." The seller paid his Homeowners Fee of $10 to help maintain the commons on the previous January 1. Title insurance will cost $194.60; no other insurance premiums are due. The commission is 6 percent due from the seller to the broker. The water meter was read, but the seller had not yet been paid. It was therefore decided that the bill would be sent to the broker and later paid by him. Consequently, $40 was put in escrow by the seller with the broker. The understanding is that if the bill is less than $40, the surplus would be given by the broker to the seller after he had paid his bill.

The following table shows the broker's receipts and disbursements:

	Receipts	Disbursements
Earnest Money	$ 1,000.00	
From Buyer at Closing	15,789.13	
To Seller at Closing		$13,733.74
Paid Title Insurance		194.60
Paid Recording Fee		2.00
Paid Documentary Fee		4.15
Paid Certificate of Taxes Fee		3.00
Paid Transfer Fee		35.00
Paid Mtg. Co. Escrow Shortage		38.64
Paid June Payment to Mtg. Co.		248.00
Paid His Own Commission		2,490.00
Holds $40 for Water Bill		40.00
	$16,789.13	$16,789.13

The closing statement in those states where the attorney closes title is in many respects a great deal simpler than in those states where the broker closes the title. Generally, the attorneys for both the seller and the purchaser prepare similar statements prior to the closing to save time at the closing.

Assume the same case as set forth above. The attorney for the purchaser is to receive a $100 fee and the attorney for the seller is to receive a $100 fee. The $194.60 paid for the title policy is to be paid by the seller. The rules of the New York Board of Real Estate are to be followed.

At the closing the attorney for the seller gives his client a closing statement.

CLOSING STATEMENT (FOR THE SELLER)

Premises: (a brief description)
Seller: *AA* and his wife, *BA*
Purchaser: *X* and his wife, *Y*
Date of Closing: May 23, 19—
Appearances at Closing: *AA* and *BA*; *X* and *Y*; Lee Brannon, Broker; John Doe, Esq., Attorney for the Purchaser; Richard Roe, Esq., Attorney for the Seller.

Purchase Price	$41,500.00	
Tax Reserves	132.18	
Homeowner's Fee	5.83	
	$41,638.01	$41,638.01
Earnest Money Paid	$ 1,000.00	
Mortgage Assumed	24,766.96	
Interest Assumed	106.81	
Taxes Assumed	305.90	
	$26,179.67	
Due Seller from Buyer	15,458.34	
	$41,638.01	$41,638.01

Disbursements for Seller by
Seller's Attorney

To Broker for Commission	$ 2,490.00	
To Title Insurance Company	194.60	
To Buyer's Attorney for Water/ Sewage Escrow	40.00	
To Myself Legal Fee	100.00	
	$ 2,824.60	

The amount of disbursements is then subtracted from the buyer's check of $15,458.34 — $2,824.60 = $12,633.74. To keep his accounts straight, the broker gives his check in the amount of $1,000 (the earnest money). The seller then has received a total of $12,633.74 + 1,000 = $13,633.74. The $100 difference between this and the previously illustrated closing statement is due to the $100 attorney fee.

At the same time, the attorney for the purchaser delivers the purchaser a closing statement containing the same information as that given in the statement above, but substituting the following list of disbursements.

Disbursements by Buyer's Attorney for the Buyer:

Recording Fee	$ 2.00
Documentary Fee	4.15
Certificate of Taxes Due	3.00
To Bank for Escrow Shortage	38.64
To Bank June Payment	248.00
Transfer Fee to Bank	35.00
Legal Fee to Myself	100.00
	$430.79

As a result of the above the buyer at the time of the closing has to put up the $15,458.34 check plus the disbursements of $430.79, totaling $15,889.13. The $100 difference between this closing statement and the previously illustrated statement is due to the attorney's fee. Three other figures should be explained. The amount of $40 given by the seller to the buyer's attorney is in his escrow account until payment of the final water/sewage bill. The $305.90 in taxes assumed by the buyer will have to be paid by him when due. The $106.81 interest assumed by the buyer will have to be paid by him when due. It should be noted that often the financial institution will demand payment of this on closing of title. In this event the $106.81 will show up as an additional disbursement by his attorney, thereby increasing the amount of the disbursements by this sum.

The table on page 589 is given to assist the student in determining whether to compute time backward from the date of closing or forward from that date. It is *not* recommended that the student learn this table because it is too complicated. It is suggested that the beginning student could occasionally use this table to check and determine whether or not he has made the correct computation.

CLOSING MORTGAGE LOANS

A prospective lender, because he is the person lending the money with the real property as security for the loan, should exercise considerable care. He may think that his mortgage is going to be a first

Computing "Backward" or "Forward" from the Date of Closing[1]

KIND OF ITEM	ENCOUNTERED	DEBIT TO	WHY?	CREDIT TO	WHY?	FIGURE
Interest accumulated	Usual	Seller	He rid himself of a debt	Buyer	He will pay cash later	Back
Interest paid in advance	Unusual	Buyer	He gets the right to use the house free of interest payments	Seller	He sold a right in addition to the house	Forward
Insurance premium paid in advance	Usual	Buyer	He bought something besides a house	Seller	He sold the future effectiveness of a policy	Forward
Insurance premium which is in arrears	Unusual	Seller	He rid himself of an accounts payable	Buyer	He will pay out cash later	Back
Rent paid in advance	Usual	Seller	The tenant made a part of the last month's rent payment for the benefit of the buyer	Buyer	The right to use this house will be denied him for the rent period	Forward
Rent in arrears	Unusual	Buyer	He bought an accounts receivable in addition to house	Seller	He sold one of his accounts receivable	Back
Taxes paid in advance	Often	Buyer	He bought the right to live in a house without paying taxes	Seller	He sold a house *plus* the right to live there without paying rent for rest of tax period	Forward
Taxes in arrears	Often	Seller	He rid himself of an accounts payable	Buyer	He will pay this money out later	Back

[1] C. Glenn Lewis, "The Broker's Three Primary Legal Instruments" (mimeo) by special permission of the author.

mortgage, but he will not actually know unless he has a title search made or an abstract of title brought up to date indicating that there are no other mortgages on the property. Nor without the abstract will he know if there are judgments, mechanic's liens, or any of the other encumbrances on the title as outlined in Chapter 9.

The closing of a mortgage loan is, in many respects, a great deal easier than the closing of a title. After the lender has been able to ascertain that there are no prior liens on the property, the important thing to be remembered is that the borrower pays all of the fees and expenses of the loan. For example, a borrower makes an application to a bank for a $25,000 mortgage on a property on which there is an existing mortgage in the amount of $4,000. The interest on the $4,000 is at 8 percent per annum and six months' interest has accrued. It is assumed that there is a prepayment clause in the $4,000 mortgage and it thus can be paid at any time. The closing statement would be substantially as follows:

Loan		$25,000.00
Less:		
Payment of Mortgage	$4,000.00	
Interest to Date	160.00	
Legal Fee for Satisfaction	25.00	
Recording Fee for Satisfaction	3.00	
Legal Fee for Bond and Mortgage	35.00	
Recording Fee for Mortgage	4.00	
Mortgagee's Title Policy	125.00	
		4,352.00
Due Borrower		$20,648.00

In those states where there is a mortgage tax, this is taken into consideration. This increases the deduction and consequently reduces the proceeds to the borrower.

In those states where the mechanic's lien relates back to the time of the commencement of the work or the contract, lending institutions often attempt to protect their loan from a lien filed after the recording of their mortgage. They do this by making the loan and holding the money in escrow. The mortgage is recorded, and the money is held by the institution until the time has elapsed for the filing of the lien.

THE BROKER'S RESPONSIBILITY

It is the broker's responsibility when he handles the closing of title to see that the transaction is consummated with a high degree of smoothness, and that all parties leave with the feeling that they have been fairly treated. The greater the knowledge of the broker, the easier it is for him to accomplish these ends. The broker's situation might be held as being analogous to that of a doctor; when a doctor has a large number of alternatives at his fingertips, the greater is the chance of survival for the patient. The same is true for the broker: the greater the number of alternatives at the broker's fingertips, the greater the chance for the survival of the transaction.

For example, earlier in this text an encroachment was defined as an overlapping. The practical aspects of this can become of great importance to the real estate broker. Assume that title is about to close and there is an encroachment discovered at the last minute. The eaves of a garage are overlapping, and the buyer decides not to go through with the transaction on the grounds that the title is unmarketable. What can the broker suggest to save the deal? The answer is: "Escrow." If the broker is aware of alternatives, he can suggest that a part of the purchase price be delivered to a third person until the seller either moves the garage or purchases the land over which the eaves hang. As an alternative, the money may be held to reimburse the buyer for doing the same things. In the first instance, when the seller has complied with the terms of the escrow agreement, the escrow agent (the holder of the money) will deliver the balance of the purchase price to the seller. In the latter case, the costs will be paid out of the escrow money and the balance, if any, turned over to the seller.

This is just one instance of smooth consummation of a transaction in terms of disposition and attitudes created by the broker in the minds of the persons involved in the transaction.

What else can the broker do with respect to smoothly closing a title?

1. Prepare accurately and thoroughly a closing statement for both the buyer and the seller and be able to explain in detail the figures on the statements to the satisfaction of all parties to the transaction.

2. Advise the seller to bring the deed from his grantor to the closing in the event that the purchaser's attorney is present at the closing and desires to inspect it in terms of property description.

3. Advise the seller to bring his tax receipts, receipts for assessments, and water charges, if any, to avoid any possible discussion in this regard.

4. Transfer insurance policies to the purchaser. If the purchaser is going to obtain insurance from another company, the broker should obtain the agent's name and telephone number from the buyer prior to the closing so that he can telephone the agent at the moment the deed is delivered in order to make certain that the house in the hands of the purchaser is covered. While this may not be the duty of the broker, it is one of those things that causes a feeling among purchasers that the broker is acting fairly and honestly.

5. Advise the seller, when necessary, to have his attorney prepare any satisfactions of judgment or mechanic's liens and to bring them to the closing in order to have these removed as exceptions to the title.

6. Advise the seller, if there are any leases, to bring to the closing a letter of introduction for the buyer to the tenants and the keys to the building. Also suggest that the seller have an affidavit prepared showing that rents have not been prepaid.

7. Advise the seller to have his attorney prepare a bill of sale covering any personal property included in the transaction.

8. Advise the seller, if the seller is acting as "attorney," to bring his power of attorney with him to the closing in the event that the attorney for the buyer desires to examine the power of attorney. This should be done even though the power of attorney may be recorded.

The above list is by no means complete, but will give the broker an idea of some of the things necessary to bring a transaction to a smooth ending. It is suggested that the broker prepare a checklist, made up in accordance with local custom, as to the necessary things that he must do in order to close a transaction. A copy of this can be inserted in the "deal" envelope to insure that everything has been done that could be done to create a feeling of confidence in the people with whom the broker is dealing.

QUESTIONS FOR REVIEW

1. Why is it advisable for all purchasers of real property to have a survey made?
2. Under what circumstances, if any, would a purchaser be justified in requesting a bill of sale at a closing?
3. What is the rule of the New York Board of Real Estate with regard to computation and apportionment of taxes?

4. Why does a seller bring his insurance policies to a closing?
5. What is meant by an *apportionment* in a title closing?

PROBLEMS

1. Prepare a closing statement for both the purchaser and the seller under the following circumstances:

   A agrees to purchase Meadowbrook from *B*. The purchase price is $36,000, $4,000 cash paid on the signing of contract. *A* agrees to take the property "subject to" a $15,000 mortgage and pay the balance in cash. The taxes are $438.00 per year payable semiannually, January 1 and July 1. The interest on the mortgage is at 8½ percent, payable quarterly, the last payment having been made to but not including July 1. The insurance premium is $272 for three years and was purchased on March 1, 1974. The title policy cost $178. The attorney for the seller charged a $162 fee, and the attorney for the purchaser charged a $147 fee. There is a recording fee of $4. Title is to close on August 18, 1974.
2. Contact a real estate board in your community and from it obtain the customs in respect to closing of titles and prepare a summary of these customs.
3. Prepare a mortgage closing statement from the following:
   (a) Amount of new loan, $15,000.
   (b) Balance of existing loan of $7,500 to be paid.
   (c) Three months' interest on existing mortgage at 7 percent per annum.
   (d) Legal fees, $25.
   (e) Title insurance policy of $75.

   The applicant for the loan is Mr. Charles, his property is Lot #32 of the Brookline Development Corporation in your town, your county, and your state. The lender is the Third National Bank of Folkstown. The holder of the $7,500 mortgage is Mr. Evans, also of your town, your county, and your state. Draw all the necessary documents from the illustrations given in previous chapters of the book.
4. *A* is selling an investment property to *B*. In the contract of sale, *A* lists the gross rental from the property at $6,000 per year. What, if anything, should *B* require from *A* at the title closing pertaining to the tenants?
5. Mr. Buyer agrees to purchase a parcel of property from Mr. Seller. Mr. Realtor is the broker. The First National Bank of Folkstown

has agreed to finance part of the transaction; namely, $5,000 on a total price of $8,000, Mr. Buyer to furnish the difference in cash. Mr. Seller agrees to furnish an abstract of title. At the closing, Mr. Realtor, Mr. Buyer, Mr. Seller, and Mr. Cashier of the bank appear. Without attempting to apportion any of the charges involved, draw a simple flow chart indicating how and what instruments pass hands, and how much money passes from hand to hand and in what manner.

SUGGESTED READINGS

Case, Frederick E. *Real Estate,* Rev. ed. Boston: Allyn and Bacon, 1962. Chapter 14.

Ring, Alfred A. *Real Estate Principles and Practices*, 7th ed. Englewood Cliffs, New Jersey: Prentice-Hall, Inc., 1972. Chapter 18.

Weimer, Arthur M., Homer Hoyt, and George F. Bloom. *Principles of Real Estate,* 6th ed. New York: The Ronald Press Company, 1972. Chapter 16.

Chapter 24

Residential Appraising

When one considers the continuing increase in owner-occupied dwelling units, the increasing need for residential appraisals is apparent. Prospective buyers, owners, institutional lenders, and governmental units appraising for condemnation purposes all have an interest in residential property valuation.

THE PROBLEM OF VALUE

An *appraisal* is an attempt to obtain a just and fair opinion or estimate of the value of a parcel of real property. One of the basic problems is to determine just what the word "value" means. William Stanley Miller, one-time president of the New York State Tax Commission, described over fifty types of "value" . . . and then admitted that the list was by no means exhaustive.

The problem of determining just what value is was pointed up in the State of Florida where the state law requires all county assessors to assess at "full cash value." The governor of the state declared that a lack of a definition of full value had handicapped efforts to enforce the full value law. The governor said: "It is different from full value, and it is not 100 percent of market value. But I cannot say just what it is."

A few days later, one of the state legislators warned that assessors had better be careful to take "speculative value" into account when they were assessing at full cash value. The state comptroller then issued a statement saying that the time element would prevent any new definition of full cash value being applied to the property tax assessments. He added that he wasn't altogether certain that any new definition of full cash value could be arrived at. He also said that the Florida Supreme Court had indicated that full cash value meant the market value and the Supreme Court of another state subsequently held that market value was actually full cash value.[1]

It can readily be seen that the problem of determining just what value is may become rather clouded and complex. Value is nebulous, whatever it is, and it has been said that "value is in the eye of the beholder." In the final analysis, a person attempting to determine value may reach a conclusion depending on his reasons for making the attempt. Remember that "value" is a noun and that invariably one will find this noun preceded by an adjective. For example, one may want to know, for his own purposes: "market value," "capitalized value," "intrinsic value," "fair value," "cash value," "book value," "nuisance value," "liquidation value," "potential value," *ad infinitum.*

Economic Concept of Value

To the economist *value* is the power of commanding commodities in exchange. This was expressed by Adam Smith in his *Wealth of Nations* when he observed that "the word 'value' has two different meanings, and sometimes expresses the utility of some particular object and sometimes the power of purchasing other goods which possession of that object conveys." The latter concept implies economic or exchange value.

This concept might be expressed as the rate at which commodities exchange for other commodities. Historically, barter was the usual mode of exchange. Today the exchange usually is indirect; that is,

[1] The *Massachusetts Supreme Court* has held that "fair" cash value and "market" value mean the same thing. There assessments are made at "fair" cash value.

one commodity is sold for money, and the money is used to pay for something else.

It should be clear that value is not necessarily determined by usefulness, utility, or importance. For example, water is most useful, and its value is great, but in most parts of the world the power of water to command commodities in exchange is low. Thus, in the economic sense the value of water is low. Another example is iron, which is more useful than gold, but expressed in terms of value and in terms of exchange, gold commands a far greater amount of money.

Value and Price

If value can be thought of as the power to command commodities in exchange, it must be distinguished from price. *Price* expresses an individual estimate of value in terms of accepted medium of exchange. If an individual says that his house sold for less than its value, he is talking about price.

One of the problems concerning the measurement of value is that one must think of the exchange power of goods in terms of money, which really means "market value." And the purchasing power of money constantly fluctuates. Therefore, market value constantly fluctuates. In a period of depression, dollars in hand can purchase more goods than in a period of inflation. Thus, in a period of depression it pays an individual to move out of things into cash, and in a period of inflation to move from cash into things. This means that during a period of depression as the purchasing power of the dollar increases (as prices tumble), an individual holding cash can purchase more units of goods than he could before. The opposite is true in a period of inflation; then it is better to buy a washing machine, because, as prices rise, the price of the washing machine will also rise (even on the secondhand market). What has all this to do with value? The point is that while prices are changing, the *value* of a good *may* remain the same. Assume, for example, that *A* owns a new washing machine priced at $100. Assume further that suddenly things are inflated so that the same machine is now priced on the market at $200. This means that the purchasing power of the dollar has halved. As far as value or the power of a good to command other goods is concerned, the *value* of *A's* washing machine has remained the same, though his dollars have halved. By selling the washing machine for which he paid a price of $100, he can now get $200 and thus command $200 worth of other goods at current prices. This means that he is able to obtain as many units as he could before the inflation. Individuals holding money during this period are able to buy only half as many units of goods.

Cost

Cost is historical and is a measure of things that happened in the past. For example, if a person says that his house cost $20,000 five years ago, its value today could conceivably be only $10,000, or it could be $40,000 if inflation were serious enough. He is thinking of the past and expenditures that have been made in the past in speaking of cost. What makes value? The thinking of people makes value, particularly when dealing with real estate. The important things are human needs and human desires. Humans need shelter. Humans desire things other than just shelter. The social, economic, and political forces bear greatly on value within a specific area, and these forces are ultimately controlled or influenced by people.

The Elements of Value

An appraiser must recognize the existence of four primary elements that influence value: (1) physical elements, (2) economic elements, (3) social elements, and (4) legal elements. Many of these are discussed in detail later in the chapter. However, the following should be noted to point up their interrelationship and interaction in reaching some sort of decision as to value.

Physical Elements. This concerns factors which can create, condition, or destroy value. For example, in determining the value of land the appraiser must consider location, size, shape, area, frontage, topsoil, drainage, contour, topography, accessibility, utilities, roads, climate, and even the beautiful or ugly view. In improvements, the appraiser must consider material, workmanship, and wear and tear on the property (physical depreciation).

Economic Elements. Here one must consider income of the property, actual or potential, the earning power of the community, prevailing rates of interest, mortgage markets and federal participation in the mortgage market, general business conditions of the nation, the state, and the locale.

Social Elements. These too affect value. Here one deals with neighborhoods, population trends, marriage rates, traffic hazards, dead-end streets, urban renewal, noise, civic attitudes, and even architectural design.

Legal Elements. Legal elements can also create, condition, and destroy values. Here one's concern is with zoning, deed restrictions, city planning or lack of city planning, condition of title, and even legislation which might restrict or change the character of the land. For example, a planned expressway might have a definite effect or value as far as a particular area is concerned.

Characteristics of Value

The characteristics of value are in a sense related to the elements of value as was outlined above. They can, however, be separated and discussed with the idea of making the concept of "value" more meaningful. These value characteristics are:

Utility. This is defined as the power of a good to render a service or fill a need. Under this definition a common nail has utility, but it must be at the right place at the right time to have value. Furthermore, nails must be relatively scarce. Thus, air has utility; it is in the right place and at the right time, but it has no "market" value because it is not scarce. The point is that often the characteristics that go to make up value must be in useful combination.

Scarcity. This is a relative term related to supply and demand. If a product has utility, is relatively scarce, and has the other characteristics of value, then the "market" price is likely to be high.

Demand. Demand can be defined in economic terms as the desire for a good or service backed by the ability to pay for the product. This in reality is what the economist calls "effective demand" in order to emphasize the difference between wants and "economic demand."

Transferability. This is a legal concept, but essential to "market value." A good may have all of the other value characteristics, but if no one has the ability or right to transfer the good to another, it is without "market value."

In many cases transferability is thought of as related to mobility, but in the case of real property, for example, it need not be. An item may have utility, be scarce, and be in demand, but may have no market value because of lack of transferability.

Two Basic Concepts Relating to Value

Although it will later become apparent that there are a number of "principles of value," it is felt that only two need be introduced here to enable the student to better grasp the idea of "value." These are:

The Substitution Principle. The *substitution principle* holds that a thing cannot be worth more than the cost of replacement. This means that the value of a thing cannot be higher than the cost necessary to replace the thing, provided the substitution can be conveniently made. For example, a seller may wish to sell his home for $41,500. A new home, similarly constructed, including more conveniences, and only a few hundred feet away is priced at $42,000. The effect of the substitution principle will lower the asking price of the first home.

The Principle of Conformity. The *principle of conformity* is the maximum value of real property found where there is a reasonable degree of homogeneity with all the standards of the area. In short, a lot must be developed much in the same way as the adjacent neighborhood. Thus, mixing up land uses leads to lesser values.

The Value of the Appraiser

The basis of the valuation as far as the practicing appraiser is concerned is market value. When it becomes necessary for him to use a different concept of value, he treats it as a special case and proceeds accordingly. What then is market value?

The American Institute of Real Estate Appraisers in its *Appraisal Terminology and Handbook* says:

Market Value: (1) As defined by the courts, the highest price estimated in terms of money which a property will bring if exposed for sale in the open market, allowing a reasonable time to find a purchaser who buys with knowledge of all uses to which it is adapted and for which it is capable of being used. (2) Frequently, it is referred to as the price at which a willing seller would sell and a willing buyer would buy, neither being under abnormal pressure. (3) It is the price expected if a reasonable time is allowed to find a purchaser if both seller and prospective buyer are fully informed.

This is the definition given to market value by professional appraisers and is the one that is used quite generally in practice, so for practical purposes our definition may be limited to it here.

Objective Versus Subjective Thinking

One important factor in real estate appraising is the need for objective thinking. It is absolutely essential insofar as possible to eliminate one's own personal prejudices when inspecting the property under consideration. It is important to think in terms of the particular location in which the property is situated and not in terms of any other location.

This was brought into sharp focus recently when the author was conducting a field trip with an appraising class. Upon approaching the home under consideration, the author asked for an estimate of its value. One of the students was a resident of a county where most of the homes are in the high-price bracket. His estimate was $27,500, while the other students put the estimate at $22,000, which was within $500 of the market value of the property. The $5,000 error on the part of this student was due to the fact that he was thinking in terms of home values in his own county instead of the area under consideration. His thinking was subjective and not objective as it should have been for a realistic appraisal.

APPROACHES TO RESIDENTIAL APPRAISING

There are three main approaches to residential appraising: the replacement cost approach, the market data approach, and the income approach. The last-named will be discussed in detail in Chapter 25.

The Replacement Cost Approach

This method of appraising residential property involves essentially determining the replacement cost of the property, as of today, and then depreciating the property in terms of its present condition. In short, replacement cost less the "used-up" value of the house equals present value. Many factors are involved in determining replacement cost and used-up value as can be seen readily by glancing at the suggested appraisal report that is reproduced and explained in detail section by section beginning on page 611.

Market Data Approach

This approach is used primarily as a check on the computations employed in the depreciated replacement cost method. Basically, it involves a comparison of the sales prices that have been obtained for like accommodations—like accommodations meaning properties similar in all respects to the one under consideration. Of course, it necessarily follows that the more sales that have taken place, the less chance of error.

The Income Approach

Through this approach net income is capitalized to determine value. Briefly, the question is, "What is the present worth of future income?" Because of its importance in the evaluation of income-producing property, it will be discussed more thoroughly in the next chapter. However, in residential property appraising, frequently an attempt is made to use a rule of thumb pertaining to income called the gross income multiplier. It is a rule of thumb based on gross income and should not be confused with the "income approach" which uses net figures. It is a useful secondary check on the other approaches to value.

The multiplier is derived by using recent sales divided by actual or estimated monthly rentals. For example, see top of page 603.

The multiplier is 115. Assuming the property under consideration rents for \$170, the estimated market value equals 115 × \$170 = \$19,550, which may be rounded off to \$19,500.

SALE	MARKET VALUE		ACTUAL OR ESTIMATED MONTHLY RENTAL		GROSS MONTHLY MULTIPLIER (rounded off)
1.	$20,000	÷	$175	=	114
2.	19,500	÷	160	=	122
3.	21,000	÷	180	=	117
4.	22,000	÷	200	=	110
Totals and Averages	$82,500		$715	Average	115

Although useful, the gross monthly multiplier contains some serious defects and must be used with care:

1. Gross income rather than net income is used. No accounting for operating or maintenance costs is included.

2. The multiplier assumes uniformity of the various properties in their operating ratios. There is an implied assumption that all real property taxes, heating costs, etc., are the same.

3. No importance is placed on the remaining economic life of the properties. Some have a longer remaining economic life than others. It is assumed here that all the properties examined are the same.

FUNDAMENTAL CONSIDERATIONS IN MAKING REAL ESTATE APPRAISALS

In the final analysis, an appraisal is based on sound judgment. This implies a need for factual data supporting the judgment. Some judgment aids are discussed below. To guide you in your study, a suggested appraisal report is provided.

Population Trends

The population of a city or town increases in importance according to the purpose for which an appraisal is made. The home buyer looks upon a house as a place to live and the city in which the property is located as a place to work. He is, therefore, not too much interested in population trends. His prime interest lies in today's worth of the building. A slightly different situation exists with an appraisal being made for a prospective investor. True, he is interested in present worth of the house under consideration, but he is also interested in anything that might affect the value of the property over a long period of time. The prime interest of the investor lies in the value of the property as security for a loan, the loan generally being repayable over a long period.

Why, then, is the investor interested in population trends? The answer to this lies in supply and demand. The investor will recognize immediately that if the population trend of a city is down and has been going down for some time, there is a good possibility of housing being thrown on the market with a consequent depression of real property values and a corresponding impairment of his security. On the other hand, if the population trend is upward, then lending institutions might be more easily persuaded to lend money on the property. The lender feels that after a period of time the demand for houses will be high and will command a high resale price should resale become necessary.

General Neighborhood Characteristics

General neighborhood characteristics help the appraiser form an opinion as to the value of the property. The neighborhood has a tremendous influence on value. Certain trends within a neighborhood should be taken not only as danger signals with regard to future value, but must also be taken into consideration in terms of present value.

For example, suppose that an otherwise fashionable district is changing into a rooming-house district. This would indicate that any further changes in that direction might conceivably affect the value of the property for residential purposes. How does one determine whether the area is becoming a rooming-house district? The answer is by a close inspection of the neighborhood, not by driving past, but by walking through the area and making careful observations.

Changes in a district can be found by making inquiries of people living in the district. If a district is changing from residential into business, note the number of new businesses, new store fronts, and so forth.

The type of residential district may be noted from any new construction in the neighborhood. The kind of new construction should be observed. Determine whether or not the neighborhood has been "kept up." For example, a dirty, unkempt aura about a neighborhood is an indication of a downward trend in the section.

One rule of thumb often helpful in appraising is that when the houses in a particular neighborhood are over twenty-five years old, that neighborhood is probably in for a period of decline.

Fire and Police Protection. The matter of fire and police protection becomes important in the appraisal of property located in suburban areas. The lack of adequate police and fire protection will undoubtedly affect the market value of the property because of a natural tendency of people to shy away from a location without these essentials. Another consideration, although a minor one, is that insurance rates in places lacking fire and police protection are generally high.

Distances to Schools, Stores, Etc. The distances to schools, stores, transportation, and churches are important to the overall appraisal picture in the same manner as fire and police protection. A lack of proximity to schools, churches, etc., will reflect on the market value of the property.

Authorized Public Improvements. In making an appraisal, it is important for one to be aware of any authorized public improvements. For example, there may not be a school in the area in which the building is located; therefore, this may previously have been taken as detrimental to the property. If, however, it is determined that a school has been authorized, this may offset previous determinations with regard to a lack of schools within a reasonable distance from the building being appraised.

The same thing might prove true when, at the moment, police and fire protection is considered inadequate. It may be that protection has been authorized by the councilmen of the town. The place to find out whether public improvements have been authorized is in the town hall or city hall, as the case may be.

Salability. The degree of salability of the property will have a direct effect upon the market value of the property and, hence, affect the appraisal. If, for example, the property is located in a neighborhood that is undesirable, the salability of the property would have a tendency to be depressed. The question of salability becomes even more important if the client is a lending institution because, again, the lender looks upon the property as security for a long-term loan. A property that is difficult to sell is a hazard, and it is the duty of the appraiser to make clear to his client any hazardous conditions that exist.

Building Description

The problems arising under building description lead to more accurate perception concerning the value of the property. Three important questions are, in part, answered here: first, the question of physical deterioration or depreciation; second, the value of any "extra features"; and third, the cost of any exterior or interior repairs which must be taken into consideration before any final value can be assigned to the building. Keeping in mind that an attempt is being made to determine depreciated replacement or replacement cost, one can then see these factors in terms of property by finding replacement cost, subtracting the depreciation, subtracting the value of repairs, adding the value of extra features, and adding the value of the land.

The value to be assigned to such extra features as the fireplace or the garage should not be too difficult to obtain from contractors specializing in this work. The cost of interior repairs or exterior repairs may easily be determined in the same way.

Here, too, one should note the workmanship and construction of the building because of the influence that this factor will have on determining the rate of depreciation.

Site Evaluation

One of the first things that an appraiser does upon visiting a property is to attempt to evaluate the site. This valuation of the site is to determine whether the land is realizing its highest and best use. That is, an evaluation is made to determine the highest and best possible utilization of that site in terms of producing the maximum future return to the owner. The evaluation of the site in terms of income production is perhaps of more value when income-producing property is being appraised, but it nevertheless does have some importance in residential appraising.

The major importance of site evaluation when appraising residential property is in determining the existence of *economic obsolescence* or the loss in value to a property due to the impairment of economic value; that is, due to a change in the character of a neighborhood. The evaluation of the site thus lays the groundwork for placing a value on the land.

Depreciation and Obsolescence

If one can determine the cost of a building when new and subtract from this the amount in terms of dollars and cents that the building has been consumed, an accurate estimate of the present value of the building can easily be determined. Suppose, for example, that the cost of a building when new was $20,000 and that it had been consumed to the extent of $4,000 worth, it is then a simple matter to state that the present value of the building is $16,000.

This consumed quantity of a used building is called depreciation. *Depreciation* is a general term covering loss of value from *any* cause. Generally, depreciation is referred to in terms of a percentage figure. In the example above it might be said that the house had depreciated 20 percent according to the appraiser's observation. Another way of saying the same thing is to state that the remaining economic life of a home after it has depreciated 20 percent is 80 percent.

It must be recognized that age alone is not the only cause of depreciation. For example, the Internal Revenue Service states that a one-family brick dwelling has an annual depreciation rate of 2 percent. Thus, the expected life of a one-family brick dwelling, under normal conditions, is 50 years. Common sense dictates that all one-family brick dwellings do not collapse at the end of 50 years like the one-horse shay. It is possible that the remaining economic life of one house may be greater than that of another. It follows then that in selecting the proper rate of depreciation, the appraiser must exercise superior judgment.

The fact that the actual age of a building does not necessarily control the rate of depreciation may readily be seen. In the suburbs within commuting distance of New York City, there are many people inhabiting homes well over 100 years old. In theory these houses should long since have been completely depreciated, but the fact remains that most of them have between 20 and 30 years of remaining economic life.

Suppose that there are two brick houses side by side, constructed by the same builder and in all respects similar. Theoretically, both houses should be completely consumed or depreciated at the end of 50 years, and therefore, should be depreciated at a theoretical rate of 2 percent per year. Suppose further that *A* and *B* purchase these houses and each moves into his respective house at the same time. *A* does absolutely nothing to improve or repair the building. On the other hand, *B* loves to putter around and each spring he paints the trim, the interior, and the screens. At the end of five years, he has a professional painter completely redecorate the place. If he discovers a leaky faucet, *B* hastens to repair it. In the fall he has his chimney cleaned and the oil burner checked.

At the end of ten years, which house would be in the better condition? Obviously *B's* home because of the excellent care *B* had given it. Would the appraiser be justified in flatly stating that because of the fact that both homes were ten years old that each is to be depreciated 20 percent, and, therefore, the *remaining economic life* of each home is 80 percent (80 percent good)? Obviously both houses would not be considered as being in the same condition and thus equally depreciated.

What then is the answer? The answer lies in observing the loss of value from each of the three causes or factors that make up depreciation. They are: (1) physical deterioration, (2) functional obsolescence, and (3) economic obsolescence.

These three factors enable the appraiser to form a judgment and to make a determination of depreciation applicable to the particular building under examination. What is meant by these three terms?

Physical Deterioration. *Physical deterioration* is the decay and natural wear and tear on a building. Dry rot sets in, the roof sags, the paint is cracked and peeling, plaster is falling from the walls, termites have weakened the structure—all of these things and many more go to make up physical deterioration. These signs of wear and tear must be looked for and carefully noted by the appraiser.

All of the elements listed above are existent or inherent in the property. To a large degree, however, the owner of the property himself has a certain amount of control over physical deterioration.

Functional Obsolescence. *Functional obsolescence* is an impairment of desirability and usefulness brought about by changes in design, art, process, and the like. These changes make a property less desirable. This is distinguished from physical deterioration in that the owner has little or no control over this type of reduction of value of his home. The owner has no control, for example, over any radical changes in architectural design of buildings. Nevertheless, the value of his building is reduced because of them unless he elects to correct the defect through modernization. A house may be *physically* sound, but the kitchen and bathroom fixtures may be old-fashioned. The fact that the fixtures are outmoded lessens the desirability of the property, and therefore reduces the value of it.

It should be remembered that functional obsolescence comes about for the most part as a result of external causes.

Economic Obsolescence. *Economic obsolescence* is the impairment of desirability or useful life of property arising from economic forces. Although the property owner may limit to a large degree both physical depreciation and functional obsolescence, he has little or no control over economic obsolescence. Economic obsolescence has to do with changes of the neighborhood and is probably the greatest cause of loss in value of real property. It is an *external* factor that causes loss of value. This is usually brought about by a running down of the neighborhood causing it to lose character, or it may be that changes inconsistent with the use of property as a residence may take place in a neighborhood. For example, a factory may be erected in a residential neighborhood, or an expressway may be constructed with resultant traffic noise. All of these things make up economic obsolescence with its consequent loss of value to homes.

In the final analysis it is the judgment of the appraiser in weighing the above factors that enables him to reach a figure representing an accurate rate of depreciation.

One important factor should always be borne in mind, namely, that the amount of accrued depreciation is always determined by observation *at the time of the appraisal.* This may seem obvious, but it is a trap into which inexperienced appraisers often fall. Just because the original value of a house has been depreciated 10 percent over a period of five years (a rate of 2 percent per annum), it does not necessarily follow that two years later it will have depreciated to the extent of 14 percent of its original value merely because it is now seven years old. Conceivably, a new owner may within two years let a building get completely in disrepair. In this case the depreciation over a two-year period might jump from 10 to 20 percent of the original value of the building or even higher. An appraiser cannot, therefore, use his files to determine the rate of depreciation of a house without a reexamination of the premises. Each time an appraisal is made, a visit to the premises is imperative because he must determine the amount of accrued depreciation by observation.

Zoning Ordinances

Zoning ordinances are laws passed by a municipality placing artificial restrictions on the use of properties lying within its jurisdiction. These laws should be, and usually are, based on land use, distribution of population, topography, meteorological data, and other pertinent information.

Generally, the zoning ordinances divide land into three main categories; namely, industrial, business, and residential properties. This means, among other things, that although a residence may be in a business or industrial zone, a business or industrial property may not encroach upon a residential zone.[2]

A zoning law may have a very marked effect upon an appraisal. The proper thing to do before making an appraisal is to examine carefully a zoning map with regard to the property under appraisal. This is an unqualified "must."

For example, suppose that the house being appraised is in an unrestricted area—unrestricted in the sense that a factory may be built alongside the property at anytime. A situation of this kind creates a condition known as a "hazard," and when such a condition exists, an appraiser might be justified in depreciating the property as much as 25 percent of its original value.

An important factor to bear in mind when examining a lot is the square footage or front footage required by the local zoning laws pertaining to the minimum area upon which a house may be built. This is not too important when the property being appraised already contains a house. It is important, however, when considering a vacant lot.

---

[2] Under the zoning laws of some cities, residences are not permitted in industrial zones.

THE REPLACEMENT COST APPROACH

The most common method of residential appraising is the replacement cost approach. When using this method the appraiser determines the square feet of the building, multiplies the square footage $\times$ the cost per square foot = replacement cost − depreciation = depreciated replacement cost.

For example, a building has 1,000 square feet at a cost per square foot of $12, effective age ten years. It has been depreciated at 2 percent per year, or 20 percent for 10 years; hence, it is 80 percent good. Thus, the depreciated replacement cost = 1,000 $\times$ $12 = $12,000 $\times$ .80 = $9,600.

Of course, the example above is oversimplified. A much more sophisticated and more accurate example is shown as follows. It should be pointed out that the replacement cost example is designed to be used with the Marshall and Swift Company's *Residential Cost Handbook*. There are a number of these published throughout the country making the appraiser's job easier in the sense that cost per square foot is readily obtainable. Many appraisers, however, rely on this same information from local builders, financial institutions, and their own office files (called plants).

In the example that follows, the building is assumed to be new. The estimate of value would be the same except for the appraiser's deduction for depreciation.

The example on page 613 shows a photo of the house under appraisement. This is a common practice on most appraisal forms. Page 614 shows a detailed drawing of the floor plan. Most appraisers are not highly skilled; hence a floor plan drawn by them would be quite rough but acceptable.

Page 615 shows the description of the building which is a must on all appraisals because it aids the appraiser in forming a judgment as to the value of the property.

Pages 616 and 617 show the area calculations and various adjustments. For example, the area is shown as 2,987 square feet. This figure is repeated on line 1 of the Appraisal Computations on the lower part of page 616. The porch area is shown on lines 16 and 17; and the garage area, 496 square feet, on line 20.

The adjustments are made by working with the residential cost handbook. Adjustments are deviations from the standard home, either better, in which case they are added to the overall cost, or less than the standard, in which case they are deducted. For example, cost basis of the porch is $3.95 a square foot, an additional $1.67 per square foot is added for the roof, plus another $.64 a square foot for the ceiling, totaling $6.26 a square foot. This is derived from page 619, which is reproduced from the cost handbook.

The Local Multiplier

One of the more perplexing things about working with any of the cost handbooks is the "local multiplier." In the example given here, it is 1.04. It could vary a great deal in different parts of the country. It simply means that a standard cost base of 100 has been established and that building costs in any city may be either greater or lower than 100. Hence, the cost figure per square foot is either adjusted upward or lowered to meet local conditions. In the example given, line 25 shows the subtotal of all building improvements as $43,405. However, line 26 indicates a multiplier of 1.04. Thus 1.04 × 43,405 = $45,141, the value for that area. Some local multipliers are shown on page 620.

How Are the Multipliers Obtained?

The services, such as Marshall and Swift, send quarterly supplements to their subscribers showing any changes in local multipliers. Thus, if in one quarter, the multiplier was 100 and if the costs in that city have increased, the next local multiplier might be 1.03. The new cost figures are obtained by a service from local contractors and financial institutions.

How Are Homes Keyed Into the Cost Handbook?

The problem is how to obtain the correct cost figures for different styles and ages of homes. The answer is that the cost handbooks are set up so that a photo of the style of the home being appraised is reproduced in the handbook and referenced to a page giving cost figures for that particular type home. For example, suppose a home 15 years old is being appraised. The appraiser looks at it and then matches it with a given photo in the book. Under the photo is the page number giving cost figures for that 15-year-old building. One would work from there on the form in the manner described above.

REPLACEMENT COST EXAMPLE

ONE AND ONE HALF STORY

Presented by

MARSHALL and SWIFT
Publication Company

1617 BEVERLY BOULEVARD ● LOS ANGELES, CALIFORNIA 90026

Copies of this material are available, without charge, to current subscribers or qualified instructors for free distribution to appraisal students.

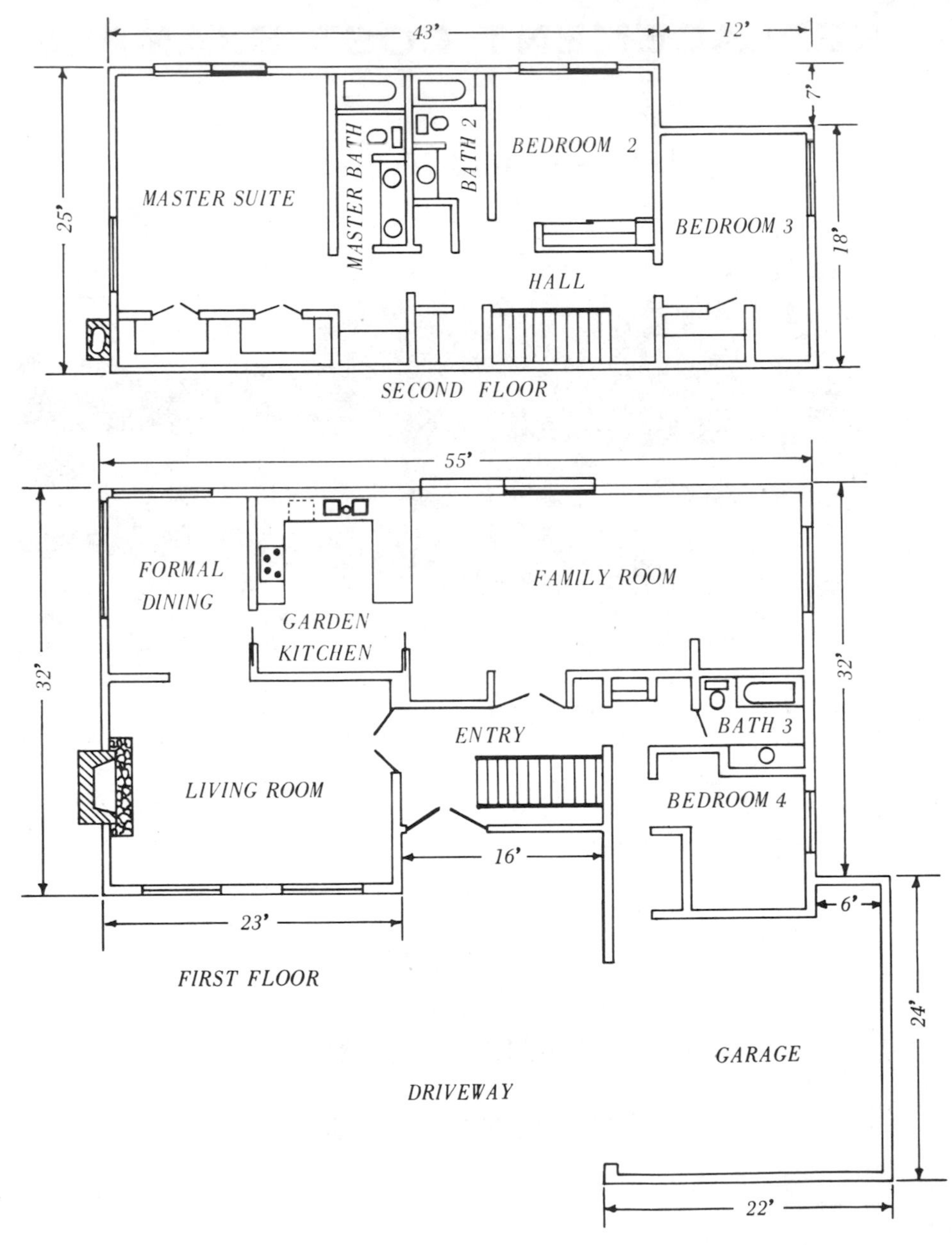
43'
12'
7'
25'
18'
MASTER SUITE
MASTER BATH
BATH 2
BEDROOM 2
BEDROOM 3
HALL
SECOND FLOOR
55'
32'
32'
FORMAL
DINING
GARDEN
KITCHEN
FAMILY ROOM
ENTRY
BATH 3
LIVING ROOM
BEDROOM 4
16'
6'
23'
FIRST FLOOR
24'
GARAGE
DRIVEWAY
22'

SUBJECT RESIDENCE DESCRIPTION

FOUNDATION:	Reinforced concrete footings and walls around perimeter and under interior bearing partitions. No abnormal soil conditions.
STRUCTURAL FRAME:	All frame members are wood. Quality of workmanship and material is good.
EXTERIOR FINISH:	Painted stucco is primary finish. Front of residence is partially covered with wood shingle siding and decorative plywood panels of good quality.
ROOF:	Good quality wood shingles over 30 lb. felt on 1"x6" spaced sheathing.
INSULATION:	4" rock wool batts placed between ceiling joists adjacent to exterior surfaces.
INTERIOR FINISH:	Plaster walls with paint and some wallpaper. Ceiling has sprayed plaster finish. Ceramic tile counter tops and splash in kitchen and cultured marble pullman tops in baths.
SASH AND DOORS:	Painted hollow core doors throughout interior, sliding glass door in breakfast area, double door front entry, sliding aluminum sash.
FLOORS:	Concrete slab on first floor and wood subfloor with carpet on second floor. Kitchen and bath floors are vinyl asbestos tile. Entry floor is terrazzo tiles.
PLUMBING:	Twelve good quality fixtures as follows: 2 tubs with shower over; 1 stall shower with ceramic tile; 3 lavatory sinks; 3 toilets; 1 kitchen sink; 1 laundry tray and washer-dryer service; 1 water heater.
CABINETS AND CLOSETS:	Adequate kitchen cabinets of good quality hardwood veneer with stain finish. Sufficient walk-in and wardrobe type bedroom closets, and shelved linen closet.
FIREPLACE:	One single, 2 story fireplace of average quality.
HEATING AND COOLING:	Gas fired forced air furnace. 5 ton refrigerated air conditioning utilizing forced air ducts with thermostat controls.
ELECTRICAL:	Flexible steel conduit, adequate outlets. Lighting fixtures are good quality.
BUILT-IN APPLIANCES:	Good quality double gas oven and range, hood and fan, garbage disposer, dishwasher and mixer-blender unit.
ATTACHED GARAGE:	Wood frame with concrete slab floor and wood shingle roof. Overhead wood door. Roof and exterior finish conform to that of house.
GENERAL QUALITY:	Residence and garage reflect good quality workmanship and materials throughout.

SQUARE FOOT APPRAISAL FORM

for use with the **RESIDENTIAL COST HANDBOOK**

Appraisal for ______ Property owner ______

Address ______

Appraiser ______ Date ______

TYPE		QUALITY		STYLE		EXTERIOR WALLS	
Conventional	☒	Low	☐	No. Stories	____	Stucco	☒
Modern	☐	Fair	☐	Split level	☐	Siding or shingle	☐
Rustic	☐	Average	☐	1½ story - Fin.	☒	Brick veneer	☐
Apartment	☐	Good	☒	1½ story - Unfin.	☐	Common brick	☐
Town house	☐	Very good	☐	End row	☐	Face brick or stone	☐
Row house	☐			Inside row	☐	Concrete block	☐

Floor areas: 1st *1,696* 2nd *1,291* 3rd ______ 4th ______ Total *2,987*

Basement area: Finished *NONE* Unfinished ______ Garage area *496* ☐ Detached ☒ Attached

Number multiple units ______ Average area per unit ______ ☐ Built-in

Porches (a) *96 SQ. FT.* (b) ______ (c) ______ Other ______

APPRAISAL COMPUTATIONS

	Quan.	Cost	+	-	Extension
1. **Compute residence basic cost:** Floor area × selected sq. ft. cost (*$12.87 x .964*)	*2,987*	*$12.41*			*$37,069*
2. Basic residence cost adjustments Lines 3-14. Describe and indicate plus or minus			+	-	
3. Roofing *WOOD SHINGLE (BASE)*					
4. Flooring 1st floor *CONCRETE SLAB W/ VINYL ASB. TILE ($-1.33 + $.49)*	*1,696*	*.84*		*–*	*1,425*
5. Flooring upper floors *WOOD SUBFLOOR W/CARPET ($-.86 + $1.10)*	*1,291*	*.24*	*+*		*310*
6. Heating *FORCED AIR, GAS (BASE) W/ REFRIG. AIR COND.*	*2,987*	*1.04*	*+*		*3,106*
7. Ceiling insulation *2ND FLOOR ONLY*	*1,291*	*.12*	*+*		*155*
8. Plumbing *12 FIXTURES (BASE = 9)*	*3*	*240*	*+*		*720*
9. Fireplace *SINGLE, 2 STORY (AVERAGE QUALITY, PAGE A-38)*	*/*	*705*	*+*		*705*
10. Built-in appliances *GAS RANGE & OVEN, EXHAUST FAN & HOOD,*					
11. *GARBAGE DISPOSER, DISHWASHER (BASE)*					
12. *MIXER-BLENDER*	*/*	*85*	*+*		*85*
13. Miscellaneous					
14.					
15. **Subtotal adj. residence cost:** Line 1 plus or minus Lines 3-14					*40,725*
16. Porches or balconies, describe *FRONT: 6'x16' = 96 SQ. FT.*					
17. *W/ STEPS @ $3.95, + ROOF @ $1.67, + CEILING @ $.64*	*96*	*6.26*			*601*
18. Basement *NONE*					
19. **Subtotal residence cost:** Total of Lines 15-18					*41,326*
20. **Garage** – sq. ft. area x selected sq. ft. cost *STUCCO*	*496*	*4.66*	*+*		*2,311*
21. Attached garage - deduct for common wall *"*	*18*	*12.91*		*-*	*232*
22. Garage roofing adjustment *NONE*					
23. Garage miscellaneous					
24. **Subtotal garage cost:** Line 20 plus or minus Lines 21-23					*2,079*
25. **Subtotal of all building improvements:** Sum of Lines 19 and 24					*43,405*
26. Current local cost of buildings: Local multiplier *1.04* x Line 25					*$45,141*
27. Depreciation: Age ____ Condition ____ Deduction ____ % of Line 26					
28. Depreciated cost of building improvements: Line 26 less Line 27					
29. Yard improvements cost: List, total, apply local multiplier and depreciate on reverse side					
30. Landscaping cost: List and compute on reverse side					
31. Lot or land value					
32. **TOTAL INDICATED VALUE** – Total of Lines 28-31					

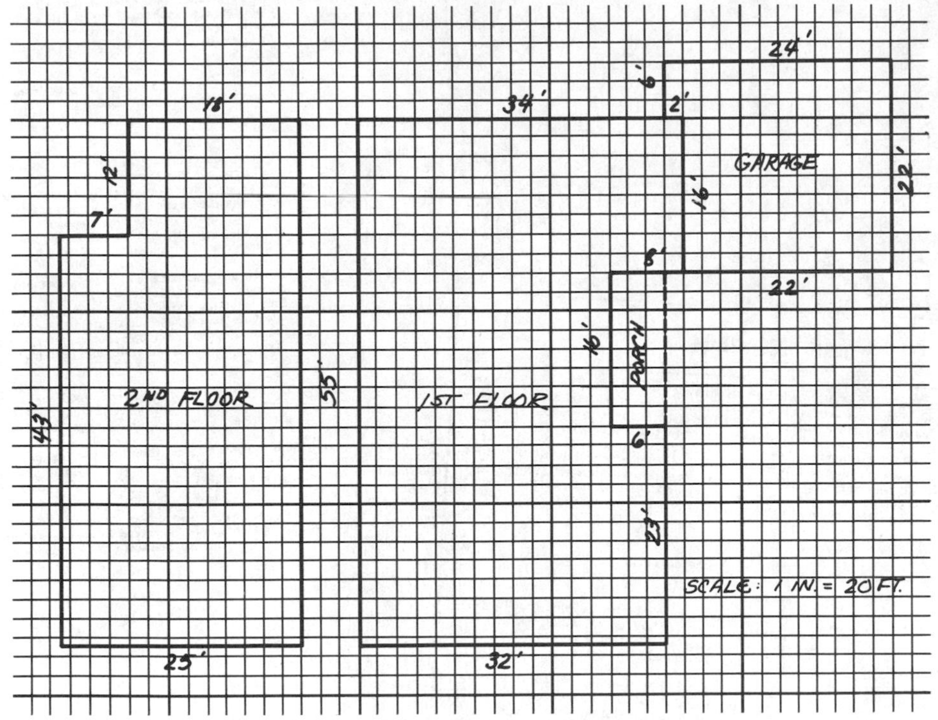

NOTES AND COMPUTATIONS

FLOOR AREA

FIRST FLOOR:	55.0' x 32.0' =	1,760 SQ. FT.
	2.0' x 16.0' =	32 " "
LESS	6.0' x 16.0' =	−96 " "
	SUB-TOTAL	1,696 SQ. FT.
SECOND FLOOR:	25.0' x 43.0' =	1,075 SQ. FT.
	12.0' x 18.0' =	216 " "
	SUB-TOTAL	1,291 SQ. FT.
	TOTAL	2,987 SQ. FT.

*NOTE: COST ADJUSTMENT – LARGE RESIDENCE EQUALS .964 (PAGE 12 OF HANDBOOK)

GARAGE AREA:	22.0' x 22.0' =	484 SQ. FT.
	2.0' x 6.0' =	12 " "
	TOTAL	496 SQ. FT.

PORCH AREA:

FRONT: 6.0' x 16.0' = 96 SQ. FT.

BASIC DESCRIPTION

Homes of Good Quality may be custom built for individual owners or mass produced in above average residential developments. Good standard materials are used throughout and workmanship is usually above average. The Good Quality homes generally exceed the minimum building requirements of lending institutions, mortgage insuring agencies and building codes. Architectural design is attractive with attention given to refinements and detail. Interiors are well finished, usually having some good quality wallpaper, wood paneling and selected fixtures. Exterior front elevations frequently have an appealing combination of ornamental materials or other refinement.

RESIDENCE

Foundation . . . . Reinforced concrete perimeter footing and wall with piers or continuous foundation under interior bearing walls.

Roof . . . . Good quality cedar shingles on wood sheathing and rafters. Roof slope averages 5/12 or less. Use Square Foot Adjustments to correct basic residence cost for other types of roofing.

Interior Walls . . . . . Taped and painted drywall having few surface imperfections; some good quality wallpaper and wood paneling; skilled workmanship throughout.

Doors, Trim and Sash . Good quality hardwood hollow core slab or panel doors; hardwood or softwood base and casing with tight mitered corners and well finished; attractive interior and exterior hardware. Well designed fenestration using good grade sash.

Floors . . . . Primary finish for first and upper story floors, select or first grade hardwood on sound wood subfloor and joists. Wood subfloor only, on second story of one and one half story residence with unfinished second floor.
Use Square Foot Adjustments to correct basic residence cost for other types of flooring and floor cover.

Plumbing . . . . Nine good quality fixtures, white or standard color, which can include any of the following: water heater, laundry tray and service, tiled stall shower; along with toilet, lavatory sink, tub with shower over, kitchen sink.
Use Lump Sum Adjustments to correct basic residence cost for more or less than nine plumbing fixtures.

Bathroom . . . . Enameled ceiling and walls or combination of enamel and wallpaper; ceramic tile or vinyl floor cover; pullman or vanity cabinet with ceramic tile or good quality plastic top and splash.

Kitchen . . . . Enameled ceiling and walls with some decorative wallpaper; vinyl tile or heavy gauge coved and patterned linoleum floor cover; ample cabinets of finished hardwood veneer with ceramic tile or good quality plastic top and splash; good quality decorative hardware.

Closets. . . . . Walk-in or large sliding door wardrobe closets; guest closet; ample linen and storage closets; good finish and hardware.

Heating. . . . . Gas fired forced air furnace with sufficient output and duct work to all main areas and baths.
Use Square Foot Adjustments to correct for other types of heating and cooling.

BASIC DESCRIPTION

Built-in Appliances . . Gas range and oven; exhaust fan and hood; garbage disposer; dishwasher. Good quality units with some custom features.
Add or deduct from Lump Sum Adjustments when applicable.

Fireplace . . . . None included in basic cost. Add from Lump Sum Adjustments when applicable.

BASEMENT

Unfinished . . . . Poured concrete or concrete block walls; concrete slab floor, smooth troweled with drain; wood or steel beams and columns supporting floor structure above; well constructed and painted softwood stairway; adequate electrical outlets and windows.
Use Lump Sum Adjustments for adding cost of plumbing fixtures or rough-in.

Finished . . . . Good quality asphalt tile or heavy gauge vinyl asbestos floor cover; walls are drywall or plywood paneling on furring strips; taped and painted drywall on ceiling; adequate heating and good lighting. No partition walls included. Cost per linear foot for interior partitioning may be computed from the Unit-in-Place Cost Section.

GARAGE . . . . Concrete slab floor and apron; good quality overhead door; conforms to residence in type, quality and construction. Compute from Garage Cost Table.

quare Foot and Lump Sum Adjustments not listed on the cost pages may be etermined by reference to Segregated Cost Section B. For detailed cost djustments or the pricing of speciality items, refer to Unit-in-Place Cost ection C.

o modify the basic residence cost for Modern or Rustic architectural degns and to adjust for larger floor areas than given in the cost tables, refer Pages 11 and 12 in the front of your Residential Cost Handbook.

Contractors overhead and profit included in all costs.

COST ADJUSTMENT-LARGE RESIDENCE

The following multipliers are provided to adjust the square foot cost factors for all residences having a floor area greater than the largest floor area given in the particular table being used. To determine the proper cost factor for a large residence:

1. Select the proper multiplier from the following schedules as indicated by the quality and square foot area of the residence being appraised.

2. Apply the multiplier selected to last cost factor given in the appropriate column of the cost table being used.

3. The cost factor thus obtained is the basic square foot cost for the subject large residence and is then adjusted and computed in the usual manner.

LOW QUALITY RESIDENCE . . . Apply multiplier to appropriate 1500 square foot cost factor.

SQ. FT. AREA	MULTIPLIER	SQ. FT. AREA	MULTIPLIER	SQ. FT. AREA	MULTIPLIER
1600	.989	2100	.969	2600	.954
1700	.984	2200	.966	2700	.951
1800	.979	2300	.963	2800	.948
1900	.975	2400	.960	2900	.945
2000	.972	2500	.957	3000	.943

FAIR QUALITY RESIDENCE . . Apply multiplier to appropriate 2400 square foot cost factor.

SQ. FT. AREA	MULTIPLIER	SQ. FT. AREA	MULTIPLIER	SQ. FT. AREA	MULTIPLIER
2500	.993	2700	.979	2900	.968
2600	.986	2800	.973	3000	.964

AVERAGE QUALITY RESIDENCE . . . Apply multiplier to appropriate 2400 squar[e] foot cost factor.

SQ. FT. AREA	MULTIPLIER	SQ. FT. AREA	MULTIPLIER	SQ. FT. AREA	MULTIPLI[ER]
2600	.985	3400	.953	4200	.933
2800	.974	3600	.947	4400	.930
3000	.965	3800	.942	4600	.927
3200	.958	4000	.937	4800	.925

GOOD QUALITY RESIDENCE . . Apply multiplier to appropriate 2400 s[quare] foot cost factor.

SQ. FT. AREA	MULTIPLIER	SQ. FT. AREA	MULTIPLIER	SQ. FT. AREA	MULT[IPLIER]
2600	.989	3600	.939	4600	
2800	[illegible]	3800	.934	4800	
3000	.964	4000	.931	5000	
3200	[illegible]	4200	.928	5200	
3400	.945	4400	.925	5400	

VERY GOOD QUALITY RESIDENCE . . Apply multiplier to appropriate 3[...] foot cost factor.

SQ. FT. AREA	MULTIPLIER	SQ. FT. AREA	MULTIPLIER	SQ. FT. AREA	
3400	.999	4400	.954	5400	
3600	.984	4600	.949	5600	
3800	.973	4800	.945	5800	
4000	.965	5000	.941	6000	
4200	.959	5200	.938	6200	

page 12

Square Foot Costs
Good Quality
(Finished 2nd Floor)

ONE AND ONE HALF STORY

RESIDENCE COSTS (per sq. ft. of total floor area)

Sq. Ft. Area	WOOD FRAME Stucco	Siding or Shingle	Brick Veneer	Sq. Ft. Area	MASONRY Common Brick	Face Brick or Stone	Concrete Block
1000	$17.17	$17.75	$18.98	1000	$19.49	$21.54	$18.70
1100	16.55	17.12	18.25	1100	18.75	20.76	18.01
1200	16.08	16.65	17.70	1200	18.19	20.16	17.45
1300	15.71	16.28	17.28	1300	17.77	19.67	17.04
1400	15.37	15.94	16.92	1400	17.40	19.27	16.67
1600	14.79	15.37	16.31	1600	16.73	18.59	16.05
1800	14.24	14.81	15.73	1800	16.15	17.93	15.51
2000	13.74	14.32	15.24	2000	15.65	17.36	14.99
2200	[illegible]	13.85	14.78	2200	15.18	16.81	14.54
2400	12.87	13.42	14.35	2400	14.72	16.29	14.09

RESIDENCE COST ADJUSTMENTS

The following cost adjustments are based on workmanship and materials that conform to the quality level of the square foot costs given above. The plus or minus signs indicate whether an item is an addition to, or a deduction from, the basic square foot cost. Cost adjustments for items not listed below may be determined by reference to the Segregated Cost Section.

SQUARE FOOT ADJUSTMENTS

ROOFING (Apply to total flr. area)
Wood shingle . . . . (base)
Wood shake . . . . [illegible]
Mission tile . . . . + .64
Asphalt shingle . . . . - .19
Built-up, large rock . . . . . . - .16

FLOORS (Apply to individual floors)
Hardwood . . . . (base)
Concrete slab only . . . . . . -1.33
Wood subfloor only . . . . . . - .86
Add for: Carpet . . . . +1.10
Vinyl asb. tile . . . . + .49

HEATING (Apply to total flr. area)
Forced air, gas . . . . (base)
Flr. or wall furnace, gas . . . . -$.36
Gravity, gas . . . . - .12
Forced air, oil . . . . + .08
Floor radiant, hot water . . . . + .99
Ceiling radiant, electric . . . + .07
Baseboard, electric . . . . . + .14
Baseboard, hot water . . . . [illegible]
Refrig. A/C using htr. duct . . +1.04

INSULATION (Ceiling area) . . + .12

LUMP SUM ADJUSTMENTS

* Indicates items included in base cost.

***PLUMBING** 9 fixtures . . . . (base)
Per fixture . . . . +or-$240
Plbg. fixture, rough-in . . . [illegible]
Tub enclosure 90

BUILT-IN APPLIANCES
*Gas range & oven, built-in . . . $400
Elec. range & oven, built-in . 455
Gas range & oven, drop-in . . . 230
Elec. range & oven, drop-in . 285
Elect. microwave oven 750

*Garbage disposer $105
*Exhaust fan & hood 115
Kitchen or bath exhaust fan . . 55
*Dishwasher . . . . [illegible]
Mixer-blender 85
Radio-intercom . . . . [illegible]
Vacuum cleaner system . . . 490
Built-in refrigerator 400

FIREPLACES Single, 2 story . . . $ 830
Double, 2 story . . 1075

PORCH COSTS

Sq. Ft. Area	Open Slab	Open W/Steps	Add For Roof	Add For Ceiling
25	$ 2.59	$ 6.88	$ 1.86	$ .74
50	2.31	[illegible]	[illegible]	[illegible]
100	1.83	3.95	1.67	.64
200	1.65	[illegible]	[illegible]	[illegible]

ADJUSTED BASEMENT COSTS

Sq. Ft. Area	Unfinished	Finished
200	$ 7.77	$10.20
400	6.08	8.11
800	4.11	5.68
1600	3.39	4.81

GARAGE COSTS (per sq. ft. of garage area)

Type	Area	Stucco	Siding or Shingle	Brick Veneer	Common Brick	Face Brick or Stone	Concrete Block
Detached	200	[illegible]	$ 7.08	$ 9.36	$ 9.87	$13.29	$ 8.31
	400	4.66	5.46	6.65	7.28	9.51	6.15
	600	[illegible]	4.58	5.76	6.32	8.28	5.37
Built-in	200	$ 4.70	$ 5.51	$ 6.92	$ 7.29	$ 9.18	$ 6.31
	400	[illegible]	4.65	5.61	5.88	7.42	5.25
Wall cost per lin. ft.		$12.91	$13.87	$18.54	$21.50	$25.60	$17.55

ATTACHED GARAGE - Compute as detached, then deduct the above cost per linear foot of common wall. **BASEMENT GARAGE** - Add lump sum to unfinished basement cost, single $485, double $595. **OPEN CARPORT** - all sizes, $3.07 per square foot. **INTERIOR FINISH** - Built-in and basement garage costs include interior finish. Add to detached and attached garage costs for interior finish as follows: Ceiling, $.73 per square foot, walls, $3.92 per linear foot.

page A-56

LOCAL MULTIPLIERS

LOCAL MULTIPLIERS . . . Apply these multipliers to the basic prices in the handbook to arrive at the up-to-date local cost.

As each cost section in the book is revised and brought up to date the Local Multipliers for that section are adjusted to the new cost base date.

Section A Multipliers apply to Square Foot Cost Section.

Section B Multipliers apply to Segregated Cost Section.

Section C Multipliers apply to Unit-in-Place Cost Section.

	SECTION A MULTIPLIERS FRAME	MASONRY	SECTION B MULTIPLIERS FRAME	MASONRY	SECTION C MULTIPLIERS FRAME	MASONRY
ALASKA						
Anchorage.....	1.48	1.57				
Juneau........	1.55	1.58	1.54	1.63		
Kenai.........	1.56	1.62	1.61	1.64	1.63	1.70
ARIZONA			1.62	1.68	1.70	1.71
Douglas.......	1.04	1.02			1.71	1.75
Flagstaff.....	1.03	1.04	1.08	1.05		
Nogales.......	1.03	1.02	1.07	1.07	1.14	1.10
Phoenix.......	1.02	1.01	1.07	1.05	1.13	1.12
Tucson........	1.02	1.01	1.06	1.04	1.13	1.10
Yuma..........	1.05	1.00	1.06	1.04	1.12	1.09
IFORNIA			1.09	1.03	1.12	1.09
ntelopeValley	1.09	1.09			1.16	1.08
kersfield...	1.10	1.10	1.14	1.13		
ythe........	1.11	1.12	1.15	1.14	1.20	1.18
te Co.......	1.10	1.12	1.16	1.16	1.21	1.19
linga.......	1.12	1.12	1.15	1.16	1.22	1.21
eka.........	1.12	1.14	1.17	1.16	1.21	1.21
sno.........	1.09	1.10	1.17	1.18	1.23	1.21
ord.........	1.09	1.10	1.14	1.14	1.23	1.23
rial Co....	1.12	1.12	1.14	1.14	1.20	1.19
....	1.10	1.10	1.17	1.16	1.20	1.19
Arrowhead	1.17	1.18	1.15	1.14	1.23	1.21
Tahoe.....	1.17	1.20	1.22	1.22	1.21	1.19
geles...	1.06	1.06	1.22	1.24	1.29	1.28
....	1.10	1.11	1.10	1.09	1.29	1.30
Co......	1.13	1.14	1.15	1.15	1.17	1.14
....	1.09	1.10	1.18	1.18	1.21	1.20
....	1.10	1.10	1.14	1.14	1.25	1.23
....	1.11	1.14	1.15	1.14	1.20	1.19
o......	1.12	1.15	1.16	1.18	1.21	1.19
....	1.12	1.12	1.17	1.19	1.22	1.23
....	1.05	1.06	1.17	1.16	1.23	1.24
ngs..	1.11	1.11	1.09	1.09	1.23	1.21
.....	1.12	1.15	1.16	1.15	1.16	1.14
.....	1.06	1.06	1.17	1.19	1.22	1.20
.....	1.10	1.11	1.10	1.09	1.23	1.24
.....	1.10	1.11	1.15	1.15	1.17	1.14
ino	1.06	1.06	1.15	1.15	1.21	1.20
...	1.07	1.08	1.10	1.09	1.21	1.20
o.	1.12	1.13	1.11	1.12	1.17	1.14
..	1.13	1.14	1.17	1.17	1.18	1.17
po	1.09	1.09	1.18	1.18	1.23	1.22
.	1.11	1.12	1.14	1.13	1.25	1.23
.	1.10	1.11	1.16	1.16	1.20	1.18
.	1.12	1.14	1.15	1.15	1.22	1.21
	1.11	1.13	1.17	1.18	1.21	1.20
	1.13	1.15	1.16	1.17	1.23	1.23
	1.12	1.15	1.18	1.19	1.22	1.22
	1.08	1.09	1.17	1.19	1.25	1.24
	1.12	1.15	1.13	1.13	1.23	1.24
	1.09	1.10	1.17	1.19	1.19	1.18
	.06	1.07	1.14	1.14	1.23	1.24
	.11	1.12	1.10	1.11	1.20	1.19
			1.16	1.16	1.17	1.15
					1.22	1.21

Square Foot Costs
Average Quality
(Finished 2nd Floor)

ONE AND ONE HALF STORY

RESIDENCE COSTS (per sq.ft. of total floor area)

WOOD FRAME Sq. Ft. Area	Stucco	Siding or Shingle	Brick Veneer	MASONRY Sq. Ft. Area	Common Brick	Face Brick or Stone	Concrete Block
1000	$13.54	$14.17	$16.04	1000	$16.37	$18.55	$15.42
1100	13.20	13.79	15.44	1100	15.78	17.79	14.86
1200	12.92	13.49	14.97	1200	15.31	17.22	14.45
1300	12.67	13.23	14.60	1300	14.92	16.74	14.10
1400	12.46	12.99	14.27	1400	14.60	16.38	13.84
1600	12.08	12.57	13.79	1600	14.12	15.82	13.38
1800	11.72	12.19	13.37	1800	13.71	15.35	12.96
2000	11.40	11.87	13.02	2000	13.33	14.93	12.59
2200	11.10	11.56	12.74	2200	13.03	14.55	12.27
2400	10.82	11.27	12.46	2400	12.73	14.20	11.96

RESIDENCE COST ADJUSTMENTS

The following cost adjustments are based on workmanship and materials that conform to the quality level of the square foot costs given above. The plus or minus signs indicate whether an item is an addition to, or a deduction from, the basic square foot cost. Cost adjustments for items not listed below may be determined by reference to the Segregated Cost Section.

SQUARE FOOT ADJUSTMENTS

ROOFING (Apply to total flr. area)
Asphalt shingle . . . . (base)
Built-up, small rock . . . . +$.16
Wood shingle . . . . + .35
Wood shake . . . . + .78
Mission tile . . . .

FLOORS (Apply to individual floors)
Hardwood . . . . (base)
Concrete slab only . . . . -$1.12
Wood subfloor only . . . . - .70
Add for: Carpet . . . . . . + .60
Vinyl asb. tile . . + .41

HEATING (Apply to total flr. area)
Forced air, gas . . . . . . (base)
Flr. or wall furnace, gas . -$.31
Gravity, gas . . . . - .10
Forced air, oil . . . . . . + .07
Glass panel, electric . . . + .03
Ceiling radiant, electric . + .06
Baseboard, electric . . . . + .13
Baseboard, hot water . . . + .47
Refrig. A/C using htr. duct + .96

INSULATION (Ceiling area) . . + .11

LUMP SUM ADJUSTMENTS

* Indicates items included in base cost.

***PLUMBING** 6 fixtures . . . (base)
Per fixture . . . . . . + or - $ 220
Plbg. fixture, rough-in . . . 85
Tub enclosure 80

BUILT-IN APPLIANCES
*Gas range & oven, built-in . $ 350
Elec. range & oven, built-in 400
Gas range & oven, drop-in . 210
Elec. range & oven, drop-in 260
Elect. microwave oven . . . 635

*Garbage disposer . . . . . . $ 90
*Exhaust hood & fan 95
Kitchen or bath exhaust fan 45
Dishwasher 260
Mixer-blender 75
Radio-intercom 180
Vacuum cleaner system . . . 455
Built-in refrigerator 360

FIREPLACES Single, 2 story . $ 705
Double, 2 story . 915

PORCH COSTS

Sq. Ft. Area	Open Slab	Open W/Steps	Add For Roof	Add For Ceiling
25	$2.41	$6.36	$1.78	$ .66
50	2.13	5.09	1.66	.61
100	1.73	3.73	1.61	.57
200	1.52	2.90	1.53	.54

ADJUSTED BASEMENT COSTS

Sq. Ft. Area	Unfinished	Finished
200	$7.48	$9.91
400	5.71	7.65
800	3.73	5.26
1600	3.20	4.61

GARAGE COSTS (per sq. ft. of garage area)

Type	Area	Stucco	Siding or Shingle	Brick Veneer	Common Brick	Face Brick or Stone	Concrete Block
Detached	200	$ 5.06	$ 6.32	$ 8.48	$ 8.97	$12.12	$ 7.52
	400	4.09	4.98	6.19	6.88	8.97	5.58
	600	3.43	4.16	5.37	5.99	7.78	4.83
Built-in	200	$ 4.08	$ 4.90	$ 6.25	$ 6.58	$ 8.32	$ 5.70
	400	3.45	4.07	5.02	5.32	6.75	4.65
Wall cost per lin. ft.		$12.30	$12.98	$17.40	$20.02	$23.79	$16.62

ATTACHED GARAGE - Compute as detached, then deduct the above cost per linear foot of common wall. **BASEMENT GARAGE** - Add lump sum to unfinished basement cost, single $445, double $550. **OPEN CARPORT** - all sizes, $2.91 per square foot. **INTERIOR FINISH** - Built-in and basement garage costs include interior finish. Add to detached and attached garage costs for interior finish as follows: Ceiling, $.67 per square foot, walls, $3.56 per linear foot.

page A-38

Segregated Costs
Foundation
Exterior Wall

FOUNDATION . . . EXTERIOR WALL

FOUNDATION . . . Apply cost to linear feet of exterior wall. The following costs include perimeter foundation only. Other foundation costs included with floor cost.

One Story Foundation Costs TYPE	LOW	FAIR	AVERAGE	GOOD	VERY GOOD
Frame-stucco or siding	$3.27	$3.62	$4.13	$4.51	$4.93
Masonry & masonry veneer	4.41	4.77	5.07	5.32	5.67
Two Story Foundation Costs					
Frame-stucco or siding	$4.94	$5.47	$6.24	$6.81	$7.44
Masonry & masonry veneer	6.66	7.20	7.66	[illegible]	8.56

Notes: *1. Abnormal soil conditions may increase cost of residential foundations as much as 50%.*
2. For one and one-half story use two story costs.
3. Increase two story costs 40% for each additional story above two stories.

EXTERIOR WALL . . . Apply costs to linear feet of exterior wall. The following costs include exterior finish, wall frame, interior finish, sash and exterior doors. Ceiling height, eight feet.

CONVENTIONAL

First story wall costs per linear foot of perimeter

TYPE	LOW	FAIR	AVERAGE	GOOD	VERY GOOD
Stucco	$15.57	$18.30	$22.71	$26.37	$31.64
Siding or shingle	16.30	18.96	23.96	[illegible]	34.15
Brick veneer	21.42	24.34	30.30	35.89	42.64
Brick	24.35	27.36	31.74	37.43	44.49
Face brick or stone	30.01	33.85	37.73	44.35	52.92
Concrete block	19.43	22.32	27.97	33.04	39.78

Note: *Add $.11 per square foot for wall insulation.*

Multistory wall cost adjustment . . . For each foot of extra height above first story, add to the first story exterior wall costs as follows:

TYPE	LOW	FAIR	AVERAGE	GOOD	VERY GOOD
Stucco	$1.52	$1.77	$2.21	$2.59	$3.09
Siding or shingle	1.59	1.85	2.34	2.77	3.35
Brick veneer	2.09	2.39	2.97	3.52	4.18
Brick	2.38	2.68	3.11	3.67	4.37
Face brick or stone	2.92	3.32	3.69	4.35	5.19
Concrete block	1.90	2.18	2.74	3.24	3.90

MODERN AND RUSTIC . . . Multiply the above conventional exterior wall costs by the following multipliers to make the costs applicable to modern and rustic homes.

ARCHITECTURAL TYPE	STUCCO	SIDING OR SHINGLES	BRICK VENEER	BRICK	FACE BRICK	CONCRETE BLOCK
Modern	1.09	1.06	1.02	1.01	.98	1.04
Rustic	1.04	1.03	1.02	1.02	1.01	1.02

GABLE WALL . . . Cost per square foot of gable wall. The following costs include gable wall structure, and exterior finish only.

TYPE	LOW	FAIR	AVERAGE	GOOD	VERY GOOD
Stucco	$ .85	$ .95	$1.11	$1.29	$1.54
Siding or shingle	.91	.98	1.18	[illegible]	1.64
Brick veneer	1.19	1.27	1.48	1.76	2.05
Brick	1.76	1.89	2.09	2.47	2.89
Face brick or stone	2.16	2.33	2.49	2.92	3.44
Concrete block	1.40	1.54	1.85	2.18	2.59

All of the above costs include a normal allowance for plans, specifications and general contractor's overhead and profit.

ROOF

Segregated Costs
Roof

CONVENTIONAL AND RUSTIC ROOFS . . . Apply costs to first floor area.
With Ceiling Joists . . . The following costs include ceiling joists, roof frame, 1" sheathing and roofing. Low to average pitch. Add $.12 per square foot if insulated.

TYPE	LOW	FAIR	AVERAGE	GOOD	VERY GOOD
Asphalt shingle	$1.30	$1.39	$1.54	$1.62	$1.81
Built-up rock	1.28	1.37	1.52	[illegible]	1.89
Wood shingle	1.43	1.57	1.72	1.88	2.15
Rigid asbestos shingle	1.62	1.79	1.94	[illegible]	2.41
Wood shakes	1.71	1.85	2.01	2.17	2.39
Mission Tile	2.15	2.28	2.47	2.66	2.87
Concrete tile	1.93	2.07	2.24	2.40	2.63

With Exposed Beam Ceiling . . . The following costs include beams, sheathing, roofing and insulation. Low to average pitch.

TYPE	LOW	FAIR	AVERAGE	GOOD	VERY GOOD
Asphalt shingle	$1.52	$1.63	$1.80	$1.92	$2.14
Built-up rock	1.49	1.60	1.78	1.94	2.18
Wood shingle	1.67	1.84	2.01	2.20	2.52
Rigid asbestos shingle	1.90	2.09	2.27	2.48	2.82
Wood shakes	1.97	2.13	2.31	2.50	2.75
Mission tile	2.34	2.49	2.69	2.90	3.13
Concrete tile (light weight)	2.16	2.32	2.51	2.69	2.95

Roof cost multipliers for steep slope: 6/12 1.04 8/12 1.11 12/12 1.31

ROOF DORMERS . . . Apply costs to linear feet, measured across face of dormer; do not include sides. Costs are for dormers with unfinished interior. Interior finish cost for dormers is automatically computed from floor, ceiling and other segregated cost tables if dormer floor area is included in total residence floor area.

TYPE	LOW	FAIR	AVERAGE	GOOD	VERY GOOD
Hip or gable roof	$22.50	$26.50	$32.00	[illegible]	$45.00
Shed roof	18.50	22.50	27.50	31.50	36.50

DERN ROOF . . . Apply costs to first floor area.
Ceiling Joists . . . (Finish ceiling applied directly to bottom of roof rafs.) The following costs include roof frame, sheathing, roofing and insuon. Flat to low pitch with typical wide overhang.

TYPE	LOW	FAIR	AVERAGE	GOOD	VERY GOOD
lt-up rock	$1.65	$1.77	$1.96	$2.18	$2.44

iling Joists . . . The following costs include ceiling joists, roof frame, ing, roofing and insulation. Low pitch with typical wide overhang.

YPE	LOW	FAIR	AVERAGE	GOOD	VERY GOOD
up rock	$1.83	$1.95	$2.18	$2.42	$2.71

sed Beams . . . The following costs include beams, sheathing, roofing lation. Flat to low pitch with typical wide overhang.

TYPE	LOW	FAIR	AVERAGE	GOOD	VERY GOOD
rock	$1.94	$2.07	$2.31	$2.57	$2.87
ceiling joists	.23	.24	.26	.30	.33

above costs include a normal allowance for plans, specifications l contractor's overhead and profit.

INTERIOR

FLOOR . . . Apply cost to total floor area. Costs include interior foundation, floor structure, main floor finish and allowance for bath, kitchen and other minor floor finishes in accordance with general quality of the house.

First Story Floor Costs

WOOD STRUCTURE	LOW	FAIR	AVERAGE	GOOD	VERY GOOD
Hardwood	$1.73	$1.84	$2.08	$2.42	$2.86
Softwood, finished	1.51	1.56	1.79	2.03	2.33
Vinyl asbestos tile	1.41	1.50	1.66	1.84	2.18
Sub-floor (for carpet)	1.12	1.23	1.38	1.56	1.89
CONCRETE SLAB					
Hardwood (in mastic)	$1.70	$1.79	$1.94	$2.10	$2.40
Asphalt tile	1.17	1.25	1.38	[illegible]	1.68
Vinyl asbestos tile	1.34	1.39	1.46	1.57	1.80
Vinyl tile or sheet	1.62	1.75	1.90	[illegible]	2.34
Colored slab	.91	.99	1.10	1.16	1.34
Bare slab (for carpet)	.77	.83	.91	.96	1.09

Upper Story Floor Costs

WOOD STRUCTURE	LOW	FAIR	AVERAGE	GOOD	VERY GOOD
Hardwood	$1.78	$1.91	$2.15	$2.49	$2.93
Softwood, finished	1.55	1.61	1.82	2.08	2.40
Vinyl asbestos tile	1.46	1.54	1.69	[illegible]	2.28
Sub-floor (for carpet)	1.15	1.27	1.42	1.61	1.95
Foamed conc. (for carpet)	1.23	1.37	1.53	[illegible]	1.98

Note: *For elevated concrete slab above basement garage use $2.33 to $2.87 per square foot according to quality. This includes supporting columns.*

CEILING . . . Apply cost to total floor area. The following costs include ceiling finish only.

TYPE	LOW	FAIR	AVERAGE	GOOD	VERY GOOD
Plaster, painted	$ .40	$ .44	$ .49	$ .54	$ .63
Plywood, painted	.35	.38	.46	.53	.61
Drywall, painted	.36	.39	.42	[illegible]	.53
Plaster, sprayed	.33	.35	.37	.39	.43
Tile, acoustic (furred)	.54	.58	.64	[illegible]	.75
Open beam (paint only)	.15	.17	.20	.23	.25

INTERIOR CONSTRUCTION . . . Apply cost to total floor area. The following costs include interior partition framing and finish, interior doors ar[...] cabinet work.

TYPE	LOW	FAIR	AVERAGE	GOOD	VERY GO[...]
One Story	$2.29	$2.81	$3.01	$3.38	$4.31
Split Level	2.14	2.56	2.83	3.17	3.9
Two Story	2.09	2.53	2.71	[illegible]	3.8
One & One Half Story	2.22	2.67	2.89	3.23	4.0
Multiple Residence	3.02	3.36	3.63	[illegible]	4.7
Town or Row House					
One Story	2.07	2.43	2.89	3.26	3.
Multi-Story	1.86	2.23	2.67	3.02	3.

STAIRWAYS . . . Apply cost to each full flight of stairs. The following cos[...] clude stair framing, finish and railings.

Interior Stairways

FRAME - FINISH	LOW	FAIR	AVERAGE	GOOD	VER[...]
Wood-softwood	$214	$264	$331	$411	$
Wood-hardwood	264	333	414	[illegible]	

Exterior Stairways

	LOW	FAIR	AVERAGE	GOOD
Wood-softwood	$155	$190	$250	$335
Wood-cement compo.	295	321	378	471
All steel	380	439	529	643

All of the above costs include a normal allowance for plans, spec[...] and general contractor's overhead and profit.

MECHANICAL . . . BUILT-INS

HEATING AND COOLING . . . Apply costs to total area being heated or cooled. Costs include all equipment, convectors and controls.

TYPE	LOW	FAIR	AVERAGE	GOOD	VERY GOOD
Forced air furnace, electric	$ .68	$ .74	$ .82	$ .93	$1.05
Forced air furnace, gas	.58	.63	.68	.79	.87
Gravity furnace, gas	.47	.53	.59	.67	.75
Floor or wall furnace, gas	.31	.33	.37	.43	.51
Baseboard, electric	.70	.76	.82	.91	1.01
Baseboard, hot water, gas	.91	1.05	1.15	1.35	1.56
Baseboard, steam, gas	.80	.94	1.13	1.33	1.58
Radiators, hot water, gas	.87	.96	1.08	1.24	1.42
Radiators, steam, gas	.69	.76	.84	.97	1.11
Floor radiant, hot water, gas	1.42	1.48	1.60	1.79	1.98
Ceiling radiant, electric	.60	.66	.73	.82	.93
Evaporative, no ducts	.21	.23	.25	.27	.30
Evaporative, w/ducts	.43	.45	.47	.50	.54
Refrigerated, using htr. duct	.82	.91	.98	1.13	1.31
COMBINED H & C					
Refrigeration & heating	$1.33	$1.46	$1.57	$1.82	$2.07
Heat pump system	1.75	1.87	[illegible]	2.27	2.51

Note: *1. Add 10% to gas heating systems if oil fired.*
2. Window type refrigerated coolers range in cost from $225 to $350 per ton capacity, including installation, depending upon size, type and local sources of supply. In determining ton capacity, a one horsepower motor produces approximately one ton of cooling. Add wiring allowance of $65 for 220 volt units. For heat pumps (reverse cycle AC) add 25%.

ELECTRICAL . . . Apply cost to total floor area. Costs include house service, wiring and light fixtures.

TYPE	LOW	FAIR	AVERAGE	GOOD	VERY GOOD
Flex (flexible steel conduit)	$ .67	$ .75	$ .86	$1.01	$1.31
Romex (non-metallic sheathed cable)	.48	.53	.60	.72	.89
B. X. (steel armored cable)	.54	.59	.68	.82	1.13
Rigid conduit	.77	.85	.98	1.21	1.55

PLUMBING . . . Apply cost to each plumbing fixture, including water heater as one fixture. The following costs include all rough and finish plumbing.

UNIT	LOW	FAIR	AVERAGE	GOOD	VERY GOOD
Avg. cost per fixture	$185	$200	$215	$235	$255
Auto. washer rough-in	70	75	85	[illegible]	110

BUILT-IN APPLIANCES . . . Apply cost to each built-in appliance. Costs include installation, extra utility outlets and cabinet work as applicable.

APPLIANCE	LOW	FAIR	AVERAGE	GOOD	VERY GOOD
Range & oven, gas (built-in)	$320	$345	$380	$415	$460
Range & oven, gas (drop-in)	200	215	240	[illegible]	290
Range & oven, electric (built-in)	360	385	435	475	510
Range & oven, elect. (drop-in)	250	270	285	315	345
Oven, electronic microwave	----	----	635	[illegible]	825
Exhaust fan and hood	65	75	95	115	145
Exhaust fan	35	40	45	[illegible]	70
Refrigerator-freezer (built-in)	290	310	360	[illegible]	455
Dishwasher	260	275	295	330	370
Mixer-blender	60	65	75	85	105
Garbage disposer	70	80	90	105	125
Radio-intercom	125	145	180	[illegible]	250
Gas incinerator	185	205	225	255	295
Vacuum cleaner system	400	415	455	490	550
Bathroom heater, electric	35	45	55	70	85

All of the above costs include a normal allowance for plans, specifications and general contractor's overhead and profit.

Segregated Costs
Porches, Attics
Fireplace

PORCHES . . . ATTICS

FIREPLACES . . . Apply cost to each fireplace. The following costs include complete fireplace as described. Double fireplaces are back-to-back with one chimney.

TYPE	LOW	FAIR	AVERAGE	GOOD	VERY GOOD
Single, one story	$465	$500	[illegible]	$660	$795
Single, two story	605	650	705	830	965
Double, one story	700	750	[illegible]	925	1070
Double, two story	815	875	920	1080	1250

PORCHES . . . Apply all costs to porch floor area.

OPEN CONCRETE PORCHES - INCLUDING PERIMETER FOUNDATION

QUALITY	25 SQ. FT.		100 SQ. FT.		200 SQ. FT.	
	WITH STEPS	SLAB	WITH STEPS	SLAB	WITH STEPS	SLAB
Low	$5.79	$2.20	$3.42	$1.48	$2.20	$1.25
Fair	6.21	2.41	3.57	1.68	2.31	1.32
Average	6.76	2.62	[illegible]	1.72	2.43	1.39
Good	7.18	2.86	3.82	1.84	2.56	1.45
Very good	7.67	2.94	[illegible]	1.95	2.68	1.51

Note: *Use $.70 per square foot for slab porches without perimeter foundation.*

OPEN WOOD PORCHES - WITH WOOD STEPS

QUALITY	25 SQ. FT.	100 SQ. FT.	200 SQ. FT.	300 SQ. FT.
Low	$2.21	$1.80	$1.53	$1.40
Fair	2.54	2.06	1.80	1.61
Average	2.87	2.34	2.15	1.87
Good	3.34	2.74	2.48	2.20
Very good	3.88	3.20	2.81	2.48

ADD FOR PORCH ROOF - (NO CEILING INCLUDED)

TYPE	LOW	FAIR	AVERAGE	GOOD	VERY GOOD
Asphalt shingle	$1.53	$1.64	$1.82	$1.81	$2.14
Built-up rock	1.51	1.62	1.79	[illegible]	2.23
Wood shingle	1.69	1.85	2.03	2.22	2.54
Rigid asbestos shingle	1.91	2.11	2.29	[illegible]	2.84
Wood shakes	2.02	2.18	2.37	2.56	2.82
Mission tile	2.54	2.69	2.91	3.14	3.39
Concrete tile (light weight)	2.28	2.44	2.64	2.83	3.10

ADD FOR PORCH CEILING

TYPE	LOW	FAIR	AVERAGE	GOOD	VERY G
Stucco	$ .58	$ .63	$ .66	[illegible]	$.
Wood	.42	.44	.47	.51	.
Hardboard	.35	.40	.43	[illegible]	.

WOOD FRAME BALCONIES - (ALSO USE THESE COSTS FOR STAIR LANDINGS)

QUALITY	WOOD FLOOR		CEMENT COMPOSITION F	
	WOOD RAIL	ORN. IRON RAIL	WOOD RAIL	ORN. IR
Low	$3.51	$4.68	$4.33	$5.
Fair	3.92	5.09	4.71	5
Average	4.24	5.46	5.23	6
Good	4.97	6.25	5.96	7
Very good	5.29	6.62	6.26	

Notes: *1. Add for balcony roofs from porch roof table above. 2. Add for plastered bal or soffit $.58 to $.79 per square foot in accordance with quality.*

ATTICS . . . Attic finish may be priced from the appropriate Segr Unit-in-Place Cost tables or the following cost range can be use $3.60 per square foot of floor area. Costs include softwood floor way, drywall ceiling and walls, wiring, and gable windows. Pl partition walls are not included and may be added from the U Cost tables.

All of the above costs include a normal allowance for plans, s and general contractor's overhead and profit.

page B-10

UNIT-IN-PLACE COSTS

Unit-in-Place Costs
Concrete Slab, Floor Cover
Hardwood, Terrazzo, Cove Base

CONCRETE STEPS

Cost per lineal foot $2.85

CONCRETE SLAB . . . Cost per sq. ft.

4" slab	$ .56
Reinforcing mesh	.08
Gravel base	.09
Vapor barrier	.06
Total	$ .79

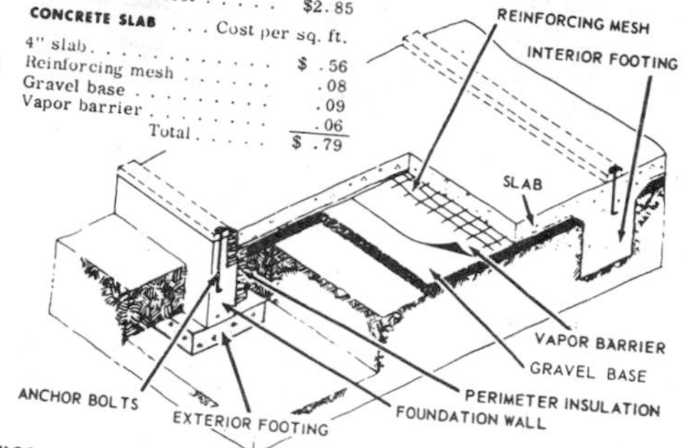

CONCRETE SLAB AND FOUNDATION

FLOOR COVER . . . Cost per square foot.

	AVG.	GOOD	EXC.		AVG.	GOOD	EXC.
Asphalt tile	$ .34	[illegible]	$ .46	Quarry tile	$2.20	$2.40	$2.60
Carpeting	.60	1.20	1.70	Rubber tile	.78	.87	1.10
Ceramic tile	2.30	[illegible]	2.85	Slab color	.11	.14	.23
Cork tile	.75	.92	1.05	Slate	1.90	2.20	2.45
Flagstone	1.70	1.95	2.20	Underlayment	.20	.24	.25
Foamed Conc	.27	.33	.37	Vinyl tile	.80	.95	1.25
Linoleum	.49	.61	.76	Vin.asb.tile	.39	.48	.64
Marble	3.90	5.15	6.20	Vinyl sheet	.74	.90	1.30

HARDWOOD . . . Cost per square foot.

	COMMON	SELECT	CLEAR
Strip, 2-1/4" x 1/2"	$ .68	$ .73	$ .82
Strip, 2-1/4" x 13/16"	.78	.86	.99
Plank, imitation, 13/16"	.93	.98	1.07
Parquet, 13/16"	.98	1.12	1.31
Parquet, ½" in mastic	.84	.94	1.12
Parquet, 13/16" in mastic	.94	1.08	1.25
Pegged and grooved, 13/16"	1.05	1.20	1.45

TERRAZZO . . . Cost per square foot. (Exclusive of base slab)

Plain, small amount	$2.25
Decorative, small amount	3.30

COVE BASE . . . Cost per lineal foot.

Ceramic tile	$1.85
Rubber topset	.55
Terrazzo	2.40
Vinyl topset	.44

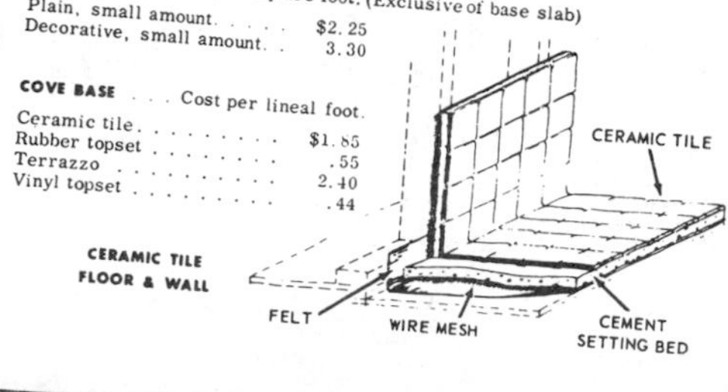

CERAMIC TILE FLOOR & WALL

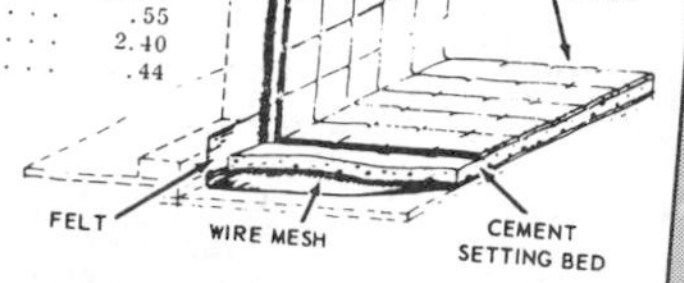

page C-5

LOCAL MULTIPLIERS

LOCAL MULTIPLIERS . . . Apply these multipliers to the basic prices in the handbook to arrive at the up-to-date local cost.

As each cost section in the book is revised and brought up to date the Local Multipliers for that section are adjusted to the new cost base date.

Section A Multipliers apply to Square Foot Cost Section.

Section B Multipliers apply to Segregated Cost Section.

Section C Multipliers apply to Unit-in-Place Cost Section.

	SECTION A MULTIPLIERS		SECTION B MULTIPLIERS		SECTION C MULTIPLIERS	
	FRAME	MASONRY	FRAME	MASONRY	FRAME	MASONRY
ALASKA						
Anchorage.....	1.48	1.57	1.54	1.63	1.63	1.70
Juneau........	1.55	1.58	1.61	1.64	1.70	1.71
Kenai.........	1.56	1.62	1.62	1.68	1.71	1.75
ARIZONA						
Douglas.......	1.04	1.02	1.08	1.05	1.14	1.10
Flagstaff.....	1.03	1.04	1.07	1.07	1.13	1.12
Nogales.......	1.03	1.02	1.07	1.05	1.13	1.10
Phoenix.......	1.02	1.01	1.06	1.04	1.12	1.09
Tucson........	1.02	1.01	1.06	1.04	1.12	1.09
Yuma..........	1.05	1.00	1.09	1.03	1.16	1.08
LIFORNIA						
ntelopeValley	1.09	1.09	1.14	1.13	1.20	1.18
akersfield...	1.10	1.10	1.15	1.14	1.21	1.19
lythe........	1.11	1.12	1.16	1.16	1.22	1.21
utte Co......	1.10	1.12	1.15	1.16	1.21	1.21
alinga......	1.12	1.12	1.17	1.16	1.23	1.21
reka........	1.12	1.14	1.17	1.18	1.23	1.23
esno........	1.09	1.10	1.14	1.14	1.20	1.19
nford.......	1.09	1.10	1.14	1.14	1.20	1.19
erial Co...	1.12	1.12	1.17	1.16	1.23	1.21
io.........	1.10	1.10	1.15	1.14	1.21	1.19
e Arrowhead	1.17	1.18	1.22	1.22	1.29	1.28
Tahoe....	1.17	1.20	1.22	1.24	1.29	1.30
Angeles...	1.06	1.06	1.10	1.09	1.17	1.14
ra........	1.10	1.11	1.15	1.15	1.21	1.20
n Co......	1.13	1.14	1.18	1.18	1.25	1.23
d........	1.09	1.10	1.14	1.14	1.20	1.19
to.......	1.10	1.10	1.15	1.14	1.21	1.19
Co.......	1.11	1.14	1.16	1.18	1.22	1.23
a Co.....	1.12	1.15	1.17	1.19	1.23	1.24
d.......	1.12	1.12	1.17	1.16	1.23	1.21
Co......	1.05	1.06	1.09	1.09	1.16	1.14
prings..	1.11	1.11	1.16	1.15	1.22	1.20
....	1.12	1.15	1.17	1.19	1.23	1.24
de.....	1.06	1.06	1.10	1.09	1.17	1.14
nto....	1.10	1.11	1.15	1.15	1.21	1.20
....	1.10	1.11	1.15	1.15	1.21	1.20
ardino	1.06	1.06	1.10	1.09	1.17	1.14
o.....	1.07	1.08	1.11	1.12	1.18	1.17
cisco.	1.12	1.13	1.17	1.17	1.23	1.22
......	1.13	1.14	1.18	1.18	1.25	1.23
bispo	1.09	1.09	1.14	1.13	1.20	1.18
Co..	1.11	1.12	1.16	1.16	1.22	1.21
bara.	1.10	1.11	1.15	1.15	1.21	1.20
....	1.12	1.14	1.17	1.18	1.23	1.23
a...	1.11	1.13	1.16	1.17	1.22	1.22
....	1.13	1.15	1.18	1.19	1.25	1.24
....	1.12	1.15	1.17	1.19	1.23	1.24
...	1.08	1.09	1.13	1.13	1.19	1.18
...	1.12	1.15	1.17	1.19	1.23	1.24
...	1.09	1.10	1.14	1.14	1.20	1.19
...	1.06	1.07	1.10	1.11	1.17	1.15
..	1.11	1.12	1.16	1.16	1.22	1.21

Segregated Costs
Garages
Carports

GARAGES . . . CARPORTS

GARAGE FOUNDATION . . . Apply costs to linear feet of exterior wall.

TYPE	LOW	FAIR	AVERAGE	GOOD	VERY GOOD
Frame-stucco or siding	$2.22	$2.41	$2.64	$2.81	$3.01
Masonry & masonry veneer	2.36	2.57	2.92	[illegible]	3.57

GARAGE EXTERIOR WALL . . . Apply costs to linear feet of exterior wall.

TYPE	LOW	FAIR	AVERAGE	GOOD	VERY GOOD
Stucco (no sheathing)	$10.45	$11.24	$11.80	$12.39	$13.59
Siding or shingle	10.97	11.65	12.46	[illegible]	14.68
Brick veneer	14.25	15.40	16.70	17.79	19.90
Brick	16.36	17.59	19.19	20.63	23.13
Face brick or stone	18.52	20.44	22.83	24.57	27.58
Concrete block	13.76	15.24	16.91	18.28	20.53

Garage Wall Interior Finish . . . If interior of garage wall is finished, add to above exterior wall cost from this table.

TYPE	LOW	FAIR	AVERAGE	GOOD	VERY GOOD
Plaster, unpainted	$2.87	$3.11	$3.47	$3.83	$4.10
Drywall, painted	2.78	3.01	3.38	3.73	3.99
Plywood, painted	3.23	3.53	3.85	4.13	4.39
Hardboard, painted	3.15	3.44	3.62	3.87	4.13

GARAGE ROOF AND CONCRETE FLOOR . . . Apply costs to total floor area.

TYPE	LOW	FAIR	AVERAGE	GOOD	VERY GOOD
Asphalt shingle	$1.56	$1.68	$1.87	$2.01	$2.14
Built-up rock-conven.	1.54	1.65	1.85	2.04	2.18
Built-up rock-modern	1.79	1.91	2.15	[illegible]	2.49
Wood shingle	1.69	1.84	2.03	2.19	2.33
Wood shakes	1.85	1.98	2.18	[illegible]	2.44
Mission tile	2.18	2.32	2.51	2.65	2.76

Garage Ceiling . . . If garage has a finished ceiling add to above garage floor and roof cost from this table. Costs include ceiling joist allowance.

TYPE	LOW	FAIR	AVERAGE	GOOD	VERY GOOD
Plaster, unpainted	$ .58	$ .61	$ .66	$ .71	$ .77
Drywall, painted	.53	.57	.62	.67	.71
Plywood, painted	.61	.63	.68	.72	.78
Hardboard, painted	.57	.60	.65	.69	.73

BUILT-IN GARAGE FLOOR . . . If residence or apartment has a built-in garage with living area above, use the following table to determine the cost of the floor and supporting columns. Add for exterior wall, wall interior finish and ceiling finish from appropriate tables above. Do not include garage foundation. Cost for foundation should be computed with residence costs from two story residence foundation table. Apply costs to square foot floor area.

TYPE	LOW	FAIR	AVERAGE	GOOD	VERY GOOD
Concrete floor	$ .78	$ .83	$ .91	$ .99	$1.11
Asphalt floor	.51	.54	.60	.64	.71

CARPORTS . . . Apply costs to square foot area of carport. The following costs include roofing, roof frame, supporting structure, painting and concrete slab.

TYPE	LOW	FAIR	AVERAGE	GOOD	VERY GOOD
Asphalt shingle	$2.28	$2.48	$2.69	$2.89	$3.09
Built-up rock-conven.	2.27	2.46	2.67	2.92	3.13
Built-up rock-modern	2.43	2.63	2.86	3.12	3.35
Wood shingle	2.40	2.61	2.82	3.03	3.25
Wood shakes	2.54	2.74	3.01	3.22	3.44
Mission tile	2.80	3.10	3.40	3.73	4.01
Deduct for asphalt floor	.27	.30	.33	.37	.41

All of the above costs include a normal allowance for plans, specifications and general contractor's overhead and profit.

page B-12

EVALUATING LAND

There are many ways of obtaining a figure for the estimated value of the lot on which a building stands. The most common method is on a comparative sales basis. As many sales figures as possible are to be obtained before a final figure of value per front foot is determined, or the total lot selling price. Having once acquired a sum per front foot, this figure is multiplied by the number of front feet to find the value of the land and this in turn is added to the replacement cost of the property. For example, suppose a house with a replacement value of $19,275.20 for the building alone is on a lot 50 × 100 and it is found that the value of the lot is $40 per front foot. The entire lot, therefore, is to be estimated at $2,000 (50 × $40). This is added to the building in the following manner:

Replacement cost	$19,275.20
Lot	2,000.00
Estimated value of lot and building	$21,275.20

It should be noted that when evaluating land, corner lots are generally considered to be more valuable than lots in the center of a block. Most appraisers consider them to be valued at an additional 10 to 15 percent over adjoining center lots. However, this is true only if the side street is paved. In the event the side street is unpaved, the chances are great that sooner or later there will be an assessment placed on the lot which will counterbalance the additional value placed on it because of location.

The comparative lot sales need not be nearby lots. They must, however, be similar and conform. It is here that one can apply the principle of conformity previously discussed. Hence the width, depth, and shape of the comparative lots should conform with the subject lot. In addition, the off-site improvements, that is, sewers, paving, etc., and restrictions must be in conformity with the subject lot.

Character of the Land

When a lot is considered by itself, the character of the land takes on a certain amount of importance. Level or gently sloping land is the most desirable. One should note carefully when examining a lot if the lot is a "dump" lot. This is a lot built up by fill over rubbish to street level. Generally, built-up lots are found on the outskirts of rapidly expanding towns and villages. This type of lot may be bad and should be depreciated because of the danger of excessive settling of any building constructed on this type of property.

Lots Below Grade

In general, lots below grade or street level are undesirable because they have a tendency to flood during rainstorms. This results in damp or flooded basements. There is apt to be difficulty, too, with sewage disposal if the lot is below grade. It may be necessary to install a sump pump on buildings placed on this type of lot in order to increase the flow of sewage to the public disposal system.

A lot that is six feet or more below the street level is usually depreciated 50 percent, while lots from one to six feet below grade are depreciated from 5 to 50 percent.

QUESTIONS FOR REVIEW

1. What is the economist's concept of value?
2. Distinguish between value and price.
3. How can value remain the same while prices change?
4. What are the three approaches to appraising?
5. Define *appraising*.
6. Explain the three factors that cause depreciation.
7. Show how you would determine value by the comparative market data approach.
8. How is it possible that "good" or "bad" schools in a neighborhood can affect the value of a nearby parcel of real property?
9. How does one determine neighborhood characteristics?
10. Why should one be aware of changes in a district?
11. Explain what is meant by the replacement cost approach in residential appraising.
12. What is meant by *remaining economic life*?
13. You are given two similar buildings to appraise. One is four years old and the other twenty-five years old. In attempting to arrive at an estimate of value, which approach would be most appropriate to use in each case?

14. What are the criticisms of using a gross multiplier in the income approach in obtaining an estimate of value?
15. How can a lack of zoning laws affect the value of property?

PROBLEMS

1. Each of the following statements represents either: (a) physical depreciation or deterioration; (b) functional obsolescence; or (c) economic depreciation or obsolescence. Indicate the type of depreciation represented and comment.
   (a) Shingles on the roof are curled and rotted from the weather.
   (b) A residential property is next to a factory. The factory was built in the neighborhood because of a lack of proper zoning regulations.
   (c) The property under examination is an old house in a neighborhood crowded with rooming houses.
   (d) The property under examination is a waterfront warehouse. The floor has a slant because the piles supporting it are rotting away.
   (e) A home contains old-fashioned bathroom fixtures and wainscoting on the kitchen walls.
   (f) A California-type (Spanish) bungalow is located in a neighborhood predominantly containing ranch-style homes.
2. Section 1027 (i) of the FHA Underwriting Manual lists the following sources of error in valuing property. Comment on each one showing how it is true:
   (a) Misconception of the objective and purpose for which the valuation is made.
   (b) Lack of judgment and experience.
   (c) Haste and carelessness.
   (d) Inadequate data or data of poor quality.
   (e) Incorrect interpretation of data.
   (f) Incorrect method of valuation.
   (g) Faulty application of correct method.
   (h) Influence on valuator.
3. Two years ago you appraised a home with an effective age of six years, and you depreciated it at 12 percent. You are now called upon to appraise the same home. You obtain new cost figures, new comparable sales figures, and depreciate at the rate of 16 percent, having determined the effective age from your old files. Can you justify this? Why or why not?

4. After examining a residential property, you arrive at the following data:

(a) Value indicated by Cost Approach		$16,330
(b) Value indicated by Income Approach		$15,760
(c) Value indicated by Market Data Approach		
(1) Arithmetic average	$16,500	
(2) Most comparable sale	16,200	
(3) Arithmetic average of sales price per square foot	15,775	
(4) Most comparable sales price per square foot	16,030	
(5) Arithmetic average sales price per room	15,450	
(6) Most comparable sales price per room	16,000	

Problem: Give an opinion of value and justify your position.

SUGGESTED READINGS

Case, Frederick E. *Real Estate,* Rev. ed. Boston: Allyn and Bacon, 1962. Chapter 8.

Kahn, Sanders A., Frederick E. Case, and Alfred Schimmel. *Real Estate Appraisal and Investment.* New York: The Ronald Press Company, 1963. Chapters 8-10.

May, Arthur A. *The Valuation of Residential Real Estate,* 2d ed. Englewood Cliffs, New Jersey: Prentice-Hall, Inc., 1953.

Ring, Alfred A. *Real Estate: Principles and Practices,* 7th ed. Englewood Cliffs, New Jersey: Prentice-Hall, Inc., 1972. Chapters 23 and 24.

Ring, Alfred A. *The Valuation of Real Estate,* 2d ed. Englewood Cliffs, New Jersey: Prentice-Hall, Inc., 1970. Chapters 9 and 13.

Chapter 25

Appraising Income Property

The basic problems encountered in the appraisal of income-producing property are nearly the same as those found in the appraisal of residential property. One of the major differences, however, is that the capitalization approach is employed to a far greater extent. For the time being, it might be said that the major concern with the appraiser of income-producing property is to determine the present worth of a stream of future income.

THE CAPITALIZATION APPROACH

In capitalizing, one is attempting to determine the present worth of future earnings. How then is this done? At any given time there is in existence a rate of interest—that is, the price of capital or the amount of rental that one expects and should receive in return for the use of his money. There also exists, at this same given period of time, the amount of money on which this interest rate is to be paid (the principal), and the amount of money which is to be paid as rent (the income). Thus, there exists the amount invested (principal), the interest rate, and the income. When given net income and a rate of interest, the problem is to convert them into value. Net income can easily be found by examining the income statement of the property owner. The income statement must be reconstructed as will be discussed later. The rate of interest can be determined by an analysis of the money market and certain other factors. Given these two figures, the third figure—value—can readily be determined by simple mathematics.

Suppose the interest rate is found to be 6 percent. Suppose further that an individual is informed that he will receive a guaranteed income from a certain vending machine of \$600 per annum. What is the *top* price that will be paid for the vending machine? In other words, what is its value? The answer becomes obvious at once—\$10,000. Mathematically, it is determined thus:

$$.06 \times X = \$600$$
$$X = \$600 \div .06$$
$$X = \$10{,}000$$

A question arises at this point. Why will an individual not pay more than \$10,000? Why not \$11,000? Since money can be invested elsewhere at 6 percent, a prudent individual with \$11,000 will invest the money in something other than a vending machine and receive a return of \$660. Anyone would be foolish to tie up an extra \$1,000 in the machine and receive less income than could be obtained from an investment of another kind.

In real estate, a capitalization rate is used in place of an interest rate. *Capitalization rate* is defined as the rate necessary to attract well-informed investors into investing their funds in real property. Now, substituting the \$600 net income after depreciation which might be received from a parcel of real property for the \$600 received from the vending machine, it can be seen by the same reasoning that the most that will be paid for the real property paying \$600 per year, with the rate at 6 percent, is \$10,000. The property will not command over that, but it certainly may command less, depending on any number of circumstances which will be pointed out.

Selecting a Capitalization Rate

One of the most important and likewise most difficult problems facing the appraiser of income property is the selection of the proper capitalization rate. An error of even one percent in either direction can result in a serious miscalculation. In the vending machine problem given above, for example, the interest rate was given as 6 percent, the net income as \$600. Therefore, the top price of the vending machine was determined to be \$10,000. Suppose that the appraiser erroneously selected 5 percent as the interest rate; then:

$$\begin{aligned} .05 \times X &= \$600 \\ X &= \$600 \div .05 \\ X &= \$12{,}000 \end{aligned}$$

In the problem above, the lowering of the interest rate by one percent resulted in a change of \$2,000, or an error of 20 percent. A *lowering* of the interest or capitalization rate then will *raise* the estimated value of the property, in this case from \$10,000 to \$12,000.

Suppose that the error in the selection of the interest or capitalization rate is 1 percent in the other direction—7 percent is chosen instead of 6 percent as it should have been; then:

$$\begin{aligned} .07 \times X &= \$600 \\ X &= \$600 \div .07 \\ X &= \$8{,}571.43 \end{aligned}$$

Thus it can be seen, if the interest or capitalization rate is *raised* incorrectly, the estimated value of the property will be *lowered*.

How then, does one determine the capitalization rate? Note that in the simple problem given above, value was determined by capitalizing at a given interest rate. The *interest rate* is defined as the rate of payment for the use of a principal sum of money. In determining the value of property in a real estate appraisal, part of the problem is solved by using the capitalization rate to capitalize the net income received from the property. Although there are several commonly used methods of determining capitalization rates, only two methods will be discussed.

Band of Investment Technique

In the band of investment technique, interest rates for partial property interests are rated by their relative importance to the total property value. A rate of interest is calculated by weighing fractional rates of mortgages and equity. The underlying assumption is that these rates can be determined from the investment market. For example, the returns on the equity interest of a property are determined in the market as well as the first and second mortgage rates. The highest risk is on the equity interest because this can be wiped out first, the intermediate risk is on the second mortgage, and the lowest risk is on the first mortgage.

Because of variations in risk, the highest rate of return is naturally on the items having the greatest risk factor. Once the rates are determined, they are weighted. For example, suppose equity holders receive a 10 percent return, the second mortgagee 9 percent, and the first mortgagee 7 percent. Assume that the equity share is 20 percent of the property value, the second mortgage 20 percent of the value, and the first mortgage 60 percent of the value; then:

PROPERTY INTEREST	PERCENT OF TOTAL PROPERTY VALUE		INTEREST	WEIGHTED INTEREST
Equity (highest risk)	20	x	10%	2.0%
Second Mortgage (intermediate risk)	20	x	9	1.8
First Mortgage (lowest risk)	60	x	7	4.2
		Capitalization rate		8.0%

In summary, the interest rates are related to relative risk. The higher the risk, the higher the rate. Hence the weighted average allocated to the three property interests gives one the 8 percent capitalization rate.

Summation Method

This is an attempt on the part of the appraiser to build up a rate by setting up the component parts which when taken together constitute an overall rate. This may be done by adding:

1. The safe rate. This usually is the rate paid by savings banks or on long-term government bonds.

2. The rate for risk. This is the amount to be paid to the investor for any risk that he is taking.

3. The rate for nonliquidity. This is the rate that is given to the investor because of the nonliquidity of real estate.

4. The rate for burden of management. This is to compensate the investor for the cost of managing the investment. This is a different fee from the fee paid for managing the property.

The sum of these factors taken together equals the capitalization rate, for example:

(1) The safe rate	3%
(2) The rate for risk	3%
(3) The rate for nonliquidity	1%
(4) Rate for burden of management	1%
Capitalization rate	8%

Building Residual Technique

In the building residual technique, a value is assigned to the land, and a fair rate of return is attributed to it. This sum is deducted from the total net income before depreciation, and the balance is capitalized to determine the value of the building. The land value is then added to the value of the building to give a final determination of value.

Assume that the net income before depreciation on a property is $10,000. Part of this income must be attributed to the land, and part must be attributed to the building. Assume further that the capitalization rate selected is 6 percent. By a comparative market data approach, the value of the land is found to be $25,000. At 6 percent this equals $1,500, that part of the net income of $10,000 which is conceived of as having been earned by the land ($25,000 value of land × .06 = $1,500 earned by land). The balance, or residual return, of $10,000 − $1,500 is $8,500, the income that is attributable to, or earned by, the improvements on the property. This $8,500 is capitalized at 6 percent to give a value to the improvements; thus:

$$.06X = \$8{,}500 \text{ (income from improvements)}$$
$$X = \$8{,}500 \div .06$$
$$X = \$141{,}666.66 \text{ (value of improvements)}$$

The $141,666.66 is the value of the improvements. This figure is then added to the value of the land to obtain the value of the land and improvements ($25,000 + $141,666.66 = $166,666.66).

It should be noted here that as yet no consideration has been made for depreciation. That is, the income has been capitalized without an allowance for depreciation of the improvements on the land. Before dealing with depreciation, net income should be figured.

Determination of Net Income

As was stated previously, it is the net income upon which the capitalization rate is applied. *Net income* is the gross income of the property minus operating expenses. However, there are other factors that must be taken into consideration. This means, first, that the net return must be figured on the basis of the property's being free and clear. When determining net income for the purpose of an appraisal, amortization of mortgage and any interest paid are to be disregarded. This becomes clear if one can conceive of a property whose entire earnings are being paid out in interest and amortization of a mortgage. The property under this assumption would show no net earnings and hence be of no value in terms of capitalization.

In determining the net income, the appraiser seeks to obtain detailed and accurate information concerning the income and operating expenses from the owner of the property. This information should be carefully analyzed and checked against available leases for any discrepancies. Tenants without leases should be queried as to the amount of rent they pay. The appraiser should also have a good idea, for example, as to the amount of fuel consumed in the type of building that he is appraising. Quite conceivably the owner might have submitted inaccurate figures which would distort the total operating costs. After having examined the books of account of the owner, the appraiser should set up an income statement in which he may, if necessary, make adjustments to arrive at net income. The owner may not have taken vacancies and repairs into consideration in his operating statement, or perhaps the appraiser might feel that other adjustments are justified. For example, there might be a public liability insurance policy with limits of only $10,000 and $20,000 on the property. The appraiser may decide that a policy with limits of $50,000 and $100,000 is more realistic for the building under consideration. In this case, the appraiser would increase the expense of operation of the property in the additional amount that a proper insurance policy would cost.

When attempting to determine the net income from a property, the appraiser is also justified in adjusting what, in his opinion, appear to be very low or very excessive rents. In general, it might be said then that in arriving at net income, the appraiser is in reality seeking the probable net income (sometimes called *stable net income*). He does this to avoid a distorted figure for net income with a consequent distortion of the value of the property.

Depreciation and Obsolescence

The depreciation affecting investment property is of the same nature as the depreciation affecting residential properties; namely, physical depreciation, functional obsolescence, and economic obsolescence. The combination of these three factors converted into a percentage figure constitutes the rate of depreciation. Basically, these rates are determined by the type of building and by the value of the construction of the building. For example, an apartment of good construction may have a useful life of fifty years, and the normal rate of future depreciation would be at 2 percent per year. However, functional and economic obsolescence may add to that figure. In the final analysis, the rate of depreciation is determined by the type of construction, the condition of the building, and the factors which make up the functional obsolescence.

Since the land itself does not usually depreciate, what is done with the figure that has been determined as the rate of depreciation for the building? [1] In income appraising, the rate of depreciation is added to the capitalization rate; this is the rate that is applied to residual income applicable to the improvements to determine the final worth of the improvements. The reason the depreciation rate is added to the capitalization rate is to provide for *future* depreciation.

In the final analysis, every investor must think of two things. First, a return *of* his capital, and secondly, a return *on* his capital. For example, if a man deposits $10,000 in a savings and loan association which pays a dividend rate of 5 percent, he certainly should

[1] The major exception to this is peat and muck soils. Mineral soils can be maintained at or near native fertility by proper management. but subsidence (loss) of the peat or muck soils cannot be prevented except by reflooding these lands and retiring them from agricultural use. These soil deposits are found in Florida, Michigan, Wisconsin, Minnesota, California, and Oregon. Roy L. Lassiter, Jr., "Subsidence and Land Values on Organic Soils," *The Appraisal Journal*, October, 1958.

be able to anticipate $500 return *on* his capital at the end of one year and he certainly must anticipate the return *of* his capital of $10,000 at the end of that time. It is no different in real estate, namely, the return *of* the capital and the return *on* the capital. But real property improvements depreciate over time. Hence a rate is added to provide for future depreciation as was pointed out above; this rate is in reality added to provide for a recapture of the capital investment over remaining economic life of the improvements.

In the light of this, reexamine the problem given above. Assume again that the income of a property is $10,000, and that the capitalization rate is 6 percent and that by a comparative method, the land is determined to be $25,000. Thus, again $1,500 of the $10,000 is attributable to the land, leaving $8,500 attributable to the improvements on the land. Here let us make a further assumption; namely, that we have determined the future depreciation rate on the property to be 2 percent per annum. Thus instead of capitalizing the $8,500 attributable to the building at 6 percent as was done previously, we now capitalize at a rate of 8 percent. The 2 percent for future depreciation is added to the 6 percent capitalization rate, giving us the 8 percent. Therefore, the value of the building is now:

.08 × X = $8,500
X = $8,500 ÷ .08
X = $106,250, value of the building
$ 25,000, value of the land
$131,250 or
$131,000, value of land and building

Land Residual Technique

The question often arises as to the inability on the part of the appraiser to obtain comparative data pertaining to the value of the land. For example, in many downtown areas, there have been no recent sales of vacant land; hence, no means of ascertaining value by comparing data is available. In this case, how can the residual returns method be employed? The answer is that the problem is done in reverse.

A value is attributed to the building based upon the cost (new) at current prices less accrued depreciation. For example, assume that a building is valued at $106,250 and the net income is $10,000, the capitalization rate is 6 percent, and 2 percent is allowed for future depreciation; then:

$106,250 × .08 = $8,500 (attributable to building)
$10,000 − $8,500 = $1,500 (attributable to land)
.06X = $1,500
X = $1,500 ÷ .06
X = $25,000 (value of the land)
106,250 (value of improvement)
$131,250 (value of land and improvement)

The resulting value of the land is a correct estimate only if the improvement represents the highest and best use of the land and if the improvement is in new condition. This process is not practical unless the land is a large part of the whole.

Property Residual Technique

A third method of solving the problem is by means of the property residual technique. In the two previous techniques an estimate was made of either the land or the building. In the property residual technique, the land and the building are treated as one for the life of the building. For example, assume that the building is valued at $106,250, then the income before depreciation is $10,000, the rate of capitalization is 6 percent, and the future depreciation is figured at 2 percent:

(1) The building is depreciated
$106,250 × .02 = $2,125

(2) Depreciation is subtracted from net income
$10,000 − $2,125 = $7,875 (attributable to the property)

(3) The net attributable to the property (after depreciation) is capitalized:

.06X = $7,875
X = $131,250 (value of the property)

HIGHEST AND BEST USE

It is necessary to inject at this point a rather subtle complication: the concept of highest and best use. *Highest and best use* is defined as "that use which is most likely to produce the greatest net return over a given period of time." [2]

The question here should be: What difference does it make? In part, the answer is that highest and best use is related to value, particularly when concerned with income-producing property. In reality, it is a major factor of fair market value. It was pointed out as early as 1894 in a Supreme Court decision that—

> the value of the property results from the use to which it is put and varies with the profitableness of that use, the present and prospective, actual and anticipated. There is no pecuniary value aside from that which results from such use—the amount and profitable character of such use determines the value.

Factors of Production and Highest and Best Use

Generally, the economist thinks that in order to produce a product, various inputs are used in combination to obtain desirable results in terms of profits. These inputs are land, labor, and capital. Briefly, in order for there to be production, labor must be paid, a payment must be made for the use of capital, and a payment must be made for the use of the land. Both labor and capital are relatively mobile. Land is fixed; therefore, labor and capital must be both profitable and paid first, and the residual is paid to the land. If the land is not put to its highest and best use, then that amount left over for the land decreases, and consequently, the value of the land also decreases because its net earnings are decreasing. For example, if a farmer produces corn, he must use land, labor, and capital. He must receive, to be prudent, a return on his capital at least equal to what he might receive in an alternative investment; he must also receive a wage at least equivalent to what he could earn elsewhere, and, for the land, there must be an amount left over at least equivalent to the market rental of the land. If this were not so, it would pay the farmer to rent out the land, work for someone else, and invest the value of his capital contribution.

If the demand for corn is low and the price is down and if the land will produce nothing else, then the value of the land will be

---

[2] *Appraisal of Real Estate* (2d ed.; Chicago: American Institute of Real Estate Appraisers, 1951), p. 40.

low. It might be that the land is located in an area suitable for a dude ranch, in which case the net income of the same land if put to this highest and best use might be high, and consequently, the value changed in two different time periods. This occurs because a residual from labor and capital can be attributed to the land use.

In practice, the problem often arises in condemnation appraisals. Suppose a profitable farm is valued at $100,000 before any taking, and suppose that farm is completely dependent on irrigation in order to produce anything. Suppose only a few acres are taken, but that these acres control the water supply, and as a result the rest of the land will soon return to desert. It is entirely conceivable that these few acres will be valued for condemnation purposes at nearly the full $100,000. Why? Because the value of the part left to the owner after the partial taking is governed largely by the best use of the owner's remainder after the taking. In this case he has virtually nothing left except desert land which is nonproductive.

Highest and Best Use and Diminishing Returns

The economist defines *diminishing returns* as an increase in some inputs relative to other comparatively fixed inputs that will cause output to increase; but after a point the extra output resulting from the same additions of inputs will become less and less. Classically, this is illustrated by again using farmland as an example. If a farmer has 100 acres of cornland and adds one man-year of labor, there results a certain output. If he adds a second laborer, the total output will probably increase, but by not so many extra bushels of corn. A third man added may still further increase output of corn, but his labor will produce still less. In other words, the fixed factor of production, the land, has decreased in proportion to the variable input, labor.

How does this relate to highest and best use, and the general problem of evaluation? The answer is that the *point of diminishing returns* is that point beyond the maximum value at which additional investment does not produce a return commensurate with the return available for that investment if put in an alternative investment opportunity. This basic concept, of course, is directly related to what real estate practitioners refer to as overimprovement and underimprovement.

Highest and Best Use and Overimprovement and Underimprovement

The concept of overimprovement and underimprovement is an important part of highest and best use and the appraiser's practical application of the law of diminishing returns. In reality, when one uses the term *underimprovement*, he is really talking about a property which is not being used to its highest and best use. Also, when one speaks of an *overimprovement*, that individual is really saying that the point of diminishing returns has been reached and that the property is not being put to its highest and best use. The effect on value of an improvement can easily be seen. For example, an individual may buy an older home and rehabilitate it. The cost of rehabilitation may be so great that the layman will say: "He'll never get his money out." By this is meant an overimprovement, the point of diminishing returns has been met and passed. Hence, even though the cost of rehabilitation may be high, the practical appraiser will give an estimate of value which may be considerably less than cost. His justification for this is, of course, that the property has been overimproved and that the property is not being put to its highest and best use.

An underimprovement works much in the same way. It is entirely conceivable that an owner of land might erect a building on his property which will bring in a relatively low income. If a residual is applied to the land in the manner described above, the underimprovement will have a tendency to drag down the value of the property because the property is not being put to its highest and best use. In practice the appraiser takes care of either the overimprovement or underimprovement by increasing the amount of *functional obsolescence.*

The economist views an underimprovement and the resulting loss of revenue as an opportunity cost. When a property *could* make \$25,000, but is making only \$10,000 because of the underimprovement, the \$15,000 possible additional revenue is a cost to society; and this cost is an opportunity cost.

Factors in the Determination of Highest and Best Use

Within the definition of highest and best use, four basic factors are implied:

1. Net return on investment after costs are met.

2. Time. Because real estate values are constantly changing, the value of any particular property must be determined as of a stated time period.

3. Location. Location is related to highest and best use in the sense that the greatest net return over a given period of time will vary with the location. For example, a vacant lot in one location may at one time represent the highest and best use if used for residential purposes. Yet, after the passage of time this same lot's highest and best use may be as a commercial property.

4. Use-density. When inspecting a site, the appraiser must ask himself this question: What types of structures are found in this area and in what numbers? This question is related to the highest and best use because the appraiser must determine the types of structures best adapted to an area. He must be careful not to forget, however, that the market value of property will fall if too many similar structures are constructed in this same area.

Depreciation on Equipment

Most modern apartment houses and motels, for example, contain certain items of equipment, such as refrigerators and gas ranges, that must be considered. The question is, of course, how and where are these items considered? Generally, they are figured by the appraiser in his arrival at a figure for *net* income. Thus, the depreciation on the items of equipment is figured in the nature of an operating expense to determine net income. To arrive at the $10,000 net income as given in the problem above, let us assume that the gross income was $11,000 and that depreciation on equipment was figured at $1,000. Thus, the $1,000 subtracted from the $11,000 would give us the net income of $10,000.

Management

At some time during his career, the appraiser will discover the sometimes startling fact that similar properties in similar locations vary tremendously in the amount of their earnings. The answer to this phenomenon usually lies in the difference between good and bad management. The appraiser is not interested in either poor or excellent management *per se*. With a change in management, the income of the property might very well change with it. It is, therefore, incumbent upon the appraiser to make his position clear when he finds a wide discrepancy in the management of a particular building with the average. This suggests then that the appraiser is interested in average income and, therefore, must make his position clear.

REPLACEMENT ANALYSIS APPROACH

The question will arise as to whether the replacement cost new less depreciation fits into the picture. In the appraisal of an income property, the answer is that it does. It is a convenient means of checking against the results obtained by the capitalization process. In appraising income property, the appraiser generally will estimate the replacement cost new by determining the number of square feet and multiplying the cost per square foot by that number. In many cases, however, it should be remembered that it is just as convenient and often more accurate to do this by the cubic foot method. After determining the replacement cost new, the appraiser determines the depreciation of the building, giving the replacement value of the improvement. This is added to the value of the land, the resulting figure being the present replacement value of improvements and land.

If the present replacement cost does not approximate the value obtained by capitalization, then the entire appraisal should be rechecked for possible error. The appraiser should be mindful that the cost approach tends to set the upper limit of value.

GUIDES FOR PREPARING THE APPRAISAL REPORT

Limiting Factors in Appraising

In appraising income property, the appraiser is given certain facts, and he obtains other facts by analysis and observation. From these facts he draws his conclusions *as judge, not advocate*. He should, therefore, in his appraisal report make his position perfectly clear. He should limit his responsibility to defending his honest and fair opinion from the facts as he sees them without bias and without personal advantage. It must be made clear in the report that the appraisal was done on the assumption that title to the property was good and marketable and that the appraiser has assumed the assessments and the taxes have been paid. The appraiser must also take no responsibility for legal matters; and, of course, he makes the statement that he has no present or contemplated future interest in the property under consideration.

Expert Testimony

In the appraisal report, the appraiser should state that no right to expert testimony is included. That is, the client does not have the right to call upon the appraiser to testify in court unless the appraiser is paid an additional fee for any appearances in court that he may make.

If the appraiser is called upon to testify in court concerning a particular property, he should be well prepared in advance and be well aware of the demands that will be made upon him. He will, of course, have many conferences with his client's attorney prior to the trial. One of the favorite tricks of opposing attorneys is to ask the expert whether or not he discussed the case with anyone prior to the trial. The answer should naturally be: "Yes, with attorney so-and-so." It is remarkable the number of people who answer this question in the negative, feeling that if they admit they discussed the case with anyone that the cause may be prejudiced. A negative answer to a question of this type makes a very bad impression on a jury.

All questions put by both attorneys must be answered fully and truthfully. The appraiser should not talk too much, nor should he volunteer an opinion. If a question cannot be answered, he should admit it rather than attempt to give an answer of which he is not certain. On cross-examination, the attorney asking the questions knows the answers, especially if they are of a technical nature and he is attempting to discredit the expert's testimony by forcing him into giving an incorrect answer. It is wise to bring notes to court. If any facts are forgotten, a witness's memory may be refreshed.

Preliminary Examination

Prior to an actual examination of the property, the appraiser should have made available to him certain necessary documents for examination. He should have before him either an abstract of title or a title report of a title insurance company. Although it is not his function to pass on title, it is his function to obtain a proper legal description of the property and to determine whether or not there are any easements or restrictions appearing in the abstract that might affect the value of the property.

If possible, the appraiser should also obtain the plans of the building. This will give him an idea as to the number of square feet or cubic feet in the building, which figure he will later use in figuring replacement cost in order to check against the value obtained by the capitalization method.

An inventory of the equipment in the building must be obtained together with the age of the equipment. This information will be checked later by observation and actual examination of the equipment. Depreciation will be figured on this equipment and the amount of the depreciation taken into consideration when determining the net income of the property.

Any leases affecting the property must be obtained and carefully examined because the income to the property is a result of those leases. Conceivably, the leases reflecting a high income of a taxpayer might be nearly at an end. It is also conceivable that the property will not warrant such tenants again. In this case the appraiser would have to adjust the probable net income of the property to reflect this loss of income in the future.

If available, a survey of the property should be obtained. One of the items of the appraisal report submitted by an appraiser is a map of the property showing its location with regard to parking lots, transportation, and other pertinent details. The survey helps in making an exact location of the property on such a map.

It goes almost without saying that the appraiser *must* obtain the books and records reflecting the financial operations of the property. The appraiser should be interested in average income rather than phenomenal income, and when possible, he should attempt to obtain these records for at least ten years back. From an examination of these records, the appraiser can, if the records go back far enough, obtain a clearer picture as to the income and expense incurred in the operation of the property. In this way, he is able to make his adjustments of the income statement more realistic and, hence, more accurate.

THE APPRAISAL REPORT

What constitutes the appraisal report to be submitted by the appraiser to his client? First, there is a title page and a table of contents. Second, there is a letter of transmittal to the client in which the value of the improvements and the value of the land is broken down and a total estimated value given for the land and the improvements. Most business property appraisal reports also contain a photograph of the property together with a detailed map of the property in relation to side streets and any nearby parking lots. There will also be included here a detailed floor sketch of the building being appraised.

In addition to the items above, the appraisal report of a store building, for example, might be outlined in great detail as indicated by the following topics.

Type of Property

A statement should be made as to whether it is or is not a typical investment property, or if there is anything unusual about the property.

Description

A legal description of the property is given. It is obtained either from the abstract of title or from the title report. If there are any easements or restrictions on the property, mention is made of them at this point.

Zoning

If the property is zoned for business, the report should so state. It is important to remember that the zoning laws must be carefully examined not only for the location of the store but also for surrounding areas. The reason for this is that there might be a grocery store on the edge of an area that is zoned for residences. In this case, the appraiser would recognize that the grocery store has a certain monopolistic value. If the income of the store is far above the average, the reason would probably be that the zoning laws prevented any competition in that particular area. In this case, there would be no phenomenal income to the store to be adjusted downward by the appraiser because under normal circumstances the monopoly created by the zoning laws would, in all probability, continue with the resulting high income to the property and a consequent reflection upon value.

Assessed Valuation

This is the total of the assessed value of the land and the assessed value of the building. It is important only in those areas where the assessed valuation of the property nearly approximates the value of the property.[3] In most areas, however, it should be remembered that the assessed valuation of a property bears little relation to the value of the property. However, in those areas in which the assessed valuation is related to the value of the property, the assessed valuation provides a figure against which the appraiser can check his ultimate estimate of value.

Type of Tenants

It will be recalled that the appraiser in most instances is attempting to forecast the probable or stable net income. Therefore, the type of tenants occupying an income property becomes of paramount importance. For example, it is often better to have chain store tenants not only because of their good credit rating, but also because their careful choice of locations is an indication of the stability of the district.

Similarly, an old established firm with a long-term lease would be a better indication of the probable net income than a new and perhaps financially insecure firm.

Transportation

Here all of the modes of transportation serving the community are listed. In many respects the economic life of a community is dependent upon its transportation facilities. This, in turn, will ultimately affect the earning capacity of the property that is under consideration.

Description of Site

Here the land upon which the improvement is built is described in terms of both its size and shape (rectangular, triangular, etc.).

[3] One might argue that, even in those areas where the assessed valuation does not approximate market value, the assessed valuation reflects the value of the property and, therefore, should be included in the report.

The topography is also described. Thus, if the land is above grade, it is mentioned here. It is here, too, that the appraiser lays part of the groundwork for any necessary later justification of the selection of a value of the land. Ordinarily, rectangular lots are more valuable than triangular lots in the same location. There are, however, some instances and some businesses that warrant an additional value for the triangular lot. For example, a supermarket may lie on a triangular lot affording good parking space and a good approach for traffic. This might justify the value placed on the triangular lot.

Parking Area

The relationship to parking areas of the building under consideration is important, especially when appraising downtown locations. All parking areas should be shown on the map of the property.

Improvements

Having already described the site in terms of its topography, attention is then turned to the improvements on the site. The improvements are described in detail, for example, a one-story retail store building with full basement. In addition, there should be a description of details including the measurement of the building, the number of stores into which it is divided, the various sizes of the stores, and any other details that might be pertinent to a thorough and proper description of the building.

Construction

This is a continuation of the description of the improvements. The type of construction from the basement to the roof is described in complete detail; that is, cement block foundation, brick or brick veneer walls, etc.

Interior

A complete breakdown is made describing the interior of the premises in detail: the type of floors, including the basement and the rest of the floors of the building; whether the walls are plaster or dry wall; the type of trim; lighting; and so forth. In addition, a statement is made as to whether repairs are needed, and an estimate is made of the cost of these repairs.

Tenancies

It will be recalled that the various leases under which the premises are held by tenants are obtained from the owner. The leases are examined and any important conclusions found from the study are made here. A statement of the amounts paid by each tenant, including the type of store being run by each of the tenants, is made. If leases are to expire soon, this must be reported in the light of the need for the appraiser to forecast the probable net income of the premises. For example, if a lease at a high rental is about to expire and the appraiser has reason to believe that the lease will not be renewed under the same terms, this should be noted here, together with its possible effect on the gross income from the property.

Equipment

Here the result of an *actual* inventory of all equipment is recorded. The inventory includes pumps, fire fighting equipment, and any other items that are subject to physical wear and tear. If the appraisal is being made on a motel or an apartment house, kitchen ranges and refrigerators ought to be included. Not only is an actual count made of the equipment, but the ages of the various items should be obtained because a depreciation charge must be made in the income statement, and many owners do not include this as an expense item. However, as far as the appraiser is concerned, this must be reflected completely and accurately.

Income Statement

Following the above items, the appraisal report contains an income statement. The income from each unit comprising the property is placed on the income statement and totaled to obtain the gross income. From the gross income the expense items, as shown by the books and records of the owner, are subtracted to obtain the net income as shown by the owner.

Keeping in mind that he is interested in *probable* or *stable* net income, the appraiser must make adjustments accordingly. Briefly, it may be shown on the appraisal report in the manner shown below.

Income Statement

OWNER'S STATEMENT				(PROBABLE OR) STABLE NET INCOME	
Income:					
Rental from stores:		$10,000.00			$10,000.00
Expenses:					
Insurance	$ 100.00			$ 300.00	
Repairs	300.00			300.00	
Taxes	600.00			600.00	
	$1,000.00	$ 1,000.00	Management	150.00	
Net Income		$ 9,000.00		$1,350.00	1,350.00
			Stable Net Income		$ 8,650.00

It will be noticed that the insurance item was changed and a figure added for management expense. In each case, the appraiser must justify the change. For example, he might have considered the amount of insurance to be too low.

The appraiser will then capitalize on the stable net income as he has determined it. This figure is the net *before* depreciation and is more realistic than the figures submitted by the owner.

Capitalization

After determining what amounts to the probable net income as shown above, the next step is to capitalize that income. Prior to actually doing this, however, the appraiser selects the capitalization rate. It is at this point in the appraisal report that the appraiser must justify the selection of the rate. This is done by analyzing the money market, the risk involved in the particular building under consideration, the nonliquidity of real estate, and for the most part what rate of return it will take to attract prudent investors to invest in similar properties. Included in this rate is the percentage to take care of *future* depreciation.

Replacement Analysis

As a check on the estimated value of the property as obtained by the capitalization method, the appraiser will use the replacement analysis approach on his appraisal report. He will determine the square feet in the building or, if he wishes, the number of cubic feet in the building, and from this calculate the replacement value of the property. After finding the value of the property new, he will depreciate this figure to obtain the replacement value of the property. It should be remembered that this figure will generally be higher than the sum obtained through the capitalization method and will represent, in all probability, the highest figure that can be obtained in an appraisal of the property.

Market Data

If similar properties have been sold recently, the appraiser can obtain from these the necessary information for still a third check on his figures; namely, the market data approach. Here he may have an excellent check on his previous determinations.

Interpretation into Value

It is at this point in the appraisal report that the appraiser correlates his information and interprets this information into the estimated value of the property. This amount is submitted to the client as the estimated value of the property.

APARTMENT HOUSE APPRAISING

The appraisal of an apartment house does not differ greatly in technique from the appraisal of any other type of income property. An adjustment must be made in the operating statement for a reserve for replacement which is deducted from the income in the nature of an expense. In addition, vacancy and collection losses must be deducted from the rental value (100 percent). This is done first to give an effective gross figure from which all other expenses (janitor, fuel, etc.) are deducted.

The amount of vacancy and collection losses vary with the type of tenancy, the property, and general economic conditions. If a steady rental is assumed for the remaining economic life of the property, the vacancy and collection losses are figured by estimating the probable average vacancy and collection loss over the remaining economic life of the property as a percentage of the 100 percent rental income of the property. If conditions are bad and vacancies are 10 percent, for example, this figure might be adjusted downward to allow for the expected average over the remaining life of the property.

In addition to this, great care must be taken to depreciate the equipment of the building to obtain a true net income. Thus, the appraiser must be extremely careful in examining the refrigerators, for example, to ascertain that they are all that the owner might say that they are.

APPRAISING LEASE INTERESTS

In a lease there are generally two parties: the lessor and the lessee. The lessor is entitled to the rent during the term of the lease and is entitled to possession at the expiration of the term. The lessee is entitled to possession of the property and anything the property will earn over and above the contractual rent that must be paid to the lessor.

It will be recalled from Chapter 7 that the lessor's right to receive back all of his interest in the property at the end of the term is called a *reversionary interest*. This interest has value, the determination of which is one of the appraiser's problems.

The problem of appraising a lease from the lessor's viewpoint consists of determining the value of the fee. The value of the fee can be determined by the capitalization of income, making the assumption that the property is free and clear of the lease or leases where a sublessee is involved.

A second method of determining the value of the fee is by the use of interest tables. When interest tables are used, the results may differ with the straight-line capitalization method for several reasons. First, capitalization is in perpetuity and assumes no termination of income. Second, the use of interest tables assumes termination in a stated number of years; for example, income is received from a property and it is assumed that the building on it has an estimated remaining economic life of ten years. In the following pages the value of a lease and the leasehold will be determined by means of interest tables.

Use of Interest Tables

The value of the fee free and clear of the lease can be determined by the use of interest tables. One of the things to be dealt with here is to determine the value of future income. If, for example, a lease nets $500 per year for ten years to the lessor and he owns the building and the land, what is the value to him of $500 per year for ten years? Does this mean that the value to him is worth $5,000 over the life of the lease? Obviously not. Will a prudent businessman pay $5,000 for the privilege of collecting $5,000 in the future? A dollar in hand today is worth a dollar; a dollar to be paid one year from now is worth less than a dollar. Why? Because there is a loss of interest during the year. The promise to pay one dollar in one year must be discounted.

If the interest rate is 4 percent and a businessman invests roughly 96 cents today, it will be worth $1 in one year. Thus, the discounted value of $1 payable in a year may fairly be said for our purpose here to be about 96 cents.

Present values may be determined by the use of interest tables. Usually the so-called Inwood table or the Hoskold table is used. The Inwood table presupposes that part of the annual return is principal and part of the return is interest. The assumption is that the part returned as principal reduces the outstanding investment. The Hoskold premises assume that a part of the principal and interest is returned annually. However, the assumption here is that the part returned as principal is reinvested in a sinking fund. Either premise can be and is used. For illustrative purposes, the Inwood table is used here.

The Problem

Assuming that the appraiser is interested in determining the value of the lease to the *lessor*, there are two questions that must be answered: (1) What is the present worth of future stable *net* rentals? and (2) What is the value of the reversionary interest to the lessor?

The Lessor's Solution

Assume that the net rental under a lease is $1,000 and that the term of the lease under examination is 10 years. What, then, is the present worth of the lease? The first step involves the determination of the present worth of $1,000 per annum for a 10-year period. The $1,000 must be discounted. The next question is, at what rate should the $1,000 be discounted? This involves the selection of the proper rate. This selection is made in much the same manner as the selection of the capitalization rate as was discussed previously in the chapter. In addition to the examination of the factors that bring about a capitalization rate, the appraiser must examine the lease to determine its reasonableness, the desirability of the property; and the adaptability of the building to the property on which it stands.

Assume that the rate selected is 6 percent. The next step is to find the present worth of a series of payments to be made in the future when the rate is 6 percent. An examination of the Inwood table below shows that 6 percent for 10 years indicates a factor of 7.360. The annual net rental is then multiplied by this factor: $1,000 × 7.360 = $7,360.

YEARS	3%	3½%	4%	4½%	5%	5½%	6%	7%	8%	YEARS
1	.971	.966	.962	.957	.952	.948	.943	.935	.926	1
2	1.913	1.900	1.886	1.873	1.859	1.846	1.833	1.808	1.783	2
3	2.829	2.802	2.775	2.749	2.723	2.698	2.673	2.624	2.577	3
4	3.717	3.673	3.630	3.588	3.546	3.505	3.465	3.387	3.312	4
5	4.580	4.515	4.452	4.390	4.329	4.270	4.212	4.100	3.993	5
6	5.417	5.329	5.242	5.158	5.076	4.996	4.917	4.767	4.623	6
7	6.230	6.115	6.002	5.893	5.786	5.683	5.582	5.389	5.206	7
8	7.020	6.874	6.733	6.596	6.463	6.335	6.210	5.971	5.747	8
9	7.786	7.608	7.435	7.269	7.108	6.952	6.802	6.515	6.247	9
10	8.530	8.317	8.111	7.913	7.722	7.538	7.360	7.024	6.710	10
11	9.253	9.002	8.760	8.529	8.306	8.093	7.887	7.499	7.139	11
12	9.954	9.663	9.385	9.119	8.863	8.619	8.384	7.943	7.536	12
13	10.635	10.303	9.986	9.683	9.394	9.117	8.853	8.358	7.904	13
14	11.296	10.921	10.563	10.223	9.899	9.590	9.295	8.745	8.244	14
15	11.938	11.517	11.118	10.740	10.380	10.038	9.712	9.108	8.559	15
16	12.561	12.094	11.652	11.234	10.838	10.462	10.106	9.447	8.851	16
17	13.166	12.651	12.166	11.707	11.274	10.865	10.477	9.763	9.122	17

A Portion of an Inwood Annuity Table

The figure, $7,360, indicates the present worth of an annual net income of $1,000 for a period of 10 years.

The next problem is to determine the value of the lessor's reversionary interest. It can be seen at this point that the present value of the income, plus the present value of the reversion, will equal the value of the leasehold from the lessor's viewpoint.

Assume that the property is now worth $10,000 and that the property value will remain constant; that is, the value of the building plus the value of the land will be worth the same at the end of the period. It should be noted that the constant value assumption is warranted only if the land has been put to the highest and best use.

An examination of the table reveals that the value of a *single* payment of $1 at 6 percent in ten years is .558395. This is the factor, and thus:

$$\$10{,}000 \times .558395 = \$5{,}583.95$$

Thus the present worth of the income and the reversion:

Present worth of income	=	$ 7,360.00
Present worth of reversion	=	5,583.95
Appraised value of lessor's interest,		$12,943.95 (which may

be rounded off to $13,000).

YEARS	4%	5%	6%	7%	8%
1	.961538	.952381	.943396	.934579	.925925
2	.924556	.907029	.889996	.873438	.857338
3	.888996	.863838	.839619	.816297	.793832
4	.854804	.822702	.792094	.762895	.735029
5	.821927	.783526	.747258	.712986	.680582
6	.790315	.746215	.704961	.666342	.630169
7	.759918	.710681	.665057	.622749	.583490
8	.730690	.676839	.627412	.582008	.540268
9	.702587	.644609	.591898	.543933	.500248
10	.675564	.613913	.558395	.508349	.463193
11	.649581	.584679	.526788	.475092	.428882
12	.624597	.556837	.496969	.444011	.397113
13	.600574	.530321	.468839	.414964	.367697
14	.577475	.505068	.442301	.387817	.340460
15	.555265	.481017	.417265	.362445	.315241
16	.533908	.458112	.393646	.338734	.291890
17	.513373	.436297	.371364	.316574	.270268

A Portion of an Annuity Table Showing the Present Value of a Single Payment of $1 at a Future Date (for Computing the Present Value of a Reversion)

QUESTIONS FOR REVIEW

1. In appraising income property, what is the relationship between income and the value of the property?
2. What is meant by the capitalization process?
3. How does an appraiser select the capitalization rate?
4. What is meant by the process of residual returns?
5. In the residual returns process, how is the value of the land determined?

6. How is net income figured in appraising income property?
7. Explain three types of obsolescence and depreciation.
8. What may raise the rate of functional obsolescence?
9. Why is the depreciation rate added to the capitalization rate?
10. If one is unable to determine the comparative value of the land, how is the residual return process employed?
11. How can management change the net income of a property?
12. Define *highest and best use*.
13. How is the concept of highest and best use related to the "law of diminishing returns"?
14. How is highest and best use related to the so-called "factors of production"?
15. Does it make a difference to the appraiser who the tenants of a property are?
16. What is meant by *replacement analysis*?
17. Why should an appraiser be interested in probable or stable net income of a property rather than in the net income as reflected by the owner's income statement?
18. What is the importance of zoning in an income property appraisal?
19. What is the Inwood method of determining interest?

PROBLEMS

1. Using the income approach, determine the value of the following property:

Estimated Annual Gross Income	$38,700
Vacancy Loss 2½ percent	967
Adjusted Gross Income	$37,733
Other Income (washing machines, etc.)	1,192
Effective Gross Income	$38,925
Expenses	12,996
Net Income Before Capital Recapture	$25,929

First Mortgages are obtainable at 70 percent of value at a rate of 8¾ percent.

Second Mortgages are obtainable at 10 percent of value at a rate of 10 percent.

Equity is at 20 percent of value and demands a 12 percent return. The value of the land and improvements (landscaping, etc.) is $51,816. The remaining economic life of the building is 33 years.

2. Some years ago, Frank Smith rented a vacant lot to the Acme Oil Company, Inc. The lease was made for a term of 25 years at a rental that netted Smith $150 per month. Under the terms of the lease, the Acme Oil Company, Inc., built a gasoline station and installed all of the necessary equipment. The lease provides that Acme can remove both the station and equipment at the expiration of the lease if they desire to do so.

   Smith dies at the end of 9 years, and the executor of his estate finds it necessary to have Smith's interest appraised for purposes of settling the estate.

   You find that the land is now worth $30,000 and feel certain that it will be worth the same at the end of the term provided in the lease.

   There is a good market for leased properties of this kind on a 6 percent net return.

   Prepare an appraisal for the executor of the estate.

3. Each of the following statements is an example of one of the three types of depreciation or obsolescence found in income properties. State the category into which they fall.

   (a) Plaster on the ceiling of an apartment is cracked, and in some places pieces have fallen from the ceiling.

   (b) A chain store has been enjoying a good business. An expressway is constructed, cutting off all access to the store.

   (c) The flooring of a warehouse is cracked from hard use.

   (d) An apartment house has its apartments laid out as follows: Living room in the front, followed by a bedroom, bath, and kitchen; a hall runs alongside these rooms which are set up in a sort of "Pullman car" arrangement.

   (e) Basement floor is cracked because building was left unattended, and the boiler froze and burst.

   (f) You are interested in appraising an apartment house that was constructed some years ago. Across the street from the house, a large modern steam laundry has been constructed.

4. The amount of economic obsolescence in a building is in proportion to the age of the building. Comment.

5. You are requested to estimate the market value of a 25-suite apartment house (including janitor suite) from data supplied based upon a comparison of the subject property with similar type apartment houses. All the suites are three rooms.

   You visit the property, have an opportunity to talk with several tenants, inspect five suites, talk with the janitor, measure the building and form an opinion as to cost, depreciation, and condition.

   The land is 50′ x 100′ and by comparison you find it to be worth \$6 per square foot. You estimate economic life at 40 years and discover that a 6½ percent return will attract purchasers to this type property.

   You then sit down to figure typical units as follows:

   Gross income—\$21.25 per room per month
   Vacancy and credit loss—5%
   Taxes—checked at courthouse, actual expense \$1,260
   Insurance—figured at 1% of effective gross income
   Management—5% of effective gross income
   Heating—\$16 per room per year
   Electric and gas—\$9 per suite (tenants are metered; this is for halls, laundry, and driers)
   Water—\$15 per suite per year
   Janitor—\$600 per year plus one suite
   Supplies, hauling, miscellaneous—\$10 per month
   Decoration—⅔ of one month's rent
   Maintenance and repairs—½ of one month's rent
   Stoves, furnished—\$100 each, 12-year life
   Refrigerators, furnished—\$220 each, 12-year life
   Payments on first mortgage—\$461 per month at 6%

   Prepare an income and expense statement based on the information above and process it to an indication of value by using the building residual method.

SUGGESTED READINGS

Appraisal of Real Property. U.S. Department of the Interior. Washington: Office of the Secretary, 1960. Chapters II and III.

Case, Frederick E. *Real Estate,* Rev. ed. Boston: Allyn and Bacon, 1962. Chapter 10.

Kahn, Sanders A., Frederick E. Case, and Alfred Schimmel. *Real Estate Appraisal and Investment.* New York: The Ronald Press Company, 1963. Chapters 12-14.

Ring, Alfred A. *Real Estate: Principles and Practices,* 7th ed. Englewood Cliffs, New Jersey: Prentice-Hall, Inc., 1972. Chapters 23 and 24.

Ring, Alfred A. *Valuation of Real Estate,* 2d ed. Englewood Cliffs, New Jersey: Prentice-Hall, Inc., 1970. Chapters 9 and 10.

Weimer, Arthur M., Homer Hoyt, and George F. Bloom. *Real Estate,* 6th ed. New York: The Ronald Press Company, 1972. Chapters 12 and 13.

Chapter 26

Subdivisions, Developments, and Condominiums

A *subdivider* is one who buys undeveloped acreage, divides it into smaller parcels, and sells it. A *developer* is one who advances the process a step further by building homes on the lots before selling them. Sometimes, in addition to homes, the developer will build a controlled shopping center which provides convenient and accessible shops for the people living in the development. In practice the terms are frequently used interchangeably.

For over one hundred years, beginning with Thomas Jefferson, subdivisions were laid down in grid fashion. The reason for this was that the surveyor's compass then in use made straight lines and right angles the easiest way to lay down a pattern on land. When Congress adopted the Government Land Survey, the grid tradition was carried on in the country north and west of the Ohio River with the formation of the 640-acre sections. By custom, then, the grid became the standard for laying out subdivisions, particularly in those areas which are now the great cities of the United States, where for the most part blocks are either 300 or 600 feet in length.

By the late 1860's, some courageous developers devised what was then considered a radical idea. The thinking began to move in the direction of recognizing natural topography together with the preservation of amenities (for example, trees) and a separation of the various urban land uses. These radical ideas were incorporated in Riverside, Illinois, in 1869; Vandergrift, Pennsylvania, in 1895; and gradually in other developments: that planning should be for entire neighborhoods, sections of cities, and for entire cities.

PRELIMINARY PROBLEMS OF THE DEVELOPER

Analyzing the Market

One must be constantly reminded of the axiom of the marketeer that "any sound marketing plan whether from the point of view of the manufacturer or the middleman begins with the consumer. . . ." It would be well for one in real estate practice to adopt that axiom as his own. In the final analysis, the real estate broker stands or falls on his ability to satisfy the needs of the consumer. If the broker is able to satisfy needs, the result will be not only great personal satisfaction but also increased profits.

Before beginning a subdivision or development, the subdivider or developer should analyze the market: study the consumer to determine his needs. He must determine whether the time is ripe for a subdivision. There are many cases when ideas that are fundamentally sound fail because the time for their promulgation is premature. For example, Suffolk County, Long Island, is dotted with subdivisions that failed during the twenties; yet, after World War II, these same areas sold rapidly. After World War II, credit was easily available, there was a pent-up demand for housing caused by increasing marriages, increasing population, high income, and improved transportation. Thus, the time was ripe for development.

The individual contemplating a subdivision or development must determine whether the time is ripe for the execution of his plans. Failure to determine this is to leave oneself open to financial catastrophe. To determine whether the time is ripe for a development, it is necessary to analyze the market as shown in Chapter 2.

Selecting a Site

Sites upon which to create a development or subdivision must be selected with the greatest possible care. Many and varied factors have to be considered. As far as possible, the site selected should be in the natural path of the city's growth. As a general rule, cities move outward from their original point along main arteries of traffic in a pattern influenced by natural and artificial barriers. Or, if the city is on a waterfront, there will be a tendency for the growth to move from the water's edge to the highlands. While these are general rules, it sometimes happens that a developer can change the direction of the natural growth of a city; however, in order to do this, a considerable expenditure for promotion must be made.

The specific problems of site selection break down into two major parts: prepurchase analysis and postpurchase operation. The purpose of the former, of course, is to select the proper site *before* investing substantial sums and to check items which may spell the difference between profit or loss. The purpose of postpurchase operation is to carry through with the subdivision plan to selling it and to a point of profit maximization.

PREPURCHASE PROCEDURES

Land Cost

This is discovered, of course, through discussion with the landowner. He will give a price on the raw land. Many subdividers begin with a simple rule of thumb. A five-to-one ratio of selling price to cost is expected to be necessary to yield a profit. That is, the subdivider asks himself the question: If I pay $500 per acre for the raw land, can I expect a return of $2,500 when this land is cut up? Of course, this rule can be, and often is, changed to conform with local practice when necessary.

Other Cost Factors

The next logical step is to prepare, either alone or with the help of a surveyor, a tentative layout to determine the number of lots. The major reason for this is that one may, in this manner, estimate the *lot* price of the improvements. In short, if road costs total $1,000 and only 10 lots are available, then the cost allocated to each lot of the road is $100. However, if 100 lots are available, then the cost of the road allocated to each lot will be only $10.

Drainage, Soil Tests, and Topography

The property should be examined for drainage. Without proper drainage the cost of developing a satisfactory solution for the drainage of street and storm waters may prove prohibitive.

Soil tests are important in areas where septic tanks are expected to be used. In those areas, the county public health departments have percolation maps indicating where septic tanks may be used. In the event that tests haven't been run on the land the developer has in mind, the health department will run the tests.

Topography is important in any development. The site should be adaptable to its proposed use. If the land is rough and hilly, thought must be given to the manner in which the roads will be laid out.

Existing Utilities

The location of utilities may govern the design of the subdivisions. In some cases the absence of gas, sewage, water, and electricity may cause the project to be abandoned. When the utility lines are reasonably near the proposed project, it is necessary to contact the utility companies to determine the cost of installing new utilities in the project. This is done with the idea of allocating the cost of the utilities on a per lot basis.

Road Costs

The cost of building roads in the project must be estimated and divided between the estimated number of lots in order to determine the cost per lot. Because the problem of roads is so great in any development, it will be discussed at length later in this chapter.

Transportation, Schools, and Shopping Districts

Easily available transportation can often make or break a development or subdivision. Therefore, it should be determined if any freeways are nearby or proposed for building in the near future. What is the bus and railroad transportation? Nearness of schools should be determined as well as shopping districts. Availability of these facilities often makes the task of the subdividers easier. In addition, the subdivider might think in terms of creating space for nearby schools and building his own shopping centers. This has been done in the larger subdivisions.

Zoning and Restrictions

Zoning laws are restrictions imposed by municipalities upon the use of property. As far as zoning laws are concerned, every prospective subdivider or developer would do well to obtain a copy of the local zoning regulations as soon as the thought of subdividing enters his mind. All land prior to purchase must be thought of in terms of existing zoning laws. The land examined might prove to be zoned for industry or business rather than for residential purposes. The land might be zoned for residential purposes when the developer had in mind a controlled shopping center along with the plans for his housing development. Rather than make plans and then be forced to change them, the developer or subdivider should determine beforehand what restrictions he must observe.

The lot sizes must be carefully examined in the light of existing zoning laws. For example, the divider might be thinking in terms of lots with a forty-foot frontage when the zoning ordinances for the city require the minimum to be 50 by 100 feet. Obviously, the developer or divider must be familiar with zoning requirements.

Not only may the size of the lot be restricted by reason of zoning ordinances, but the height and the area of the building on the lot may be controlled also. For example, a typical ordinance may state the following requirements:

> HEIGHT—In the "A" Residential District, no building, hereafter erected or altered, shall exceed thirty-five (35) feet or three (3) stories. . . .
>
> . . . "A" Building Area—In the "A" Residential District, the total building area shall not exceed twenty-five (25) percent of the total lot area.[1]

Restrictions to be placed on a development are governed somewhat by the subdivider himself. A common restriction has to do with

---

[1] Building Ordinance of the Town of Brookhaven, N. Y., Ordinance No. 15, effective March 16, 1937, and as subsequently amended. This ordinance is typical of many throughout the country.

the distance that buildings must be set back from the street. Others may limit the number of stories of the houses or determine whether flat-roofed houses are permissible. In most developments there is a restriction in the deed that permits occupancy only by a single family.

The reason for these restrictions is to promote harmony in the neighborhood, which in turn makes the task of selling the property easier, and adds to the reputation of the subdivider or developer.

The *Underwriting Manual* of the FHA offers the following recommendation regarding restrictive covenants:

> The protection afforded by suitable covenants is of primary importance in areas which lack the benefit of adequate and effective zoning. In properly zoned areas protective covenants are an important supplementary aid in maintaining neighborhood character and values. The extent of zoning protection is limited to governmental exercises of the police powers of maintaining and promoting public health, safety, and welfare. Protective covenants, being agreements between private parties, can go much further in meeting the needs of a particular development and in providing maximum possible protection.[2]

Financing

The availability of proper financing should be investigated. If the developer is thinking in terms of FHA or VA, he should contact a mortgage banker or other suitable source of funds and determine what the FHA and/or VA requirements and specifications are. This is particularly appropriate in the event the developer is planning a rather large development.

Purchase, Option, or Escrow? After having determined from the preliminary survey as outlined on the preceding pages that the development is practical, some developers will make an outright purchase of the land and continue with the subdivision. However, it would appear more practical—depending, of course, upon the bargaining position of the subdivider—either to take an option on the property, as is done in most states, or enter into a conditional escrow transaction as is done in California.

---

[2] FHA, *Underwriting Manual,* Sec. 1354, Art. 4.

The reasons for the option or conditional escrow are to receive a more firm commitment on financing, to prepare a final *tentative* map which must be approved by the planning commission and, in California, by the Real Estate Department. Then the final map must be approved. And finally, the time period will enable one to be released from obligation if FHA or VA requirements become so restrictive as to make the project impractical.

In California, a conditional escrow is used in place of the option. There the escrow agreement on subdivisions is generally from 60 to 90 days. Basically, this is the same as the option and the purchaser enters into the agreement upon certain express conditions, that is, that he can get proper financing, and if he fails to obtain the necessary financing, then he is released from the obligation to purchase.

Generally, when financing is assured and the title company reports the title is in good order, the developer will either exercise his option or close his conditional escrow and proceed with the subdivision.

The important thing to note is that much can be done to determine the practicability of a subdivision before much money is invested in the transaction.

The Rolling Option. Many of the larger developers and subdividers use what they have labeled "the rolling option." It is simply a device to free capital and minimize risk. For example, a subdivider may have in mind to subdivide 150 acres. He may, if he chooses, purchase the 150 acres and subdivide it all at one time. However, if he does this, he ties up a large amount of capital and faces a risk of loss in the event the project fails. Consequently, to avoid this he simply enters into an option agreement with the seller of the land which could be substantially as follows: he purchases 50 acres outright and is given an option to buy the second 50 within a stated time; then he has a further option to buy the third 50-acre tract within a stated time. Thus, if he fails on the first 50-acre project, he is not obligated to buy the second 50-acre tract. If things go well, he will subdivide the whole tract, exercising options as he goes.

THE NEED FOR GENERAL PLANNING

Some developers are distressed by what they regard as insufferable delays of planning "red tape." Others feel that communities are placing undue cost burdens upon them. Yet, one developer built a large development, and then it was discovered that not a single foot of space had been left for schools, whereupon five acres of brand new homes had to be knocked down for the invasion of suburbia's children. In suburban Rochester, New York, a builder built a 640-home development without a sewer system. Almost immediately the inhabitants were engulfed by septic tank effluent. Subsequently, the health officials stepped in and ordered the installation of a sewage system—at a cost. And at Portuguese Bend, south of Los Angeles, 156 homes ranging in cost from $25,000 to $50,000 slid down the hillside after having floated on a sea of septic tank effluent. No one had discovered that the shale beneath was unable to absorb the sewage effluent. In 1953, 350 homes were sold in a Long Island development; six years later these homes were condemned by the State of New York for an expressway. For lack of planning the taxpayers were forced to carry an additional burden.[3] These are but a few instances of hundreds which demonstrate both social and money costs of poor planning.

Does good planning pay? More often than not it does, for both the developer and the taxpayer. A study of a square mile of Trenton, New Jersey, has shown that under proper planning $450,000 could have been saved in street improvement costs and sixty-five acres set aside for recreation and other purposes. This, without a cent's loss to landowners and developers.

The United States Savings and Loan League suggests that land planning pays because: (1) it cuts development costs by requiring less lineal feet of streets, less curbing, less cutting and grading (by respecting the contours of the land); (2) it secures investment for generations and preserves the tax base through protection of property values and property rights; (3) it eliminates the misuse of property, thus preventing damage to the health, safety, and convenience of the community as a whole; (4) it eliminates hazardous or other unsatisfactory conditions that depress property values; (5) it saves municipal government unnecessary expense by providing suitable sites for schools and parks at a time when land values are low; (6) finally, its total effect is to take speculating out of subdividing.[4]

---

[3] Edward Higbee, *The Squeeze—Cities Without Space* (New York: William Morrow and Company, Apollo Edition, 1960), pp. 127-130.

[4] *Land Planning,* p. 7.

Planning the Subdivision

People buy property in subdivisions near cities because they want to get out of the city. They want to build in the "country." For that reason, successful subdividers attempt to retain as much of the country in the subdivision as possible. Wide streets and winding roads where possible, coupled with trees and foliage, make the subdivision attractive to people who have been reared in the cities. Lots must be laid out as attractively as possible, both in size and physical appearance. Some subdivisions have parks and playground areas to make them more attractive to the buyer with children.

In planning subdivisions these principles should be observed: [5]

1. Street intersections should be at right angles to minimize traffic hazards. Lots with double frontage are uneconomical and undesirable and should be avoided. Bad and Good designs are:

Bad Good

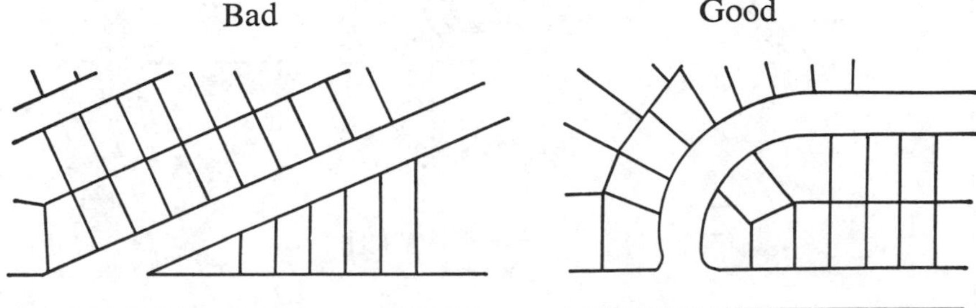

2. Intersections of minor streets with arterial or collector streets should be held to a minimum to avoid hazard and delay:

Bad Good

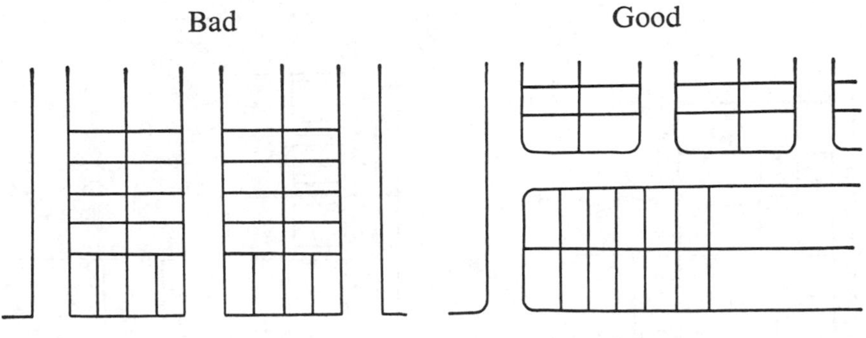

[5] Designs from "Control of Land Subdivisions," State of New York, Department of Commerce.

3. Dead-end streets should be avoided:

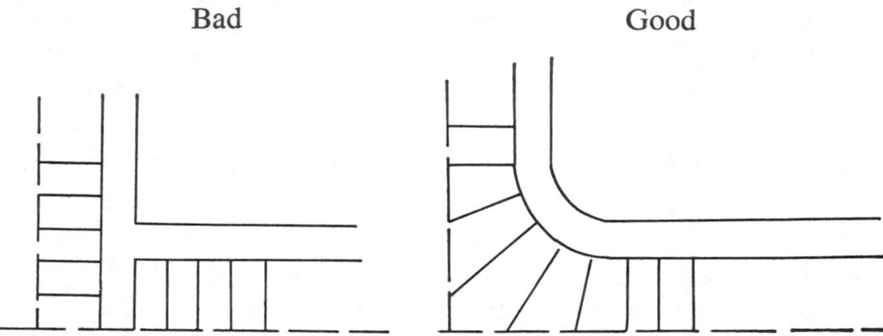

4. Street jogs with center-line offsets of less than 125 feet should be avoided:

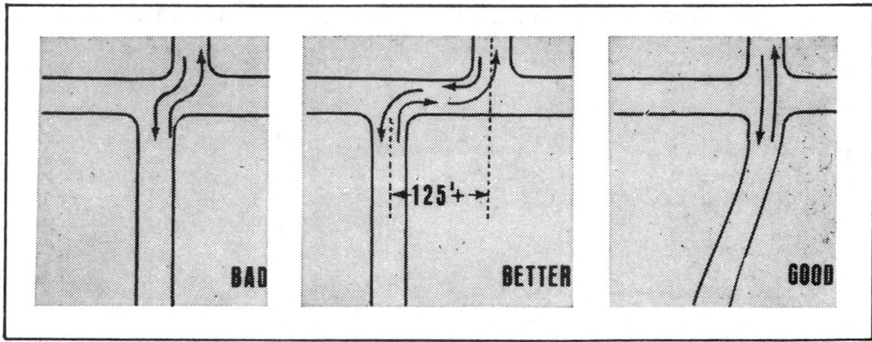

5. Corner lots require greater widths than interior lots in order to provide proper setback of the dwellings from the side street:

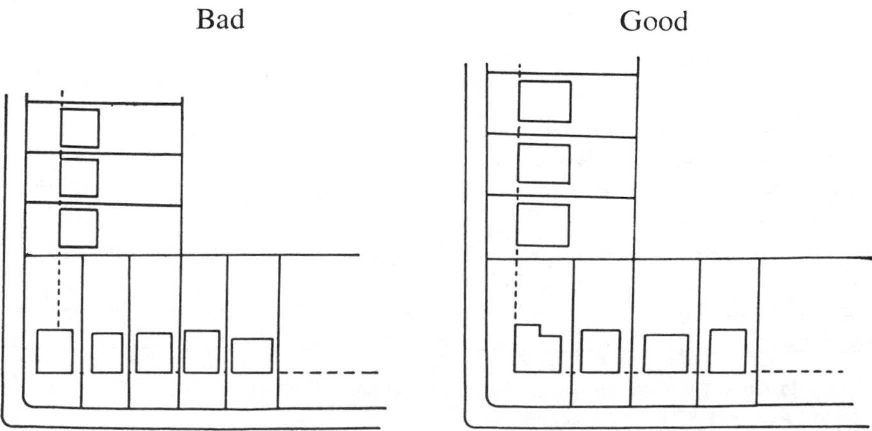

The following illustration shows good and bad planning and includes some of the principles illustrated above: [6]

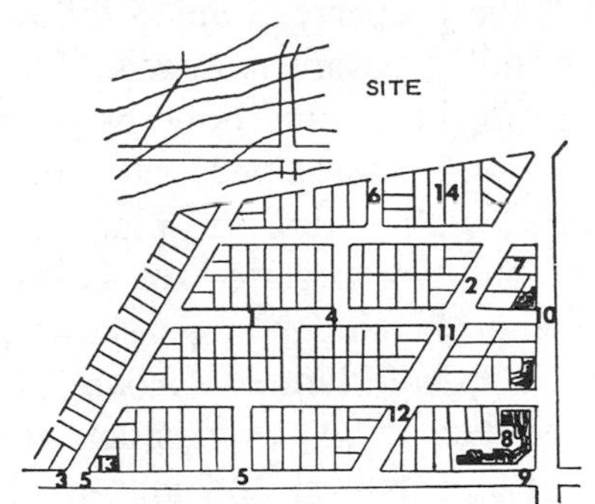

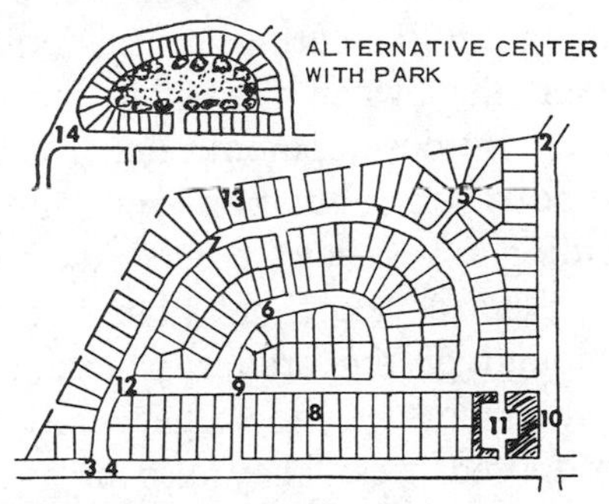

POOR PLANNING and what is wrong with it:
1 Gridiron street pattern without purpose.
2 Heavy traffic within subdivision.
3 Angular intersections.
4 Non-abutting cross streets.
5 Numerous subdivision entrance streets.
6 Dead-end streets.
7 Small, uneconomical blocks.
8 Ribbon shopping districts.
9 No off-street parking space.
10 Stores amid residences.
11 Lots not perpendicular to streets.
12 Angular lots.
13 Small corner lots.
14 Deep lots.

GOOD PLANNING and what is good about it:
1 Curved street pattern adds subdivision appeal.
2 Heavy traffic diverted.
3 Safe, perpendicular intersections.
4 Few subdivision entrance streets.
5 Quiet street.
6 Local streets for local traffic only.
7 Streets fit topography.
8 Long, economical blocks.
9 Cross walks in long blocks.
10 Organized shopping center.
11 Off-street parking space.
12 Wide corner lots.
13 Lots perpendicular to streets.
14 Provision for interior park.

It is interesting to note, when analyzing the above recommendations, that nearly every suggestion either provides the subdivider with a good selling point or tends to save him money. At the same time the community is benefited. For example, a properly planned subdivision will have no heavy through traffic, an important factor in selling to people with children.

The Planned Urban Development

The planned urban development (PUD) is a development incorporating a variety of uses planned and developed as a unit. Such development may be that of individual lots or may have common recreation or open space surrounding clustered buildings. Typically, common land is an essential element.[7]

---

[6] *Ibid,* p. 42.

[7] Many communities require that the functional open space, exclusive of parking or streets be 25 percent of the total acreage.

To create a PUD, the owner must outline the development plan. If approved by the Planning Board (and/or City Council, depending on the location) a *tentative* rezoning of the property is made following a public hearing. At this point no building permit is issued. However, the owner must bind the property to those conditions listed in the final development plan. A final rezoning is then given. After this, subdivision regulations must be complied with (filing the plat, providing for streets, etc.). At this point building permits are issued.

The development plan referred to above includes maps showing enough of the area surrounding the proposed Planned Urban Development to show the relationship of the PUD to existing and proposed uses. They also must show existing natural and man-made features and existing zoning of adjacent property. In addition, the applicant must show the types, locations, densities, and acreage consumed by all the land uses. A written statement is also required outlining the present ownership of all the land involved in the PUD, an expected schedule of beginning and completion, and a statement of intent concerning the provision of water, sewer, and highway improvements.[8]

FINANCIAL PROBLEMS OF THE DEVELOPER

Financing the Subdivision or Development

The problem of financing the subdivision or development is a difficult one. Banks, the normal place for financing real estate transactions, usually will not lend money on raw acreage. They will, however, make building loans after construction has begun on the property. Therefore, the subdivider or developer has to employ one or more of the following financing methods:

1. He finances the purchase and development costs out of his own pocket. This, of course, requires a substantial outlay on the part of the subdivider. The Housing and Home Finance Agency suggests the following as collateral security for a business loan: contractor's equipment, personal automobile, equity in residence, warehouse inventory, marketable securities, assignment of contract payments and mortgage proceeds, land holdings, and trucks.

---

[8] Some zoning regulations state: "The proposed unit development shall be under single development control through one owner, corporation, or agency." But this varies from place to place.

2. The purchase of the raw land is partially financed by the seller by means of a purchase money mortgage that the seller takes back, plus a down payment in cash paid by the purchaser.

3. Sometimes the subdivider will obtain an option to purchase the property. This is generally done when the owner has begun a subdivision of his own, but has, for any one of a number of reasons, failed to carry it out to completion. The roads are usually laid and the lots surveyed. The person employing the option takes it on the lots and proceeds to build, purchasing the lots one at a time under the terms of the option.

4. A developer may purchase the land, file the plat, cut the necessary roads, and begin building one house with his own money. After reaching the required stage of construction, he may then obtain a building loan from a bank.

5. The subdivider or developer may form a syndicate embracing a number of persons, each of whom puts up part of the cash, and each of whom shares in the profits.

6. Sometimes a corporation is formed and stock is sold for the purpose of raising the required cash.

OTHER PROBLEMS OF THE DEVELOPER

Filing the Plat

As a result of the actions of some incompetent and unscrupulous subdividers, most states have enacted stringent laws regulating the subdividing of real property.

A map must be filed together with certain other legal requirements which are discussed later. The first problem is to have a map made by a competent, licensed surveyor. In most cases this map, or *plat* as it is called, must first be approved by the town, county, or city planning board, or sometimes by the city commissioners. It is suggested that the name of a surveyor to do the job be obtained from the planning consultant, city commissioner, or whoever first approves the plat. In this manner, much trouble regarding the acceptance of the plat can be avoided.

If the owner of a parcel of raw land has a map made and sells from an unrecorded map by a lot and block description, most of the states provide that each lot sold or conveyed in that manner shall result in a fine to the person selling. This does not, however, preclude an owner from having a map made and selling parcels by a metes and bounds description.

The most complicated situation in filing a plat is the number of bodies which must approve the filing. Sometimes when a map is being filed, it must have approval not only from the county officials but also from the township officials.

Before beginning the subdivision, or perhaps even before the acquisition of the raw land, the subdivider should inquire about the requirements of the town planning board. Although the requirements vary, in general they have to do with building the road to proper specifications. For example, some townships require that the road-cut be made to a width of fifty feet, and oiled to a width of at least forty feet. These requirements vary from township to township, but in any event there will be some road-building specifications that have to be followed. The specifications not only will call for the road to be cut to a specified width, but they will also specify the method of applying the oil: the number of gallons of a specified grade per square yard, the number of coats of oil, and the amount of the "blotter coat" of sand that must be applied. In some areas it is necessary to place a bond with the town board to insure that the road will be built in accordance with the specifications set down by the board. The bond is usually two thirds of the cost of building the road and is posted in cash or "the equivalent thereof." As the road is built, it is inspected by the town supervisor of highways and if it is not built according to specifications, the bond money is used by the township to complete properly the building of the road.

When the plat is approved by the town board and a bond is furnished to insure the proper building of the road, the map is filed with the proper county official, generally the county clerk. In most states an abstract covering at least twenty years must be filed with the map. In addition, most places require that a certificate be obtained from the county treasurer showing that all of the taxes due and payable on the land have been paid as of the date of filing. Some counties specify the size of the map to be filed. In some areas of the country, especially those areas where there is no city water or sewage system, approval must be obtained from the local board of health for sewage disposal and water supply systems. For example, when it is necessary that a well be drilled on the property, it is often required by the health department that the cesspool or septic tank to be constructed for sewage disposal be built at least seventy-five feet from the well. This, too, will vary from county to county, but generally a minimum distance of seventy-five feet is required from the water system to the sewage disposal system. These requirements for filing the plat are general throughout the United States, although there are local variations that must be checked.

Implied Warranties in Homes

More and more state courts are holding builders liable for defects in home building. As one writer put it, the law has evolved to the incongruous state where "it offers greater protection to the purchaser of a seventy-nine-cent dog leash than it does to the purchaser of a $40,000 home. If the dog leash is defective, the purchaser can get his money back and he may be able to recover damages if he loses his dog because of the defective leash. If the purchaser of the house is required to replace the heating unit two months after the purchase, he probably has no recourse against the seller. Quality is generally at the risk of the buyer of real property, absent an express warranty or fraud." [9]

This old rule is changing. In a leading case the builder-vendor was held liable on an implied warranty for damages resulting from water seeping into the basement of the house. The court said, "Where a person holds himself out as specially qualified to perform work of a particular character there is an implied warranty that the work shall be done in a reasonably good and workmanlike manner and that the completed product or structure shall be reasonably fit for its intended purpose." (Waggoner v. Midwestern Development, Inc., 154 N.W. 2d 803 [S.D. 1967])

Furthermore in at least one state lenders have been held liable for defective housing. "As a result of the decision in Connor v. Great Western Federal Savings and Loan Assn., 447 P. 2d. 609 (Cal. 1968), a new trail . . . has been blazed. The law may no longer allow lending institutions to slither into a sanctuary after having unleashed and sponsored an irresponsible developer." [10]

---

[9] Haskell, *The Case For an Implied Warranty of Quality in the Sales of Real Property,* 53 Georgetown L.J. 633 (1965), quoted by William Schwartz, *Defective Housing: The Fall of Caveat Emptor,* 33 Journal of the American Trial Lawyers Association, 122 (1970).

[10] Schwartz, *ibid.,* p. 138.

Land Sales Full Disclosure Act

As a result of fraudulent land sales, Congress passed the Land Sales Full Disclosure Act in 1972. Basically, the Act requires the seller of subdivided property to make a full, complete, and accurate disclosure of all relevant information about the property *prior* to the consummation of the sale to the buyer of the land. The Act protects the buyer against fraudulent and deceptive sales practices by providing civil and criminal remedies against the land developer and the sales agent for willful violations of the Act.

The following is a list of the most common violations of the Act and the remedies that can be applied either by the purchaser or the Government.[11]

PROHIBITED PRACTICE	REMEDIES	PARTY LIABLE
1. "Property Report" not furnished purchaser prior to sale	Rescission, or Suit for damages Criminal Action	Developer or Agent
2. Contract does not contain Notice of Rescission Right of purchaser, and it is not explained to the purchaser	Rescission, or Suit for damages Criminal Action	Developer or Agent
3. Property Report furnished contains untrue statement or omission of a material fact	Suit for damages Criminal Action	Developer or Agent
4. Lot sold to purchaser during period of time Statement of Record was either suspended or had not received an effective date from H.U.D.	Suit for Damages Criminal Action	Developer or Agent
5. Lot sold by fraudulent or deceptive advertising, or misrepresentation, which was relied on by the purchaser.	Suit for damages Criminal Action	Developer or Agent

NOTE: These prohibited practices could support **class actions** under Rule 23 of the Federal Rules of Civil Procedure. Class actions allow individual purchasers to join together in a single cause of action. Salesmen should appreciate the fact that every purchaser is not helpless against the developer but under the proper circumstances, has the strength of all the purchasers combined.

[11] William B. Ingersoll with Special Contributions by Stuart M. Block, "Federal Laws Affecting Land Sales Practices," the *Land Developer*. Vol. I. No. 7 (November-December, 1972).

Land developers are required to file a Statement of Record with the Office of Interstate Land Sales Registration (OILSR), Department of Housing and Urban Development. The Statement of Record details information which is summarized in a document called the *Property Report,* which must be given to the prospective purchaser prior to a sale. It contains such things as: name and location of developer and subdivision; effective date of the report; road distances to nearby communities; financial terms and refund policies, if any; mortgages and liens; protection, if any, afforded the buyer in case of financial default of the developer; leasing arrangements; taxes and special assessments to be paid by the buyer; escrow and title arrangements, plus any restrictions, easements, covenants and their effects on the buyer; recreational facilities available and expected dates of completion of proposed ones; availability or lack of utilities and services, such as trash collection, sewers, water supply; any need for drainage and fill before the land can be used for building; presence of schools, medical facilities, shopping, and transportation or proposed dates of availability of such services; number of homes now occupied; accessibility of lots by roads.

If there is any material misrepresentation or if the *Property Report* is not distributed, both the developer and the salesman can be jailed for five years, fined $5,000, and be subject to a civil suit by the buyer.

If a buyer has not seen the site, he has 48 hours after the delivery of the property report to rescind the contract.

State Land Use Regulations

Many states have and most states will move into the area of land use regulations because of full disclosure and environmental considerations.

For example, in 1963 California revised its subdivision laws based on the principle of full disclosure. In that year the legislature gave the California Real Estate Department power to withhold public report of subdivisions unless subdividers gave certain detailed information. The real estate commission requires proof of title; interest contracted for; satisfactory demonstration that adequate financial arrangements have been made for off-site improvements and community facilities; and specific information indicating that parcels of land can, indeed, be used in the way in which they are intended.

As soon as California strengthened its laws, some unscrupulous developers moved to neighboring states. In 1964, California added an additional law that gives the real estate department power to refuse out-of-state advertising if it feels that such advertising constitutes an investment danger to its citizens. In that year Nevada, New Mexico, and Oregon passed laws patterned after California. Other states are moving in that direction at the urging of President Nixon, who believes land is a precious resource that must be controlled in its use. The states, in his opinion, are uniquely qualified to regulate land use because they are closer to regional problems than the federal government and are more aloof from local problems and tax bases than the counties.

This, coupled with an awareness that uncontrolled development has had a shattering impact on the environment, has led to environmental "impact" laws—and more to come in the future. For example, California's Environmental Quality Act of 1970 requires the state agencies to publish detailed reports on the environmental impact of their projects. However, in a recent court decision (Friends of Mammoth Mountain v. Mono County), the California Court ruled the Act also applied to private developers, saying, "To limit the operation of the E.Q.A. solely to what are essentially public works projects would frustrate the effectiveness of the Act." [12]

Other states can be expected to follow the California decision either by statutes or by court decisions.

CONDOMINIUMS [13]

In 1970, 20 percent of housing starts in California were condominiums. In the same year 40 percent of the starts in Florida were condominiums. Thus, it seems appropriate that it be dealt with in considerable detail.

What is it? *Webster's Third New International Dictionary* defines *condominium* as:

---

[12] Quoted in *Time* (January 1, 1973), p. 45.

[13] Much of this discussion has been adapted by the author from an unpublished paper done by one of the author's students, Allen Porter, entitled "Condominiums."

> Common ownership by two or more persons holding undivided fractional shares in the same property and having the right to alienate their shares resembling tenancy in common in Anglo-American law rather than joint tenancy with its right of survivorship.

Briefly, the condominium is an ownership in fee simple by an individual of a single unit in a multi-unit structure, coupled with ownership of an undivided interest in the land and other elements of the structure held in common with other unit owners of the building. The fee simple ownership of the single unit generally applies to the airspace between the walls and between the floors and ceilings. If the walls are for the support of the building or are in common with another unit, they belong in the category called "common elements." Generally, the common elements consist of the land beneath the buildings, yards, service installations, and community entrances and exits. In the final analysis, a person owns his own unit in fee and is a co-owner with others in the common elements.

Rights and Obligations

There are three main documents creating rights and obligations of the co-owners. These are the declaration, the map (or area plot plan), and the conveyance.

The Declaration. The *declaration* defines the rights and obligations of the co-owners, and defines the rules and regulations under which the condominium must operate.

Generally the contents of the declaration consists of twenty parts:

1. Legal description of the land upon which the condominium sits.
2. Definition and description of the condominium unit, usually according to state statute. For example, Colorado defines a condominium unit as an "individual airspace unit together with interest in the common elements appurtenant to such unit." [14]
3. A description of the common elements. State legislation recognizes certain elements as common elements. If there is a

[14] *Colorado Revised Statutes of 1953,* 118-15-2.

desire to make one of these elements not a common element or to add to the list of common elements, a statement to that effect must be made in the declaration. For example, common elements under Colorado statutes and most states are:

a. The land on which a building or buildings are located.
b. The foundations, columns, girders, beams, supports, main walls, roofs, halls, corridors, lobbies, stairs, stairways, fire escapes, entrances, and exits of such building or buildings.
c. The basements, yards, gardens, parking areas, and storage spaces.
d. The premises for the lodging of custodians or persons in charge of the property.
e. Installations of central services, such as power, light, gas, hot and cold water, heating, refrigeration, central air conditioning, and incinerating.
f. The elevators, tanks, pumps, motors, fans, compressors, ducts, and in general all apparatus and installations existing for common use.
g. Such community and commercial facilities as may be provided for in the declaration.
h. All other parts of the property necessary or convenient to its existence, maintenance, and safety, or normally in common use.

4. A description of the limited common elements. Colorado statute defines limited common elements as "those common elements designated in the declaration as reserved for the use by fewer than all the owners of the individual airspace units." [15]
5. Provision for reciprocal easements.
6. Provision for the administration of the property by an association or cooperative of owners.
7. Provision for assessments to establish a fund for the payment of common expenses. Common expenses covered by the assessment should include at least the following: taxes, insurance, water, heat, recreational facilities, repairs and service.
8. Method of collection for the common fund.

[15] *Colorado Revised Statutes of 1953,* 118-15-3b.

9. Remedies and procedure for collection of assessments.
10. Imposition of lien to insure collection of funds.
11. Provision for procedure or the enforcement of the lien.
12. Provision for insurance covering both common and units.
    a. How insurance for common units is to be paid.
    b. How insurance for units is to be paid.
    c. Requirement of insurance by unit owners.
13. Provision for rights of individual owner in respect to interior surfaces of the unit.
14. Provision restricting the use to which a condominium may be put.
15. Provision restricting partition by condominium units. For example, the Colorado statute governs such provision: "If such declaration . . . restricts partition of the common elements, the rules or laws known as the rule against perpetuities and the rule prohibiting unlawful restraints on alienation shall not be applied to defeat or limit any such provision."
16. Provision against animals, or certain types of animals.
17. Provision describing how common facilities are to be used.
18. Provision for relative rights and obligations of the co-owners in case of destruction, either partial or total.
19. Provision limiting individual owners from subleasing units. The limitation is usually that approval of the sublessee by the condominium management, or co-owners, or other designated group must first be made. This allows control as to the type of people living in the condominium. For example, Windsor Gardens permits families only where the head of the household is over fifty.
20. Provision for amendment procedure to the declaration.

In some declarations not all the provisions listed above will be used. In other declarations additional and different provisions may be used. The use of these provisions is for the benefit of the entire condominium.

A set of bylaws to govern operation of the building might be used in place of some provision in the declaration. The bylaws need not be recorded and will constitute an agreement binding upon the unit owners.

The Map. The map is necessary to describe a condominium unit in a form complying to adequate legal description. The map must describe the unit both horizontally and vertically. The map is a means to describe an individual unit, and when filed, units can be sold by such descriptions as registered on the map.

Basically, there are three methods for making a map:

1. Subdivision plat: Use of a three-dimension drawing of the entire building, which allows for both vertical and horizontal description.
2. Apartment survey: Describing the apartments as being all of that airspace or area on the land upon which the building or buildings are located which lies between two horizontal planes, the lower of which has an elevation of . . . feet, the upper of which has an elevation of . . . . feet, and the vertical lines of which are bounded and described.
3. A system which is a variation of metes and bounds.

The Conveyance. The same forms of conveyance can be used for condominiums as are used for any other type of real property interest. Basically, the form will be the same except for certain provisions which are required, and it must meet required rules of formality in order to be legal. The conveyances will probably cover:

1. Description of airspace which is to be subject of ownership.
2. Description of areas that are to be subject of exclusive right to use and occupancy.
3. Rights to use other common elements or common facilities.
4. Exception of the other airspaces and undivided interest.
5. Reserve to the grantor the right to convey similar interests to other parties.
6. Right to additional construction or improvement of common elements by grantor.
7. Right to reserve space for construction.
8. Any other provisions which may be deemed necessary.

Financing the Condominium

The major breakthrough in the area of financing came in September, 1963, when the National Housing Act, Section 234, went into effect. This act enabled the FHA to insure mortgages on condominiums and gave a strong impetus to the movement in condominium ownership.

Probably the most important lenders in the condominium field are the savings and loan associations, the national banks, insurance companies, and mortgage bankers. Generally, most of the different loan institutions impose, or have imposed on them, regulations restricting loans. General restrictions regarding condominium loans are:

1. Owner must have 100% title to his unit. Title must be a fee simple.
2. Owner must be able to pay his own taxes, or may have to make monthly payments to a tax reserve.
3. Insurance requirements are usually very important in the case of condominiums.
4. A first lien is generally required.

Condominiums may have higher interest rates than single-unit structures because there may be some additional risks and costs associated with condominium loans, which are not associated with regular home loans. One of the most prevalent risks in condominium loans is that of the quality of management operating the condominium. Under a home loan the lender has recourse if the owner lets the house deteriorate, and the lender may have recourse against the owner of an individual unit in a condominium if the owner lets the unit itself deteriorate. But the lender usually does not have any control over the management, who may let the common elements fall into a state of waste, impairing the lender's security. If a lender must foreclose and take over a condominium unit, his expenses would be higher than in taking over a house of equal price because he must continue to pay expenses for common elements which are not present in a home. Furthermore, there is a moral obligation to keep up the unit because it may create a detriment to the rest of the condominium if not kept up. Servicing loans for a condominium are generally higher than for a home of equal price. Appraisals and inspections will generally be more costly than for a home because the entire condominium must be appraised as well as the individual unit. Also statutes and regulations governing condominiums and loans require extra legal and engineering services that are not required with regular home loans.

QUESTIONS FOR REVIEW

1. When selecting a site for a subdivision, what pertinent points must the subdivider examine?
2. Why is zoning important to a developer?
3. Subdivision planning pays both the subdivider and the community. Discuss.
4. Explain the "rule of thumb" used by subdividers in estimating the necessary return per dollar of outlay for acreage.
5. Explain in detail the legal requirements of filing a map or plat.
6. Explain how the maintenance of common spaces is handled in condominiums.
7. Why might the interest rates be higher for financing a condominium than for a single-family residence?
8. How is a PUD different from an ordinary subdivision?
9. What prompted the federal government to enact the Land Sales Full Disclosure Act?
10. What is the *rolling option* and how is it used?

PROBLEM

1. You are given the opportunity to purchase a parcel of land 2,000 feet deep with a 290-foot frontage on a main highway. The only approach to the property is from the main highway because there is wooded area on either side of the parcel. The owner tells you that the purchase price is $24,000. The parcel is located 5 miles from the outskirts of a small but growing city. From previous investigations you feel that there is a need for more housing in the area. There is no water or sewage, but in that section of the country most people drill their own wells and build their own septic tanks anyway, so that doesn't bother you too much. Electricity is available. You speak to the town engineer who recommends an old friend as a surveyor. The surveyor to whom you speak about the project states that if you decide to go through with the idea, the Town Planning Board would be happier if you cut a road parallel to the main highway, 1,000 feet back from the main highway. In addition, he tells you that the planning board will refuse to accept the plat unless you have a "fifty-foot turnaround" at the far end of any proposed road. You are told that this means a circle with a fifty-foot radius.

Upon studying the zoning ordinance, you find that the property is located in what is called the "C" Residence District. You discover upon further reading that it states:

> "C" Size of Lot-Area—In the "C" Residential District, no building shall be erected or altered on a lot of any area less than five thousand (5,000) square feet, or upon a lot having a frontage of less than fifty (50) feet.
>
> . . . In the "C" Residence District the total building area shall not exceed thirty-five (35) percent of the total lot area. . . .
>
> . . . In the "C" Residence District, the required front yard shall be at least twenty-five (25) feet. . . .
>
> In the "C" Residence District, there shall be two (2) side yards, one (1) on each side of the building, the total aggregate of both sides to be eighteen (18) feet and no one (1) side to be less than eight (8) feet wide. . . .

After examining the ordinance, you decide that if you do go through with the deal, you should sell some of the lots. Then if things go well, you might try building houses. After all, your finances are limited—you have only $10,000 in cash. The zoning ordinance also reveals to you that you must have a minimum of a 50-foot cut for a road. A road-building contractor tells you that when you begin to build your road, you must deposit two thirds of the cost with the Town Planning Board to insure that the road will be built according to their standards. This deposit must be in cash. The roadbuilding contractor assures you that he can and will build the road at a cost of $3 per lineal foot.

You approach the owner and he agrees to sell you the property for $24,000. He will require $5,000 cash and will take back a purchase money mortgage in the amount of $19,000. It will be a blanket mortgage with a partial release clause calling for the payment of $200 per lot toward the purchase price on the first ten lots sold. The mortgage is for three years at 8 percent.

(a) Draw a diagram showing the maximum number of lots, size of lots, roads, and turnaround.

(b) Determine the price of the lots at four times the average cost of the land and the cost of the road. Each lot is priced the same. You call the subdivision "Greenacres."

(c) Prepare a classified advertisement to be inserted in the local papers. You have decided to sell the lots for cash.

(d) You sell ten lots and then decide to build homes on the remainder of the property. What do you obtain from the mortgagee at this point?

(e) An architect submits plans to you for a house having dimensions of 42′ x 30′. It is a popular ranch-type house, but you reject the drawings. Why?

(f) You finally select a house that you believe will sell for $20,500. You go to your banker and arrange to finance the building. What does the banker ask you to give him as security for a proposed loan?

(g) The cost to you of the house including the lot is $17,500. You find a buyer and take him to a bank which agrees to give him a loan of $16,000. What takes place at the closing?

(h) List any restrictions that you might want in the deeds given by you to the lot purchasers and to the home purchasers.

SUGGESTED READINGS

Ring, Alfred H. *Real Estate Principles and Practices*, 7th ed. Englewood Cliffs, New Jersey: Prentice-Hall, Inc., 1972. Chapter 25.

Smith, Halbert C., Carl J. Tschappat, and Ronald L. Racster. *Real Estate and Urban Development.* Homewood, Illinois: Richard D. Irwin, Inc., 1973. Chapter 13.

Weimer, Arthur M., Homer Hoyt, and George F. Bloom. *Real Estate,* 6th ed. New York: The Ronald Press Company, 1972. Chapters 14 and 15.

Chapter 27

The City as an Economic Base

Following the lead of a few progressive and farsighted city executives, an increasing number of city planners, real estate executives, and economists are beginning to recognize the importance of base studies. Implicit in this recognition is the awareness that the economic well-being of the individual citizen, as well as the growth and financial strength of the city, is to a large degree determined by the economic health of the community. For this reason more and more base studies are being made. In many instances the results have brought about "agonizing reappraisals" followed by needed corrective action.

BASE STUDIES IN RELATION TO A CITY

There have been numerous definitions of the so-called "economic base." Often the definitions depend upon the objective of those studying the economic base of cities and regions. Marketing people, for example, are interested in sales potentials within an area; city planners are interested in terms of predicting future land use. One of the most useful concepts, however, seems to be that an *economic base* is: "The export activities of a community that bring in its net earnings and enable it to continue as an independent entity."[1] In short, it is the selected base or area in relation to the United States as a whole.[2] We can also say that it is a city or sharply defined area studied from the point of view of money inflows versus money outflows. For purposes of illustration, one can think of a city into which no money flows and in which all necessities of life have to be purchased from outside the city. In such a case it can be safely concluded that over a given period of time (the time at which all of the inhabitants run out of funds), the city will slowly die. Perhaps this is not so absurd. Virginia City, Montana, was at one time a prosperous city of 10,000 inhabitants with four daily newspapers and numerous hangings resulting from the overconscientious activities of the local Committee of Vigilance. The city exported gold in great quantities and imported food and sometimes other dubious necessities of life. However, when Alder Gulch finally gave up the last of its gold, the city died, having nothing further to export to the outside world and being forced to live completely off imports. When this happened, the population decreased rapidly until only a handful of people, whose descendants now live completely off tourism, were left.

As noted previously, then, the base must be sharply defined, whether it be the city itself or a metropolitan area because, after all, the area under study can encompass the entire United States. The Bureau of the Census has recognized this problem by providing population data and other statistical data for the city by three types of definitions:

1. The corporate city proper
2. The urbanized area; that is, the area determined by cutting off the "city" at the point where urban characteristics stop and rural characteristics begin
3. The standard metropolitan statistical area

Another way of thinking of money inflow versus outflow is in terms of the mercantilist concept of foreign trade with regard to a nation. The mercantilist writers of the seventeenth and eighteenth

[1] Richard B. Andrews, "Mechanics of the Urban Economic Base," *Land Economics,* XXIX (May, 1953).

[2] "Oskaloosa *v.* the United States," *Fortune,* Vol. 17, No. 4 (April, 1938), pp. 55ff.

centuries considered that a nation in order to prosper needed what they called a "favorable" balance of trade. This meant that a nation's exports had to exceed its imports. This also meant that as a result of the excess of exports over imports, a nation's gold supply increased. In a sense it might be said that a city with a "favorable" economic base is a city in which its exports exceed its imports. This cannot be thought of only in terms of exports of goods but also in terms of exports of services. Thus, a dormitory city may be prosperous even though its exports may consist only of executive talent employed in another city.

Purposes of Base Studies

As was indicated, different groups prepare base studies for different reasons. Yet, in spite of an announced objective by any particular group, one basic purpose of the study is an attempt to forecast the future economic growth of the community in terms of population and employment. There has recently been an increasing awareness on the part of responsible community executives and businessmen of the growing competitive struggle between communities. Implicit in this is the recognition by these men that growth in terms of increased employment and population depends on exporting more than is imported. As has been suggested by Professor Seyfried: "Goods and services exported from the community to the nation or world outside will bring in additional income and this additional income will enlarge the purchasing power of the community. Enlarged purchasing power of the community results in an expansion of productive facilities necessary to meet the increased demands of the population. In turn, increased productive facilities lead to a rise in employment, hence more population." [3]

The practical significance of a base study to the real estate practitioner is to be found in the effects of all this on property values. He is interested in the economic base because in a dying city values naturally decline; and in a growing area, with increased demand for real property, values will almost universally increase.

---

[3] Warren R. Seyfried, "Predicting the Economic Growth Potential of the Community," *The Appraisal Journal,* Part I, Vol. XVI, No. 1 (January, 1958), p. 55.

Groups Interested in Economic Base Studies

As has been suggested, there are many groups which may have an interest in forecasting population and economic growth. Some of these are:

The Chamber of Commerce. One of the functions of a local chamber of commerce is to maintain and develop the economy of the community. One of the methods by which this is done is by attracting new industry into the community. Many of the more enlightened local chamber executives attempt to do this by preparing a base study. In this way they feel that they have a more concrete "package" to present to interested business executives. They rightly feel that facts and figures are more impressive than empty talk concerning an area. Thus, in this sense, the base study may be considered a selling device to sell manufacturing firms on a particular location.

Communities Involved in Highway Programs. It has been the sad experience of many communities in the past that their economy has been virtually destroyed by express highway programs that bypass their communities. This experience has been limited to small communities depending on tourism and truck traffic for a greater part of their economic existence. The practical problem generally raised is that the city fathers of these communities have realized too late the effect that the express or limited-access highway will have on the community. Even when they have realized the gravity of the situation in time, they have made little or no headway with the persons in charge of highway planning because they have been unable to substantiate their petitions and pleas with hard facts. Some of the more forward-looking of the smaller communities have, by means of base studies, been able to show the future effect of the bypass on the local economy. Thus armed, they have been able to persuade the planners to have interchanges connecting them with the expressway, thereby saving their economy to some degree.[4]

Appraisers. One of the fundamentals of the appraisal process is the prediction of economic conditions for the nation, region, and the

[4] Salem, Ohio, is an example whereby failure to provide an interchange injured the economy of the community.

community. Thus, base studies are of prime importance for appraisers. It has been suggested by Professor Paul Wendt that since it is necessary for the appraiser to forecast future incomes for industrial, commercial, and residential property, he must understand the structure of that economy.[5] It appears that an analysis of the community's economic base is more important when the capitalization of income method of approach is employed.

City Governments. City governments are interested in base studies for many purposes, most important of which is the prediction of future tax revenues. The major single source of income to local governments, amounting to nearly 50 percent of the total, is from the real property tax. The real property tax is based on a concept of value. While it is true that this concept of value varies from locality to locality, nevertheless some sort of value is attributed to the real property within an area as the base for the tax. Because values change as the economic status of the community changes, it becomes necessary for local governments to make long-range predictions as to future income from taxes. Hence, to do the job properly, an accurate analysis of the community's economic base should be prepared. This is done too often, however, by "guesstimates" rather than by means of a more rational analytical approach, particularly in the smaller communities.

Marketeers. Those persons interested in the marketing of consumer and industrial goods are interested in economic base studies. The major question raised by these individuals is: What is the relationship of area "A" to the rest of the United States? In other words, if the gross national product decreases, will the buying power in area "A" increase, remain the same, decrease in proportion, or decrease at a faster rate? Or if the gross national product increases, will the buying potential in area "A" increase in the same proportion, increase at a faster rate, decrease, or remain the same? There is a recognition that economic change is usually not uniform throughout the country. Therefore, certain areas, even under adverse general economic conditions, might fare better than other areas. Accordingly, it might pay certain manufacturers to concentrate their selling efforts

[5] Paul F. Wendt, *Real Estate Appraisal* (New York: Henry Holt and Co., 1956), p. 76 *et seq.*

in areas that reflect a greater stable potential buying power for their products.

Real Estate Brokers. Brokers, particularly those interested in industrial real estate, often find economic base studies a must. Before an industry goes into a new area, management will raise questions as to the availability of skilled and unskilled labor, labor rates, transportation, taxes, availability of sufficient industrial water supply, and sometimes climate. In Florida and California, for example, part of their booming industrial growth is the result of excellent climate. Labor seems to prefer warmer areas. In addition, the heating costs saved often play an important part in the decision to locate the plant in an area with a warm climate.

EMPLOYMENT AND INCOME WITHIN THE BASE

Types of Employment Within the Base

The two major types of employment within a community are called primary and secondary, or service, employment.[6]

Primary employment is that employment which brings purchasing power into the base from outside. *Secondary employment* refers to those employment opportunities supported by those engaged in primary employment.[7]

In essence, it is from primary employment that money flows into the base area. The service, or secondary, employment activities feed off those engaged in primary employment; for example, retail trade within the defined base, local construction, and the like.[8] It follows then that the secondary employment is contingent upon the amount and composition of the primary employment. It would appear that the composition of income in primary employment should also be considered. In other words, if all of the income from primary employment flows into the hands of those in extremely high income brackets,

[6] Richard R. Ratcliff, *Urban Land Economics* (New York: McGraw-Hill Book Company, 1949), p. 42.

[7] Richard B. Andrews, *op. cit.* Divides the two types of employment into: (1) basic employment; and (2) service employment. Essentially, they are defined the same way as defined by Professor Ratcliff in his classic cited above.

[8] There is a question as to the effect on growth resulting from autonomous *new investment.* (New in the Keynesian sense.)

it might be that spending on secondary employment might be lower than if the same amount of income were spread over a greater number of individuals in lower income brackets. This is the result of a larger marginal propensity to save, plus the fact that many larger consumption expenditures of high-income groups are often made outside their immediate environs.

As a result of the primary employment, a ratio is created between primary employment and secondary employment. For example, a study might show a ratio of primary employment to secondary employment of 1:1.54 in Denver, which means that for every 100 persons employed in primary employment there are 154 employed in secondary employment, or a total of 254 employed.

For purposes of predicting future population growths and economic activity within the community, it can be said that if primary employment grows, the general rule is that secondary employment will grow in a ratio to it. For illustrative purposes, assume the ratio is 1:1. One primarily employed person results in one secondarily employed person. On the basis of this, one can project future population growth. In making a projection, the individuals concerned with the prediction generally consider three possibilities; that is, high, medium, and low. Thus in projecting for 1985, one might consider primary employment in a community to be a high of 30,000, a medium of 20,000, and a low of 10,000. With a one-to-one ratio this would mean that secondary employment would be a high of 30,000, a medium of 20,000, and a low of 10,000. If each category is added together to obtain a *total* employment in the base, then the high total employed would be 60,000, the medium total would be 40,000, and the low total would be 20,000. The question would now remain: What is to be the projected total population, including women, children, and unemployed? Here, too, a ratio is employed. This ratio is based on figures obtained from the last available census data. Suppose that for every person employed there are three individuals in the community. The ratio would then be one employed to three unemployed persons. In this case the *total population* of the base for 1985 might be projected as a high of 180,000 (3 × 60,000), a medium of 120,000 (3 × 40,000), and a low of 60,000 (3 × 20,000).

As a word of caution, one cannot assume that in all instances the secondary type of employment will be completely dependent on the primary type of employment. For example, primary employment will often fail to grow as expected because of lags in secondary employment. If a community fails to provide proper facilities, industrial expansion will be slowed down because labor forces will refuse to migrate to this area. One of the reasons for the phenomenal industrial growth in Florida came about in just the opposite way. Amenities and facilities for recreation were previously developed to take care of tourism. This sort of thing created a situation favorable for the migration of labor once plants were constructed or proposed in that state. It should also be noted that ratios between primary and secondary employment do not necessarily remain constant.

The Form of Income

Income in the base may be in the form of wages, salaries, dividends, royalties, pensions, rents, insurance, interest, and profits. Of course, income to the individual may be received in one or any combination of these forms.

Sources of Income

The Census breaks employment in industry studies into different categories. The table below shows the results of a chamber of commerce study in Las Cruces, New Mexico. Included therein is the number employed in ten categories and the percent of the total in each of the categories.

SOURCE OF EMPLOYMENT	NUMBER EMPLOYED	PERCENT OF TOTAL
1. All Other	1,850	15
2. Manufacturing	800	6
3. Mining	1,600	13
4. Contract Construction	725	5
5. Trans., Comm., Elec., Gas, & S.S.	850	7
6. Wholesale & Retail Trade	2,550	21
7. Finance, Ins., & Real Estate	275	2
8. Service	1,225	10
9. Government	1,150	9
10. Agriculture	1,450	12
Total	12,475	100

There are several reasons for this sort of breakdown, the major one being the ability to determine more strongly a position with regard to establishing primary and secondary employment as the result of a particular industry. In addition, as will be subsequently discussed, diversification of industry within the base might prove important in the event of recession or depression. What is suggested, then, is that all the sources of income within the base must be identified, first in terms of numbers employed in the various categories and, secondly, in terms of percentages of these to the total.

Primary and Secondary Sources of Employment and Income

In wholesale and retail trade some of the income flows into the base as the result of the base having a trading area outside the immediate confines of the area. It is entirely conceivable, for example, that most of the business done by retail stores comes from outside the base. Thus, part of the employment in the retail stores would constitute primary employment and some would constitute service employment. As was suggested above, it is important to break down the figures into primary employment and secondary employment in order to determine the ratios and, consequently, to make population projections. One question remains: If total employment in wholesaling and retailing is X numbers, how much of X is attributable to primary employment, and how much is attributable to secondary employment?

The most accurate method of determining whether sales in wholesaling and retailing come from within or without the base is to analyze each sale. This, of course, would prove nearly impossible. Hence, compromise is in order. This is done in the following manner. Data are obtained as to the number of workers per 1,000 of population in the United States engaged in wholesaling and retailing.[9] For example, assume the ratio of 100 persons engaged in wholesaling and retailing to every 1,000 of population exists in the United States. Suppose that in the base under study there are 150 persons per 1,000 population engaged in wholesaling and retailing. In this case, it is assumed then that 100 persons per 1,000 receive income from within

---

[9] W. G. Pinnell, *An Analysis of the Economic Base of Evansville, Indiana* (1954), Indiana University, School of Business, pp. 30-31.

the community and 50 persons serve those from without the community. This means, then, that if the population is only 1,000 persons, those in wholesaling and retailing engaged in primary and secondary, or service, employment would break down as follows:

	BASIC OR PRIMARY EMPLOYMENT	SERVICE OR SECONDARY EMPLOYMENT
Wholesaling and Retailing	50	100

The same sort of problem arises with regard to manufacturing, except that it becomes even more complex. One of the problems is that some of the manufactured products are consumed within the area. If this be so, then it follows that no money flows into the base from the outside. If *A* is employed by a service station and purchases a washing machine manufactured inside the defined base, what would be the effect on secondary employment? To determine this, certain basic assumptions are generally made: (a) the area consumes its proportionate share of total production based on its percentage of the total population, and (b) refinements are made; that is, if products are obviously not intended for local consumption, they are eliminated and refinements are made with regard to the truth or falsity of the assumption that local goods will be universally consumed by local inhabitants.

For example, part of the analysis of manufacturing is to break down and examine manufacturing, for the base might produce heavy industry drill presses, washing machines, etc. The drill presses may obviously all be shipped to the outside world. Assume that 900 persons are engaged in the manufacture of drill presses and 100 are engaged in the manufacture of washing machines. Thus, manufacturing employs 1,000. All the income from the drill presses flows into the community, thus 900 of the 1,000 are clearly employed in primary employment. What about the 100 engaged in the manufacture of washing machines some of which are consumed within the community? How many are primarily employed and how many are secondarily employed? Assume they manufacture and sell 1,000 machines per year and assume national production of all washing machines is 10,000 per year and that local residents buy 100 machines per year. Then the base consumes one percent of total machines produced in the nation during the year. For purposes of *approximating* secondary employment, it can be said that there is one person of the 100 employed in the manufacture of washing machines in secondary employment. In practical operation, however, it is almost impossible to determine the exact number of machines sold during the year within the base. Therefore, if the total population of the area is 5,000 and one person out of every 50 purchased a machine during the year, it would be assumed that 100 machines would be consumed in the area and that one person was engaged in secondary employment, based on the previously explained percentages. In real life, each person purchasing a washing machine in the base does not consume local products; therefore, further refinements are made in the nature of approximations. These refinements are necessary in order to make the breakdown between primary employment and secondary employment more realistic. In practice it is often necessary to arrive at these refinements by intuition.

This technique has been called the base-ratio or location quotient technique. Reduced to a formula it is:

$$\frac{\text{X}}{\text{total local employment}} = \frac{\text{national employment in industry I}}{\text{total national employment}}$$

When one solves for X, one finds the numbers necessary in industry I to supply the base needs. To summarize, assume X is 3,000, the amount necessary for the locality (really based on the rest of the nation). If there are 5,000 employed in industry I in the base, then it is assumed that the surplus employees (2,000) are engaged in export activity.

The Extractive Industries

Some areas rely heavily for their primary employment on the extractive industries. For example, Butte, Montana, relies heavily on copper mining. Other areas rely on lumbering—certain sections of the states of Washington and Oregon, for example. In these areas, a problem arises with respect to predicting the future of these natural resources. If it is felt that the natural resources will be depleted within the foreseeable future, this must be taken into consideration in predicting population growths. In addition, in this day of rapid technological advances the question of substitutability of synthetics and/or other extractive products for the natural resources of the base must be raised. For example, aluminum is frequently being substituted for steel; the wide use of plastics for garbage pails and other articles has decreased the demand for zinc and other metals.

LOCAL ECONOMIC STABILITY

In a base analysis one of the major questions that needs to be raised is: To what extent is the primary employment within the base tied to fluctuations in national income and employment? For example, as a general rule the automobile industry is seriously affected when the demand for new cars decreases during a period of recession. Thus, when primary employment is hurt, the secondary employment is likewise hurt. It has been said that the primary industries thus become the local area's link to the national economy.[10]

The question is, of course, how closely is primary employment within a base tied in with the nation as a whole? The answer depends mainly on two things: (1) the nature of the goods and services produced and (2) the diversification of production in the local area.

The Nature of the Goods and Services Produced

A fact long recognized by economists is that different types of products have widely different ranges of fluctuations. Luxury versus necessity and heavy industrial machinery versus light consumer goods are both examples of this. In the case of the former, during a depression, an individual may be forced into a diet of fatback and hominy grits and away from beef and milk. During a period of depression or recession, a woman might be forced into temporary contentment with the purchase of a less costly perfume though she would prefer an expensive scent. The point is that a base engaged in the manufacture of expensive perfume for the outside world can expect to be more seriously hurt economically during a period of recession than an area manufacturing a lower quality perfume which sells at a much lower price.

---

[10] C. Rapkin, L. Winnick, and D. M. Blank, *Housing Market Analysis: A Study of Theory and Methods* (Washington: Housing and Home Finance Agency, 1953), p. 45.

In the case of a base engaged in manufacturing basic and heavy industrial machinery, fluctuations during downswings in the cycle are even more vicious and injurious. Part of this phenomenon in the heavy industrial goods industry is explained by the *acceleration principle*. This means that a given change in the demand for consumer goods causes a greater change in the demand for capital goods. For example, suppose a manufacturer of consumer goods uses 10 machines and each machine produces 100 units of the good; thus, total output for the factory is 1,000 units. Assume also that physical depreciation is at the rate of 10 percent per year or, for purposes of illustration, one machine per year wears out. Under these conditions the manufacturer of the machine receives an order for one replacement machine per year. Suppose, then, that the business of the consumer goods factory increases 50 percent or the demand for his products increases from 1,000 units to 1,500 units. This means that he will have to order an additional six machines, one for natural wear and tear and five to fulfill orders for the increased demand. Initially this means that as the production of consumer goods increases 50 percent, the demand for the manufacture of the industrial good increases 500 percent. Suppose the following year the manufacture of the consumer goods business remains the same—1,500 units. Then the manufacturer will order only 1½ machines to take care of wear out. This means, then, that the manufacturer of the heavy machine will find his business has declined nearly 85 percent. To make it worse, assume that the producer of the consumer goods in the following year finds his business has slipped to 1,000 units, or back to where it was before. Now he still wears out one machine per year, but he will probably replace this with one of the five idle machines and will order nothing from the manufacturer of the industrial machine. Thus, the manufacturer might have to close his plant or lay off workers engaged in primary employment.

Some of these relationships are suggested in the following table adapted from a similar table prepared by the United States Department of Commerce. It shows the percent change in expenditures of disposable income, with the effect of the trend held constant.

This table suggests, among other things, that if disposable income goes down one percent, the expenditures for boats goes down 3.1 percent. Also, with a one percent decline in disposable income, expenditures for electricity go down only .2 percent.

TABLE I

ABOVE-AVERAGE SENSITIVITY	COEFFICIENT OF SENSITIVITY
Durable Goods	
Boats and Pleasure Craft	3.1
Luggage	1.9
Furniture	1.4
Nondurable Goods	
Flower Seeds and Potted Plants	1.6
Stationery and Writing Supplies	1.4
Services	
Admissions: Legitimate Theatre and Opera	1.9
Fur Storage and Repairs	1.6
AVERAGE SENSITIVITY	
Durable Goods	
Ophthalmic Products and Orthopedic Appliances	.8
Nondurable Goods	
Toys and Sport Supplies	1.0
Services	
Admissions Professional Baseball	.9
Beauty Parlor Service	.8
BELOW-AVERAGE SENSITIVITY	
Durable Goods	
China, Glassware, Tableware, and Utensils	.7
Nondurable Goods	
Drug Preparations and Sundries	.6
Gasoline and Oil	.5
Services	
Funeral and Burial Services	.6
Water	.2
Electricity	.2

Diversification of Production in the Local Area

This deals with the effect on the local economy of diversification in industries giving rise to primary employment. For example, at one time the little town of Mauch Chunk (now Jim Thorpe) in Pennsylvania depended for its existence on one industry, namely, repair yards for the Lehigh Valley Coal and Navigation Company. When the railroad moved its repair yards, the entire economy of the community collapsed. With the breakdown of the local economy, real estate values rapidly decreased, contrary to the national trend. The question raised is: If that same community had had many diversified primary industries bringing in the same total revenue, would the economy have suffered as greatly?

There appears to be a relationship between instability of local areas and the degree of concentration of industry within the area. In the recession of 1957 and 1958, for example, Detroit suffered greatly as a result of depressed conditions in the automotive industry. At the same time, other areas whose source of primary employment was diversified seemed relatively isolated from depressed business conditions. As a general rule, but only as a general rule, one can conclude that the larger the number of products produced in an area, the more stable the local economy is likely to be. However, this generalization is also governed by the *type* of product produced within the base. Again, an area may be heavily diversified, but if it is highly diversified in the production of heavy industrial goods, the mere diversification will not necessarily lead to greater stability.

FURTHER AREAS OF INVESTIGATION

In addition to analyzing types of employment within the base, sources of income, and local economic stability, it is also necessary to analyze a more complete inventory of local economic resources. This inventory consists of a number of general areas with appropriate subdivisions. The most important of these are: [11] [12]

Population and the Labor Force

A long-term population trend of the base under study should be obtained to determine whether there have been population increases, decreases, or if it has been static. These figures must be compared with long-term trends of the United States and should also be compared with trends of cities of similar size and composition. The sex and age of the local population should be analyzed against national figures. The reason for this is that an area might be extremely deficient in male population of age suitable for the work force. The

---

[11] W. G. Pinnell, *op. cit.*, p. 35.

[12] Edward K. Smith, "A Guide to Economic Base Studies for Local Communities," The Bureau of Business and Economic Research, Northeastern University, Boston, Mass., 1955.

population figures of the area are further analyzed in terms of race, citizenship, and place of birth. The education of the population is also examined in terms of numbers of school years completed. The reason for this is that the highly complex methods of modern production call for a literate work force.

The labor force itself is a matter to be scrutinized from the point of view of relative size (compared with the rest of the United States); sex is examined in terms of relationship of female to male workers, from which one might conclude that the male labor force is not being utilized to its fullest capacity. The various occupations of the labor force are examined. This is important in determining the training and skills of the work force. Lastly, figures must be obtained for the professional and technical workers of the community—teachers, lawyers, and nurses, for instance.

Remember that all of these figures should be compared with those of cities of similar size and with the United States as a whole. It is meaningless to state that a city has a skilled labor force of 2,000 males; this figure has meaning only when it is determined how this number compares with that of cities of similar size.

Transportation, Power, and Natural Resources

Any transportation facilities available to the community should be studied. A major question that must be answered concerns freight rates. Studies must be made of the rates of all types of transportation facilities, with particular emphasis on rates of raw materials and semifabricated goods shipped into the community. These costs must be compared with those of communities engaged in the manufacture of similar products.

Future highway plans should also be examined to determine the impact on industry and housing. Off-street parking facilities for downtown areas should be studied, too, to determine the impact of lack of facilities on retail trade. For example, one might determine that a certain amount of retail trade comes from outside the urban area, but an off-street parking study might point up the fact that the retail trade area is losing part of its potential as the result of lack of parking space.

Power resources must be studied and analyzed. For example, industries requiring a great deal of electric power will have a tendency to move to areas where that type of power is the cheapest. An example of this is the growth of the aluminum industry in the so-called Inland Empire (that area surrounding Spokane, Washington). Hence, it is important to obtain comparative rates on electricity and gas. If there are foreseeable plans for the increase of power in the area, they should be noted also.

Natural resources have a tremendous effect on the growth potential of a base area. Industrial water supplies should be noted and compared with similar cities. Generally, as a city grows, water requirements also tend to rise. In some areas it is vital that conservation methods be studied in order to avoid inhibiting the growth of the area. Minerals in the area of the base should be studied and broken down by type with estimates of the amounts and ease of extraction. Where relevant, agriculture in the area surrounding the base must be studied. There are many cities in the United States that serve as a service center for an agricultural area. Often the fortunes of the base community are tied to the agricultural economic conditions of the surrounding area. It is therefore important to note farm employment, crop values, specific crops and their long-term potentials, and farm purchases within the base.

The Urban Plant

The inventory of the urban plant consists of an inventory of housing, both private and rented, together with the availability of land and the immediate prospects for increasing dwelling units. In addition, other types of community facilities must be noted, including such things as hospitals, educational institutions, facilities such as fire and police protection, together with the recreational and cultural facilities which the community affords.

Financial Resources

Here one attempts to determine the status of local financial institutions. Have savings in the community been increasing or decreasing over a period of the past ten years? What sort of loan funds are available: short-term, intermediate, or long-term loans? An inquiry should also be made as to the interest rates paid by both business and individuals for the use of these funds. If possible it should be determined whether any local funds are available for more speculative ventures, either from special-type institutions or individuals.

Local Taxation and Expenditures

The local tax structure must be determined and compared with similar cities. Often this sort of thing will lead an industry to locate in the area under study. Some people maintain that industry is being driven out in some states because of high property taxes. What are the expenditures in the area for schools, fire protection, and other municipal facilities? All figures obtained should be compared with those of similar cities.

Sources of Information

In order to obtain data for the inventory suggested, a great deal of work must be done. Help can be had from the census reports, local newspapers, chambers of commerce, civic organizations, planning officials, and tax offices. Useful private publications such as *Sales Management* and *Standard Rate and Data Guide* are also available. These publications, which are published annually, contain much of the information necessary for the area. The most important resource for obtaining information, though, is plenty of legwork. With a little luck the base analyst is often able to receive aid from civic organizations for this work.

SOME SHORTCOMINGS OF BASE STUDIES

To date all the methods of studying the city as an economic base are admittedly imperfect. But as one critic has put it, "However, to be only critical is tantamount to substituting nothing for something in a situation which demands action." [13]

---

[13] Charles E. Ferguson, "Statics, Dynamics, and the Economic Base," Ralph Pfouts, ed., *The Techniques of Urban Analysis* (Trenton, New Jersey: Chandler-Davis Publishing Company, 1960), pp. 338-339.

Criticisms of Base-Ratio Techniques

The relation between primary and secondary employment may not predict the consequences of development of new employment. One reason for this is that it fails to consider the impact which such employment may have on imports. For example, a new firm which sells all its output locally may provide goods that were formerly imports. Therefore, this *local* employment can be as effective in terms of putting money into the base as would be *export* employment, if it cuts off exports.

Export-local employment variation among cities or in a given city "at different points in time arises out of the fact that similar amounts of employment may represent far different amounts of income. Thus, export industries made up predominantly of employees receiving high wages and salaries may induce more secondary employment than low-income industries of similar size." [14] Here the problem is really whether an annual salary of $10,000 will induce as much secondary employment as two individuals receiving $5,000 per year each.

QUESTIONS FOR REVIEW

1. Define the term *economic base.*
2. List the three ways the Bureau of the Census gives statistical data for a city.
3. Why should real estate practitioners be interested in economic base studies?
4. Define the terms *primary employment* and *secondary employment* as they are used by students of economic base studies.
5. What is meant by the ratio of primary employment to secondary employment?
6. How does an economic base relying chiefly on income from the extractive industries present a special problem in conducting a base analysis?
7. What has product diversification to do with local economic stability?
8. What is the *acceleration principle?*

---

[14] "The Export-Local Employment Relationship in the Metropolitan Area," *Monthly Review,* Federal Reserve Bank of Kansas City (March, 1960), p. 3.

9. How does the acceleration principle affect local economic stability?
10. List and explain four important areas that must be investigated when making an economic base study. Do not include types of employment, sources of income, or local economic stability and diversification in your answer.

PROBLEM

1. You are given the following figures on an economic base: primary employment, 15,550; secondary employment, 33,280.
   (a) Determine the ratio.
   (b) A new factory engaged in primary employment is moving into the base and intends to employ 350 persons. What can you say about the possible future population growth in town, the demand for labor, and the demand for real estate?

SUGGESTED READINGS

Ring, Alfred H. *Real Estate Principles and Practices,* 7th ed. Englewood Cliffs, New Jersey: Prentice-Hall, Inc., 1972. Chapter 1.

Smith, Halbert C., Carl J. Tschappat, and Ronald L. Racster. *Real Estate and Urban Development.* Homewood, Illinois: Richard D. Irwin, Inc., 1973. Chapter 13.

Weimer, Arthur M., Homer Hoyt, and George F. Bloom. *Real Estate,* 6th ed. New York: The Ronald Press Company, 1972. Chapter 8.

Chapter 28

City Planning and Zoning

The poet Dante when asked, "Where didst thou see Hell?" is reputed to have answered: "In the city around me." Plato, on the other hand, viewed the city as a place where men lead a common life for a noble end.

The true picture of a city is probably somewhere between these two extremes. But one thing is certain, cities can no longer be allowed to grow without some sort of guidance. In recognition of this, much emphasis in recent years has been directed toward the subject of city planning.

THE NEED FOR CITY PLANNING

The city is a dynamic, pulsating, ever-changing thing. Economic, social, political, and even natural forces contribute to the sometimes dramatic, sometimes subtle changes that are wrought. For example, in certain of the hard-coal regions of Pennsylvania, because of a decrease in the demand for coal, the mines have come to a virtual standstill. The area wears an aura of perpetual depression; the homes are shabby and fast-decaying because of the economic forces at work.

In many areas people move, for the sake of their children, to suburban areas springing up on the fringes of every large city. These social forces change the complexion of the city, within and without. Suburban service industries, schools, churches, and recreational facilities are in demand in order to meet the needs of the people.

A holocaust in the nature of a tornado or flood changes the city's picture in those areas unfortunate enough to suffer from such events. The movements of people have made and are making fresh demands on disturbed politicians. Little by little, the need for city planning and for orderly city growth is being impressed upon the minds of politicians, and in many parts of the country city planning has resulted sometimes, unfortunately, only because without planning the city's survival has been threatened—not because it is the logical thing to do.

Planning implies a certain amount of control over the utilization of land. In the past, cities have grown without controls. Within the city proper and at the fringes this has led to many of the current problems. For example, within the city no provisions were made historically for off-street parking. Prior to the advent of the automobile, modern traffic and parking problems naturally could not have been foreseen. Today, however, the parking problem has grown acute. Surveys have indicated that further parking at curbs in some areas is impossible. In many cities this has produced serious economic problems. Purchasing power that is actually expended, not just potential purchasing power, determines the importance of downtown business districts. If these downtown business districts are unable to absorb the increasing auto traffic of shoppers, then business in these locations suffers accordingly.

Outside the historical borders of cities, serious problems also have arisen due to lack of control over growth. Many subdivisions that were laid out in the twenties have actually prevented orderly city growth. Lots were often sold without proper provision for utilities and streets. Lots were too small for desirable community living. These communities have suffered from this type of operation.

For many years these patterns of land use have been growing in an uncontrolled manner. It is true that some control was maintained by use of police power in the form of building codes to prevent fires and actual structural collapse, and there were some injunctions issued to prevent nuisances.[1] However, control was at a minimum.

The problem of uncontrolled growth and the need for city planning were brought into sharp focus as the result of the Chicago World's Fair in 1893. The emphasis then was to provide a more attractive appearance for cities, to provide open spaces for parks, and to further provide civic centers. In short, the emphasis was on the so-called "city-beautiful." The idea of the "city-beautiful" was crystallized in 1908 with the publication of Daniel H. Burnham's *Plan of Chicago*. The *Plan* chiefly stressed beautiful public works structures and paid little attention to the economic and social aspects of the city. This lack was the major deficiency of early city planning concepts.[2] Still, a useful function was served in the sense that it generated popular support for planning in the direction of the "city-practical." This latter concept leaned more toward widening of streets and the general modernization of public utilities. Today, of course, planning goes much further.

DEVELOPMENT OF CITY PLANNING

Enabling Acts

Cities are conceived of as having received their municipal powers from the state. For example, under the laws of some states, an area with as little population as 125 may become a city. The citizens of the area, after voting on the issue, may seek to become an "incorporated" city. The municipality is granted a charter from the state much like a business corporation is granted a charter or certificate of incorporation. Like the incorporated business, the incorporated city must operate within the scope of the powers specifically granted by the charter. In short, powers are *delegated* to the cities by the states. Cities cannot operate outside these delegated powers without subjecting themselves to legal action by citizens who might believe their constitutional rights have been invaded.

---

[1] Ernest M. Fisher and Robert M. Fisher, *Urban Real Estate* (New York: Henry Holt and Company, 1954), pp. 434-437.

[2] Richard L. Nelson and Frederick T. Aschman, *Real Estate and City Planning* (New York: Prentice-Hall, Inc., 1956), p. 181.

Historically, this had a serious impact on city planning. The city could not alter its official plan without specific action on the part of the state legislature. This sort of action was hard to come by in the face of the volume of other legislation faced by the typical state legislature. With increasing industrial activity and the growth of more complex problems in urban areas after World War I, legislatures began giving municipalities more control over their own affairs. Specifically, state legislatures began passing enabling acts. An *enabling act* permits municipalities to establish planning agencies if they desire.

Many states pattern their enabling acts after the model act devised for the Department of Commerce by a committee of experts in 1928. Although the acts vary from state to state, most of them follow the same general pattern.

Planning Commissions

Enabling acts provide for the establishment of a *planning commission*. Membership on the commission varies from state to state. Generally, there are from five to fifteen members. The members are appointed by the mayor, city council, or the city manager with the consent of the city council. Often the mayor and councilmen sit as *ex officio* members of the commission. In some states, the statute requires membership on the commission be in part lay citizens. The model act referred to above provides in addition to the mayor, one member of the city council, one administrative official selected by the mayor, and six lay members.

The function of the planning commission is to prepare a plan or plans for the development or redevelopment of the community. The underlying theory is that proper planning will be the guide to the growth of the municipality and that it protects citizens of the city from influences which would adversely affect both residential properties and investment properties.

Geographical Scope of Planning

The problem raised here is whether or not the city is limited by its boundaries with regard to planning. Usually the enabling acts recognize the impracticability of having planning stop at the city's edge. Some enabling acts give authority to the city planning commission as far out as six miles from the edge of the city provided they do not extend into the boundaries of another city.

The model act provides for making plans for as far beyond the city limits as the commission thinks bears a close relationship to the planning of the city itself. In short, it recognizes that planning must be looked at as a whole unit and cannot be limited by arbitrary boundaries which might have come about as the result of historical accident. Conditions outside the city limits affect conditions within.

Capital Improvements

Only a few enabling acts carry with them a provision for capital improvement programing. However, some states, notably New Jersey, provide: "In the preparation of the master plan the planning board shall give due consideration to the probable ability of the municipality to carry out, over a period of years, the various projects embraced in the plan without imposition of unreasonable financial burdens. . . ."

This suggests that the commissions make suggestions as to public improvements which are in keeping with such city plans as they are developed. It further suggests the necessity of planning commissions looking into the future and anticipating what public structures will be necessary to harmonize with their overall plan, and to implement these future plans by anticipating necessary financial requirements.

The Master Plan

Most enabling acts give much space to what is commonly referred to as the master plan. Section seven of the Standard City Planning Enabling Act of 1928, refers to the *master plan* as follows:

> The plan shall be made with the general purpose of guiding and accomplishing a coordinated, adjusted, and harmonious development of the municipality and its environs which will, in accordance with present and future needs, best promote health, safety, morals, order, convenience, property, and general welfare, as well as efficiency and economy in the process of development; including among other things adequate provisions for traffic, the promotion of safety from fire and other damages, adequate provision for light and air, the promotion

> of the healthful and convenient distribution of the population, the promotion of good civic design and arrangement, wise and efficient expenditure of public funds, and the adequate possession of public utilities and other public requirements.

One of the difficult problems with a master plan is that it sometimes becomes obsolete as soon as it is completed. The more competent city planners attempt to look upon the plan as a thing which must exist over time, and not as a balance sheet which gives a photographic picture as of a moment of time.

The master plan is generally envisioned as planning in six broad areas: [3]

1. Source of information. One of the first steps in planning is to develop a source of information. This is a survey of the city in terms of present conditions and probable future growth. It includes economic activity, population growth, composition of population in terms of age groupings, breakdown of the labor force, and the like. Channels of movement, that is, both traffic within the city and modes of transportation to and from the city, are considered. Public facilities, physical resources, and liabilities are also considered. This facet of city planning was examined in greater detail in Chapter 26.

2. A program for correction. If the survey of the city reveals liabilities in the nature of blighted spots or fire and health hazards, provisions are made in the master planning for correcting these defects where possible.

3. An indicator of goals. It is suggested that the plan should contain indications of what the community wants in terms of the city. For example, if the community wants parks, the plan should contain provision for parks.

4. An estimate of the future. Here are considered the variables affecting the physical development of the community; for example, estimates of industrial growth, future age, and composition of the population.

5. A technique for coordination. The purpose of this function of master planning is to prevent one group from working against the other, as a school board versus a zoning board. The school board might consider a certain parcel of real property desirable for the

---

[3] Charles M. Haar, "The Master Plan," *Law and Contemporary Problems,* Volume 20, No. 2 (Spring, 1955), p. 355 *et seq.*

location of a new high school, while the zoning board might consider a school located on that particular spot highly undesirable. The master plan, it has been said, "represents a recognition of the fact that the value of each specific thing is determined only in relation to things outside itself, and that, therefore, one must have a guide to things outside in order to make intelligent decisions about the specific thing." [4]

6. A device for stimulating public interest and responsibility. In brief, one of the functions of the planning commission is to sell the master plan to the public. This often requires the preparation of several alternative plans. The plan cannot function without public support; therefore, if the public refuses to accept one plan, compromise plans must be presented for possible acceptance.

Obtaining the Public's Cooperation

One of the major problems met in practice by city planners is the need for obtaining public cooperation to implement the master plan. Some private interests will be injured and will object to the plan and, hence, resist adoption of the plan. Suppose, for example, that the plan calls for more off-street parking. It is conceivable that certain influential individuals will be financially injured as a result of this move on the part of the city. Or suppose that the plan calls for proper sewage and roads in subdivisions at the fringe of the city. This may cause short-run financial injury to an "in and out" operator. Often these persons will object to the plan, and they cannot be blamed, especially if it means financial hardship.

One method of dealing with these problems, although often not necessarily the best method, is through the police power. The *police power* is the power of the government to regulate land use in the interest of the public welfare.

The concept of the police power is broad and has been subject to much legal interpretation which has increased the scope of the concept. "With the growth and development of the State, the police power necessarily develops, within reasonable bounds, to meet changing conditions." [5]

---

[4] Alfred Bettman, *American Society of Planning Officials,* Conference in Planning Problems and Administration (1940), p. 60.

[5] *City of Aurora* v. *Robert Burns,* 319 Ill. 93,149 N.E. 784 at 788.

Legislatures quick to recognize the broad scope of the concept of the police power will often, when drawing a bill, specifically insert in the law that the public welfare is of chief concern. The courts have gone along with this sort of declaration and, in interpreting legislation of this type, have sought to implement the legislative enactments.

In the final analysis the use of the police power involves a certain amount of control over the use of private property. It is recognized that more often than not the use of the police power is the only method by which private interests obstructing the implementation of the master plan can be dislodged. However, a better way, when possible, is to attempt to influence by sound reasoning and thus obtain the cooperation of those individuals opposing the city plan.

It has been suggested that if the plan is properly drawn, "those whose investments demand long-term stability, will be anxious to conform voluntarily to plans dedicated to desirable economic and social goals. . . . Perhaps of even more importance . . . is the ability of planning activity to anticipate and point up opportunities for investment that will at the same time help achieve the objectives of the city plan." [6]

Financing the Plan

Like many good things, city planning costs money. Therefore, another major problem in putting the city plan in operation is financing the plan. Although it can be easily demonstrated by planners that planning will pay off in the long run, many people, especially taxpayers, believe, as Lord Keynes, that in the long run we will all be dead. Often, immediate beneficial aspects of some of the phases of planning can be demonstrated in order to induce the taxpayer to burden himself with the costs. For example, the monetary beneficial aspects of off-street parking can be readily demonstrated. Dramatic evidence is available. In Quincy, Massachusetts, from 1941 to 1949, the city spent $823,000 for off-street parking for 560 cars in the central business district. This expenditure was financed by the sale of general obligation bonds. Total assessments of adjacent property increased from about 5.5 million in 1941 to nearly 9 million

[6] Richard L. Nelson and Frederick T. Aschman, *op. cit.*, p. 199.

in 1951. This meant an annual increase in revenue to the city amounting to $155,000, enough to amortize the cost of the project in six years.

Retail store sales in the area increased rapidly. One store reported an increase from $70 per square foot in 1949 to $168 in 1952. Another store reported an increase of 225 percent in revenue from retail sales in five years.[7]

Other effects on increased earnings by business establishments, taxes, and assessments can readily be demonstrated. In addition, one can show how the anticipated benefits will increase the value of the land. The financial problem appears to be only one of the problems involved, but an important one in the area of putting the plan in operation. It is more important perhaps than certain legal and social problems which are certain to arise.

The Future Scope of Planning

Tunnard[8] states that most Americans will in the future live in fifteen great, sprawling, nameless communities. The great American city which has no name has the following characteristics:

1. 25 to 35 million people
2. 1/6th to 1/4th of the total population
3. One half of the economic power of the *entire world.*

The city of great size will extend from the Old Post Road in Bangor, Maine, to Norfolk, Virginia, covering a span of over 600 miles. This, too, is the area referred to by Gottmann as "Megalopolis."[9]

Tunnard points out that the United States is on the way to creating a "man-made mess." We cannot afford to continue to have planning take place on a city or local basis without regard for the region. He cites power lines, clearings for gas pipelines, oil storage tanks, all cutting across the landscape in haphazard fashion; strings

---

[7] *Parking Guide for Cities,* U. S. Department of Commerce (Washington, D. C., 1956), p. 63.

[8] Christopher Tunnard, "America's Super Cities," *Harpers,* Vol. 217, No. 1299 (August, 1958), pp. 59-65.

[9] Jean Gottmann, *Megalopolis* (New York: The Twentieth Century Fund, 1961).

of houses cutting themselves off from the very landscape their owners moved out to enjoy; new roads being built without regard to topography or existing order, merely to solve the mounting traffic snarls or to take advantage of the least costly rights of way.

Tunnard outlines four major problems of the superregion:

1. To see that the fringe housing is properly located and does not become a jerry-built slum.
2. To determine a rational use of land on a broad scale.
3. To design a highway network that makes industry, decentralized offices, and regional commercial centers accessible to more people.
4. To provide a vastly increased recreational system of parks and reservations.

It is probably true that our great population explosion will result in a number of supercities. If so, the implication for future planning is that it will be needed outside of city and county lines. Furthermore, many students of regionalism feel that there is a need for some type of interstate planning, which suggests a new type of federalism across state lines. Failure to plan for the sprawling interurbia may very well result in the predicted "man-made mess."

ZONING

Zoning means the division of a municipality or county into districts for the purpose of regulating the location and use of buildings, land, and building construction. The regulation is brought about through rules which constitute the exercise of the police power. These rules and regulations are uniform with respect to each class or kind of building or land within each district but may differ between districts. Land use or building use is controlled by the municipality.

Generally, the zoning powers conferred by the state zoning laws upon a municipality may be exercised within the municipality. Those zoning powers conferred upon a county may be exercised within the unincorporated areas of the county.

In addition, the zoning laws give authority to the proper local officials to bring action to prevent or restrain the construction, alteration, or repair of any building, or use or occupancy of any building or land in violation of the zoning regulations. For example, if an individual wishes to alter a large residence in a residential area to a small apartment house, the owner must first obtain permission of the proper zoning officials. If the owner proceeds without having first obtained permission, the zoning officials may proceed in court and obtain an order to restrain that individual from continuing with the alteration. Often, too, persons violating zoning regulations may be subject to fine and imprisonment.

Most zoning regulations actually predate the master plans now in effect, or they are used in many areas in the absence of a master plan. In places where the master plan is in effect, the zoning regulations are used in conjunction with the comprehensive plan and effectively aid the implementation of the plan.

Primary Zoning Purposes

There are basically five primary purposes of zoning,[10] which take the form of protection for the public. These usually consist of:

1. Protection against aesthetic nuisances. Things that may constitute "eye-sores" are to be avoided. For example, in some areas zoning regulations specifically prohibit "eye-sores" in the nature of junkyards, except in specifically designated areas. In many cases the zoning regulations go a step further and provide that those engaged in the junk business must provide a fence of "at least eight feet in height" around the junkyard. Some areas, too, have specifically provided for regulation of billboards. In 1911, an important court decision establishing the police power with regard to zoning for aesthetic purposes was decided in a case involving the prohibition of billboards. The court said: Billboards "endanger the public health, promote immorality, constitute hiding places and retreats for criminals. . . . The evidence shows, and common observation teaches us, that the grounds in the rear thereof are being constantly used as privies and a dumping ground for all kinds of waste . . . the evidence also shows that behind these obstructions the lowest form of prostitution and other acts of immorality are frequently carried on, almost under the public gaze." [11]

---

[10] Norman Williams, "Planning, Law, and Democratic Living," *Law and Contemporary Problems,* Vol. 20 (Spring, 1955), pp. 332 *et seq.*

[11] *St. Louis Gunning Advertising Co.* v. *St. Louis,* 137 S.W. 929.

2. Protection of morals. Zoning regulations may be specifically provided for protection of morals. For example, the use of certain types of business buildings used for purposes leading to immorality may be limited. In this sense, in specified areas buildings which may be used for poolrooms may be prohibited.

3. Protection against psychological nuisances. An example of zoning as protection against psychological nuisance may be the limitation of funeral parlors to certain specified areas. Cemeteries and crematoriums may also be relegated to specified locations by virtue of zoning regulations.

4. Protection against physical danger. The public is protected against physical danger by zoning laws. For example, in some places special areas are allocated for necessary arsenals, fireworks factories, and other types of industries that might endanger the public and where potential danger exists. Recently, some parts of the country have been quick to amend their zoning regulations to protect the public against accidents that might arise from atomic energy installations.

5. Protection of light, air, and open space. This is the type of regulation that leads to yard and building height regulations. Buildings often are regulated in size in accordance with the size of the lot that they are intended to occupy.

The Interrelationship of Planning and Zoning

In England zoning and planning are spoken of as if indivisible. In the United States, however, they are spoken of as separate entities. This has led to much debate and discussion over the question of whether zoning can be or should be done without a master plan. It is generally accepted that zoning can be best done when incorporated as part of a comprehensive master plan. However, it is realized that many of the smaller communities have no master plan and therefore do control land uses by means of zoning ordinances alone.

General Zoning Ordinance Forms

The classic form of zoning is three-dimensional. The three categories are residential, business or commercial, and industrial. However, modern zoning goes beyond the classic form. New York City has 15 zoning districts and 18 different use groupings. The use groupings provide for four groups of areas for retail and commercial uses.

One of the major goals of zoning is an attempt to obtain a certain amount of homogeneity in each of the areas. Therefore, in all three categories, there is often a need for subdividing the categories. For example, a city may be zoned in terms of "A" Residential District, "B" Residential District, and so forth. There may be a minimum 100-front-foot lot required in the "A" zone, while the minimum for the "B" zone may be only 50 feet. Thus the homogeneity is achieved in each zone. This may continue in terms of height of homes, number of families to each home, and many other factors which limit the land use but are thought to be desirable.

Some residential zoned areas may permit an overlapping into commercial enterprise which is free from possible nuisance or is of a professional nature. For example, dressmaking, millinery, or similar handicrafts are often permitted in residential areas. Often, too, such professions as doctors, dentists, and lawyers are permitted in these locations. In the case of the dressmaker, however, any public display of goods is usually prohibited. In the residential area, it is customary to prohibit any sign or advertisement larger than six by twelve inches and bearing anything but the name and occupation (by words only) of the practitioner.

It is interesting to note that in these areas real estate brokers' advertising signs are generally limited in size and number. For example, there may be a limitation in the size of the sign to 24 square feet and only one sign permitted to each 500 feet of frontage on the highway or highways on which the property fronts.

One of the major problems in planning a residential zone is that of traffic generating. In short, the use of the land will often determine the amount of traffic in the area. For example, those areas containing apartment houses result in more intensive land use than single-family zones. This intensive land use increases the amount of traffic in the area. It is obvious, too, that those areas containing commercial enterprise or industry are likely to generate still more traffic. Thus, it appears that planners will tend to exclude traffic generators from residential areas. This is one of the major reasons for excluding apartment houses in areas containing predominantly single-family homes. At the same time, capable planners will tend to locate retail districts in locations that will efficiently service adjoining residential districts and also minimize traffic congestion.

It can be readily appreciated, then, that the classic three-dimensional zoning cannot be approached without much thought. Modern planners go further than residential, commercial, and industrial classifications. In residential areas thought must be given to traffic generation, lot size, and size and height of the buildings (or bulk regulations). Whether to include or exclude professions from the area or possibly to permit "resident-industry" to come into the area must also be determined.

In the commercial classification, modern planners are forced to raise questions as to what sort of commerce shall be permitted. Off-street parking and its effects upon the city's retail structure must be considered; height of buildings and the entry of "light industry" into the business zone are other problems which must also be solved. Often planners have difficulty in determining just what "light industry" is.

Historically, the industrial zone was often arbitrarily relegated to areas along the docks or railroad tracks of the city. At the time this worked quite effectively. However, with the increase in truck and air transportation there has been a movement of some industries to the so-called industrial park areas. Here new problems are raised for planners. While in the past planners were not too much concerned with the percentage of the lot occupied by a factory, present-day practice concerns itself with such problems as minimum front, rear, and side yards of industrial concerns. In addition, the effect of industry on nearby residential areas is also a matter of concern. For example, some industries, by their very nature, produce noxious odors. Planning commissions are forced to think of prevailing winds and the effect the odors will have on nearby residential districts. It can be concluded that as cities and fringe areas become more complex, so do the problems of the planners.

Exclusionary Zoning

Exclusionary zoning, sometimes called "snob zoning," is designed to keep out housing for low- or even moderate-income groups. To do this minimum lot sizes as well as minimum floor space specifications have been mandated. For purposes of illustration, an exaggeration is used. Suppose a city or county passed a zoning ordinance stating that the minimum lot size should be 15 acres. In this case land costs would be raised to the level that the general welfare would not be fostered or promoted and hence would probably be unconstitutional as exclusionary.[12]

The point is that by excessively raising the lot size the cost of the land is raised, hence the cost of the home, hence the "exclusion." For example, *without* exclusionary zoning, as a result of inflation and supply and demand during the period 1960-70, an average house lot in Boston rose from $3,690 to $9,210; Dayton, Ohio, from $3,589 to $8,228; metropolitan Washington, D.C., from $4,353 to $9,268.[13]

If the sizes of these lots were raised, it can easily be seen that they may be exclusionary and hence discriminatory against low-income and medium-income groups.

Zoning Practice

The zoning, or city planning, commission is an administrative body, and as such is governed in its actions by administrative law. In most areas there exists a board of appeals which has jurisdiction over zoning cases brought before it *after* the appellants have been heard by the planning board or planning commission. A person who feels that he has been aggrieved, and can so demonstrate, may appeal a decision of the planning board of appeals to the courts. An example of an improper action on the part of the board might be in the case of the board arbitrarily prohibiting the admission of vital evidence in the hearing before the board. It should be noted that an individual appealing a decision of the board cannot appear before the courts before his administrative remedies have been exhausted. That is, he must first appear before the planning commission, then appeal to the board of appeals in those areas where it exists, and only after that may he go into court.

Nonconforming Use

All zoning ordinances provide for what is commonly called a *nonconforming use*, a structure used in violation of a zoning regulation which was a lawful use at the time of the enactment of the

---

[12] *National Land and Investment Co. et al.* v. *Kohn et al.*, 419 Pa. 504. The court also stated that the desire of many residents of keeping the area the way it was did not rise to the level of public welfare.

[13] *Savings and Loan News*, Vol. 91, No. 30 (November 6, 1970).

zoning ordinance. In short, zoning regulations cannot be retroactive. For example, if an individual were using a large barn in the rear of his property for a truck garage at the time of the passage of the ordinance, he may continue to use it as a truck garage even though the area has been classified as a residential district.

Generally, the regulations state if the nonconforming use is discontinued for a period of time (often 3 years), then any future use must be made in conformance with the rest of the zoned area. Often, too, the zoning ordinance will state that if the building is destroyed by fire or other causes to the extent of a certain percentage of its value, it cannot be repaired unless it conforms with the regulations.

A person seeking a change in the zoning regulations cannot do it easily. First he must submit a petition to the zoning board requesting the change. After this a notice is published in a local newspaper, the time length varying from state to state. This notice calls for a public hearing on the proposed change. One of the major reasons for requiring a public hearing is to make it more difficult for politicians to impose pressure on the board. At the hearing, those favoring the change and those against the change may be heard. After this the board renders its decision. Certain minor variances can be made in some states without a public hearing.

BUILDING CODES

Although not strictly falling into the category of city planning and zoning, building codes should be mentioned because of their close relationship with planning and zoning. *Building codes* are municipal ordinances limiting private property rights by regulating the construction and occupancy of buildings. For the most part there are variances in the codes from city to city, although there is now a movement to somewhat standardize the building codes by geographical area; for example, the Southern Building Code. Most of the codes relate to sanitary requirements, structural safety, number of windows required per room, fireproofing, and the like. In most areas having building codes, a builder is first required to obtain a building permit before proceeding with new construction and also certain types of alterations. In these areas of the country there are regularly appointed, and sometimes elected, building inspectors who determine whether the codes have been complied with. Generally, an application for a certificate of occupancy is filed simultaneously with the issuance of the building permit. The *certificate of occupancy* is a statement issued by the building inspector stating that the building code and/or zoning regulations have been complied with. In this manner the zoning boards are able to exercise greater control over the enforcement of the regulations. In the event that the building code and/or zoning regulations are not complied with, the building inspector will not issue the certificate. The real estate practitioner should be aware of the importance of the certificate of occupancy, because often financial institutions require a certified copy of the certificate before they will close a mortgage loan.

QUESTIONS FOR REVIEW

1. How does uncontrolled growth raise problems for cities?
2. How does the idea of the "city-beautiful" differ from modern concepts of city planning?
3. What is an *enabling act?*
4. How may future needs for planning lead to a new form of federalism?
5. Give the general pattern that enabling acts follow.
6. What is a *master plan?*
7. List the six broad areas incorporated in a master plan.
8. What is the concept of the police power, and how is it related to city planning?
9. How is zoning related to city planning?
10. What is meant by *traffic generating*, and how does it affect planning of residential zones?
11. What is a *noncomforming use*?
12. How are building codes related to city planning?
13. The county passes a zoning regulation requiring that builders may build only single-family residences on five acres or more. Comment on the possible invalidity of this regulation.
14. What is the purpose of planned urban development?

PROBLEMS

1. One of the many surveys that must be done in connection with city planning is on the parking problem. Using the following five headings, attempt to make a checklist of items for a parking survey:

(a) Street parking facilities and their use
(b) Present off-street parking facilities and their use
(c) Potential off-street parking sites
(d) Demand for street and off-street parking facilities
(e) Economics of off-street parking facilities of different types; for example, parking lots, wall-less garages, underground garages, etc.

One example in the checklist under item one above might be "relation to business"; another, "interference with moving traffic"; and so on.

2. A report for the city of Worcester, Massachusetts, suggests that the planners turn the heart of the city's central business district into an exclusive pedestrian area, prohibiting all vehicular traffic on downtown Main Street and streets abutting. The common vehicles would have access to the central business district by way of a high-speed distribution loop. The elevated loop would permit an uninterrupted movement of pedestrians along the Main Street Mall. Opening off the loop would be one of a series of garages planned for the downtown area.
   (a) Comment in detail.
   (b) Suppose an individual objected to the overhead loop. What action might the city take?

3. The Worcester plan calls for a high expenditure of funds. If the major objective is to increase sales and fight off the encroachment of the outlying shopping center, what may be a major problem even if the project is completed?

SUGGESTED READINGS

Case, Frederick E. *Real Estate,* Rev. ed. Boston: Allyn and Bacon, 1962. Chapter 27.

Ring, Alfred H. *Real Estate Principles and Practices,* 7th ed. Englewood Cliffs, New Jersey: Prentice-Hall, Inc., 1972. Chapter 26.

Weimer, Arthur M., Homer Hoyt, and George F. Bloom. *Real Estate,* 6th ed. New York: The Ronald Press Company. Chapter 6.

Chapter 29

Public Housing, Urban Renewal, and Rehabilitation

According to the Bureau of the Census, *substandard housing units* are either (a) dilapidated or (b) lack or have shared complete plumbing facilities. A unit is dilapidated if, because of either inadequate original construction or deterioration, it is below the generally accepted standard for housing and should be torn down or extensively repaired or rebuilt.

In August of 1973 the Bureau of the Census released figures indicating nearly 3.2 million substandard dwelling units in the United States. At the present rate of building (about 2.4 million units a year), it would take nearly 18 months just to replace substandard housing without building a single new unit.

The Report of the President's Committee on Urban Housing has estimated the need for new and rehabilitated housing units at 26 million from 1968 to 1978. Of this number, six million would have to be subsidized in one way or another.[1]

---

[1] Report of the President's Committee on Urban Housing (Kaiser Report), *A Decent House* (Washington: U.S. Government Printing Office, 1968), p. 39.

THE PROBLEM OF SUBSTANDARD HOUSING

Aside from a humane desire to improve housing, the real cost of slums and blighted areas is high. Many local housing authorities and planning commissions have conducted studies which suggest that the costs of servicing slum areas are ten to one compared with taxes collected from these areas. In short, for every $100 spent on community services in slum areas only $10 is returned to the city in the form of taxes.

In a situation so vast and complex as the slum problem one is apt to become lost in a maze of statistics and be unable to see the forest for the trees. Sometimes a pinpoint view helps visualize the problem. In New York City in 1960, for instance, a bill was passed to prohibit families with children under sixteen from moving into single rooms without separate bathroom and kitchen facilities. Families living in those rooms were scheduled to vacate such rooms by 1965. At the time the bill was signed, the mayor proudly announced that if necessary the City of New York would buy the single-room tenements and restore them to their original use as apartment buildings. At the time the bill was passed, there were 755 such buildings housing 45,000 families. In addition, there were 14,000 former one- and two-family houses that were renting out single rooms to an unknown number of families. Unfortunately, the mayor's budget permitted the restoration of only 24 of the buildings and relocation of 1,300 families per year. At that rate, it was estimated that it would take 50 to 100 years for the city to wipe out the backlog.[2]

Causes of Slums and Blight

Cities are dynamic in the sense that there is within the boundaries and on the outskirts continual movement. Professor Paul Wendt lists three major causes of blight and slum growth. The first is the financial problem of the cities. The second is shown by the fact that the major source of slums is reputed to be the "cumulative obsolescence" in streets, transportation services, schools, and other public facilities within cities. The third cause of slums is the result of nearly half a century of chronic housing shortage.[3]

---

[2] Edward Higbee, *The Squeeze—Cities Without Space* (New York: William Morrow and Company, Apollo Edition, 1960), p. 36.

[3] Paul F. Wendt, *Housing Policy* (Berkeley, California: The University of California Press, 1963), p. 197.

To this list might be added lack of foresight in creating proper building codes and effective city planning. In addition there appears to be some laxity on the part of politicians in the enforcing of housing and zoning codes and sanitary ordinances in those cities where appropriate laws are already on the books. To help eliminate slum and blighted areas, several programs, both public and private, have been devised. A discussion of these programs forms the rest of this chapter.

PUBLIC HOUSING

In 1892, Congress first entered the field of housing by appropriating the sum of $20,000 to finance a survey of slums in large cities. Since that time, particularly in recent years, the federal government has played a more active role in the area of housing. Between 1892 and 1932, little was done in the broad area now commonly referred to as "public housing." However, in 1932 direct federal aid for residential construction was provided for in the Emergency Relief and Construction Act of 1932. This Act empowered the then potent Reconstruction Finance Corporation to make loans to "state-regulated" limited-dividend corporations. These corporations were limited as to rents they could charge tenants. Within the first year of the Act, Knickerbocker Village in New York City was the only project authorized.

In 1933, Congress passed the National Recovery Act, which, in its housing aspects, went many steps further than the Act of 1932. The latter Act provided for the "construction, reconstruction, alteration, or repair under public regulation or control of low-rent housing and slum clearance projects." Under this Act, administrative power passed from the RFC to the Public Works Administration.

The PWA was authorized to grant 25- to 35-year loans up to 85 percent of value at 4 percent interest to limited-dividend corporations. Only seven loans were made to such corporations by the end of the first year. In February, 1934, the PWA began acquiring land and directing its own projects. Between 1934 and November of 1937, the PWA initiated 51 projects in 39 localities which provided for 21,652 families at a cost of about $130 million.

In 1937, Congress passed the United States Housing Act. Under the terms of the Act, the Housing Division of the PWA was transferred to the United States Housing Authority. More important, the

1937 Act provided for what amounted to formal recognition of public housing. The Act made special provision for the construction of public housing which, however, was to be under the jurisdiction of local housing authorities. The Housing Authority had the power to make loans to local housing authorities up to 90 percent of the cost and, in addition, to pay annual subsidies sufficient to meet carrying charges on the loans. Local governments made annual contributions equal to 20 percent of federal contributions. These local contributions were generally in the form of tax abatements. Specifically, the Act provided that: "The state, city, county, or other political subdivision in which the project is situated shall contribute, in the form of cash or tax remissions, general or special, or tax exemptions at least 20 per centum of the annual contributions herein provided."

The increased scope of the Act of 1937, including the tax abatement provisions, served to widen the rapidly growing breach between those favoring public housing and those who opposed it. However, the urgency of World War II, together with the virtual halt of residential construction, temporarily quieted the conflict between the "housers" and their opponents. After World War II, and continuing to date, open hostilities have been renewed, fuel having been added to the fire with the passage of the Housing Act of 1949 and many of its subsequent amendments.

The Housing Act of 1949

Title I of the Housing Act of 1949 provides for financial assistance by the federal government for the clearance of slum and blighted areas. Title I was approved by Congress within the framework of the National Housing Policy contained in the Housing Act of 1949. The essence of the National Housing Policy is that the Housing and Home Finance Agency and its constituent agencies or other agencies of the federal government having responsibilities in the field of housing will encourage and assist: (a) the production of housing of sound standards of design, construction, livability, and size for adequate family life; (b) the reduction of costs of housing without sacrifice of such sound standards; (c) the use of new designs, materials, techniques, and methods in residential construction; the use of standardized dimensions and methods of assembly of homebuilding materials and equipment; and the increase of efficiency in residential construction and maintenance; (d) the development of well-planned, integrated, residential neighborhoods and the development and redevelopment of communities; and (e) stabilization of the housing industry at a high volume of construction.[4]

Local Aspects of Public Housing

Federal assistance for public housing cannot be had without the request of the locality for assistance. The initiation and carrying out of a project lies in the hands of a local public agency. A *local public agency* is defined as "any state, county, municipality, or other governmental agency or public body which is authorized to undertake the project for which assistance is sought." [5]

The first step, then, for a locality in moving toward a public housing project is to create a local housing authority. Housing authorities are nonprofit corporations created under state law for the principal purpose of building, owning, and operating public housing projects. It should be kept in mind that the states must first, through legislative action, create the framework for the appointments of the local housing authority. Each local housing authority is governed by five local commissioners who serve without pay and who are appointed by the mayor or other governing body.

Financial Aspects of Public Housing

The key to any part of public housing is, of course, adequate financing of the project. Thus, the major federal function in a public housing project is to lend financial assistance to a community. Title I of the Act permits assistance for four types of areas:

1. A slum area or a deteriorated or deteriorating area predominantly residential in character.
2. Any other deteriorated or deteriorating area which is to be developed or redeveloped for predominantly residential uses.
3. Land which is predominantly open and which, because of obsolete platting, diversity of ownership, deterioration of structures or of site improvements, or otherwise, substantially arrests the sound

---

[4] *A Guide to Slum Clearance and Urban Redevelopment,* Housing and Home Finance Agency, Revised (Washington, D. C., 1950), p. 2.

[5] *Ibid.,* p. 2.

growth of the community and which is to be developed for predominantly residential uses.

4. Open land necessary for sound community growth which is to be developed for predominantly residential uses.[6]

The financial assistance may be of three different types—advances of funds for surveys and plans, temporary loans, and permanent financing.

Advances of Funds for Surveys and Plans in Preparation of a Project. These advances usually consist of two types: (1) a preliminary advance and (2) a final advance.

The *preliminary advance* may be used only for surveys and other activities necessary to identify one or more project areas for redevelopment and to obtain information in support of an application for a final advance. The *final advance* is made only in connection with a properly identified project area. The money obtained must be used to finance detailed studies and plans necessary in preparation for a temporary loan and capital grant.

Temporary Loans. The *temporary loan* is a short-term loan of federal funds. This enables the local authority to finance the acquisition of land in an eligible project and to make the land available for redevelopment in accordance with the plan. At this step the local authority may obtain a loan from private sources instead of using federal funds. The security given to private sources for this type of loan is a guarantee by the PHA that sufficient funds will be made available for payment of these loans.

Permanent Financing. After completion of the project, the temporary financing is replaced with permanent financing. Debenture bonds are sold to private investors through investment bankers, and the temporary loans are paid off. These bonds are particularly attractive to private investors because they are tax exempt and are guaranteed by the federal government as to both principal and interest. These bonds are amortized from rents received from tenants in the project. In the event the rental income falls short of the necessary interest and amortization charges, the federal government makes up

[6] *Ibid.*, p. 6.

the difference by means of a subsidy. The subsidy will be discussed more fully later in this chapter because it is one of the bones of contention between those favoring public housing and those opposing it.

Eligibility for Occupancy

Public housing is designed for low-income groups. To be eligible for public housing the family income must be low enough to make the family unable to obtain decent accommodations in the private housing market. The head of the family must not be a member of a subversive organization. He or she must also be a citizen of the United States. Except for veterans, these families must, at the time of making application for housing, be residing in a substandard dwelling unit, or must be living in crowded conditions, or must be in a position of being forced to move due to causes beyond their control.

The maximum income for admission and continued occupancy is determined by the local housing authority and varies from city to city. Generally, each family is required to pay not less than 20 percent of its income for rent including utilities. Rent includes charges for light, cooking fuel, water, refrigeration, and other utilities. The local authorities are charged with the responsibility of not only verifying the income of applicants prior to admission but also of conducting reexamination of income at least once each year to determine eligibility for continued occupancy.

Under the law the top rental for admission must be at least 20 percent *below* the rents at which private enterprise is providing a substantial supply of available standard housing, either new or old (for similar housing).

Frequently, those who meet the income and other requirements for public housing as enumerated above, are often disqualified for other reasons, such as undesirable families (police records, alcoholism, illegitimacy, rent delinquency, etc.) and families *too* large.

Investigations have further suggested that although some 52 percent of those who are about to be displaced from slums are eligible for public housing, only 20 percent actually move into public housing. Many reject public housing because: (a) they want to stay in the old neighborhood whether public housing is there or not; (b) they feel a stigma is attached to public housing; (c) they refuse to abide by the rules that go with public housing; (d) they dislike the physical characteristics of public housing; and (e) they appear to like living in slums. Many of the planners and urban renewal administrators are middle-class individuals who often have difficulty in understanding that many slum dwellers may not wish to adopt a middle-class way of life.[7]

The Pros and Cons of Public Housing

Does Public Housing Compete With Private Enterprise? The opponents of public housing maintain that direct government investment in housing acts as a deterrent to private investment in low-income rental housing. It is pointed out by the opponents of public housing that traditionally low-income groups eventually occupy housing originally built for higher income groups. This is done by a filtering down process. In addition, one of the fears of those opposing public housing is that once public housing (or a form of subsidized housing) has been built for low-income groups, then persons in middle-income groups might also demand some form of public housing. The results of this could, of course, prove disastrous to the private-enterprise system.

The proponents of public housing are equally emphatic in their claims that public housing does not interfere with private enterprise. It is stated that the housing authorities must fix their maximum entrance rental in low-rent projects at more than 20 percent below the lowest rental at which private enterprise can profitably provide standard housing. They further point out that many low-income families have had to live in slums because they could not afford good, privately owned housing, used or new.

Is Public Housing Subsidized Housing? Opponents of public housing claim that public housing is subsidized. Moreover, they say that this is only a step toward socialism, and this in turn will lead to a totalitarian state.

The proponents of public housing freely admit that there is a subsidy involved in the public housing program. However, they point out that the subsidy is paid only when needed to assist in paying

[7] Martin Millspaugh, "Problems and Opportunities of Relocation," *Law and Contemporary Problems,* Vol. 26, No. 1 (Winter, 1961), pp. 6-36.

principal and interest on the bonds. To date, in no year has the full subsidy as authorized by Congress been required.

In response to the accusation against public housing as being socialistic, the proponents of public housing, in essence, put forth the argument that minimum standards of decent housing are important for the preservation of democracy. They raise the question as to whether or not more people are driven to the "isms" as a result of poor housing than would be the case if they were able to have decent housing.

To qualify as tenants under the public housing program families or individuals must possess income eligibility and fall within one of the following categories:

1. Elderly (at least one spouse aged 62 years or more).
2. Physically handicapped.
3. Occupant of substandard housing.
4. Displaced by government action.
5. Occupant or former occupant of a home which suffered destruction or extensive damage in a disaster area, so determined by the Small Business Administration, subsequent to April 1, 1965.

Elderly and physically handicapped persons will not qualify if they possess assets more than twice the annual income limits established for their eligibility for rent supplements. Others will not qualify if their assets exceed 150 percent of such income limits.

The Rent Supplement. Under the Housing Act of 1965, clearly a subsidy has been enacted. This is highly controversial. Under the law an eligible tenant pays 25 percent of his net income in rent and the federal government makes up the difference. For example, a person earning $4,000 per year pays his landlord $1,000. If the rent is $1,200 per year, the government pays the extra $200. If the tenant's income rises to $4,800 per year, the tenant pays the entire $1,200.

The 25 percent of net income is defined as gross income less (a) $300 of the earnings of each member of the family less than 18 years of age, (b) expense of prolonged illness, and (c) expense of taking care of children of a working mother.

There are income limits depending on the size of the family. For example, a 12-person family can earn $7,300 per year and be subsidized, while a two-person family can earn only $4,000 per year and be subsidized. It should be noted that income limitations vary with each county in the United States. In high-cost areas, the family income may be higher.

In January, 1973, this program was suspended by executive order for 18 months. At the time of suspension, it was doubtful whether the program would resume.

Model Cities

Technically, the "model cities" program, the Demonstration Cities and Metropolitan Development Act was passed in 1966. At the time, due to violent "demonstrations" in a number of cities in the United States, frightened bureaucrats hurriedly changed the name from "Demonstration Cities" to "Model Cities." As envisioned by the Act, a city applying for federal aid would select a single blighted area and submit an overall plan for rejuvenation. The project would include housing for different income groups and the public health, education, recreation, welfare, and transportation services necessary to "change the total environment." Beyond these guidelines it was up to the city officials to determine precisely what was to be built.

Does Public Housing Create Ghettos? Opponents of public housing strongly argue that public housing creates ghettos of low-income subsidized groups. In addition, it is put forth that it creates an isolated minority group that could easily become prey to unscrupulous local politicians who use them to gain their own ends.

The proponents point out that slums may in effect be ghettos anyway—ghettos of low-income groups. Further, they are quick to point out that local politicians use these people to gain whatever expedient matter that may interest them.[8]

Special Problems of Public Housing

A number of questions have arisen relating to public housing. These might be termed special problems of public housing, and it is felt that they should be mentioned in passing.

[8] *The New York Times,* Oct. 12, 1958, reporting a Public Housing Administration study stated, "Many persons feel there is a social stigma attached to living in public housing projects." This was found to be the major reason why people move out of public housing. The second major reason was that people felt the rents were unreasonably high even though subsidized.

New Housing. Essentially, the problem is whether or not *new* housing should be provided for the lowest income groups in society.[9] Professor Wendt points out that traditionally housing needs of low-income groups in the United States have been provided through a filtering down process of used homes formerly occupied by middle- and upper-income groups. The filtering down process is analogous to the passing down of used automobiles to low-income groups. It is pointed out that if high volumes of new housing for middle- and upper-income groups are produced and if the filtering down process worked efficiently, the housing standards of lower income groups would be raised.

Taxes. Public housing is exempt from local taxes. In order to pay their fair share of municipal costs, most local authorities make voluntary payments in lieu of taxes. These payments usually amount to 10 percent of the shelter rents paid by tenants. *Shelter rent* is the gross rent charged less the cost of utility services.

Referendum. Under Public Law 176, approved July 31, 1953, local voters have the opportunity to accept or reject public housing. The law prohibits the use of funds for projects when they have been disapproved by "the governing body of the locality, and the people have voted against any such low-rent housing projects. . . ."

In 1971 the Supreme Court upheld the validity of a required referendum on public housing. A suit was brought against the San Jose Housing Authority charging that Article 34 of the California Constitution, which required the referendum, violated the 14th Amendment of the U.S. Constitution by discriminating against low-income persons and minority groups, but the Supreme Court held otherwise.

URBAN RENEWAL

In 1953, the President's Advisory Committee on Governmental Housing Policies and Programs found that new slums were being formed faster than old ones were cleared, and called for a program to prevent as well as clear slums. In January, 1954, President Eisenhower, acting on the Committee's recommendations, called on Congress for legislation that would aid localities to: (1) prevent the

[9] *Ibid.*, pp. 24-25.

spread of blight into good areas; (2) rehabilitate and conserve areas that could be economically restored; and (3) continue clearance and redevelopment of areas that could not be saved.

The Housing Act of 1954 was the response of Congress to the President's plea. The Act provided for a new total approach to end blight as well as clear slums through using a range of community, private, and federal resources. The new approach is called *urban renewal.*

At the outset it should be clearly understood that the major difference between what is known broadly as "urban renewal" and other slum clearance programs is that *private enterprise* plays a most active part in urban renewal. As such, the program has had the approval of the NATIONAL ASSOCIATION OF REALTORS.

The Community Workable Program

Urban renewal begins with what is known as the "workable program." This is a plan of action for and by the community itself. It is a survey of a community's total problem and its own blueprint for effective action to combat slums and blight. In short, it is a program concerned not only with treating existing blight but also with protecting and preserving the community as a whole against the threat of blight.

One of the criticisms of the program is that nowhere in the Act is "community" defined; therefore it is argued that the concentration of urban renewal is in the central cities rather than in metropolitan areas, of which central cities are only a part. To a certain degree this is overcome by Section 701 of the Act of 1959, which authorizes grants to statewide, metropolitan, and regional planning agencies. These grants shall be used to plan for "entire urban areas having common or related urban development problems.[10]

For the most part this fails to solve the problem for the simple reason that planning agencies working on a broad basis do not exist in many cases.

Elements of the Workable Program. The practical and immediate objective of the workable program is to qualify for certain federal financial aids. To qualify for these aids, the community must,

[10] 40 U.S.C.A. Section 441 (Supp. 1959).

through its chief executive, submit a workable program for certification to the Housing and Home Finance Administrator. The community must commit itself to attain seven objectives within a reasonable length of time. These are:

1. Adequate local codes and ordinances, effectively enforced.
2. A comprehensive plan for development of the community.
3. Analysis of blighted neighborhoods to determine treatment needed.
4. Adequate administrative organization to carry out an urban renewal program.
5. Ability to meet financial requirements.
6. Responsibility for adequately rehousing families displaced by urban renewal and other governmental activities.
7. Citizen participation.

Using the Program. The program takes two basic forms, one being renewal and the other rehabilitation. Essentially, the renewal program involves clearance of slum structures and complete rebuilding. The rehabilitation consists of improving already existing structures. The purpose of the former is to remove urban decay and the latter to rebuild and to retard further decay. In the case of rehabilitation, private enterprise (individual property owners as well as businessmen) renews existing structures, while the community improves run-down neighborhood parks, playgrounds, schools, and other detrimental influences that might have caused the neighborhood to deteriorate.

Federal Assistance for Urban Renewal

To carry out the program, most communities may need the assistance of the federal government in any one or a combination of ways. Assistance may be needed in community planning, project clearance, redevelopment or rehabilitation, and in the rehousing of displaced persons. This assistance usually takes the form of monetary aids. These aids to communities are administered by the Urban Renewal Administration. The URA Commissioner allocates funds for local use and prescribes policies under which urban renewal technicians in the Housing and Home Finance Agency regional offices assist communities undertaking urban renewal. The monetary assistance can be in the form of: (1) planning advances, (2) temporary loans, or (3) capital grants.

Planning Advances. Funds may be obtained to finance surveys and planning work necessary before actual operations in the project can get under way. Advances are also authorized for urban surveys to determine whether urban renewal projects will be feasible and also for preliminary planning for general neighborhood areas which are to be renewed in various stages over a period of not more than ten years.

Temporary Loans. These loans are made to the community for the purpose of acquiring slum land or structures. In addition, funds are available for use in clearing the site and preparing the area for redevelopment or rehabilitation.

Capital Grants. After land has been acquired and has been made ready for redevelopment or rehabilitation, it is disposed of to private enterprise or to public bodies. It must be sold for its fair value for the uses called for in the workable urban renewal plan. The difference between the return received from the disposition of the land and the total cost of carrying out the project is its net cost. The government agrees to pay two thirds of this net cost through a capital grant. The city pays at least one third of this net cost through cash, land, public facilities, demolition, or other work contributed to the project operation.

Problems of Displaced Families

Any program of renewal or rehabilitation means that many persons will be unable to find adequate housing as the result of demolition. Many of these persons lack the means of obtaining housing on the normal market. Several things are done to comply with the provisions of the law requiring that decent, safe, and sanitary housing be available to these families. Special assistance has been provided by the federal government. This assistance takes the following forms:

Low-Rent Public Housing. Where displaced families are unable to obtain decent housing on the private market, the Public Housing Administration, with the approval of the local governing body, can contract to make development loans and pay annual subsidies for public housing units.

Relocation Payments. Originally, payments up to $100 for an individual or family and up to $2,000 for a business concern, could be made by local redevelopment agencies and added to the federal grant for the project to cover necessary moving expenses and other direct losses of property resulting from displacement from the project area.

The average cost of the first 16,500 family payments was $65.22. Happily, the Internal Revenue Service ruled that this was not taxable income. The payments are not due until *after* the property is acquired in an urban renewal project. Businessmen receive a maximum of $3,000 for moving expenses and, although the average payments are about $1,100, there have been some cases (printing plants and warehouses) where the moving bill ran to $30,000. The difference was borne by the businessman.

Effectiveness of the Program

Urban renewal is likely to stay with us for a long time. "In terms of expenditures, problems of this type are likely to claim the tax funds in amounts only lower than amounts for defense and education." [11]

In spite of, or perhaps because of, the size and complexity of the program, it apparently has not worked as well as its advocates have hoped. In some cities, for example, the rate of decay is moving faster than renewal.

The red tape of urban renewal is formidable. In some cases five to seven years have been needed to *process* an urban renewal application. The legal paths through which a private developer must tread are almost unbelievable. "Counsel for the prospective redeveloper will soon find an urban redevelopment project is 'just another real estate deal' in the same limited sense that Alfonso's first evening with Lucretia Borgia was 'just another blind date.' " [12] For example, the cost of presenting a competitive bid will run from $35,000 to $50,000 with a chance of one in five or ten of actually getting the property.[13] (There are six different methods of bidding and nine bid

---

[11] Arthur M. Weimer, "Would a Regional Bank System Help Urban Renewal?" *Business Horizons,* Vol. 3, No. 4 (Winter, 1960), p. 88.

[12] Eli Goldston, Allan Oakley Hunter, and Guido A. Rothruff, Jr., "Urban Redevelopment—The Viewpoint of Counsel of a Private Redeveloper," *Law and Contemporary Problems,* Vol. XXVI, No. 1 (Winter, 1961), p. 119.

[13] Editorial, "The City as an End Product," *Architectural Forum* (May, 1960), p. 91.

documents to be examined by an attorney.) Even greater legal problems arise if the bid is accepted.

In some cases interstate highway programs run through slum areas without any planning or coordination with urban renewal authorities. The highway programs fail to provide for family relocation and in many instances create new slums. In some areas the federal government locates and enlarges military installations oblivious of the impact on urban redevelopment.

One of the major problems is the lack of coordination among federal programs in the urban areas . . . "urban renewal is parceled out to the redevelopment agency, expressway construction to the state highway department, civil defense to the director of civil defense, and so on. Each moves in the direction that seems best from its limited viewpoint." [14]

Although progress has been slow and difficult, there has been some clearing and aiding of slums. In a situation which demands action, something is better than nothing. Perhaps the time has come to reexamine the entire Urban Renewal Program and the Acts and their amendments with a view to placing the program under one head with the coordination and cooperation of federal, state, and local agencies. It might be appropriate also to provide for a simpler path on which the redeveloper can wend his weary way.

REHABILITATION

Rehabilitation moves hand in glove with urban renewal. It is big business by any standard of measurement. Each year between $11 and $12 billion is spent for nonfarm home improvements, additions and alterations, maintenance and repairs. Moreover, rehabilitation can perform a useful social function by cleaning up and preventing additional blighted and slum areas. One of the best examples of this type of conservation is the 350-block "Back of the Yards" area in Chicago. This has been labeled by former FHA Commissioner Julian H. Zimmerman as "the best community in the nation."

In that area 125,000 people of twenty-one nationalities live predominantly on 25′ by 125′ lots. In 1941, 8,000 homes in the area

[14] Richard H. Leach, "The Federal Urban Renewal Program: A Ten-Year Critique," *Law and Contemporary Problems,* Vol. XXV, No. 4 (Autumn, 1960), p. 785.

were guilty of 3,600 building code violations. Through good neighborhood leadership and the cooperation of the savings and loan institutions, more than 6,500 of these homes have been modernized and brought up to code standards. Whereas from 1946 to 1953 only six new homes were built in the area, since that time 500 new homes have been constructed and currently another 200 are planned.[15]

Not only does the Housing Act contemplate urban renewal, but it also includes rehabilitation and as such the FHA is authorized under Title II, Section 220 to insure loans in certified slum and urban renewal areas. In addition to the federal assistance, there has been some state aid given to rehabilitation. New York, for example, has an act authorizing cities to adopt ordinances providing that any increase in assessed valuation resulting from alterations and improvements to *certain multiple* dwellings which eliminate unhealthy or dangerous conditions will be exempt from local property taxes for a period up to twelve years.

Some cities have also contributed to urging rehabilitation in slum areas. Some of these cities are New Orleans; Oakland (California); and Cleveland (Ohio), where the Cleveland Development Foundation was organized on a charitable basis. Among other things the foundation—with private funds—assists in financing rehabilitation costs in hardship cases.

BUSINESS ASPECTS OF REHABILITATION

It has been demonstrated time and time again that rehabilitation, particularly for those practitioners engaged in management, has increased the earnings of rehabilitated properties. Consequently, where it can be demonstrated that earnings have increased, it can also be shown that the value of the property has increased.

A practitioner may approach the problem of rehabilitation from a number of viewpoints. First, he may wish to increase his management income by rehabilitating a property. Second, he may be interested in purchasing a run-down property, rehabilitating it, and then either keeping the property for investment purposes or selling the property at a profit. In either case, however, the problem involves several steps.

---

[15] *Savings and Loan News,* Vol. LXXXIII, No. 7 (July, 1962), p. 32.

The Survey

Many of the management firms interested in rehabilitation conduct an extensive survey of blighted areas. The individuals working for these firms search for structurally sound properties that will readily lend themselves to rehabilitation and modernization. Justifiable items of modernization are noted. That is, only those items which will yield an increased return commensurate with the necessary expense are thought of in the proposed rehabilitated building. For example, in some properties complete bathrooms are visualized; in others only toilets are included in the proposed modernization plans. One must guard against overimprovement.

After a preliminary survey has been made, the management firm approaches the owner with one or two purposes in mind: to negotiate (a) a selling agency agreement or (b) a management agreement on the basis of the outlined rehabilitation program.

It is demonstrated to the owner that modernization and repairs will bring increased revenue more than justifying the cost and the management fee. In addition, most firms engaged in this type of business use before-and-after photos to show what they have done on other properties. Pictures are also taken on the subject property showing the "before" condition. These are particularly effective where the owner of the subject property is an absentee owner.

TOWARD SOLVING THE SLUM PROBLEM

The answer to this most pressing and complex problem is not easy, if indeed there is an answer. Some advocate solutions which range from family subsidies, rent certificates, 100 percent financing to businessmen building low-cost housing, and raising the income-earning ability of low-income groups through additional training and education. Another suggested possibility is lowering of building costs by using cheaper material and standardization.

The cities and the metropolitan areas need help desperately. They seem to be bent on their own destruction by building expressways. then increasing taxes to heights which force the businessman to leave, thus reducing the tax base. People of high incomes are forced to move to the suburbs, their places being taken by lower-income groups. Approximately 25 percent of the budgets of major cities is for welfare and about 20 percent for education. In 1958 the former commissioner of housing stated that the people of any city without a comprehensive plan of action under way by 1960 at the latest would face municipal bankruptcy by 1965. Unfortunately, many cities have already fallen into that predicted state.

Thomas Reid, one-time civic affairs director of the Ford Motor Company, told the National Assembly of Mayors, "While we have a million more slum dwellers than we have farm dwellers, the allocation of federal expenditure is $3,000 per farm family and only $84 per urban slum family."

Perhaps in recognition of this, the Ford Foundation made grants to a number of universities to help develop urban counterparts of the agricultural research, education, and extension programs of the land-grant colleges. These grants will perhaps train urban agents to help in rehabilitation for the homeowner. More important, they may be able to assist in the much-needed coordination between agencies for an effective urban renewal program. Time is running out for the metropolitan areas and the inhabitants thereof. Urbo-phrentis is already upon us.[16]

QUESTIONS FOR REVIEW

1. What is a *substandard house*?
2. List the three major causes of blight and slum growth.
3. Write a brief history of public housing.
4. Explain the local aspects of public housing.
5. Under Title I of the Housing Act of 1949 provision is made for financial assistance to the community; list and explain three types of loans and advances of funds to a community.
6. List the pros and cons of public housing.
7. How does the concept of urban renewal differ from public housing?
8. What is a *relocation payment* in urban renewal?
9. What is *rehabilitation*?
10. What is meant by the term "survey" as used by those interested in rehabilitation?

---

[16] *Urbo-phrentis* is a coined term which suggests that urban dwellers are developing strangely singular physical and psychological characteristics.

PROBLEM

1. Many writers in the area of real estate feel that the modular home or prefab will solve the nation's acute housing shortage. But at least one writer feels this is by far an oversimplification. Richey [17] points out that: (a) Because of high overhead the net savings on a factory-built house amounts to about $340 per home exclusive of freight charges. (b) Building codes differ between states and even between areas within a particular state. (For example, roofs must be different between different parts of a state to take into account different snow loads within the state.) (c) Frequently, where a home is completely factory assembled with wiring and plumbing covered at the factory, local building inspectors have insisted upon removing cabinets and sheetrock to inspect the buildings.

   Discuss ways in which these objections might be overcome.

SUGGESTED READINGS

Ratcliff, Richard A. *Real Estate Analysis.* New York: McGraw-Hill Book Company, 1961. Chapter 13.

Ring, Alfred H. *Real Estate Principles and Practices,* 7th ed. Englewood Cliffs, New Jersey: Prentice-Hall, Inc., 1972. Chapter 26.

Smith, Halbert C., Carl J. Tschappat, and Ronald L. Racster. *Real Estate and Urban Development.* Homewood, Illinois: Richard D. Irwin, Inc., 1973. Chapter 18.

Weimer, Arthur M., Homer Hoyt, and George F. Bloom. *Real Estate,* 6th ed. New York: The Ronald Press Company, 1972. Chapter 6.

[17] Clyde W. Richey, "Reduced Construction Cost—A Solution to the Housing Crisis?" *Real Estate Topics* (Boulder, Colorado: Graduate School of Business Administration, University of Colorado, Fall, 1970).

Appendix A

REALTOR®

CODE OF ETHICS

NATIONAL ASSOCIATION OF REALTORS®

Preamble

UNDER all is the land. Upon its wise utilization and widely allocated ownership depend the survival and growth of free institutions and of our civilization. The REALTOR® is the instrumentality through which the land resource of the nation reaches its highest use and through which land ownership attains its widest distribution. He is a creator of homes, a builder of cities, a developer of industries and productive farms.

Such functions impose obligations beyond those of ordinary commerce. They impose grave social responsibility and a patriotic duty to which the REALTOR® should dedicate himself, and for which he should be diligent in preparing himself. The REALTOR®, therefore, is zealous to maintain and improve the standards of his calling and shares with his fellow-REALTORS® a common responsibility for its integrity and honor.

In the interpretation of his obligations, he can take no safer guide than that which has been handed down through twenty centuries, embodied in the Golden Rule:

"Whatsoever ye would that men would do to you, do ye even so to them."

Accepting this standard as his own, every REALTOR® pledges himself to observe its spirit in all his activities and to conduct his business in accordance with the following Code of Ethics:

Part I
Relations to the Public

ARTICLE 1.
The REALTOR® should keep himself informed as to movements affecting real estate in his community, state, and the nation, so that he may be able to contribute to public thinking on matters of taxation, legislation, land use, city planning and other questions affecting property interests.

ARTICLE 2.
It is the duty of the REALTOR® to be well informed on current market conditions in order to be in a position to advise his clients as to the fair market price.

ARTICLE 3.
It is the duty of the REALTOR® to protect the public against fraud, misrepresentation or unethical practices in the real estate field.

He should endeavor to eliminate in his community any practices which could be damaging to the public or to the dignity and integrity of the real estate profession. The REALTOR® should assist the board or commission charged with regulating the practices of brokers and salesmen in his state.

ARTICLE 4.
The REALTOR® should ascertain all pertinent facts concerning every property for which he accepts the agency, so that he may fulfill his obligation to avoid error, exaggeration, misrepresentation, or concealment of pertinent facts.

ARTICLE 5.
The REALTOR® should not be instrumental in introducing into a neighborhood a character of property or use which will clearly be detrimental to property values in that neighborhood.

ARTICLE 6.
The REALTOR® should not be a party to the naming of a false consideration in any document, unless it be the naming of an obviously nominal consideration.

ARTICLE 7.
The REALTOR® should not engage in activities that constitute the practice of law and should recommend that title be examined and legal counsel be obtained when the interest of either party requires it.

ARTICLE 8.
The REALTOR® should keep in a special bank account, separated from his own funds, monies coming into his possession in trust for other persons, such as escrows, trust funds, client's monies and other like items.

ARTICLE 9.
The REALTOR® in his advertising should be especially careful to present a true picture and should neither advertise without disclosing his name, nor permit his salesmen to use individual names or telephone numbers, unless the salesman's connection with the REALTOR® is obvious in the advertisement.

ARTICLE 10.
The REALTOR®, for the protection of all parties with whom he deals, should see that financial obligations and commitments regarding real estate transactions are in writing, expressing the exact agreement of the parties; and that copies of such agreements, at the time they are executed, are placed in the hands of all parties involved.

Part II
Relations to the Client

ARTICLE 11.
In accepting employment as an agent, the REALTOR® pledges himself to protect and promote the interests of the client. This obligation of absolute fidelity to the client's interest is primary, but it does not relieve the REALTOR® from the obligation of dealing fairly with all parties to the transaction.

ARTICLE 12.
In justice to those who place their interests in his care, the REALTOR® should endeavor always to be

informed regarding laws, proposed legislation, governmental orders, and other essential information and public policies which affect those interests.

ARTICLE 13.
Since the REALTOR® is representing one or another party to a transaction, he should not accept compensation from more than one party without the full knowledge of all parties to the transaction.

ARTICLE 14.
The REALTOR® should not acquire an interest in or buy for himself, any member of his immediate family, his firm or any member thereof, or any entity in which he has substantial ownership interest, property listed with him, or his firm, without making the true position known to the listing owner, and in selling property owned by him, or in which he has such interest, the facts should be revealed to the purchaser.

ARTICLE 15.
The exclusive listing of property should be urged and practiced by the REALTOR® as a means of preventing dissension and misunderstanding and of assuring better service to the owner.

ARTICLE 16.
When acting as agent in the management of property, the REALTOR® should not accept any commission, rebate or profit on expenditures made for an owner, without the owner's knowledge and consent.

ARTICLE 17.
The REALTOR® should not undertake to make an appraisal that is outside the field of his experience, unless he obtains the assistance of an authority on such types of property, or unless the facts are fully disclosed to the client. In such circumstances the authority so engaged should be so identified and his contribution to the assignment should be clearly set forth.

ARTICLE 18.
When asked to make a formal appraisal of real property, the REALTOR® should not render an opinion without careful and thorough analysis and interpretation of all factors affecting the value of the property. His counsel constitutes a professional service.

The REALTOR® should not undertake to make an appraisal or render an opinion of value on any property where he has a present or contemplated interest unless such interest is specifically disclosed in the appraisal report. Under no circumstances should he undertake to make a formal appraisal when his employment or fee is contingent upon the amount of his appraisal.

ARTICLE 19.
The REALTOR® should not submit or advertise property without authority, and in any offering, the price quoted should not be other than that agreed upon with the owners as the offering price.

ARTICLE 20.
In the event that more than one formal written offer on a specific property is made before the owner has accepted an offer, any other formal written offer presented to the REALTOR®, whether by a prospective purchaser or another broker, should be transmitted to the owner for his decision.

Part III
Relations to His Fellow-REALTOR®

ARTICLE 21.
The REALTOR® should seek no unfair advantage over his fellow-REALTORS® and should willingly share with them the lessons of his experience and study.

ARTICLE 22.
The REALTOR® should so conduct his business as to avoid controversies with his fellow-REALTORS®. In the event of a controversy between REALTORS® who are members of the same local board, such controversy should be arbitrated in accordance with regulations of their board rather than litigated.

ARTICLE 23.
Controversies between REALTORS® who are not members of the same local board should be submitted to an arbitration board consisting of one arbitrator chosen by each REALTOR® from the real estate board to which he belongs or chosen in accordance with the regulations of the respective boards. One other member, or a sufficient number of members to make an odd number, should be selected by the arbitrators thus chosen.

ARTICLE 24.
When the REALTOR® is charged with unethical practice, he should place all pertinent facts before the proper tribunal of the member board of which he is a member, for investigation and judgment.

ARTICLE 25.
The REALTOR® should not voluntarily disparage the business practice of a competitor, nor volunteer an opinion of a competitor's transaction. If his opinion is sought, it should be rendered with strict professional integrity and courtesy.

ARTICLE 26.
The agency of a REALTOR® who holds an exclusive listing should be respected. A REALTOR® cooperating with a listing broker should not invite the cooperation of a third broker without the consent of the listing broker.

ARTICLE 27.
The REALTOR® should cooperate with other brokers on property listed by him exclusively whenever it is in the interest of the client, sharing commissions on a previously agreed basis. Negotiations concerning property listed exclusively with one broker should be carried on with the listing broker, not with the owner, except with the consent of the listing broker.

ARTICLE 28.
The REALTOR® should not solicit the services of an employee or salesman in the organization of a fellow-REALTOR® without the knowledge of the employer.

ARTICLE 29.
Signs giving notice of property for sale, rent, lease or exchange should not be placed on any property by more than one REALTOR®, and then only if authorized by the owner, except as the property is listed with and authorization given to more than one REALTOR®.

ARTICLE 30.
In the best interest of society, of his associates and of his own business, the REALTOR® should be loyal to the real estate board of his community and active in its work.

CONCLUSION

The term REALTOR® has come to connote competence, fair dealing and high integrity resulting from adherence to a lofty ideal of moral conduct in business relations. No inducement of profit and no instructions from clients ever can justify departure from this ideal, or from the injunctions of this Code.

The Code of Ethics was adopted in 1913. Amended at the Annual Convention in 1924, 1928, 1950, 1951, 1952, 1955, 1956, 1961, and 1962.

Appendix B

The following form may be used for trade-ins, as outlined in Chapter 19, "Selling."

TRADE-IN AGREEMENT
SUGGESTED BY

MIAMI BOARD OF REALTORS
1390 N. W. 7th Street
Miami, Florida

S. C. BLUH COMPANY
Mortgage Bankers
269 Giralda Avenue
Coral Gables, Florida

(Sample)
AGREEMENT

THIS AGREEMENT, Made this ____________ day of ____________, by and between ____________, hereinafter known as Broker, and John Smith and Mary Smith, husband and wife ____________, hereinafter called owners, WITNESSETH:

WHEREAS, the Owners hereto have simultaneously, with the execution of this agreement, entered into a Contract of Real Estate Purchase for a residence property at (new home), the Contract is of same date herewith.

AND WHEREAS, the Owners desire to sell and dispose of their present residence property for the purpose of paying a portion of the said Contract price and the Broker is willing to guarantee the sale value of said present Residence Property and to apply the same upon said Contract price;

NOW, THEREFORE, it is agreed by and between the parties hereto as follows:

1. That the Broker guarantees to the Owners that the Broker will sell their property known as: (address of old home), in the City of ____________ hereinafter called Property, on or before (90) days from date hereof for a minimum net sale value to the Owners of ($) hereinafter called Purchase Price. Represented and determined by a sale price of ($), less amount required to pay off mortgage of ($), leaving an equity of ($). Owners represent these figures as the approximate amount owing on mortgage(s) and other lien(s) on the property. Difference shall be adjusted at time of closing of newly purchased property.

2. That the Owners have simultaneously herewith received such minimum sale value of said Property by way of Credit upon said Contract in the sum of ($).

3. The Broker shall use his best effort to sell said Property for the best price and upon the best terms obtainable, and the Owners agree to sell and convey to such purchaser as may offer the best price and terms for said Property, obtained by the Broker, provided the Purchase Price shall be not less than ($) net to the Owners, and the terms of sale satisfactory.

4. In the event that a purchaser is obtained for said Property for a contract price that, after the payment of 7% real estate commission, will leave a net Purchase Price equal to or more than ($), then it is agreed that of such Purchase Price the sum of ($) cash shall be turned over to the Broker in consideration of the credit of like amount previously given on said Contract, as above provided:

5. In the event that no purchaser is obtained for said Property on satisfactory price and terms that will yield a Purchase Price to the Owners of not less than said ($) on or before (90) days from date hereof and prior to possession by the Owners, the Owners will have two options: Option No. 1—To convey to the Broker (subject to same conditions of sale under Article No. 6 hereof) the said Property in full payment of the credit provided for in said Contract as above set forth and up to the full sum of ($); or Option No. 2—Pay such funds as required to perform under said contract and retain title to said Property free of any further obligations under this agreement;

6. Said Property, at (old home), in the City of ____________, shall be sold subject to the taxes due and payable as of closing, and thereafter. All appurtenances, including appliances, screens, venetian blinds, awnings, permanently installed mirrors and linoleum, now used on said Property, to go with the Property, and on making such sale, the Owners shall furnish an Abstract of Title to the Property showing a good and merchantable title and free from all liens and encumbrances, excepting current taxes and mortgage balance as heretofore set out.

7. If the Owners elect to transfer title of said Property to the Broker, the transfer (unless otherwise agreed upon in writing by the parties hereto) shall be made not later than ____________ days from date hereof, or if possession is taken of new home purchased at (new home) prior to ____________ days from date, then an executed deed for said Property shall be held in escrow until end of said (90 days) and the Owners shall pay all maintenance costs, fuel, utilities, interest and insurance until possession is given. IT IS MUTUALLY AGREED BY and between the parties hereto, that the time of payment, or the cancellation (by exercising Option No. 2 in Article No. 5) as provided herein, shall be essence of this agreement; and that all the covenants and agreements herein contained shall extend to and be obligatory upon the heirs, executors, administrators and assigns of the respective parties.

IN WITNESS WHEREOF, the Broker and the Owners have signed their names the day first written above.

NAME OF BROKER:

By: ______________________________ ______________________________

Title *Owners*

Trade-In Agreement

Appendix C

OIL AND GAS LEASE

AGREEMENT, Made and entered into the 22d day of April, 19--, by and between John Redden of Gresham, Oregon, hereinafter called lessor (whether one or more), and Oregon Oil Company, hereinafter called lessee

WITNESSETH: That the said lessor, for and in consideration of One and 00/100 ($1) - Dollars, cash in hand paid, the receipt of which is hereby acknowledged, and of the covenants and agreements hereinafter contained on part of lessee to be paid, kept and performed, has granted, demised, leased and let and by these presents does grant, demise, lease and let unto the said lessee for the sole and only purpose of mining and operating for oil and gas and of laying pipe lines, and of building tanks, power stations and structures thereon to produce, save and take care of said products, all that certain tract of land situate in the County of Multnomah, State of Oregon, described as follows, to-wit:

(here follows a complete legal description)

of Section 8, Township T. 6 N., Range R. 1 E., and containing 160 acres, more or less. It is agreed that this lease shall remain in force for a term of 5 years from this date, and as long thereafter as oil or gas or either of them is produced from said land by lessee.

In consideration of the premises the said lessee covenants and agrees:

1st. To deliver to the credit of lessor, free of cost, in the pipeline to which lessee may connect wells on said land, the equal one-eighth part of all oil produced and saved from the leased premises.

2nd. To pay lessor one-eighth (1/8) of the gross proceeds each year, payable quarterly, for the gas from each well where gas only is found, while the same is being used off the premises, and if used in the manufacture of gasoline a royalty of one-eighth (1/8), payable monthly at the prevailing market rate for gas; and lessor to have gas free of cost from any such well for all stoves and all inside lights in the principal dwelling on said land during the same time, by making lessor's own connections with the well at lessor's own risk and expense.

3rd. To pay lessor for gas produced from any oil well and used off the premises or in the manufacture of gasoline or any other product a royalty on one-eighth (1/8) of the proceeds, at the mouth of the well, payable monthly at the prevailing market rate.

If no well be commenced on said land or within the boundaries of the lands described as follows:

(here follows a description of these boundaries)

on or before the 22d day of April, 19--, this lease shall terminate as to both parties unless the lessee shall on or before that date pay or tender to the lessor or to the lessor's credit in the First National Bank at Sixth and Main Streets, or its successors, which shall continue as the depository regardless of changes in the ownership of said land, the sum of One and 00/100 ($1) - Dollars, which shall operate as a rental and cover the privilege of deferring the commencement of a

An Oil and Gas Lease

well for 6 months from said date. In like manner and upon like payments or tenders, the commencement of a well may be further deferred for like periods of the same number of months successively. And it is understood and agreed that the consideration first recited herein, the down payment, covers not only the privileges granted to the date when said first rental is payable as aforesaid, but also the lessee's option of extending that period as aforesaid, and any and all other rights conferred.

Should the first well drilled on the above described land be a dry hole, then, and in that event, if a second well is not commenced on said land within twelve months from the expiration of the last rental period for which rental has been paid, this lease shall terminate as to both parties, unless the lessee on or before the expiration of said twelve months shall resume the payments of rentals, in the same amount and in the same manner as hereinbefore provided. And it is agreed that upon the resumption of the payments of rentals as above provided, that the last preceding paragraph hereof governing the payment of rentals and the effect thereof, shall continue in force just as though there had been no interruption in the rental payments, and if the lessee shall commence to drill a well within the term of this lease or any extension thereof, the lessee shall have the right to drill such well to completion with reasonable diligence and dispatch, and if oil or gas, or either of them, be found in paying quantities, this lease shall continue and be in force with like effect as if such well has been completed within the term of years first mentioned.

If said lessor owns a less interest in the above described land than the entire and undivided fee simple estate therein, then the royalties and rentals herein provided for shall be paid the said lessor only in the proportion which lessor's interest bears to the whole and undivided fee.

Lessee shall have the right to use, free of cost, gas, oil and water produced on said land for lessee's operations thereon, except water from the wells of lessor.

When requested by lessor, lessee shall bury lessee's pipelines below plow depth.

No well shall be drilled nearer than 200 feet to the house or barn now on said premises without written consent of lessor.

Lessee shall pay for damages caused by lessee's operations to growing crops on said land.

Lessee shall have the right at any time to remove all machinery and fixtures placed on said premises, including the right to draw and remove casing.

If the estate of either party hereto is assigned—and the privilege of assigning in whole or in part is expressly allowed—the covenants hereof shall extend to their heirs, executors, administrators, successors or assigns, but no change in the ownership of the land or assignments of rental or royalties shall be binding on the lessee until after the lessee has been furnished with a written transfer or assignment or a true copy thereof; and it is hereby agreed that in the event this lease shall be assigned as to a part or as to parts of the above described lands and the assignee or assignees of such part or parts shall fail or make default in the payment of the proportionate part of the rents due from him or them, such default shall not operate to defeat or affect this lease in so far as it covers a part or parts of said lands upon which the said lessee or any assignee thereof shall make due payment of said rental.

Lessor hereby warrants and agrees to defend the title to the lands herein described, and agrees that the lessee shall have the right at any time to redeem for lessor, by payment, any mortgages, taxes or other liens on the above described lands, in the event of default of payment by lessor, and be subrogated to the rights of the holder thereof, and the undersigned lessors, for themselves and their heirs, successors, and assigns, hereby surrender and release all right of dower and homestead in the premises described herein, in so far as said right of dower and homestead may in any way affect the purposes for which this lease is made, as recited herein.

IN WITNESS WHEREOF, we sign this the 22d day of April , 19--.
Witnesses:

/s/ John H. Small, Notary Public　　　/s/ John Redden
　　　/s/ Edward Ellis for
Acknowledgment　　　Oregon Oil Company

Stevens-Ness Law Publishing Company, Portland, Oregon

An Oil and Gas Lease (Concluded)

Appendix D

MONTHLY PAYMENTS NECESSARY TO AMORTIZE A LOAN OF $1,000

No. of Years	Annual Interest Rate								
	5%	5½%	6%	6½%	7%	7½%	8%	8½%	9%
5	$18.88	$19.11	$19.34	$19.57	$19.81	$20.04	$20.28	$20.52	$20.76
6	16.11	16.34	16.58	16.81	17.05	17.29	17.54	17.78	18.03
7	14.14	14.38	14.61	14.85	15.10	15.34	15.59	15.84	16.09
8	12.66	12.90	13.15	13.39	13.64	13.89	14.14	14.40	14.65
9	11.52	11.76	12.01	12.26	12.51	12.77	13.02	13.28	13.55
10	10.61	10.86	11.11	11.36	11.62	11.87	12.14	12.40	12.67
11	9.87	10.12	10.37	10.63	10.89	11.15	11.42	11.69	11.96
12	9.25	9.51	9.76	10.02	10.29	10.56	10.83	11.10	11.38
13	8.74	8.99	9.25	9.52	9.79	10.06	10.33	10.62	10.90
14	8.29	8.55	8.82	9.09	9.36	9.64	9.92	10.20	10.49
15	7.91	8.18	8.44	8.72	8.99	9.27	9.56	9.85	10.15
16	7.58	7.85	8.12	8.40	8.68	8.96	9.25	9.55	9.85
17	7.29	7.56	7.84	8.12	8.40	8.69	8.99	9.29	9.59
18	7.04	7.31	7.59	7.87	8.16	8.45	8.75	9.06	9.37
19	6.81	7.08	7.37	7.65	7.95	8.24	8.55	8.86	9.17
20	6.60	6.88	7.17	7.46	7.76	8.06	8.37	8.68	9.00
25	5.85	6.16	6.45	6.76	7.07	7.39	7.72	8.06	8.40
30	5.37	5.68	6.00	6.33	6.66	7.00	7.34	7.69	8.05

The amortization table above is the most convenient table with which to work. For example, assume a 20-year mortgage at 6 percent in the amount of $10,000. From the percentage column the rate can be seen to be $7.17 per $1,000. Thus, $7.17 × 10 = $71.70 monthly payments to amortize the mortgage over a 20-year period.

Index

A

B

D

N

O

Q

R

S

T

U

V

W

Z